Windows NT®/2000® ADSI Scripting for System Administration

Thomas Eck

M T P

MACMILLAN
TECHNICAL
PUBLISHING
U·S·A

Windows NT®/2000® ADSI Scripting for System Administration

By Thomas Eck

Published by:
MTP
201 West 103rd Street
Indianapolis, IN 46290

Copyright © 2000 by MTP

All rights reserved. No part of this book shall be reproduced, stored in a retrieval system, or transmitted by any means, electronic, mechanical, photocopying, recording, or otherwise, without written permission from the publisher. No patent liability is assumed with respect to the use of the information contained herein. Although every precaution has been taken in the preparation of this book, the publisher and author(s) assume no responsibility for errors or omissions. Neither is any liability assumed for damages resulting from the use of the information contained herein.

International Standard Book Number: 1-57870-219-4

Library of Congress Catalog Card Number: 99-63276

Printed in the United States of America

First Printing: March, 2000

03 02 01 00   7 6 5 4 3 2

Interpretation of the printing code: The rightmost double-digit number is the year of the book's printing; the rightmost single-digit number is the number of the book's printing. For example, the printing code 00-1 shows that the first printing of the book occurred in 2000.

Trademarks

All terms mentioned in this book that are known to be trademarks or service marks have been appropriately capitalized. MTP cannot attest to the accuracy of this information. Use of a term in this book should not be regarded as affecting the validity of any trademark or service mark.

Windows NT, Windows 2000, ADSI, Exchange Server, Visual Basic, Site Server, and InterDev are registered trademarks of Microsoft Corporation.

Netscape Directory Server is a registered trademark of Netscape Corporation.

Entrust PKI is a registered trademark of Entrust Corporation.

Warning and Disclaimer

Every effort has been made to make this book as complete and as accurate as possible, but no warranty or fitness is implied. The information provided is on an "as is" basis. The author and the publisher shall have neither liability nor responsibility to any person or entity with respect to any loss or damages arising from the information contained in this book.

Publisher
David Dwyer

Associate Publisher
Brad Koch

Executive Editor
Al Valvano

Acquisitions Editor
Karen Wachs

Development Editor
Shannon Leuma

Managing Editor
Gina Brown

Product Marketing Manager
Stephanie Layton

Project Editors
Alissa Cayton
Kristy Knoop

Copy Editor
Daryl Kessler

Indexer
Cheryl Lenser

Technical Editors
David Gore
Brendan McTague

Proofreader
Debbie Williams

Compositor
Amy Parker

Overview

Introduction

- Part I **Preparing for Programmatic Administration**
  - 1 Overview of the Active Directory Service Interfaces (ADSI)
  - 2 Making the Transition: Multi-Tier Development for System Administrators
- Part II **Exploring the ADSI Service Providers: Windows NT**
  - 3 Container Enumeration Methods and Programmatic Domain Account Policy Manipulation
  - 4 Programmatic User Account Manipulation
  - 5 Programmatic Group Manipulation
  - 6 Programmatic Computer and Service Manipulation
  - 7 Programmatic File and Print Resource Management
- Part III **Exploring the ADSI Service Providers: IIS**
  - 8 Programmatic Management of the IIS Metabase
  - 9 Programmatic Management of Web Site Properties
  - 10 Programmatic Management of FTP Site Properties
- Part IV **Exploring the ADSI Service Providers: LDAP**
  - 11 Programmatic Management of LDAP Infrastructures
  - 12 Programmatic Management of the Windows 2000 Active Directory
- Part V **Appendixes**
  - A VBScript Code Reference
  - B ADSI 2.5 Programmer's Reference
  - C Further Reading
  - Index

Table of Contents**

	Introduction	xx
Part I	**Preparing for Programmatic Administration**	**1**
1	**Overview of the Active Directory Service Interfaces (ADSI)**	**3**

    ADSI Abstracts Namespace Manipulation 5
        Abstraction Technology 6
        ADSI Versus Native Vendor Namespace API Performance 8
    Practical Usage of ADSI 8
        Shadowing Business Workflow Processes 9
        Enforcing Naming Standards 10
        Automating System Management 10
        Property Cache 11
        Namespace Searches 13
        Security Objects 14
    Interface Support 14
    Applied Theory: Using ADSI to Migrate from
    Windows NT 4.0 to Windows 2000 16
    Summary 17

2	**Making the Transition: Multi-Tier Development for System Administrators**	**19**

    Why Visual Basic? 20
        Visual Basic Defines Datatypes in Variable Declarations 20
        Visual Basic Allows Multi-Tier Development 20
        Visual Basic Separates Business Logic from Application
            Logic with COM 21
        COM Allows Code Reuse 22
    Establishing the Development Environment 22
    Configuring the Visual Basic Environment 23
    Testing Code Segments in a Non-Critical Environment 26
    Using ADSI and Visual Basic Interactively 27
    Developing a COM Server Using Visual Basic and ADSI 28
        Testing the COM Server Using Visual Basic 31
        Instantiating the COM Object from a VBScript
            Active Server Page 32
        Creating a Delegation Model Using DCOM 34
        Running COM Components in MTS 34
    Summary 38

| Part II | Exploring the ADSI Service Providers: Windows NT | 41 |

3 Container Enumeration Methods and Programmatic Domain Account Policy Manipulation 43

Enumerating Domains in the Windows NT Namespace 44
    Enumerating Domains Using Visual Basic 44
Managing Windows NT Domain Properties 44
    Binding Domains Using Visual Basic 45
    Querying and Setting a New Value for
      AutoUnlockInterval... 46
    Querying and Setting a New Value for
      LockoutObservationInterval 47
    Querying and Setting a New Value for
      MaxBadPasswordsAllowed 48
    Querying and Setting a New Value for MaxPasswordAge 49
    Querying and Setting a New Value for MinPasswordAge 50
    Querying and Setting a New Value for
      MinPasswordLength 51
    Querying and Setting a New Value for
      PasswordHistoryLength 52
Enumerating Objects Within a Domain or Computer 53
    Enumerating a Generic Container 53
    Applying Filters for Enumeration 54
Creating and Deleting Objects Using IADsContainer 55
    Adding and Removing Computer Accounts............................... 56
    Adding, Removing, and Renaming User Accounts 57
    Adding and Removing Groups 59
Creating the NTContainerManagement Class Module 60
    Using the Functions in NTContainerManagement...................... 64
    Using the Functions in NTContainerManagement...................... 66
Summary 69

4 Programmatic User Account Manipulation 71

User Object Binding Syntax 72
    User Object Binding Syntax Using Visual Basic 72
Managing User Account Properties 72
    Manipulating the User FullName Property 73
    Manipulating the Description Property 74
    Manipulating User Passwords 76
    Manipulating a User Flag 77
    Manipulating the User Must Change Password
      at Next Logon Status Flag 79
    Manipulating the User Cannot Change Password
      Status Flag.. 81
    Manipulating the Password Never Expires Status Flag.............. 82

      Manipulating the Account Disabled Status Flag 83
      Manipulating the Account Locked Out Status Flag 85
  Manipulating User Environment Profiles 87
      Manipulating a User Profile Path 87
      Manipulating the LoginScript Property 88
      Manipulating a Home Directory Path 89
      Manipulating the Home Directory Mapping 90
  Manipulating User Login Hours 91
      Querying User Logon Hours Using Visual Basic 91
  Manipulating a User Login Workstation 92
      Querying Login Workstations Using Visual Basic 93
      Adding a New Login Workstation to the LoginWorkstations
        Property Using Visual Basic 93
      Removing an Existing Login Workstation from the
        LoginWorkstations Property Using Visual Basic 94
  Manipulating Account Properties 95
      Querying the Account Expiration Date Using Visual Basic 95
      Setting the Account Expiration Date Using Visual Basic 96
      Querying the Account Type Using Visual Basic 97
  Manipulating the Parameters Property 98
  ADSI Exposed Properties that Cannot Be Manipulated
   Using Standard GUI Tools 99
      Querying the BadLoginCount Property Using Visual Basic 99
      Querying LastLogin for a Given Machine
        Using Visual Basic 100
      Querying LastLogoff for a Given Machine
        Using Visual Basic 100
      Querying PasswordMinimumLength for a
        User Account Using Visual Basic 101
      Querying PasswordRequired for a User Account Using
        Visual Basic 101
      Setting PasswordRequired for a User Account
        Using Visual Basic 102
      Querying User Password Age Using Visual Basic 102
  Creating the NTUserManagement Class Module 105
      Using the Functions in NTUserManagement 110
  Summary 113

5 Programmatic Group Manipulation   115

  Windows NT Security Group Administration 115
      Group Binding 116
      Adding Users to a Group 117
      Removing Users from a Group 117
      Enumerating Members of a Group 118
      Querying User Membership in a Group 118
      Querying and Setting Group Description Field Values 120

       Enumerating Individual User Group Membership 122
    Using Groups to Manage File System Security 123
       Creating an Inheritance Structure 124
       Creating the NTGroupManagement Class Module 126
       Using the Functions in NTGroupManagement........................128
    Summary..129

6 Programmatic Computer and Service Manipulation   131

    Querying Computer Properties: The IADsComputer Interface..........131
       Querying the Computer Owner Using Visual Basic.................132
       Querying the Registered Organization Using Visual Basic........132
       Querying the Computer Operating System
          Using Visual Basic...133
       Querying the Computer Operating System
          Version Using Visual Basic 133
       Querying the Computer Processor Type Using
          Visual Basic..134
       Querying the Installed HAL on Windows NT
          Using Visual Basic...134
    Querying and Manipulating Computer Services:
       The IADsService Interface..135
       Enumerating Installed Services on a Specific
          Computer Using Visual Basic 135
       Binding to Services Using Visual Basic..136
       Querying Service Dependencies Using Visual Basic....................136
       Setting a New Service Dependency Using Visual Basic 137
       Querying Service Display Name Using Visual Basic 138
       Setting a New Service Display Name Using Visual Basic 140
       Querying Host Computer Property Using Visual Basic..............140
       Querying Service Executable Path Using Visual Basic................141
       Setting New Service Executable Path Using Visual Basic 141
       Querying Service Account Name Using Visual Basic 142
       Querying Service Start Type Using Visual Basic........................143
       Setting Service Start Type Using Visual Basic............................144
    Querying and Manipulating Service Operations:
       The IADsServiceOperations Interface 145
       Enumerating Service Status Using Visual Basic..........................145
       Starting a Service Using Visual Basic 146
       Stopping a Service Using Visual Basic..147
       Pausing a Service Using Visual Basic..148
       Continuing a Paused Service Using Visual Basic.......................148
       Setting New Service Password Using Visual Basic 149
    Creating the NTComputerManagement Class Module 150
       Using the Functions in NTComputerManagement 156
    Summary 158

7	Programmatic File and Print Resource Management	161
	Managing File Resources	162
	Binding the LanmanServer Container Using Visual Basic	162
	Enumerating Shares on a System Using Visual Basic	162
	Binding to a Specific File Share Using Visual Basic	163
	Querying the File Share Current User Count Using Visual Basic	163
	Querying the File Share Description (Comment Field) Using Visual Basic	164
	Setting a New File Share Description Using Visual Basic	165
	Querying the File Share Host Computer Using Visual Basic	165
	Querying the File Share Maximum Users Property Value Using Visual Basic	166
	Setting a New Value for the File Share Maximum Users Property Value Using Visual Basic	167
	Querying the File Share Path Property Value Using Visual Basic	167
	Creating a Share Programmatically Using Visual Basic	168
	Removing a Share Using Visual Basic	168
	Managing File Sessions	169
	Enumerating User Sessions Using Visual Basic	169
	Managing Individual Sessions Using Visual Basic	170
	Disconnecting a Single User Session Using Visual Basic	171
	Disconnecting All User Sessions Using Visual Basic	171
	Managing Open Resources	172
	Enumerating Open Resources Using Visual Basic	172
	Examining the Properties of a Single Open Resource Using Visual Basic	174
	Managing Print Resources	174
	Enumerating Print Queues Using Visual Basic	175
	Binding a Specific Print Queue Using Visual Basic	175
	Querying Print Queue Properties Using Visual Basic	176
	Managing Print Queues Programmatically Using Visual Basic	177
	Creating the NTResourceManagement Class Module	184
	Using the Functions in NTResourceManagement	194
	Summary	200
Part III	**Exploring the ADSI Service Providers: IIS**	**201**
8	Programmatic Management of the IIS Metabase	203
	IIS Metabase Structure	204
	Examining the Structure of the IIS Metabase Using Visual Basic	204

The IIsComputer Object..206
    Backing Up the IIS Metabase Using Visual Basic.....................206
    Manipulating Maximum IIS Network Bandwidth....................208
    MIME Mapping Management..210
IIS Site Logging 213
    Logging Provider Support in Each IIS Service.......................213
    Enable Logging..213
    Active Log Format...214
    Advanced Log Format Properties 216
    W3C Extended Log File Provider Properties 218
    ODBC Log Provider Properties 220
Programmatic Site Management..223
    Enumerating WWW Virtual Sites on an IIS
        Server Using Visual Basic 223
    Enumerating FTP Virtual Sites on an IIS Server
        Using Visual Basic..224
    Finding the Index Number for a Site Based on the
        ServerComment Property Using Visual Basic 225
    Creating a New Web Site Using Visual Basic..........................225
    Creating a New FTP Site Using Visual Basic 227
    Deleting a Site By Referencing the ServerComment
        Property Using Visual Basic..227
    Deleting an FTP Site Using Visual Basic 229
    Creating a New Virtual Directory Using Visual Basic..............229
    Creating a New FTP Virtual Directory Using Visual Basic 230
    Removing an Existing Virtual Directory Using Visual Basic 230
    Removing an Existing FTP Virtual Directory
        Using Visual Basic..231
    Managing Web Directories and Files Using Visual Basic 231
Programmatic Site Operations...233
    Querying Site Status Using Visual Basic..................................233
    Starting a Site Using Visual Basic..235
    Stopping a Site Using Visual Basic..235
    Pausing a Site Using Visual Basic..235
    Continuing a Paused Site Using Visual Basic 236
    Creating the IIsSiteManagement Class Module...................236
    Using the Functions in IIsSiteManagement 249
Summary...259

9   Programmatic Management of Web Site Properties   261

Virtual Site Binding..262
Virtual Directory Binding..262
Property Inheritance...263

Programmatically Administering the Web Site
Property Sheet..267
    Web Site Identification..268
    Connections...272
Programmatically Administering the Web Operators
Property Sheet..274
    Querying Operators Using Visual Basic....................................275
    Setting a New Operator Using Visual Basic.............................275
    Removing an Operator Using Visual Basic..............................276
Programmatically Administering the Web Performance
Property Sheet..276
    Performance Tuning 277
    Enable Bandwidth Throttling 278
    Connection Configuration 279
Programmatically Administering the Home Directory
Property Sheet..279
    Local Home Directory..280
    Remote Home Directory..281
    Access Permissions and Content Control for
      Local and Remote Home Directories 283
    Web Application Configuration..284
    HTTP URL Redirection..288
Programmatically Administering the Documents Property Sheet........291
    Enable Default Document 291
    Enable Document Footer...293
Programmatically Administering the Directory Security
Property Sheet..294
    Authentication Methods...295
    Secure Communications 299
    Restricting Access by IP Address 301
    Setting New IP Address Restrictions Using Visual Basic...........303
Programmatically Administering the HTTP Headers
Property Sheet..305
    Content Expiration...305
    Custom HTTP Headers 307
    Platform for Internet Content Selection (PICS) Ratings.............308
    MIME Type Management 310
Creating the IIsWebManagement Class Module..................................312
    Using the Functions in IIsWebManagement.............................326
Summary..334

10 Programmatic Management of FTP Site Properties 337
Determining Property Inheritance 337
Programmatically Administering the FTP Site
  Property Sheet..339
    Manipulating Site Identification Properties................................340
    Manipulating Connection Properties 343
    Manipulating Connection Timeout..344
Programmatically Administering the Security Accounts
  Property Sheet..344
    Configuring Anonymous Connection 345
    FTP Site Operators 348
Programmatically Administering the Messages
  Property Sheet..349
    Greeting Message 350
    Exit Message 351
    Maximum Connections Message..352
Programmatically Administering the Home Directory
  Property Sheet..353
    Local Home Directory..353
    Remote Home Directory..354
    Directory Access Permissions..356
    Directory Listing Style 357
Programmatically Administering the Directory Security
  Property Sheet..359
    Querying Current IP Address Restrictions Using
      Visual Basic 360
    Setting New IP Address Restrictions Using Visual Basic..........361
  Creating the IIsFTPManagement Class Module 362
    Using the Functions in IIsFTPManagement 371
Summary..374

Part IV Exploring the ADSI Service Providers: LDAP 375

11 Programmatic Management of LDAP Infrastructures 377
A Brief Overview of LDAP Technology and Terminology..................378
  What Is LDAP? 378
  The Informational Model: What Can Be Placed
    into an LDAP Directory? 378
  The Naming Model: How Is the Data Organized? 379
  The Functional Model: Accessing and Updating Data..............380
  The Security Model: Controlling Unauthorized
    Access to Entries and Attributes..381
Available LDAP APIs 381
Commercial Products Supporting LDAP..382
Applied Theory: Installing the Netscape Directory Server................382

Manipulating an LDAP Directory Using ADSI 385
    Discovering the Architecture of an Existing LDAP
      Directory Using Visual Basic 387
    Querying Entry Attributes with ADSI Using Anonymous
      Access in Visual Basic 387
    Querying Entry Attributes with ADSI Using Alternate
      Credentials in Visual Basic 388
    Modifying Entry Attributes Using ADSI in Visual Basic 388
    Creating a New Entry Using ADSI in Visual Basic 389
    Removing an Entry Using ADSI in Visual Basic 389
Using ADO to Search an LDAP Directory Using Visual Basic 390
Managing Microsoft Exchange Mailboxes and Distribution
  Lists Using ADSI's LDAP Provider 391
    Creating a New Exchange Mailbox Using Visual Basic 391
    Removing an Existing Exchange Mailbox Using
      Visual Basic 394
    Adding a Distribution List Member Using Visual Basic 394
    Removing a Distribution List Member Using Visual Basic 395
    Determining the Distribution List Owner Using
      Visual Basic 395
Creating the LDAPObjectManagement Class Module 396
    Using the Functions in LDAPObjectManagement 399
Creating the ExchangeObjectMgt Class Module 401
    Using the Functions in ExchangeObjectMgt 404
Summary 405

12 Programmatic Management of the Windows 2000 Active Directory   407

Active Directory Terminology Primer 408
Binding to Objects in the Active Directory 410
    Binding to the Root DS Entry (RootDSE) Using
      Visual Basic 411
    Binding to an Active Directory Object Using Alternate
      Credentials 412
    Searching the Entire Forest Using the Global Catalog
      and Visual Basic 413
Manipulating Objects in the Active Directory 415
    Displaying All User Class Objects in the Active
      Directory Using Visual Basic 415
    Displaying All Group Class Objects in the Active
      Directory Using Visual Basic 416
    Displaying All Computer Class Objects in the
      Active Directory Using Visual Basic 416

Creating Objects in the Active Directory..417
    Creating Objects in the Active Directory Using
        Visual Basic..417
    Displaying Object Classes and Associated Mandatory
        Attributes Using Visual Basic..418
    Removing Objects from the Active Directory Using Visual Basic.......419
    Deleting an Entire Branch of a Directory Tree
        Using Visual Basic...419
    Renaming Objects in the Active Directory Using
        Visual Basic..420
    Moving Objects Within a Tree Using Visual Basic....................420
Managing Security for Objects in the Active Directory.....................421
    Constants Used in ACEs..422
    Basic Active Directory Security Administration........................425
    Advanced Topics in Active Directory Security
        Manipulation..432
Creating the ADObjectManagement Class Module............................435
    Using the Functions in ADObjectManagement..........................450
Summary..452

Part V Appendixes   455

A VBScript Code Reference   457
Chapter 3: Container Management Code 457
Chapter 4: User Management Code 463
Chapter 5: Group Management Code..479
Chapter 6: Computer and Service Management Code 481
Chapter 7: File and Print Service Management Code 490
Chapter 8: IIS Site Operations Code 500
Chapter 9: IIS Web Site Operations Code 514
Chapter 10: IIS FTP Site Operations Code 533
Chapter 11: LDAP Infrastructure Management Code 543
Chapter 12: Windows 2000 Management Code 549

B ADSI 2.5 Programmer's Reference   565
AccessControlEntry Interface 565
AccessControlList 570
IADs Interface 571
IADsCollection 573
IADsComputer 574
IADsContainer 580
IADsDeleteOps Interface 581
IADsDomain 582
IADsFileService 586

  IADsFileServiceOperations 592
  IADsFileShare 596
  IADsGroup 600
  IADsLocality 603
  IADsMembers 607
  IADsO Interface 607
  IADsOU Interface 611
  IADsOpenDSObject 614
  IADsPrintJob 615
  IADsPrintJobOperations 620
  IADsPrintQueue 624
  IADsPrintQueueOperations 629
  IADsResource 633
  IADsService 636
  IADsServiceOperations 642
  IADsSession 646
  IADsUser 649
  Custom WinNT Properties 662
  WinNTSystemInfo 662

C Further Reading 663
  Active Directory Design and Administration 663
  Active Directory Service Interfaces (ADSI) 664
  Active Server Page (ASP) Scripting 665
  ActiveX Data Objects 666
  Lightweight Directory Access Protocol (LDAP) 666
  Visual Basic 667

About the Author

Thomas Eck (ASE, CCA, CNA, GCA, MCDBA, MCSD, MCSE+I) is a specialist with Perot Systems Corporation in the Global Financial Services industry division. Currently, he is working as a Systems Architect and project manager on contract with a major European investment bank. His unique role at the bank allows him to define the global implementation standards employed for the bank's intranet and extranet Web infrastructure. As part of this role, he leads a group charged with the research and development of new and innovative ways to solve workflow and interoperability issues using Web and thin-client technology. Additionally, Thomas provides support and consultation to the various global development, engineering, and deployment teams within the bank environment.

Outside the office, Thomas has served as a contributing author and editor of several titles for Osborne McGraw-Hill and Charles River Media, and also contributes regularly to *MCP Magazine*.

When he is not engulfed in writing, work, or studying for an industry certification exam, Thomas and his wife can usually be found spending time with family, traveling, going to the theater, or creating fabulous culinary creations at their home near Chicago.

Thomas always welcomes questions and feedback regarding his work—if you want to reach him directly, feel free to drop him a note at thomas.eck@ps.net.

About the Technical Reviewers

These reviewers contributed their considerable hands-on expertise to the entire development for *Windows NT/2000 ADSI Scripting for System Administration*. As the book was being written, these dedicated professionals reviewed all the material for technical content, organization, and flow. Their feedback was critical to ensuring that *Windows NT/2000 ADSI Scripting for System Administration* fits our reader's need for the hightest quality technical information.

David Gore, an MCSE+I, has been working in the Information Technology field since 1977. He has been involved with the management, planning, engineering/architecture, and administration of a variety of large-scale systems. For the last six years, he has been working extensively with a wide range of Microsoft products such as NT 4.0 and 2000, Exchange, SMS, SQL, Proxy Server, Site Server, IIS, and Visual Basic, to name a few. He currently resides in Naperville, IL, with his wife and son.

Brendan McTague is a senior systems engineer with the Global Financial Services division of Perot Systems Corporation. He currently manages a cross-platform internet engineering team for the investment division of a major European bank. Brendan graduated with a bachelor of science degree in computer science from Temple University; he has been working with Windows NT for more than five years, and received his MCSE in July, 1995. When not working, Brendan prefers to spend his time with his wife and child in their home outside Chicago.

Dedication
This book is dedicated to my wife, Jeanne, with whom each passing day reminds me that love truly is boundless.

Acknowledgments
There are so many people who have made this book possible; however, three extraordinary women come to mind that have truly helped craft this title as it reads today.

First and foremost on any list of extraordinary women is my wife, Jeanne, whose patience with the long nights in the laboratory, delayed meals, and lost time together during our first year of marriage made this writing experience possible. Without your continuous support and encouragement throughout this project, this book and all the other endeavors in my life could never be possible.

I would also like to express my utmost gratitude to Karen Wachs for her patience and professionalism throughout the duration of this project. When questions arose, you were always there to make the decision, address my concerns, and encourage me to keep progressing. Your expertise in the publishing, technical, and project management arenas was absolutely essential to the successful completion of this title. You are truly an outstanding person, and it was an honor for me to work with a professional of such high caliber on this project.

Capping this list of these extraordinary women is Shannon Leuma, who is perhaps one of the best development editors one could have the privilege of working with. The time you spent coordinating with the technical reviewers helped me organize the text into a more cohesive and readable body of work. Your unmatched attention to detail and your seemingly infinite supply of constructive comments helped transform this text into a work that the entire project team could be proud of.

To my technical reviewers and fellow coworkers at the bank, Brendan McTague and Dave Gore, I would like to thank you for your help both in and out of the office. Your feedback and frank criticism of each chapter provided invaluable insight to enhance the quality of this text. In particular, I would like to express my gratitude to Brendan for his role in bringing this title to fruition. His introduction to Al Valvano and Jen Garrett began my relationship with New Riders.

Additionally, I would like to thank the other outstanding professionals at New Riders with whom I came into contact during the course of this project, including Gina Brown, Alissa Cayton, and Kristy Knoop for coordinating the efforts to edit and compose the final text.

To all the other people at New Riders who contributed their time to this book, who have the often-thankless job of working behind the scenes to produce the titles we rely on as professionals, I would also like to extend my expressions of gratitude.

Finally, I would like to thank Richard Ault at Microsoft for helping me get through some of the more complex elements of programmatic administration early in my experience with ADSI and the product's lifecycle. It truly was an honor to have someone of your caliber take the time to review my text in its entirety before going to press. Your experience with ADS, and detailed comments throughout each chapter truly helped assure that the text was both technically accurate and comprehensive enough to be valuable to even the most advanced readers.

Tell Us What You Think!

As the reader of this book, *you* are our most important critic and commentator. We value your opinion and want to know what we're doing right, what we could do better, what areas you'd like to see us publish in, and any other words of wisdom you're willing to pass our way.

As the Executive Editor for the Networking team at New Riders Publishing, I welcome your comments. You can fax, email, or write me directly to let me know what you did or didn't like about this book— as well as what we can do to make our books stronger.

Please note that I cannot help you with technical problems related to the topic of this book, and that due to the high volume of mail I receive, I might not be able to reply to every message.

When you write, please be sure to include this book's title and author, as well as your name and phone or fax number. I will carefully review your comments and share them with the author and editors who worked on the book.

Fax: 317-581-4663
Email: nrpfeedback@newriders.com

Mail: Al Valvano
Executive Editor
Networking
New Riders Publishing
201 West 103rd Street
Indianapolis, IN 46290 USA

Introduction

Who Should Read This Book?

Unlike other titles, this book does not attempt to present many theories behind the technologies you are working with, but rather delves directly into working code segments that can save you countless hours through automation of redundant tasks.

The practical nature of this book targets an advanced- to expert-level audience comprised of system administrators, application developers, and, to a lesser extent, IT management. If you are new to administration, you may want to use this book in conjunction with the more conventional texts described in Appendix C, "Further Reading."

For the system administrator, this book provides the code that is required to automate the most common administrative tasks in Windows NT, Internet Information Server, LDAP directory implementations, Microsoft Exchange Server, and Windows 2000 Active Directory namespace infrastructures. If you are new to using Visual Basic, be sure to work through the exercises found in Chapter 2, "Making the Transition: Multi-Tier Development for System Administrators," to bring you up to speed.

For the application developer, this book provides the Visual Basic code that is required to perform system-level administrative functions using a relatively simple API. It is also well suited for Web developers; the author's COM-based approach allows code to be reused in VBScript, JavaScript, or any other language that supports automation.

For the IT manager, this book helps put into perspective what can and cannot be done programmatically when you are trying to formulate a strategy or solution for your customer's problem.

No matter which category you fall into, you will find a plethora of administrative examples that are ready to implement in your environment.

Prerequisites

To gain the best use of this book, you will require the following:

- A Windows NT or Windows 2000 client
- A namespace in which you can safely test your code

If you want to develop COM objects in Visual Basic, you will also require the use of Visual Basic 5.0 (Professional or Enterprise editions) or higher.

> **Note**
>
> *If you do not have access to Visual Basic, you can use the VBScript segments in Appendix A, "VBScript Code Reference," together with IIS (a free download from Microsoft) and an ASCII text editor to break into programmatic administration.*
>
> *Additionally, if you have any of the Microsoft Office suite installed, you may also be able to use Excel or Access to work with these segments in the included Visual Basic for Applications environment.* ◆

Part I
Preparing for Programmatic Administration

1   Overview of the Active Directory Service Interfaces (ADSI)

2   Making the Transition: Multi-Tier Development for System Administrators

Overview of the Active Directory Service Interfaces (ADSI)

The job description of a system administrator rarely includes reference to the tedious tasks that are inherently part of the responsibilities of most support professionals. To have time for the more interesting aspects of their jobs, many administrators turn to scripting languages to automate monotonous tasks. While Microsoft included several command-line utilities in the original release of Windows NT, these tools were somewhat limited in terms of functionality and offered the administrator no option but to run these scripts from a command prompt. Although this may be adequate for scripts intended for limited internal use, shelling to a command prompt is a far from acceptable solution for inclusion in a Graphical User Interface (GUI) application. Thus, to access additional functionality not included in the command-line tools, or to avoid the need to shell to a command prompt, developers were forced to directly access the appropriate Application Programming Interface (API) to perform the desired action.

Whereas most C++ programmers are intimately familiar with manipulating APIs, most system administrators familiar with shell scripting or even Visual Basic found themselves in some rather uncharted territory. Administrators wishing to automate tasks beyond the functionality provided by the command-line tools had no choice but to turn to third-party tools, to use direct API calls, or to wait for someone else to develop an easier method to automate the administrative tasks at hand.

Soon, a number of products appeared to rescue the administrator from this seemingly impossible situation. For administrators familiar with Perl scripting, the AdminMisc extensions allowed user and domain management using a relatively simple scripting language. However, while these extensions work well for managing the Windows NT environment, they do not fit into Microsoft's current strategic direction for administering Windows environments. And although shell scripting is extremely effective, it does not fit in well with today's GUI application development standards, nor can it easily scale to fit the needs of larger enterprises. Countless other products, including WinBatch and Kixtart, were developed to help perform some of the more difficult tasks such as Registry manipulation, but still lack the robustness required for today's enterprises.

For many years, competing operating system vendors maintained a significant advantage over Microsoft by implementing robust directory services supporting LDAP, X.500, and even proprietary directory services such as Novell's Netware Directory Service (NDS). Critics of the Windows NT environment often pointed to the "flat" architecture of the Security Account Manager (SAM) database as leading a long list of flaws preventing Windows NT 4.0 from sharing the spotlight with UNIX in the enterprise-level operating system market.

Responding to the need for a true directory services solution, Microsoft began supporting the industry-standard Lightweight Directory Access Protocol (LDAP), first in Microsoft Exchange 5.0 and later in Site Server and Windows 2000. In keeping with Microsoft's recent marketing and product naming standards, the directory services architecture found in Windows 2000 was named the *Active Directory*.

Due to the central role the Active Directory plays in administration and support of the Windows 2000 operating system, a robust development environment supporting the Active Directory is essential to help automate workflow processes and administrative tasks in Windows 2000. Although Microsoft could have restricted customization of the Active Directory to experienced C++ developers, the company instead decided to make manipulation of the Active Directory as easy to automate as any Visual Basic for Applications (VBA)-enabled application.

Using the *Active Directory Service Interfaces (ADSI)* libraries, managing a Windows NT or Windows 2000 namespace has now been brought down to the level of even the most novice developer. By trading in the significantly complex API calls needed previously for a simple set of procedures that can manipulate the environment, programmatic administration of a namespace is now well within the reach of a systems administrator.

However, despite the release of ADSI in February 1997, few people paid much attention to the product (nor its predecessor, OLE-DS). Microsoft's work with directory services would not be well publicized until the Windows 2000 development effort matured and Microsoft's commitment to developing an enterprise namespace was embraced by the public. While the name "Active Directory Service Interfaces" might imply that the product solely supports the

Active Directory, ADSI fully supports programmatic control of administrative tasks in Windows NT 4.0. Additionally, ADSI supports the following:

- Administration of the Microsoft Exchange Server (using the LDAP service provider)
- Novell bindery products, using the NWCOMPAT service provider
- Novell NDS products using the NDS ADSI service provider
- All LDAP-compliant directory service infrastructures (LDAP V2 and up, Microsoft Site Server personalization and membership directory, and so on)
- Windows 2000's Active Directory
- The Internet Information Server (IIS) Metabase

Although extremely powerful, ADSI is accessible to developers and administrators familiar with either Visual Basic or C++, as well as those who are familiar with the "lighter" versions of these languages, such as VBScript and JavaScript. In addition, ADSI is supported on other automation controllers, including Perl and Rexx, and allows administrators to use any language supporting Object Linking and Embedding (OLE) automation with the ADSI Component Object Model (COM) objects. Whether you are developing a natively compiled executable, COM object, Web application, or even as part of a login script using Windows Scripting Host (WSH), ADSI provides a relatively simple interface to automate most every enterprise administration task.

Should an enterprise decide to upgrade to Windows 2000 today or in the distant future, adoption of ADSI will prove an invaluable investment by supporting the automation of workflow processes and reducing tedious administrative tasks. ADSI's simple cross-language nature enables rapid development of customized applications and allows more robust login scripts to be created, thus providing better support for any organization's infrastructure.

ADSI Abstracts Namespace Manipulation

Despite common misconception among many system administrators, ADSI is not a programming language. It is rather a collection of COM objects that allows programmatic manipulation of any supported namespace. ADSI thus provides a layer of abstraction between a programming language and the processes required to manipulate a namespace. This abstraction is taken a step further when using OLE automation controllers, such as Visual Basic, which are able to automate the creation of the underlying OLE code. Visual Basic can make all necessary IDispatch interface calls, leaving the developer free to concentrate on the business logic of the application rather than the inner workings of COM.

To provide a non-technical example of this abstraction technique, assume you have hired a translator who speaks fluent English, Spanish, German, French, and Italian. Although you are fluent only in English, with this translator at your side, you now have the ability to communicate with almost anyone you might encounter in your travels about Western Europe. Because ADSI knows how to speak to Windows NT, LDAP, and NDS/Bindery namespaces, ADSI can be viewed in a similar fashion to this translator. ADSI can also manipulate the IIS Metabase, third-party products, and even custom namespaces by implementing custom-developed service providers and extensions to directory service schema.

> **Note**
>
> *The database schema is responsible for defining the available fields for storing data. "Extending" the schema refers to the definition of additional fields in which to store custom information, such as a field to hold the serial number of a Security Dynamics access token given to an employee, or other enterprise-specific data.*
>
> *For a non-technical example, consider the U.S. Postal system. The post office defines the following address schema to assure proper delivery of a letter:*
>
> Name
>
> Address
>
> City, State ZIP
>
> Postage Amount
>
> *Sometimes, however, we must extend the schema to include an apartment number, floor location, or mail stop to further describe the recipient's location.* ◆

Abstraction Technology

The concept of generating code that can span multiple products or even multiple vendors is not new to developers familiar with the Windows platform development process. Just as the Telephony Application Programming Interface (TAPI) masks the low-level language required to access a telephony device, ADSI provides an interface to mask the required API calls to perform the requested actions in multiple namespaces. In TAPI, a modem vendor is responsible for supplying a device driver that complies with the TAPI standard. Thus, an application developer working on a telephony application can forget about the hundreds of modem types available on the market today and instead write code that will work with any TAPI-compliant hardware.

Microsoft has not limited this concept of abstraction only to hardware devices. The same abstraction technology can be found when writing mail applications using the Messaging Application Program Interface (MAPI) interface, and even database connectivity when using the Open Database Connectivity (ODBC) interfaces. Using ADSI, this abstraction permits a developer to learn only the syntax specific to each ADSI provider instead of learning the API calls necessary to manipulate each individual namespace.

By the very nature of this abstraction, ADSI allows corporate developers to establish management applications with little concern over future infrastructure decisions that might otherwise force the application into a major redevelopment effort or extinction. To give a brief example of this concept, consider the following Visual Basic code that creates a user in the Windows NT namespace:

```
Dim Container as IADsContainer 'Establish Container variable of type
↪IADsContainer
Dim User as IADsUser 'Establish NewUser variable of type IADsUser

'Bind to the WinNT namespace and instantiate the ADSNT.DLL object if it is not
↪active:
Set Container = GetObject("WinNT://UserDomain")

'Create a new user in the namespace:
Set User = Container.Create("User","TEck")

'Write the information to the namespace
User.SetInfo
```

Although the WinNT provider still functions properly in Windows 2000, to perform a user creation directly in the proper container within the Active Directory, examine the following Visual Basic code:

```
Dim Container as IADsContainer 'Establish Container variable of type
↪IADsContainer
Dim User as IADsUser 'Establish NewUser variable of type IADsUser

'Bind to the LDAP namespace and instantiate the ADSLDP.DLL object if it is not
↪active:
Set Container = GetObject("LDAP://ldap_server/OU=Engineering,DC=PerotSystems,
↪DC=COM")

'Create a new user in the namespace:
Set User = Container.Create("User","cn=Teck")
User.Put("sAMAccountName", "Teck")

'Write the information to the namespace
User.SetInfo
```

Even if you are not familiar with Visual Basic, you can see that the code segments for the WinNT and LDAP namespaces are strikingly similar. Notice that while the arguments passed for binding the namespace and defining the user may differ between the WinNT and LDAP providers (because of the requirement to specify the location of the object within the directory), the syntax used to manipulate the ADSI interfaces is nearly identical. The parameters differ per ADSI service provider to accommodate the requirements of each underlying directory service. Unlike the flat architecture found in the WinNT namespace, the LDAP service provider allows the administrator to explicitly define the location within the namespace in which to create the user object.

Without ADSI, you would need to learn how to manipulate each namespace vendor's API to create a new user, resulting in longer development times and reduced adaptability to changes in the enterprise infrastructure. In today's heterogeneous environment, such a task would inevitably result in a huge learning curve for an administrator simply wishing to automate a few manual tasks, and probably would negate any benefits derived from such an automation exercise. ADSI clearly lowers the bar to enable almost any administrator (even those new to programmatic administration methods) to develop custom administration applications for his or her organization.

If careful planning and good programming practices are exercised when developing applications utilizing ADSI, a single code base can be established that can span any of the ADSI provider namespaces without future code modification.

ADSI Versus Native Vendor Namespace API Performance

Whether discussing technical architecture or the non-technical aspects of daily life, logic dictates that the introduction of each layer of abstraction should significantly decrease the overall performance (or efficiency) of a system. Microsoft claims that despite the layer of abstraction ADSI provides between the application and the native API, the performance delta between using native API calls and using ADSI is negligible. Although this may seem questionable, the negligible performance degradation experienced when using ADSI is due to the efficiency of the routing layer that handles calls between the application and the raw processes to manipulate each respective namespace. For most administrators, the relative ease of ADSI far outweighs any slight performance advantages the native API calls might maintain.

Practical Usage of ADSI

In addition to allowing closer ties with existing workflow processes, the multi-tier nature of ADSI's architecture allows you to quickly and easily convert theoretical principles into practical applications. Whether these principles center on creating a more efficient internal workflow process, or you simply have a requirement to be able to quickly search a given namespace, ADSI can help.

In the sections that follow, you will take a more in-depth look at some of the more significant practical applications of ADSI, including the following:
- Shadowing business workflow processes
- Enforcing naming standards
- Automating system management

You will also explore the way ADSI employs property caches, conducts namespace searches, and utilizes security.

Shadowing Business Workflow Processes

Just as you might prefer clothing that has been tailored to fit your body shape, today's enterprise demands applications that combine the advantages of shrink-wrapped functionality with the ability to tailor the application to suit the needs of the business. Microsoft and other vendors have clearly responded to these demands, and many new office automation applications on the market today offer the ability to modify default behavior and automate the use of such products through VBA.

Before Web-based applications became possible, internal workflow processes often were required to change to fit the flow of the application. In such cases, software vendors were sculpting business processes, rather than following the more logical approach that business requirements should instead drive the application development effort.

With the advent of COM support in Web server applications, robust Web applications can be rapidly developed to exactly shadow the workflow processes of *any* business unit. Using COM objects, you can easily separate application logic from business logic, thus creating an application that is both flexible and easy to modify. In addition, Web-based applications offer the following advantages:

- User interface images can be modified to match current corporate marketing collateral and aesthetic standards
- Managers can consolidate multiple tools into a single common interface, thus reducing the user learning curve required to use the application effectively

By studying a business workflow, a developer can create an application that automates several of the processes contained within the workflow and exactly shadows existing business processes.

To better understand how ADSI fits into the workflow, suppose a new employee has joined your company. To be effective on her first day of work, she requires desk space, a telephone, a workstation, and accounts in the NT, Exchange, Novell, and UNIX namespaces. Using ADO, you can write a script to capture data from the human resources database, and subsequently create accounts in the LDAP directory, NDS, Exchange, and the Windows NT SAM. Using this data with each appropriate ADSI service provider, you can automatically assign group and distribution list membership to this new user based on the data found in the HR database.

Enforcing Naming Standards

Before the introduction of ADSI, there was little that could be done to incorporate business rules into Windows NT administrative workflows. For example, suppose all workstation accounts created in resource domains are required to be eight characters long, begin with "WKS," and follow a naming standard based upon the business unit the device is assigned to.

Although a common requirement, the default Windows NT tools could provide no method for enforcing such a standard. Neither Server Manager nor User Manager enables you to specify any custom-defined standards for the fields in the SAM, and in turn a user can create accounts that do not accurately follow the naming standards established for the enterprise.

Using ADSI, however, an HTML or Visual Basic form can be developed to enforce a pre-defined naming standard before creating the account.

Automating System Management

Quite often, administrative tasks must be performed upon every workstation in a region, or occasionally, upon the entire enterprise. Whether it is the addition of a new file system share or changing the password of the local administrator account on every machine in the domain, these tasks are very well suited to scripting efforts using ADSI.

To better understand the extent to which ADSI supports system management in the enterprise, consider the following types of management that can be automated using ADSI:

- Domain management
- Exchange Mailbox management
- File session management
- Group management
- IIS Metabase management
- Print management
- Service management
- File Share management
- User management

The following Visual Basic code segment illustrates the power of ADSI by enumerating all computer accounts in the domain and setting the local "administrator" account password to a known value:

```
On Error Resume Next

Dim TargetDomain as String
Dim ADsPath as String
Dim Domain as IADsContainer
Dim Computer as IADsComputer
Dim LocalAdminAccount as IADsUser

TargetDomain = "Resource_Domain_Name"
ADsPath = "WinNT://" & TargetDomain
Set Domain = GetObject(ADsPath)
Domain.Filter=Array("Computer")

For Each Computer in Domain
    Set LocalAdminAccount = GetObject("WinNT://" & TargetDomain & "/" &
    ↳Computer.Name & "/administrator,user")
    LocalAdminAccount.SetPassword ("Tweek@Coffee")
    If Err.Number=0 then Debug.Print "Local administrator password changed on "
    ↳& Computer.Name
    Err.Number = 0
Next
```

In just a few lines of Visual Basic code, you are able to change the local administrator password for every Windows NT workstation in a given resource domain. Consider for a moment how long this would take if you were required to do it manually using User Manager. This same concept can be applied in many ways, allowing the addition of a new "workstation administrators" group in the user domain to be added to the local administrators group on each machine, or perhaps removing a group from all machines in a given resource domain.

These are just a few small examples of the benefits of administrative function automation; as you study each chapter in this book, you will invariably think of dozens of applications to help tackle a particular administrative issue in your enterprise.

Property Cache

In an effort to reduce the amount of time spent traversing the network to retrieve and set properties, ADSI employs a *property caching* model. Every ADSI interface derived from the IADs interface supports this caching model through the GetInfo and SetInfo methods.

GetInfo

The `GetInfo` method is called each time a request for new data is made from the directory. If you wish to retrieve the value of the `FullName` field in the SAM for user Eckth, use the following Visual Basic code:

```
Dim User as IADsUser
Set User = GetObject("WinNT://Domain/Eckth,user")
Debug.Print "The Full Name value for user EckTh is: " & User.FullName
```

Although `User.GetInfo` was never *explicitly* called, any property retrieved from the directory will *implicitly* call the `GetInfo` method. If you reference `User.FullName` again elsewhere in your code, ADSI will return the value held in the property cache rather than performing another lookup in the directory.

SetInfo

ADSI also exposes the `SetInfo` method in the IADs interface to reduce the required number of directory write events. If you are creating a new object in a namespace, you can set several properties upon creation of the object, yet only one write operation will be performed upon the directory. Like the Windows Registry, most directories have been optimized for fast queries, but in exchange for this optimization, sport relatively poor write performance. To minimize network traffic, ADSI's property cache allows you to perform a single write operation, which is best utilized by restricting the number of calls to the `SetInfo` method.

Consider the following Visual Basic code:

```
Dim Container As IADsContainer
Dim User As IADsUser

Set Container = GetObject("WinNT://Domain_Name")
Set User = Container.Create("User", "EckTh")
User.FullName = "Thomas E. Eck"
User.Description = "PSC, Chicago, Intranet Engineering"

User.SetInfo
```

In the preceding example, you create the user, populate the full name field, and write the description field. The only time the directory is ever updated is when `User.SetInfo` is called.

GetInfo/SetInfo Combination

Although the necessity of the `SetInfo` method is rather obvious, the explicit use of the `GetInfo` method may not be quite as clear. Using a combination of the `GetInfo` and `SetInfo` methods found in most ADSI interfaces, a crude transaction server can be implemented.

Consider the following Visual Basic code as an example:

```
Dim User as IADsUser
Dim Retval as Boolean

Set User=GetObject("WinNT://Domain/TEck,user")
User.FullName = "Thomas Eck"
User.Description = "PSC, Stamford, Intranet Engineering"

Retval = MsgBox("Are you sure you wish to change the Fullname, and Description
➥Values for user TEck?", vbYesNo + vbCritical + vbDefaultButton2, ➥"Confirm
Action")

If Retval = vbYes Then
    User.SetInfo 'Commit the transaction to the directory
Else
    User.GetInfo 'Rollback the trans/Repopulate cache with old values.
End If
```

In the preceding example, the property cache is populated with some new values for your test account, but before committing the information to the directory, the user has a chance to roll back the transaction. If the user cancels the changes, the GetInfo method is called explicitly to repopulate the property cache with the old values for the user.

If the transaction is canceled without the explicit call to GetInfo, any subsequent calls to User.FullName or User.Description would reflect the changes that were supposed to be abandoned because the property cache still holds these values.

Namespace Searches

ADSI can act as an OLE-DB provider to allow native database queries to be performed using ActiveX Data Objects (ADO) against directory service namespaces. Considering that queries are the most often performed action on any directory structure, the ability to query a directory as a native OLE-DB source can be a powerful feature. Using ADSI in this way, you can design extremely robust directory service applications that take advantage of result sets derived from table joins between a directory service and an external database.

Unfortunately, the use of ADSI as an OLE-DB provider is only supported when querying against LDAP and NDS namespaces. To search the Windows NT namespace, you must instead enumerate the domain and then manipulate the result set using conditionals. Enumeration examples using ADSI can be found throughout this book, whereas the use of ADSI as an OLE-DB provider is only covered in Chapter 11, "Programmatic Management of LDAP Infrastructures" due to the fact that searches using ADO are only possible in LDAP namespaces.

Security Objects

ADSI provides interfaces for both authorization and authentication against the Active Directory using either NTLM or Kerberos as the authentication method. This incredibly powerful feature enables developers to script secure single-signon solutions using ADSI to authenticate against the Active Directory or another LDAP infrastructure. ADSI allows a secure single-signon mechanism to be brought to every aspect of the enterprise, including intranet and extranet applications. Authentication against the Active Directory using ADSI is covered in more detail in Chapter 12, "Programmatic Management of the Windows 2000 Active Directory."

Interface Support

Although ADSI is easier to use than the corresponding native API calls and allows for more efficient code creation, you must understand the aspects of each namespace that can be manipulated using ADSI. ADSI provides a consistent interface across all namespaces, but certain functionality may be supported only by a particular service provider.

The following table lists the interfaces supported by each ADSI service provider. For a complete reference of individual properties and methods found within each interface and supportability within each namespace, see Appendix B, "ADSI 2.5 Programmer's Reference." For additional provider support information, you may also want to visit http://msdn.microsoft.com.

> **Note**
>
> In Table 1.1, items shown in **bold** are of significant importance to the system administrator.
>
> \+ The plus symbol indicates that at least one element of the interface is supported in the namespace.
>
> \- The minus symbol indicates that this interface is not supported in this namespace. ♦

Table 1.1 Interface Support for Default ADSI Service Providers.

Interface	WinNT	LDAP	NDS	NWCOMPAT
IADs	+	+	+	+
IADsAccessControlEntry	-	+	+	-
IADsAccessControlList	-	+	+	-
IADsAcl	-	-	+	-
IADsBackLink	-	-	+	-
IADsCaseIgnoreList	-	-	+	-
IADsClass	+	+	+	+
IADsCollection	+	-	-	+

Interface Support

Interface	WinNT	LDAP	NDS	NWCOMPAT
IADsComputer	+	-	-	+
IADsComputerOperations	+	-	-	+
IADsContainer	+	+	+	+
IADsDeleteOps	-	+	-	-
IADsDomain	+	-	-	-
IADsEmail	-	-	+	-
IADsExtension	+	+	-	+
IADsFaxNumber	-	-	+	-
IADsFileService	+	-	-	+
IADsFileServiceOperations	+	-	-	+
IADsFileShare	+	-	-	+
IADsGroup	+	+	+	+
IADsHold	-	-	+	-
IADsLargeInteger	-	+	-	-
IADsLocality	-	+	+	-
IADsMembers	+	+	+	+
IADsNamespaces	+	+	+	+
IADsNetAddress	-	-	+	-
IADsO	-	+	+	-
IADsOU	-	+	+	-
IADsObjectOptions	-	+	-	-
IADsOctetList	-	-	+	-
IADsOpenDSObject	+	+	+	-
IADsPath	-	-	+	-
IADsPathname	+	+	+	+
IADsPostalAddress	-	-	+	-
IADsPrintJob	+	-	-	+
IADsPrintJobOperations	+	-	-	+
IADsPrintQueue	+	+	+	+
IADsPrintQueueOperations	+	+	+	+
IADsProperty	+	+	+	+
IADsPropertyEntry	+	+	+	+
IADsPropertyList	+	+	+	+
IADsPropertyValue	+	+	+	+
IADsPropertyValue2	+	+	+	+
IADsReplicaPointer	-	-	+	-

continues ▶

Table 1.1 continued

Interface	WinNT	LDAP	NDS	NWCOMPAT
IADsResource	+	-	-	-
IADsSecurityDescriptor	-	+	+	-
IADsService	+	-	-	-
IADsServiceOperations	+	-	-	-
IADsSession	+	-	-	-
IADsSyntax	+	+	+	+
IADsTimeStamp	-	-	+	-
IADsTypedName	-	-	+	-
IADsUser	+	+	+	+
IDirectoryObject	-	+	+	-
IDirectorySearch	-	+	+	-

Applied Theory: Using ADSI to Migrate from Windows NT 4.0 to Windows 2000

Exploiting the directory service provider abstraction methods found in the ADSI COM objects, ADSI lends itself to becoming an extremely powerful tool to aid the migration from the Windows NT user domain SAM to Windows 2000's Active Directory.

Unlike the Windows NT SAM, the Active Directory can become the central information store for all pertinent employee data. By extending the schema of the Active Directory to add enterprise-specific data fields to each user record, you now have the ability to allow consolidation of multiple external data stores into a single location. In this regard, select data from the corporate Human Resources database can be stored in the Active Directory to allow the creation of extremely robust directory service enabled applications.

Many third-party domain migration tools simply do not account for any fields beyond those originally contained in the NT SAM. If the Active Directory is to become a central repository for user information, these tools provide little functionality beyond the simple creation of a new user object in the Active Directory. To populate the extended fields of the Active Directory, a second process must be instantiated to pull data from an external database source, creating additional development effort.

Rather than investing in third-party migration products (most of which use ADSI) for a one-time migration, forward-thinking managers should instead task internal development teams to learn to use ADSI with Visual

Basic. In the same process used to create a user object in the Active Directory, the extended attributes of each object can be populated with information from an external source, such as the Human Resources database or virtually any ODBC-compliant database platform. Such a scripting effort would reduce the efforts required to later populate this information in the directory after using these third-party utilities. In addition, the time invested to learn ADSI will provide not only for the migration process itself, but also will allow administrators to provide better support for the enterprise *after* the migration.

Summary

Using ADSI, administrators and developers have the tool set required to rapidly build applications that interact with LDAP IIS and Windows NT namespaces. Before the release of ADSI, programmatic manipulation of namespaces was primarily reserved for advanced developers with knowledge of the API calls required to manipulate each namespace. By implementing ADSI as a set of COM objects, Microsoft has enabled the use of high-level automation controllers such as Visual Basic, Perl, Rexx, JavaScript, and VBScript to be used for programmatic namespace manipulation. By allowing such languages to be used, the level of development skill required to use ADSI has been lowered to match the programming talents found in the skill sets of many advanced system administrators.

After learning how to use ADSI in Visual Basic-based COM servers, you can greatly reduce the amount of time spent performing repetitive tasks on multiple objects in any given namespace. Using ADSI enumeration, you can perform operations upon an entire class of objects within a namespace.

Beyond enumeration, it is also possible to join data from external database applications with data contained in the Active Directory or another LDAP namespace using ADSI as an OLE-DB provider. This allows the creation of extremely robust directory applications to service the enterprise, whether for search operations or namespace object attribute manipulation.

ADSI provides the developer and administrator with a set of functions enabling the transformation of theoretical principles to those existing in the practical world. Concepts we have talked about for several years but could never properly implement (such as single-signon), can now be made possible using ADSI and the Active Directory.

Regardless of the directory service infrastructure implemented in your enterprise, taking the time to learn how to use ADSI will surely prove to be an invaluable timesaving investment.

2
Making the Transition: Multi-Tier Development for System Administrators

In the following chapters, you will be presented with code segments and exercises you can use to assemble a fully customized administrative application for your enterprise. As an expert in systems administration, you might be familiar with the topics being discussed, but you might lack some of the development skills required to create a working administrative application. In this chapter, we explore the configuration of the development environment to help you create working applications from the code segments presented in this book. In addition, we will discuss some of the advantages of jumping into the deep end of Visual Basic development by using ADSI in *Component Object Model* (COM) objects.

Although we will discuss some of the fundamental elements of Visual Basic programming and COM development, this chapter is not intended as a comprehensive guide to programming in Visual Basic. If you are new to development, you should examine a text dedicated to Visual Basic so that you can master the fundamental concepts of the language. Many excellent resources about Visual Basic and COM development are available, several of which are described in Appendix C, "Further Reading."

This chapter is an overview of the capabilities of Visual Basic. Although several ADSI code segments are included in the exercises, these are meant only to demonstrate a particular concept—do not be alarmed that the code may seem foreign to you at this point. The chapters that follow will give you a more in-depth discussion of Visual Basic-based ADSI development.

With the disclaimers regarding the scope of this chapter out of the way, we can now get down to the business at hand, which is to show you the power of ADSI, Visual Basic, and COM.

Why Visual Basic?

Although the word "basic" is contained within its title, the power of applications that are built using this robust development environment is anything but rudimentary. Although many administrators think of Visual Basic in terms of crude custom-developed database front-ends, Microsoft Office macros, shareware applications, and those dreadful VBRUNXXX.DLL's, which are required to support older Visual Basic applications, today's Visual Basic development environment can be used to build extremely sophisticated, yet easy to develop, multi-tier applications. With the recent proliferation of Web technology, forward-thinking developers and IT managers are trading in the resource-hungry, network-intensive, natively compiled applications of yesteryear in favor of thinner, easily customized, Web-based applications.

Most other ADSI texts focus on ADSI in *Active Server Page (ASP)* scripts. Although the use of ADSI code directly within an ASP is quick and easy to implement, some problems are inherent in this particular employment, and are discussed in the following sections.

Visual Basic Defines Datatypes in Variable Declarations

As you learn about ADSI, you will become familiar with the datatypes passed in and out of ADSI's methods. To focus purely on ASP scripting using VBScript masks the true datatypes used with each function—as VBScript uses the variant datatype for all variables in the language.

Datatypes play a tremendous role in resource allocation for an application; thus, to display only VBScript robs you of a solid understanding of the datatypes used with ADSI. If you have ever tried converting an application from VBScript to Visual Basic, you know that this can be a daunting task if you do not have a solid programming background. Unless you continue to use variants for all datatypes (a shameless waste of system resources!) you will have an extremely difficult time getting your code to work unless you know the proper datatypes for each argument and return value. By viewing all code examples in this text in Visual Basic, you will gain a better understanding of the datatypes used with ADSI.

Visual Basic Allows Multi-Tier Development

Another problem with implementing ADSI code strictly within ASP is that application logic is intermingled with business logic. This makes it difficult to determine which function is supporting business logic and which function is supporting the proper execution of the application.

This presents particular problems when an organization merges with another entity and business rules change. For example, a recently merged corporation may decide to change its user account-naming standard. If the code to enforce the naming standard is intermingled with the code that actually performs user account creation, the system administrator must test every element in the page to assure that the development effort did not break the core application logic. This may sound trivial, but there has to be a better way to deal with an extremely complex page containing hundreds or thousands of lines of code.

There is indeed a better way, and it is called the *Component Object Model* (COM).

Visual Basic Separates Business Logic from Application Logic with COM

What the rest of the industry refers to as "*n*-tier" (2-tier, 3-tier, 4-tier, and so on) architecture, Microsoft labels with their own moniker: Windows DNA. No matter what you call it, the concept is simple: Efficient application architectures are founded upon separation of business logic and application logic.

Many applications and operating systems use this same concept, including almost every recent release of Microsoft software. The Office product line allows you to "drive" individual office automation applications from Visual Basic using the object model exposed by the office automation suite's type library. If you have ever created a stored procedure in SQL Server or called a batch file from inside another, you can understand the benefits of a procedural approach to programming.

To translate this into a nontechnical example: Imagine that you own a retail store in a shopping center. At the end of the day, you must perform 25 tasks to secure the store and close out the day's business. To help your employees, you create a checklist of items that need to be completed to close the store. After the list is written and distributed, you can simply tell your employees to "close" the store, and they will walk through the 25 steps on the checklist.

This approach makes it easy to perform repetitive or complex tasks within a single atomic unit that can be called using a single command. This concept is the fundamental premise of the Component Object Model (COM). Using COM, you can now provide the correct way to instantiate your object and reference the functions to the Web developer's call, encapsulating all ADSI code within your COM server. Should the underlying infrastructure of your organization change, you can easily change the code in the COM server without requiring the Web developers to redevelop the ASP that references the COM object.

To continue the store example: If you decided to change the store-closing procedure, you could update the task list to reflect the changes, but still tell employees to "close" the store. In this way, you can change the underlying store-closing procedures, but still reference the tasks at hand with a single command.

Visual Basic allows you to create COM objects quickly and easily by compiling code as an ActiveX DLL, and modifying the way subroutines and functions are defined—for example, private versus public procedures or referencing variables by value instead of by reference. The creation of ActiveX DLL's is discussed in the "Developing a COM Server Using Visual Basic and ADSI" section found later in this chapter.

COM Allows Code Reuse

By compiling code into COM objects, Web developers can use any language they choose—as long as the Web server supports it and the scripting language supports automation. If you create a COM object in Visual Basic, you can then allow VBScript developers to reference your object using only a few lines of code. If your Web developers use JavaScript, they too can share the same object. If you want to run an ADSI function within a Windows Scripting Host (WSH) application, you can also use the functions contained within a Visual Basic-developed COM object.

Without COM, the alternative is rather grim: Every time you want to create a user in a new application, you will have to break out this text and write up the appropriate script. Instead, if you choose to use COM, you can create a reusable component library that allows developers to select their functions by instantiating the proper class module and subsequently calling the appropriate function within the COM server.

Establishing the Development Environment

Regardless of the development strategy you choose to pursue, you must install ADSI before using any of this text's code in a Windows NT environment.

> **Note**
>
> *Windows 2000 includes the latest version of ADSI in the base build and does not require separate installation of the ADSI libraries.* ◆

Simply navigate to http://www.microsoft.com/adsi to obtain the ADSI 2.5 installation routine for your operating system and processor architecture.

> **Note**
>
> *If you will be running your ADSI scripts from IIS Active Server Pages on Windows NT 4.0, you must also install the ADSI libraries on your Web server(s).* ♦

If you are using ActiveX Data Objects (ADO) to query the Active Directory or a native LDAP namespace, you may also want to obtain the latest Microsoft Data Access Components (MDAC) release from Microsoft at http://www.microsoft.com/data.

If you want to develop your code as COM objects, you must install Visual Basic on your development workstation. Although VB5 fully supports the creation of COM objects, VB6 offers several enhancements to the language and integration with Microsoft Transaction Server (MTS).

> **Note**
>
> *You must use the Visual Basic Professional edition or the Enterprise edition to create COM objects. Visual Basic Learning Edition does not include the capability to compile native code, which is essential to COM server development.*
>
> *To create COM components for Alpha systems, you must compile your objects using the Enterprise version of Visual Basic on an Alpha development workstation.* ♦

To implement code directly in an ASP, you simply need a text editor (such as Notepad), IIS 3.0 or higher, and ADSI installed on the Web server.

> **Note**
>
> *For examples of each chapter's Visual Basic code segments in VBScript ASP format, refer to the Code Reference Library available in Appendix A, "VBScript Code Reference" and in electronic format from this book's Web site,* http://www.newriders.com/adsi. ♦

Configuring the Visual Basic Environment

With Visual Basic and ADSI installed, you can create a Visual Basic project template that speeds testing and modification of the code segments found in the following chapters. You can start a new project and configure the environment each time manually using the steps outlined in Exercise 2.1, or you can save it as a template to be used when creating a new project that utilizes ADSI.

Exercise 2.1   *Creating a Visual Basic Project Template*

1. Begin by launching Visual Basic.

> **Note**
>
> *For purposes of this exercise, all example images were shot using Visual Basic 6.0 Enterprise on a Windows NT 4.0 Workstation. However, the same steps should apply for either VB 5.0 or VB 6.0.* ♦

2. A dialog box prompts you to create a new project. Create a new project based on the Standard EXE template (see Figure 2.1).

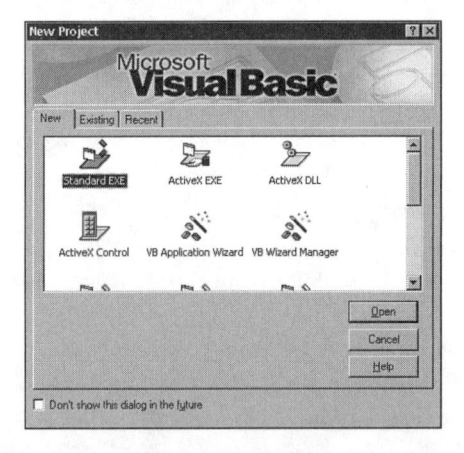

Figure 2.1   *Creating a New Project in Visual Basic.*

> **Note**
>
> *If you disabled this dialog box from presenting on start up, or recently closed another project, simply click File, New Project, and select the Standard EXE icon.* ♦

3. Add a command button to Form1 that will be used to launch the code for testing in your environment (see Figure 2.2). The layout and configuration of the form is unimportant; a simple command button added to the form is adequate.

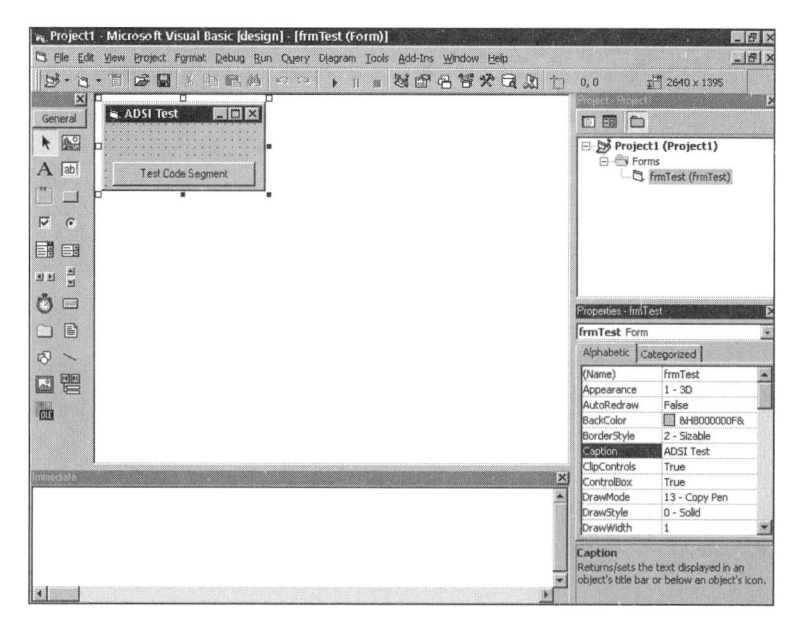

Figure 2.2 *Create a Test Form.*

4. Name the command button *cmdTest*, because the examples that follow will depend on this exact nomenclature within the form.

5. After you arrange the objects on the form, set a reference to the Active DS Type Library (see Figure 2.3). To do this, click Project from the menu bar, then select References.... If you do not see the "Active DS Type Library" entry in the list of references, make sure the ADSI 2.5 libraries are properly installed on your workstation.

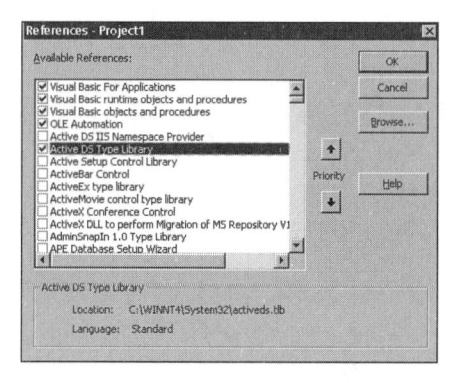

Figure 2.3 *Set a Reference to the Active DS Type Library.*

continues ▶

Exercise 2.1 *continued*

6. Save the form and project for future use. If you plan to do a significant amount of work with ADSI, you can save the project to the Template\Projects directory, which creates an entry in the New Project dialog box. Taking such an action will allow you to create a new project with the reference set and form created immediately upon launching Visual Basic.

Testing Code Segments in a Non-Critical Environment

Establishing a test environment is critical to the successful development of large-scale ADSI operations that invoke the SetInfo method of the IADs interface. It is far too risky to develop ADSI code that can affect the entire scope of your administrative rights within a production environment.

If you have access to a test environment, you will want to make sure that you test your code segments there before attempting to use your code in a production domain. You wield an incredible amount of power with ADSI and Visual Basic—a small coding error can yield potentially catastrophic results reaching to the farthest extent of your administrative privileges in the enterprise. A loop operation to delete all accounts in the user domain may take only a few moments to execute, but could create many hours of work for the disaster recovery team if performed accidently.

Although the underlying APIs still enforce the rules within each namespace, Windows NT depends largely on the administrative tool user interfaces to prevent unexpected results. A malformed ADSI statement could potentially create an object in the namespace that you are unable to delete or access using the GUI tools. This makes an even more compelling case for maintaining a disparate testing and development environment.

If you do not have a formal test environment, set up an isolated PDC that you do not mind re-staging if you corrupt the namespace with a malformed procedure. The only way to reduce the risk of making catastrophic mistakes in a production environment is to assure that your code works as expected in a testing environment.

> **Warning**
>
> *Take time now to establish a proper development and test environment before continuing with the following exercises.* ♦

Using ADSI and Visual Basic Interactively

Microsoft places a tremendous amount of stock in the Microsoft Management Console (MMC) for Windows 2000 administration due to the ability to create custom snap-ins and utilize a common User Interface (UI) for all administrative functions. While the MMC makes great strides in the areas of usability and maintainablilty, it still doesn't allow you to perform tasks on large quantities of objects in the enterprise. Many administrators needing to perform ad hoc administration on thousands of machines (such as adding a new user domain global group to the Administrators local group on each machine in a domain) will find Visual Basic an ideal environment from which they can issue commands responsible for performing such tasks.

Just as Command-Shell scripting works well for automating administrative tasks, you can harness the power of the Visual Basic/ADSI development environment to execute ad hoc administrative tasks in the enterprise.

Exercise 2.2   *Using the Visual Basic IDE as an Administrative Console*

You can test a very simple bit of code that will allow you to enumerate all user accounts defined on a given machine. Although this is not an enterprise-wide code example, it demonstrates how an interactive administration session might use ADSI and VB.

1. Double-click the command button in your code test form. This enables you to write code for the command button's Click event.

2. Insert the indented code so that the code window looks similar to the following:

```
Private Sub cmdTest_Click()
    Dim User As IADsUser
    Dim Container As IADsContainer
    Dim ContainerName As String

    ContainerName = "Computer_Name"

    Set Container = GetObject("WinNT://" & ContainerName)
    Container.Filter = Array("User")
    For Each User In Container
        Debug.Print User.Name
    Next
End Sub
```

3. Replace the ContainerName variable assignment with the NetBIOS name of a machine you want to enumerate. If the name of the target machine is *DEVNYC8521,* then the variable assignment would be
   ```
   ContainerName = DEVNYC8521
   ```

continues ▶

Exercise 2.2   continued

4. Press F5 to run your code.

The Immediate Window displays the usernames of all defined accounts on the target machine.

> **Note**
>
> When enumerating local accounts on member servers and workstations, you can speed up the process significantly by adding the name of the resource domain in the binding string. The syntax to use for the preceding example is
>
>   ContainerName = "ResourceDomain/MachineName" ◆

Although you are displaying the names of the user accounts in the Immediate Window for this exercise, you could easily replace the Debug.Print statement with an operation on each account, such as forcing the password to expire, and so on.

Additionally, you could add a domain enumeration function to enumerate each machine in a resource domain, locate the administrator account, and reset the password to a known value—assuming you have rights to do so. This can be handy for revoking administrative rights for users who know the local administrator password on their NT workstation.

Imagine how much time you can save by using the Visual Basic development environment to issue commands that reach hundreds or even thousands of objects in a given domain. The next time you need to perform an action on a large number of objects, consider using ADSI in the Visual Basic IDE to perform the task.

> **Warning**
>
> With such an increase in power comes a significant increase in the risk you pose to your enterprise when developing new code. If you do not have a test environment in which to run your code, be extremely careful before using your code in a domain-wide operation that writes to a production namespace. ◆

Developing a COM Server Using Visual Basic and ADSI

Although many administrators will soon feel comfortable performing large-scale administrative tasks interactively using Visual Basic, many situations may require a more formal environment from which to initiate their code.

This environment may be a Visual Basic application or even a Web page.

To allow code reuse and increased stability of Web applications, you can compile a COM server to contain your administrative tasks. Once compiled, developers using a variety of languages can utilize the functions within the object.

In Exercise 2.3, you will explore the creation of a simple COM server that generates a new user account in the Windows NT namespace.

Exercise 2.3   *Creating an ActiveX DLL for Account Creation*

1. To eliminate multiple compiles during the development effort, begin by pasting the following code into the Click event procedure for the testing application created earlier. If code exists behind the command button, paste over the top of it, creating the following subroutine:

   ```
   Private Sub cmdTest_Click()
       Dim Container As IADsContainer
       Dim ContainerName As String
       Dim User As IADsUser
       Dim NewUser As String
       
       ContainerName = "Computer_Name"
       
       Set Container = GetObject("WinNT://" & ContainerName)
       NewUser = "ADSI_Test_01"
       Set User = Container.Create("User", NewUser)
       User.SetInfo
   End Sub
   ```

2. After replacing the ContainerName variable assignment with the name of the target computer name, run the code segment using the F5 key. Click the proper command button once to test the code. Close the form.

3. Launch User Manager and select the target computer to examine the machine's local SAM. Alternatively, you can launch User Manager from a command line as follows:
   ```
   usrmgr \\Computer_Name
   ```

   You should see a new user account named *ADSI_Test_01*. Delete this account and return to Visual Basic.

   You have now proven that the Visual Basic code creates a new user account in your environment. Next you will create a procedure from this code, so that it can be used more effectively.

   If the code did not execute successfully, make sure your user account has administrative rights on the workstation or server you are targeting.

continues ▶

Exercise 2.3   *continued*

4. In the General Declarations section, (the top of the code window), add the following:
   ```
   Private Sub CreateUser(ContainerName As String, NewUser As String)
       Dim Container As IADsContainer
       Dim User As IADsUser
       Set Container = GetObject("WinNT://" & ContainerName)
       Set User = Container.Create("User", NewUser)
       User.SetInfo
   End Sub
   ```
   Notice that the ContainerName and NewUser variable declarations and assignments have been removed. The subroutine is now responsible for declaring the variables. The calling statement is responsible for assigning values to the variables.

5. Next, modify the Click event code for cmdTest to call the new subroutine:
   ```
   Private Sub cmdTest_Click()
       Call CreateUser("Computer_Name", "New_User_To_Create")
   End Sub
   ```

6. Replace the *Computer_Name* and *New_User_To_Create* placeholders with the appropriate values and run the code. Click the command button once to test the code and verify that the account was created properly.

   With this procedure in place, you can now reuse the code anywhere you want in the form—as many times as you need, simply by assuring that unique values are passed in for the new user account name.

> **Note**
>
> *Notice that you are not using the form and command button for anything other than calling the procedure. This is a vital concept, as COM servers cannot have any form of graphical user interface. In this example, the form represents the client, and the procedure is on its way to becoming a method defined in a COM server.* ◆

Next, you can modify the procedure code to complete its metamorphosis into a COM server.

7. To begin this procedure, you must first change the declaration of the Sub to be *Public*:
   ```
   Public Sub CreateUser(ContainerName As String, NewUser As String)
   ```

8. Next, you must ensure that data passed in using arguments is passed by value and not by reference (as is the default for Visual Basic):
   ```
   Public Sub CreateUser(ByVal ContainerName As String, ByVal NewUser As
   ↪String)
   ```

9. Copy the entire CreateUser procedure onto the clipboard so that you can insert it into a new class module, which will become your first COM server.
10. Close the current Visual Basic project without saving.
11. Open a New Project, but this time select the ActiveX DLL Project Template.
12. Paste the code into the class module's code window. Rename the project *ADSI_COM* and the class module *UserMgmt*. Meaningful names for projects and class modules is essential in COM development, because these become part of the name required to instantiate the object.

Note

You can put additional class modules into a single ActiveX DLL to allow logical grouping of administrative functions. For example, you could easily create an additional class module for group management, and another for managing services. This is the strategy that will be employed for the COM server creation exercises throughout this text. ◆

Because you are in a new project, you must set a reference to the Active DS Type Library, as performed previously for the Standard EXE project.

13. Click the File menu, then select Make ADSI_COM.DLL... Specify the location for the finished DLL. Visual Basic compiles a new DLL containing the CreateUser function. Close the *ADSI_COM* project.

Note

Notice that only the procedure's first line changed between the code segments used in the Standard EXE project and the ActiveX DLL. ◆

If the code compiles without error, you have compiled your first COM Server using Visual Basic.

Testing the COM Server Using Visual Basic

With your first COM server developed (or using the precompiled COM server from the Web site), you can now look at how the COM server affects development of Visual Basic client applications.

Exercise 2.4   *Using a Custom COM Server in a Visual Basic Project*

1. To test your first ADSI COM server, create a new project based on the Standard EXE template project. Click Project, References. Notice that ADSI_COM appears in the list. Set a reference to this object.
2. Add a command button to the form. Double-click the button, and type the following code into the click event for Command1:

```
Private Sub Command1_Click()
    Dim FirstCOM As ADSI_COM.UserMgmt
    Set FirstCOM = New ADSI_COM.UserMgmt
    Call FirstCOM.CreateUser("ComputerName", "ADSI_COM_Test1")
End Sub
```

If you have Auto List Members enabled, a dialog box appears when you type Call_FirstCOM. The dialog box shows you that a method named CreateUser is available. In addition, when you open the left parenthesis, the proper syntax displays to enable proper use of the CreateUser method.

> *Tip*
>
> *If you have not already done so, replace the* ComputerName *variable declaration with the name of the target machine.* ◆

3. Run the project and click the Command1 command button to test the COM server. Verify that the user account was created using User Manager.
4. If the account named *ADSI_COM_Test1* appears in the list of accounts, you have successfully created an account using your first COM object developed with Visual Basic and ADSI.

Instantiating the COM Object from a VBScript Active Server Page

As businesses evolve into multi-national entities, the development model of these organizations must also evolve to adapt to the bandwidth limitations of WAN communications.

HTML development allows organizations to share rich multimedia applications with remote sites across even the slowest network connection. Content arrives at the client as text and graphic images to be rendered using client resources. This thin-client model is what most organizations are focusing on for new applications as the model scales well and is relatively simple to implement despite the constant evolution of the business.

As such, this text would be far from complete to ignore the desire for readers to implement ADSI functions in a Web environment. While we have been focusing on Visual Basic as the development environment for all code utilizing ADSI, you can easily instantiate a COM object from an ASP, taking full advantage of the power of ADSI from an ASP.

Exercise 2.5 *Instantiating the ADSI_COM.DLL Object from an Active Server Page Script*

1. If you want to use this COM object from IIS, copy the ADSI_COM.DLL to the IIS server. Then, from the server console, open a command window and navigate to the DLL's location. Type the following command to register the DLL:

   ```
   REGSVR32 ADSI_COM.DLL
   ```

   If the registration is successful, a dialog box appears, stating:

   ```
   DllRegisterServer in ADSI_COM.DLL succeeded.
   ```

2. With the proper registry entries now made, you can instantiate the object from an ASP, as follows:

   ```
   <%@ Language=VBScript %>
   <%Dim FirstCOM
   Set FirstCOM = Server.CreateObject("ADSI_COM.UserMgmt")
   Call FirstCOM.CreateUser("Computer_Name","ADSI_COM_ASP1")
   Response.Write Err.Number
   %>
   ```

3. Save the ASP file and set the NTFS permissions so that only Administrators and System can read the file.

4. Verify that either Basic or NTLM authentication is enabled using Internet Service Manager.

5. Test the page using any HTML browser. If a 0 is returned, you successfully created a new user named ADSI_COM_ASP1.

   Although this is a simple example, you should begin to see the power and ease of COM development when combined with an ASP. With a bit of imagination, you can easily add a form to collect the name of the server on which to create the user account and verify that the user account name follows the naming standard for the enterprise. After instantiating the COM server, only a single line of code is needed to actually create a user account.

> **Tip**
>
> *Be sure to set the NTFS permissions on the file so that only Administrators and System have access to the file. If the anonymous account has access to the ASP, the anonymous user account credentials are used. A General Access Denied error message displays, and the operation fails (unless the anonymous account is in the Administrators group).*
>
> *If you receive a General Access Denied message, the problem is usually in NTFS permissions and/or the IIS authentication mode used for the ASP.* ✦

Creating a Delegation Model Using DCOM

If you want non-administrative users to perform administrative tasks in a namespace, you must give users the ability to impersonate another identity when accessing resources.

If you do not care about the security of your enterprise, you could add the anonymous user account to the administrators group, which establishes this impersonation. While functional, taking such an approach allows crafty users to query the IIS Metabase and find the value of the password assigned to this account, thus obtaining the use of a privileged account in the enterprise. Additionally, this opens a floodgate of potential hacking against your enterprise from a Web client.

For those who value the security of their enterprise, more secure methods for impersonating an account identity must be sought. By adding Microsoft Transaction Server (MTS) and the Distributed Component Object Model (DCOM) into the picture, you can run your ADSI-based functions under a different user account—allowing the basis for a delegated administration model.

> **Note**
>
> MTS is a free component (included in the Windows NT Option Pack) and is installed as an integral component of IIS. Although most people think of MTS as simply providing database transaction support, it is also the best method to allow IIS in-process components to participate in DCOM.
>
> Advanced usage of MTS and DCOM is well outside the scope of this text, much less a chapter on COM development. If you want to find more information about these innovation-enabling technologies, check out Appendix C "Further Reading". ♦

Imagine being able to allow your help desk users to reset passwords, disable accounts, or clear an account lockout condition without granting them membership in the "Account Operators," "Domain Admins," or equivilent security group for the user domain. If you have too many administrators in your organization, you can use ADSI, COM, and MTS to create a delegation model that alleviates this risk-laden condition.

Running COM Components in MTS

To avoid running ADSI functions using a privileged account, you can create a delegation model. This model lets users perform administrative tasks without actually being an administrator. For Windows 2000 enterprises, this is usually accomplished using the Active Directory; however, many Windows NT users may want to allow greater levels of granularity to their enterprise administration model.

To further prove the power of COM, Exercise 2.6 will allow you to run the ADSI_COM.DLL COM server you created earlier under an administrative account identity.

Exercise 2.6 *Establishing a Delegation Model Using Microsoft Transaction Server and the Distributed Component Object Model*

1. To begin using MTS, you must first create a new package to run the COM server in (see Figure 2.4).

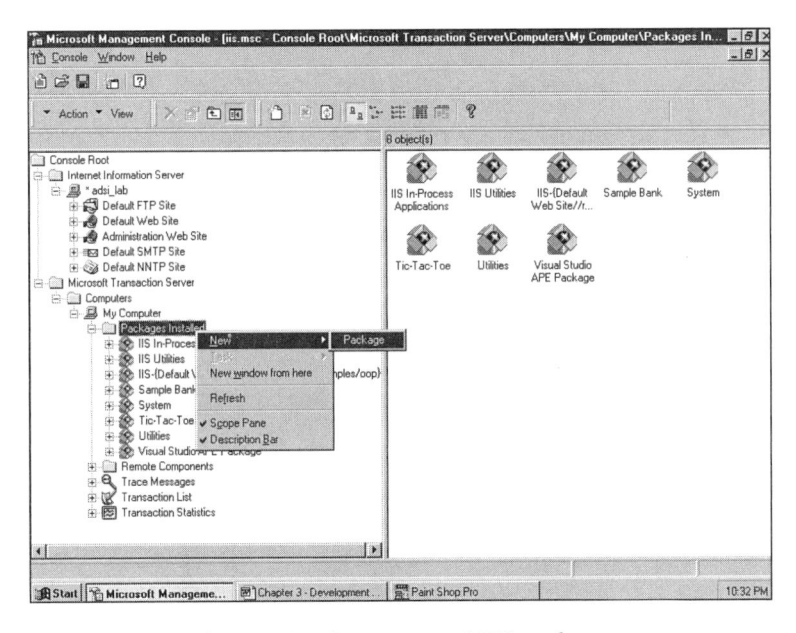

Figure 2.4 *Create a new MTS package.*

2. Open Internet Service Manager, and locate the Microsoft Transaction Server snap-in folder. Expand the folders until you get to the Packages Installed folder. Right-click the folder, select New, Package.

Tip

If you need to install a package on multiple servers, you can export existing packages. Then use the Install pre-built package feature in the Package Wizard (see Figure 2.5) to perform the import. ◆

continues ▶

Exercise 2.6   *continued*

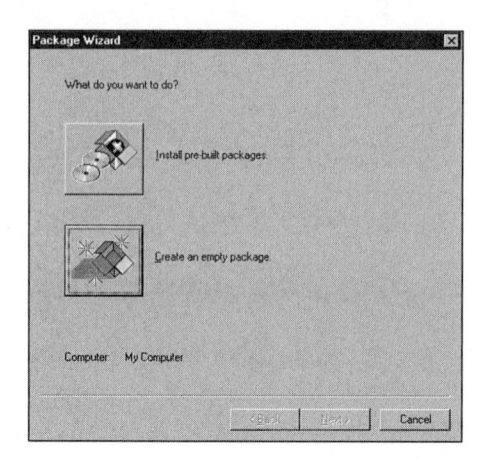

Figure 2.5   *Creating an MTS Package Using the Package Wizard.*

For purposes of this example, you should create an empty package (see Figure 2.6).

Figure 2.6   *Creating an empty package.*

3. Select a descriptive name for the MTS package. This name has no programmatic meaning. It is there strictly as a container for COM components and bears no meaning when components are instantiated from the client application.

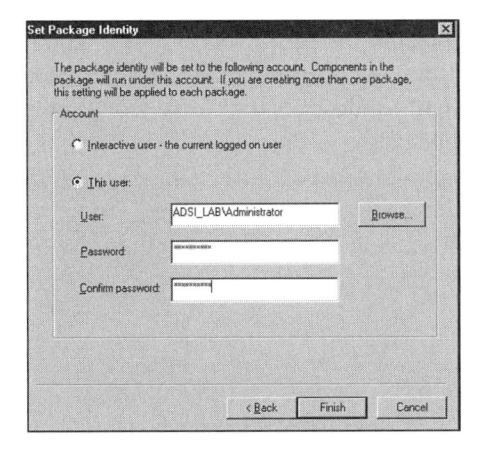

Figure 2.7 *Setting the Package Identity.*

4. If you want to run the components contained within this package under an alternate identity (thus establishing a delegation model), you can do so by specifying the account to use in the Package Identity dialog box. In most cases, you should always use a privileged account for the package identity.

> **Warning**
>
> *If you assign a privileged account to this identity, non-administrative users can use the functions in the COM server. Although this may be desirable in many cases, you should consider all ramifications before taking such an action.* ◆

5. Click Finish to complete the package creation.

   With the package created, you must now populate the package with COM components.

6. Open the new package, and navigate to the Components folder. Right-click the folder, select New, Component.

   If you have already registered the component, you can import it into the package by selecting the *Import components that are already registered* command button.

   For most cases, however, the path of the .DLL is known and can be easily located in the file system. After clicking the Install New Components command button, click the Add Files command button to browse the file structure for the COM server.

7. After you locate the server, click Finish to finalize the installation of the COM server.

To prevent unauthorized use of the COM server, you may want to assign MTS roles to the individual class modules within the COM server. MTS allows you to assign Windows NT security groups to the roles, which are then assigned to each class in the component.

In addition, you might want to use some form of group verification in the COM server to prevent unauthorized use of the procedures contained in the object. This ultimately creates the most granular administrative model available, as each function can then require specific group membership before executing.

> **Note**
>
> A delegated COM server example is included on this book's Web site: http://www.newriders.com/adsi. ♦

Using the technique presented in Exercise 2.6, you have allowed the functions of the COM server to run under a different identity without changing a single line of client code, thus allowing non-administrative users to create a new user account.

When instantiating the object from an ASP, the referenced class module will run under MTS context—improving the stability and increasing the variety of options available to the systems developer.

Summary

In addition to the capability to create COM objects, Visual Basic is an ideal language to help you learn ADSI, as you will need to know the datatypes required and returned by each of the ADSI interface properties and methods.

Also, the Visual Basic IDE allows you to issue commands to production and test environments to perform administrative tasks on a single machine or the entire enterprise. If you require the ability to perform an administrative task on multiple machines, you may soon find yourself launching Visual Basic instead of the MMC to issue the commands. The time spent developing a simple script can yield tremendous returns on your time investment if the number of machines is significantly large.

Although ADSI is at home when it is implemented directly in an ASP, some significant advantages to encapsulating ADSI code in a COM server are

- The reduction of interdependence of business and application code in applications.
- The capability to share code between developers, regardless of development language.
- The capability to impersonate a privileged account to create a delegation model using MTS/DCOM.

Although the exercises in this chapter have merely scratched the surface of COM server development in Visual Basic, hopefully you discovered how easy it is to create a COM object and the many advantages of doing so.

If you do not have access to Visual Basic or do not want to implement your code segments in a COM server, you still have several options. You can download a precompiled COM server from http://www.newriders.com/adsi or you can implement code directly in an ASP by using the VBScript examples found in Appendix A.

In addition, all code examples can be downloaded from http://www.newriders.com/adsi to save the time of inputting the examples by hand. No matter which development strategy you select, by the end of this book, you should have little doubt that ADSI is one of the most important advancements to help enable efficient large-scale enterprise administration.

Part **II**

Exploring the ADSI Service Providers: Windows NT

3 Container Enumeration Methods and Programmatic Domain Account Policy Manipulation

4 Programmatic User Account Manipulation

5 Programmatic Group Manipulation

6 Programmatic Computer and Service Manipulation

7 Programmatic File and Print Resource Management

3

Container Enumeration Methods and Programmatic Domain Account Policy Manipulation

By combining the enumeration code segments found in this chapter with the code found in all chapters in Part II, "Exploring the ADSI Service Providers: Windows NT," of this text, you can quickly create applications that can manipulate either the entire enterprise or just a small subset of the Windows NT namespace.

Used alone, enumeration functions provide little additional information than that found in User Manager or Server Manager. However, when used recursively or when combined with the object manipulation code segments found in this text, you can reduce tedious manual tasks to just a few lines of code.

The IADsDomain interface allows programmatic manipulation of the account policy for a given domain. Just as you can programmatically manipulate the password age or password history length for a single user account using the IADsUser interface, you can also query and modify the default account lockout policy, password age, password length, and so on, that apply to all user accounts in a specific domain.

This chapter will explore the programmatic methods required to manipulate these functions using script written in the Visual Basic Integrated Development Environment (IDE). In particular, we will take a look at the following:

- Enumerating domains in the Windows NT namespace
- Managing Windows NT domain properties
- Enumerating objects within a domain or computer
- Creating and removing objects using IADsContainer

Enumerating Domains in the Windows NT Namespace

Using ADSI, it is surprisingly simple to obtain the entire list of Windows NT domains in the enterprise. This is performed by binding to the WinNT: namespace identifier, then using a *For...Each* loop to enumerate all the members visible to your machine.

This enumeration process can be especially useful upon initialization of a Visual Basic or Web-based administration application. By allowing the user to choose the target domain from a drop-down combo box, you will reduce typographical errors and increase ergonomic efficiency of the application by eliminating the multiple keystrokes required to enter the name of the domain to be managed. This also allows you to implement more efficient code, as there is little need to perform significant error checking on a target domain that was passed into a function using such an enumeration process.

Enumerating Domains Using Visual Basic

You can display all domains in the Windows NT namespace by using the following Visual Basic code:

```
Dim NameSpace as IADsContainer
Dim Domain as IADs

Set NameSpace = GetObject("WinNT:")

For Each Domain in Namespace
    Debug.Print Domain.Name
Next
```

Tip

When implemented upon initialization of a custom administrative application, using the previous code in combination with a drop-down combo box or tree-view control can be an especially effective mechanism to select the domain to be managed. ♦

Managing Windows NT Domain Properties

After the user has chosen the domain to be managed, you can manipulate the default account policy settings for the domain. The properties found in the IADsDomain interface directly correlate to those found in the Account Policy dialog box in User Manager for Domains. The Account Policy dialog box is shown in Figure 3.1.

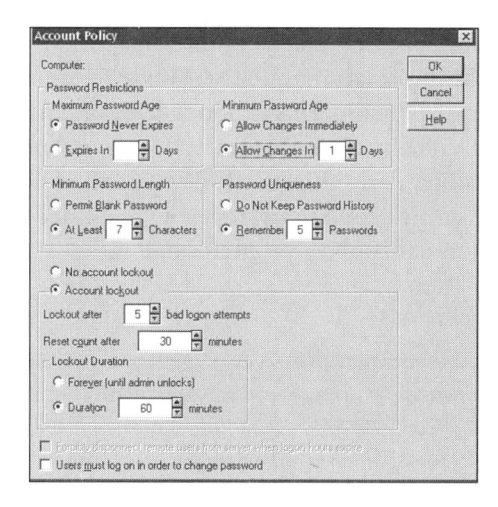

Figure 3.1 *Account Policy dialog box in User Manager for Domains.*

Binding Domains Using Visual Basic

Before you can manipulate the properties of the domain, you must first bind to the domain container object. Use the following Visual Basic code to bind the domain prior to manipulating any of the account policy properties for the domain:

```
Dim Domain as IADsDomain
Dim DomainName as String
DomainName = "Domain_Name_To_Manage"
Set Domain = GetObject("WinNT://DomainName, domain")
```

If you plan to set or query the values for multiple properties in a single domain, you need to bind the domain only once within the lifetime of the function.

> *Note*
>
> *The binding operation can be costly in terms of application performance, so use bindings judiciously to maximize overall application responsiveness. Binding performance is substantially increased by specifying the class name with the object, as follows:* `GetObject("WinNt://DomainName, domain")`. ♦

If the code will set the values of multiple properties, you need to call the SetInfo method only once during the lifetime of the code segment. Again, following this course of action will yield better application performance due to decreased network traffic because the write operation performed on the namespace is executed only once.

If you must touch several domains in the same script, use the SetInfo method to write the information to the SAM before beginning the binding operation on the new domain. This action will ensure that the proper data was written to the domain before beginning to repopulate the property cache with information derived from the new domain.

By binding and writing to the directory only once per managed domain, you will achieve optimal application performance.

> ### Security Considerations
> *An account with administrative privileges in the bound domain is required to query or set all properties used for account policy manipulation. A run-time automation error (usually -2147023570/8007052e) will be returned if the user account does not have sufficient privileges when attempting to query or set these properties.* ♦

Querying and Setting a New Value for *AutoUnlockInterval*

The AutoUnlockInterval property of the IADsDomain interface allows you to set the amount of time to wait before automatically resetting the account lockout status flag on a locked-out user account. In User Manager's Account Policy dialog box, this interface programmatically manipulates the *Lockout Duration* parameter.

Querying *AutoUnlockInterval* Using Visual Basic

By dimensioning a long datatype variable, you can use the following Visual Basic code to find the number of seconds a user will be required to wait before an account lockout condition is reset automatically:

```
Dim Domain as IADsDomain
Dim DomainName as String
DomainName = "Domain_Name_To_Manage"
Set Domain = GetObject("WinNT://" & DomainName)

Dim RetVal as Long
RetVal = Domain.AutoUnlockInterval
Debug.Print RetVal
```

Setting a New Value for *AutoUnlockInterval* Using Visual Basic

If you wish to change the amount of time a user must wait before the user account is automatically unlocked, assign the AutoUnlockInterval property a new value (in seconds) and use the SetInfo method to write the changes back to the namespace:

```
Dim Domain as IADsDomain
Dim DomainName as String
DomainName = "Domain_Name_To_Manage"
Set Domain = GetObject("WinNT://" & DomainName)
```

```
Dim NewValue as Integer
NewValue = 7200
Domain.AutoUnlockInterval = NewValue
Domain.SetInfo
```

By setting the `AutoUnlockInterval` property to 7,200 and returning to User Manager for Domains, the new value for Lockout Duration is now 120 minutes. Although the Account Policy dialog box shows the value in minutes, the IADsDomain `AutoUnlockInterval` property expects the value assigned to this property to be entered in seconds.

Tip

To set the lockout duration to Forever (Until Admin Unlocks), set the value of the `AutoUnlockInterval` *property to -1 in your code.* ◆

Querying and Setting a New Value for *LockoutObservationInterval*

The `LockoutObservationInterval` property determines the amount of time the domain controller will keep count of bad login attempts for the domain before resetting a user's `BadLoginCount` value back to 0. This value directly correlates to the Reset Count After *n* Minutes setting in the Account Policy dialog box.

Querying *LockoutObservationInterval* Using Visual Basic

Like the `AutoUnlockInterval` property, the `LockoutObservationInterval` is stored in seconds. To ensure that you do not overflow the integer datatype, you should always store this value using a long datatype.

Consider the following Visual Basic code to query the time window during which Windows NT will increment the BadLoginCount counter:

```
Dim Domain as IADsDomain
Dim DomainName as String
DomainName = "Domain_Name_To_Manage"
Set Domain = GetObject("WinNT://" & DomainName)

Dim RetVal as Long
RetVal = Domain.LockOutObservationInterval
Debug.Print RetVal
```

Setting a New Value for *LockoutObservationInterval* Using Visual Basic

If you want to change the amount of time Windows NT monitors bad login attempts in the domain, you can set a new value for the `LockoutObservationInterval` property using the following Visual Basic code:

```
Dim Domain as IADsDomain
Dim DomainName as String
DomainName = "Domain_Name_To_Manage"
Set Domain = GetObject("WinNT://" & DomainName)
```

```
Dim NewValue as Long
NewValue = 1800
Domain.LockoutObservationInterval = NewValue
Domain.SetInfo
```

> **Tip**
>
> By setting this value to 1800, the domain controller will reset its count of bad login attempts for all user accounts after 30 minutes has elapsed. ♦

Querying and Setting a New Value for *MaxBadPasswordsAllowed*

Coupled with the `LockoutObservationInterval` property, the `MaxBadPasswordsAllowed` value establishes the number of bad password attempts allowed before locking out the account. This value correlates to the Lockout After *n* Bad Logon Attempts setting in the Account Policy dialog box.

Querying *MaxBadPasswordsAllowed* Using Visual Basic

Using the following Visual Basic code, a value between 0 and 999 will be returned, representing the number of logons a user can attempt before the account is locked out:

```
Dim Domain as IADsDomain
Dim DomainName as String
DomainName = "Domain_Name_To_Manage"
Set Domain = GetObject("WinNT://" & DomainName)

Dim RetVal as Integer
RetVal = Domain.MaxBadPasswordsAllowed
Debug.Print RetVal
```

Setting a New Value for *MaxBadPasswordsAllowed* Using Visual Basic

To set a new value for the number of bad logon attempts for a given domain, simply assign a new integer value to the `MaxBadPasswordsAllowed` property. This assignment can be performed directly (`Domain.MaxBadPasswordsAllowed = 4`) or indirectly by assigning a variable to the property.

Use the following Visual Basic code to set a new value for the number of bad logon attempts for a given domain:

```
Dim Domain as IADsDomain
Dim DomainName as String
DomainName = "Domain_Name_To_Manage"
Set Domain = GetObject("WinNT://" & DomainName)
```

```
Dim NewValue as Integer
NewValue = 5
Domain.MaxBadPasswordsAllowed = NewValue
Domain.SetInfo
```

Querying and Setting a New Value for *MaxPasswordAge*

To prevent risks associated with users retaining passwords indefinitely, most enterprises enforce a password expiration policy for the domain. You can programmatically manipulate the Maximum Password Age setting found in the User Manager for the Domains Account Policy dialog box using the MaxPasswordAge property of the IADsDomain interface.

Querying *MaxPasswordAge* Using Visual Basic

Consider the following Visual Basic code to find how many days a user can retain a password before it expires:

```
Dim Domain as IADsDomain
Dim DomainName as String
DomainName = "Domain_Name_To_Manage"
Set Domain = GetObject("WinNT://" & DomainName)

Dim RetVal as Long
RetVal = Domain.MaxPasswordAge
RetVal = RetVal / 86400
Debug.Print RetVal
```

> *Note*
>
> *Despite the fact that User Manager for Domains uses days as the unit of measure for this property, the* MaxPasswordAge *property is set using the number of seconds until the password expires.*
>
> *To quickly convert the number of days to seconds, simply multiply the number of days until password expiration by 86,400 and use the resulting number to set the property value. Conversely, to convert the queried value for* MaxPasswordAge *back into the number of days, simply divide the result by 86,400.*
>
> *If you wish to allow all users to retain passwords for an infinite amount of time, set the* MaxPasswordAge *property to -1.* ◆

Setting a New Value for *MaxPasswordAge* Using Visual Basic

If you want passwords to expire at a regular interval for users in the domain, you can assign a value to the MaxPasswordAge property of the IADsDomain interface using the following Visual Basic code:

```
Dim Domain as IADsDomain
Dim DomainName as String
DomainName = "Domain_Name_To_Manage"
Set Domain = GetObject("WinNT://" & DomainName)
```

```
Dim NewValue as Long
NewValue = 2592000
Domain.MaxPasswordAge = NewValue
Domain.SetInfo
```

Querying and Setting a New Value for *MinPasswordAge*

Just as you can force a user to change his or her password at specified intervals, you can also force retention of a chosen password for a specific duration. If your enterprise forces password uniqueness, you should also take advantage of the Windows NT Minimum Password Age setting. This property prevents users from overriding the password history setting by forcing the user to retain a password for a specified amount of time.

Querying *MinPasswordAge* Using Visual Basic

Use the following Visual Basic code to find the minimum amount of time a user must wait before a new password can be chosen:

```
Dim Domain as IADsDomain
Dim DomainName as String
DomainName = "Domain_Name_To_Manage"
Set Domain = GetObject("WinNT://" & DomainName)

Dim RetVal as Long
RetVal = Domain.MinPasswordAge
RetVal = RetVal / 86400
Debug.Print RetVal
```

Setting a New Value for *MinPasswordAge* Using Visual Basic

Use the following Visual Basic code to force users to wait a specified amount of time before changing their account password:

```
Dim Domain as IADsDomain
Dim DomainName as String
DomainName = "Domain_Name_To_Manage"
Set Domain = GetObject("WinNT://" & DomainName)

Dim NewValue as Long
NewValue = 0
Domain.MinPasswordAge = NewValue
Domain.SetInfo
```

> **Tip**
>
> Once again, the `MinPasswordAge` property is stored using seconds as the unit of measure. To allow users to change passwords immediately, set this value to 0. ◆

Querying and Setting a New Value for *MinPasswordLength*

Using the `MinPasswordLength` property of the IADsDomain interface, you can manipulate the Minimum Password Length field found in the Account Policy dialog box in User Manager for Domains. This setting forces all domain users to use passwords greater than or equal to the length specified by this setting.

Most enterprises force users to use at least six characters for all passwords in order to increase the time required for brute-force password-cracking utilities to obtain a user's password. Although there are many other factors contributing to the ease with which such tools can determine a password, extending the length of all user account passwords is a good first step to prevent compromise of a domain user account.

> **Tip**
>
> *Ideally, the best protection against brute-force hash comparison utilities is to encrypt the SAM using the* `SYSKEY` *utility, to physically secure any emergency repair disks created with the* `-s` *parameter, and to limit physical access to all domain controllers.* ♦

Querying *MinPasswordLength* Using Visual Basic

To find the number of characters required for passwords used on all domain user accounts, use the following Visual Basic code:

```
Dim Domain as IADsDomain
Dim DomainName as String
DomainName = "Domain_Name_To_Manage"
Set Domain = GetObject("WinNT://" & DomainName)

Dim RetVal as Long
RetVal = Domain.MinPasswordLength
Debug.Print RetVal
```

Setting a New Value for *MinPasswordLength* Using Visual Basic

By assigning a value to the `MinPasswordLength` property of the IADsDomain interface, you can establish the minimum number of characters required for all domain passwords. This setting does not force current users that do not comply with the value of this property to change their passwords, but simply enforces all new password changes to use at least the number of characters specified by the `MinPasswordLength` property.

Use the following Visual Basic code to set a new value for `MinPasswordLength`:

```
Dim Domain as IADsDomain
Dim DomainName as String
DomainName = "Domain_Name_To_Manage"
Set Domain = GetObject("WinNT://" & DomainName)
```

```
Dim NewValue as Long
NewValue = 7
Domain.MinPasswordLength = NewValue
Domain.SetInfo
```

> **Tip**
>
> *If you wish to allow blank passwords to be used in the domain, set the value of* `MinPasswordLength` *to –1.* ◆

Querying and Setting a New Value for *PasswordHistoryLength*

`PasswordHistoryLength` sets the number of passwords Windows NT will store for each user in the domain. This security feature prevents users from using the same password for each password change performed. Programmatically manipulating this value will cause changes to be seen immediately in the Password Uniqueness data field in User Manager's Account Policy dialog box.

Querying *PasswordHistoryLength* Using Visual Basic

To find out how many user passwords will be "remembered" by Windows NT, use the following Visual Basic code:

```
Dim Domain as IADsDomain
Dim DomainName as String
DomainName = "Domain_Name_To_Manage"
Set Domain = GetObject("WinNT://" & DomainName)

Dim RetVal as Long
RetVal = Domain.PasswordHistoryLength
Debug.Print RetVal
```

Setting a New Value for *PasswordHistoryLength* Using Visual Basic

If you wish to force users to use unique passwords for each password change performed, use the following Visual Basic code to set a new value to the IADsDomain `PasswordHistoryLength` property:

```
Dim Domain as IADsDomain
Dim DomainName as String
DomainName = "Domain_Name_To_Manage"
Set Domain = GetObject("WinNT://" & DomainName)

Dim NewValue as Long
NewValue = 3
Domain.PasswordHistoryLength = NewValue
Domain.SetInfo
```

When performing a password change request, Windows NT will check to make sure the new password you are requesting does not equal the value of any of the last passwords used, up to the value of `PasswordHistoryLength`.

Tip

To disable password history, set the `PasswordHistoryLength` *property to –1.* ◆

Enumerating Objects Within a Domain or Computer

After you have obtained the name of the domain (or a member server/workstation) using enumeration, you will most likely wish to view the objects within the specified container. To retrieve the contents of the domain container, simply bind to the container object itself. You can then use a *For...Each* loop to retrieve the contents of the container for display or manipulation.

This enumeration method will return the entire contents of any SAM—whether it is the SAM on a domain controller, member server, or workstation.

Enumerating a Generic Container

To best understand the concept of container enumeration, imagine a file cabinet containing photographs from each of the vacations you have taken during your life. You might have a drawer (representing a container) with file folders labeled with each of the locations you have visited (also containers). Within each of these folders, you have placed each of the photos of your trip.

When you enumerate a container, you select a container and look through all the objects within it. In the vacation photograph example, this would be analogous to selecting a file folder and examining each of the photos in it one by one. When you enumerate the "container" in this way, you view all objects within it—whether they are images of your spouse, scenic photos, or even those photos you took with the camera strap blocking the subject.

Enumerating a Generic Container Using Visual Basic

Use the following Visual Basic code to enumerate all objects within any container:

```
Dim Container as IADsContainer
Dim ContainerName as String
ContainerName = "Container_Name_To_Manage"
Set Container = GetObject("WinNT://" & ContainerName)
```

```
Dim LeafObject as IADs
For Each LeafObject in Container
    Debug.Print LeafObject.Name
Next
```

> **Tip**
>
> To enumerate a domain, simply replace the Container_Name_To_Manage variable assignment with a valid domain name. To enumerate a workstation or member server, specify the domain name and computer name as Domain_Name/Computer_Name. ♦

Applying Filters for Enumeration

The previous code segments will return objects of all classes contained within the domain (or local SAM database), as they do not specify which type of objects you seek within the given container. If these code segments were run against a domain containing many objects, the returned result set is likely to be much larger than you require. To help reduce the size of the result set returned from such queries, ADSI allows specification of a filter to be used for the enumeration process.

In the case of a domain object in the Windows NT namespace, these filters may include user accounts, groups, computer accounts, services, or just about any object class. Applying a filter to the enumeration process may substantially increase the performance of the query and often provides better use of system resources.

To continue the photography example, if you wished to show the photographs of your recent vacation to a colleague, you would likely remove all images you deem members of the "flawed" or "boring" classes.

Enumerating User Accounts Using Visual Basic

By setting the IADsContainer `Filter` property to an array containing the string `"User"`, you can narrow the enumeration of a container down to objects belonging to the User class. Use the following Visual Basic code as a guide:

```
Dim Container as IADsContainer
Dim ContainerName as String
ContainerName = "Container_Name_To_Manage"
Set Container = GetObject("WinNT://" & ContainerName)

Container.Filter = Array("User")
Dim User as IADsUser
For Each User in Container
    Debug.Print User.Name
Next
```

Enumerating Computer Accounts Using Visual Basic
By changing the IADsContainer Filter property to "Computer," you can enumerate all computer accounts defined in the Windows NT SAM. Use the following Visual Basic code as a guide:

```
Dim Container as IADsContainer
Dim ContainerName as String
ContainerName = "Container_Name_To_Manage"
Set Container = GetObject("WinNT://" & ContainerName)

Container.Filter = Array("Computer")
Dim Computer as IADsComputer
For Each Computer in Container
     Debug.Print Computer.Name
Next
```

Enumerating Groups Using Visual Basic
If you wish to enumerate all groups defined in the Windows NT SAM, you can easily do so using the following Visual Basic code:

```
Dim Container as IADsContainer
Dim ContainerName as String
ContainerName = "Container_Name_To_Manage"
Set Container = GetObject("WinNT://" & ContainerName)

Container.Filter = Array("Group")
Dim Group as IADsGroup
For Each Group in Container
     Debug.Print Group.Name
Next
```

> *Tip*
>
> *The preceding code example shows all group objects and does not distinguish between local and global groups. If you wish to view only local groups, you can set the IADsContainer* Filter *property to* `"Array("LocalGroup")"`.
>
> *Likewise, if you wish to view all global groups in the domain, you can set the IADsContainer* Filter *property to* `"Array("GlobalGroup")"`. ♦

Creating and Deleting Objects Using IADsContainer
As a container object, a domain must expose the ability to create and remove objects within the container. Whether managing a resource domain or a user domain, the Create and Delete methods of the IADsContainer interface allow addition and removal of computer accounts, user accounts, and groups in the domain.

> **Note**
>
> *An account with administrative privileges in the bound domain is required to add or remove objects in the domain container. A run-time error (-2147023570/8007052e) will be returned if the user account does not have sufficient privileges when attempting to add or remove an object from the domain container.* ♦

Adding and Removing Computer Accounts

For any Windows NT machine to participate in domain security, it must first have a computer account created in the resource domain. Typically, the creation of such an account is performed using Server Manager.

Using ADSI, you can perform the addition and removal of machine accounts with the distinct advantage of being able to script and automate the creation/removal of new machine accounts.

Adding a New Computer Account Using Visual Basic

Contrary to popular understanding, a computer account is actually a user account with a few exceptions:

- The object must be created using the "computer" class.
- The object must have the user flag ADS_UF_WORKSTATION_TRUST_ACCOUNT (0x1000) set.
- The initial password for the account must be set to the name of the machine in lower case.

Use the following Visual Basic code to create a new computer account in the domain:

```
Dim Container as IADsContainer
Dim ContainerName as String
Dim ComputerAccount as IADsUser
ContainerName = "Container_Name_To_Manage"
Set Container = GetObject("WinNT://" & ContainerName)

Dim Computer as IADsComputer
Dim NewComputer as String
NewComputer = "Computer_Account_To_Create"

Set Computer = Container.Create("Computer", UCase(NewComputer))
Computer.SetInfo

Set ComputerAccount = GetObject("WinNT://" & ContainerName & "/" & NewComputer &
↪"$,user")
ComputerAccount.Put "UserFlags", (ComputerAccount.Get("UserFlags") Or &H1000)
ComputerAccount.SetPassword (LCase(NewComputer))
ComputerAccount.SetInfo
```

> **Note**
>
> *Notice that three bindings are taking place in this example. After binding the container, a new computer object is created and written to the namespace. Then, the new object is bound as a user object and several user account properties are set to allow the machine to join the domain.* ◆

Removing a Computer Account Using Visual Basic

To remove a computer account, simply bind to the container object and call the `Delete` method on the account to remove it from the container.

Unlike the `Create` method, deletions are performed immediately and do not require a call to the `SetInfo` method to commit the change to the SAM.

```
Dim Container as IADsContainer
Dim ContainerName as String
ContainerName = "Container_Name_To_Manage"
Set Container = GetObject("WinNT://" & ContainerName)

Dim ComputerToRemove as String
ComputerToRemove = "Computer_Account_To_Remove"

Call Container.Delete("Computer", ComputerToRemove)
```

Adding, Removing, and Renaming User Accounts

Using the IADsContainer and IADsUser objects, you can begin the process of creating a new user in the domain. This process is similar to creating a new user account using User Manager for Domains without setting any of the extended properties for the account (such as full name, description, group membership, password, and so on). These properties will be covered in great detail in Chapter 4, "Programmatic User Account Manipulation".

Although the variable names and data types are changed to accommodate the class of the new object, the syntax used to create a new user or group is nearly identical for each class. Additionally, you can rename user accounts using the IADsContainer `MoveHere` method.

Adding a New User Account Using Visual Basic

After binding to the container, you can simply call the IADsContainer `Create` method to establish a new object in the container. Use the following Visual Basic code to add a new user account:

```
Dim Container as IADsContainer
Dim ContainerName as String
ContainerName = "Container_Name_To_Manage"
Set Container = GetObject("WinNT://" & ContainerName)
```

```
Dim User as IADsUser
Dim NewUser as String
NewUser = "User_Account_To_Create"

Set User = Container.Create("User", NewUser)
User.SetInfo
```

> **Tip**
>
> *If you wish to set properties of the user object, such as the description or full name associated with the account, you should do so before calling the IADs* SetInfo *method. Note that* set password *is an immediate operation. The account must exist before attempting any password manipulation function calls. See Chapter 4 for more information on User Account property manipulation.* ◆

Removing a User Account Using Visual Basic

Unlike the addition of a new object in a container, removal of an object from a container requires only a call to the Delete method of the IADsContainer interface. Use the following Visual Basic code to remove a user account:

```
Dim Container as IADsContainer
Dim ContainerName as String
ContainerName = "Container_Name_To_Manage"
Set Container = GetObject("WinNT://" & ContainerName)

Dim UserToRemove as String
UserToRemove = "User_Account_To_Remove"
Call Container.Delete("User", UserToRemove)
```

Renaming a User Account Using Visual Basic

Because each account is identified by its security identifier (SID), Windows NT allows you to easily rename user accounts. To do this programmatically, simply use the IADsContainer MoveHere method to change the name of the account. Although the name has changed, the SID has remained the same, leaving all access control lists (ACLs) intact. Use the following Visual Basic code to rename a user account:

```
Dim Container As IADsContainer
Dim ContainerName As String
Dim OldName As String
Dim User As IADsUser
Dim NewUser As IADsUser
Dim NewName As String
OldName = "Old_Account_Name"
NewName = "New_Account_Name"
ContainerName = "Target_Domain_Name"
```

```
Set Container = GetObject("WinNT://" & ContainerName)
Set User = GetObject("WinNT://" & ContainerName & "/" & OldName & ",user")
Set NewUser = Container.MoveHere(User.ADsPath, NewName)
Set User = Nothing
```

Adding and Removing Groups

Once again, by making a simple change to the name of the class of object to be manipulated, the same code can be reused for group creation and deletion.

You can determine the default group type by looking at the type of object that is bound. For example, if you bind to a local workstation SAM, you are permitted only to create a local group, and thus this is the default group type created when the Create method of IADsContainer is called.

By default, a domain controller binding will yield the creation of a global group when the Create method is called. To prevent such ambiguity when creating groups, you can assign an ADSI constant to the GroupType attribute to explicitly state which group type you wish to create.

Adding a New Local Group Using Visual Basic

To add a local group on a domain controller, member server, or workstation, set the GroupType parameter to ADS_GROUP_TYPE_LOCAL_GROUP (0x4) after calling the Create method of the IADsContainer interface. Use the following Visual Basic code to add a new local group:

```
Dim Container as IADsContainer
Dim ContainerName as String
ContainerName = "Container_Name_To_Manage"
Set Container = GetObject("WinNT://" & ContainerName)

Dim Group as IADsGroup
Dim NewGroup as String
NewGroup = "Requested_Groupname"

Set Group = Container.Create("Group", NewGroup)
Group.Put "groupType", 4
Group.SetInfo
```

Adding a New Global Group Using Visual Basic

Just as you can specify that the group to be created should belong to the LocalGroup class, you can create global groups on domain controllers by specifying the ADS_GROUP_TYPE_GLOBAL_GROUP (0x2) parameter when creating a new group object in the container. Use the following Visual Basic code to add a new global group:

```
Dim Container as IADsContainer
Dim ContainerName as String
ContainerName = "Container_Name_To_Manage"
Set Container = GetObject("WinNT://" & ContainerName)
```

```
Dim Group as IADsGroup
Dim NewGroup as String
NewGroup = "Requested_Groupname"

Set Group = Container.Create("Group", NewGroup)
Group.Put "groupType", 2
Group.SetInfo
```

> **Note**
>
> *Despite the difference in classes, Windows NT does not allow the coexistence of a local group and a global group with the same name.* ♦

Removing a Group Using Visual Basic

In the removal process, Windows NT does not care if the group object is a local group or a global group, so you need not specify an explicit group class. In these cases, the generic "Group" class will not yield any ambiguity when binding to the group object that you wish to remove. Use the following Visual Basic code to remove a group:

```
Dim Container as IADsContainer
Dim ContainerName as String
ContainerName = "Container_Name_To_Manage"
Set Container = GetObject("WinNT://" & ContainerName)

Dim GroupToRemove as String
GroupToRemove = "Group_To_Remove"
Call Container.Delete("Group", GroupToRemove)
```

Creating the NTContainerManagement Class Module

In this section, you will begin the first of many exercises throughout Part II that will ultimately yield the creation of the NTAdmin.DLL COM server.

By using a class module for the creation of new objects in a container and the manipulation of domain properties, you can easily separate business logic from application logic. This approach is desirable if you want to create code that you can reuse for any administrative application you might be working on.

In keeping with today's n-tier development standards, you can create a COM object containing all the container and domain property manipulation code found in this chapter. The creation of a COM server is desirable if you want to use this code with a non-administrative account (delegated administration) or if you wish to incorporate additional logic into a single atomic function.

Exercise 3.1 *Creating NTAdmin.DLL: Domain and Container Management Functions*

1. Create a new ActiveX DLL Visual Basic project.
2. Set a reference to the Active DS Type Library by clicking the Project menu, selecting References..., and placing a checkmark next to the Active DS Type Library entry. Click the OK command button to exit the References–Project1 dialog box.
3. Rename Project1 as **NTAdmin**.
4. Rename the Class1 class module as **NTContainerManagement**.
5. Enter the following code into the General Declarations section of the class module:

```
Public Function EnumerateNamespace() As Variant
    On Error Resume Next
    Dim Domain As IADs
    Dim NewElement() As Variant
    Dim NameSpace As IADsContainer
    Dim i As Long
    Set NameSpace = GetObject("WinNT:")
    For Each Domain In NameSpace
        i = UBound(NewElement) + 1
        ReDim Preserve NewElement(i)
        NewElement(i) = Domain.Name
    Next
    EnumerateNamespace = NewElement
End Function

Public Function QueryDomainProp(ByVal DomainName As String, ByVal PropertyName As
➥String) As Long
    Dim Domain As IADsDomain
    Dim ADsPath As String
    ADsPath = "WinNT://" & DomainName
    Set Domain = GetObject(ADsPath)
    Select Case UCase(PropertyName)
        Case "AUTOUNLOCKINTERVAL"
            QueryDomainProp = Domain.AutoUnlockInterval
        Case "LOCKOUTOBSERVATIONINTERVAL"
            QueryDomainProp = Domain.LockoutObservationInterval
        Case "MAXBADPASSWORDSALLOWED"
            QueryDomainProp = Domain.MaxBadPasswordsAllowed
        Case "MAXPASSWORDAGE"
            QueryDomainProp = Domain.MaxPasswordAge
        Case "MINPASSWORDAGE"
            QueryDomainProp = Domain.MinPasswordAge
        Case "MINPASSWORDLENGTH"
            QueryDomainProp = Domain.MinPasswordLength
        Case "PASSWORDHISTORYLENGTH"
            QueryDomainProp = Domain.PasswordHistoryLength
    End Select
```

continues ▶

Exercise 3.1 *continued*

```
End Function

Public Function SetDomainProp(ByVal DomainName As String, ByVal PropertyName As
⇢String, ByVal NewValue As Long) As Boolean
    Dim Domain As IADsDomain
    Dim ADsPath As String
    Dim SetDomainPropStatus As Long
    ADsPath = "WinNT://" & DomainName
    Set Domain = GetObject(ADsPath)
    Select Case UCase(PropertyName)
        Case "AUTOUNLOCKINTERVAL"
            Domain.AutoUnlockInterval = NewValue
            Domain.SetInfo
        Case "LOCKOUTOBSERVATIONINTERVAL"
            Domain.LockoutObservationInterval = NewValue
            Domain.SetInfo
        Case "MAXBADPASSWORDSALLOWED"
            Domain.MaxBadPasswordsAllowed = NewValue
            Domain.SetInfo
        Case "MAXPASSWORDAGE"
            Domain.MaxPasswordAge = NewValue
            Domain.SetInfo
        Case "MINPASSWORDAGE"
            Domain.MinPasswordAge = NewValue
            Domain.SetInfo
        Case "MINPASSWORDLENGTH"
            Domain.MinPasswordLength = NewValue
            Domain.SetInfo
        Case "PASSWORDHISTORYLENGTH"
            Domain.PasswordHistoryLength = NewValue
            Domain.SetInfo
    End Select
    If Err = 0 Then SetDomainProp = True
End Function

Public Function CreateContainerObject(ByVal ContainerName As String, ByVal
⇢ObjectClass As String, ByVal ObjectName As String) As Boolean
    Dim Container As IADsContainer
    Dim ADsPath As String
    ADsPath = "WinNT://" & ContainerName
    Set Container = GetObject(ADsPath)
    Select Case UCase(ObjectClass)
        Case "USER"
            Dim User As IADsUser
            Set User = Container.Create("User", ObjectName)
            User.SetInfo
        Case "GLOBALGROUP"
            Dim GlobalGroup As IADsGroup
            Set GlobalGroup = Container.Create("Group", ObjectName)
            GlobalGroup.Put "groupType", ADS_GROUP_TYPE_GLOBAL_GROUP
```

```
                GlobalGroup.SetInfo
            Case "LOCALGROUP"
                Dim LocalGroup As IADsGroup
                Set LocalGroup = Container.Create("Group", ObjectName)
                LocalGroup.Put "groupType", ADS_GROUP_TYPE_LOCAL_GROUP
                LocalGroup.SetInfo
            Case "COMPUTER"
                Dim Computer As IADsComputer
                Dim ComputerAccount As IADsUser
                Set Computer = Container.Create("Computer", UCase(ObjectName))
                Computer.SetInfo
                Set ComputerAccount = GetObject("WinNT://" & ContainerName & "/"
                ↪& ObjectName & "$,user")
                ComputerAccount.Put "UserFlags", (ComputerAccount.Get("UserFlags")
                ↪Or &H1000)
                ComputerAccount.SetPassword (LCase(ObjectName))
                ComputerAccount.SetInfo
        End Select
        If Err = 0 Then CreateContainerObject = True
End Function

Public Function DeleteContainerObject(ByVal ContainerName As String, ByVal
↪ObjectClass As String, ByVal ObjectName As String) As Boolean
    Dim Container As IADsContainer
    Dim ADsPath As String
    ADsPath = "WinNT://" & ContainerName
    Set Container = GetObject(ADsPath)
    Call Container.Delete(ObjectClass, ObjectName)
    If Err = 0 Then DeleteContainerObject = True
End Function
Public Function RenameUserAccount(ByVal ContainerName As String, ByVal
↪OldUserName As String, ByVal NewUserName As String) As Boolean
    On Error Resume Next
    Dim Container As IADsContainer
    Dim User As IADsUser
    Set Container = GetObject("WinNT://" & ContainerName)
    Set User = GetObject("WinNT://" & ContainerName & "/" & OldUserName &
    ↪",user")
    If Err.Number = 0 Then
        Call Container.MoveHere(User.ADsPath, NewUserName)
    End If
    If Err.Number = 0 Then
        RenameUserAccount = True
    Else
        RenameUserAccount = False
    End If
End Function

Public Function EnumerateContainer(ByVal ContainerName As String, Optional ByVal
↪Filter As String) As Variant
    On Error Resume Next
    Dim LeafObject As IADs
    Dim Container As IADsContainer
```

continues ▶

Exercise 3.1   *continued*

```
        Dim i As Long
        Dim NewElement() As Variant
        Set Container = GetObject("WinNT://" & ContainerName)
        If Filter <> " Then
            Container.Filter = Array(Filter)
        End If
        For Each LeafObject In Container
            i = UBound(NewElement) + 1
            ReDim Preserve NewElement(i)
            NewElement(i) = LeafObject.Name
        Next
        EnumerateContainer = NewElement
    End Function
```

6. Compile the code as NTAdmin.DLL.
7. Save and close the NTAdmin project.

> **Tip**
>
> *If you do not want to share your code between applications, you can enter the preceding code into a code module in any Visual Basic application.* ◆

> **Tip**
>
> *You can download the Visual Basic 6.0 project or pre-compiled version of NTAdmin.DLL from* http://www.newriders.com/adsi. ◆

Using the Functions in NTContainerManagement

With the NTContainerManagement class module created, you can access the functions contained in the class module from any programming language that supports OLE automation, including Visual Basic, VBScript, and JavaScript.

After the NTContainerManagement class module has been instantiated, you can reduce domain management to a single line of code by referencing the methods (`SetDomainProp`, `EnumerateContainer`, and so on) in the class module.

Instantiating NTAdmin.NTContainerManagement Using Visual Basic

Before you can use the new class module in your programming environment, you must instantiate the object.

First, you must set a reference to NTAdmin. From the Project menu, select References..., and then scroll through the list to find NTAdmin.

> *Tip*
>
> *If you are using a different machine from the one on which the NTAdmin.DLL was compiled, you must copy the DLL to the machine and run REGSVR32 NTAdmin.DLL to register the DLL.* ◆

With a reference now established to NTAdmin.DLL, you can instantiate the object in your code, as follows:

```
Dim ContainerManagement As NTAdmin.NTContainerManagement
Set ContainerManagement = New NTAdmin.NTContainerManagement
```

You can now use all seven methods of the object by simply typing `ContainerManagement.Method`. If you have AutoListMembers enabled for the Visual Basic IDE, Visual Basic will automatically show you the names and syntax for each of the public methods in the class module.

Instantiating NTContainerManagement in a VBScript Active Server Page

Begin by copying the NTAdmin.DLL to your IIS server. From the server console, register NTAdmin.DLL using REGSVR32. If you want to use the DLL in a delegated administration environment, create an MTS package and specify a privileged account for the package identity.

With the DLL now registered, create a new ASP page and use the following VBScript code to instantiate the object:

```
Dim ContainerManagement
Set ContainerManagement = Server.CreateObject("NTAdmin.NTContainerManagement")
```

The methods of the object can now be called simply by typing `ContainerManagement.Method`.

Instantiating NTContainerManagement from a JavaScript Active Server Page

If the NTAdmin.DLL has not been copied to the IIS server, follow the previous example.

After the DLL has been registered, you can use the following JavaScript code in an Active Server Page to instantiate the NTAdmin.NTContainerManagement component:

```
var ContainerManagement =
↪Server.CreateObject("NTAdmin.NTContainerManagement");
```

Using the Functions in NTContainerManagement

Use Table 3.1 to help you use the proper syntax for each of the methods of the NTContainerManagement interface:

Table 3.1   NTContainerManagement Method Syntax

Action	Syntax
Enumerate Domains	For Each Item in ContainerManagement.↪EnumerateNamespace Debug.Print Item Next
Create Computer Account	RetVal = ↪ContainerManagement.CreateContainer↪Object("Domain_Name", "Computer", ↪"Computer_Name")
Create User Account	RetVal = ↪ContainerManagement.CreateContainer↪Object("Domain_Name", "User", ↪"User_Name")
Create Global Group	RetVal = ↪ContainerManagement.CreateContainer↪Object("Domain_Name", "GlobalGroup", ↪"Group_Name")
Create Local Group	RetVal = ↪ContainerManagement.CreateContainer↪Object("Domain_Name", "LocalGroup", ↪"Group_Name")
Delete Computer Account	RetVal = ↪ContainerManagement.DeleteContainer↪Object("Domain_Name", "Computer", ↪"Computer_Name")
Delete User Account	RetVal = ↪ContainerManagement.DeleteContainer↪Object("Domain_Name", "User", ↪"User_Name")
Delete Group	RetVal = ↪ContainerManagement.DeleteContainer↪Object("Domain_Name", "Group", ↪"Group_Name")

Creating the NTContainerManagement Class Module

Action	Syntax
Query `AutoUnlockInterval`	`RetVal = ContainerManagement.QueryDomainProp ("Domain_Name", "AutoUnlockInterval")`
Query `LockoutObservationInterval`	`RetVal = ContainerManagement.QueryDomainProp ("Domain_Name", "LockoutObservationInterval")`
Query `MaxBadPasswordsAllowed`	`RetVal = ContainerManagement.QueryDomainProp ("Domain_Name", "MaxBadPasswordsAllowed")`
Query `MaxPasswordAge`	`RetVal = ContainerManagement.QueryDomainProp ("Domain_Name", "MaxPasswordAge")`
Query `MinPasswordAge`	`RetVal = ContainerManagement.QueryDomainProp ("Domain_Name", "MinPasswordAge")`
Query `MinPasswordLength`	`RetVal = ContainerManagement.QueryDomainProp ("Domain_Name", "MinPasswordLength")`
Query `PasswordHistoryLength`	`RetVal = ContainerManagement.QueryDomainProp ("Domain_Name", "PasswordHistoryLength")`
Set `AutoUnlockInterval`	`RetVal = ContainerManagement.SetDomainProp ("Domain_Name", "AutoUnlockInterval", New_Value)`
Set `LockoutObservationInterval`	`RetVal = ContainerManagement.SetDomainProp ("Domain_Name", "LockoutObservationInterval", New_Value)`
Set `MaxBadPasswordsAllowed`	`RetVal = ContainerManagement.SetDomainProp ("Domain_Name", "MaxBadPasswordsAllowed", New_Value)`
Set `MaxPasswordAge`	`RetVal = ContainerManagement.SetDomainProp ("Domain_Name", "MaxPasswordAge", New_Value)`
Set `MinPasswordAge`	`RetVal = ContainerManagement.SetDomainProp ("Domain_Name", "MinPasswordAge", New_Value)`

continues ▶

Action	Syntax

Set `MinPasswordLength`	`RetVal =`
	`↳ContainerManagement.SetDomainProp`
	`↳("Domain_Name", "MinPasswordLength",`
	`↳New_Value)`

Set `PasswordHistoryLength`	`RetVal =`
	`↳ContainerManagement.SetDomainProp`
	`↳("Domain_Name", "PasswordHistory`
	`↳Length", New_Value)`

Rename User Account	`RetVal =`
	`↳ContainerManagement.RenameUserAccount`
	`↳("Domain_Name","Old_Account",`
	`↳"New_Account")`

Enumerate All Domain Objects	`For Each Item in ContainerManagement.`
	`↳EnumerateContainer("Domain_Name")`
	`    Debug.Print Item`
	`Next`

Enumerate Users in a Domain	`For Each Item in ContainerManagement.`
	`↳EnumerateContainer("Domain_Name",`
	`↳"User")`
	`    Debug.Print Item`
	`Next`

Enumerate All Groups in a Domain	`For Each Item in ContainerManagement.`
	`↳EnumerateContainer("Domain_Name",`
	`↳"Group")`
	`    Debug.Print Item`
	`Next`

Enumerate Global Groups in a Domain	`For Each Item in ContainerManagement.`
	`↳EnumerateContainer("Domain_Name",`
	`↳"GlobalGroup")`
	`    Debug.Print Item`
	`Next`

Enumerate Local Groups in a Domain	`For Each Item in`
	`↳ContainerManagement.EnumerateContainer`
	`↳("Domain_Name","LocalGroup")`
	`    Debug.Print Item`
	`Next`

Enumerate Computer Accounts in a Domain	`For Each Item in ContainerManagement.`
	`↳EnumerateContainer("Domain_`
	`↳Name","Computer")`
	`    Debug.Print Item`
	`Next`

Summary

Using the IADs, IADsContainer, and IADsDomain interfaces, the developer or administrator can begin an administrative application workflow by creating scripts that enumerate all domains within the WinNT: namespace. After the user selects a domain to manage, he or she can then manage the account policy of the domain itself, or can further enumerate the contents of the container.

One of the most useful elements in an administrative workflow application is the ability to create and delete objects in a container. Computers, users, local groups, and global groups are easily created and removed from the domain by calling the Create and Delete methods of the IADsContainer interface.

To simplify the code required to perform additions and deletions in a given container, a Visual Basic class module can be created to allow your code to be used from any programming language supporting OLE automation. These functions allow a single line of code to be used in an application to create or delete any class of object or to manage the properties of the domain.

By coupling the enumeration methods used in this chapter with the programmatic object manipulation techniques discussed in the later chapters of Part II, extremely robust administrative applications can be developed with minimal effort.

4
Programmatic User Account Manipulation

In the majority of enterprises, the mundane workflow processes are those most prone to process omission errors. Using programmatic methods, development-savvy administrators can create workflow applications that perform all of the actions required to create a new account, thus eliminating errors resulting from process omission.

To help you develop these administrative workflow applications, this chapter explores programmatic manipulation of user account properties, including the following:

- Managing and manipulating user account properties
- Manipulating the user environment profile
- Manipulating user logon hours and workstations
- Manipulating the user parameter field

You will also use ADSI to expose the values assigned to properties that cannot be manipulated using standard GUI tools, such as the times of the user's last login and logoff.

Whether the application to be built is part of an existing business process or is simply part of a cache of administrative time saving utilities, Visual Basic and ADSI provide an incredibly robust platform on which to build your next administrative automation project.

Finally, in this chapter you will continue the creation of the NTAdmin.DLL COM server application you started in Chapter 3, "Container Enumeration Methods and Programmatic Domain Account Policy Manipulation."

User Object Binding Syntax

When binding a user object, you can specify the User class at the end of the binding string to designate the class of the object to be manipulated. Specifying the class of the object eliminates any ambiguity surrounding the type of object to bind and increases overall performance of the binding operation.

User Object Binding Syntax Using Visual Basic

Use the following Visual Basic code to bind to an existing user account in the domain:

```
Dim User as IADsUser
Dim UserName as String
Dim UserDomain as String
UserDomain = "Target_User_Domain"
UserName = "Target_User_Name"
Set User = GetObject("WinNT://" & UserDomain & "/" & UserName & ",user")
```

Managing User Account Properties

Of all of the interfaces in the Windows NT service provider, the IADsUser interface provides the greatest number of properties and methods to programmatically manipulate user accounts. The great number of exposed properties and methods involved should be of little surprise to even a novice systems administrator, as the majority of daily administrative tasks are focused around user account management. Using the IADsUser interface, you can build applications and scripts that tie together the administrative processes previously performed using individual, manual steps.

When creating a new user account, you typically have a default set of groups for which the user requires membership, as well as a home directory to create. In addition, the user home directory must be shared and permissions applied to allow it to be mapped from a login script and to restrict unauthorized access. After entering the appropriate user name, full name, and description, you should also populate the profile path and home directory path fields in the SAM to let Windows NT know where it should look to find the user's home directory and roaming profile. Finally, the information regarding the new user account must be distributed to the user (or more likely his or her manager) in a secure, efficient manner. By passing information from ADSI to an application that utilizes an object model (such as Outlook), this too can be accomplished using programmatic methods.

Investing time in the creation of a script to automate workflow processes is sure to increase customer satisfaction because the automated workflow processes will no longer be prone to the errors encountered in the manual workflow process. Using the methods and properties implemented in the IADsUser interface, you can manipulate almost all of the configurable options available in the User Properties dialog box in User Manager for Domains.

Manipulating the User *FullName* Property

As shown in Figure 4.1, when creating a new account, most enterprises set an appropriate value for the Full Name data field to help identify the user account. This is typically limited to the user's first and last name and perhaps the middle initial if applicable.

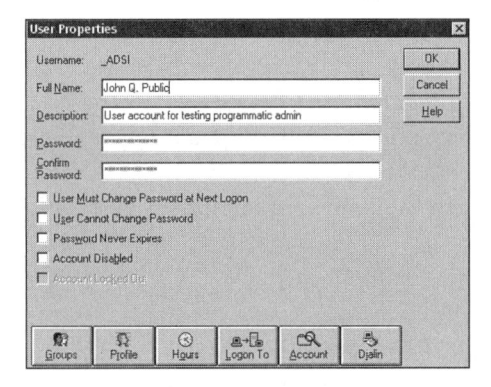

Figure 4.1 *User Properties dialog box in User Manager for Domains.*

Some enterprises may choose to implement this field as a field-delimited record to incorporate better interoperability with programmatic methods for manipulating the SAM. By taking such an approach, you can create Web-based tools that can parse down the field into individual elements providing Active Directory-like properties for Windows NT environments.

Querying the User *FullName* Property Using Visual Basic

To return the bound user's full name as a string, use the following Visual Basic code:

```
Dim User as IADsUser
Dim UserName as String
Dim UserDomain as String
UserDomain = "Target_User_Domain"
UserName = "Target_User_Name"
Set User = GetObject("WinNT://" & UserDomain & "/" & UserName & ",user")

Dim RetVal as String
RetVal = User.Fullname
Debug.Print RetVal
```

Setting a New Value for the User *FullName* Property Using Visual Basic
To set a new value for the bound user's Full Name field in the SAM, use the following Visual Basic code:

```
Dim User as IADsUser
Dim UserName as String
Dim UserDomain as String
Dim NewFullName as String
UserDomain = "Target_User_Domain"
UserName = "Target_User_Name"
NewFullName = "New_Value_For_Full_Name_Field"
Set User = GetObject("WinNT://" & UserDomain & "/" & UserName & ",user")

User.Fullname = NewFullname
User.SetInfo
```

Manipulating the *Description* Property

The Description property allows you to enter data regarding the employee, including geographic location of the account owner, department, cost center, employee identification number, or any other information about the user you desire.

> *Note*
>
> *If a naming standard is not currently in place for this field, you should consider forcing its data to comply with a specific delimited standard to improve the ability to query the data. Without the attributes of the Active Directory available to Windows NT users, the ability to target a specific group of users is limited. By implementing meaningful field-delimited data in the* Description *(and* FullName*) properties, you can significantly increase the power of programmatic administration functions.* ♦

Querying the *Description* Property Using Visual Basic
To return the currently bound user object's Description property as a string, use the following Visual Basic code:

```
Dim User as IADsUser
Dim UserName as String
Dim UserDomain as String
UserDomain = "Target_User_Domain"
UserName = "Target_User_Name"
Set User = GetObject("WinNT://" & UserDomain & "/" & UserName & ",user")

Dim RetVal as String
RetVal = User.Description
Debug.Print RetVal
```

Setting a New Value for the *Description* Property Using Visual Basic
To set a new value for a user's Description property, use the following Visual Basic code:

```
Dim User as IADsUser
Dim UserName as String
Dim UserDomain as String
Dim NewDescription as String
UserDomain = "Target_User_Domain"
UserName = "Target_User_Name"
NewDescription = "New_Value_For_Description_Field"
Set User = GetObject("WinNT://" & UserDomain & "/" & UserName & ",user")

User.Description = NewDescription
User.SetInfo
```

Note

If you want to query an individual element within the contents of a field-delimited property, use the following Visual Basic code:

```
Dim User as IADsUser
Dim UserName as String
Dim UserDomain as String
Dim Delimiter As String
UserDomain = "Target_User_Domain"
UserName = "Target_User_Name"
Delimiter = "|"
Set User = GetObject("WinNT://" & UserDomain & "/" & UserName & ",user")
Dim RetVal as String
RetVal = User.Description
Dim FirstDelim As Integer
Dim DescriptionLength As Integer
Dim ParsedElement As String
Dim TerminalCondition As Boolean
StartPosition = 1
While TerminalCondition <> True
    FirstDelim = InStr(1, RetVal, Delimiter)
    If FirstDelim = 0 Then
        TerminalCondition = True
    Else
        DescriptionLength = Len(RetVal)
        ParsedElement = Left(RetVal, FirstDelim - 1)
        Debug.Print Trim(ParsedElement)
        RetVal = Right(RetVal, (DescriptionLength - FirstDelim))
    End If
Wend
Debug.Print Trim (RetVal) ◆
```

Manipulating User Passwords

One of the most common administrative tasks for any help desk or access control group administrator is user account password management. This involves resetting a password to a known value and forcing the user to change the password on his next login.

Users also participate in these activities by entering their current password and entering a new value for their password. Unlike an explicit password set operation, these operations can be performed simply with knowledge of the current password by using a user-level privilege account.

Querying a User Password Stored in the SAM

It is important to note that this field in the SAM cannot be accessed programmatically by *any* tool, including ADSI. If you want to find the value of a user password, you must instead use a brute-force password hash comparison utility such as L0phtCrack or one of the many other tools available on the Internet for such purposes.

Setting a New Value for a User Password Using Visual Basic

To use the SetPassword method, the calling user need not know the original user password, but must possess administrative rights in the domain to perform the action.

If you want to reset a user password without knowing the original password, use the following code:

```
Dim User as IADsUser
Dim UserName as String
Dim UserDomain as String
UserDomain = "Target_User_Domain"
UserName = "Target_User_Name"
Set User = GetObject("WinNT://" & UserDomain & "/" & UserName & ",user")

Dim NewPassword as String
NewPassword = "Superm@n99"
Call User.SetPassword(NewPassword)
```

> *Note*
>
> Obviously, you should replace the value of Superm@n99 *with a password of your choosing. This value can be populated using any string value that does not violate Windows NT's rules for valid passwords.* ♦

Changing a User Password Using Visual Basic

When users change passwords, they must enter both the current password as well as the new password they desire to use. This simple security method enables non-administrative users to change their own passwords without having any more than simple user-level privileges in the domain. Use the following Visual Basic code to change the password for a user account where the current password is known:

```
Dim User as IADsUser
Dim UserName as String
Dim UserDomain as String
UserDomain = "Target_User_Domain"
UserName = "Target_User_Name"
Set User = GetObject("WinNT://" & UserDomain & "/" & UserName & ",user")
Dim NewPassword as String
Dim OldPassword as String
NewPassword = "Superm@n26"
OldPassword = "B@tm@n74!"
Call User.ChangePassword(OldPassword, NewPassword)
```

Tip

When using a Web server to implement password changes, to ensure that passwords are not sent over the wire in clear text between the Web server and the client, all pages dealing with user password information should be encrypted using a Secure Sockets Layer (SSL) connection. ♦

Manipulating a User Flag

To find the status of user flags in the SAM, use the Get method of the IADs interface to retrieve the flag setting. Unlike other properties manipulated using ADSI, these properties require a bit of work to query and set because they are manipulated using bitwise operators. The following table defines some constants that represent the hex values of four of the five status flags shown in User Manager:

0x00002	ADS_UF_ACCOUNTDISABLE
0x00010	ADS_UF_LOCKOUT
0x00040	ADS_UF_PASSWD_CANT_CHANGE
0x10000	ADS_UF_DONT_EXPIRE_PASSWD

> **Note**
>
> Notice that there is no flag for the User Must Change Password at Next Logon setting. This is because this setting is not controlled by a user flag, but rather is controlled simply by setting the `PasswordExpired` property to 1 for the user account. ♦

There are many user flags available to the developer for manipulation and control of a user account. A complete listing of ADSI constants can be found in Appendix B, "ADSI 2.5 Programmer's Reference."

To set and query these hex values, use the Or, Xor, and And operators to manipulate these flags in the following general manner:

- The Or operator is used to initially set a bit (as in the case of a new account creation).
- The Xor operator is used to toggle the status of the flag (from enabled to disabled, or vice-versa).
- The And operator is used to query the value held in the SAM.

Querying the Value of a User Flag Using Visual Basic

To find the value of a specific flag using Visual Basic, use the following general syntax:

```
Dim User as IADsUser
Dim UserName as String
Dim UserDomain as String
UserDomain = "Target_User_Domain"
UserName = "Target_User_Name"
Set User = GetObject("WinNT://" & UserDomain & "/" & UserName & ",user")

Dim Flags As Long
Flags = User.Get("UserFlags")
If (Flags And &H10000) <> 0 Then
    Debug.Print "The specified user account is configured so that the password
➥never expires."
End If
```

> **Note**
>
> Notice you are "And-ing" the `0x10000` hex value (Password Never Expires) with the user flags and then evaluating the result of the operation. If anything other than 0 is returned, you can be sure that the Password Never Expires status flag is set for the bound account. ♦

Toggling a User Flag Using Visual Basic

Likewise, you can toggle these flags by using the Put method and the Xor operator to modify the bit to its complement. Consider the following Visual Basic code:

```
Dim User as IADsUser
Dim UserName as String
Dim UserDomain as String
UserDomain = "Target_User_Domain"
UserName = "Target_User_Name"
Set User = GetObject("WinNT://" & UserDomain & "/" & UserName & ",user")

Dim Flags As Long
Flags = User.Get("UserFlags")
User.Put "UserFlags", (Flags Xor &H10000)
User.SetInfo
```

After finding the value of UserFlags you perform an Xor operation on the current UserFlags property to toggle the bit value. Next, you write the new value back into the directory with the SetInfo method.

> *Tip*
>
> *By simply changing the Xor operator to an Or operator, you can use the preceding code to set the initial value of a status flag.* ♦

Manipulating the User Must Change Password at Next Logon Status Flag

In most cases, after you reset a password, the User Must Change Password at Next Logon status flag should be set to ensure that the default password does not become the new password for the user account.

You may want to incorporate this functionality in the password change procedure code if the security policy for your enterprise dictates that even IT personnel are not permitted to have knowledge of user account password information.

> *Note*
>
> *Behind the scenes, Windows NT expires the password to force the user to change the account password upon next logon. For this reason, NT does not allow you to set this flag and the Password Never Expires flag at the same time. Although this is obvious when using the User Manager GUI (due to the error dialog box raised), when using programmatic methods to manipulate properties and methods, this is not nearly as apparent.* ♦

Querying the User Must Change Password at Next Logon Status Flag Using Visual Basic

To find the current value of the `PasswordExpired` user flag, use the following Visual Basic code:

```
Dim User as IADsUser
Dim UserName as String
Dim UserDomain as String
UserDomain = "Target_User_Domain"
UserName = "Target_User_Name"
Set User = GetObject("WinNT://" & UserDomain & "/" & UserName & ",user")

Dim PasswordExpired As Integer
PasswordExpired= User.Get("PasswordExpired")
If PasswordExpired = 1 Then
    Debug.Print "The user account is configured so that the password must be
➥changed on next logon."
Else
    Debug.Print "The user will NOT be required to change the account password on
➥next logon."
End If
```

> *Note*
>
> *If the* `PasswordExpired` *property returns a value of 1 when queried, the password has expired and must be changed upon next logon. If the value of* `PasswordExpired` *returns 0, the password has not yet expired.* ♦

Setting a New Value for the User Must Change Password at Next Logon Status Flag Using Visual Basic

To expire a user account password immediately, set the `PasswordExpired` property to a value of 1, as shown in the following Visual Basic code:

```
Dim User as IADsUser
Dim UserName as String
Dim UserDomain as String
UserDomain = "Target_User_Domain"
UserName = "Target_User_Name"
Set User = GetObject("WinNT://" & UserDomain & "/" & UserName & ",user")
Dim PasswordExpired As Integer
User.Put "PasswordExpired", 1
User.SetInfo
```

> *Tip*
>
> *In this case, you are using the IADs* `Put` *method to force a new value for the* `PasswordExpired` *property for the user account. If you want to remove the* `PasswordExpired` *bit for a user account, simply set this property value to 0.* ♦

Manipulating the User Cannot Change Password Status Flag

Although this flag is not often used by enterprises for user accounts (frequent user password changes should be encouraged), it can nevertheless be programmatically manipulated. Using the user flag bitwise operations described previously, this bit can be queried, set, and toggled.

Querying the User Cannot Change Password Status Flag Using Visual Basic

To prevent users from having the right to change their own passwords, use the following Visual Basic code:

```
Dim User as IADsUser
Dim UserName as String
Dim UserDomain as String
UserDomain = "Target_User_Domain"
UserName = "Target_User_Name"
Set User = GetObject("WinNT://" & UserDomain & "/" & UserName & ",user")

Dim Flags As Long
Flags = User.Get("UserFlags")
If (Flags And &H00040) <> 0 Then
    Debug.Print "The specified user account is configured so that the password
 cannot be changed."
End If
```

Setting the Value for the User Cannot Change Password Status Flag Using Visual Basic

There may be cases (such as when creating a new account) where you must ensure that the value of this bit is set to a specific value. Use the following Visual Basic code to explicitly set the User Cannot Change Password status flag in the SAM:

```
Dim User as IADsUser
Dim UserName as String
Dim UserDomain as String
UserDomain = "Target_User_Domain"
UserName = "Target_User_Name"
Set User = GetObject("WinNT://" & UserDomain & "/" & UserName & ",user")

Dim Flags As Long
Flags = User.Get("UserFlags")
User.Put "UserFlags", Flags OR &H00040
User.SetInfo
```

Toggling the Value for the User Cannot Change Password Status Flag Using Visual Basic

To toggle the value of the User Cannot Change Password status flag, you can use the following Visual Basic code:

```
Dim User as IADsUser
Dim UserName as String
Dim UserDomain as String
UserDomain = "Target_User_Domain"
UserName = "Target_User_Name"
Set User = GetObject("WinNT://" & UserDomain & "/" & UserName & ",user")

Dim Flags As Long
Flags = User.Get("UserFlags")
User.Put "UserFlags", Flags XOR &H00040
User.SetInfo
```

Manipulating the Password Never Expires Status Flag

When creating a service account, it is always advisable to set the ADS_UF_DONT_EXPIRE_PASSWORD user flag on the account to prevent service startup failures due to password synchronization issues. By setting this flag, the specified account is not subject to the maximum password age setting in the domain's account policy configuration, and will not be forced to change passwords on a periodic basis.

Querying the Password Never Expires Status Flag Using Visual Basic

To query the current password expiration policy affecting the bound user account, use the following Visual Basic code:

```
Dim User as IADsUser
Dim UserName as String
Dim UserDomain as String
UserDomain = "Target_User_Domain"
UserName = "Target_User_Name"
Set User = GetObject("WinNT://" & UserDomain & "/" & UserName & ",user")

Dim Flags As Long
Flags = User.Get("UserFlags")
If (Flags And &H10000) <> 0 Then
    Debug.Print "The specified user account is configured so that the password
↪never expires."
End If
```

Setting the Password Never Expires Status Flag Using Visual Basic
To allow a user account to be unaffected by the maximum password age restrictions in the domain (if applicable), use the following Visual Basic code to explicitly set the ADS_UF_DONT_EXPIRE_PASSWORD bit:

```
Dim User as IADsUser
Dim UserName as String
Dim UserDomain as String
UserDomain = "Target_User_Domain"
UserName = "Target_User_Name"
Set User = GetObject("WinNT://" & UserDomain & "/" & UserName & ",user")

Dim Flags As Long
Flags = User.Get("UserFlags")
User.Put "UserFlags", Flags OR &H10000
User.SetInfo
```

Toggling the Password Never Expires Status Flag Using Visual Basic
To toggle the current value of the Password Never Expires field in the user's SAM record, use the following Visual Basic code:

```
Dim User as IADsUser
Dim UserName as String
Dim UserDomain as String
UserDomain = "Target_User_Domain"
UserName = "Target_User_Name"
Set User = GetObject("WinNT://" & UserDomain & "/" & UserName & ",user")

Dim Flags As Long
Flags = User.Get("UserFlags")
User.Put "UserFlags", Flags XOR &H10000
User.SetInfo
```

Manipulating the Account Disabled Status Flag

ADS_UF_ACCOUNTDISABLE is a user flag that can be raised in the SAM record for any user account. The IADsUser interface also implements this functionality as a property for easier manipulation.

Note

If you prefer to use bitwise operators, you can manipulate the Account Disabled user flag using the same techniques as shown for the Password Never Expires flag. Simply change the hex value passed as an argument of the IADs Put *method from 0x10000 (&H10000) to 0x2 (&H2).* ♦

Querying the Account Disabled Status Flag Using Visual Basic and the *AccountDisabled* Property

To enable easier manipulation of the Account Disabled status flag, Microsoft exposed the AccountDisabled property in the IADsUser interface. Use the following Visual Basic code to determine whether an account is currently enabled or disabled:

```
Dim User as IADsUser
Dim UserName as String
Dim UserDomain as String
UserDomain = "Target_User_Domain"
UserName = "Target_User_Name"
Set User = GetObject("WinNT://" & UserDomain & "/" & UserName & ",user")

Dim RetVal as Boolean
RetVal = User.AccountDisabled
Debug.Print RetVal
```

Setting a New Value for the Account Disabled Status Flag Using Visual Basic and the *AccountDisabled* Property

To enable or disable a user account, simply set the IADsUser AccountDisabled property to the proper Boolean value, as shown in the following Visual Basic code:

```
Dim User as IADsUser
Dim UserName as String
Dim UserDomain as String
UserDomain = "Target_User_Domain"
UserName = "Target_User_Name"
Set User = GetObject("WinNT://" & UserDomain & "/" & UserName & ",user")

Dim NewValue as Boolean
NewValue = False
User.AccountDisabled = NewValue
User.SetInfo
```

> #### Enumerating a Domain to Report All Disabled Accounts Using Visual Basic
>
> In some enterprises, it may be useful to generate a list of all accounts that are currently disabled for auditing purposes. To perform such an action, simply enumerate all user accounts in a given domain (or local SAM) and use a conditional to display any accounts that are currently disabled.
>
> Consider the following Visual Basic code to generate a report of all disabled accounts for a given domain:
>
> ```
> Dim Domain As IADsContainer
> Dim DomainName as String
> Dim UserAccount As IADsUser
> Dim Counter As Integer
> ```

```
Counter = 0
DomainName = "Target_Domain_Name"
Set Domain = GetObject("WinNT://" & DomainName)
Domain.Filter = Array("User")
Debug.Print "The following accounts are disabled in domain: " & Domain.Name
For Each UserAccount In Domain
    If UserAccount.AccountDisabled = True Then
        Debug.Print UserAccount.Name
        Counter = Counter + 1
    End If
Next
If Counter = 1 Then
    Debug.Print "Only 1 user account in the " & Domain.Name & " domain is
➥disabled."
Else
    Debug.Print Counter & " user accounts are disabled in the " & Domain.Name & "
➥domain."
End If ◆
```

Manipulating the Account Locked Out Status Flag

Depending on the Account Policy configuration for the domain, account lockout conditions can be a tremendous burden on system administrators. As part of the IADsUser interface, you can both query and reset account lockout conditions.

> *Tip*
>
> *As was the case with the* AccountDisabled *property, the Account Lockout user flag can also be manipulated using bitwise operators.* ◆

Querying the Account Locked Out Status Flag Using Visual Basic and the *IsAccountLocked* Property

To find out if a user account has been locked out, use the following Visual Basic code:

```
Dim User as IADsUser
Dim UserName as String
Dim UserDomain as String
UserDomain = "Target_User_Domain"
UserName = "Target_User_Name"
Set User = GetObject("WinNT://" & UserDomain & "/" & UserName & ",user")

Dim RetVal as Boolean
RetVal = User.IsAccountLocked
Debug.Print RetVal
```

Unlocking a User Account Using Visual Basic and the *IsAccountLocked* Property

To unlock a currently locked-out user account, use the following Visual Basic code:

```
Dim User as IADsUser
Dim UserName as String
Dim UserDomain as String
UserDomain = "Target_User_Domain"
UserName = "Target_User_Name"
Set User = GetObject("WinNT://" & UserDomain & "/" & UserName & ",user")
If User.IsAccountLocked = True Then
    User.IsAccountLocked = False
    User.SetInfo
End If
```

> **Note**
>
> *Despite the hours of entertainment derived from locking out the user accounts held by your manager and teammates, Microsoft does not allow you to set the* `IsAccountLocked` *property to True in the release version of ADSI 2.5.* ♦

Resetting All Locked-Out User Accounts for a Domain

The following code enumerates all user accounts in the domain and resets all accounts to an enabled state:

```
Dim Domain As IADsContainer
Dim UserAccount As IADsUser
Dim Counter As Integer
Dim DomainName as String
Counter = 0
DomainName = "Target_Domain_Name"
Set Domain = GetObject("WinNT://" & DomainName)
Domain.Filter = Array("User")
For Each UserAccount In Domain
    If UserAccount.IsAccountLocked = True Then
        Debug.Print UserAccount.Name
        UserAccount.IsAccountLocked = False
        UserAccount.SetInfo
        Counter = Counter + 1
    End If
Next
If Counter = 1 Then
    Debug.Print "Only 1 user account in the " & Domain.Name & " domain was
↪unlocked."
Else
    Debug.Print Counter & " user accounts were unlocked in the " & Domain.Name &
↪" domain."
End If
```

If this script is run on a regular basis, there is little reason to continue permitting lockout conditions to exist in the domain. Be sure to consult with your security organization before implementing such code. ♦

Manipulating User Environment Profiles

Using ADSI, you can programmatically manipulate the User Environment Profile and Home Directory parameters for any given user account (as shown in Figure 4.2). This can be handy in cases where the server responsible for home directories or user profile storage is renamed or consolidated and all existing users must have their profiles modified to reflect the changes.

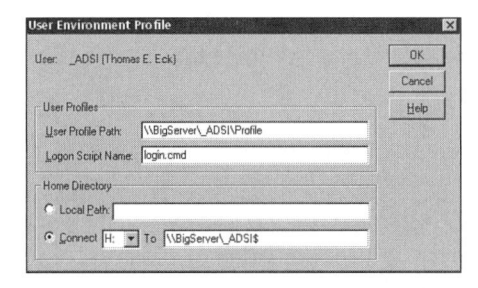

Figure 4.2 *User Environment Profile dialog box in User Manager for Domains.*

With ADSI, the administrator can quickly write a few lines of code and adapt gracefully to the ever-changing minds of management without drastically affecting the amount of free time available for the more interesting projects that may present themselves. Ultimately, the goal of any development-savvy systems administrator should be to create scripts that increase proactive monitoring of conditions in the domains, as well as quickly adapt to the inevitable changes of the modern enterprise.

Manipulating a User Profile Path

Using the IADsUser interface and the Windows NT service provider, you can manipulate the User Profile Path entry in a user account SAM entry.

Querying the User Profile Path Using Visual Basic

To find the current value used by Windows NT to specify the location of a user's profile, use the following Visual Basic code:

```
Dim User as IADsUser
Dim UserName as String
Dim UserDomain as String
UserDomain = "Target_User_Domain"
```

```
UserName = "Target_User_Name"
Set User = GetObject("WinNT://" & UserDomain & "/" & UserName & ",user")

Dim RetVal as String
RetVal = User.Profile
Debug.Print RetVal
```

Setting a New User Profile Path Using Visual Basic

To set a new value for a user's profile path, use the following Visual Basic code:

```
Dim User as IADsUser
Dim UserName as String
Dim UserDomain as String
Dim NewValue as String
UserDomain = "Target_User_Domain"
UserName = "Target_User_Name"
NewValue = "New_User_Profile_Path"
Set User = GetObject("WinNT://" & UserDomain & "/" & UserName & ",user")

User.Profile = NewValue
User.SetInfo
```

Manipulating the *LoginScript* Property

Just as you can query and set the value of the Profile property for any given user account, you can also manipulate the value of the LoginScript property.

Querying the *LoginScript* Property Using Visual Basic

Use the following Visual Basic code to find the login script currently in use for the bound user account:

```
Dim User as IADsUser
Dim UserName as String
Dim UserDomain as String
UserDomain = "Target_User_Domain"
UserName = "Target_User_Name"
Set User = GetObject("WinNT://" & UserDomain & "/" & UserName & ",user")

Dim RetVal as String
RetVal = User.LoginScript
Debug.Print RetVal
```

Setting the *LoginScript* Property Using Visual Basic

To specify a new login script for the bound user object, use the following Visual Basic code:

```
Dim User as IADsUser
Dim UserName as String
Dim UserDomain as String
```

```
UserDomain = "Target_User_Domain"
UserName = "Target_User_Name"
Set User = GetObject("WinNT://" & UserDomain & "/" & UserName & ",user")

Dim NewValue as String
NewValue = "NewLoginScript.CMD"
User.LoginScript = NewValue
User.SetInfo
```

Manipulating a Home Directory Path

Like many of the most commonly configured properties of a user record in the SAM, the Home Directory Path entry is manipulated using a property of the IADsUser interface.

Querying the Home Directory Path Using Visual Basic

To find the UNC path associated with the user's home directory, use the following Visual Basic code:

```
Dim User as IADsUser
Dim UserName as String
Dim UserDomain as String
UserDomain = "Target_User_Domain"
UserName = "Target_User_Name"
Set User = GetObject("WinNT://" & UserDomain & "/" & UserName & ",user")

Dim RetVal as String
RetVal = User.HomeDirectory
Debug.Print RetVal
```

Setting a New Home Directory Path Using Visual Basic

If you need to change the location of a user's home directory you can programmatically manipulate the user's SAM record to reflect the change. Consider the following Visual Basic code:

```
Dim User as IADsUser
Dim UserName as String
Dim UserDomain as String
Dim NewValue as String
UserDomain = "Target_User_Domain"
UserName = "Target_User_Name"
NewValue = "New_Home_Directory_Path_Value"
Set User = GetObject("WinNT://" & UserDomain & "/" & UserName & ",user")

User.HomeDirectory = NewValue
User.SetInfo
```

Manipulating the Home Directory Mapping

Although `HomeDirectory` is exposed as a property of the IADsUser interface, to manipulate the Home Directory Mapping entry in the SAM, you must use the IADs `Get` method to access the `HomeDirDrive` property.

Querying the Home Directory Mapping Using Visual Basic

To find the drive letter used to map a user's home directory, use the following Visual Basic code:

```
Dim User as IADsUser
Dim UserName as String
Dim UserDomain as String
UserDomain = "Target_User_Domain"
UserName = "Target_User_Name"
Set User = GetObject("WinNT://" & UserDomain & "/" & UserName & ",user")

Dim RetVal as String
RetVal = User.Get("HomeDirDrive")
Debug.Print RetVal
```

Setting a New Home Directory Mapping Using Visual Basic

To change the drive letter used to map a user's home directory, use the following Visual Basic code:

```
Dim User as IADsUser
Dim UserName as String
Dim UserDomain as String
Dim NewValue as String
UserDomain = "Target_User_Domain"
UserName = "Target_User_Name"
NewValue = "New_Value_For_Home_Directory_Drive"
Set User = GetObject("WinNT://" & UserDomain & "/" & UserName & ",user")

User.Put("HomeDirDrive", NewValue)
User.SetInfo
```

> *Tip*
>
> To set the drive letter used for the home directory mapping, pass in the drive letter and a colon as a string value (such as `"H:"`).
>
> If you want to specify a local path for the home directory, simply set the `HomeDirDrive` property to a null string:
>
> ```
> User.Put("HomeDirDrive", "")
> ```
> ◆

Manipulating User Login Hours

As shown in Figure 4.3, Windows NT allows you to define specific times during which a user will have access to domain resources. With a bit of programming knowledge and a whole lot of patience, you can query and set the values of the User Logon hours field in a user SAM record using the LoginHours property of the IADsUser interface.

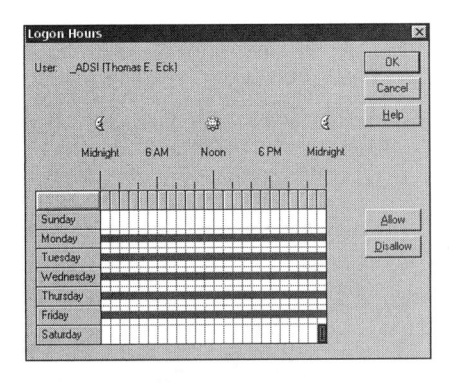

Figure 4.3 *User Logon Hours dialog box in User Manager for Domains.*

ADSI returns a variant array that can be stepped through using a *For...Each* loop. In this array, a total of 21 values will be returned (7 days made up of 24 bits each). ADSI returns values ranging from 0 to 255, each representing a specific set of hours in the day. If you are weak with binary math (as most of us are!) this will certainly prove to be a significantly difficult endeavor.

For the purpose of discussion in this text, most administrators will most likely want to query only whether an account has any user logon hours that may be restricting the user from logging on.

By taking this true/false approach to querying the logon hours for a user record, only values of less than 255 will prevent a user from logging in. If you enumerate all values in search of those of less than 255, you can quickly determine whether the user account has any time restrictions placed upon it. This eliminates the need to relearn the binary math principles that are required to manipulate this field.

Querying User Logon Hours Using Visual Basic

Use the following Visual Basic code segment as a guide to determine if a user account has logon hour restrictions placed upon it:

```
Dim User as IADsUser
Dim UserName as String
Dim UserDomain as String
UserDomain = "Target_User_Domain"
UserName = "Target_User_Name"
```

```
Set User = GetObject("WinNT://" & UserDomain & "/" & UserName & ",user")
Dim TimeEntry As Variant
Dim Restriction As Integer
For Each TimeEntry In User.LoginHours
    If TimeEntry < 255 Then Restriction = 1
Next
If Restriction = 1 Then
    Debug.Print "User account " & UserDomain & "\" & UserName & " has time
    ↪restrictions placed upon it."
Else
    Debug.Print "There are no time restrictions affecting user account " &
    ↪UserDomain & "\" & UserName & "."
End If
```

> **Note**
>
> *This code should be run only for domain accounts; local SAMs do not define logon hours for an account.* ◆

Manipulating a User Login Workstation

As shown in Figure 4.4, Windows NT allows the administrator the ability to restrict login to a specific group of machines. This can be helpful for restricting service accounts or preventing users from roaming to other workstations in the enterprise.

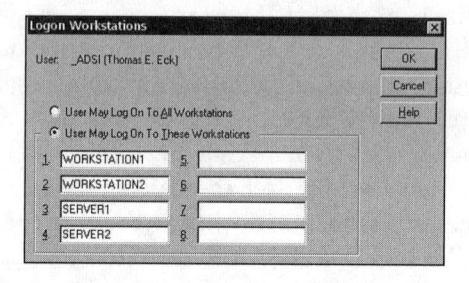

Figure 4.4 *User Logon Workstations dialog box in User Manager for Domains.*

The `LoginWorkstations` property of the IADsUser interface will return a variant array containing the machines for which user logon will be limited. If this property is set for a user account, the user may only interactively log on to the machines specified in the array assigned to this property.

This property should be set when configuring service accounts to keep users from using these often privileged accounts elsewhere in the enterprise if they should happen to know the password for the account.

Querying Login Workstations Using Visual Basic

Using the now familiar *For...Each* loop to enumerate the contents of the variant array of strings, you can return the values of all workstations for which a user account is limited. Consider the following Visual Basic code segment to perform this action:

```
On Error Resume Next
Dim User as IADsUser
Dim UserName as String
Dim UserDomain as String
Dim Workstation as Variant
UserDomain = "Target_User_Domain"
UserName = "Target_User_Name"
Set User = GetObject("WinNT://" & UserDomain & "/" & UserName & ",user")

If User.LoginWorkstations = "" then
    For Each Workstation in User.LoginWorkstations
        Debug.Print Workstation
    Next
Else
    Debug.Print User.LoginWorkstations
End If
```

Adding a New Login Workstation to the *LoginWorkstations* Property Using Visual Basic

To add a new logon workstation, you must set the value of the LoginWorkstations property to an array of strings representing the workstations to which the user account will be limited.

Use the following Visual Basic code to add a single entry to the array in the IADsUser LoginWorkstations property:

```
On Error Resume Next
Dim TargetUserDomain As String
Dim TargetUserName As String
Dim Value As String
Dim User As IADsUser
Dim Workstation As Variant
Dim NewElement() As Variant
Dim i As Long
Dim EmptyArray As Integer
    Dim Entry As Variant
Dim ValueAlreadyExists As Integer
TargetUserDomain = "Target_User_Domain"
TargetUserName = "Target_User_Name"
Value = "New_Login_Workstation_To_Add"
Set User = GetObject("WinNT://" & TargetUserDomain & "/" & TargetUserName &
↪",user")
If IsArray(User.LoginWorkstations) = True Then
For Each Entry In User.LoginWorkstations
        i = UBound(NewElement) + 1
        ReDim Preserve NewElement(i)
```

```
            NewElement(i) = Entry
            If Entry = "" Then EmptyArray = 1
            If Entry = Value Then ValueAlreadyExists = 1
        Next
        If EmptyArray = 1 Then
            User.LoginWorkstations = Array(Value)
            User.SetInfo
        Else
            If ValueAlreadyExists <> 1 Then
                i = UBound(NewElement) + 1
                ReDim Preserve NewElement(i)
                NewElement(i) = Value
                User.LoginWorkstations = NewElement
                User.SetInfo
            End If
        End If
    Else
        If User.LoginWorkstations <> Value Then
            User.LoginWorkstations = Array(User.LoginWorkstations, Value)
            User.SetInfo
        End If
    End If
End If
```

Removing an Existing Login Workstation from the *LoginWorkstations* Property Using Visual Basic

To remove an entry from an existing LoginWorkstations array, you can use the following Visual Basic code as a guide:

```
On Error Resume Next
Dim TargetUserDomain As String
Dim TargetUserName As String
Dim Value As String
Dim User As IADsUser
Dim Workstation As Variant
Dim NewElement() As Variant
Dim i As Long
TargetUserDomain = "Target_User_Domain"
TargetUserName = "Target_User_Name"
Value = "Login_Workstation_To_Remove"
Set User = GetObject("WinNT://" & TargetUserDomain & "/" & TargetUserName & _
",user")
If IsArray(User.LoginWorkstations) = True Then
    Dim Entry As Variant
    For Each Entry In User.LoginWorkstations
        If Value <> Entry Then
            i = UBound(NewElement) + 1
            ReDim Preserve NewElement(i)
            NewElement(i) = Entry
        End If
    Next
    User.LoginWorkstations = NewElement
    User.SetInfo
```

```
        Else
            If User.LoginWorkstations = Value Then
                User.LoginWorkstations = Array("")
                User.SetInfo
            End If
        End If
```

Manipulating Account Properties

As shown in Figure 4.5, the User Manager GUI allows the administrator to set an account expiration date and define if the account is permitted to participate in cross-domain security.

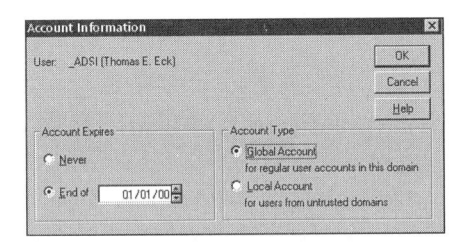

Figure 4.5 *Account Information dialog box in User Manager for Domains.*

Using ADSI, you can manipulate both of these elements programmatically using the AccountExpirationDate property of the IADsUser interface and raising the ADS_TEMP_DUPLICATE_ACCOUNT user flag for the target user account.

Querying the Account Expiration Date Using Visual Basic

To query the SAM to find the account expiration date, simply examine the AccountExpirationDate property of the IADsUser interface using the following code:

```
On Error Resume Next
Dim User as IADsUser
Dim UserName as String
Dim UserDomain as String
UserDomain = "Target_User_Domain"
UserName = "Target_User_Name"
Set User = GetObject("WinNT://" & UserDomain & "/" & UserName & ",user")

Dim AccountExpirationDate as Date
AccountExpirationDate = User.AccountExpirationDate
Debug.Print AccountExpirationDate
```

> **Note**
>
> In this example, you instruct Visual Basic to skip over any errors if they are found. If the user account does not define an expiration date, ADSI will raise an error stating that the property could not be found in the cache. Please note that this error handler affects the scope of an entire procedure. If you are a "sloppy," one-procedure kind of developer, you may find unexpected results with this option turned on. For best results, wrap the previous procedure in a function, passing in all required user variable data as arguments. Taking such an action will prevent the error handler from affecting the entire code module.
>
> With the error handler turned on, if the account has not defined an account expiration date, ADSI will return a value of 0, which is equivalent to 12:00:00 AM in the date datatype. ◆

Setting the Account Expiration Date Using Visual Basic

In cases where an enterprise uses contractors or temporary employees, or wants to make sure an employee's account access is cut off on his or her termination date, the AccountExpirationDate can be modified to disable login on a specified date.

> **Note**
>
> It is important to note that the date in the SAM will not match the date in the GUI because the GUI specifies the last day the user has access (for example, the user retains access up until 23:59:59 on the date in the GUI). ◆

To set a new account expiration date for a user account, simply set the AccountExpirationDate variable in the following Visual Basic code with a meaningful date:

```
Dim User as IADsUser
Dim UserName as String
Dim UserDomain as String
UserDomain = "Target_User_Domain"
UserName = "Target_User_Name"
Set User = GetObject("WinNT://" & UserDomain & "/" & UserName & ",user")

Dim AccountExpirationDate as Date
AccountExpirationDate = #mm/dd/yyyy#
User.AccountExpirationDate = AccountExpirationDate
User.SetInfo
```

> **Tip**
>
> If you want to remove an existing expiration date (configure the account so that it never expires), simply set the AccountExpirationDate property to #12:00:00#. ◆

Querying the Account Type Using Visual Basic

One of the more subtle configuration options available to Windows NT administrators is the ability to create either global or local accounts. By default, all user accounts are *global* accounts, which have the ability to access resources in multiple domains. *Local* accounts are limited to the domain in which they were created.

There are a few rare instances in which a local account may be desirable, such as when a user does not require access to remote domains, or when you must grant a user from an untrusted domain (temporary) access to the resources of a domain. These occasions may be few and far between; nevertheless, ADSI allows query and manipulation of this field.

As with all user flags, simply use the And operator to query the current status of the flag. If the return value is anything other than 0, the ADS_UF_TEMP_DUPLICATE_ACCOUNT flag is set for the account, as in the following Visual Basic code:

```
Dim User as IADsUser
Dim UserName as String
Dim UserDomain as String
UserDomain = "Target_User_Domain"
UserName = "Target_User_Name"
Set User = GetObject("WinNT://" & UserDomain & "/" & UserName & ",user")

Dim Flags As Long
Flags = User.Get("UserFlags")
If (Flags And &H100) <> 0 Then
    Debug.Print "Local Account"
Else
    Debug.Print "Global Account"
End If
```

Using ADSI, you can also change the account type from a global account (default account type) to a local account. Perform this action by toggling the ADS_TEMP_DUPLICATE_ACCOUNT (0x100) user flag in the target user's SAM record.

Notice in these examples that you must call the SetInfo method twice to set the ADS_TEMP_DUPLICATE_ACCOUNT (0x100) or ADS_NORMAL_ACCOUNT (0x200) user flag. Windows NT does not allow a user account to define both flags simultaneously, so you must first remove the conflicting user flag before attempting to reclassify the user account type.

Configuring a Global Account as a Local Account Using Visual Basic

Using the following Visual Basic code, you can easily disable the ability of an existing account to cross domain trusts by changing it to become a local account:

```
Dim User as IADsUser
Dim UserName as String
Dim UserDomain as String
```

```
UserDomain = "Target_User_Domain"
UserName = "Target_User_Name"
Set User = GetObject("WinNT://" & UserDomain & "/" & UserName & ",user")
Dim Flags As Long
Flags = User.Get("UserFlags")
If (Flags And &H200) <> 0 Then
    User.Put "UserFlags", Flags Xor &H200
    User.SetInfo
    Flags = User.Get("UserFlags")
    User.Put "UserFlags", Flags Xor &H100
    User.SetInfo
End If
```

Configuring a Local Account as a Global Account Using Visual Basic
If someone has already configured an account to be a local account but you now want to reclassify the account as global, you can configure the account to cross domain trusts by setting the NORMAL_ACCOUNT user flag, as follows:

```
Dim User as IADsUser
Dim UserName as String
Dim UserDomain as String
UserDomain = "Target_User_Domain"
UserName = "Target_User_Name"
Set User = GetObject("WinNT://" & UserDomain & "/" & UserName & ",user")
Dim Flags As Long
Flags = User.Get("UserFlags")
If (Flags And &H100) <> 0 Then
    User.Put "UserFlags", Flags Xor &H100
    User.SetInfo
    Flags = User.Get("UserFlags")
    User.Put "UserFlags", Flags Xor &H200
    User.SetInfo
End If
```

Manipulating the *Parameters* Property

Microsoft has given the developer a storage area that can be accessed by calling the IADs Get method on the Parameters custom user property of the Windows NT service provider. This field is where the Citrix/Terminal Server profile paths, as well as user-specific RAS information, are stored.

> **Note**
>
> *This may be exciting news for those seeking the answers to programmatic manipulation of the Terminal Server/Citrix WinFrame-specific profile parameters. This field is very difficult to manipulate using Visual Basic and ADSI, however, and thus will not be covered in this text. If you wish to programmatically manipulate*

these parameters, see `http://msdn.microsoft.com/isapi/msdnlib.idc?the URL=/library/psdk/termserv/wtsapi_9hgu.htm` *for information on the WTS API*

For those seeking to manipulate RAS configuration parameters, you can use an additional DLL found in the ADSI Resource Kit to manipulate these properties. A link to the ADSI Resource kit distribution is contained in the Web site accompanying this text at `http://www.newriders.com/adsi`. ✦

ADSI Exposed Properties that Cannot Be Manipulated Using Standard GUI Tools

There are several properties that were not directly implemented into the standard Windows NT GUI tools that can be accessed using ADSI. Many of these properties are used as internal counters, fail to yield useful information, or can be accessed by manipulating the properties of the parent container, but are interesting to examine nonetheless.

Querying the *BadLoginCount* Property Using Visual Basic

Using the `BadLoginCount` property of the IADsUser interface, you can examine the counter used to determine the number of bad logins encountered for any given user account on a specific domain controller or machine.

The system uses this counter to determine whether the account lockout threshold has been met for an account. Although there is little or no need in most environments to query this value, ADSI still exposes this read-only property for you to query upon. Use the following Visual Basic code to view the number of incorrect login attempts for a given user account:

```
On Error Resume Next
Dim User as IADsUser
Dim UserName as String
Dim UserDomain as String
UserDomain = "Target_User_Domain"
UserName = "Target_User_Name"
Set User = GetObject("WinNT://" & UserDomain & "/" & UserName & ",user")

Dim RetVal as Integer
RetVal = User.BadLoginCount
Debug.Print RetVal
```

> *Note*
>
> *If this property does not contain an integer, an error will be returned by ADSI claiming that the property could not be found in the property cache. Once again, you can use VB's* `On Error Resume Next` *error handler to avoid fatal termination of your application.* ✦

Querying *LastLogin* for a Given Machine Using Visual Basic

This property can be very useful when querying a local machine account database, but can yield unexpected results when binding to domain controllers in large domains containing multiple Backup Domain Controllers (BDCs). This seemingly inaccurate data is derived from the fact that a user can be authenticated on any BDC in the Windows NT domain authentication architecture. Use the following code to determine a user's last login on a member server or workstation:

```
On Error Resume Next
Dim User as IADsUser
Dim UserName as String
Dim UserDomain as String
UserDomain = "Target_User_Domain"
UserName = "Target_User_Name"
Set User = GetObject("WinNT://" & UserDomain & "/" & UserName & ",user")

Dim RetVal as Date
RetVal = User.LastLogin
Debug.Print RetVal
```

> *Note*
>
> *If the user has never logged into the domain (or on the domain controller servicing the request), ADSI will return an error, thus terminating the application or script.* ◆

Querying *LastLogoff* for a Given Machine Using Visual Basic

In addition to obtaining the date of a user's last login, you can also determine the date of a user's last logoff. Once again, this may not provide the expected result when used against a domain controller in enterprises with more than one domain controller.

Using similar Visual Basic code to what we used for LastLogin, you can also query a user's last logoff event, as follows:

```
Dim User as IADsUser
Dim UserName as String
Dim UserDomain as String
UserDomain = "Target_User_Domain"
UserName = "Target_User_Name"
Set User = GetObject("WinNT://" & UserDomain & "/" & UserName & ",user")

Dim RetVal as Date
RetVal = User.LastLogoff
Debug.Print RetVal
```

Querying *PasswordMinimumLength* for a User Account Using Visual Basic

To query the minimum password length for an individual user account, simply display the value of the `PasswordMinimumLength` property, as follows:

```
Dim User as IADsUser
Dim UserName as String
Dim UserDomain as String
UserDomain = "Target_User_Domain"
UserName = "Target_User_Name"
Set User = GetObject("WinNT://" & UserDomain & "/" & UserName & ",user")

Dim RetVal as Integer
RetVal = User.PasswordMinimumLength
Debug.Print RetVal
```

> *Note*
>
> *Although it may be desirable to set individual minimum lengths for user accounts, this is not permitted using the Windows NT service provider. Using the Windows NT provider, you can query only the minimum password length field.*
>
> *This value is actually derived from the parent container (in this case, the domain) and will violate the DS schema rules if you attempt to change this property on individual user accounts.*
>
> *This property can be useful for eliminating a second binding to the domain container if you need to query the minimum password length during the course of manipulating a user object.* ◆

Querying *PasswordRequired* for a User Account Using Visual Basic

Unlike the `PasswordMinimumLength` property, you can selectively require a password for individual user accounts without violating the DS schema rules. This can be useful for overriding the domain account policy for this setting to create a guest or generic login.

To determine whether a password is required for an existing user account, use the following Visual Basic code:

```
Dim User as IADsUser
Dim UserName as String
Dim UserDomain as String
UserDomain = "Target_User_Domain"
UserName = "Target_User_Name"
Set User = GetObject("WinNT://" & UserDomain & "/" & UserName & ",user")

Dim RetVal as Boolean
RetVal = User.PasswordRequired
Debug.Print RetVal
```

Setting *PasswordRequired* for a User Account Using Visual Basic

Use the following Visual Basic code to permit an individual user account to use a blank password:

```
Dim User as IADsUser
Dim UserName as String
Dim UserDomain as String
UserDomain = "Target_User_Domain"
UserName = "Target_User_Name"
Set User = GetObject("WinNT://" & UserDomain & "/" & UserName & ",user")

Dim NewValue as Boolean
NewValue = True
User.PasswordRequired = NewValue
User.SetInfo
```

Querying User Password Age Using Visual Basic

By default, Windows NT does not allow an administrator to specify a different maximum password age for privileged accounts. Programmatically, however, you can write a service or application that enumerates the members of a group, examines the password age for each user contained in the group, and then sets the PasswordExpired bit for each account with a password age longer than a specified value.

Although some security organizations allow 60- to 90-day password ages (or more) for business users, this exposes the organization to greater risk from the use of password-cracking utilities on administrative accounts.

Using the following code, you can effortlessly enforce a 30-day maximum password age for all users in the "Domain Admins" group:

```
Dim Group As IADsGroup
Dim GroupName As String
Dim GroupDomain As String
GroupDomain = "Target_Domain"
GroupName = "Domain Admins"
Set Group = GetObject("WinNT://" & GroupDomain & "/" & GroupName & ",group")
Dim Member As Variant
Dim User As IADsUser
For Each Member In Group.Members
    Set User = GetObject("WinNT://" & GroupDomain & "/" & Member.Name & ",user")
    If User.Get("PasswordAge") > 2592000 Then
        If (User.Get("UserFlags") And &H10000) = 0 Then
            Debug.Print Member.Name

            'If you wish to perform a query only, comment out the following
            ⇒two lines:
            User.Put "PasswordExpired", CLng(1)
            User.SetInfo
        End If
    End If
Next
```

Note

As with most values in the SAM, the time unit used for the `PasswordAge` *custom property is in seconds.* ◆

Querying Machine Password Age

Chapter 3 examined the creation of a computer account. This process involved multiple bindings—one to create the object in the computer container, another to the newly created computer object so it could be written to the directory, and a third to a user object to manipulate the user flags and password value.

The fact that computer accounts are actually just hidden user accounts opens up a wide variety of interesting possibilities for storing additional data about a machine. You can use the unpopulated string fields for a machine account to store data about the primary user of the machine or the physical location of the machine. More importantly, however, you can find out when the machine last authenticated with the domain, which can be valuable data for those tasked with cleaning up a resource domain SAM.

Most administrators are good at placing files into directories. When it comes to removing these items, however, these same administrators often wait until catastrophe strikes (such as running out of disk space) on the off chance that the data might be required for future reference.

Just as file servers continue to host files no longer in use, in most enterprise resource domains, Server Manager lists computer accounts that have been off the network for months. Administrators are usually reluctant to remove these accounts for fear that the removal might cause a user (and thus the administrator) significant hardship by doing so.

When you created the computer account initially, recall that you set an initial password. As part of the secure channel that is set up between the domain controller and the workstation, this password will be changed on a regular basis. By combining this bit of knowledge with a query on the `PasswordAge` property for a computer account, you can programmatically determine which machines have not been on the network for a specified period of time.

As referenced in Microsoft KB article Q197478, machine account passwords are changed every seven days by default. If your enterprise has not disabled this functionality, (see Q154501 for more information about how to disable this security feature) you can use the following code to determine which machines have not changed their passwords in the last seven days. In theory, any machine that has a password older than seven days can be considered to be off the network. To be safe, a more reasonable value should be chosen (perhaps 90 or 180 days) to accommodate mobile users who may not utilize network connectivity on a regular basis.

continues ▶

▶ *continued*

Consider the following code to determine which computer accounts have not been on the network in over 180 days:

```
Dim Container As IADsContainer
Dim TargetDomain as String
TargetDomain = "Domain_In_Which_To_Find_Old_Machine_Accounts"
Set Container = GetObject("WinNT://" & TargetDomain)
Dim Member As Variant
Dim Computer As IADsUser
Container.Filter = Array("Computer")
For Each Member In Container
    Set Computer = GetObject("WinNT://" & TargetDomain & "/" & Member.Name & "$,user")
        If Computer.Get("PasswordAge") > 15552000 Then
            Debug.Print Computer.ADsPath & " " & Computer.Get("PasswordAge")
        End If
Next
```

If you change the Debug.Print statement to call Container.Delete, use care to ensure that only workstation/member server accounts are removed.

Wrapping the call to Container.Delete with a conditional testing for the ADS_UF_WORKSTATION_TRUST_ACCOUNT user flag, as follows, can perform this safely:

```
Dim Container As IADsContainer
Dim TargetDomain as String
TargetDomain = "Domain_In_Which_To_Find_Old_Machine_Accounts"
Set Container = GetObject("WinNT://" & TargetDomain)
Dim Member As Variant
Dim Computer As IADsUser
Dim Flags as Variant
Container.Filter = Array("Computer")
For Each Member In Container
    Set Computer = GetObject("WinNT://" & TargetDomain & "/" & Member.Name & ↵"$,user")
        If Computer.Get("PasswordAge") > 15552000 Then
            Flags = Computer.Get("UserFlags")
            If (Flags And &H1000) <> 0 Then
                Call Container.Delete("computer", Member.Name)
            End If
        End If
Next ◆
```

Warning

The PDC does not change passwords every seven days; do not delete the PDC account!

The preceding code will permanently delete old machine accounts in the domain. If you are not careful (omitting the user flag conditional, for instance), you can delete the account for the PDC, which does not change passwords every seven days.

Make sure you use a `Debug.Print` *statement before actually deleting the old accounts to be sure you are not eliminating valid workstations or servers from the domain. Although workstation accounts can simply be re-created, domain controller accounts cannot without significant difficulty.* ◆

Creating the NTUserManagement Class Module

In this section, you continue the creation of the NTAdmin.DLL COM server application started in Chapter 3.

Just as in previous chapters, a class module within an ActiveX DLL will handle the manipulation of the IADsUser interface.

Exercise 4.1 *Creating NTAdmin.DLL: User Account Management Functions*

1. Open the NTAdmin ActiveX DLL Visual Basic project that was started in Chapter 3. You can also download the project from http://www.newriders.com/adsi.

2. If you are adding to the NTAdmin project, add a new class module to the project. If this is a new project, make sure to set a reference to Active DS Type Library.

3. Name the new module **NTUserManagement**.

   Enter the following code into the General Declarations section of the class module:

   ```
   Public Function QueryUserProperty(ByVal TargetUserDomain As String, ByVal
   ⇒TargetUserName As String, ByVal PropertyToQuery As String) As Variant
       On Error Resume Next
       Dim User As IADsUser
       Set User = GetObject("WinNT://" & TargetUserDomain & "/" & TargetUserName &
   ⇒",user")
       Select Case UCase(PropertyToQuery)
           Case "FULLNAME"
               QueryUserProperty = User.FullName
           Case "DESCRIPTION"
               QueryUserProperty = User.Description
           Case "ACCOUNTDISABLED"
               QueryUserProperty = User.AccountDisabled
           Case "ISACCOUNTLOCKED"
               QueryUserProperty = User.IsAccountLocked
           Case "PROFILE""
               QueryUserProperty = User.Profile
           Case "LOGINSCRIPT"
               QueryUserProperty = User.LoginScript
           Case "HOMEDIRECTORY"
               QueryUserProperty = User.HomeDirectory
           Case "HOMEDIRDRIVE"
               QueryUserProperty = User.Get("HomeDirDrive")
           Case "LOGINHOURS"
               Dim TimeEntry As Variant
   ```

continues ▶

Exercise 4.1 *continued*

```
                    Dim Restriction As Integer
                    For Each TimeEntry In User.LoginHours
                        If TimeEntry < 255 Then Restriction = 1
                    Next
                    If Restriction = 1 Then
                        QueryUserProperty = False
                    Else
                        QueryUserProperty = True
                    End If
                Case "ACCOUNTEXPIRATIONDATE"
                    QueryUserProperty = User.AccountExpirationDate
                Case "ACCOUNTTYPE"
                    Dim Flags As Long
                    Flags = User.Get("UserFlags")
                    If (Flags And &H100) <> 0 Then
                        QueryUserProperty = "LOCAL"
                    Else
                        QueryUserProperty = "GLOBAL"
                    End If
                Case "BADLOGINCOUNT"
                    QueryUserProperty = User.BadLoginCount
                Case "LASTLOGIN"
                    QueryUserProperty = User.LastLogin
                Case "LASTLOGOFF"
                    QueryUserProperty = User.LastLogoff
                Case "PASSWORDEXPIRED"
                    QueryUserProperty = User.Get("PasswordExpired")
                Case "PASSWORDMINIMUMLENGTH"
                    QueryUserProperty = User.PasswordMinimumLength
                Case "PASSWORDREQUIRED"
                    QueryUserProperty = User.PasswordRequired
                Case "PASSWORDAGE"
                    QueryUserProperty = User.Get("PasswordAge")
        End Select
End Function

Public Function SetUserProperty(ByVal TargetUserDomain As String, ByVal
↪TargetUserName As String, ByVal PropertyToQuery As String, ByVal NewValue As
↪Variant) As Boolean
        On Error Resume Next
        Dim User As IADsUser
        Set User = GetObject("WinNT://" & TargetUserDomain & "/" & TargetUserName &
        ↪",user")
        Select Case UCase(PropertyToQuery)
            Case "FULLNAME"
                User.FullName = NewValue
            Case "DESCRIPTION"
                User.Description = NewValue
            Case "ACCOUNTDISABLED"
                User.AccountDisabled = NewValue
            Case "ISACCOUNTLOCKED"
```

Creating the NTUserManagement Class Module   107

```
                    User.IsAccountLocked = NewValue
            Case "PROFILE"
                    User.Profile = NewValue
            Case "LOGINSCRIPT"
                    User.LoginScript = NewValue
            Case "HOMEDIRECTORY"
                    User.HomeDirectory = NewValue
            Case "HOMEDIRDRIVE"
                    Call User.Put("HomeDirDrive", NewValue)
            Case "ACCOUNTEXPIRATIONDATE"
                    User.AccountExpirationDate = NewValue
            Case "ACCOUNTTYPE"
                    Dim Flags As Long
                    Flags = User.Get("UserFlags")
                    If (Flags And &H200) <> 0 Then
                        User.Put "UserFlags", Flags Xor &H200
                        User.SetInfo
                        Flags = User.Get("UserFlags")
                        User.Put "UserFlags", Flags Xor &H100
                    Else
                        If (Flags And &H100) <> 0 Then
                            User.Put "UserFlags", Flags Xor &H100
                            User.SetInfo
                            Flags = User.Get("UserFlags")
                            User.Put "UserFlags", Flags Xor &H200
                        End If
                    End If
            Case "PASSWORDEXPIRED"
                    Call User.Put("PasswordExpired", NewValue)
            Case "PASSWORDREQUIRED"
                    User.PasswordRequired = NewValue
        End Select
        User.SetInfo
        If Err.Number = 0 Then SetUserProperty = True Else SetUserProperty = False
End Function

Public Function ChangeUserPassword(ByVal TargetUserDomain As String, ByVal
➥TargetUserName As String, ByVal OldPassword As String, ByVal NewPassword As
➥String) As Boolean
    Dim User As IADsUser
    Set User = GetObject("WinNT://" & TargetUserDomain & "/" & TargetUserName &
    ➥",user")
    Call User.ChangePassword(OldPassword, NewPassword)
    If Err.Number = 0 Then ChangeUserPassword = True Else ChangeUserPassword =
    ➥False
End Function

Public Function SetUserPassword(ByVal TargetUserDomain As String, ByVal
➥TargetUserName As String, ByVal NewPassword As String) As Boolean
    Dim User As IADsUser
    Set User = GetObject("WinNT://" & TargetUserDomain & "/" & TargetUserName &
    ➥",user")
```

continues ▶

Exercise 4.1 *continued*

```
            Call User.SetPassword(NewPassword)
            If Err.Number = 0 Then SetUserPassword = True Else SetUserPassword = False
End Function

Public Function UserFlag(ByVal TargetUserDomain As String, ByVal TargetUserName _
➥As String, ByVal Action As String, ByVal UserFlagConstant As String) As Boolean
        Dim User As IADsUser
        Dim Flags As Long
        Set User = GetObject("WinNT://" & TargetUserDomain & "/" & TargetUserName & _
➥",user")
        Flags = User.Get("UserFlags")
        Select Case UCase(UserFlagConstant)
            Case "PASSWD_CANT_CHANGE"
                Select Case UCase(Action)
                    Case "SET"
                        User.Put "UserFlags", Flags Or &H40
                        User.SetInfo
                        If Err.Number = 0 Then UserFlag = True Else UserFlag = _
                        ➥False
                    Case "QUERY"
                        If (Flags And &H40) <> 0 Then
                            UserFlag = True
                        Else
                            UserFlag = False
                        End If
                    Case "TOGGLE"
                        User.Put "UserFlags", Flags Xor &H40
                        User.SetInfo
                        If Err.Number = 0 Then UserFlag = True Else UserFlag = _
                        ➥False
                End Select
            Case "DONT_EXPIRE_PASSWD"
                Select Case UCase(Action)
                    Case "SET"
                        User.Put "UserFlags", Flags Or &H10000
                        User.SetInfo
                        If Err.Number = 0 Then UserFlag = True Else UserFlag = _
                        ➥False
                    Case "QUERY"
                        If (Flags And &H10000) <> 0 Then
                            UserFlag = True
                        Else
                            UserFlag = False
                        End If
                    Case "TOGGLE"
                        User.Put "UserFlags", Flags Xor &H10000
                        User.SetInfo
                        If Err.Number = 0 Then UserFlag = True Else UserFlag = _
                        ➥False
                End Select
        End Select
End Function
```

Creating the NTUserManagement Class Module   109

```
Public Function SetLogonWorkstations(ByVal TargetUserDomain As String, ByVal
↪TargetUserName As String, ByVal Action As String, ByVal Value As String) As
↪Boolean
    On Error Resume Next
    Dim User As IADsUser
    Dim Workstation As Variant
    Dim NewElement() As Variant
    Dim i As Long
    Dim Entry As Variant
    Dim EmptyArray As Integer
    Dim ValueAlreadyExists As Integer
    Set User = GetObject("WinNT://" & TargetUserDomain & "/" & TargetUserName &
↪",user")
    Select Case UCase(Action)
        Case "ADD"
            If IsArray(User.LoginWorkstations) = True Then
                For Each Entry In User.LoginWorkstations
                    i = UBound(NewElement) + 1
                    ReDim Preserve NewElement(i)
                    NewElement(i) = Entry
                    If Entry = "" Then EmptyArray = 1
                    If Entry = Value Then ValueAlreadyExists = 1
                Next
                If EmptyArray = 1 Then
                    User.LoginWorkstations = Array(Value)
                    User.SetInfo
                Else
                    If ValueAlreadyExists <> 1 Then
                        i = UBound(NewElement) + 1
                        ReDim Preserve NewElement(i)
                        NewElement(i) = Value
                        User.LoginWorkstations = NewElement
                        User.SetInfo
                    End If
                End If
            Else
                If User.LoginWorkstations <> Value Then
                    User.LoginWorkstations = Array(User.LoginWorkstations,
↪Value)
                    User.SetInfo
                End If
            End If
        Case "REMOVE"
            If IsArray(User.LoginWorkstations) = True Then
                For Each Entry In User.LoginWorkstations
                    If UCase(Value) <> UCase(Entry) Then
                        i = UBound(NewElement) + 1
                        ReDim Preserve NewElement(i)
                        NewElement(i) = Entry
                    End If
                Next
                User.LoginWorkstations = NewElement
                User.SetInfo
```

continues ▶

Exercise 4.1 *continued*

```
                    Debug.Print "here" & Err.Number
                Else
                    If User.LoginWorkstations = Value Then
                        User.LoginWorkstations = Array("")
                        User.SetInfo
                    End If
                End If
        End Select
        If (Err.Number = 0 Or Err.Number = 9 Or Err.Number = 92) Then
            SetLogonWorkstations = True
        Else
            SetLogonWorkstations = False
        End If
End Function

Public Function EnumerateLogonWorkstations(ByVal TargetUserDomain As String,
➥ByVal TargetUserName As String) As Variant
    On Error Resume Next
    Dim User As IADsUser
    Dim Workstation As Variant
    Dim NewElement() As Variant
    Dim i As Long
    Set User = GetObject("WinNT://" & TargetUserDomain & "/" & TargetUserName &
➥",user")
    If User.LoginWorkstations = "" Then
        For Each Workstation In User.LoginWorkstations
            i = UBound(NewElement) + 1
            ReDim Preserve NewElement(i)
            NewElement(i) = Workstation
        Next
        EnumerateLogonWorkstations = NewElement
    Else
        EnumerateLogonWorkstations = Array(User.LoginWorkstations)
    End If
End Function
```

4. Compile the code as NTAdmin.DLL.
5. Save and close the NTAdmin project.

> **Tip**
>
> *You can download the Visual Basic 6.0 project or a pre-compiled version of NTAdmin.DLL from* http://www.newriders.com/adsi. ◆

Using the Functions in NTUserManagement

With the NTUserManagement class module created, you can access this function from any programming language that supports OLE automation, including Visual Basic, VBScript, and JavaScript.

> **Tip**
>
> *To instantiate the object, follow the appropriate syntax found in Chapter 3. Substitute the NTUserManagement class name where necessary.* ♦

Use Table 4.1 to help you use the proper syntax for each of the methods of the NTUserManagement interface:

Table 4.1 NTUserManagement *Method Syntax*

Action	Syntax
Query User Full Name	QueryUserProperty("Target_User_Domain", ➥"Target_User_Name","FullName")
Query User Description	QueryUserProperty("Target_User_Domain", ➥"Target_User_Name","Description")
Determine if Account is Disabled or Enabled	QueryUserProperty("Target_User_Domain", ➥"Target_User_Name","AccountDisabled")
Determine Account Lockout Status	QueryUserProperty("Target_User_Domain", ➥"Target_User_Name","IsAccountLocked")
Query User Profile Path	QueryUserProperty("Target_User_Domain", ➥"Target_User_Name","Profile")
Query Login Script	QueryUserProperty("Target_User_Domain", ➥"Target_User_Name","LoginScript")
Query Home Directory Path	QueryUserProperty("Target_User_Domain", ➥"Target_User_Name","HomeDirectory")
Query Home Directory Drive Mapping	QueryUserProperty("Target_User_Domain", ➥"Target_User_Name","HomeDirDrive")
Query Existence of Login Hour Restrictions	QueryUserProperty("Target_User_Domain", ➥"Target_User_Name","LoginHours")
Query Account Expiration Date	QueryUserProperty("Target_User_Domain", ➥"Target_User_Name","AccountExpirationDate")
Query Account Type (local or global)	QueryUserProperty("Target_User_Domain", ➥"Target_User_Name","AccountType")
Query Bad Login Count	QueryUserProperty("Target_User_Domain", ➥"Target_User_Name","BadLoginCount")
Query Last Login	QueryUserProperty("Target_User_Domain", ➥"Target_User_Name","LastLogin")
Query Last Logoff	QueryUserProperty("Target_User_Domain", ➥"Target_User_Name","LastLogoff")
Query Password Expired	QueryUserProperty("Target_User_Domain", ➥"Target_User_Name","PasswordExpired")
Query Password Minimum Length	QueryUserProperty("Target_User_Domain", ➥"Target_User_Name","PasswordMinimumLength")
Query Password Required	QueryUserProperty("Target_User_Domain", ➥"Target_User_Name","PasswordRequired")

continues ▶

Table 4.1   continued

Action	Syntax
Query Password Age	`QueryUserProperty("Target_User_Domain",` `↳"Target_User_Name","PasswordAge")`
Set User Full Name	`SetUserProperty("Target_User_Domain",` `↳"Target_User_Name","FullName","NewValue")`

Set User Description	`SetUserProperty("Target_User_Domain",`
	`↳"Target_User_Name","Description",`
	`↳"NewValue")`

Set Account Disabled Bit	`SetUserProperty("Target_User_Domain",` `↳"Target_User_Name","AccountDisabled",True)`
Reset Account Lockout	`SetUserProperty("Target_User_Domain",` `↳"Target_User_Name","IsAccountLocked",True)`
Set User Profile Path	`SetUserProperty("Target_User_Domain",` `↳"Target_User_Name","Profile","NewValue")`
Set Login Script	`SetUserProperty("Target_User_Domain",` `↳"Target_User_Name","LoginScript","NewValue")`

Set Home Directory Path	`SetUserProperty("Target_User_Domain",`
	`↳"Target_User_Name","HomeDirectory",`
	`↳"NewValue")`

Set Home Directory Drive Mapping	`SetUserProperty("Target_User_Domain",`
	`↳"Target_User_Name","HomeDirDrive",`
	`↳"NewValue")`

Set Account Expiration Date	`SetUserProperty("Target_User_Domain",`
	`↳"Target_User_Name","AccountExpirationDate",`
	`↳#NewValue#)`

Toggle Account Type	`SetUserProperty("Target_User_Domain",` `↳"Target_User_Name","AccountType","")`
Set Password Expired	`SetUserProperty("Target_User_Domain",` `↳"Target_User_Name","PasswordExpired",True)`
Set Password Required	`SetUserProperty("Target_User_Domain",` `↳"Target_User_Name","PasswordRequired",True)`

Change User Password	`ChangeUserPassword("Target_User_Domain",`
	`↳"Target_User_Name","Old_Password","New_`
	`↳Password")`

Set User Password	`SetUserPassword("Target_User_Domain",` `↳"Target_User_Name","New_Password")`

Query "User Cannot Change Password" bit	`UserFlag("Target_User_Domain",`
	`↳"Target_User_Name","Query",`
	`↳"PASSWD_CANT_CHANGE")`

Set "User Cannot Change Password" bit	`UserFlag("Target_User_Domain","Target_User_` `↳Name","Set","PASSWD_CANT_CHANGE")`
Toggle "User Cannot Change Password" bit	`UserFlag("Target_User_Domain","Target_User_` `↳Name","Toggle","PASSWD_CANT_CHANGE")`

Action	Syntax
Query "Password Never Expires" bit	`UserFlag("Target_User_Domain","Target_User_`↪`Name","Query","DONT_EXPIRE_PASSWD")`
Set "Password Never Expires" bit	`UserFlag("Target_User_Domain",`↪`"Target_User_Name","Set","DONT_EXPIRE_`↪`PASSWD")`
Toggle "Password Never Expires" bit	`UserFlag("Target_User_Domain",`↪`"Target_User_Name","Toggle","DONT_EXPIRE_`↪`PASSWD")`
Add Logon Workstation	`SetLogonWorkstations("Target_User_Domain",`↪`"Target_User_Name","Add","New_Logon_`↪`Workstation")`
Remove Logon Workstation	`SetLogonWorkstations("Target_User_`↪`Domain","Target_User_Name","Remove",`↪`"Workstation_To_Remove")`

Enumerate Logon Workstations	`For Each Item In EnumerateLogonWorkstations`↪`("Target_User_Domain","Target_User_Name")`
	`    Debug.Print Item`
	`Next`

Summary

Using the IADsUser interface, you can manipulate the majority of the most common administrative tasks performed on a daily basis. Combining enumeration functions with the properties and methods of the IADsUser interface, you can perform extremely powerful queries and account manipulation procedures on a container object and its contents.

The IADsUser interface applies not only to user accounts, but also to computer accounts. This opens a wealth of possibilities, including the ability to query machine password age. Additionally, you can populate unused fields with the name of the primary user, business unit, and physical location of the machine to create extremely powerful directed administration procedures.

Using the password age for a user account, you can force users with privileged accounts to change their passwords more frequently than standard user accounts. Taking such an action is highly recommended if the default domain password policy allows password ages of greater than 30 days to minimize the risk of compromises from password-cracking utilities. Ultimately, encrypting the SAM using SysKey is the best protection against compromise from such utilities.

With the ADSI IADsUser interface, it is also possible to query fields and counters that are not visible using standard Windows NT GUI tools such as BadLoginCount, LastLogin, and LastLogoff for an individual user account.

With the code samples throughout this text and a bit of practice with the ADSI IADsUser interface, you can create extremely powerful user management tools using Visual Basic.

5
Programmatic Group Manipulation

Managing groups and group membership is typically the core operation for administrators tasked with managing file system security. With Visual Basic, you can use methods of the IADsGroup and IADsUser interfaces to query and manipulate groups in the Windows NT namespace. By employing the code segments in this chapter, you can also access the SAM to create applications that use the default authentication and access control mechanisms for managing Windows NT security. Using this system is more desirable than using JET (MS_Access) databases, the Registry, or other insecure data stores to house application security information.

In addition to basic group-membership manipulation, this chapter will explore a proven best-practice method for managing file system security when you require extremely granular access to the files and directories that make up the structure of an NT File System (NTFS) partition.

You will also continue the creation of the NTAdmin.DLL COM server application you started in Chapter 3, "Container Enumeration Methods and Programmatic Domain Account Policy Manipulation."

Windows NT Security Group Administration

The IADsGroup interface supports full management of group objects in domains or in the individual SAMs used on member servers and NT workstations. Using the IADsGroup interface (see Figure 5.1), you can perform the following functions in a Windows NT namespace:

- Add members to any given group.
- Remove members from any given group.
- Enumerate the members of a group.

- Query whether a given user belongs to a group.
- Query or set the description for any given group.

By adding the Groups method of the IADsUser interface to the above methods, you can also

- Enumerate all groups to which a specific user object has been assigned.

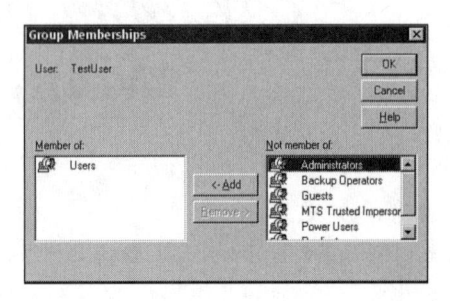

Figure 5.1 *Group Memberships dialog box in User Manager for Domains.*

Group Binding

To manipulate a group object using ADSI, you must first bind to the desired group object. In general, the following syntax is used to perform the binding:

```
GetObject("WinNT://" & DomainName & "/" & GroupName & ",group")
```

Notice that you specified the object class as part of the binding string. This yields better performance than the equivalent classless binding string.

> *Tip*
>
> *Although it is an optional parameter, the class name should always be specified as part of the binding string to avoid ambiguity and to improve binding performance.* ♦

Group Binding Using Visual Basic

To bind a group object using Visual Basic, use the following example as a guide:

```
Dim Group as IADsGroup
Dim GroupName as String
Dim GroupDomain as String
GroupDomain = "Target_Group_Domain"
GroupName = "Target_Group_Name"
Set Group = GetObject("WinNT://" & GroupDomain & "/" & GroupName & ",group")
```

To perform a binding to a group object in your environment, simply replace the assignments for `GroupDomain` and `GroupName` with the appropriate values for your enterprise. With the object bound, you can now manipulate the exposed properties and methods of the IADsGroup interface.

Adding Users to a Group

For most administrators, the addition of user accounts to security groups is bound to enter into his or her daily agenda on a regular basis. To help facilitate these actions in the namespace, the IADsGroup interface exposes the `Add` method for manipulation of group memberships.

To add a new member to a currently bound group object, use the following general syntax:

```
Group.Add(ADsPath of User Object)
```

Tip

You can explicitly state the `ADsPath` *of the user (*`WinNT://Domain/User`*), or you can bind to a user object and then pass in the* `ADsPath` *property value to the* `Add` *method of the IADsGroup interface.* ◆

Adding Users to a Group Using Visual Basic

To add a user to an existing Windows NT security group, use the folowing Visual Basic code:

```
Dim Group as IADsGroup
Dim GroupName as String
Dim GroupDomain as String
Dim User as IADsUser
Dim UserName as String
Dim UserDomain as String
GroupName = "Target_Group_Name"
GroupDomain = "Target_Group_Domain"
UserName = "Target_User_Name"
UserDomain = "Target_User_Domain"
Set User = GetObject("WinNT://" & UserDomain & "/" & UserName & ",user")
Set Group = GetObject("WinNT://" & GroupDomain & "/" & GroupName & ",group")
Group.Add(User.ADsPath)
Group.SetInfo
```

Removing Users from a Group

Not surprisingly, the IADsGroup interface also implements a method to remove users from a group. The `Remove` method follows a very similar syntax to the `Add` method of the IADsGroup interface:

```
Group.Remove(ADsPath of User Object)
```

Removing Users from a Group Using Visual Basic

To remove an existing group member from the bound group, use the following Visual Basic code:

```
Dim Group as IADsGroup
Dim GroupName as String
Dim GroupDomain as String
Dim User as IADsUser
Dim UserName as String
Dim UserDomain as String
GroupName = "Target_Group_Name"
GroupDomain = "Target_Group_Domain"
UserName = "Target_User_Name"
UserDomain = "Target_User_Domain"
Set User = GetObject("WinNT://" & UserDomain & "/" & UserName & ",user")
Set Group = GetObject("WinNT://" & GroupDomain & "/" & GroupName & ",group")
Group.Remove(User.ADsPath)
```

Enumerating Members of a Group

Using User Manager, you can enumerate the members of a group in order to help you decide whether to add or remove an account to a particular group.

Enumerating Members of a Group Using Visual Basic

Using the following Visual Basic code, you can enumerate all users with membership in the bound security group:

```
Dim Group as IADsGroup
Dim GroupName as String
Dim GroupDomain as String
GroupName = "Target_Group_Name"
GroupDomain = "Target_Group_Domain"
Set Group = GetObject("WinNT://" & GroupDomain & "/" & GroupName & ",group")

For Each Member in Group.Members
     Debug.Print Member.Name
Next
```

Querying User Membership in a Group

The `IsMember` method will return a Boolean value indicating whether the user account passed as an argument belongs to the currently bound group. This is useful for positively verifying that a group addition action was completed successfully, or for testing a user's group membership before performing an action.

Tip

By itself, the IsMember *method simply returns a Boolean result, providing little value unless it is combined with a conditional to perform some action based upon the results of this test. This conditional may test to see if the user belongs to a specific group and then add the account if* IsMember *returns a false condition. You can also create a conditional to query if a user belongs to a specific administrative group before allowing the application to continue.* ♦

Querying User Membership in a Group Using Visual Basic

Use the following Visual Basic code to verify that a user belongs to a specific security group:

```
Dim Group as IADsGroup
Dim GroupName as String
Dim GroupDomain as String
Dim User as IADsUser
Dim UserName as String
Dim UserDomain as String
GroupName = "Target_Group_Name"
GroupDomain = "Target_Group_Domain"
UserName = "Target_User_Name"
UserDomain = "Target_User_Domain"
Set User = GetObject("WinNT://" & UserDomain & "/" & UserName & ",user")
Set Group = GetObject("WinNT://" & GroupDomain & "/" & GroupName & ",group")
RetVal = Group.IsMember(User.ADsPath)
Debug.Print RetVal
```

Note

Notice that first the user account is bound and then the ADsPath *of the user object is passed in to the* IsMember *method. This is done for two reasons. The first is simply that you want to make sure the account exists before attempting to verify group membership. Secondly, on non-domain controllers, unless the resource domain is explicitly specified, ADSI will return an incorrect result. The use of the* ADsPath *property as the argument to the* IsMember *method is the ideal way to accurately determine if a user belongs to a given security group.* ♦

Note

When using the IsMember *method to verify group membership, it is important to note that a False condition will be returned if a user's membership is enjoyed through global group membership. To prevent this, you may wish to examine the object class for each member of the group, bind to any global groups, and use the* IsMember *method at that level to verify group membership.* ♦

> **Further Exploration:** *Using the* `IsMember` *Method to Control Rendering of Interface Elements in Active Server Pages*
>
> One of the most useful methods of the IADsGroup interface for the Web developer is the `IsMember` method. While many of the ADSI functions are only accessible by privileged user accounts, both privileged and non-privileged user accounts can receive a result from a call to the `IsMember` method.
>
> For Web developers who frequently work with pages secured by Windows NT Challenge/Response or Basic Authentication, this property can enable some interesting enhancements to a Web interface. Although you can use other objects from Microsoft (such as PermChk) to perform similar duties, the `IsMember` method is an efficient and simple method for controlling the rendering of Web pages based on a user's group membership in a given SAM database.
>
> Using the `IsMember` method in an Active Server Page, you can actually turn on and off interface elements based on a user's group membership. This can avoid the use of cookies, user preference databases, and can even prevent support calls when a user clicks a link to an item he or she does not have the proper permission to access.
>
> Consider the following scenario to help illustrate the power of the `IsMember` method in Active Server Page (ASP) scripting:
>
> The management team has determined that senior managers in the firm should be able to edit employee performance evaluations using a new intranet application. In an effort to keep the user interface as simple as possible, the intranet development team decides that the link enabling document editing should be available only to those users who actually have rights to edit the performance evaluation documents.
>
> Using the `IsMember` method of the IADsGroup interface, the developer can simply query the SAM to find out whether the user is in the senior managers group, and render the link accordingly.
>
> Unlike client-side script, ASPs will hide all conditionals and code used for generating the resulting HTML from user view. If the conditional evaluating the return value is `False`, the link simply will not show up in the client-side source code, and thus will not be rendered. The end result is a user interface that is tailored specifically to a user's actual permissions in the environment, providing greater simplicity and elegance in the interface implementation. ◆

Querying and Setting Group Description Field Values

In the SAM record of each local and global group, there exists an optional field that allows you to enter a description defining the function of the group. If you implement group descriptions using a meaningful naming standard (such as the owner of the group, the function of the group, or the name of the application served by the group), group description field queries can provide an especially powerful search mechanism when combined with ADSI's group enumeration methods.

Using the Description property of the IADsGroup interface, it is possible to query and set the value for the description field for any group.

Querying Group Description Field Value Using Visual Basic
Using Visual Basic, we can query the value of the description field using the following syntax:

```
Dim Group as IADsGroup
Dim GroupName as String
Dim GroupDomain as String
Dim RetVal as String
GroupDomain = "Target_Group_Domain"
GroupName = "Target_Group_Name"
Set Group = GetObject("WinNT://" & GroupDomain & "/" & GroupName & ",group")
RetVal = Group.Description
Debug.Print RetVal
```

Setting New Group Description Field Value Using Visual Basic
Just as you can query the value of the description field for any given group, you can also set a new value for the field programmatically.

Tip

The ability to programmatically manipulate the description field can be useful for application setup routines that require a group to be created, or for appending information to an existing group description field. ♦

Use the following Visual Basic code to set a new value for the description field on a single group:

```
Dim Group as IADsGroup
Dim GroupName as String
Dim GroupDomain as String
Dim RetVal as String
GroupDomain = "Target_Group_Domain"
GroupName = "Target_Group_Name"
GroupDescription = "Target_Group_Description"
Set Group = GetObject("WinNT://" & GroupDomain & "/" & GroupName & ",group")
Group.Description = GroupDescription
Group.SetInfo
```

If you need to append the value of the description field to accommodate new information in your group description naming standard, simply perform a query of the current value, concatenate the old value with the amendment, and then write the new description back into the directory. This process is detailed as follows using Visual Basic:

```
Dim Group as IADsGroup
Dim OriginalValue as String
Dim ValueToAppend as String
Dim NewValue as String
Dim GroupName as String
Dim GroupDomain as String
Dim RetVal as String
GroupDomain = "Target_Group_Domain"
GroupName = "Target_Group_Name"
Set Group = GetObject("WinNT://" & GroupDomain & "/" & GroupName & ",group")
OriginalValue = Group.Description
ValueToAppend = " (Owner=NT Engineering)"

NewValue = OriginalValue & ValueToAppend
Group.Description = NewValue
Group.SetInfo
```

Enumerating Individual User Group Membership

Using User Manager, you have the ability not only to view all groups in a given domain, but you can also view the groups for which a specific user account has been assigned.

Although you have seen that the IADsGroup interface exposes the Members method to return all the users for a given group, you may also want to enumerate all groups for which a given user belongs. To perform this action, simply call upon the Groups method of the IADsUser interface to return a variant array containing all groups to which the specified user account belongs.

Enumerating Individual User Group Membership Using Visual Basic

To enumerate individual user group membership, you must first bind to the user account for which you seek group membership information. Following the binding, use a *For...Each* loop to step through each item in the collection returned by the call to the Groups method, as follows:

```
Dim User as IADsUser
Dim Group as IADsGroup
Dim UserDomain as String
Dim UserName as String
UserDomain = "Target_User_Domain"
UserName = "Target_User_Name"
```

```
Set User = GetObject("WinNT://" & UserDomain & "/" & UserName & ",user")
For Each Group in User.Groups
    Debug.Print Group.Name
Next
```

Using Groups to Manage File System Security

When it comes to permissioning a file system, Microsoft has a very specific method that aims to reduce risk and simplify administration. Careful adherence to this technique will allow programmatic manipulation of file structure permissions using ADSI.

Unfortunately, most enterprises deviate from the file-permissioning guidelines set forth by Microsoft because they *appear* overly complicated to maintain. Microsoft recommends the following strategy for managing Windows NT security groups:

1. Place all user accounts into global groups in the user domain.
2. Add these global groups to a local group in the resource domain.
3. Apply permissions to resources by modifying the Access Control List (ACL) to include an Access Control Entriy (ACE) for the local group.

In most enterprises, however, practice all-too-often dictates that a conglomerate of user accounts be added directly to the ACLs for specific files in the file system as well as global groups added to ACLs on directories, and other severe departures are made from Microsoft's best practice advice.

There is a whole list of reasons why you should follow the advice from the folks in Redmond, but perhaps the most compelling reason is for pure administrative elegance. If you always use the "users in globals, globals in locals, permission resources using locals" strategy, after a directory has been set up, you should not need to add or remove ACEs in the resource's ACL.

If you have ever had someone (or worse yet, *been* the someone) in the system administration group apply a new ACL to a high level in the file system (such as the entire drive) and then propagate the changes throughout the file structure, you are well aware of the benefits gained by eliminating the need for direct ACL manipulation. By simply creating a group for each directory that requires unique permissions, you can eliminate all ACL management after the file structure has been created.

Consider the following directory structure:

```
D:\
D:\Data
D:\Data\MSOfficeData
D:\Data\VisualStudioData
D:\Apps
D:\Apps\MSOffice
D:\Apps\VisualStudio
```

In most enterprises, users requiring access to a specific directory are granted access through modification of the ACL to include an ACE for the user account or perhaps a global group that the user belongs to. Although you could easily grant a user access to both the D:\Apps\MSOffice and D:\Data\MSOfficeData directories in this manner, you must grant this access in more than one place at a time. While this may seem trivial in the two-directory example shown here, it is rather significant when an application requires permissions in 10–20 directories for proper operation.

Creating an Inheritance Structure

You can gain significantly more control over the file system by simply creating one local group on the file server for each directory in the structure. If users require differing levels of access (Read-Only, Change, Full Control, or No Access) you can create several local groups per directory to accommodate these variances in access levels.

Beginning at the root of the filespace, grant the *D_Drive* groups (assuming it is indeed the D: drive you are permissioning) access, and propagate the changes down the entire structure. Continue down all directories in the tree until you have applied every local group to every directory requiring unique permissions in the file system.

What you have now created is an inheritance structure in which a user granted access at a point high up in the directory structure (such as the D: drive) has access to this resource and everything below it. Likewise, a user granted access in the middle of the structure can see everything below where the account group membership allows, but cannot access anything above.

Consider Table 5.1 as an example of the ACLs for the MSOffice application directory.

Table 5.1   Establishing a File System Inheritence Structure

Resource	Local Group	Access Level
D:	D_Drive_FC	Full Control
	D_Drive_CH	Change
	D_Drive_RO	Read Only
D:\Apps	D_Drive_FC	Inherited (Full Control)
	D_Drive_CH	Inherited (Change)
	D_Drive_RO	Inherited (Read Only)
	D_Apps_FC	Full Control
	D_Apps_CH	Change Control
	D_Apps_RO	Read Only
D:\Apps\MSOffice	D_Drive_FC	Inherited (Full Control)
	D_Drive_CH	Inherited (Change)

Resource	Local Group	Access Level
	D_Drive_RO	Inherited (Read Only)
	D_Apps_FC	Inherited (Full Control)
	D_Apps_CH	Inherited (Change)
	D_Apps_RO	Inherited (Read Only)
	D_Apps_MSOffice_FC	Full Control
	D_Apps_MSOffice_CH	Change
	D_Apps_MSOffice_RO	Read Only

It is clear from this table that users belonging to the *D_Apps_MSOffice_RO* group will have read-only access to the D:\Apps\MSOffice directory, but cannot access anything in the D:\Apps level of the file structure, nor will they enjoy access to D:\Apps\VisualStudio.

If we create an *MSOffice_Users* global group in the user domain, we can add this group to the appropriate local groups on the server (such as *D_Apps_MSOffice* and *D_Data_MSOfficeData*). This eliminates the need to assign explicit permissions to both of these directories for each user account requiring access.

Next, by adding user accounts to the *MSOffice_Users* global group in the user domain, any user account belonging to this group will enjoy access to both the application and data directories associated with MSOffice.

> **Note**
>
> *This may seem to be a significant amount of work to initially implement, but there are immense benefits to this method of file system security management, including the capability to manage file system security using ADSI.* ◆

By avoiding direct manipulation of the ACLs on individual resources, you eliminate a significant amount of risk from incorrectly modified ACLs that were propagated down the directory structure from a higher-level directory. An administrator should manage *group memberships* on a regular basis, *not* ACLs.

> **Note**
>
> *To help set up a new file server using this method, a script is available in the sample code for this book to help create and manage the directories and groups using this security administration method.*
>
> *You can find this script at* http://www.newriders.com/adsi. ◆

Application developers should carefully consider this method; it can allow extremely granular access to files and resources in addition to simplifying administration. Rather than describing the ACLs required for the application to run and still retain a secure environment (or, worse yet, not apply any security to the file system at all), the developer can create groups and CACLS scripts to initially deploy the application.

Creating the NTGroupManagement Class Module

In this section, you continue the creation of the NTAdmin.DLL COM server application you started in Chapter 3.

Just as in all previous chapters, manipulation of the IADsGroup interface (and one method of the IADsUser interface) is handled by a class module within an ActiveX DLL.

Exercise 5.1   *Creating NTAdmin.DLL: Group Management Functions*

1. Open the NTAdmin ActiveX DLL Visual Basic project that was started in Chapter 3. You can also download the project from http://www.newriders.com/adsi.

2. If you are adding to the NTAdmin project, add a new class module to the project. If this is a new project, make sure to set a reference to Active DS Type Library.

3. Name the new module **NTGroupManagement**.

4. Enter the following code into the General Declarations section of the class module:

```
Public Function ManageGroup(ByVal TargetGroupDomain As String, ByVal
➥TargetGroupName As String, ByVal TargetUserDomain As String, ByVal
➥TargetUserName As String, ByVal Action As String) As Boolean
    Dim Group As IADsGroup
    Dim User As IADsUser
    Set User = GetObject("WinNT://" & TargetUserDomain & "/" & TargetUserName &
➥",user")
    Set Group = GetObject("WinNT://" & TargetGroupDomain & "/" & TargetGroupName
➥& ",group")
    Select Case UCase(Action)
        Case "ADD"
            Group.Add (User.ADsPath)
        Case "REMOVE"
            Group.Remove (User.ADsPath)
    End Select
    Group.SetInfo
    If Err.Number = 0 Then ManageGroup = True Else ManageGroup = False
End Function

    Public Function EnumerateGroupMembers(ByVal TargetGroupDomain As String, ByVal
➥TargetGroupName As String) As Variant
        On Error Resume Next
        Dim Group As IADsGroup
        Dim NewElement() As Variant
        Dim i As Long
        Set Group = GetObject("WinNT://" & TargetGroupDomain & "/" & TargetGroupName
```

Creating the NTGroupManagement Class Module   127

```
        ⇒& ",group")
        For Each Member In Group.Members
                i = UBound(NewElement) + 1
                ReDim Preserve NewElement(i)
                NewElement(i) = Member.Name
        Next
        EnumerateGroupMembers = NewElement
End Function

Public Function VerifyGroupMembership(ByVal TargetGroupDomain As String, ByVal
⇒TargetGroupName As String, ByVal TargetUserDomain As String, ByVal
⇒TargetUserName As String) As Boolean
        Dim Group As IADsGroup
        Dim User As IADsUser
        Set User = GetObject("WinNT://" & TargetUserDomain & "/" & TargetUserName &
    ⇒",user")
        Set Group = GetObject("WinNT://" & TargetGroupDomain & "/" & TargetGroupName
    ⇒& ",group")
        VerifyGroupMembership = Group.IsMember(User.ADsPath)
End Function

Public Function QueryGroupDescription(ByVal TargetGroupDomain As String, ByVal
⇒TargetGroupName As String) As String
        Dim Group As IADsGroup
        Set Group = GetObject("WinNT://" & TargetGroupDomain & "/" & TargetGroupName
    ⇒& ",group")
        QueryGroupDescription = Group.Description
End Function

Public Function SetGroupDescription(ByVal TargetGroupDomain As String, ByVal
⇒TargetGroupName As String, ByVal NewDescription As String) As Boolean
        Dim Group As IADsGroup
        Set Group = GetObject("WinNT://" & TargetGroupDomain & "/" & TargetGroupName
    ⇒& ",group")
        Group.Description = NewDescription
        Group.SetInfo
        If Err.Number = 0 Then SetGroupDescription = True Else SetGroupDescription =
    ⇒False
End Function
```

5. Compile the code as *NTAdmin.DLL*.
6. Save and close the NTAdmin project.

Tip

You can download the Visual Basic 6.0 project or a pre-compiled version of NTAdmin.DLL from http://www.newriders.com/adsi ◆

Using the Functions in NTGroupManagement

With the NTGroupManagement class module created, you can access this function from any programming language that supports OLE automation, including Visual Basic, VBScript, and JavaScript.

> **Tip**
>
> *To instantiate the object, follow the appropriate syntax found in Chapter 3. Substitute the NTGroupManagement class name where necessary.* ♦

Use Table 5.2 to help you use the proper syntax for each of the methods of the NTGroupManagement interface.

Table 5.2 NTGroupManagement *Method Syntax.*

Action	Syntax
Add a member to a group	Debug.Print ↪ManageGroup("Group_Target_Domain", ↪"Target_Group_Name", ↪"Target_UserDomain", ↪"Target_UserName", "Add")
Remove a member from a group	Debug.Print ↪ManageGroup("Group_Target_Domain", ↪"Target_Group_Name", ↪"Target_UserDomain", ↪"Target_UserName", "Remove")
Enumerate all users in a group	For Each Item In ↪EnumerateGroupMembers("Group_Target_ ↪Domain", "Target_Group_Name") Debug.Print Item Next
Verify user membership in a given group	Debug.Print ↪VerifyGroupMembership("Group_Target_ ↪Domain", "Target_Group_Name", ↪"Target_UserDomain", ↪"Target_UserName")
Query the description for a given group	Debug.Print ↪QueryGroupDescription("Group_Target_ ↪Domain", "Target_Group_Name")
Set a new description for a given group	Debug.Print ↪SetGroupDescription("Group_Target_ ↪Domain", "Target_Group_Name", ↪"New_Group_Description")

Summary

Using the methods of the IADsGroup and IADsUser interfaces, developers can create applications that rely upon the Windows NT SAM for managing application security rather than other methods, such as the Registry or external databases for access control and authentication. In addition, the systems administrator can script all group management activities.

In a properly managed file system, you can also use ADSI to manage permissions on directories and access to applications. Although ADSI cannot be used to directly modify the ACLs on a given resource without the ADSI Resource Kit extension DLLs, it is ideally suited to managing the group memberships for group ACEs within each ACL.

Beyond the creation of new groups and addition of group members, the potential for extension of default functionality is limited only by your own creativity. With a small amount of programming knowledge and the Active Directory Service Interfaces, the ability to script tedious group administration tasks can result in a reduction of risk to the computing environment, more efficient administration techniques, and maybe even a chance for you to go home on time.

6

Programmatic Computer and Service Manipulation

In addition to basic namespace manipulation, ADSI provides developers and administrators with a powerful set of programmatic interfaces for querying and manipulating attributes of computers throughout the enterprise.

The read-only properties exposed by the Windows NT service provider in the IADsComputer interface are well suited to controlling program flow to assure a machine meets certain administrator/developer-specified criteria, such as restricting an application to run on Windows NT only.

The IADsService interface allows you to modify the default behavior of installed services, including the ability to change the display name and path to the service executable.

Lastly, using the IADsServiceOperations interface, you can start, stop, pause, continue, and query the status of installed services for any given machine.

This chapter will cover the use of these three interfaces as they relate to the Windows NT service provider.

Querying Computer Properties: The IADsComputer Interface

Using the IADsComputer interface you can query various properties of a machine, including the Hardware Abstraction Layer (HAL) in use and the owner and registered organization of the machine. Unlike Registry editing tools used to manipulate these properties, all properties of ADSI's IADsComputer interface found within the Windows NT service provider are read-only.

For this reason, this interface is well suited for gathering statistics about the enterprise or controlling program flow, as opposed to the programmatic enterprise administration you have been performing in previous chapters. If you wish to manipulate the values of the interface properties, you will have to use traditional methods, such as REGEDT32.

By combining enumeration functions with IADsComputer property queries, you can generate reports regarding the status of an upgrade, or determine older technology in use in the environment by examining the appropriate properties.

> **Tip**
>
> As described in Chapter 3, "Container Enumeration Methods and Programmatic Domain Account Policy Manipulation," a "Computer" filter on the IADsContainer interface can allow all computers in a resource domain to be enumerated. ♦

Querying the Computer Owner Using Visual Basic

You can derive a computer's primary user by querying the RegisteredOwner string in the Registry. While you can use REGEDIT/REGEDT32 to query a single remote Registry for these values, you can use ADSI to perform this query on large quantities of machines using the following Visual Basic code with an enumeration function:

```
Dim Computer as IADsComputer
Dim ComputerName as String
Dim ComputerDomain as String
ComputerDomain = "Target_Computer_Domain"
ComputerName = "Target_Computer_Name"
Set Computer= GetObject("WinNT://" & ComputerDomain & "/" & ComputerName &
↪",computer")

Dim RetVal as String
RetVal = Computer.Owner
Debug.Print RetVal
```

Querying the Registered Organization Using Visual Basic

Using similar Visual Basic code to that which was used to query the computer owner, you can query the RegisteredOrganization string value in the Registry, as follows:

```
Dim Computer as IADsComputer
Dim ComputerName as String
Dim ComputerDomain as String
ComputerDomain = "Target_Computer_Domain"
ComputerName = "Target_Computer_Name"
```

```
Set Computer= GetObject("WinNT://" & ComputerDomain & "/" & ComputerName &
↳",computer")

Dim RetVal as String
RetVal = Computer.Division
Debug.Print RetVal
```

Querying the Computer Operating System Using Visual Basic

You can also find the current name of the operating system for any given machine using the following Visual Basic code:

```
Dim Computer as IADsComputer
Dim ComputerName as String
Dim ComputerDomain as String
ComputerDomain = "Target_Computer_Domain"
ComputerName = "Target_Computer_Name"
Set Computer= GetObject("WinNT://" & ComputerDomain & "/" & ComputerName &
↳",computer")

Dim RetVal as String
RetVal = Computer.OperatingSystem
Debug.Print RetVal
```

> *Note*
>
> When run against a Windows NT workstation, this code segment simply returns the string Windows NT. ◆

Querying the Computer Operating System Version Using Visual Basic

In conjunction with the OperatingSystemVersion property of the IADsComputer interface, you can also find the version number of Windows for any given machine using the following Visual Basic code:

```
Dim Computer as IADsComputer
Dim ComputerName as String
Dim ComputerDomain as String
ComputerDomain = "Target_Computer_Domain"
ComputerName = "Target_Computer_Name"
Set Computer= GetObject("WinNT://" & ComputerDomain & "/" & ComputerName &
↳",computer")

Dim RetVal as String
RetVal = Computer.OperatingSystemVersion
Debug.Print RetVal
```

> **Note**
>
> *This code will output the major and minor revision numbers of the installed operating system, for instance* `4.0` *for Windows NT Workstation 4.0.* ◆

Querying the Computer Processor Type Using Visual Basic

Using the `Processor` property of the IADsComputer interface, you can determine the processor architecture (Alpha or x86) as well as the family, model, and stepping of the installed processor(s). Use the following Visual Basic code to determine the processor architecture:

```
Dim Computer as IADsComputer
Dim ComputerName as String
Dim ComputerDomain as String
ComputerDomain = "Target_Computer_Domain"
ComputerName = "Target_Computer_Name"
Set Computer= GetObject("WinNT://" & ComputerDomain & "/" & ComputerName &
↵",computer")

Dim RetVal as String
RetVal = Computer.Processor
Debug.Print RetVal
```

> **Note**
>
> *This code will output the processor type (x86 or Alpha) as well as the family, model, and stepping of the processor, such as* `x86 Family 5 Model 4 Stepping 3`. ◆

Querying the Installed HAL on Windows NT Using Visual Basic

Despite its name, the `ProcessorCount` property does not yield an integer representing the physical number of processors installed in the system, but rather shows the HAL in use on the system. Use the following Visual Basic code to query the HAL in use:

```
Dim Computer as IADsComputer
Dim ComputerName as String
Dim ComputerDomain as String
ComputerDomain = "Target_Computer_Domain"
ComputerName = "Target_Computer_Name"
Set Computer= GetObject("WinNT://" & ComputerDomain & "/" & ComputerName &
↵",computer")

Dim RetVal as String
RetVal = Computer.ProcessorCount
Debug.Print RetVal
```

Querying and Manipulating Computer Services: The IADsService Interface

ADSI exposes two interfaces for managing services in Windows NT: IADsService and IADsServiceOperations. The IADsService interface is responsible for manipulating the configuration of an installed service, whereas the IADsServiceOperations interface provides the bulk of service-related administration. In this section, we will take a look at the IADsService interface. Using this interface, you can do the following:

- Enumerate services installed on a given machine.
- Query and set service dependencies.
- Modify the naming, paths, and behavior of installed services.
- Query the status of a specific service.

Enumerating Installed Services on a Specific Computer Using Visual Basic

As shown in Figure 6.1, to display a list of services installed on a computer, you can simply open the Services applet in control panel. If you want to generate a list of all services on a given machine, you can easily do so by binding to the computer object, then narrow the result set to just services using the IADsContainer `Filter` property.

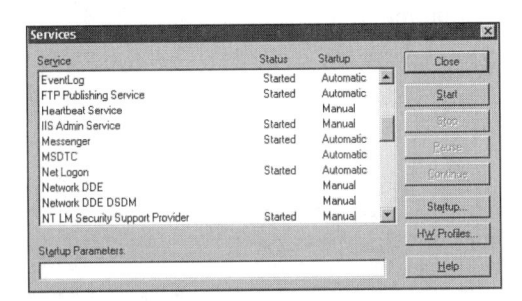

Figure 6.1 *Windows NT Control Panel Services applet.*

By combining this enumeration process with the properties and methods of the IADsService and IADsServiceOperations interfaces, you can quickly write administrative applications without ever referring to a native API reference manual.

Consider the following Visual Basic code to generate a list of services on a given machine:

```
Dim Computer as IADsComputer
Dim ComputerName as String
Dim ComputerDomain as String
ComputerDomain = "Target_Computer_Domain"
ComputerName = "Target_Computer_Name"
Set Computer = GetObject("WinNT://" & ComputerDomain & "/" & ComputerName & ⤶",computer")

Computer.Filter = Array("service")
Dim Service As IADsService
For Each Service In Computer
    Debug.Print Service.Name
Next
```

Tip

While in the For...Next loop, you can easily call upon any of the IADsService properties or methods to display or modify information related to each individual service. ♦

Binding to Services Using Visual Basic

If you know the programmatic name (usually the name of the service executable) of the service you want to manipulate, you can bind directly to the service for further manipulation and queries. Consider the following Visual Basic code to form the basis of these queries and manipulations:

```
Dim Computer as IADsComputer
Dim ComputerName as String
Dim ComputerDomain as String
Dim Service As IADsService
Dim TargetService as String
TargetService = "Target_Service_Name"
ComputerDomain = "Target_Computer_Domain"
ComputerName = "Target_Computer_Name"
Set Computer = GetObject("WinNT://" & ComputerDomain & "/" & ComputerName & ⤶",computer")
Set Service = Computer.GetObject("service", TargetService)
```

Querying Service Dependencies Using Visual Basic

Windows NT allows the developer/administrator the ability to define dependent services for any given service. If you attempt to stop a service upon which other services are dependent, these services will also be stopped.

To discover which services are dependent on a specific service, use the following Visual Basic code:

```
On Error Resume Next
Dim Computer as IADsComputer
Dim ComputerName as String
Dim ComputerDomain as String
Dim Service As IADsService
Dim TargetService as String
TargetService = "Target_Service_Name"
ComputerDomain = "Target_Computer_Domain"
ComputerName = "Target_Computer_Name"
Set Computer = GetObject("WinNT://" & ComputerDomain & "/" & ComputerName & ⮠",computer")
Set Service = Computer.GetObject("service", TargetService)

If IsArray(Service.Dependencies) = True Then
    Dim Entry As Variant
    For Each Entry In Service.Dependencies
        Debug.Print Entry
    Next
Else
    Debug.Print Service.Dependencies
End If
```

Upon examining the code, you can see that the list of dependencies is returned as an array, which you can then enumerate to display each individual dependent service.

Tip

For an example of the behavior of the dependency property, look at the relationship between the IISADMIN and W3SVC services. On machines with IIS installed, if you stop the IIS ADMIN service, this action will force a dialog box querying whether you also want to stop the WWW publishing service (W3SVC). When you examine the Dependencies *property of the W3SVC service, you see that the IISADMIN service is defined as a dependency of the W3SVC.* ♦

Setting a New Service Dependency Using Visual Basic

If a new service was just installed and you want to define a new dependency for the service, this is easily performed using ADSI. Consider the following Visual Basic code to perform this action:

```
On Error Resume Next
Dim Computer As IADsComputer
Dim Service As IADsService
Dim NewElement() As Variant
Dim i As Long
Dim EmptyArray As Integer
Dim DependencyAlreadyExists As Integer
```

```
    Dim ComputerDomain As String
    Dim TargetComputer As String
    Dim TargetService As String
    Dim NewDependency As String
    TargetService = "Target_Service_Name"
    ComputerDomain = "Target_Computer_Domain"
    TargetComputer = "Target_Computer_Name"
    NewDependency = "mssqlserver"
    Set Computer = GetObject("WinNT://" & ComputerDomain & "/" & TargetComputer &
    ⇒",computer")
    Set Service = Computer.GetObject("service", TargetService)

    If IsArray(Service.Dependencies) = True Then
        Dim Entry As Variant
        For Each Entry In Service.Dependencies
            i = UBound(NewElement) + 1
            ReDim Preserve NewElement(i)
            NewElement(i) = Entry
            If Entry = "" Then EmptyArray = 1
            If Entry = NewDependency Then DependencyAlreadyExists = 1
        Next
        If EmptyArray = 1 Then
            Service.Dependencies = Array(NewDependency)
            Service.SetInfo
        Else
            If DependencyAlreadyExists <> 1 Then
                i = UBound(NewElement) + 1
                ReDim Preserve NewElement(i)
                NewElement(i) = NewDependency
                Service.Dependencies = NewElement
                Service.SetInfo
            End If
        End If
    Else
        If Service.Dependencies <> NewDependency Then
            Service.Dependencies = Array(Service.Dependencies, NewDependency)
            Service.SetInfo
        End If
    End If
```

Querying Service Display Name Using Visual Basic

When manipulating an installed service, you may notice that the name used for binding the service does not match the name displayed in the Services dialog box. Windows NT allows the administrator/developer to define an additional entry for each service to reference the service in a more friendly way. The service name property is a short name used for programmatic identification of the service that matches the name of the service executable. The service display name property is a string that can be defined to enable a more friendly method for manipulating services using GUI tools.

Querying and Manipulating Computer Services: The IADsService Interface 139

To query the display name for a given service, use the following Visual Basic code:

```
Dim Computer as IADsComputer
Dim ComputerName as String
Dim ComputerDomain as String
Dim Service As IADsService
Dim TargetService as String
TargetService = "Target_Service_Name"
ComputerDomain = "Target_Computer_Domain"
ComputerName = "Target_Computer_Name"
Set Computer = GetObject("WinNT://" & ComputerDomain & "/" & ComputerName &
↳",computer")
Set Service = Computer.GetObject("service", TargetService)

Debug.Print Service.DisplayName
```

If you cannot easily derive the name of a service from its display name, use the following Visual Basic code to return the name in the Visual Basic IDE's Immediate window:

```
Dim Computer as IADsComputer
Dim ComputerName as String
Dim ComputerDomain as String
Dim StringToFind as String
ComputerDomain = "Target_Computer_Domain"
ComputerName = "Target_Computer_Name"
StringToFind = "Display_Name_To_Find"
Set Computer = GetObject("WinNT://" & ComputerDomain & "/" & ComputerName &
↳",computer")
Computer.Filter = Array("service")

Dim Service As IADsServiceFor Each Service In Computer
    If InStr(Service.DisplayName, StringToFind) <> 0 Then
        Debug.Print Service.Name; " = "; Service.DisplayName
    End If
Next
```

After finding the service name from the display name, simply use the service name to manipulate the bound service.

> *Tip*
>
> *If you convert the preceding code segment to a function, you can pass the results into other service-related functions in a single line of Visual Basic code, as follows:*
> ```
> Dim Computer as IADsComputer
> Dim ComputerName as String
> Dim ComputerDomain as String
> Dim Service As IADsService
> Dim TargetService as String
> Dim ServiceDisplayName as String
> ```
>
> *continues* ▶

▶ *continued*

```
ServiceDisplayName = "Display_Name_of_Service"
ComputerDomain = "Target_Computer_Domain"
ComputerName = "Target_Computer_Name"
TargetService = GetServiceName(ServiceDisplayName, ComputerDomain, ComputerName)
Set Computer = GetObject("WinNT://" & ComputerDomain & "/" & ComputerName & _
",computer")
Set Service = Computer.GetObject("service", TargetService)
Debug.Print Service.HostComputer

Public Function GetServiceName(DisplayName as String, ComputerDomain as String, _
ComputerName as String) as String
    Dim Computer as IADsComputer
    Set Computer = GetObject("WinNT://" & ComputerDomain & "/" & ComputerName & _
",computer")
    Computer.Filter = Array("service")
    Dim Service As IADsService
    For Each Service In Computer
        If InStr(Service.DisplayName, DisplayName) <> 0 Then
            GetServiceName = Service.Name
        End If
    Next
End Function ◆
```

Setting a New Service Display Name Using Visual Basic

If you no longer wish to retain the name previously assigned to a service, you can easily redefine it by setting a new value to the `DisplayName` property. Use the following Visual Basic code to perform this task:

```
Dim Computer as IADsComputer
Dim ComputerName as String
Dim ComputerDomain as String
Dim Service As IADsService
Dim TargetService as String
Dim NewDisplayName as String
TargetService = "Target_Service_Name"
ComputerDomain = "Target_Computer_Domain"
ComputerName = "Target_Computer_Name"
NewDisplayName = "New_Service_Display_Name"
Set Computer = GetObject("WinNT://" & ComputerDomain & "/" & ComputerName & _
",computer")
Set Service = Computer.GetObject("service", TargetService)

Service.DisplayName = NewDisplayName
Service.SetInfo
```

Querying Host Computer Property Using Visual Basic

The `HostComputer` property defines the `ADsPath` of the machine hosting the executable used for the service. In most cases, the `HostComputer` property will match the `ADsPath` of the currently bound computer object.

Use the following Visual Basic code to return the value of the `HostComputer` property:

```
Dim Computer as IADsComputer
Dim ComputerName as String
Dim ComputerDomain as String
Dim Service As IADsService
Dim TargetService as String
TargetService = "Target_Service_Name"
ComputerDomain = "Target_Computer_Domain"
ComputerName = "Target_Computer_Name"
Set Computer = GetObject("WinNT://" & ComputerDomain & "/" & ComputerName &
↵",computer")
Set Service = Computer.GetObject("service", TargetService)

Debug.Print Service.HostComputer
```

> *Note*
>
> *This property cannot be set programmatically using ADSI.* ✦

Querying Service Executable Path Using Visual Basic

Windows NT services are executables that can be run outside of the current user's context. Each service maintains the path of its executable, which can be queried by examining the `Path` property of a bound service object. Use the following Visual Basic code to determine the path to the executable for the bound service:

```
Dim Computer as IADsComputer
Dim ComputerName as String
Dim ComputerDomain as String
Dim Service As IADsService
Dim TargetService as String
TargetService = "Target_Service_Name"
ComputerDomain = "Target_Computer_Domain"
ComputerName = "Target_Computer_Name"
Set Computer = GetObject("WinNT://" & ComputerDomain & "/" & ComputerName &
↵",computer")
Set Service = Computer.GetObject("service", TargetService)

Debug.Print Service.Path
```

Setting New Service Executable Path Using Visual Basic

If you wish to move the executable associated with a service, you can potentially do so without reinstalling the service. Simply manipulate the `Path` property of the IADsService interface after moving the executable image within the file system.

> **Note**
>
> *Although you can modify the* Path *property while the service is running, the change will not take affect until the service has been cycled.* ♦

Use the following Visual Basic code to change the path to the service executable:

```
Dim Computer as IADsComputer
Dim ComputerName as String
Dim ComputerDomain as String
Dim Service As IADsService
Dim TargetService as String
Dim NewServicePath as String
TargetService = "Target_Service_Name"
ComputerDomain = "Target_Computer_Domain"
ComputerName = "Target_Computer_Name"
NewServicePath = "New_Path_To_Executable"
Set Computer = GetObject("WinNT://" & ComputerDomain & "/" & ComputerName &
↪",computer")
Set Service = Computer.GetObject("service", TargetService)

Service.Path = NewServicePath
Service.SetInfo
```

Querying Service Account Name Using Visual Basic

All services run under the context of another user account. Whether the account is explicitly defined or is simply the LocalSystem account, it is run outside the current user context. This allows services to run even when a user is not logged in and to perform privileged operations when a non-privileged account is currently logged in.

Using the GUI, if you click the Startup button in the Service dialog box, you can determine the user account associated with any given service (see Figure 6.2). Using the IADsService interface, you can also perform this same query programmatically.

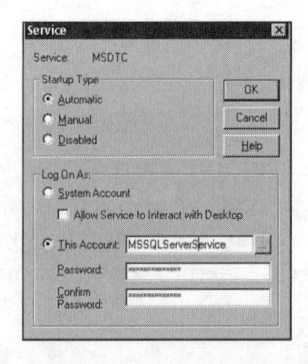

Figure 6.2 *Service dialog box in Services Windows NT Control Panel applet.*

To query which account is being used for a service, simply display the value of the ServiceAccountName property of the IADsService interface. The following Visual Basic code demonstrates this process:

```
Dim Computer as IADsComputer
Dim ComputerName as String
Dim ComputerDomain as String
Dim Service As IADsService
Dim TargetService as String
TargetService = "Target_Service_Name"
ComputerDomain = "Target_Computer_Domain"
ComputerName = "Target_Computer_Name"
Set Computer = GetObject("WinNT://" & ComputerDomain & "/" & ComputerName & ➥",computer")
Set Service = Computer.GetObject("service", TargetService)

Debug.Print Service.ServiceAccountName
```

Tip

Combined with an enumeration function, you can find the service account used with all services on a given machine. ◆

Note

This property cannot be set programmatically using ADSI. ◆

Querying Service Start Type Using Visual Basic

You can query the method used to start the service by examining the ServiceStart property of the IADsService interface. Five constants can be used, but only the last three in Table 6.1 are commonly used in Windows NT.

Table 6.1 Service Start Type Constants

Constant	Value
ADS_SERVICE_BOOT_START	0
ADS_SERVICE_SYSTEM_START	1
ADS_SERVICE_AUTO_START	2
ADS_SERVICE_DEMAND_START	3
ADS_SERVICE_DISABLED	4

Warning

If you attempt to set a value that is not in the table (such as 5), an error will occur. ◆

Using the preceding table and the following Visual Basic code, you can determine the startup type for any service running on a system:

```
Dim Computer as IADsComputer
Dim ComputerName as String
Dim ComputerDomain as String
Dim Service As IADsService
Dim TargetService as String
TargetService = "Target_Service_Name"
ComputerDomain = "Target_Computer_Domain"
ComputerName = "Target_Computer_Name"
Set Computer = GetObject("WinNT://" & ComputerDomain & "/" & ComputerName &
↪",computer")
Set Service = Computer.GetObject("service", TargetService)

Select Case Service.StartType
    Case 0
        Debug.Print "BOOT"
    Case 1
        Debug.Print "SYSTEM"
    Case 2
        Debug.Print "AUTOMATIC"
    Case 3
        Debug.Print "MANUAL"
    Case 4
        Debug.Print "DISABLED"
End Select
```

Setting Service Start Type Using Visual Basic

You can also set a new startup type for a service by passing in a new integer value representing one of the startup type constants. Use the following Visual Basic code to programmatically manipulate the startup method for a service:

```
Dim Computer as IADsComputer
Dim ComputerName as String
Dim ComputerDomain as String
Dim Service As IADsService
Dim TargetService as String
TargetService = "Target_Service_Name"
ComputerDomain = "Target_Computer_Domain"
ComputerName = "Target_Computer_Name"
Set Computer = GetObject("WinNT://" & ComputerDomain & "/" & ComputerName &
↪",computer")
Set Service = Computer.GetObject("service", TargetService)

'Use 4 to disable the service, 3 for Manual startup or 2 to AutoStart the service
Service.StartType = 4
Service.SetInfo
```

> *Note*
>
> *Notice that you are assigning the* StartType *property to an integer as represented in the table of constants shown in the earlier section "Querying Service Start Type Using Visual Basic."* ◆

Querying and Manipulating Service Operations: The IADsServiceOperations Interface

If you are developing Web-based administration consoles for the help desk or building scripts to aid product deployment, you can also programmatically start, stop, pause, continue, or change a service account password for an installed service using the IADsServiceOperations interface.

> *Note*
>
> *By combining the service enumeration functions with the* Status *property, you can query the status of all installed services to determine the current state of each individual service on a machine.* ◆

In this section, we will take a look at the IADsServiceOperations interface. Using this interface, you can do the following:

- Enumerate service status.
- Query the status of a specific service.
- Start, stop, continue, pause, or disable an installed service.
- Set a new service password.

Enumerating Service Status Using Visual Basic

If you want to emulate the Services Control Panel applet (or Server Manager's service manipulation interface) in a custom application, you must begin by enumerating the installed services on a target machine and then classifying the status of each service.

Use Table 6.2 as a reference for the IADsService status constants.

Table 6.2 Service Staus Constants

Constant	Integer Value
ADS_SERVICE_STOPPED	1
ADS_SERVICE_START_PENDING	2
ADS_SERVICE_STOP_PENDING	3
ADS_SERVICE_RUNNING	4
ADS_SERVICE_CONTINUE_PENDING	5
ADS_SERVICE_PAUSE_PENDING	6
ADS_SERVICE_PAUSED	7
ADS_SERVICE_ERROR	8

By querying the status property of the IADsServiceOperations interface, Visual Basic returns an integer representing whether the service is stopped, running, paused, pending an operation, or in error.

> *Tip*
>
> *You can make the return value a bit friendlier by using a case statement to present a string value to the user.* ◆

Consider the following Visual Basic code as an example of service status enumeration:

```
Dim Computer As IADsComputer
Dim ComputerName As String
Dim ComputerDomain As String
ComputerDomain = "Target_Computer_Domain"
ComputerName = "Target_Computer_Name"
Set Computer = GetObject("WinNT://" & ComputerDomain & "/" & ComputerName & ↵",computer")
Computer.Filter = Array("service")
Dim Service As IADsServiceOperations
Dim ServiceStatus As String

For Each Service In Computer
    Select Case Service.Status
        Case 1
            ServiceStatus = "Stopped"
        Case 2
            ServiceStatus = "Start Pending"
        Case 3
            ServiceStatus = "Stop Pending"
        Case 4
            ServiceStatus = "Running"
        Case 5
            ServiceStatus = "Continue_Pending"
        Case 6
            ServiceStatus = "Pause_Pending"
        Case 7
            ServiceStatus = "Paused"
        Case 8
            ServiceStatus = "Error"
    End Select
    Debug.Print Service.Name & vbTab & ServiceStatus
Next
```

Starting a Service Using Visual Basic

There may be times when you want to query the status of a critical service and then respond automatically if it is found to be in a stopped or paused state. Additionally, you may want to enumerate a resource domain and enable or start a service (such as the scheduler service) without having to "visit" each machine using Server Manager.

Using the following Visual Basic code, you can programmatically start an installed, enabled service:

```
Dim Computer as IADsComputer
Dim ComputerName as String
Dim ComputerDomain as String
Dim Service As IADsService
Dim TargetService as String
TargetService = "Target_Service_Name"
ComputerDomain = "Target_Computer_Domain"
ComputerName = "Target_Computer_Name"
Set Computer = GetObject("WinNT://" & ComputerDomain & "/" & ComputerName &
↳",computer")
Set Service = Computer.GetObject("service", TargetService)

If Service.Status = 1 Then
    Service.Start
    Debug.Print "The " & Service.Name & " service has been started."
Else
    If Service.Status = 4 Then
        Debug.Print "The " & Service.Name & " service is already started."
    Else
        Debug.Print "The " & Service.Name & " service could not be started."
    End If
End If
```

Tip

If a service is installed but currently disabled, you will not be able to start it. Before attempting to start the service, you must set the StartType *property to either 2 or 3.* ♦

Stopping a Service Using Visual Basic

If you wish to stop a running service, use the following Visual Basic code:

```
Dim Computer as IADsComputer
Dim ComputerName as String
Dim ComputerDomain as String
Dim Service As IADsService
Dim TargetService as String
TargetService = "Target_Service_Name"
ComputerDomain = "Target_Computer_Domain"
ComputerName = "Target_Computer_Name"
Set Computer = GetObject("WinNT://" & ComputerDomain & "/" & ComputerName &
↳",computer")
Set Service = Computer.GetObject("service", TargetService)

If Service.Status = 4 Then
```

```
            Service.Stop
            Debug.Print "The " & Service.Name & " service has been stopped."
      Else
            If Service.Status = 1 then
                  Debug.Print "The " & Service.Name & " service is already stopped."
            Else
                  Debug.Print "The " & Service.Name & " service could not be stopped."
            End If
      End If
```

Pausing a Service Using Visual Basic

If a service supports the ability to be paused (such as Schedule, Server, or NetLogon) you can pause a service using the following Visual Basic code:

```
Dim Computer as IADsComputer
Dim ComputerName as String
Dim ComputerDomain as String
Dim Service As IADsService
Dim TargetService as String
TargetService = "Target_Service_Name"
ComputerDomain = "Target_Computer_Domain"
ComputerName = "Target_Computer_Name"
Set Computer = GetObject("WinNT://" & ComputerDomain & "/" & ComputerName &
↪",computer")
Set Service = Computer.GetObject("service", TargetService)

If Service.Status = 4 Then
      Service.Pause
      Debug.Print "The " & Service.Name & " service has been paused."
Else
      If Service.Status = 7 Then
            Debug.Print "The " & Service.Name & " service is already paused."
      Else
            Debug.Print "The " & Service.Name & " service could not be paused."
      End If
End If
```

Tip

A critical error will be issued if the service does not support the Pause *method. Verify that the bound service supports the ability to be paused using Control Panel; or use the On Error Resume Next statement to handle the error gracefully.* ♦

Continuing a Paused Service Using Visual Basic

If a service is currently paused, you can return the service to a running state using the following Visual Basic code:

```
Dim Computer as IADsComputer
Dim ComputerName as String
Dim ComputerDomain as String
Dim Service As IADsService
```

```
Dim TargetService as String
TargetService = "Target_Service_Name"
ComputerDomain = "Target_Computer_Domain"
ComputerName = "Target_Computer_Name"
Set Computer = GetObject("WinNT://" & ComputerDomain & "/" & ComputerName &
↵",computer")
Set Service = Computer.GetObject("service", TargetService)

If Service.Status = 7 Then
    Service.Continue
    Debug.Print "The " & Service.Name & " service has been unpaused."
Else
    If Service.Status = 4 Then
        Debug.Print "The " & Service.Name & " service is already running."
    End If
End If
```

Setting New Service Password Using Visual Basic

Although the IADsServiceOperations interface provides you with a great deal of useful techniques for manipulating a service, from a security perspective, one of the most useful is the inclusion of the SetPassword method. Assuming the service account does not have any other dependencies (such as a DCOM identity), you can finally write an application to change the password of a service account with little concern about the service failing to start due to a login failure.

To set the password to be used with the ServiceAccountName property, use the following Visual Basic code:

```
Dim Computer as IADsComputer
Dim ComputerName as String
Dim ComputerDomain as String
Dim Service As IADsService
Dim TargetService as String
Dim NewPassword as String
TargetService = "Target_Service_Name"
ComputerDomain = "Target_Computer_Domain"
ComputerName = "Target_Computer_Name"
NewPassword = "New_Password"
Set Computer = GetObject("WinNT://" & ComputerDomain & "/" & ComputerName &
↵",computer")
Set Service = Computer.GetObject("service", TargetService)
Service.SetPassword(NewPassword)
Service.SetInfo
```

Tip

After programmatically changing the password for a service account in the SAM (using the IADsUser interface), you can easily call the preceding code segment for each service that depends on the account to synchronize the login information between the account and the service. ◆

Creating the NTComputerManagement Class Module

In this section, you will continue the creation of the NTAdmin.DLL COM server application started in Chapter 3.

Just as we have done in all previous chapters, the manipulation of the IADsComputer, IADsService, and IADsServiceOperations interfaces will be handled by a class module within an ActiveX DLL.

Exercise 6.1 *Creating NTAdmin.DLL: Computer and Service Management Functions*

1. Open the NTAdmin ActiveX DLL Visual Basic project that was started in Chapter 3. You can also download the project from http://www.newriders.com/adsi.

2. If you are adding to the NTAdmin project, add a new class module to the project. If this is a new project, make sure to set a reference to Active DS Type Library.

3. Name the new module `NTComputerManagement`.

4. Enter the following code into the General Declarations section of the class module:

```
Public Function QueryComputerProperty(ByVal TargetDomain As String, ByVal
➥TargetComputer As String, ByVal PropertyToQuery As String) As String
    On Error Resume Next
    Dim Computer As IADsComputer
    Set Computer = GetObject("WinNT://" & TargetDomain & "/" & TargetComputer &
➥",computer")
    Select Case UCase(PropertyToQuery)
        Case "DIVISION"
            QueryComputerProperty = Computer.Division
        Case "OPERATINGSYSTEM"
            QueryComputerProperty = Computer.OperatingSystem
        Case "OPERATINGSYSTEMVERSION"
            QueryComputerProperty = Computer.OperatingSystemVersion
        Case "OWNER"
            QueryComputerProperty = Computer.Owner
        Case "PROCESSOR"
            QueryComputerProperty = Computer.Processor
        Case "PROCESSORCOUNT"
            QueryComputerProperty = Computer.ProcessorCount
    End Select
End Function

Public Function QueryServiceProperty(ByVal TargetDomain As String, ByVal
➥TargetComputer As String, ByVal TargetService As String, ByVal PropertyToQuery
➥As String) As String
    On Error Resume Next
    Dim Computer As IADsComputer
    Dim Service As IADsService
    Set Computer = GetObject("WinNT://" & TargetDomain & "/" & TargetComputer &
➥",computer")
    Set Service = Computer.GetObject("service", TargetService)
```

Creating the NTComputerManagement Class Module   151

```
        Select Case UCase(PropertyToQuery)
            Case "STARTTYPE"
                Dim StartType As String
                Select Case Service.StartType
                    Case 0
                        StartType = "Boot_Start"
                    Case 1
                        StartType = "System_Start"
                    Case 2
                        StartType = "Automatic"
                    Case 3
                        StartType = "Manual"
                    Case 4
                        StartType = "Disabled"
                End Select
                QueryServiceProperty = StartType
            Case "DISPLAYNAME"
                QueryServiceProperty = Service.DisplayName
            Case "HOSTCOMPUTER"
                QueryServiceProperty = Service.HostComputer
            Case "PATH"
                QueryServiceProperty = Service.Path
            Case "SERVICEACCOUNTNAME"
                QueryServiceProperty = Service.ServiceAccountName
        End Select
End Function

Public Function QueryServiceDependencies(ByVal TargetDomain As String, ByVal
➥TargetComputer As String, ByVal TargetService As String) As Variant
    On Error Resume Next
    Dim Computer As IADsComputer
    Dim Service As IADsService
    Dim NewElement() As Variant
    Dim i As Long
    Set Computer = GetObject("WinNT://" & TargetDomain & "/" & TargetComputer &
➥",computer")
    Set Service = Computer.GetObject("service", TargetService)
    If IsArray(Service.Dependencies) = True Then
        Dim Entry As Variant
        For Each Entry In Service.Dependencies
            i = UBound(NewElement) + 1
            ReDim Preserve NewElement(i)
            NewElement(i) = Entry
        Next
        QueryServiceDependencies = NewElement
    Else
        QueryServiceDependencies = Array(Service.Dependencies)
    End If
End Function

Public Function SetServiceProperty(ByVal TargetDomain As String, ByVal
➥TargetComputer As String, ByVal TargetService As String, ByVal PropertyToSet As
➥String, ByVal NewValue As Variant) As Boolean
    Dim Computer As IADsComputer
```

continues ▶

Exercise 6.1 *continued*

```
    Dim Service As IADsService
    Set Computer = GetObject("WinNT://" & TargetDomain & "/" & TargetComputer &
↳",computer")
    Set Service = Computer.GetObject("service", TargetService)
    Select Case UCase(PropertyToSet)
        Case "STARTTYPE"
            Service.StartType = NewValue
            Service.SetInfo
        Case "DISPLAYNAME"
            Service.DisplayName = NewValue
            Service.SetInfo
        Case "PATH"
            Service.Path = NewValue
            Service.SetInfo
        Case "SERVICEACCOUNTNAME"
            Service.ServiceAccountName = NewValue
            Service.SetInfo
    End Select
    If Err.Number = 0 Then
        SetServiceProperty = True
    Else
        SetServiceProperty = False
    End If
End Function

Public Function AddServiceDependency(ByVal TargetDomain As String, ByVal
↳TargetComputer As String, ByVal TargetService As String, ByVal NewDependency As
↳String) As Boolean
    On Error Resume Next
    Dim Computer As IADsComputer
    Dim Service As IADsService
    Dim NewElement() As Variant
    Dim i As Long
    Dim EmptyArray As Integer
    Dim DependencyAlreadyExists As Integer
    Set Computer = GetObject("WinNT://" & TargetDomain & "/" & TargetComputer &
↳",computer")
    Set Service = Computer.GetObject("service", TargetService)
    If IsArray(Service.Dependencies) = True Then
        Dim Entry As Variant
        For Each Entry In Service.Dependencies
            i = UBound(NewElement) + 1
            ReDim Preserve NewElement(i)
            NewElement(i) = Entry
            If Entry = "" Then EmptyArray = 1
            If Entry = NewDependency Then DependencyAlreadyExists = 1
        Next
        If EmptyArray = 1 Then
            Debug.Print "empty"
            Service.Dependencies = Array(NewDependency)
            Service.SetInfo
```

Creating the NTComputerManagement Class Module

```
            Else
                If DependencyAlreadyExists <> 1 Then
                    i = UBound(NewElement) + 1
                    ReDim Preserve NewElement(i)
                    NewElement(i) = NewDependency
                    Service.Dependencies = NewElement
                    Service.SetInfo
                End If
            End If
        Else
            If Service.Dependencies <> NewDependency Then
                Service.Dependencies = Array(Service.Dependencies, NewDependency)
                Service.SetInfo
            End If
        End If
        Debug.Print Err.Number & " " & Err.Description
        If Err.Number = 0 Or Err.Number = 9 Or Err.Number = 92 Then
            AddServiceDependency = True
        Else
            AddServiceDependency = False
        End If
End Function

Public Function RemoveServiceDependency(ByVal TargetDomain As String, ByVal
➥TargetComputer As String, ByVal TargetService As String, ByVal
➥DependencyToRemove As String) As Boolean
    On Error Resume Next
    Dim Computer As IADsComputer
    Dim Service As IADsService
    Dim NewElement() As Variant
    Dim i As Long
    Dim EntryCounter As Integer
    Set Computer = GetObject("WinNT://" & TargetDomain & "/" & TargetComputer &
    ➥",computer")
    Set Service = Computer.GetObject("service", TargetService)
    If IsArray(Service.Dependencies) = True Then
        Dim Entry As Variant
        For Each Entry In Service.Dependencies
            If Entry <> DependencyToRemove Then
                EntryCounter = EntryCounter + 1
                i = UBound(NewElement) + 1
                ReDim Preserve NewElement(i)
                NewElement(i) = Entry
            End If
        Next
        Select Case EntryCounter
            Case 0
                Service.Dependencies = Array("")
            Case 1
                Service.Dependencies = Entry
            Case EntryCounter > 1
                Service.Dependencies = NewElement
        End Select
```

continues ▶

Exercise 6.1 *continued*

```
            Service.SetInfo
        Else
            If Service.Dependencies = DependencyToRemove Then
                Service.Dependencies = Array("")
                Service.SetInfo
            End If
        End If
        If Err.Number = 0 Or Err.Number = 9 Then
            RemoveServiceDependency = True
        Else
            RemoveServiceDependency = False
        End If
    End Function

    Public Function EnumerateServices(ByVal TargetDomain As String, ByVal
    ⇒TargetComputer As String, ByVal WithStatus As Boolean) As Variant
        On Error Resume Next
        Dim Computer As IADsComputer
        Dim Service As IADsService
        Dim ServiceStatus As String
        Dim NewElement() As Variant
        Dim i As Long
        Set Computer = GetObject("WinNT://" & TargetDomain & "/" & TargetComputer &
        ⇒",computer")
        Computer.Filter = Array("service")
        For Each Service In Computer
            i = UBound(NewElement) + 1
            ReDim Preserve NewElement(i)
            If WithStatus = True Then
                Select Case Service.Status
                    Case 1
                        ServiceStatus = "Stopped"
                    Case 2
                        ServiceStatus = "Start Pending"
                    Case 3
                        ServiceStatus = "Stop Pending"
                    Case 4
                        ServiceStatus = "Running"
                    Case 5
                        ServiceStatus = "Continue Pending"
                    Case 6
                        ServiceStatus = "Pause Pending"
                    Case 7
                        ServiceStatus = "Paused"
                    Case 8
                        ServiceStatus = "Error"
                End Select
                NewElement(i) = Service.Name & vbTab & ServiceStatus
            Else
                NewElement(i) = Service.Name
            End If
        Next
```

Creating the NTComputerManagement Class Module   155

```vb
            EnumerateServices = NewElement
    End Function

    Public Function ServiceOperations(ByVal TargetDomain As String, ByVal
    ⇒TargetComputer As String, ByVal TargetService As String, ByVal ServiceOperation
    ⇒As String) As Boolean
        Dim Computer As IADsComputer
        Dim Service As IADsServiceOperations
        Set Computer = GetObject("WinNT://" & TargetDomain & "/" & TargetComputer &
        ⇒",computer")
        Set Service = Computer.GetObject("service", TargetService)
        Select Case UCase(ServiceOperation)
            Case "START"
                If Service.Status = 1 Then
                    Service.Start
                End If
            Case "STOP"
                If Service.Status = 4 Then
                    Service.Stop
                End If
            Case "CONTINUE"
                If Service.Status = 7 Then
                    Service.Continue
                End If
            Case "PAUSE"
                If Service.Status = 4 Then
                    Service.Pause
                End If
        End Select
        If Err.Number = 0 Then
            ServiceOperations = True
        Else
            ServiceOperations = False
        End If
    End Function

    Public Function SetServiceAccountPassword(ByVal TargetDomain As String, ByVal
    ⇒TargetComputer As String, ByVal TargetService As String, NewPassword As String)
    ⇒As Boolean
        Dim Computer As IADsComputer
        Dim Service As IADsServiceOperations
        Set Computer = GetObject("WinNT://" & TargetDomain & "/" & TargetComputer &
        ⇒",computer")
        Set Service = Computer.GetObject("service", TargetService)
        Call Service.SetPassword(NewPassword)
        If Err.Number = 0 Then
            SetServiceAccountPassword = True
        Else
            SetServiceAccountPassword = False
        End If
    End Function
```

5. Compile the code as NTAdmin.DLL.
6. Save and close the NTAdmin project.

> **Tip**
>
> You can download the Visual Basic 6.0 project or a pre-compiled version of NTAdmin.DLL from http://www.newriders.com/adsi. ♦

Using the Functions in NTComputerManagement

With the NTComputerManagement class module created, you can access this function from any programming language that supports OLE automation, including Visual Basic, VBScript, and JavaScript.

> **Tip**
>
> To instantiate the object, follow the appropriate syntax found in Chapter 3. Substitute the NTComputerManagement class name where necessary. ♦

Use Table 6.3 to help you use the proper syntax for each of the methods of the NTComputerManagement interface.

Table 6.3 NTComputerManagement *Method Syntax.*

Action	Syntax
Query Computer Division	QueryComputerProperty("Domain_Name", ↪"Computer_Name", "Division")
Query Registered Organization	QueryComputerProperty("Domain_Name", ↪"Computer_Name", "Owner")
Query Operating System Name	QueryComputerProperty("Domain_Name", ↪"Computer_Name", "OperatingSystem")
Query Operating System Version	QueryComputerProperty("Domain_Name", ↪"Computer_Name", ↪"OperatingSystemVersion")
Query Processor Type	QueryComputerProperty("Domain_Name", ↪"Computer_Name", "Processor")
Query Installed HAL	QueryComputerProperty("Domain_Name", ↪"Computer_Name", "ProcessorCount")
Enumerate Installed Services	For Each Item In ↪EnumerateServices("Domain_Name", ↪"Computer_Name", False) Debug.Print Item Next
Query Service Start Type	QueryServiceProperty("Domain_Name", ↪"Computer_Name", ↪"Service_Name","StartType")
Query Service Display Name	QueryServiceProperty("Domain_Name", ↪"Computer_Name", ↪"Service_Name","DisplayName")
Query Service Host Computer	QueryServiceProperty("Domain_Name", ↪"Computer_Name", ↪"Service_Name","HostComputer")

Action	Syntax

Query Service Executable Path	`QueryServiceProperty("Domain_Name",`
	`↪"Computer_Name",`
	`↪"Service_Name","Path")`

Query Service Account Name	`QueryServiceProperty("Domain_Name",`
	`↪"Computer_Name",`
	`↪"Service_Name","ServiceAccountName")`

Query Service Dependencies	`For Each Item In`
	`↪QueryServiceDependencies("Domain_Name",`
	`↪"Computer_Name", "Service_Name")`
	    `Debug.Print Item`
	`Next`

Set Service Startup Type	`SetServiceProperty("Domain_Name",`
	`↪"Computer_Name", "Service_Name",`
	`↪"StartType", 2)`
	
	`Valid values for the integer are:`
	`0 - Boot_Start, 1 - System_Start, 2`
	`↪- Automatic_Start, 3-`
	`↪Manual_Start, 4 - Disabled`

Set Service Display Name	`SetServiceProperty("Domain_Name",`
	`↪"Computer_Name", "Service_Name",`
	`↪"DisplayName", "New_Display_Name")`

Set Service Executable Path	`SetServiceProperty("Domain_Name",`
	`↪"Computer_Name", "Service_Name",`
	`↪"Path", "New_Path")`

Set Service Account Name	`SetServiceProperty("Domain_Name",`
	`↪"Computer_Name", "Service_Name",`
	`↪"ServiceAccountName",`
	`↪"Service_Account_Name")`

Add Service Dependency	`AddServiceDependency("Domain_Name",`
	`↪"Computer_Name", "Service_Name",`
	`↪"New_Dependency")`

Remove Service Dependency	`RemoveServiceDependency("Domain_Name",`
	`↪"Computer_Name", "Service_Name",`
	`↪"Dependency_To_Remove")`

Enumerate Services	`For Each Item In`
	`↪EnumerateServices("Domain_Name",`
	`↪"Computer_Name", False)`
	    `Debug.Print Item`
	`Next`

Enumerate Services with Service Status	`For Each Item In`
	`↪EnumerateServices("Domain_Name",`
	`↪"Computer_Name", True)`

continues ▶

Table 6.3   continued

Action	Syntax
	Debug.Print Item
	Next
Start a Stopped Service	ServiceOperations("Domain_Name", "Computer_Name", "Service_Name", "Start")
Stop a Running Service	ServiceOperations("Domain_Name", "Computer_Name", "Service_Name", "Stop")
Pause a Running Service	ServiceOperations("Domain_Name", "Computer_Name", "Service_Name", "Pause")
Continue a Paused Service	ServiceOperations("Domain_Name", "Computer_Name", "Service_Name", "Continue")
Change Service Password	SetServiceAccountPassword ("Domain_Name", "Computer_Name", "Service_Name", "New_Password")

Summary

Using the IADsComputer, IADsService, and IADsServiceOperations interfaces, the administrator can easily perform ad hoc queries of important properties on individual machines as well as manipulate the services on any machine or group of machines in the enterprise.

The IADsComputer interface provides vital information about the machines in a resource domain, including the operating system installed and the HAL currently in use. In addition to collecting information about the enterprise, you can incorporate these functions into an application to limit execution based on a given set of parameters such as specifying that the application can be run on Windows NT 4.0 or higher or only on a multi-processor machine.

Using the IADsService interface, you can modify the default configuration of a service, such as the path to the executable, and query for dependent services. You can even change the display name of a service, thus modifying the way an administrator would see the service in the services list.

Using the IADsServiceOperations interface, you can create an application that enables synchronization between the password stored in the SAM and the password used to start the service. For those creating Web-based administrative consoles (perhaps for recycling a print spooler on the corporate technical support desk), the IADsServiceOperations interface also enables you to start the services on any machine in the enterprise.

As with the other chapters in Part II, "Exploring the ADSI Service Providers: Windows NT," all code segments found in the text were concatenated into an easy-to-implement class module in the NTAdmin.DLL ActiveX DLL (COM server) project started in Chapter 3. This DLL can then be instantiated from any programming language that supports automation, including Visual Basic, VBScript, and JavaScript.

By adding these services to your programmatic administration toolbox, you can reduce the tedium associated with performing administrative tasks upon large groups of Windows NT machines.

7
Programmatic File and Print Resource Management

In addition to managing users, groups, domain level properties, and system services, you can also harness the power of ADSI to manipulate file and print resources on machines throughout your enterprise.

Using the IADsFileService, IADsFileServiceOperations, and IADsFileShare interfaces, you can enumerate and manage existing shares on a particular machine, or combine these interfaces with the IADsContainer interface to create a new file share.

After a share is created, you can view and manage the sessions that are associated with each open resource. By loading the contents of the dynamic IADsSession interface into a collection (using ADSI's IADsCollection interface) you can programmatically view and remove user sessions connected to each file share.

ADSI's IADsPrintQueue and IADsPrintQueueOperations interfaces allow you to enumerate and manage established print queues. To view and manage the print jobs within a queue, you can use the IADsPrintJob and IADsPrintJobOperations interfaces.

By using these interfaces and the code in this chapter, you can create administrative applications for managing the following:

- File resources
- File sessions
- Open resources
- Printing resources

Finally, in this chapter you will continue the creation of the NTAdmin.DLL COM server application started in Chapter 3, "Container Enumeration Methods and Programmatic Domain Account Policy Manipulation."

Managing File Resources

Using the IADsFileService, IADsFileServiceOperations, IADsFileShare, IADsSession, and IADsContainer interfaces, you can programmatically create and remove file shares. You can also use these interfaces to view the open sessions and resources managed by a file service, in similar fashion to a computer's properties in Server Manager.

Whether you are creating a Web interface for the management of shares, sessions, and resources, or are creating a share that is part of a larger process automation workflow, ADSI provides an easy method for performing share management tasks.

Binding the LanmanServer Container Using Visual Basic

To enumerate the shares on a machine, you must first bind to the LanmanServer container on a specific computer. This process is exemplified in the following Visual Basic code segment:

```
Dim FileService As IADsFileService
Dim ComputerName As String
Dim ComputerDomain As String
ComputerDomain = "Target_Computer_Domain"
ComputerName = "Target_Computer_Name"
Set FileService = GetObject("WinNT://" & ComputerDomain & "/" & ComputerName &
↪"/LanmanServer,fileservice")
```

Enumerating Shares on a System Using Visual Basic

As shown in Figure 7.1, using the Stop Sharing menu entry in Windows File Manager (winfile.exe), you can enumerate all shares on the local machine. Alternatively, you can use the Network Neighborhood icon to show all non-hidden shares for a local or remote computer.

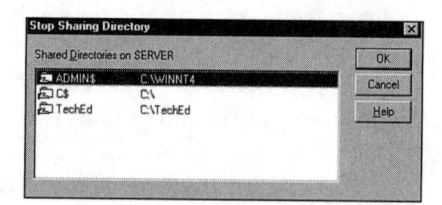

Figure 7.1 *Share Enumeration using Windows NT File Manager.*

To derive this information programmatically, you can use ADSI to bind the LanmanServer container and then use a *For...Each* loop to enumerate all non-administrative shares on any machine.

To perform this task, use the following Visual Basic code:

```vb
Dim FileService As IADsFileService
Dim FileShare As IADsFileShare
Dim ComputerName As String
Dim ComputerDomain As String
ComputerDomain = "Target_Computer_Domain"
ComputerName = "Target_Computer_Name"
Set FileService = GetObject("WinNT://" & ComputerDomain & "/" & ComputerName &
↪"/LanmanServer")
For Each FileShare In FileService
    Debug.Print FileShare.Name
Next
```

> **Note**
>
> After running this code, any hidden shares (those with a "$" appended to the name) created by the user are listed, but system hidden shares (IPC$, ADMIN$, C$, and so on) are not shown. While these shares are indeed hidden from enumeration, you can still bind and manipulate them using the techniques in this chapter. ◆

Binding to a Specific File Share Using Visual Basic

If you want to bind to a specific service on a machine, first bind the LanmanServer container, and then bind to the name of one of the leaf objects within the container.

To perform this task, use the following Visual Basic code segment as a guide:

```vb
Dim FileShare As IADsFileShare
Dim ComputerName As String
Dim ComputerDomain As String
Dim ShareName as String
ComputerDomain = "Target_Computer_Domain"
ComputerName = "Target_Computer_Name"
ShareName = "Target_Share_Name"
Set FileShare = GetObject("WinNT://" & ComputerDomain & "/" & ComputerName &
↪"/LanmanServer/" & ShareName & ",fileshare")
```

Querying the File Share Current User Count Using Visual Basic

By clicking the Shares command button in the computer properties dialog box of Server Manager, you can view the number of users for a particular shared resource on a machine. By querying the `CurrentUserCount` property of the IADsFileShare interface, you can examine this value programmatically. This is valuable for collecting software usage statistics, deciding whether to take down a file server, or simply satisfying basic curiosity.

Use the following Visual Basic code to determine the number of users currently connected to the target share:

```
Dim FileShare As IADsFileShare
Dim ComputerName As String
Dim ComputerDomain As String
Dim ShareName as String
Dim RetVal as String
ComputerDomain = "Target_Computer_Domain"
ComputerName = "Target_Computer_Name"
ShareName = "Target_Share_Name"
Set FileShare = GetObject("WinNT://" & ComputerDomain & "/" & ComputerName &
➥"/LanmanServer/" & ShareName)
RetVal = FileShare.CurrentUserCount
Debug.Print RetVal
```

Note

This property is read-only; the system is responsible for updating the value assigned to this property. ◆

Querying the File Share Description (Comment Field) Using Visual Basic

Using the Share As option in Windows File Manager (winfile.exe) or the Sharing option in the Windows NT Explorer (shown in Figure 7.2), you can view and set the comment for a share hosted on a system.

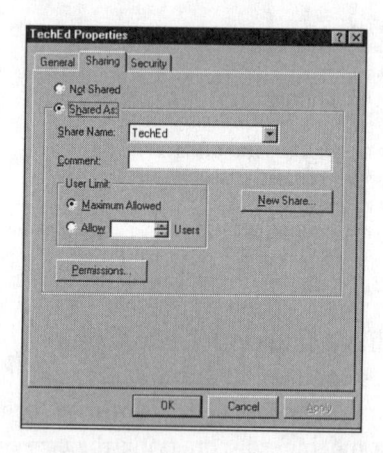

Figure 7.2 *Share dialog box in Windows NT Explorer.*

Likewise, you can set the Description property of the IADsFileShare to enter this data from your favorite programming environment, as shown in the following Visual Basic code:

```
Dim FileShare As IADsFileShare
Dim ComputerName As String
Dim ComputerDomain As String
Dim ShareName as String
Dim RetVal as String
ComputerDomain = "Target_Computer_Domain"
ComputerName = "Target_Computer_Name"
ShareName = "Target_Share_Name"
Set FileShare = GetObject("WinNT://" & ComputerDomain & "/" & ComputerName &
➥"/LanmanServer/" & ShareName)
RetVal = FileShare.Description
Debug.Print RetVal
```

Tip

If your enterprise uses delimited fields for the description values on servers, you can parse the data using Visual Basic. Use the user description field parsing code segment in Chapter 4, "Programmatic User Account Manipulation," as a guide. ♦

Setting a New File Share Description Using Visual Basic

To programmatically set a new description for a file share, use the following Visual Basic code:

```
Dim FileShare As IADsFileShare
Dim ComputerName As String
Dim ComputerDomain As String
Dim ShareName as String
Dim NewFileShareDescription as String
ComputerDomain = "Target_Computer_Domain"
ComputerName = "Target_Computer_Name"
ShareName = "Target_Share_Name"
NewFileShareDescription = "New_File_Share_Description"
Set FileShare = GetObject("WinNT://" & ComputerDomain & "/" & ComputerName &
➥"/LanmanServer/" & ShareName)
FileShare.Description = NewFileShareDescription
FileShare.SetInfo
```

Querying the File Share Host Computer Using Visual Basic

On occasion you may want to verify that the file share you are manipulating belongs to a particular host. To perform this action using ADSI, simply query the value of the HostComputer property as shown in the following Visual Basic code segment:

```
Dim FileShare As IADsFileShare
Dim ComputerName As String
Dim ComputerDomain As String
```

```
Dim ShareName as String
ComputerDomain = "Target_Computer_Domain"
ComputerName = "Target_Computer_Name"
ShareName = "Target_Share_Name"
Set FileShare = GetObject("WinNT://" & ComputerDomain & "/" & ComputerName &
↪"/LanmanServer/" & ShareName)
Debug.Print FileShare.HostComputer
```

> **Note**
>
> After running this code segment, you will notice that the ADsPath of the host is returned.
>
> This value should be considered read-only; you cannot create a share on your machine that references a remote host. ◆

Querying the File Share Maximum Users Property Value Using Visual Basic

As shown in Figure 7.2, Windows NT allows you to configure the maximum number of users allowed to connect to a shared resource.

By default, ADSI creates a share that can be used by an unlimited number of users. In some cases, you may want to limit the number of connections to the share. To query the current value assigned to the `MaxUserCount` property, use the following Visual Basic code:

```
Dim FileShare As IADsFileShare
Dim ComputerName As String
Dim ComputerDomain As String
Dim ShareName as String
ComputerDomain = "Target_Computer_Domain"
ComputerName = "Target_Computer_Name"
ShareName = "Target_Share_Name"
Set FileShare = GetObject("WinNT://" & ComputerDomain & "/" & ComputerName &
↪"/LanmanServer/" & ShareName)
Debug.Print FileShare.MaxUserCount
```

> **Tip**
>
> If the return value is −1, an unlimited number of users can access the share. ◆

Setting a New Value for the File Share Maximum Users Property Value Using Visual Basic

To programmatically assign a new value to the `MaxUserCount` property of a share, use the following Visual Basic code:

```
Dim FileShare As IADsFileShare
Dim ComputerName As String
Dim ComputerDomain As String
Dim ShareName as String
Dim NewFileShareMaximumUsers as Integer
ComputerDomain = "Target_Computer_Domain"
ComputerName = "Target_Computer_Name"
ShareName = "Target_Share_Name"
NewFileShareMaximumUsers = Maximum_Users_Value
Set FileShare = GetObject("WinNT://" & ComputerDomain & "/" & ComputerName &
➥"/LanmanServer/" & ShareName)
FileShare.MaxUserCount = NewFileShareMaximumUsers
FileShare.SetInfo
```

Querying the File Share Path Property Value Using Visual Basic

In the GUI environment, there are many ways to find the path for a share; however, as shown in Figure 7.3, you can display all shares for a particular machine in a single dialog box using Server Manager. To see which path is associated with a particular share name using programmatic methods, you can simply query the `Path` property of the bound share.

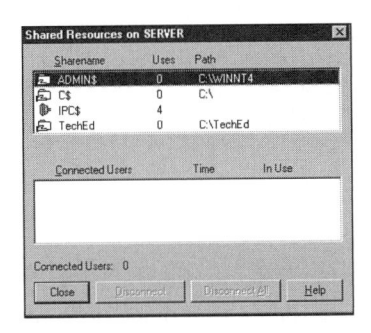

Figure 7.3 *Viewing the physical path associated with a share using Windows NT Server Manager.*

Use the following Visual Basic code to determine the path associated with a specific share:

```
Dim FileShare As IADsFileShare
Dim ComputerName As String
Dim ComputerDomain As String
Dim ShareName as String
ComputerDomain = "Target_Computer_Domain"
ComputerName = "Target_Computer_Name"
```

```
ShareName = "Target_Share_Name"
Set FileShare = GetObject("WinNT://" & ComputerDomain & "/" & ComputerName &
↳"/LanmanServer/" & ShareName)
Debug.Print FileShare.Path
```

Creating a Share Programmatically Using Visual Basic

To create a new share, call the `Create` method of the IADsContainer interface to create a new entry in the LanmanServer container. Before calling the IADs `SetInfo` method, you must first assign the IADsFileShare `Path` property to the value of the physical path you desire the share to reference. This is the only mandatory property for a new share; however, you may want to set a value for the description/comment field at the same time.

Use the following Visual Basic code to create a new share on a host and set the description/comment field to a specific string:

```
Dim Container As IADsContainer
Dim FileShare As IADsFileShare
Dim ComputerName As String
Dim ComputerDomain As String
Dim ShareName as String
Dim NewFileSharePath as String
Dim NewFileShareDescription as String
ComputerDomain = "Target_Computer_Domain"
ComputerName = "Target_Computer_Name"
ShareName = "Target_Share_Name"
NewFileSharePath = "Path_To_Share"
NewFileShareDescription = "File_Share_Comment"
Set Container = GetObject("WinNT://" & ComputerDomain & "/" & ComputerName &
↳"/LanmanServer")
Set FileShare = Container.Create("fileshare", ShareName)
FileShare.Path = NewFileSharePath
FileShare.Description = NewFileShareDescription
FileShare.MaxUserCount = -1
FileShare.SetInfo
```

Removing a Share Using Visual Basic

If you no longer require a share on a machine, you can bind to the LanmanServer container and remove the object representing the share you wish to remove.

To do this, after binding the LanmanServer container, simply call the `Delete` method of the IADsContainer interface, as shown in the following Visual Basic code:

```
Dim Container As IADsContainer
Dim ComputerName As String
Dim ComputerDomain As String
Dim ShareName as String
Dim RetVal as Integer
```

```
ComputerDomain = "Target_Computer_Domain"
ComputerName = "Target_Computer_Name"
ShareName = "Target_Share_Name"
Set Container = GetObject("WinNT://" & ComputerDomain & "/" & ComputerName &
↪"/LanmanServer")
Call Container.Delete("fileshare", ShareName)
```

Managing File Sessions

As shown in Figure 7.4, with Server Manager you can view all sessions associated with a particular resource by clicking the Users button in the Properties For dialog box. Using the IADsFileServiceOperations and IADsSession interfaces, you can also view this data programmatically.

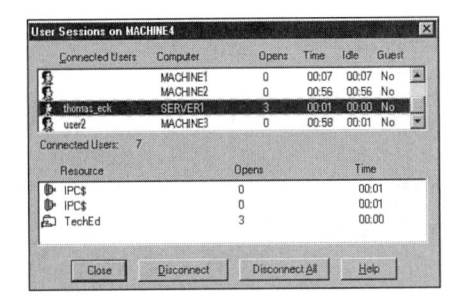

Figure 7.4 *Session enumeration using Windows NT Server Manager.*

The ability to monitor inbound connections can be useful in many ways for an application developer. For developing HTML versions of standard Windows NT administrative tools, the ability to re-create this dialog box using ADSI adds to the richness of your administrative application. This same function could be applied to determine the number of inbound connections to a particular machine for product licensing purposes.

> **Note**
>
> Not surprisingly, all properties of the IADsSession interface are read-only; they are dynamically manipulated by the system, not the user. ◆

Enumerating User Sessions Using Visual Basic

To view all active connections to a specific machine, first bind to the LanmanServer container and then enumerate the session objects contained within.

The following Visual Basic code enumerates all sessions to a given machine as well as the user responsible for the connection, the computer from which they are associated, and the connect and idle times (in seconds):

```
Dim FileService As IADsFileServiceOperations
Dim ComputerName As String
Dim ComputerDomain As String
Dim Session As IADsSession
ComputerDomain = "Target_Computer_Domain"
ComputerName = "Target_Computer_Name"
Set FileService = GetObject("WinNT://" & ComputerDomain & "/" & ComputerName &
➥"/LanmanServer")
For Each Session In FileService.Sessions
    Debug.Print "Session Name:" & Session.Name & " established by User: " &
➥Session.User & _
" from Computer: " & Session.Computer & " Connect Time: " & Session.ConnectTime &
➥_
" Idle Time: " & Session.IdleTime
Next
```

In the preceding code example, all the exposed properties of the IADsSession interface in the Windows NT service provider were displayed. Let's look at the function of each one in a bit more detail:

- **User.** This property describes the user who instantiated the connection.
- **Computer.** This property specifies the computer name of the connected user's computer.
- **ConnectTime.** This property specifies the number of seconds that have elapsed since the connection was opened.
- **IdleTime.** This property describes the time elapsed since the user last initiated an action on the connection.
- **Name.** This property is a dual interface with the IADs interface and is required for binding to an individual session.

Managing Individual Sessions Using Visual Basic

Unlike the majority of interfaces in ADSI, the IADsSession interface is created dynamically. To overcome this minor obstacle, you must use the IADsCollection interface to add and remove objects from the collection. This enables you to manage user sessions.

Additionally, the ability to query a single user session can improve performance significantly over enumeration methods on network file servers where there are likely to be hundreds (if not thousands) of sessions open.

Use the following Visual Basic code to bind to a specific user session:

```
Dim FileService As IADsFileServiceOperations
Dim ComputerName As String
Dim ComputerDomain As String
Dim Session As IADsSession
```

```
Dim Collection As IADsCollection
Dim UserSessionName As String
Dim UserSession As IADsSession
ComputerDomain = "Target_Computer_Domain"
ComputerName = "Target_Computer_Name"
UserSessionName = "Target_Session"
Set FileService = GetObject("WinNT://" & ComputerDomain & "/" & ComputerName &
↳"/LanmanServer")
Set Collection = FileService.Sessions
Set UserSession = Collection.GetObject(UserSessionName)
```

Disconnecting a Single User Session Using Visual Basic

As an administrator, there may be occasions when you need to disconnect a single user from a shared resource. Using Server Manager, this is easily performed by simply clicking the Disconnect button while the desired session is highlighted in the User Sessions dialog box. You can also perform this task programmatically by removing the desired session from the collection. To perform this task using Visual Basic, use the following code:

```
Dim FileService As IADsFileServiceOperations
Dim ComputerName As String
Dim ComputerDomain As String
Dim Session As IADsSession
Dim Collection As IADsCollection
Dim UserSessionName As String
ComputerDomain = "Target_Computer_Domain"
ComputerName = "Target_Computer_Name"
UserSessionName = "Target_Session"
Set FileService = GetObject("WinNT://" & ComputerDomain & "/" & ComputerName &
↳"/LanmanServer")
Set Collection = FileService.Sessions
Collection.Remove (UserSessionName)
```

> *Tip*
>
> *Windows NT/2000 will transparently reconnect the user session when the client requests the resource again. This code is best executed immediately before the action requiring you to disconnect the user session, such as backing up an open file or updating a .DLL that is currently in use by a remote user.* ♦

Disconnecting All User Sessions Using Visual Basic

Server Manager also allows you to remove all user sessions. To perform this task programmatically, combine the task of removing an item from the collection with an enumeration function to remove all items within the collection.

Use the following Visual Basic code to disconnect all user sessions from a given server:

```
Dim FileService As IADsFileServiceOperations
Dim ComputerName As String
Dim ComputerDomain As String
Dim Session As IADsSession
Dim Collection As IADsCollection
ComputerDomain = "Target_Computer_Domain"
ComputerName = "Target_Computer_Name"
Set FileService = GetObject("WinNT://" & ComputerDomain & "/" & ComputerName &
➥"/LanmanServer")
Set Collection = FileService.Sessions
For Each Session In Collection
     Collection.Remove (Session.Name)
Next
```

Managing Open Resources

For each user session, there are resources associated with the open connection. If a user is using an Access database, the associated .MDB file is considered an open resource in Server Manager. Using ADSI, you can enumerate all files currently in use, and subsequently view the user and lock count information for each open resource.

The ability to disconnect a user from a resource can be an important feature to administrators charged with data migration tasks where the file they want to move may be in use. When file access is denied because of an exclusive lock on the file by a user, often the only way for an administrator to gain access to the file is to simply disconnect the user from the resource.

> **Note**
>
> Unfortunately, the ability to perform this task using ADSI is not implemented in release 2.5 of the ADSI libraries. ◆

Enumerating Open Resources Using Visual Basic

As shown in Figure 7.5, you can use the GUI to enumerate all open resources on a given machine. To perform this same function using ADSI, simply use a *For...Each...Next* loop to enumerate the contents of the IADsResource collection.

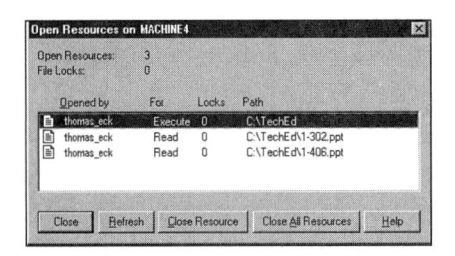

Figure 7.5 *Open Resources dialog box in Windows NT Server Manager.*

Use the following Visual Basic code to enumerate all open resources on a given machine:

```
Dim FileService As IADsFileServiceOperations
Dim ComputerName As String
Dim ComputerDomain As String
Dim Resource As IADsResource
ComputerDomain = "Target_Computer_Domain"
ComputerName = "Target_Computer_Name"
Set FileService = GetObject("WinNT://" & ComputerDomain & "/" & ComputerName &
➥"/LanmanServer")
For Each Resource In FileService.Resources
    Debug.Print "ResourceID: " & Resource.Name & " Resource: " & Resource.Path &
    ➥" Opened by: " & _
Resource.User & " Lock Count: " & Resource.LockCount
Next
```

> **Note**
>
> *The Debug.Print statement shows all properties of the IADsResource interface in the Windows NT service provider that you can examine.* ◆

Let's look at each individual property of the IADsResource interface:

- **Name.** This property is the system-generated name assigned to the resource. This is essential for identifying the resource within a collection for manipulation.
- **Path.** This property is the physical path of the open resource.
- **User.** This property is the user who holds the resource open.
- **LockCount.** This property is the number of locks on the resource.

Examining the Properties of a Single Open Resource Using Visual Basic

Windows NT dynamically assigns the Name property to the open resources on a machine, making it impossible to take any sort of educated guess as to what the proper way to identify the resource might be. To overcome this minor obstacle, simply combine a conditional with the enumeration function shown in the previous section, "Enumerating Open Resources Using Visual Basic," to filter data down to a specific user and resource.

Use the following Visual Basic code to show all open resources for a particular user:

```
Dim FileService As IADsFileServiceOperations
Dim ComputerName As String
Dim ComputerDomain As String
Dim ResourceUser As String
Dim ResourcePath As String
Dim Resource As IADsResource
Dim Collection As IADsCollection
ComputerDomain = "Target_Computer_Domain"
ComputerName = "Target_Computer_Name"
ResourceUser = "Target_Username"
Set FileService = GetObject("WinNT://" & ComputerDomain & "/" & ComputerName &
➥"/LanmanServer")
Set Collection = FileService.Resources
Debug.Print "User " & ResourceUser & " has the following resources open:"
For Each Resource In Collection
      If Resource.User = ResourceUser Then
            Debug.Print Resource.Path
      End If
Next
```

Tip

By changing the conditional statement and the contents of the ResourceUser variable, you can show a list of all users currently associated with an open resource, or even show all files that currently have locks on them. ◆

Managing Print Resources

Despite efforts to achieve a truly paperless office, all users still require access to print devices. Unfortunately, these mechanical marvels seem to host the largest number of service calls, perhaps because of the high number of moving parts, or simply because of the number of users sharing the device. Although ADSI certainly can't help when the toner is low or a paper jam occurs, it is well suited to help you manage both the print queue and print jobs associated with a network printing device.

Enumerating Print Queues Using Visual Basic

In most well-organized enterprises, one or several servers are tasked with the job of hosting print queues. Even in the most well-managed enterprise, someone will depart from the established policies and create a print queue somewhere it does not belong.

To discover such departures from standards by showing all print queues for all machines in a given domain, combine the print queue enumeration example shown in this section with the container enumeration functions for computer accounts.

> *Note*
>
> *Be prepared: This can take some time in large resource domains.* ♦

If you already know the name of a print server on the network, use the following Visual Basic code to find the names of all queues hosted on the machine:

```
Dim ComputerName As String
Dim ComputerDomain As String
Dim Container as IADsContainer
Dim PrintQueue as IADsPrintQueue
ComputerDomain = "Target_Computer_Domain"
ComputerName = "Target_Computer_Name"
Set Container = GetObject("WinNT://" & ComputerDomain & "/" & ComputerName)
Container.Filter = Array("PrintQueue")
For Each PrintQueue In Container
      Debug.Print PrintQueue.Name
Next
```

Binding a Specific Print Queue Using Visual Basic

You could enumerate an entire machine and use a conditional to find a specific queue, assuming the exact name of the queue is known. A much more appropriate method, however, would be simply to bind directly to the queue object itself.

To do this, use the following Visual Basic code:

```
Dim ComputerName As String
Dim ComputerDomain As String
Dim PrintQueueName as String
Dim PrintQueue as IADsPrintQueue
ComputerDomain = "Target_Computer_Domain"
ComputerName = "Target_Computer_Name"
PrintQueueName = "Target_Print_Queue"
Set PrintQueue = GetObject("WinNT://" & ComputerDomain & "/" & ComputerName & "/"
↪& PrintQueueName & ",printqueue")
```

Querying Print Queue Properties Using Visual Basic

Using the IADsPrintQueue interface, you can query the properties of an existing print queue (see Table 7.1).

Table 7.1   IADsPrintQueue Properties

Property	Description	Return Datatype
BannerPage	Used to get/set the path to the file used to separate print jobs.	String
Datatype	Specifies the type of data that can be processed by the queue. Usually this should be "RAW."	String
DefaultJobPriority	The default priority assigned to new print jobs.	Integer
Description	The free-text comment field associated with the queue.	String
Location	A free-text field used to describe the physical location of the printer.	String
Model	The name of the print driver used for this queue.	String
Name	The programmatic name of the printer.	String
PrintDevices	Defines the paths to other printers in the printer pool.	Variant
PrinterPath	Specifies the path to a printer.	String
PrintProcessor	The print processor associated with this queue. Usually set to "winprint."	String
Priority	The priority associated with the print queue. An administrator can create a high-priority print queue for small print jobs and another, low-priority, off-hours-only queue for printing large documents and booklets.	Integer
StartTime	Establishes the lower bound of the valid time for use with this queue.	Date
UntilTime	Establishes the upper bound of the valid time for use with this queue.	Date

You can examine each of the properties in the preceding table (except PrintDevices) by using syntax similar to the following:

```
Dim ComputerName As String
Dim ComputerDomain As String
Dim PrintQueueName as String
Dim PrintQueue as IADsPrintQueue
Dim RetVal as String
ComputerDomain = "Target_Computer_Domain"
ComputerName = "Target_Computer_Name"
```

```
PrintQueueName = "Target_Print_Queue"
Set PrintQueue = GetObject("WinNT://" & ComputerDomain & "/" & ComputerName & "/"
↳& PrintQueueName)
RetVal = PrintQueue.Model
Debug.Print RetVal
```

> **Warning**
>
> *When dimensioning the return value (RetVal in this example), be sure to specify the proper datatype associated with the property to avoid type mismatch errors.* ♦

To manipulate the `PrintDevices` property (which returns a variant array of strings), use the following Visual Basic code:

```
Dim ComputerName As String
Dim ComputerDomain As String
Dim PrintQueueName as String
Dim PrintQueue as IADsPrintQueue

Dim Item as Variant
ComputerDomain = "Target_Computer_Domain"
ComputerName = "Target_Computer_Name"
PrintQueueName = "Target_Print_Queue"
Set PrintQueue = GetObject("WinNT://" & ComputerDomain & "/" & ComputerName & "/"
↳& PrintQueueName)
If IsArray(PrintQueue.PrintDevices) Then
    For Each Item In PrintQueue.PrintDevices
        Debug.Print Item
    Next
Else
    Debug.Print PrintQueue.PrintDevices
End If
```

Managing Print Queues Programmatically Using Visual Basic

The IADsPrintQueueOperations interface allows the administrator to query the status of a queue, pause and resume operation of a queue, and examine the current list of print jobs in a queue. This can be incredibly useful for building applications that will allow inexperienced help desk staff to diagnose print server issues using a Web interface or custom application.

Querying Queue Status Using Visual Basic

Using the IADsPrintQueueOperations interface, you can query the current status of the queue. By implementing the following Visual Basic code, you can return the value of the IADsPrintQueueOperations Status method to find the current status of a print queue:

```
Dim PrintQueue As IADsPrintQueueOperations
Dim ComputerName As String
Dim ComputerDomain As String
Dim PrintQueueName As String
Dim RetVal As Long
```

```
ComputerDomain = "Target_Computer_Domain"
ComputerName = "Target_Computer_Name"
PrintQueueName = "Target_Print_Queue"
Set PrintQueue = GetObject("WinNT://" & ComputerDomain & "/" & ComputerName & "/"
➥& PrintQueueName)
RetVal = PrintQueue.Status
Debug.Print RetVal
```

To make it easier to decipher the status return codes, you may want to include a list of constants (using Table 7.2 as a guide) in your code module.

Table 7.2 Print Queue Status Constants

Constant	Value
ADS_PRINTER_READY	0x0
ADS_PRINTER_PAUSED	0x1
ADS_PRINTER_PENDING_DELETION	0x2
ADS_PRINTER_ERROR	0x3
ADS_PRINTER_PAPER_JAM	0x4
ADS_PRINTER_PAPER_OUT	0x5
ADS_PRINTER_MANUAL_FEED	0x6
ADS_PRINTER_PAPER_PROBLEM	0x7
ADS_PRINTER_OFFLINE	0x8
ADS_PRINTER_IO_ACTIVE	0x100
ADS_PRINTER_BUSY	0x200
ADS_PRINTER_PRINTING	0x400
ADS_PRINTER_OUTPUT_BIN_FULL	0x800
ADS_PRINTER_NOT_AVAILABLE	0x1000
ADS_PRINTER_WAITING	0x2000
ADS_PRINTER_PROCESSING	0x4000
ADS_PRINTER_INITIALIZING	0x8000
ADS_PRINTER_WARMING_UP	0x10000
ADS_PRINTER_TONER_LOW	0x20000
ADS_PRINTER_NO_TONER	0x40000
ADS_PRINTER_PAGE_PUNT	0x80000
ADS_PRINTER_USER_INTERVENTION	0x100000
ADS_PRINTER_OUT_OF_MEMORY	0x200000
ADS_PRINTER_DOOR_OPEN	0x400000
ADS_PRINTER_SERVER_UNKNOWN	0x800000
ADS_PRINTER_POWER_SAVE	0x1000000

Pausing a Print Queue Using Visual Basic

There may be occasions when you want to pause the print queue to perform service on the printer, or perhaps to build up a few jobs in the queue to explore programmatic print job management.

To pause a print queue, call the Pause method of the IADsPrintQueueOperations interface after binding the queue. Use the following Visual Basic code as a guide to pause a queue:

```
Dim PrintQueue As IADsPrintQueueOperations
Dim ComputerName As String
Dim ComputerDomain As String
Dim PrintQueueName As String
Dim RetVal As Long
ComputerDomain = "Target_Computer_Domain"
ComputerName = "Target_Computer_Name"
PrintQueueName = "Target_Print_Queue"
Set PrintQueue = GetObject("WinNT://" & ComputerDomain & "/" & ComputerName & "/"
↩& PrintQueueName)
PrintQueue.Pause
```

> *Note*
>
> *The* Pause *and* Resume *methods take a few moments to take effect. Do not make a call to the IADsPrintQueueOperations* Status *property immediately following one of these actions, for the property may not yet reflect the change.* ◆

Resuming a Print Queue Using Visual Basic

To resume the print queue after it has been in a paused state, use the following code to bring the queue back to normal operations:

```
Dim PrintQueue As IADsPrintQueueOperations
Dim ComputerName As String
Dim ComputerDomain As String
Dim PrintQueueName As String
Dim RetVal As Long
ComputerDomain = "Target_Computer_Domain"
ComputerName = "Target_Computer_Name"
PrintQueueName = "Target_Print_Queue"
Set PrintQueue = GetObject("WinNT://" & ComputerDomain & "/" & ComputerName & "/"
↩& PrintQueueName)
PrintQueue.Resume
```

Enumerating Print Jobs in a Print Queue Using Visual Basic

Using the Windows NT 4.0 GUI, you can view print queues and jobs by double-clicking the desired printer in the Printers folder, as shown in Figure 7.6. By using a *For...Each...Next* loop to enumerate the contents of the variant array passed back from the PrintJobs method of the IADsPrintQueueOperations interface, you can view contents and properties of individual jobs contained within the queue programmatically.

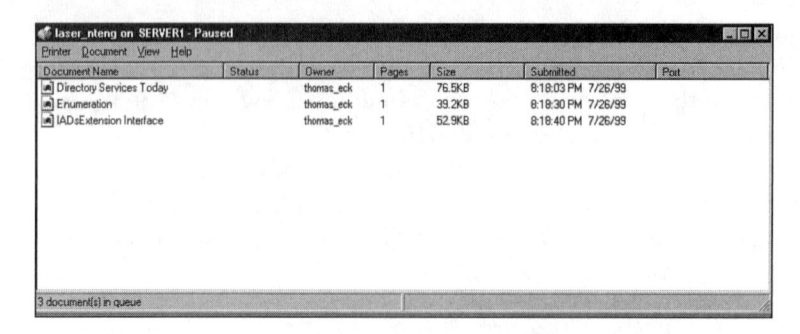

Figure 7.6 *Contents of a Windows NT print queue.*

Use the following Visual Basic code to display the programmatic ID, document name, document owner, and total page count of print jobs in a given queue:

```
Dim PrintQueue As IADsPrintQueueOperations
Dim ComputerName As String
Dim ComputerDomain As String
Dim PrintQueueName As String
Dim PrintJob as IADsPrintJob
ComputerDomain = "Target_Computer_Domain"
ComputerName = "Target_Computer_Name"
PrintQueueName = "Target_Print_Queue"
Set PrintQueue = GetObject("WinNT://" & ComputerDomain & "/" & ComputerName & "/"
↳& PrintQueueName)
For Each PrintJob in PrintQueue.PrintJobs
    Debug.Print PrintJob.Name & " " & PrintJob.Description & " " & PrintJob.User
    ↳& " " & PrintJob.TotalPages
Next
```

In addition to the programmatic identifier, document name, document owner, and total pages submitted that you examined in the previous example, there are many more properties you can examine for a particular print job. Use the Table 7.3 as a guide.

Table 7.3 IADsPrintJob Properties

Method/Property	Description	Read Only?	Return Datatype
Description	The title of the document	No	String
HostPrintQueue	The ADsPath of the host queue	Yes	String
Notify	The userid of the user to notify when printing has completed	No	String
Priority	The priority of the job in the queue	No	Integer

Managing Print Resources   181

Method/Property	Description	Read Only?	Return Datatype
Size	The size (in bytes) of the submitted job	Yes	Long
StartTime	The earliest time for the job to be printed	No	Date
TimeSubmitted	The time the job was submitted to the queue	Yes	Date
TotalPages	The total number of pages to be printed	Yes	Long
UntilTime	The latest time for the job to be printed	No	Date
User	The owner of the print job	Yes	String

You can simply use a Debug.Print statement (use the code from the preceding "Querying Print Queue Properties Using Visual Basic" section as a guide) to list all of these properties on a single line, or you can store each one in a variable of the appropriate datatype.

Changing the Priority of a Queued Print Job for a Specific Username Using Visual Basic

You can actually manipulate the non-read-only properties using the IADsPrintJob interface.

Consider the following Visual Basic code that will raise the priority of any job in the queue bearing a specific username to a priority value of 99:

```
Dim PrintQueue As IADsPrintQueueOperations
Dim ComputerName As String
Dim ComputerDomain As String
Dim PrintQueueName As String
Dim PrintJob as IADsPrintJob
Dim UserToPrioritize as String
ComputerDomain = "Target_Computer_Domain"
ComputerName = "Target_Computer_Name"
PrintQueueName = "Target_Print_Queue"
UserToPrioritize = "User_To_Elevate_Priority"
Set PrintQueue = GetObject("WinNT://" & ComputerDomain & "/" & ComputerName & "/"
↪& PrintQueueName)
For Each PrintJob in PrintQueue.PrintJobs
    If PrintJob.User = UserToPrioritize Then
        PrintJob.Priority = 99
        PrintJob.SetInfo
    End If
Next
```

Additional Properties Provided by the IADsPrintJobOperations Interface

There are many properties exposed by the IADsPrintJob interface. However, you cannot discover any real-time information about the current status of a print job within the queue, such as position, time elapsed since the job began printing, or the number of pages that have already been printed. To find out this information, you can dimension a variable of type IADsPrintJobOperations to discover these extended, time-sensitive properties.

These properties can be accessed just like those of the IADsPrintJob interface—by using a debug statement or storing the returned values of each query in an appropriately dimensioned variable.

To help determine the proper usage of these properties, use Table 7.4.

Table 7.4 IADsPrintJob Operations Properties and Methods

Method/Property	Description	Read Only?	Return Datatype
PagesPrinted	The number of pages of the job that have already been printed	Yes	Long
Position	The position of the currently selected job in the queue	No	Long
Status	The current status of the job	Yes	Paused (1)
			Error (2)
			Deleting (4)
			Printing (10)
			Offline (20)
			PaperOut (40)
			Printed (80)
			Deleted (100)
TimeElapsed	The time (in seconds) that the job has been being serviced by the printer	Yes	Long

Removing Jobs from the Print Queue Using Visual Basic

Occasionally, there is a need to delete a print job that has been placed in the print queue. ADSI can perform the task almost effortlessly, using the IADsCollection interface. This interface stores the contents of the collection returned by the PrintJobs method of the IADsPrintQueueOperations interface. With the print jobs stored in the collection, you can remove specific jobs.

To perform this task, you must first know the programmatic ID of the job to delete. This is an integer or long integer value that uniquely identifies the document to be printed in the queue. To find the programmatic ID of the job, find it from the Name property of any object dimensioned of type IADsPrintJob.

Consider the following Visual Basic code that will remove all print jobs submitted by a particular user:

```
Dim PrintQueue As IADsPrintQueueOperations
Dim PrintJob As IADsPrintJob
Dim ComputerName As String
Dim ComputerDomain As String
Dim PrintQueueName As String
Dim Collection As IADsCollection
Dim UserToRemove as String
ComputerDomain = "Target_Computer_Domain"
ComputerName = "Target_Computer_Name"
PrintQueueName = "Target_Print_Queue"
UserToRemove = "User_To_Remove_From_Queue"
Set PrintQueue = GetObject("WinNT://" & ComputerDomain & "/" & ComputerName & "/" 
➥& PrintQueueName)
Set Collection = PrintQueue.PrintJobs
For Each PrintJob In PrintQueue.PrintJobs
    If PrintJob.User = UserToRemove Then
        Collection.Remove (CStr(PrintJob.Name))
    End If
Next
```

Purging All Print Job Entries from the Queue Using Visual Basic

There are two approaches to removing all entries from a print queue. You can use the code from the previous section without the conditional to limit it to just a single user, or you can simply call the Purge method of the IADsPrintQueueOperations interface. In general, enumeration functions are expensive in terms of system resources, so the Purge method is likely to be a better choice if you want to indiscriminately remove all jobs from a queue. Additionally, it is important to note that the PrintJobs method of the IADsPrintQueue interface takes a snapshot of the current jobs in the queue. As such, it may be possible for the jobs to be processed during the course of processing, causing binding errors. These errors are also eliminated by the Purge method.

Use the following Visual Basic code segment to remove all entries from a specific print queue:

```
Dim PrintQueue As IADsPrintQueueOperations
Dim ComputerName As String
Dim ComputerDomain As String
Dim PrintQueueName As String
Dim RetVal As Long
```

```
ComputerDomain = "Target_Computer_Domain"
ComputerName = "Target_Computer_Name"
PrintQueueName = "Target_Print_Queue"
Set PrintQueue = GetObject("WinNT://" & ComputerDomain & "/" & ComputerName & "/"
↪& PrintQueueName)
PrintQueue.Purge
```

Creating the NTResourceManagement Class Module

In this section, you will continue the creation of the NTAdmin.DLL COM server application started in Chapter 3.

Exercise 7.1 *Continuing the Creation of the NTAdmin.DLL COM Server Application: The NTResourceManagement Module*

1. Open the NTAdmin ActiveX DLL Visual Basic project that was started in Chapter 3. You can also download the project from http://www.newriders.com/adsi.

2. If you are adding to the NTAdmin project, add a new class module to the project. If this is a new project, make sure to set a reference to Active DS Type Library.

3. Name the new module **NTResourceManagement**.

4. Enter the following code into the General Declarations section of the class module:

```
Public Function EnumerateShares(ByVal TargetComputerDomain As String, ByVal
↪TargetComputerName As String) As Variant
    On Error Resume Next
    Dim FileService As IADsFileService
    Dim FileShare As IADsFileShare
    Dim NewElement() As Variant
    Dim i As Integer
    Set FileService = GetObject("WinNT://" & TargetComputerDomain & "/" &
TargetComputerName & "/LanmanServer")
    For Each FileShare In FileService
        i = UBound(NewElement) + 1
        ReDim Preserve NewElement(i)
        NewElement(i) = FileShare.Name
    Next
    EnumerateShares = NewElement
End Function

Public Function ManageShareProperty(ByVal TargetComputerDomain As String, ByVal
↪TargetComputerName As String, ByVal TargetShareName As String, ByVal Action As
↪String, ByVal ShareProperty As String, Optional ByVal NewValue As Variant) As
↪Variant
    Dim FileShare As IADsFileShare
    Set FileShare = GetObject("WinNT://" & TargetComputerDomain & "/" &
    ↪TargetComputerName & "/LanmanServer/" & TargetShareName)
```

Creating the NTResourceManagement Class Module   185

```
        Select Case UCase(Action)
            Case "QUERY"
                Select Case UCase(ShareProperty)
                    Case "CURRENTUSERCOUNT"
                        ManageShareProperty = FileShare.CurrentUserCount
                    Case "DESCRIPTION"
                        ManageShareProperty = FileShare.Description
                    Case "HOSTCOMPUTER"
                        ManageShareProperty = FileShare.HostComputer
                    Case "MAXUSERCOUNT"
                        ManageShareProperty = FileShare.MaxUserCount
                    Case "PATH"
                        ManageShareProperty = FileShare.Path
                End Select
            Case "SET"
                If NewValue <> " Then
                    Select Case UCase(ShareProperty)
                        Case "DESCRIPTION"
                            FileShare.Description = NewValue
                        Case "MAXUSERCOUNT"
                            FileShare.MaxUserCount = NewValue
                    End Select
                    FileShare.SetInfo
                    If Err.Number = 0 Then ManageShareProperty = True
                End If
        End Select
End Function

Public Function ManageShares(ByVal TargetComputerDomain As String, ByVal
➥TargetComputerName As String, ByVal TargetShareName As String, ByVal Action As
➥String, Optional ByVal SharePath As String, Optional ByVal ShareComment As
➥String) As Boolean
    Dim Container As IADsContainer
    Dim FileShare As IADsFileShare
    Set Container = GetObject("WinNT://" & TargetComputerDomain & "/" &
    ➥TargetComputerName & "/LanmanServer")
    Select Case UCase(Action)
        Case "CREATE"
            If SharePath <> " Then
                Set FileShare = Container.Create("fileshare",
                ➥TargetShareName)
                FileShare.Path = SharePath
                FileShare.Description = ShareComment
                FileShare.MaxUserCount = -1
                FileShare.SetInfo
            End If
        Case "REMOVE"
            Call Container.Delete("fileshare", TargetShareName)
    End Select
    If Err.Number = 0 Then ManageShares = True
End Function
```

```
Public Function EnumerateSessions(ByVal TargetComputerDomain As String, ByVal
↪TargetComputerName As String) As Variant
    On Error Resume Next
    Dim FileService As IADsFileServiceOperations
    Dim Session As IADsSession
    Dim NewElement() As Variant
    Dim i As Integer
    Set FileService = GetObject("WinNT://" & TargetComputerDomain & "/" &
    ↪TargetComputerName & "/LanmanServer")
    For Each Session In FileService.Sessions
        i = UBound(NewElement) + 1
        ReDim Preserve NewElement(i)
        NewElement(i) = "Session Name:" & Session.Name & " established by User:
        ↪" & Session.User & _
        " from Computer: " & Session.Computer & " Connect Time: " & 
        ↪Session.ConnectTime & _
        " Idle Time: " & Session.IdleTime
    Next
    EnumerateSessions = NewElement
End Function

Public Function DisconnectSession(ByVal TargetComputerDomain As String, ByVal
↪TargetComputerName As String, ByVal TargetUserSession As String) As Boolean
    Dim FileService As IADsFileServiceOperations
    Dim Session As IADsSession
    Dim Collection As IADsCollection
    Set FileService = GetObject("WinNT://" & TargetComputerDomain & "/" &
    ↪TargetComputerName & "/LanmanServer")
    Set Collection = FileService.Sessions
    If UCase(TargetUserSession) <> "ALL" Then
        Collection.Remove (TargetUserSession)
    Else
        For Each Session In Collection
            Collection.Remove (Session.Name)
        Next
    End If
    If Err.Number = 0 Then DisconnectSession = True
End Function

Public Function EnumerateOpenResources(ByVal TargetComputerDomain As String,
↪ByVal TargetComputerName As String) As Variant
    On Error Resume Next
    Dim FileService As IADsFileServiceOperations
    Dim Resource As IADsResource
    Dim NewElement() As Variant
    Dim i As Integer
    Set FileService = GetObject("WinNT://" & TargetComputerDomain & "/" &
    ↪TargetComputerName & "/LanmanServer")
    For Each Resource In FileService.Resources
        i = UBound(NewElement) + 1
        ReDim Preserve NewElement(i)
        NewElement(i) = "ResourceID: " & Resource.Name & " Resource: " &
        ↪Resource.Path & " Opened by: " & _
```

```
            Resource.User & " Lock Count: " & Resource.LockCount
        Next
        EnumerateOpenResources = NewElement
    End Function

    Public Function EnumeratePrintQueues(ByVal TargetComputerDomain As String, ByVal
    ↪TargetComputerName As String) As Variant
        On Error Resume Next
        Dim Container As IADsContainer
        Dim PrintQueue As IADsPrintQueue
        Dim NewElement() As Variant
        Dim i As Integer
        Set Container = GetObject("WinNT://" & TargetComputerDomain & "/" &
        ↪TargetComputerName)
        Container.Filter = Array("PrintQueue")
        For Each PrintQueue In Container
           Debug.Print PrintQueue.Name
            i = UBound(NewElement) + 1
            ReDim Preserve NewElement(i)
            NewElement(i) = PrintQueue.Name
        Next
        EnumeratePrintQueues = NewElement
    End Function

    Public Function ManagePrintQueueProperty(ByVal TargetComputerDomain As String,
    ↪ByVal TargetComputerName As String, TargetPrintQueue As String, ByVal
    ↪QueuePropertyName As String, ByVal Action As String, Optional ByVal NewValue As
    ↪Variant) As Variant
        'On Error Resume Next
        Dim PrintQueue As IADsPrintQueue
        Dim NewElement() As Variant
        Dim i As Integer
        Dim Item As Variant
        Set PrintQueue = GetObject("WinNT://" & TargetComputerDomain & "/" &
        ↪TargetComputerName & "/" & TargetPrintQueue)
        Select Case UCase(Action)
            Case "QUERY"
                Select Case UCase(QueuePropertyName)
                    Case "BANNERPAGE"
                        ManagePrintQueueProperty = PrintQueue.BannerPage
                    Case "DATATYPE"
                        ManagePrintQueueProperty = PrintQueue.Datatype
                    Case "DEFAULTJOBPRIORITY"
                        ManagePrintQueueProperty = PrintQueue.DefaultJobPriority
                    Case "DESCRIPTION"
                        ManagePrintQueueProperty = PrintQueue.Description
                    Case "LOCATION"
                        ManagePrintQueueProperty = PrintQueue.Location
                    Case "MODEL"
                        ManagePrintQueueProperty = PrintQueue.Model
                    Case "NAME"
                        ManagePrintQueueProperty = PrintQueue.Name
                    Case "PRINTDEVICES"
```

```
                    If IsArray(PrintQueue.PrintDevices) Then
                        For Each Item In PrintQueue.PrintDevices
                            i = UBound(NewElement) + 1
                            ReDim Preserve NewElement(i)
                            NewElement(i) = PrintQueue.Name
                        Next
                        ManagePrintQueueProperty = NewElement
                    Else
                        ManagePrintQueueProperty = PrintQueue.PrintDevices
                    End If
                Case "PRINTERPATH"
                    ManagePrintQueueProperty = PrintQueue.PrinterPath
                Case "PRINTPROCESSOR"
                    ManagePrintQueueProperty = PrintQueue.PrintProcessor
                Case "PRIORITY"
                    ManagePrintQueueProperty = PrintQueue.Priority
                Case "STARTTIME"
                    ManagePrintQueueProperty = PrintQueue.StartTime
                Case "UNTILTIME"
                    ManagePrintQueueProperty = PrintQueue.UntilTime
            End Select
        Case "SET"
            If NewValue <> " Then
                Select Case UCase(QueuePropertyName)
                    Case "BANNERPAGE"
                        PrintQueue.BannerPage = NewValue
                    Case "DATATYPE"
                        PrintQueue.Datatype = NewValue
                    Case "DEFAULTJOBPRIORITY"
                        PrintQueue.DefaultJobPriority = NewValue
                    Case "DESCRIPTION"
                        PrintQueue.Description = NewValue
                    Case "LOCATION"
                        PrintQueue.Location = NewValue
                    Case "MODEL"
                        PrintQueue.Model = NewValue
                    Case "PRINTDEVICES"
                        If IsArray(NewValue) Then
                            For Each Item In NewValue
                                i = UBound(NewElement) + 1
                                ReDim Preserve NewElement(i)
                                NewElement(i) = Item
                            Next
                            PrintQueue.PrintDevices = NewElement
                        Else
                            PrintQueue.PrintDevices = NewValue
                        End If
                    Case "PRINTPROCESSOR"
                        PrintQueue.PrintProcessor = NewValue
                    Case "PRIORITY"
                        PrintQueue.Priority = NewValue
                    Case "STARTTIME"
                        PrintQueue.StartTime = NewValue
```

```
                        Case "UNTILTIME"
                            PrintQueue.UntilTime = NewValue
                    End Select
                End If
                PrintQueue.SetInfo
                If Err.Number = 0 Then ManagePrintQueueProperty = True
        End Select
End Function

Public Function ManagePrintQueueOperations(ByVal TargetComputerDomain As String,
➥ByVal TargetComputerName As String, TargetPrintQueue As String, ByVal Action As
➥String) As Variant
    Dim PrintQueue As IADsPrintQueueOperations
    Set PrintQueue = GetObject("WinNT://" & TargetComputerDomain & "/" &
    ➥TargetComputerName & "/" & TargetPrintQueue)
    Select Case UCase(Action)
        Case "STATUS"
            Select Case PrintQueue.Status
                Case 0
                    ManagePrintQueueOperations = "Ready"
                Case 1
                    ManagePrintQueueOperations = "Paused"
                Case 2
                    ManagePrintQueueOperations = "Pending Deletion"
                Case 3
                    ManagePrintQueueOperations = "Error"
                Case 4
                    ManagePrintQueueOperations = "Paper Jam"
                Case 5
                    ManagePrintQueueOperations = "Paper Out"
                Case 6
                    ManagePrintQueueOperations = "Manual Feed"
                Case 7
                    ManagePrintQueueOperations = "Paper Problem"
                Case 8
                    ManagePrintQueueOperations = "Offline"
                Case 100
                    ManagePrintQueueOperations = "IO Active"
                Case 200
                    ManagePrintQueueOperations = "Busy"
                Case 400
                    ManagePrintQueueOperations = "Printing"
                Case 800
                    ManagePrintQueueOperations = "Output Bin Full"
                Case 1000
                    ManagePrintQueueOperations = "Not Available"
                Case 2000
                    ManagePrintQueueOperations = "Waiting"
                Case 4000
                    ManagePrintQueueOperations = "Processing"
                Case 8000
                    ManagePrintQueueOperations = "Initializing"
                Case 10000
                    ManagePrintQueueOperations = "Warming Up"
```

```
                        Case 20000
                            ManagePrintQueueOperations = "Toner Low"
                        Case 40000
                            ManagePrintQueueOperations = "No Toner"
                        Case 80000
                            ManagePrintQueueOperations = "Page Punt"
                        Case 100000
                            ManagePrintQueueOperations = "User Intervention"
                        Case 200000
                            ManagePrintQueueOperations = "Out of Memory"
                        Case 400000
                            ManagePrintQueueOperations = "Door Open"
                        Case 800000
                            ManagePrintQueueOperations = "Server Unknown"
                        Case 1000000
                            ManagePrintQueueOperations = "Power Save"
                    End Select
            Case "PAUSE"
                PrintQueue.Pause
                If Err.Number = 0 Then ManagePrintQueueOperations = True
            Case "RESUME"
                PrintQueue.Resume
                If Err.Number = 0 Then ManagePrintQueueOperations = True
            Case "PURGE"
                PrintQueue.Purge
                If Err.Number = 0 Then ManagePrintQueueOperations = True
        End Select
End Function

Public Function EnumeratePrintJobs(ByVal TargetComputerDomain As String, ByVal
➥TargetComputerName As String, TargetPrintQueue As String) As Variant
    On Error Resume Next
    Dim PrintQueue As IADsPrintQueueOperations
    Dim PrintJob As IADsPrintJob
    Dim NewElement() As Variant
    Dim i As Integer
    Set PrintQueue = GetObject("WinNT://" & TargetComputerDomain & "/" &
➥TargetComputerName & "/" & TargetPrintQueue)
    For Each PrintJob In PrintQueue.PrintJobs
        i = UBound(NewElement) + 1
        ReDim Preserve NewElement(i)
        NewElement(i) = PrintJob.Name & " " & PrintJob.Description & " " &
➥PrintJob.User & " " & PrintJob.TotalPages
    Next
    EnumeratePrintJobs = NewElement
End Function

Public Function ManagePrintJob(ByVal TargetComputerDomain As String, ByVal
➥TargetComputerName As String, TargetPrintQueue As String, ByVal TargetPrintJob
➥As String, ByVal Action As String, Optional ByVal PrintJobProperty As String,
➥Optional ByVal NewValue As Variant) As Variant
    Dim PrintQueue As IADsPrintQueueOperations
    Dim PrintJob As IADsPrintJob
```

Creating the NTResourceManagement Class Module   191

```
        Dim PrintJobOperation As IADsPrintJobOperations
        Dim PJCollection As IADsCollection
        Set PrintQueue = GetObject("WinNT://" & TargetComputerDomain & "/" &
        ↪TargetComputerName & "/" & TargetPrintQueue)
        Select Case UCase(Action)
            Case "QUERY"
                Select Case UCase(PrintJobProperty)
                    Case "DESCRIPTION"
                        For Each PrintJob In PrintQueue.PrintJobs
                            If PrintJob.Name = TargetPrintJob Then
                                ManagePrintJob = PrintJob.Description
                            End If
                        Next
                    Case "HOSTPRINTQUEUE"
                        For Each PrintJob In PrintQueue.PrintJobs
                            If PrintJob.Name = TargetPrintJob Then
                                ManagePrintJob = PrintJob.HostPrintQueue
                            End If
                        Next
                    Case "NOTIFY"
                        For Each PrintJob In PrintQueue.PrintJobs
                            If PrintJob.Name = TargetPrintJob Then
                                ManagePrintJob = PrintJob.Notify
                            End If
                        Next
                    Case "PRIORITY"
                        For Each PrintJob In PrintQueue.PrintJobs
                            If PrintJob.Name = TargetPrintJob Then
                                ManagePrintJob = PrintJob.Priority
                            End If
                        Next
                    Case "SIZE"
                        For Each PrintJob In PrintQueue.PrintJobs
                            If PrintJob.Name = TargetPrintJob Then
                                ManagePrintJob = PrintJob.Size
                            End If
                        Next
                    Case "STARTTIME"
                        For Each PrintJob In PrintQueue.PrintJobs
                            If PrintJob.Name = TargetPrintJob Then
                                ManagePrintJob = PrintJob.StartTime
                            End If
                        Next
                    Case "TIMESUBMITTED"
                        For Each PrintJob In PrintQueue.PrintJobs
                            If PrintJob.Name = TargetPrintJob Then
                                ManagePrintJob = PrintJob.TimeSubmitted
                            End If
                        Next
                    Case "TOTALPAGES"
                        For Each PrintJob In PrintQueue.PrintJobs
                            If PrintJob.Name = TargetPrintJob Then
                                ManagePrintJob = PrintJob.TotalPages
```

```
                End If
            Next
        Case "UNTILTIME"
            For Each PrintJob In PrintQueue.PrintJobs
                If PrintJob.Name = TargetPrintJob Then
                    ManagePrintJob = PrintJob.UntilTime
                End If
            Next
        Case "USER"
            For Each PrintJob In PrintQueue.PrintJobs
                If PrintJob.Name = TargetPrintJob Then
                    ManagePrintJob = PrintJob.User
                End If
            Next
        Case "PAGESPRINTED"
            For Each PrintJobOperation In PrintQueue.PrintJobs
                If PrintJobOperation.Name = TargetPrintJob Then
                    ManagePrintJob = 
                    ↪PrintJobOperation.PagesPrinted
                End If
            Next
        Case "POSITION"
            For Each PrintJobOperation In PrintQueue.PrintJobs
                If PrintJobOperation.Name = TargetPrintJob Then
                    ManagePrintJob = PrintJobOperation.Position
                End If
            Next
        Case "STATUS"
            For Each PrintJobOperation In PrintQueue.PrintJobs
                If PrintJobOperation.Name = TargetPrintJob Then
                    Select Case PrintJobOperation.Status
                        Case 1
                            ManagePrintJob = "Paused"
                        Case 2
                            ManagePrintJob = "Error"
                        Case 4
                            ManagePrintJob = "Deleting"
                        Case 10
                            ManagePrintJob = "Printing"
                        Case 20
                            ManagePrintJob = "Offline"
                        Case 40
                            ManagePrintJob = "Paper Out"
                        Case 80
                            ManagePrintJob = "Printed"
                        Case 100
                            ManagePrintJob = "Deleted"
                    End Select
                End If
            Next
        Case "TIMEELAPSED"
            For Each PrintJobOperation In PrintQueue.PrintJobs
                If PrintJobOperation.Name = TargetPrintJob Then
```

Creating the NTResourceManagement Class Module   193

```
                        ManagePrintJob = PrintJobOperation.TimeElapsed
                    End If
                Next
        End Select
    Case "SET"
        Select Case UCase(PrintJobProperty)
            Case "DESCRIPTION"
                For Each PrintJob In PrintQueue.PrintJobs
                    If PrintJob.Name = TargetPrintJob And NewValue <> "
                    ↪Then
                        PrintJob.Description = NewValue
                        PrintJob.SetInfo
                    End If
                Next
            Case "NOTIFY"
                For Each PrintJob In PrintQueue.PrintJobs
                    If PrintJob.Name = TargetPrintJob And NewValue <> "
                    ↪Then
                        PrintJob.Notify = NewValue
                        PrintJob.SetInfo
                    End If
                Next
            Case "PRIORITY"
                For Each PrintJob In PrintQueue.PrintJobs
                    If PrintJob.Name = TargetPrintJob And NewValue <> "
                    ↪Then
                        PrintJob.Priority = NewValue
                        PrintJob.SetInfo
                    End If
                Next
            Case "STARTTIME"
                For Each PrintJob In PrintQueue.PrintJobs
                    If PrintJob.Name = TargetPrintJob And NewValue <> "
                    ↪Then
                        PrintJob.StartTime = NewValue
                        PrintJob.SetInfo
                    End If
                Next
            Case "UNTILTIME"
                For Each PrintJob In PrintQueue.PrintJobs
                    If PrintJob.Name = TargetPrintJob And NewValue <> "
                    ↪Then
                        PrintJob.UntilTime = NewValue
                        PrintJob.SetInfo
                    End If
                Next
            Case "POSITION"
                For Each PrintJobOperation In PrintQueue.PrintJobs
                    If PrintJobOperation.Name = TargetPrintJob And
                    ↪NewValue <> " Then
                        PrintJobOperation.Position = NewValue
                        PrintJobOperation.SetInfo
                    End If
```

```
                    Next
                End Select
                If Err.Number = 0 Then ManagePrintJob = True
            Case "REMOVE"
                Set PJCollection = PrintQueue.PrintJobs
                For Each PrintJob In PrintQueue.PrintJobs
                    If PrintJob.Name = TargetPrintJob Then
                        PJCollection.Remove (CStr(PrintJob.Name))
                    End If
                Next
                If Err.Number = 0 Then ManagePrintJob = True
        End Select
End Function
```

5. Compile the code as NTAdmin.DLL.
6. Save and close the NTAdmin project.

> **Tip**
>
> You can download the Visual Basic 6.0 project or a pre-compiled version of NTAdmin.DLL from http://www.newriders.com/adsi. ◆

Using the Functions in NTResourceManagement

With the NTResourceManagement class module created, you can access this function from any programming language that supports OLE automation, including Visual Basic, VBScript, and JavaScript.

> **Tip**
>
> To instantiate the object, follow the appropriate syntax found in Chapter 3. Substitute the NTResourceManagement class name where necessary. ◆

Use Table 7.5 to help you use the proper syntax for each of the methods of the NTResourceManagement interface.

Table 7.5   NTResourceManagement Method Syntax

Action	Syntax
Enumerate Shares	For Each Share In EnumerateShares ↪("Computer_Domain", "Computer_Name") Debug.Print Share Next
Query Current User Count for a Share	Debug.Print ManageShareProperty ↪("Computer_Domain", "Computer_Name", ↪"Share_Name", "Query", ↪"CurrentUserCount")

Creating the NTResourceManagement Class Module

Action	Syntax
Query Description/Comment for a Share	`Debug.Print ManageShareProperty` ↳`("Computer_Domain", "Computer_Name",` ↳`"Share_Name", "Query", "Description")`
Query the Host Computer for a Share	`Debug.Print ManageShareProperty` ↳`("Computer_Domain", "Computer_Name",` ↳`"Share_Name", "Query", "HostComputer")`
Query the Maximum User Count for a Share	`Debug.Print ManageShareProperty` ↳`("Computer_Domain", "Computer_Name",` ↳`"Share_Name", "Query", "MaxUserCount")`
Query the Path Associated with a Share	`Debug.Print ManageShareProperty` ↳`("Computer_Domain", "Computer_Name",` ↳`"Share_Name", "Query", "Path")`
Set New Description for a Share	`Debug.Print ManageShareProperty` ↳`("Computer_Domain", "Computer_Name",` ↳`"Share_Name", "Set", "Description",` ↳`"New_Description")`
Set New Maximum User Count for a Share	`Debug.Print ManageShareProperty` ↳`("Computer_Domain", "Computer_Name",` ↳`"Share_Name", "Set", "MaxUserCount",` ↳`-1)`
Create a New File Share	`Debug.Print ManageShares("Computer_` ↳`Domain", "Computer_Name",` ↳`"Share_Name", "Create", "C:\Path",` ↳`"New Share Comment")`
Remove an Existing File Share	`Debug.Print ManageShares("Computer_` ↳`Domain", "Computer_Name",` ↳`"Share_Name", "Remove")`

Enumerate Sessions	`For Each Session In EnumerateSessions`
	↳`("Computer_Domain", "Computer_Name")`
	    `Debug.Print Session`
	`Next`

Disconnect a User Session	`Debug.Print DisconnectSession` ↳`("Computer_Domain", "Computer_Name",` ↳`"Session_Name")`

Enumerate Open Resources on a Specific Machine	`For Each OpenResource In`
	↳`EnumerateOpenResources`
	↳`("Computer_Domain", "Computer_Name")`
	    `Debug.Print OpenResource`
	`Next`

Enumerate Print Queues on a Specific Server	`For Each PrintQueue In`
	↳`EnumeratePrintQueues("Computer_`
	↳`Domain", "Computer_Name")`
	    `Debug.Print PrintQueue`
	`Next`

continues ▶

▶ *continued*

Action	Syntax
Query Queue Properties	`Debug.Print ManagePrintQueueProperty`↵`("Computer_Domain", "Computer_Name",`↵`"Printer_Name", "BannerPage", "Query")`
	`Debug.Print ManagePrintQueueProperty`↵`("Computer_Domain", "Computer_Name",`↵`"Printer_Name", "Datatype", "Query")`
	`Debug.Print ManagePrintQueueProperty`↵`("Computer_Domain", "Computer_Name",`↵`"Printer_Name", "DefaultJobPriority",`↵`"Query")`
	`Debug.Print ManagePrintQueueProperty`↵`("Computer_Domain", "Computer_Name",`↵`"Printer_Name", "Description",`↵`"Query")`
	`Debug.Print ManagePrintQueueProperty`↵`("Computer_Domain", "Computer_Name",`↵`"Printer_Name", "Location", "Query")`
	`Debug.Print ManagePrintQueueProperty`↵`("Computer_Domain", "Computer_Name",`↵`"Printer_Name", "Model", "Query")`
	`Debug.Print ManagePrintQueueProperty`↵`("Computer_Domain", "Computer_Name",`↵`"Printer_Name", "Name", "Query")`

	`If IsArray(ManagePrintQueueProperty`↵`("Computer_Domain", "Computer_Name",`↵`"Printer_Name", "PrintDevices",`↵`"Query")) Then`
	
	`    For Each Device In`↵`ManagePrintQueueProperty("Computer_`↵`Domain", "Computer_Name",`↵`"Printer_Name", "PrintDevices",`↵`"Query")`
	
	`        Debug.Print Device`
	`    Next`
	`Else`
	
	`    Debug.Print`↵`ManagePrintQueueProperty("Computer_`↵`Domain", "Computer_Name",`↵`"Printer_Name", "PrintDevices",`↵`"Query")`
	
	`End If`

	`Debug.Print ManagePrintQueueProperty`↵`("Computer_Domain", "Computer_Name",`↵`"Printer_Name", "PrinterPath",`↵`"Query")`

Action	Syntax

	`Debug.Print ManagePrintQueueProperty`
	`↪"Computer_Domain", "Computer_Name",`
	`↪"Printer_Name", "PrintProcessor",`
	`↪"Query")`

	`Debug.Print ManagePrintQueueProperty`
	`↪("Computer_Domain", "Computer_Name",`
	`↪"Printer_Name", "Priority", "Query")`

	`Debug.Print ManagePrintQueueProperty`
	`↪("Computer_Domain", "Computer_Name",`
	`↪"Printer_Name", "StartTime", "Query")`

	`Debug.Print ManagePrintQueueProperty`
	`↪("Computer_Domain", "Computer_Name",`
	`↪"Printer_Name", "UntilTime", "Query")`

Set Properties	`Debug.Print ManagePrintQueueProperty`
	`↪("Computer_Domain", "Computer_Name",`
	`↪"Printer_Name", "BannerPage", "Set",`
	`↪"pscript.sep")`

	`Debug.Print ManagePrintQueueProperty`
	`↪("Computer_Domain", "Computer_Name",`
	`↪"Printer_Name", "Datatype", "Set",`
	`↪"RAW")`

	`Debug.Print ManagePrintQueueProperty`
	`↪("Computer_Domain", "Computer_Name",`
	`↪"Printer_Name",`
	`↪"DefaultJobPriority", "Set", 50)`

	`Debug.Print ManagePrintQueueProperty`
	`↪("Computer_Domain", "Computer_Name",`
	`↪"Printer_Name", "Description",`
	`↪"Set", "Queue_Description")`

	`Debug.Print ManagePrintQueueProperty`
	`↪("Computer_Domain", "Computer_Name",`
	`↪"Printer_Name", "Location", "Set",`
	`↪"Printer_Location")`

	`Debug.Print ManagePrintQueueProperty`
	`↪("Computer_Domain", "Computer_Name",`
	`↪"Printer_Name", "Model", "Set",`
	`↪"Driver Description")`

	`Debug.Print ManagePrintQueueProperty`
	`↪("Computer_Domain", "Computer_Name",`
	`↪"Printer_Name", "PrintDevices",`
	`↪"Set", "Port")`

	`Debug.Print ManagePrintQueueProperty`
	`↪("Computer_Domain", "Computer_Name",`
	`↪"Printer_Name", "PrintProcessor",`
	`↪"Set", "WinPrint")`

continues ▶

▶ *continued*

Action	Syntax
	`Debug.Print ManagePrintQueueProperty` ↳`("Computer_Domain", "Computer_Name",` ↳`"Printer_Name", "Priority", "Set",` ↳`"Priority")`
	`Debug.Print ManagePrintQueueProperty` ↳`("Computer_Domain", "Computer_Name",` ↳`"Printer_Name", "StartTime", "Set",` ↳`#Start_Time#)`
	`Debug.Print ManagePrintQueueProperty` ↳`("Computer_Domain", "Computer_Name",` ↳`"Printer_Name", "UntilTime", "Set",` ↳`#End_Time#)`
Query Print Queue Status	`Debug.Print ManagePrintQueueOperations` ↳`("Computer_Domain", "Computer_Name",` ↳`"Printer_Name", "Status")`
Pause a Print Queue	`Debug.Print ManagePrintQueueOperations` ↳`("Computer_Domain", "Computer_Name",` ↳`"Printer_Name", "Pause")`
Resume a Print Queue	`Debug.Print ManagePrintQueueOperations` ↳`("Computer_Domain", "Computer_Name",` ↳`"Printer_Name", "Resume")`
Purge All Jobs from Queue	`Debug.Print ManagePrintQueueOperations` ↳`("Computer_Domain", "Computer_Name",` ↳`"Printer_Name", "Purge")`
Query Print Job Properties	`Debug.Print ManagePrintJob` ↳`("Computer_Domain", "Computer_Name",` ↳`"Printer_Name", "Job_Number",` ↳`"Query", "Description")`
	`Debug.Print ManagePrintJob("Computer_` ↳`Domain", "Computer_Name",` ↳`"Printer_Name", "Job_Number",` ↳`"Query", "HostPrintQueue")`
	`Debug.Print ManagePrintJob("Computer_` ↳`Domain", "Computer_Name",` ↳`"Printer_Name", "Job_Number",` ↳`"Query", "Notify")`
	`Debug.Print ManagePrintJob("Computer_` ↳`Domain", "Computer_Name",` ↳`"Printer_Name", "Job_Number",` ↳`"Query", "Priority")`
	`Debug.Print ManagePrintJob("Computer_` ↳`Domain", "Computer_Name",` ↳`"Printer_Name", "Job_Number",` ↳`"Query", "Size")`

Action	Syntax
	`Debug.Print ManagePrintJob("Computer_`↵`Domain", "Computer_Name",`↵`"Printer_Name", "Job_Number",`↵`"Query", "StartTime")`
	`Debug.Print ManagePrintJob("Computer_`↵`Domain", "Computer_Name",`↵`"Printer_Name", "Job_Number",`↵`"Query", "TimeSubmitted")`
	`Debug.Print ManagePrintJob("Computer_`↵`Domain", "Computer_Name",`↵`"Printer_Name", "Job_Number",`↵`"Query", "TotalPages")`
	`Debug.Print ManagePrintJob("Computer_`↵`Domain", "Computer_Name",`↵`"Printer_Name", "Job_Number",`↵`"Query", "UntilTime")`
	`Debug.Print ManagePrintJob("Computer_`↵`Domain", "Computer_Name",`↵`"Printer_Name", "Job_Number",`↵`"Query", "User")`
	`Debug.Print ManagePrintJob("Computer_`↵`Domain", "Computer_Name",`↵`"Printer_Name", "Job_Number",`↵`"Query", "PagesPrinted")`
	`Debug.Print ManagePrintJob("Computer_`↵`Domain", "Computer_Name",`↵`"Printer_Name", "Job_Number",`↵`"Query", "Position")`
	`Debug.Print ManagePrintJob("Computer_`↵`Domain", "Computer_Name",`↵`"Printer_Name", "Job_Number",`↵`"Query", "Status")`
	`Debug.Print ManagePrintJob("Computer_`↵`Domain", "Computer_Name",`↵`"Printer_Name", "Job_Number",`↵`"Query", "TimeElapsed")`
Set Print Job Property	`Debug.Print ManagePrintJob("Computer_`↵`Domain", "Computer_Name",`↵`"Printer_Name", "Job_Number", "Set",`↵`"Description", "New_Description")`
	`Debug.Print ManagePrintJob("Computer_`↵`Domain", "Computer_Name",`↵`"Printer_Name", "Job_Number", "Set",`↵`"Notify", "User_To_Notify")`

continues ▶

▶ *continued*

Action	Syntax

	`Debug.Print ManagePrintJob("Computer_`
	`↪Domain", "Computer_Name",`
	`↪"Printer_Name", "Job_Number", "Set",`
	`↪"Priority", New_Job_Priority)`

	`Debug.Print ManagePrintJob("Computer_`
	`↪Domain", "Computer_Name",`
	`↪"Printer_Name", "Job_Number", "Set",`
	`↪"StartTime", #StartTime#)`

	`Debug.Print ManagePrintJob("Computer_`
	`↪Domain", "Computer_Name",`
	`↪"Printer_Name", "Job_Number", "Set",`
	`↪"UntilTime", #EndTime#)`

	`Debug.Print ManagePrintJob("Computer_`
	`↪Domain", "Computer_Name",`
	`↪"Printer_Name", "Job_Number", "Set",`
	`↪"Position", PositionInQueue)`

Remove a Job from the Queue	`Debug.Print ManagePrintJob`
	`↪("Computer_Domain", "Computer_Name",`
	`↪"Printer_Name", "Job_Number",`
	`↪"Remove")`

Summary

This chapter explored the various resource management administrative functions ADSI enables you to manipulate using programmatic methods.

Using the IADsFileService, IADsFileServiceOperations, and IADsFileShare interfaces, you can easily enumerate and manage file shares for any machine in the enterprise. Add in the IADsSession and IADsCollection interfaces, and you can manage user sessions programmatically.

To manage print operations, you can easily use the IADsPrintQueue, IADsPrintQueueOperations, IADsPrintJob, and IADsPrintJobOperations interfaces to create applications to perform such duties.

With a bit of creativity and careful thought about what administrative functions affect your time the most each day, a quick ADSI script may be just the recipe needed to get you home before dinner.

Part III

Exploring the ADSI Service Providers: IIS

8   Programmatic Management of the IIS Metabase

9   Programmatic Management of Web Site Properties

10   Programmatic Management of FTP Site Properties

8

Programmatic Management of the IIS Metabase

Although most Windows NT administrative functions can be performed programmatically, some functions are unexposed to programmatic manipulation (such as setting the permissions on a share) or are too difficult to perform easily using script (such as login hours manipulation).

However, the Internet Information Server (IIS) 4.0 ADSI service provider implements a robust object model that allows you to manipulate almost every function in the IIS 4.0 Internet Service Manager Microsoft Management Console (MMC) snap-in. Just as the Windows Registry controls the configuration and operation of the Windows NT environment, the IIS Metabase is the namespace responsible for configuring IIS.

If you loaded the HTML Internet Service Manager when you installed the Windows Option Pack, look through the ASP samples in the %SystemRoot%\System32\InetSrv\IISAdmin directory. You will notice the object instantiations look surprisingly like the ADsPath binding strings you use to bind objects in the Windows NT service provider. This is because Microsoft chose ADSI as the strategic interface for programmatic IIS Metabase manipulation. Just as you can bind to the Windows NT SAM using the Windows NT namespace identifier, you can also manipulate the IIS Metabase by referencing the IIS ADSI service provider in the binding string.

This chapter will explore how you can use the power of ADSI to script IIS administrative tasks. Because of the robust object model implemented in IIS, this chapter covers topics germane to the entire server, including the following:

- The IIS Metabase structure
- The IIsComputer object
- IIS site logging
- Programmatic site management
- Programmatic site operations

In this chapter, you will also begin the first of several exercises that will ultimately yield the creation of the IISAdmin.DLL COM server.

IIS Metabase Structure

Whereas Windows NT uses the Registry to store its application configuration data, IIS derives its configuration from the IIS Metabase. Like the Windows Registry, the Metabase is a binary format file containing a hierarchical structure used to configure the IIS server.

> **Note**
>
> To view the IIS Metabase, use the MetaEdit utility contained in the IIS Resource Kit, or use ADSI to recursively enumerate the structure of the Metabase. ♦

Examining the Structure of the IIS Metabase Using Visual Basic

By understanding the structure of the IIS Metabase, you can better understand how to create the binding string required to access a specific container or leaf object in the namespace. Figure 8.1 shows the high-level structure of the IIS Metabase.

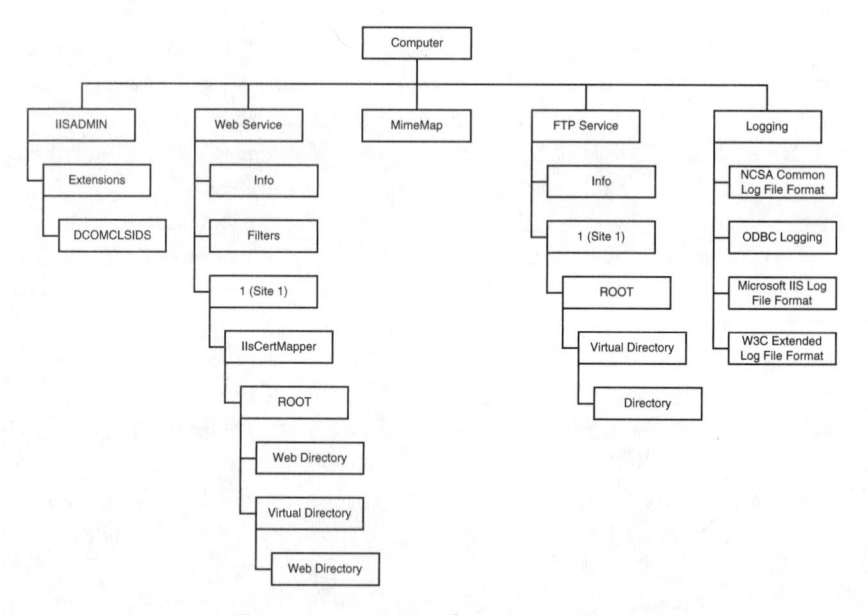

Figure 8.1 *IIS Metabase structure.*

This same diagram can be derived programmatically using ADSI and Visual Basic. If you want to view the structure of the IIS Metabase one layer at a time, use the following Visual Basic code to show each child layer in the hierarchy:

```
Dim Parent As IADs
Dim Child As IADs
Dim StartingPoint As String
Dim RetVal as String
StartingPoint = "IIS_Server_Name"
Set Parent = GetObject("IIS://" & StartingPoint)
For Each Child In Parent
  RetVal = Child.Name
  Debug.Print RetVal
Next
```

For example, if you want to view the contents of the W3SVC container, you can do so by assigning the StartingPoint variable to *Server_Name/W3SVC*. If you use *Server_Name/W3SVC* as the starting point, something similar to the following output will be displayed:

```
Filters
1
Info
2
```

On your system, there may be additional integers shown (depending on the number of Web sites you have), but most likely, the site associated with the integer value 1 is the "Default Web Site."

Based on the results displayed in the immediate window, you can then select a new starting point to show the next layer. Change the starting point to *Server_Name/W3SVC/1* and something similar to the following will be displayed:

```
ROOT
IIsCertMapper
```

Within the ROOT container, you have access to a wide range of properties that affect the site. In this manner, you can keep peeling away layers of the Metabase hierarchy until you arrive at the point in the namespace where you want to administer, which in many cases will be within the ROOT container.

> *Tip*
>
> *If you prefer, you can write a recursive function that will enumerate every node in the tree from a specific starting point. An example of such a function is included at* www.newriders.com/adsi.
>
> *While it is not needed for binding a site, you may want to examine the Metabase structure as it pertains to each of your servers.* ♦

The IIsComputer Object

The IIsComputer object exists at the top of the IIS Metabase hierarchy. In the Internet Service Manager snap-in for the MMC, this object can be presented graphically by right-clicking the name of the server and choosing Properties.

Using the IIsComputer interface, you can programmatically manage Metabase backups, throttle server bandwidth globally across all Web and FTP sites, and manage the default MIME-type entries for the server.

Backing Up the IIS Metabase Using Visual Basic

Before you begin programmatic administration of an IIS server, it is a *very* good idea to force a backup of the Metabase just in case you do something you might regret.

In general, the following syntax is used to perform a backup of the IIS Metabase:

```
IIsComputerObj.Backup BackupLocation, BackupVersion, BackupFlags
```

The `BackupLocation` parameter specifies the name of the file that will be stored in the %SystemRoot%\System32\Inetsrv\Metaback directory.

Using the `BackupVersion` parameter, you can specify whether you wish to create a new backup file or simply replace the highest version backup file in the directory. The `BackupVersion` parameter can be one of the following flags:

Flag	Description
MD_BACKUP_HIGHEST_VERSION	This flag replaces the highest backup version for the backup specified in the `BackupLocation` parameter.
MD_BACKUP_NEXT_VERSION	This flag creates a Metabase backup using the next available version number.

The `BackupFlags` parameter specifies how the backup should be performed and can be set to one of the following flags:

Flag	Description
MD_BACKUP_SAVE_FIRST	This flag performs a SaveData operation before the backup.
MD_BACKUP_FORCE_BACKUP	This flag performs the backup regardless of a failed MD_BACKUP_SAVE_FIRST operation.
MD_BACKUP_OVERWRITE	If there is an existing backup that is the same version as the one that is about to be saved, this flag overwrites the existing backup.

Armed with this background knowledge, you can now begin a backup of the IIS Metabase from Visual Basic, using the following code:

```
Dim IIsComputer As IADs
Dim Flags As Long
Dim TargetComputer as String
TargetComputer = "Target_Server_Name"
Flags = (MD_BACKUP_SAVE_FIRST Or MD_BACKUP_FORCE_BACKUP)
Set IIsComputer = GetObject("IIS://" & TargetComputer)
IIsComputer.Backup "MyBackup10", MD_BACKUP_NEXT_VERSION, Flags
```

Enumerating Existing Backups Using Visual Basic
To verify that the backup did indeed occur, you can enumerate all backups using the EnumBackups method of the IIsComputer interface.

Consider the following Visual Basic code to enumerate all existing Metabase backups:

```
On Error Resume Next
Dim IIsComputer As IADs
Dim TargetComputer As String
Dim Version, Index, TermCond As Integer
Dim Location As Variant
Dim UTCDate As Variant
TargetComputer = "Target_Server_Name"
Set IIsComputer = GetObject("IIS://" & TargetComputer)
Do While TermCond <> 1
  IIsComputer.EnumBackups ", Index, Version, Location, UTCDate
  If Err.Number <> 0 Then
    Exit Do
  End If
  Debug.Print Location & " Version: " & Version & " " & UTCDate
  Index = Index + 1
Loop
```

Restoring an Existing Metabase Backup Using Visual Basic
After you have completed a backup of the IIS Metabase, you can practice the procedure to restore the settings using programmatic methods. To perform this task, call the Restore method of the IIsComputer interface with the backup location and desired version information passed as arguments.

Consider the following Visual Basic code to help you restore the IIS Metabase after a successful backup:

```
Dim IIsComputer As IADs
Dim TargetComputer As String
Dim BackupLocation As String
TargetComputer = "Target_Server_Name"
BackupLocation = "Backup_Location_On_Target_Server"
Set IIsComputer = GetObject("IIS://" & TargetComputer)
IIsComputer.Restore BackupLocation, MD_BACKUP_HIGHEST_VERSION, 0
```

> **Tip**
>
> *To apply changes to the Metabase after a restore, you may have to reboot the server.* ♦

Deleting an Existing Metabase Backup Using Visual Basic

After testing the functionality of programmatic Metabase backup methods, you may want to clean up your server by removing all old backup files.

Use the `DeleteBackup` method of the IIsComputer object in Visual Basic to delete an existing Metabase backup file, as follows:

```
Dim IIsComputer As IADs
Dim TargetComputer As String
Dim BackupLocation As String
TargetComputer = "Target_Server_Name"
BackupLocation = "Backup_Location"
Set IIsComputer = GetObject("IIS://" & TargetComputer)
IIsComputer.DeleteBackup BackupLocation, MD_BACKUP_HIGHEST_VERSION
```

> **Tip**
>
> *Using the previous code, the system will delete the last backup performed in the specified backup location. If combined with the enumeration example, you can easily delete all existing backups programmatically.*
>
> *Additionally, you can replace the MD_BACKUP_HIGHEST_VERSION flag with the actual version number of a backup if you want to remove only a specific Metabase backup.* ♦

Manipulating Maximum IIS Network Bandwidth

As shown in Figure 8.2, IIS allows you to limit the bandwidth allocated to the File Transfer Protocol (FTP) and Web services on the IIS server using the `MaxBandwidth` property of the IIsComputer interface. This can be especially useful when a server, such as a departmental intranet server, also performs several duties, such as acting as a file server or mail server.

> **Note**
>
> *Limiting the bandwidth can also be helpful in development environments. Usability testers and developers can obtain rough estimates of the effect of a slow Wide Area Network (WAN) link on the overall client experience when navigating the production Web site. All too often, Web designers create incredibly creative, aesthetically pleasing sites but forget that some visitors will be viewing the site at much slower connection speeds than the LAN speed connection used for development.* ♦

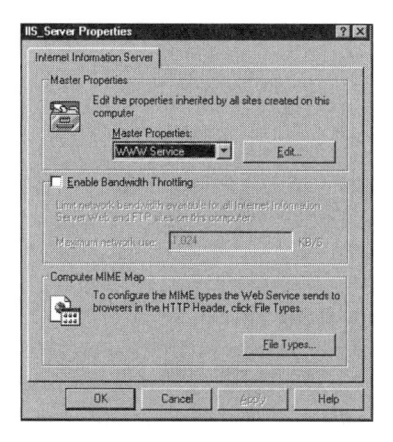

Figure 8.2 *IIS Server global properties.*

Querying *MaxBandwidth* Using Visual Basic
Use the following Visual Basic code to view the current running configuration for the MaxBandwidth property:

```
Dim IIsComputer As IADs
Dim TargetComputer as String
Dim RetVal as Long
TargetComputer = "Target_Server_Name"
Set IIsComputer = GetObject("IIS://" & TargetComputer)
RetVal = IIsComputer.MaxBandwidth
Debug.Print RetVal
```

If bandwidth throttling is not currently in use, a value of –1 will be returned.

Tip

The value returned is in bytes. If you want to view the information in KB (as the Internet Service Manager shows it), divide this value by 1024 before displaying it. ◆

Setting a New Value for *MaxBandwidth* Using Visual Basic
Using the following Visual Basic code, you can specify a new value in bytes for the bandwidth throttling setting for an IIS server:

```
Dim IIsComputer As IADs
Dim TargetComputer as String
Dim NewValue as Long
TargetComputer = "Target_Server_Name"
NewValue = New_Throttle_Value_In_Bytes
Set IIsComputer = GetObject("IIS://" & TargetComputer)
IIsComputer.MaxBandwidth = NewValue
IIsComputer.SetInfo
```

> **Warning**
>
> Although the Internet Service Manager dialog box shows that the change was made to the Metabase, you must cycle the Web publishing service in order for the change to take affect. To cycle the Web service using programmatic methods, follow the service start and stop procedures found in Chapter 6, "Programmatic Computer and Service Manipulation." ♦

MIME Mapping Management

Using the Internet Service Manager MMC snap-in or programmatic methods, you can modify the MIME types sent to browsers in HTTP headers. IIS allows the global definition of MIME types for the server, but also allows individual sites to override the settings if a particular site requires a MIME type that differs from the global setting.

Viewing the List of Current Server-Defined MIME Type Mappings Using Visual Basic

Using the following Visual Basic code, you can enumerate the MIME types inherited by all Web sites:

```
Dim IIsComputer As IADs
Dim TargetComputer as String
Dim MimeMapping as Variant
TargetComputer = "Target_Server_Name"
Set IIsComputer = GetObject("IIS://" & TargetComputer & "/MimeMap")
Debug.Print "Registered File Types:"
For Each MimeMapping in IISComputer.MimeMap
    Debug.Print "Extension: " & MimeMapping.Extension & " MIME Content Type: " & MimeMapping.MimeType
Next
```

Adding a New Server-Defined MIME Mapping Using Visual Basic

If you plan to implement a new document type that you want to associate with an application for all sites on a particular server, you can add a new MIME type at the server level.

Use the following Visual Basic code to create a new MIME mapping to be used by all sites on the IIS server:

```
Dim IIsComputer As IADs
Dim TargetComputer As String
Dim MimeMapping As Variant
Dim NewMimeMapping As Variant
Dim MimeExtension As String
Dim MimeType As String
Dim i As Integer
TargetComputer = "Target_Server_Name"
MimeExtension = "New_MIME_Extension"
```

```
MimeType = "New_MIME_Type"
Set IIsComputer = GetObject("IIS://" & TargetComputer & "/MimeMap")
NewMimeMapping = IIsComputer.GetEx("MimeMap")
i = UBound(NewMimeMapping) + 1
ReDim Preserve NewMimeMapping(i)
Set NewMimeMapping(i) = CreateObject("MimeMap")
NewMimeMapping(i).MimeType = MimeType
NewMimeMapping(i).Extension = MimeExtension
IIsComputer.PutEx ADS_PROPERTY_UPDATE, "MimeMap", NewMimeMapping
IIsComputer.SetInfo
```

Tip

To use the preceding code to create a new MIME type for all files with the extension .TEE with Microsoft Word, simply assign the MimeExtension *variable to ".TEE" and the* MimeType *variable to* "application/msword"*.* ♦

Removing a Server-Defined MIME Mapping Using Visual Basic
Although it's easy to place objects into an array, it's a bit trickier to delete them. When you think of deleting an object, you typically specify its name in some form of delete operation. However, when manipulating objects in an array, you have no way of specifically identifying individual objects within the array.

Early in life, you learned that if you did not want to include someone in an activity, it was far easier to fail to tell her where you were going rather than to specifically state that you didn't want her company. This kindergarten principle can be applied to programming efforts: If you want to delete a MIME type, you can create a new array that resembles the old one, but without the MIME type you want to delete, using a conditional to delete the mapping.

Warning

If you have not made a recent backup of the Metabase, you may want to do so before running this code. If you do not want to use the programmatic methods described earlier, you can also use the Internet Service Manager to create the backup. No matter how you intend to perform the backup, creating a backup of the Metabase before running this procedure is strongly recommended. ♦

The following Visual Basic code combines parts of the MIME type enumeration function you examined earlier (in the section "Viewing the List of Current Server-Defined MIME Type Mappings Using Visual Basic") as well as the MIME type definition code from the last example:

```
Dim IIsComputer As IADs
Dim TargetComputer As String
Dim MimeMapping As Variant
Dim MapToDelete As String
Dim NewMimeMapping As Variant
Dim i As Integer
MapToDelete = "Extension_To_Delete_From_MIME_Map"
TargetComputer = "Target_Server_Name"
Set IIsComputer = GetObject("IIS://" & TargetComputer & "/MimeMap")
NewMimeMapping = IIsComputer.MimeMap
For Each MimeMapping In IIsComputer.MimeMap
    If MimeMapping.Extension <> MapToDelete Then
        ReDim Preserve NewMimeMapping(i)
          Set NewMimeMapping(i) = CreateObject("MimeMap")
        NewMimeMapping(i).MimeType = MimeMapping.MimeType
        NewMimeMapping(i).Extension = MimeMapping.Extension
        i = i + 1
    End If
Next
Dim MimeItem As Variant
For Each MimeItem In NewMimeMapping
    Debug.Print MimeItem.MimeType
Next
IIsComputer.PutEx ADS_PROPERTY_UPDATE, "MimeMap", NewMimeMapping
'IIsComputer.SetInfo
```

Note

Notice that the last line is commented out. Before you write your new array to the namespace, make absolutely sure that the new array exists and is filled with all previous data (less the extension you specified to be deleted). Check that a list of extensions is returned in the immediate window before writing the new array to the namespace.

After you have verified your code is working as expected, remove the For...Each loop just before the commented line and delete the apostrophe before the IIsComputer.SetInfo *line to allow the changes to be written to the IIS Metabase.* ♦

Warning

If an error occurs that results in an empty array being written to the Metabase, you will lose all defined MIME types and will have to restore the Metabase using the restore procedure described previously. ♦

IIS Site Logging

With IIS, you have a host of options available for configuring site access logs. These logs are useful for auditing site access, for use with trend analysis tools (such as WebTrends), or even for replaying a specific historical event with the IIS Log Replay utility for troubleshooting.

Four logging providers are included with IIS 4.0:

- Microsoft IIS Log File Format
- NCSA Common Log File Format
- ODBC Logging
- W3C Extended Log File Format

Logging Provider Support in Each IIS Service

The ability to log user activities is common to all IIS services; however, each IIS service maintains its own set of supported logging providers.

Use Table 8.1 to determine which log formats are supported in each IIS service:

+ The plus symbol indicates that the log file format is supported by the service.

- The minus symbol indicates that the log file format is not supported by the service.

Table 8.1 Service Support for Log File Formats

Logging Provider	WWW Service	FTP Service	SMTP Service	NNTP Service
Microsoft IIS Log File Format	+	+	+	+
NCSA Common Log File Format	+	-	+	+
ODBC Logging	+	+	+	+
W3C Extended Log File Format	+	+	+	+

Enable Logging

To begin, logging must be enabled for the site. In the Internet Service Manager, click the check box captioned Enable Logging. Using Visual Basic, the process is also fairly simple—you simply modify the `LogType` property's value to log access to the site.

> *Tip*
>
> *For each code example, although the W3SVC IIS service is used in the binding string, you can easily substitute the appropriate service provider name (such as MSFTPSVC, SmtpSvc, or NNTPSVC) into the string.* ♦

Querying Current Logging Status Using Visual Basic

Use the following Visual Basic code to determine whether logging is enabled for a particular site:

```
Dim Site As IADs
Dim ServerName As String
Dim SiteIndex As Long
ServerName = "IIS_Server_Name"
SiteIndex = Site_Index_Value
Set Site = GetObject("IIS://" & ServerName & "/W3SVC/" & SiteIndex)
Debug.Print Site.LogType
```

Setting Logging Status Using Visual Basic

To enable logging for a particular site, set the value of the `LogType` property to 1. To disable logging for the site, set the property to 0.

Use the following Visual Basic code as a guide for your efforts:

```
Dim Site As IADs
Dim ServerName As String
Dim SiteIndex As Long
ServerName = "IIS_Server_Name"
SiteIndex = Site_Index_Value
Set Site = GetObject("IIS://" & ServerName & "/W3SVC/" & SiteIndex)
Site.LogType = 1
Site.SetInfo
```

Active Log Format

Using the `LogPluginCLSID` property of each IIS service provider object, you can query and toggle the active log format used for logging client requests. The IIS Metabase refers to this object by class ID (CLSID), not by name. This makes life rather interesting because you must relate names to CLSIDs in order to query or select the active log format.

By binding the Web server's logging object, you can find the names and CLSIDs of all installed providers. After you have obtained this information, you then have enough data to relate CLSIDs to friendly names anywhere the CLSID is returned from a property `Get` statement.

Querying Active Log Format Using Visual Basic

Use the following Visual Basic code to determine the active log file format for a given resource:

```
Dim Site As IADs
Dim Log As IADs
Dim ServerName As String
Dim SiteIndex As Long
ServerName = "IIS_Server_Name"
SiteIndex = Site_Index_Value
Set Site = GetObject("IIS://" & ServerName & "/W3SVC/" & SiteIndex)
```

IIS Site Logging

```
Set Log = GetObject("IIS://" & ServerName & "/logging")
For Each Item In Log
  If Site.LogPluginCLSID = Item.LogModuleID Then
    Debug.Print Item.Name
  End If
Next
```

Setting Active Log Format Using Visual Basic

If you want to set the log format programmatically, you must know either the CLSID or the friendly name of the logging object to be able to assign a new provider.

In the following code example, you'll pass in the friendly name (it must be exact) to assign the new logging provider using Visual Basic:

```
Dim Site As IADs
Dim Log As IADs
Dim ServerName As String
Dim SiteIndex As Long
Dim NewLogFormatName As String
ServerName = "IIS_Server_Name"
SiteIndex = Site_Index_Value
NewLogFormatName = "NCSA Common Log File Format"
'NewLogFormatName = "ODBC Logging"
'NewLogFormatName = "Microsoft IIS Log File Format"
'NewLogFormatName = "W3C Extended Log File Format"
Set Site = GetObject("IIS://" & ServerName & "/W3SVC/" & SiteIndex)
Set Log = GetObject("IIS://" & ServerName & "/logging")
For Each Item In Log
    If Item.Name = NewLogFormatName Then
        Site.LogPluginCLSID = Item.LogModuleID
        Site.SetInfo
    End If
Next
```

Tip

To enumerate the logging provider names on your machine, use the following Visual Basic code:

```
Dim Log As IADs
Dim ServerName As String
ServerName = "IIS_Server_Name"
Set Log = GetObject("IIS://" & ServerName & "/logging")
For Each Item In Log
   Debug.Print Item.Name
Next ◆
```

Advanced Log Format Properties

Each log provider exposes properties that allow you to manipulate extended information specific to the provider. In the case of ASCII text file-based logging, this may include the collection period and log path. In the case of the ODBC logging provider, you can specify the Data Source Name (DSN), table name, and user credentials.

Each provider maintains a unique configuration. In this section, you will examine each provider and explore the programmatic mechanism to manipulate the extended properties.

Log Period and Path Property Configuration for ASCII-Based Log Providers
Both the Microsoft IIS Log File Format and NCSA Common Log File Format providers create an ASCII text file containing a variety of information, which is not user-configurable. The only configurable parameters for these providers are the collection period and directory to be used to store the logs (see Figure 8.3).

The W3C Extended Log File Format log provider extends the logging configuration options beyond simple file path and collection period properties to include the ability to specify the events you wish to view in the log.

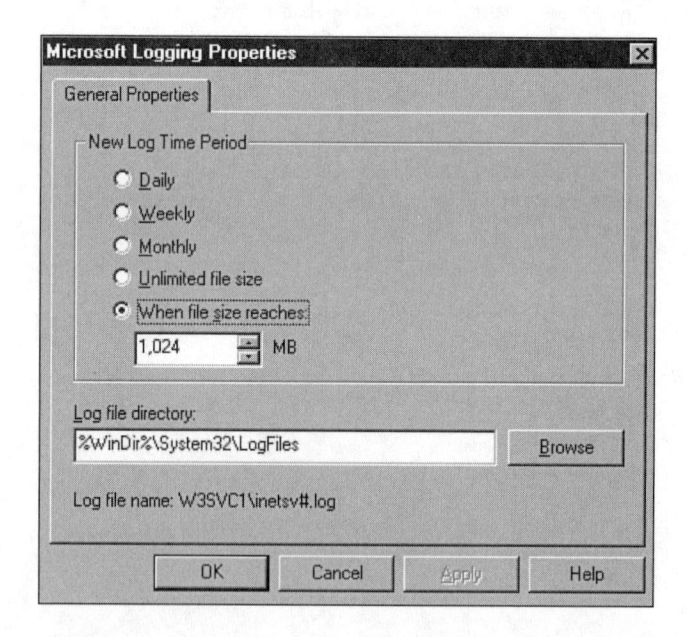

Figure 8.3 *Microsoft Logging Properties dialog box. (Similar to NCSA Common Log File Format and W3C Extended Log File Format General Properties tab.)*

To query or set the log collection period, you can manipulate the `LogFilePeriod` property of the bound service provider object.

Querying New Log Time Period Using Visual Basic
IIS uses four integers to represent the collection period for log files:

Integer	Time Period
0	Unlimited
1	Daily
2	Weekly
3	Monthly

To query this property, simply examine the current value of the `LogFilePeriod` property, as shown in the following Visual Basic code:

```
Dim Site As IADs
Dim ServerName As String
Dim SiteIndex As Long
ServerName = "IIS_Server_Name"
SiteIndex = Site_Index_Value
Set Site = GetObject("IIS://" & ServerName & "/W3SVC/" & SiteIndex)
Debug.Print Site.LogFilePeriod
```

Setting New Log Time Period Using Visual Basic
To set a new log file collection period, use the following Visual Basic code:

```
Dim Site As IADs
Dim ServerName As String
Dim SiteIndex As Long
Dim NewLogFilePeriod As Integer
ServerName = "IIS_Server_Name"
SiteIndex = Site_Index_Value
NewLogFilePeriod = 1
Set Site = GetObject("IIS://" & ServerName & "/W3SVC/" & SiteIndex)
Site.LogFilePeriod = NewLogFilePeriod
Site.SetInfo
```

Closing Logs Based on File Size
In addition to closing chronology-based logs, you can also close log files based on the size of the file. To do this, simply assign the `LogFileTruncateSize` property to the maximum size of the file you wish to create.

After the log has reached the specified size, the server opens a new log file. This can be especially handy for archiving logs to removable media where a specific size may be needed to get the log to fit on the disk.

Querying Maximum Log File Size Using Visual Basic

Consider the following Visual Basic code to query the log file truncation point:

```
Dim Site As IADs
Dim ServerName As String
Dim SiteIndex As Long
ServerName = "IIS_Server_Name"
SiteIndex = Site_Index_Value
Set Site = GetObject("IIS://" & ServerName & "/W3SVC/" & SiteIndex)
Debug.Print Site.LogFileTruncateSize
```

Setting Maximum Log File Size Using Visual Basic

To set a new maximum size for a log file, use the following Visual Basic code:

```
Dim Site As IADs
Dim ServerName As String
Dim SiteIndex As Long
Dim NewLogFileSize As Long
ServerName = "IIS_Server_Name"
SiteIndex = Site_Index_Value
NewLogFileSize = 1048576
Set Site = GetObject("IIS://" & ServerName & "/W3SVC/" & SiteIndex)
Site.LogFileTruncateSize = NewLogFileSize
Site.SetInfo
```

> **Note**
>
> To *truncate the log at the specified size, you must also set the* `LogFilePeriod` *property to 0.* ◆

W3C Extended Log File Provider Properties

Of all the log file providers, the W3C Extended Log File Format provides the most detailed and configurable set of options for which data you include in your log files (see Figure 8.4). In addition to the basic file path and collection period information, you can also choose from as many as 20 different parameters to make your logs as detailed or basic as you wish.

IIS Site Logging 219

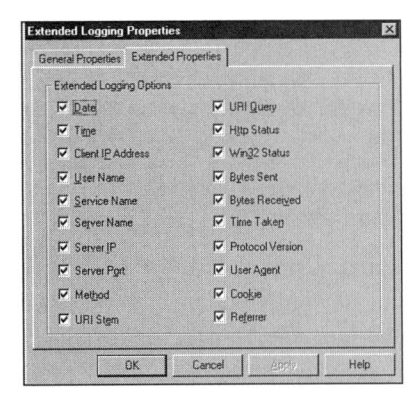

Figure 8.4 *W3C Extended Logging Properties dialog box.*

> **Note**
>
> *Each extended logging option uses a Boolean value to describe its state.*
>
> *Additionally, it is important to note that some options are not utilized by all IIS providers.* ◆

Querying Extended Logging Options Using Visual Basic
Use the following code to generate a table of these parameters in the Immediate window of the Visual Basic IDE:

```
Dim Site As IADs
Dim ServerName As String
Dim SiteIndex As Long
ServerName = "IIS_Server_Name"
SiteIndex = Site_Index_Value
Set Site = GetObject("IIS://" & ServerName & "/W3SVC/" & SiteIndex)
Debug.Print "Log Date: " & vbTab & vbTab & vbTab & Site.LogExtFileDate
Debug.Print "Log Time: " & vbTab & vbTab & vbTab & Site.LogExtFileTime
Debug.Print "Log Client IP Address: " & vbTab & Site.LogExtFileClientIp
Debug.Print "Log User Name: " & vbTab & vbTab & Site.LogExtFileUserName
Debug.Print "Log Service Name: " & vbTab & vbTab & Site.LogExtFileSiteName
Debug.Print "Log Server Name: " & vbTab & vbTab & Site.LogExtFileComputerName
Debug.Print "Log Server IP: " & vbTab & vbTab & Site.LogExtFileServerIp
Debug.Print "Log Server Port: " & vbTab & vbTab & Site.LogExtFileServerPort
Debug.Print "Log Method: " & vbTab & vbTab & vbTab & Site.LogExtFileMethod
Debug.Print "Log URI Stem: " & vbTab & vbTab & vbTab & Site.LogExtFileUriStem
Debug.Print "Log URI Query: " & vbTab & vbTab & vbTab & Site.LogExtFileUriQuery
Debug.Print "Log Http Status: " & vbTab & vbTab & Site.LogExtFileHttpStatus
Debug.Print "Log Win32 Status: " & vbTab & vbTab & Site.LogExtFileWin32Status
Debug.Print "Log Bytes Sent: " & vbTab & vbTab & Site.LogExtFileBytesSent
Debug.Print "Log Bytes Received: " & vbTab & Site.LogExtFileBytesRecv
```

continues ▶

▶ *continued*

```
Debug.Print "Log Time Taken: " & vbTab & vbTab & Site.LogExtFileTimeTaken
Debug.Print "Log Protocol Version: " & vbTab & Site.LogExtFileProtocolVersion
Debug.Print "Log User Agent: " & vbTab & vbTab & Site.LogExtFileUserAgent
Debug.Print "Log Cookie: " & vbTab & vbTab & vbTab & Site.LogExtFileCookie
Debug.Print "Log Referrer: " & vbTab & vbTab & vbTab & Site.LogExtFileReferer
```

Setting Extended Logging Options Using Visual Basic

Use the following code as a guide to specify the extended logging options for the W3C Extended Log File Format log provider:

```
Dim Site As IADs
Dim ServerName As String
Dim SiteIndex As Long
ServerName = "IIS_Server_Name"
SiteIndex = Site_Index_Value
Set Site = GetObject("IIS://" & ServerName & "/W3SVC/" & SiteIndex)
Site.LogExtFileDate = True
Site.LogExtFileTime = True
Site.LogExtFileClientIp = True
Site.LogExtFileUserName = True
Site.LogExtFileSiteName = True
Site.LogExtFileComputerName = True
Site.LogExtFileServerIp = True
Site.LogExtFileServerPort = True
Site.LogExtFileMethod = True
Site.LogExtFileUriStem = True
Site.LogExtFileUriQuery = True
Site.LogExtFileHttpStatus = True
Site.LogExtFileWin32Status = True
Site.LogExtFileBytesSent = True
Site.LogExtFileBytesRecv = True
Site.LogExtFileTimeTaken = True
Site.LogExtFileProtocolVersion = True
Site.LogExtFileUserAgent = True
Site.LogExtFileCookie = True
Site.LogExtFileReferer = True
Site.SetInfo
```

ODBC Log Provider Properties

If you want to view the log file using an ASP, you can set up an ODBC database to handle all logging requests (see Figure 8.5).

Although the ODBC log file provider makes viewing access logs from the Web extremely easy (using ADO in an ASP directly to the logging table), it comes at the cost of performance. ODBC logging has the worst performance of all logging providers available in the default installation of IIS. It should not be used unless you plan to implement a Web-based tool for monitoring site access logs or have a specific reason to use it.

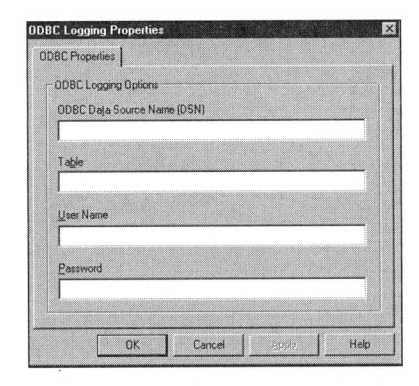

Figure 8.5 *ODBC Logging Properties dialog box.*

To enable ODBC logging, you must first use an ODBC-compliant database platform (such as Access, SQL Server, Oracle, or Sybase) to create a table with the fields as shown in Table 8.2.

Table 8.2 *Field Definitions for ODBC Log Format Tables*

Field Name	DataType
ClientHost	varchar(255)
Username	varchar(255)
LogTime	Datetime
Service	varchar(255)
Machine	varchar(255)
ServerIP	varchar(50)
ProcessingTime	Int
BytesReceived	Int
BytesSent	Int
ServiceStatus	Int
Win32Status	Int
Operation	varchar(255)
Target	varchar(255)
Parameters	varchar(255)

Next, you must set up a system DSN on the IIS Server to point to the database. If the database requires user credentials, these credentials can be specified in the IIS ODBC log properties. With the logging environment established, you can now configure IIS to begin using the ODBC database for logging.

> **Note**
>
> To configure ODBC logging, only four properties must be assigned:
> - The DSN to use (LogOdbcDataSource)
> - The name of the table (LogOdbcTableName)
> - The username required to access the table (LogOdbcUsername)
> - The associated password for the username (LogOdbcPassword) ♦

Querying ODBC Logging Information Using Visual Basic

To query the ODBC logging configuration parameters, use the following Visual Basic code:

```
Dim Site As IADs
Dim ServerName As String
Dim SiteIndex As Long
ServerName = "IIS_Server_Name"
SiteIndex = Site_Index_Value
Set Site = GetObject("IIS://" & ServerName & "/W3SVC/" & SiteIndex)
Debug.Print Site.LogOdbcDataSource
Debug.Print Site.LogOdbcPassword
Debug.Print Site.LogOdbcTableName
Debug.Print Site.LogOdbcUserName
```

Setting ODBC Logging Information Using Visual Basic

To modify an existing site's ODBC logging configuration, use the following Visual Basic code:

```
Dim Site As IADs
Dim ServerName As String
Dim SiteIndex As Long
Dim ODBC_DSN As String
Dim DBPassword As String
Dim TableName As String
Dim UserName As String
ODBC_DSN = "Name_of_Data_Source_to_Use_With_ODBC_Logging"
DBPassword = "DB_Access_Credential"
TableName = "Logging_Table_in_DB"
UserName = "DB_Access_Credential"
ServerName = "IIS_Server_Name"
SiteIndex = Site_Index_Value
Set Site = GetObject("IIS://" & ServerName & "/W3SVC/" & SiteIndex)
Site.LogOdbcDataSource = ODBC_DSN
Site.LogOdbcPassword = DBPassword
Site.LogOdbcTableName = TableName
Site.LogOdbcUserName = UserName
Site.SetInfo
```

Programmatic Site Management

One of the most valuable features in ADSI's IIS support is the ability to programmatically create, delete, and manage WWW, FTP, Simple Mail Transport Protocol (SMTP), and Network News Transfer Protocol (NNTP) sites.

Whereas most enterprises create a home directory for every account in the enterprise, tomorrow's users may also each have a virtual directory to share their information via the user-friendly Web interface that has become familiar to everyone. Without a programmatic method for performing such tasks, this could be an unbearable administrative burden on those charged with managing such environments.

The following sections explore the enumeration, creation, and manipulation of IIS sites for the WWW and FTP services.

Enumerating WWW Virtual Sites on an IIS Server Using Visual Basic

Before you can begin manipulating a site, you must first learn what sites are defined for a particular server. To do this, use the enumeration function shown earlier in the chapter (in the section "Examining the Structure of the IIS Metabase Using Visual Basic") with a slight modification to the binding string, as shown in the following Visual Basic code:

```
Dim Parent As IADs
Dim Child As IADs
Dim ServerName As String
Dim RetVal as String
ServerName = "IIS_Server_Name"
Set Parent = GetObject("IIS://" & ServerName & "/W3SVC")
For Each Child In Parent
    If IsNumeric(Child.Name) then
        RetVal = Child.Name
        Debug.Print RetVal
    End If
Next
```

After running this code segment, you quickly notice that the names of the sites on the machine do not appear using their friendly names as they do in the Internet Service Manager. Instead, you see Filters, Info, and then a series of integers. The integers represent the programmatic IDs for the sites on the server. Whereas machines may be able to easily cope with integers, human beings tend to prefer more friendly identifiers, forcing us to account for this in our code.

To show the results of the enumeration to the user, use the IIsWebServer ServerComments property to display the friendly name associated with the site as follows:

```
Dim Parent As IADs
Dim Child As IADs
Dim ServerName As String
ServerName = "IIS_Server_Name"
Set Parent = GetObject("IIS://" & ServerName & "/W3SVC")
For Each Child In Parent
    If IsNumeric(Child.Name) then
        Debug.Print "ProgrammaticID: " & Child.Name & vbTab & "Friendly Name: "
        ↪& Child.ServerComment
    End If
Next
```

> **Note**
>
> *The friendly name cannot be used to identify the object programmatically—it is merely a property, as the user profile path is for a user object. In fact, you can create two sites with exactly the same friendly name.* ◆

Enumerating FTP Virtual Sites on an IIS Server Using Visual Basic

Use the following Visual Basic code to display the integer value and the value of each associated ServerComment property value for each site defined in the Metabase:

```
Dim Parent As IADs
Dim Child As IADs
Dim ServerName As String
ServerName = "IIS_Server_Name"
Set Parent = GetObject("IIS://" & ServerName & "/MSFTPSVC")
For Each Child In Parent
    If IsNumeric(Child.Name) Then
        Debug.Print Child.Name & vbTab & " - " & vbTab & Child.ServerComment
    End If
Next
```

> **Tip**
>
> *Notice that the code for the Web and FTP services is nearly identical, with the exception being the name of the container specified by the binding string. Simply changing the container will perform similar functionality for each of the IIS services (W3SVC, MSFTPSVC, NNTPSVC, and SmtpSvc).*
>
> *If you want to apply the code in this section to the SMTP or NNTP services, begin by changing the binding string to reflect the proper IIS service.* ◆

Finding the Index Number for a Site Based on the *ServerComment* Property Using Visual Basic

Sites are generally known by name and not by index number, leaving the user in a difficult situation when trying to manipulate a site. To alleviate this issue, use the following Visual Basic code to return the index value for a site given an existing `ServerComment`:

```
Dim Sites As IADs
Dim Site As IADs
Dim SearchTerm As String
Dim Counter As Integer
Dim IndexValue As Long
Dim ServerName as String
SearchTerm = "Site_Description_String"
ServerName = "IIS_Server_Name"
Counter = 0
Set Sites = GetObject("IIS:\\" & ServerName & "\w3svc")
For Each Site In Sites
    If IsNumeric(Site.Name) Then
        If LCase(Site.ServerComment) = LCase(SearchTerm) Then
            Counter = Counter + 1
            IndexValue = Site.Name
        End If
    End If
Next
Select Case Counter
    Case 0
        Debug.Print "The referenced site could not be found.  Please enter a
        ↪new search term."
    Case 1
        Debug.Print "The index value for site '" & SearchTerm & "' is " &
        ↪IndexValue
    Case Is > 1
        Debug.Print "More than one site uses the value '" & SearchTerm & "' for
        ↪the &" _
        ; "ServerComments property.  Assure all values are unique before
        ↪continuing."
End Select
```

Creating a New Web Site Using Visual Basic

Another advantage to programmatic IIS administration is the ability to have developers create a site installation script that quickly and easily creates the site, sets all required security and configuration settings, and even starts the new site. This can be especially useful when implementing a new site across multiple nodes in a front-end Web server cluster, or when developers want to ease the burden placed on the administrative staff when bringing up new sites.

It all starts with the creation of a new site. In the previous section, you learned that sites are not defined by friendly names (as they are in the Internet Service Manager), but rather by an index number.

Consider the following Visual Basic code, which allows you to create a new site (virtual Web server) in IIS:

```
On Error Resume Next
Dim Parent As IADsContainer
Dim Child As IADs
Dim NewSite As IADs
Dim NewRoot As IADs
Dim ServerName As String
Dim Index As Long
Dim SiteName As String
Dim SitePath As String
SiteName = "Friendly_Site_Name"
ServerName = "IIS_Server_Name"
SitePath = "Site_Path"
Set Parent = GetObject("IIS://" & ServerName & "/W3SVC")
For Each Child In Parent
    If IsNumeric(Child.Name) Then
        If Index < Child.Name Then
            Index = Child.Name
        End If
    End If
Next
Index = Index + 1
Set NewSite = Parent.Create("IIsWebServer", Index)
NewSite.ServerComment = SiteName
NewSite.SetInfo
Set NewRoot = NewSite.Create("IIsWebVirtualDir", "Root")
NewRoot.Path = SitePath
NewRoot.SetInfo
```

Using the preceding code example, you can create a site and root virtual directory pointing to a specific directory.

> **Tip**
>
> Although this works well for basic configurations, you typically want to install more than one site per IP address. This is best accomplished using host headers or an alternate TCP port. To add a new host header or alternate TCP port, you must manipulate the `ServerBindings` property of the bound site.
>
> Property manipulation is covered in detail for each of the IIS Web and FTP services in Chapter 9 "Programmatic Management of Web Site Properties," and Chapter 10 "Programmatic Management of FTP Site Properties," respectively. ♦

Creating a New FTP Site Using Visual Basic

In the following Visual Basic code example, you can specify an alternate IP address and TCP port by removing the comment designator (apostrophe) and assigning a valid and unique IP address and TCP port pairing for the site.

To allow the site to be bound to any unassigned IP address, simply set the IP address to an empty string.

```
Dim Parent As IADsContainer
Dim Child As IADs
Dim NewSite As IADs
Dim NewRoot As IADs
Dim ServerName As String
Dim Index As Long
Dim SiteName As String
Dim SitePath As String
Dim SiteIPAddress as String
Dim SiteTCPPort As Long
SiteName = "Friendly_Site_Name"
ServerName = "IIS_Server_Name"
SitePath = "Site_Path"
SiteIPAddress = ""
SiteTCPPort = "21"
'SiteIPAddress = "xxx.xxx.xxx.xxx"
'SiteTCPPort = "TCP_Port_for_Server"
Set Parent = GetObject("IIS://" & ServerName & "/MSFTPSVC")
For Each Child In Parent
        If IsNumeric(Child.Name) Then
                If Index < Child.Name Then
                        Index = Child.Name
                End If
        End If
Next
Index = Index + 1
Set NewSite = Parent.Create("IIsFTPServer", Index)
NewSite.ServerComment = SiteName
NewSite.ServerBindings = Array(SiteIPAddress & ":" & SiteTCPPort & ":")
NewSite.SetInfo
Set NewRoot = NewSite.Create("IIsFTPVirtualDir", "Root")
NewRoot.Path = SitePath
NewRoot.SetInfo
```

Deleting a Site By Referencing the *ServerComment* Property Using Visual Basic

When deleting a site, you do not want to make a mistake as to which one you *really* meant to delete. In a non-clustered production environment, deleting the wrong site could be a real career-limiting move.

One of the most frustrating parts of programmatic IIS administration is dealing with the index number rather than the friendly name of the site. Although you can create multiple sites with identical names in the Internet Service Manager, this truly defies logic and good administrative practice.

Even if you decide to take such an approach, remember that besides looking at content, there is no way to determine one site from another.

Assuming you have unique `ServerComment` properties for each site on the server, you can combine the site enumeration function (described earlier in the section "Viewing the List of Current Server-Defined MIME Type Mappings Using Visual Basic") with a conditional that tests the `ServerComment` property for a known string. This allows you to use the `ServerComment` field as an identifier for managing the site.

You can use the following Visual Basic code to pass in this friendly name, find out the corresponding index number of the site, and delete the site from the Metabase:

```
Dim Sites As IADs
Dim Site As IADs
Dim SearchTerm As String
Dim Counter As Integer
Dim IndexValue As Long
Dim ServerName as String
SearchTerm = "Site_Description_String"
ServerName = "IIS_Server_Name"
Counter = 0
Set Sites = GetObject("IIS:\\" & ServerName & "\w3svc")
For Each Site In Sites
    If IsNumeric(Site.Name) Then
        If LCase(Site.ServerComment) = LCase(SearchTerm) Then
            Counter = Counter + 1
            IndexValue = Site.Name
        End If
    End If
Next
Select Case Counter
    Case 0
        Debug.Print "The referenced site could not be found.  Please enter a
        ↦new search term."
    Case 1
        Call Sites.Delete("IIsWebServer", IndexValue)
        Set Sites = Nothing
        Debug.Print "Site '" & SearchTerm & "' was deleted successfully."
    Case Is > 1
        Debug.Print "More than one site uses the value '" & SearchTerm & "' for
        ↦the " _
; "ServerComments property.  Assure all values are unique before continuing."
End Select
```

This code verifies the uniqueness of the `ServerComment` property value before performing the deletion. This eliminates any ambiguity and keeps you from having to update your resume if you happen to miss correcting a non-unique `ServerComment` property assignment in a production environment.

> **Warning**
>
> *If you choose to use the* `ServerComment` *field as an identifier for sites, be sure to verify that all sites on the server maintain unique values for the* `ServerComment` *field.* ✦

Deleting an FTP Site Using Visual Basic

By simply changing the binding string, you can programmatically delete an FTP site. Use the following Visual Basic code to perform this task:

```
Dim Sites As IADs
Dim Site As IADs
Dim SearchTerm As String
Dim Counter As Integer
Dim IndexValue As Long
Dim ServerName As String
SearchTerm = "Site_Description_String"
ServerName = "IIS_Server_Name"
Counter = 0
Set Sites = GetObject("IIS:\\" & ServerName & "\MSFTPSVC")
For Each Site In Sites
    If IsNumeric(Site.Name) Then
        If LCase(Site.ServerComment) = LCase(SearchTerm) Then
            Counter = Counter + 1
            IndexValue = Site.Name
        End If
    End If
Next
Select Case Counter
    Case 0
        Debug.Print "The referenced site could not be found.  Please enter a
        ↳new search term."
    Case 1
        Call Sites.Delete("IIsFTPServer", IndexValue)
        Set Sites = Nothing
        Debug.Print "Site '" & SearchTerm & "' was deleted successfully."
    Case Is > 1
        Debug.Print "More than one site uses the value '" & SearchTerm & "' for
        ↳the " & ServerComments & _
" property.  Assure all values are unique before continuing."
End Select
```

Creating a New Virtual Directory Using Visual Basic

When creating a new site, you must create a root virtual directory to assign to the site's `Path` property. If this step is ignored, the site will be unmanageable in the MMC or through programmatic methods until the `Path` property is set to a valid path.

In addition to the root virtual directory, a site can also contain virtual directories that can be accessed by the client at http://sitename/virtual_directory. These directories can exist anywhere in the file system and need not be a child path of the root virtual directory path. Unlike virtual sites, virtual directories use a friendly name for their programmatic identifier in the binding string.

Use the following Visual Basic code to create a new virtual directory under the default Web site:

```
Dim Parent as IADs
Dim NewVDir As IADs
Dim ServerName As String
Dim VDirPath As String
Dim VDirName As String
Dim Index As Long
ServerName = "IIS_Server_Name"
VDirPath = "Path_for_New_Virtual_Directory"
VDirName = "Name_For_Virtual_Directory"
Index = Site_Index_Integer
Set Parent = GetObject("IIS://" & ServerName & "/W3SVC/" & Index & "/ROOT")
Set NewVDir = Parent.Create("IIsWebVirtualDir", VDirName)
NewVDir.SetInfo
NewVDir.Path = VDirPath
NewVDir.SetInfo
```

Creating a New FTP Virtual Directory Using Visual Basic

Using the following Visual Basic code, you can quickly and easily implement a new virtual directory to organize your FTP site in a more logical fashion:

```
Dim Parent As IADs
Dim NewVDir As IADs
Dim ServerName As String
Dim VDirPath As String
Dim VDirName As String
Dim Index As Long
ServerName = "IIS_Server_Name"
VDirPath = "Path_for_New_Virtual_Directory"
VDirName = "Name_For_Virtual_Directory"
Index = Site_Index_Integer
Set Parent = GetObject("IIS://" & ServerName & "/MSFTPSVC/" & Index & "/ROOT")
Set NewVDir = Parent.Create("IIsFTPVirtualDir", VDirName)
NewVDir.SetInfo
NewVDir.Path = VDirPath
NewVDir.SetInfo
```

Removing an Existing Virtual Directory Using Visual Basic

There may be occasions when you require a technique to perform the deletion of an existing virtual directory. To accomplish this task, simply use the IADsContainer Delete method to remove the entry in the Metabase for the virtual directory.

Consider the following Visual Basic code to remove an existing virtual directory:

```
Dim Parent As IADsContainer
Dim ServerName As String
Dim VDirName As String
Dim Index As Long
ServerName = "IIS_Server_Name"
VDirName = "Name_For_Virtual_Directory"
Index = Site_Index_Value
Set Parent = GetObject("IIS://" & ServerName & "/W3SVC/" & Index & "/ROOT")
Call Parent.Delete("IIsWebVirtualDir", VDirName)
Set Parent = Nothing
```

Removing an Existing FTP Virtual Directory Using Visual Basic

With a simple change to the binding string, existing virtual directories on FTP sites can be removed.

Use the following Visual Basic code as a guide for removing an existing virtual directory from an FTP site:

```
Dim Parent As IADsContainer
Dim ServerName As String
Dim VDirName As String
Dim Index As Long
ServerName = "IIS_Server_Name"
VDirName = "Name_For_Virtual_Directory"
Index = Site_Index_Value
Set Parent = GetObject("IIS://" & ServerName & "/MSFTPSVC/" & Index & "/ROOT")
Call Parent.Delete("IIsFTPVirtualDir", VDirName)
```

Managing Web Directories and Files Using Visual Basic

Unlike a virtual directory entry, folders and files in the file system will not automatically synchronize with the Metabase. To bind to a directory that exists in the file system underneath a Web site's virtual directory, you must first create an entry in the Metabase. Although this may seem like a terrific amount of effort, keep in mind that the IIS Metabase hierarchy supports inheritance. This allows you to define a set of properties at a higher level (such as a virtual directory or file system directory) and have the property trickle down to all child nodes in the tree. Consequently, you must define an entry in the Metabase only for each departure from the inherited property values.

Most directory service designers try to derive designs that minimize the need to block inheritance as much as possible. Armed with this knowledge, you should try to persuade the Web developers in your organization to design the physical directory structure using a flat structure where possible to reduce the need to change inherited properties for each directory on the site.

By creating an entry in the Metabase for each directory or file requiring a unique permission or property assignment, you can bind and manage the properties for the resource.

Although the Internet Service Manager shows Web file and folder entries and allows manipulation of the properties for all of these entities, an entry is not made into the Metabase unless there is a change in the inherited configuration for the entity.

To see what is actually being stored in the Metabase, use the following Visual Basic code to enumerate the entities under a virtual directory:

```
Dim VirtualDirectory As IADs
Dim ServerName As String
Dim Index As Long
ServerName = "IIS_Server_Name"
Index = Site_Index_Value
Set VirtualDirectory = GetObject("IIS://" & ServerName & "/W3SVC/" & Index & "/ROOT")
For Each Item In VirtualDirectory
    Debug.Print Item.Name
Next
```

> **Note**
>
> This code will display all the entries in the default Web site's root virtual directory. If you compare the results found in the ISM and those in the immediate window, you quickly see the disparity. If you were to attempt to bind to default.asp and it did not have an entry in the Metabase, the operation would fail. To account for this, you must place entries in the Metabase for file system objects that should maintain different properties from those inherited from the parent object. ◆

Adding an Entry in the Metabase for a File System Directory Using Visual Basic

By enumerating the contents of the parent container, you now see that there is an entry for the file system directory specified.

Use the following Visual Basic code to define a change in the inherited properties for a Web directory:

```
Dim VirtualDirectory As IADs
Dim WebDir As IADs
Dim ServerName As String
Dim FileName As String
Dim Index As Long
Dim VirtualDirectoryName As String
ServerName = "IIS_Server_Name"
DirName = "Directory_Name_To_Enter"
Index = Site_Index
Set VirtualDirectory = GetObject("IIS://" & ServerName & "/W3SVC/" & Index & "/ROOT")
Set WebDir = VirtualDirectory.Create("IIsWebDirectory", DirName)
WebDir.SetInfo
```

Adding an Entry in the Metabase for a File in the File System Using Visual Basic

In addition to specifying unique properties for an entire virtual directory or Web directory, there may also be times when you desire the ability to set a unique property at the file level.

Use the following Visual Basic code to add a new entry in the Metabase for an individual Web file in the file system:

```
Dim VirtualDirectory As IADs
Dim WebFile As IADs
Dim ServerName As String
Dim FileName As String
Dim Index As Long
Dim VirtualDirectoryName As String
ServerName = "IIS_Server_Name"
FileName = "File_Name_To_Enter"
Index = Site_Index
Set VirtualDirectory = GetObject("IIS://" & ServerName & "/W3SVC/" & Index & "/ROOT")
Set WebFile = VirtualDirectory.Create("IIsWebFile", FileName)
WebFile.SetInfo
```

Note

If you were to enumerate the virtual directory contents after adding entries for individual directories or files, you would see that an entry was made for the file you just referenced. This enables you to bind and manipulate the file just as any other object in the namespace. ◆

Programmatic Site Operations

Using ADSI, you can query the status of a site to verify that it is indeed running. This can be especially handy in cases where you wish to write a service or application to monitor a site, or when you need to cycle the site for Metabase changes to take affect.

Querying Site Status Using Visual Basic

To query a site, simply query the ServerState property for the bound object. The property will return an integer representing the current status of the site, as follows:

Return Code	Status
1	Starting
2	Started

continues ▶

▶ *continued*

Return Code	Status
3	Stopping
4	Stopped
5	Pausing
6	Paused
7	Continuing

Use the preceding chart and the following Visual Basic code to query the state of an existing IIS site:

```
Dim Site As IADs
Dim ServerName As String
Dim Index As Long
ServerName = "IIS_Server_Name"
Index = Site_Index_Value
Set Site = GetObject("IIS://" & ServerName & "/W3SVC/" & Index)
Select Case Site.ServerState
    Case 1
        Debug.Print "Starting"
    Case 2
        Debug.Print "Started"
    Case 3
        Debug.Print "Stopping"
    Case 4
        Debug.Print "Stopped"
    Case 5
        Debug.Print "Pausing"
    Case 6
        Debug.Print "Paused"
    Case 7
        Debug.Print "Continuing"
End Select
```

Note

Those familiar with the Windows Load Balancing Service (WLBS) already know that one major weakness in the product is the inability to monitor running services under Windows NT Server 4.0.

When run on Windows NT Server 4.0, WLBS will re-converge the cluster upon heartbeat failure, but cannot detect if a service or site has gone offline.

Using the code in this section, a service can be written that allows you to monitor the entire W3SVC or critical sites and re-converge the cluster if the monitored site is in any state other than starting or started. ◆

Starting a Site Using Visual Basic

After creating a new IIS site and configuring all associated properties, you will likely wish to programmatically start the site. This is easily accomplished by calling the Start method of the appropriate site object.

Consider the following Visual Basic code sample to start the site:

```
Dim Site As IADs
Dim ServerName As String
Dim Index As Long
ServerName = "IIS_Server_Name"
Index = Site_Index_Value
Set Site = GetObject("IIS://" & ServerName & "/W3SVC/" & Index)
If Site.ServerState = 4 or Site.ServerState = 3 Then
    Site.Start
    Debug.Print "Request to start site " & Site.ServerComment & " was issued."
End If
```

Tip

To start an FTP, SMTP, or NNTP site, simply change the name of the IIS service in the binding string. ◆

Stopping a Site Using Visual Basic

To stop a site, call the Stop method of the bound site object.

Use the following Visual Basic code to bind a specific site and stop publication of the site:

```
Dim Site As IADs
Dim ServerName As String
Dim Index As Long
ServerName = "IIS_Server_Name"
Index = Site_Index_Value
Set Site = GetObject("IIS://" & ServerName & "/W3SVC/" & Index)
If Site.ServerState = 2 or Site.ServerState = 1 Then
    Site.Stop
    Debug.Print "Request to stop site " & Site.ServerComment & " was issued."
End If
```

Pausing a Site Using Visual Basic

The Pause method of the bound site object allows you to pause operations of the server temporarily. This forces all new connections to the server to be denied. Note that existing connections are not disturbed.

Use the following Visual Basic code to programmatically pause a bound Web server:

```
Dim Site As IADs
Dim ServerName As String
Dim Index As Long
ServerName = "IIS_Server_Name"
Index = Site_Index_Value
Set Site = GetObject("IIS://" & ServerName & "/W3SVC/" & Index)
If Site.ServerState = 1 or Site.ServerState = 2 Then
    Site.Pause
    Debug.Print "Request to pause site " & Site.ServerComment & " was issued."
End If
```

Continuing a Paused Site Using Visual Basic

To restore a paused server, simply call the Continue method of the bound site object to bring the site back online.

Use the following Visual Basic code to restore a paused site:

```
Dim Site As IADs
Dim ServerName As String
Dim Index As Long
ServerName = "IIS_Server_Name"
Index = Site_Index_Value
Set Site = GetObject("IIS://" & ServerName & "/W3SVC/" & Index)
If Site.ServerState = 6 or Site.ServerState = 5 Then
    Site.Continue
    Debug.Print "Request to continue paused site " & Site.ServerComment & " was
➥issued."
End If
```

Creating the IIsSiteManagement Class Module

In this section, you will begin the first of several exercises throughout Part III "Exploring the ADSI Service Providers: IIS," that will ultimately yield the creation of the IISAdmin.DLL COM server.

> *Tip*
>
> *You can download the Visual Basic 6.0 project or pre-compiled version of IISAdmin.DLL from* http://www.newriders.com/adsi. ◆

Exercise 8.1 *Creating IISAdmin.DLL: Site Management Functions*

1. Open a new ActiveX DLL Visual Basic project.
2. Set a reference to the Active DS Type Library by clicking the Project menu, References…, and placing a check mark next to the Active DS Type Library entry. Click the OK command button to exit the References–Project1 dialog box.
3. Rename the project Project1 as **IIsAdmin**.
4. Rename the Class1 class module as **IIsSiteManagement**.
5. Enter the following code into the General Declarations section of the class module:

```
Public Function BackupOperations(ByVal TargetComputer As String, ByVal Action As
➥String, Optional ByVal BackupName As String) As Variant
    On Error Resume Next
    Dim IIsComputer As IADs
    Set IIsComputer = GetObject("IIS://" & TargetComputer)
    Select Case UCase(Action)
        Case "BACKUP"
            Dim Flags As Long
            Flags = (MD_BACKUP_SAVE_FIRST Or MD_BACKUP_FORCE_BACKUP)
            IIsComputer.Backup BackupName, MD_BACKUP_NEXT_VERSION, Flags
            If Err.Number = 0 Then BackupOperations = True
        Case "ENUMERATE"
            Dim Version, Index, TermCond As Integer
            Dim Location As Variant
            Dim UTCDate As Variant
            Dim NewElement() As Variant
            Dim i As Long
            Do While TermCond <> 1
                IIsComputer.EnumBackups "", Index, Version, Location, UTCDate
                If Err.Number <> 0 Then
                    Exit Do
                End If
                i = UBound(NewElement) + 1
                ReDim Preserve NewElement(i)
                NewElement(i) = Location & vbTab & Version & vbTab & UTCDate
                Index = Index + 1
                Err.Number = 0
            Loop
            BackupOperations = NewElement
        Case "RESTORE"
            Call IIsComputer.Restore(BackupName, MD_BACKUP_HIGHEST_VERSION, 0)
            If Err.Number = 0 Then BackupOperations = True
        Case "DELETE"
            Call IIsComputer.DeleteBackup(BackupName, MD_BACKUP_HIGHEST_VERSION)
            If Err.Number = 0 Then BackupOperations = True
    End Select
End Function
Public Function MaxBandwidth(ByVal TargetComputer As String, ByVal Action As String,
```

continues ▶

Exercise 8.1 *continued*

```
➥Optional ByVal NewThrottleValue As Long) As Variant
    Dim IIsComputer As IADs
    Set IIsComputer = GetObject("IIS://" & TargetComputer)
    Select Case UCase(Action)
        Case "QUERY"
            MaxBandwidth = IIsComputer.MaxBandwidth
        Case "SET"
            IIsComputer.MaxBandwidth = NewThrottleValue
            IIsComputer.SetInfo
            If Err.Number = 0 Then MaxBandwidth = True
    End Select
End Function

Public Function MIMETypeManagement(ByVal TargetComputer As String, ByVal Action As
➥String, Optional ByVal MIMEExtension As String, Optional ByVal MIMEType As String) As
➥Variant
    On Error Resume Next
    Dim IIsComputer As IADs
    Set IIsComputer = GetObject("IIS://" & TargetComputer & "/MimeMap")
    Select Case UCase(Action)
        Case "ENUMERATE"
            Dim MimeMapping As Variant
            Dim NewElement() As Variant
            Dim i As Long
            For Each MimeMapping In IIsComputer.MimeMap
                i = UBound(NewElement) + 1
                ReDim Preserve NewElement(i)
                NewElement(i) = MimeMapping.Extension & vbTab &
                ➥MimeMapping.MIMEType
            Next
            MIMETypeManagement = NewElement
        Case "ADD"
            If MIMEType <> " And MIMEExtension <> " Then
                Dim NewMimeMapping As Variant
                NewMimeMapping = IIsComputer.GetEx("MimeMap")
                i = UBound(NewMimeMapping) + 1
                ReDim Preserve NewMimeMapping(i)
                Set NewMimeMapping(i) = CreateObject("MimeMap")
                NewMimeMapping(i).MIMEType = MIMEType
                NewMimeMapping(i).Extension = MIMEExtension
                IIsComputer.PutEx ADS_PROPERTY_UPDATE, "MimeMap", NewMimeMapping
                Err.Number = 0
                IIsComputer.SetInfo
                If Err.Number = 0 Then MIMETypeManagement = True
            Else
                MIMETypeManagement = False
            End If
        Case "REMOVE"
            If MIMEExtension <> " Then
```

Creating the IIsSiteManagement Class Module   239

```
                    Dim MapToDelete As String
                    Dim MimeItem As Variant
                    NewMimeMapping = IIsComputer.MimeMap
                    For Each MimeMapping In IIsComputer.MimeMap
                        If MimeMapping.Extension <> MIMEExtension Then
                            ReDim Preserve NewMimeMapping(i)
                            Set NewMimeMapping(i) = CreateObject("MimeMap")
                            NewMimeMapping(i).MIMEType = MimeMapping.MIMEType
                            NewMimeMapping(i).Extension = MimeMapping.Extension
                            i = i + 1
                        End If
                    Next
                    IIsComputer.PutEx ADS_PROPERTY_UPDATE, "MimeMap", NewMimeMapping
                    Err.Number = 0
                    IIsComputer.SetInfo
                    If Err.Number = 0 Then MIMETypeManagement = True
                Else
                    MIMETypeManagement = False
                End If
        End Select
End Function

Public Function SiteLogging(ByVal TargetComputer As String, ByVal IIsService As String,
➥ByVal SiteIndex As Integer, ByVal Action As String, ByVal LoggingProperty As String,
➥Optional ByVal NewValue) As Variant
    Dim Site As IADs
    Dim Item As Variant
    Select Case UCase(IIsService)
        Case "WWW"
            Set Site = GetObject("IIS://" & TargetComputer & "/W3SVC/" & SiteIndex)
        Case "FTP"
            Set Site = GetObject("IIS://" & TargetComputer & "/MSFTPSVC/" &
            ➥SiteIndex)
        Case "SMTP"
            Set Site = GetObject("IIS://" & TargetComputer & "/SMTPSVC/" &
            ➥SiteIndex)
        Case "NNTP"
            Set Site = GetObject("IIS://" & TargetComputer & "/NNTPSVC/" &
            ➥SiteIndex)
    End Select
    Select Case UCase(Action)
        Case "QUERY"
            Select Case UCase(LoggingProperty)
                Case "LOGGINGENABLED"
                    SiteLogging = Site.LogType
                Case "LOGTYPE"
                    Dim Log As IADs
                    Set Log = GetObject("IIS://" & TargetComputer & "/logging")
                    For Each Item In Log
                        If Site.LogPluginCLSID = Item.LogModuleID Then
                            SiteLogging = Item.Name
                        End If
                    Next
```

continues ▶

Exercise 8.1 *continued*

```
                    Case "LOGFILEPERIOD"
                        SiteLogging = Site.LogFilePeriod
                    Case "TRUNCATESIZE"
                        SiteLogging = Site.LogFileTruncateSize
                End Select
            Case "SET"
                Select Case UCase(LoggingProperty)
                    Case "LOGGINGENABLED"
                        Site.LogType = NewValue
                        Site.SetInfo
                    Case "LOGTYPE"
                        Set Log = GetObject("IIS://" & TargetComputer & "/logging")
                        Dim NewLogFormatName As String
                        Select Case UCase(NewValue)
                            Case "NCSA"
                                NewValue = "NCSA Common Log File Format"
                            Case "ODBC"
                                NewValue = "ODBC Logging"
                            Case "IIS"
                                NewValue = "Microsoft IIS Log File Format"
                            Case "W3C"
                                NewValue = "W3C Extended Log File Format"
                        End Select
                        For Each Item In Log
                            If Item.Name = NewValue Then
                                Site.LogPluginCLSID = Item.LogModuleID
                                Site.SetInfo
                            End If
                        Next
                    Case "LOGFILEPERIOD"
                        Site.LogFilePeriod = NewValue
                        Site.SetInfo
                    Case "TRUNCATESIZE"
                        Site.LogFilePeriod = 0
                        Site.LogFileTruncateSize = NewValue
                        Site.SetInfo
                End Select
                If Err.Number = 0 Then SiteLogging = True
        End Select
End Function

Public Function ExtendedLogProperty(ByVal TargetComputer As String, ByVal IIsService As
↪String, ByVal SiteIndex As Integer, ByVal Action As String, ByVal LoggingProperty As
↪String, Optional ByVal NewValue) As Variant
    Dim Site As IADs
    Select Case UCase(IIsService)
        Case "WWW"
            Set Site = GetObject("IIS://" & TargetComputer & "/W3SVC/" & SiteIndex)
        Case "FTP"
            Set Site = GetObject("IIS://" & TargetComputer & "/MSFTPSVC/" &
            ↪SiteIndex)
```

Creating the IlsSiteManagement Class Module   241

```
            Case "SMTP"
                Set Site = GetObject("IIS://" & TargetComputer & "/SMTPSVC/" &
                ⇒SiteIndex)
            Case "NNTP"
                Set Site = GetObject("IIS://" & TargetComputer & "/NNTPSVC/" &
                ⇒SiteIndex)
        End Select
        Select Case UCase(Action)
            Case "QUERY"
                Select Case UCase(LoggingProperty)
                    Case "DATE"
                        ExtendedLogProperty = Site.LogExtFileDate
                    Case "TIME"
                        ExtendedLogProperty = Site.LogExtFileTime
                    Case "CLIENTIP"
                        ExtendedLogProperty = Site.LogExtFileClientIp
                    Case "USERNAME"
                        ExtendedLogProperty = Site.LogExtFileUserName
                    Case "SERVICENAME"
                        ExtendedLogProperty = Site.LogExtFileSiteName
                    Case "SERVERNAME"
                        ExtendedLogProperty = Site.LogExtFileComputerName
                    Case "SERVERIP"
                        ExtendedLogProperty = Site.LogExtFileServerIp
                    Case "SERVERPORT"
                        ExtendedLogProperty = Site.LogExtFileServerPort
                    Case "METHOD"
                        ExtendedLogProperty = Site.LogExtFileMethod
                    Case "URISTEM"
                        ExtendedLogProperty = Site.LogExtFileUriStem
                    Case "URIQUERY"
                        ExtendedLogProperty = Site.LogExtFileUriQuery
                    Case "HTTPSTATUS"
                        ExtendedLogProperty = Site.LogExtFileHttpStatus
                    Case "WIN32STATUS"
                        ExtendedLogProperty = Site.LogExtFileWin32Status
                    Case "BYTESSENT"
                        ExtendedLogProperty = Site.LogExtFileBytesSent
                    Case "BYTESRECEIVED"
                        ExtendedLogProperty = Site.LogExtFileBytesRecv
                    Case "TIMETAKEN"
                        ExtendedLogProperty = Site.LogExtFileTimeTaken
                    Case "PROTOCOLVERSION"
                        ExtendedLogProperty = Site.LogExtFileProtocolVersion
                    Case "USERAGENT"
                        ExtendedLogProperty = Site.LogExtFileUserAgent
                    Case "COOKIE"
                        ExtendedLogProperty = Site.LogExtFileCookie
                    Case "REFERRER"
                        ExtendedLogProperty = Site.LogExtFileReferer
                End Select
```

continues ▶

Exercise 8.1 *continued*

```
Case "SET"
    Select Case UCase(LoggingProperty)
        Case "DATE"
            Site.LogExtFileDate = NewValue
            Site.SetInfo
        Case "TIME"
            Site.LogExtFileTime = NewValue
            Site.SetInfo
        Case "CLIENTIP"
            Site.LogExtFileClientIp = NewValue
            Site.SetInfo
        Case "USERNAME"
            Site.LogExtFileUserName = NewValue
            Site.SetInfo
        Case "SERVICENAME"
            Site.LogExtFileSiteName = NewValue
            Site.SetInfo
        Case "SERVERNAME"
            Site.LogExtFileComputerName = NewValue
            Site.SetInfo
        Case "SERVERIP"
            Site.LogExtFileServerIp = NewValue
            Site.SetInfo
        Case "SERVERPORT"
            Site.LogExtFileServerPort = NewValue
            Site.SetInfo
        Case "METHOD"
            Site.LogExtFileMethod = NewValue
            Site.SetInfo
        Case "URISTEM"
            Site.LogExtFileUriStem = NewValue
            Site.SetInfo
        Case "URIQUERY"
            Site.LogExtFileUriQuery = NewValue
            Site.SetInfo
        Case "HTTPSTATUS"
            Site.LogExtFileHttpStatus = NewValue
            Site.SetInfo
        Case "WIN32STATUS"
            Site.LogExtFileWin32Status = NewValue
            Site.SetInfo
        Case "BYTESSENT"
            Site.LogExtFileBytesSent = NewValue
            Site.SetInfo
        Case "BYTESRECEIVED"
            Site.LogExtFileBytesRecv = NewValue
            Site.SetInfo
        Case "TIMETAKEN"
            Site.LogExtFileTimeTaken = NewValue
            Site.SetInfo
```

Creating the IIsSiteManagement Class Module 243

```
                    Case "PROTOCOLVERSION"
                            Site.LogExtFileProtocolVersion = NewValue
                            Site.SetInfo
                    Case "USERAGENT"
                            Site.LogExtFileUserAgent = NewValue
                            Site.SetInfo
                    Case "COOKIE"
                            Site.LogExtFileCookie = NewValue
                            Site.SetInfo
                    Case "REFERRER"
                            Site.LogExtFileReferer = NewValue
                            Site.SetInfo
                End Select
                If Err.Number = 0 Then ExtendedLogProperty = True
        End Select
End Function

Public Function ODBCLogging(ByVal TargetComputer As String, ByVal IIsService As String,
➥ByVal SiteIndex As Integer, ByVal Action As String, ByVal LoggingProperty As String,
➥Optional ByVal NewValue) As Variant
        Dim Site As IADs
        Select Case UCase(IIsService)
                Case "WWW"
                        Set Site = GetObject("IIS://" & TargetComputer & "/W3SVC/" & SiteIndex)
                Case "FTP"
                        Set Site = GetObject("IIS://" & TargetComputer & "/MSFTPSVC/" &
                            ➥SiteIndex)
                Case "SMTP"
                        Set Site = GetObject("IIS://" & TargetComputer & "/SMTPSVC/" &
                            ➥SiteIndex)
                Case "NNTP"
                        Set Site = GetObject("IIS://" & TargetComputer & "/NNTPSVC/" &
                            ➥SiteIndex)
        End Select
        Select Case UCase(Action)
                Case "QUERY"
                        Select Case UCase(LoggingProperty)
                                Case "DSN"
                                        ODBCLogging = Site.LogOdbcDataSource
                                Case "PASSWORD"
                                        ODBCLogging = Site.LogOdbcPassword
                                Case "USERNAME"
                                        ODBCLogging = Site.LogOdbcTableName
                                Case "TABLENAME"
                                        ODBCLogging = Site.LogOdbcUserName
                        End Select
                Case "SET"
                        Select Case UCase(LoggingProperty)
                                Case "DSN"
                                        Site.LogOdbcDataSource = NewValue
                                        Site.SetInfo
                                Case "PASSWORD"
                                        Site.LogOdbcPassword = NewValue
                                        Site.SetInfo
```

continues ▶

Exercise 8.1   *continued*

```
                    Case "USERNAME"
                        Site.LogOdbcTableName = NewValue
                        Site.SetInfo
                    Case "TABLENAME"
                        Site.LogOdbcUserName = NewValue
                        Site.SetInfo
                End Select
                If Err.Number = 0 Then ODBCLogging = True
        End Select
    End Function

    Public Function EnumerateSites(ByVal TargetComputer As String, ByVal IIsService As
    ⮑String) As Variant
        On Error Resume Next
        Dim Parent As IADs
        Dim Child As IADs
        Dim NewElement() As Variant
        Dim i As Long
        Select Case UCase(IIsService)
            Case "WWW"
                Set Parent = GetObject("IIS://" & TargetComputer & "/W3SVC")
            Case "FTP"
                Set Parent = GetObject("IIS://" & TargetComputer & "/MSFTPSVC")
            Case "SMTP"
                Set Parent = GetObject("IIS://" & TargetComputer & "/SMTPSVC")
            Case "NNTP"
                Set Parent = GetObject("IIS://" & TargetComputer & "/NNTPSVC")
        End Select
        For Each Child In Parent
            If IsNumeric(Child.Name) Then
                i = UBound(NewElement) + 1
                ReDim Preserve NewElement(i)
                NewElement(i) = Child.Name & vbTab & Child.ServerComment
            End If
        Next
        EnumerateSites = NewElement
    End Function

    Public Function CreateSite(ByVal TargetComputer As String, ByVal IIsService As String,
    ⮑ByVal SiteName As String, ByVal SitePath As String) As Boolean
        Dim Parent As IADs
        Dim Child As Variant
        Dim NewSite As IADs
        Dim NewRoot As IADs
        Dim Index As Integer
        Select Case UCase(IIsService)
            Case "WWW"
                Set Parent = GetObject("IIS://" & TargetComputer & "/W3SVC")
            Case "FTP"
                Set Parent = GetObject("IIS://" & TargetComputer & "/MSFTPSVC")
            Case "SMTP"
                Set Parent = GetObject("IIS://" & TargetComputer & "/SMTPSVC")
```

Creating the IIsSiteManagement Class Module   245

```
            Case "NNTP"
                Set Parent = GetObject("IIS://" & TargetComputer & "/NNTPSVC")
        End Select
        For Each Child In Parent
            If IsNumeric(Child.Name) Then
                If Index < Child.Name Then
                    Index = Child.Name
                End If
            End If
        Next
        Index = Index + 1
        Select Case UCase(IIsService)
            Case "WWW"
                Set NewSite = Parent.Create("IIsWebServer", Index)
                NewSite.ServerComment = SiteName
                NewSite.SetInfo
                Set NewRoot = NewSite.Create("IIsWebVirtualDir", "Root")
                NewRoot.Path = SitePath
                Err.Number = 0
                NewRoot.SetInfo
            Case "FTP"
                Set NewSite = Parent.Create("IIsFTPServer", Index)
                NewSite.ServerComment = SiteName
                NewSite.SetInfo
                Set NewRoot = NewSite.Create("IIsFTPVirtualDir", "Root")
                NewRoot.Path = SitePath
                Err.Number = 0
                NewRoot.SetInfo
        End Select
        If Err.Number = 0 Then CreateSite = True
End Function

Public Function DeleteSite(ByVal TargetComputer As String, ByVal IIsService As String,
↪ByVal SiteName As String) As Boolean
        Dim Parent As IADs
        Dim Child As Variant
        Dim NewSite As IADs
        Dim Counter As Integer
        Dim IndexValue As Long
        Select Case UCase(IIsService)
            Case "WWW"
                Set Parent = GetObject("IIS://" & TargetComputer & "/W3SVC")
            Case "FTP"
                Set Parent = GetObject("IIS://" & TargetComputer & "/MSFTPSVC")
        End Select
        Counter = 0
        For Each Child In Parent
            If IsNumeric(Child.Name) Then
                If LCase(Child.ServerComment) = LCase(SiteName) Then
                    Counter = Counter + 1
                    IndexValue = Child.Name
                End If
            End If
        Next
```

continues ▶

Exercise 8.1 *continued*

```
            If Counter = 1 Then
                Select Case UCase(IIsService)
                    Case "WWW"
                        Call Parent.Delete("IIsWebServer", IndexValue)
                    Case "FTP"
                        Call Parent.Delete("IIsFTPServer", IndexValue)
                End Select
                Set Parent = Nothing
            End If
            If Err.Number = 0 Then DeleteSite = True
        End Function

        Public Function EnumerateDirectory(ByVal TargetComputer As String, ByVal IIsService As
        ⇒String, ByVal SiteIndex As Integer, ByVal RelativePath As String) As Variant
            On Error Resume Next
            Dim Parent As IADs
            Dim Child As Variant
            Dim NewElement() As Variant
            Dim i As Long
            Select Case UCase(IIsService)
                Case "WWW"
                    Set Parent = GetObject("IIS://" & TargetComputer & "/W3SVC/" & SiteIndex
                        ⇒& "/ROOT" & RelativePath)
                Case "FTP"
                    Set Parent = GetObject("IIS://" & TargetComputer & "/MSFTPSVC/" &
                        ⇒SiteIndex & "/ROOT" & RelativePath)
                Case "SMTP"
                    Set Parent = GetObject("IIS://" & TargetComputer & "/SMTPSVC/" &
                        ⇒SiteIndex & "/ROOT" & RelativePath)
                Case "NNTP"
                    Set Parent = GetObject("IIS://" & TargetComputer & "/NNTPSVC/" &
                        ⇒SiteIndex & "/ROOT" & RelativePath)
            End Select
            For Each Child In Parent
                i = UBound(NewElement) + 1
                ReDim Preserve NewElement(i)
                NewElement(i) = Child.Name
            Next
            EnumerateDirectory = NewElement
        End Function

        Public Function CreateVirDir(ByVal TargetComputer As String, ByVal IIsService As
        ⇒String, ByVal SiteIndex As Integer, ByVal VDirName As String, ByVal VDirPath As
        ⇒String) As Boolean
            Dim Parent As IADs
            Dim NewVDir As IADs
            Select Case UCase(IIsService)
                Case "WWW"
                    Set Parent = GetObject("IIS://" & TargetComputer & "/W3SVC/" & SiteIndex
                        ⇒& "/Root")
                    Set NewVDir = Parent.Create("IIsWebVirtualDir", VDirName)
```

Creating the IIsSiteManagement Class Module 247

```
            Case "FTP"
                Set Parent = GetObject("IIS://" & TargetComputer & "/MSFTPSVC/" &
                ⮕SiteIndex & "/Root")
                Set NewVDir = Parent.Create("IIsFTPVirtualDir", VDirName)
            Case "NNTP"
                Set Parent = GetObject("IIS://" & TargetComputer & "/NNTPSVC/" &
                ⮕SiteIndex & "/Root")
                Set NewVDir = Parent.Create("IIsNNTPVirtualDir", VDirName)
        End Select
        NewVDir.SetInfo
        NewVDir.Path = VDirPath
        Err.Number = 0
        NewVDir.SetInfo
        If Err.Number = 0 Then CreateVirDir = True
End Function

Public Function DeleteVirDir(ByVal TargetComputer As String, ByVal IIsService As
⮕String, ByVal SiteIndex As Integer, ByVal VDirName As String) As Boolean
    Dim Parent As IADs
    Select Case UCase(IIsService)
        Case "WWW"
            Set Parent = GetObject("IIS://" & TargetComputer & "/W3SVC/" & SiteIndex
            ⮕& "/Root")
            Call Parent.Delete("IIsWebVirtualDir", VDirName)
        Case "FTP"
            Set Parent = GetObject("IIS://" & TargetComputer & "/MSFTPSVC/" &
            ⮕SiteIndex & "/Root")
            Call Parent.Delete("IIsFTPVirtualDir", VDirName)
        Case "NNTP"
            Set Parent = GetObject("IIS://" & TargetComputer & "/NNTPSVC/" &
            ⮕SiteIndex & "/Root")
            Call Parent.Delete("IIsNntpVirtualDir", VDirName)
    End Select
    Set Parent = Nothing
    If Err.Number = 0 Then DeleteVirDir = True
End Function

Public Function CreateWebDirEntry(ByVal TargetComputer As String, ByVal SiteIndex As
⮕Integer, ByVal RelativePath As String, ByVal NewEntry As String) As Boolean
    Dim VirtualDirectory As IADs
    Dim WebDir As IADs
    Set VirtualDirectory = GetObject("IIS://" & TargetComputer & "/W3SVC/" & SiteIndex
    ⮕& "/ROOT" & RelativePath)
    Set WebDir = VirtualDirectory.Create("IIsWebDirectory", NewEntry)
    WebDir.SetInfo
    If Err.Number = 0 Then CreateWebDirEntry = True
End Function

Public Function DeleteWebDirEntry(ByVal TargetComputer As String, ByVal SiteIndex As
⮕Integer, ByVal RelativePath As String, ByVal EntryToDelete As String) As Boolean
    Dim VirtualDirectory As IADsContainer
    Set VirtualDirectory = GetObject("IIS://" & TargetComputer & "/W3SVC/" & SiteIndex
    ⮕& "/ROOT" & RelativePath)
```

continues ▶

Exercise 8.1 *continued*

```
        Call VirtualDirectory.Delete("IIsWebDirectory", EntryToDelete)
        If Err.Number = 0 Then DeleteWebDirEntry = True
End Function

Public Function CreateWebFileEntry(ByVal TargetComputer As String, ByVal SiteIndex As
↪Integer, ByVal RelativePath As String, ByVal NewEntry As String) As Boolean
        Dim VirtualDirectory As IADs
        Dim WebFile As IADs
        Set VirtualDirectory = GetObject("IIS://" & TargetComputer & "/W3SVC/" & SiteIndex
        ↪& "/ROOT" & RelativePath)
        Set WebFile = VirtualDirectory.Create("IIsWebFile", NewEntry)
        WebFile.SetInfo
        If Err.Number = 0 Then CreateWebFileEntry = True
End Function

Public Function DeleteWebFileEntry(ByVal TargetComputer As String, ByVal SiteIndex As
↪Integer, ByVal RelativePath As String, ByVal EntryToDelete As String) As Boolean
        Dim VirtualDirectory As IADs
        Set VirtualDirectory = GetObject("IIS://" & TargetComputer & "/W3SVC/" & SiteIndex
        ↪& "/ROOT" & RelativePath)
        Call VirtualDirectory.Delete("IIsWebFile", EntryToDelete)
        If Err.Number = 0 Then DeleteWebFileEntry = True
End Function

Public Function SiteOperations(ByVal TargetComputer As String, ByVal IIsService As
↪String, ByVal SiteIndex As Integer, ByVal Operation As String) As Variant
        Dim Site As IADs
        Dim SiteStatus As Integer
        Select Case UCase(IIsService)
            Case "WWW"
                Set Site = GetObject("IIS://" & TargetComputer & "/W3SVC/" & SiteIndex)
            Case "FTP"
                Set Site = GetObject("IIS://" & TargetComputer & "/MSFTPSVC/" &
                ↪SiteIndex)
            Case "SMTP"
                Set Site = GetObject("IIS://" & TargetComputer & "/SmtpSvc/" &
                ↪SiteIndex)
            Case "NNTP"
                Set Site = GetObject("IIS://" & TargetComputer & "/NNTPSVC/" &
                ↪SiteIndex)
        End Select
        SiteStatus = Site.Status
        Select Case UCase(Operation)
            Case "START"
                If SiteStatus = 4 Or SiteStatus = 3 Then
                    Site.Start
                    If Err.Number = 0 Then SiteOperations = True
                End If
            Case "STOP"
                If SiteStatus = 2 Or SiteStatus = 1 Then
                    Site.Stop
```

Creating the IIsSiteManagement Class Module   249

```
                If Err.Number = 0 Then SiteOperations = True
            End If
        Case "CONTINUE"
            If SiteStatus = 6 Or SiteStatus = 5 Then
                Site.Continue
                If Err.Number = 0 Then SiteOperations = True
            End If
        Case "PAUSE"
            If SiteStatus = 1 Or SiteStatus = 2 Then
                Site.Pause
                If Err.Number = 0 Then SiteOperations = True
            End If
        Case "QUERY"
            Select Case SiteStatus
                Case 1
                    SiteOperations = "Starting"
                Case 2
                    SiteOperations = "Started"
                Case 3
                    SiteOperations = "Stopping"
                Case 4
                    SiteOperations = "Stopped"
                Case 5
                    SiteOperations = "Pausing"
                Case 6
                    SiteOperations = "Paused"
                Case 7
                    SiteOperations = "Continuing"
            End Select
    End Select
End Function
```

6. Compile the code as IIsAdmin.DLL.
7. Save and close the IIsAdmin project.

Tip

If you do not wish to share your code between applications, you can enter the preceding code into a code module in any Visual Basic application. ♦

Using the Functions in IIsSiteManagement

With the IIsSiteManagement class module created, you can access its functions from any programming language that supports OLE automation, including Visual Basic, VBScript, and JavaScript.

> **Tip**
>
> *To instantiate the object, follow the appropriate syntax found in Chapter 3 "Container Enumeration Methods and Programmatic Domain Account Policy Manipulation." Substitute the IIsAdmin DLL name and IIsSiteManagement class name where necessary.* ♦

Use Table 8.3 to help you use the proper syntax for each of the methods of the IIsSiteManagement interface.

Table 8.3   Syntax Reference for IIsSiteManagement

Action	Syntax
Enumerate Metabase Backups	For Each Item In Obj.BackupOperations ↳("IIS_Server_Name", "Enumerate") Debug.Print Item Next
Create Metabase Backup	Call Obj.BackupOperations ↳("IIS_Server_Name", "Backup", ↳"Metabase_BackupName")
Restore Metabase Backup	Call Obj.BackupOperations ↳("IIS_Server_Name", "Restore", ↳"Metabase_BackupName")
Delete Metabase Backup	Call Obj.BackupOperations ↳("IIS_Server_Name", "Delete", ↳"Metabase_BackupName")
Query Maximum Server Bandwidth	Debug.Print Obj.MaxBandwidth ↳("IIS_Server_Name", "Query")
Set Maximum Server Bandwidth	Call Obj.MaxBandwidth("IIS_Server_Name", ↳"Set", 1024000)
Enumerate Global MIME Types	For Each Item In Obj.MIMETypeManagement ↳("IIS_Server_Name", "Enumerate") Debug.Print Item Next
Add New Global MIME Type	Call Obj.MIMETypeManagement ↳("IIS_Server_Name", "Add", ".Extension", ↳"Application/Type")
Remove Global MIME Type	Call Obj.MIMETypeManagement ↳("IIS_Server_Name", "Remove", ↳".Extension")
Query Logging Enabled	Debug.Print Obj.SiteLogging ↳("IIS_Server_Name", "WWW", 1, "Query", ↳"LoggingEnabled") Debug.Print Obj.SiteLogging ↳("IIS_Server_Name", "FTP", 1, "Query", ↳"LoggingEnabled") Debug.Print Obj.SiteLogging ↳("IIS_Server_Name", "SMTP", 1, "Query", ↳"LoggingEnabled")

Creating the IIsSiteManagement Class Module 251

Action	Syntax
	Debug.Print Obj.SiteLogging ↳("IIS_Server_Name", "NNTP", 1, "Query", ↳"LoggingEnabled")
Set Logging Enabled	Call Obj.SiteLogging("IIS_Server_Name", ↳"WWW", 1, "Set", "LoggingEnabled", 1)
	Call Obj.SiteLogging("IIS_Server_Name", ↳"FTP", 1, "Set", "LoggingEnabled", 1)
	Call Obj.SiteLogging("IIS_Server_Name", ↳"SMTP", 1, "Set", "LoggingEnabled", 1)
	Call Obj.SiteLogging("IIS_Server_Name", ↳"NNTP", 1, "Set", "LoggingEnabled", 1)
Query Logging Provider	Debug.Print Obj.SiteLogging ↳("IIS_Server_Name", "WWW", 1, "Query", ↳"LogType")
	Debug.Print Obj.SiteLogging ↳("IIS_Server_Name", "FTP", 1, "Query", ↳"LogType")
	Debug.Print Obj.SiteLogging ↳("IIS_Server_Name", "SMTP", 1, "Query", ↳"LogType")
	Debug.Print Obj.SiteLogging ↳("IIS_Server_Name", "NNTP", 1, "Query", ↳"LogType")
Set Logging Provider	Call Obj.SiteLogging("IIS_Server_Name", ↳"WWW", 1, "Set", "LogType", "ODBC")
	Call Obj.SiteLogging("IIS_Server_Name", ↳"FTP", 1, "Set", "LogType", "IIS")
	Call Obj.SiteLogging("IIS_Server_Name", ↳"SMTP", 1, "Set", "LogType", "NCSA")
	Call Obj.SiteLogging("IIS_Server_Name", ↳"NNTP", 1, "Set", "LogType", "W3C")
Query Log File Period	Debug.Print Obj.SiteLogging ↳("IIS_Server_Name", "WWW", 1, "Query", ↳"LogFilePeriod")
	Debug.Print Obj.SiteLogging ↳("IIS_Server_Name", "FTP", 1, "Query", ↳"LogFilePeriod")
	Debug.Print Obj.SiteLogging ↳("IIS_Server_Name", "SMTP", 1, "Query", ↳"LogFilePeriod")
	Debug.Print Obj.SiteLogging ↳("IIS_Server_Name", "NNTP", 1, "Query", ↳"LogFilePeriod")

continues ▶

Table 8.3   continued

Action	Syntax
Set Log File Period	`Call Obj.SiteLogging("IIS_Server_Name",` `↳"WWW", 1, "Set", "LogFilePeriod", 0)`
	`Call Obj.SiteLogging("IIS_Server_Name",` `↳"FTP", 1, "Set", "LogFilePeriod", 1)`
	`Call Obj.SiteLogging("IIS_Server_Name",` `↳"SMTP", 1, "Set", "LogFilePeriod", 2)`
	`Call Obj.SiteLogging("IIS_Server_Name",` `↳"NNTP", 1, "Set", "LogFilePeriod", 3)`

Query Log File Truncate Size	`Debug.Print Obj.SiteLogging`
	`↳("IIS_Server_Name", "WWW", 1, "Query",`
	`↳"TruncateSize")`

	`Debug.Print Obj.SiteLogging`
	`↳("IIS_Server_Name", "FTP", 1, "Query",`
	`↳"TruncateSize")`

	`Debug.Print Obj.SiteLogging`
	`↳("IIS_Server_Name", "SMTP", 1, "Query",`
	`↳"TruncateSize")`

	`Debug.Print Obj.SiteLogging`
	`↳("IIS_Server_Name", "NNTP", 1, "Query",`
	`↳"TruncateSize")`

Set Log File Truncate Size	`Call Obj.SiteLogging("IIS_Server_Name",` `↳"WWW", 1, "Set", "TruncateSize", 1048576)`
	`Call Obj.SiteLogging("IIS_Server_Name",` `↳"FTP", 1, "Set", "TruncateSize", 1048576)`
	`Call Obj.SiteLogging("IIS_Server_Name",` `↳"SMTP", 1, "Set", "TruncateSize", 1048576)`
	`Call Obj.SiteLogging("IIS_Server_Name",` `↳"NNTP", 1, "Set", "TruncateSize", 1048576)`

Query W3C Extended Properties (Substitute FTP, SMTP or NNTP as appropriate)	`Debug.Print Obj.ExtendedLogProperty`
	`↳("IIS_Server_Name", "WWW", 1, "Query",`
	`↳"Date")`

	`Debug.Print Obj.ExtendedLogProperty`
	`↳("IIS_Server_Name", "WWW", 1, "Query",`
	`↳"Time")`

	`Debug.Print Obj.ExtendedLogProperty`
	`↳("IIS_Server_Name", "WWW", 1, "Query",`
	`↳"ClientIP")`

	`Debug.Print Obj.ExtendedLogProperty`
	`↳("IIS_Server_Name", "WWW", 1, "Query",`
	`↳"Username")`

	`Debug.Print Obj.ExtendedLogProperty`
	`↳("IIS_Server_Name", "WWW", 1, "Query",`
	`↳"ServiceName")`

	`Debug.Print Obj.ExtendedLogProperty`
	`↳("IIS_Server_Name", "WWW", 1, "Query",`
	`↳"ServerName")`

Creating the IIsSiteManagement Class Module 253

Action	Syntax
	`Debug.Print Obj.ExtendedLogProperty`↵`("IIS_Server_Name", "WWW", 1, "Query",`↵`"ServerIP")`
	`Debug.Print Obj.ExtendedLogProperty`↵`("IIS_Server_Name", "WWW", 1, "Query",`↵`"ServerPort")`
	`Debug.Print Obj.ExtendedLogProperty`↵`("IIS_Server_Name", "WWW", 1, "Query",`↵`"Method")`
	`Debug.Print Obj.ExtendedLogProperty`↵`("IIS_Server_Name", "WWW", 1, "Query",`↵`"URIStem")`
	`Debug.Print Obj.ExtendedLogProperty`↵`("IIS_Server_Name", "WWW", 1, "Query",`↵`"URIQuery")`
	`Debug.Print Obj.ExtendedLogProperty`↵`("IIS_Server_Name", "WWW", 1, "Query",`↵`"HttpStatus")`
	`Debug.Print Obj.ExtendedLogProperty`↵`("IIS_Server_Name", "WWW", 1, "Query",`↵`"Win32Status")`
	`Debug.Print Obj.ExtendedLogProperty`↵`("IIS_Server_Name", "WWW", 1, "Query",`↵`"BytesSent")`
	`Debug.Print Obj.ExtendedLogProperty`↵`("IIS_Server_Name", "WWW", 1, "Query",`↵`"BytesReceived")`
	`Debug.Print Obj.ExtendedLogProperty`↵`("IIS_Server_Name", "WWW", 1, "Query",`↵`"TimeTaken")`
	`Debug.Print Obj.ExtendedLogProperty`↵`("IIS_Server_Name", "WWW", 1, "Query",`↵`"ProtocolVersion")`
	`Debug.Print Obj.ExtendedLogProperty`↵`("IIS_Server_Name", "WWW", 1, "Query",`↵`"UserAgent")`
	`Debug.Print Obj.ExtendedLogProperty`↵`("IIS_Server_Name", "WWW", 1, "Query",`↵`"Cookie")`
	`Debug.Print Obj.ExtendedLogProperty`↵`("IIS_Server_Name", "WWW", 1, "Query",`↵`"Referrer")`
Set W3C Extended Properties (Substitute FTP, SMTP or NNTP as appropriate)	`Call Obj.ExtendedLogProperty`↵`("IIS_Server_Name","WWW", 1, "Set",`↵`"Date", False)`

continues ▶

Table 8.3 continued

Action	Syntax

	`Call Obj.ExtendedLogProperty`
	`↪("IIS_Server_Name", "WWW", 1, "Set",`
	`↪"Time", False)`

	`Call Obj.ExtendedLogProperty`
	`↪("IIS_Server_Name", "WWW", 1, "Set",`
	`↪"ClientIP", False)`

	`Call Obj.ExtendedLogProperty`
	`↪("IIS_Server_Name", "WWW", 1, "Set",`
	`↪"Username", False)`

	`Call Obj.ExtendedLogProperty`
	`↪("IIS_Server_Name", "WWW", 1, "Set",`
	`↪"ServiceName", False)`

	`Call Obj.ExtendedLogProperty`
	`↪("IIS_Server_Name", "WWW", 1, "Set",`
	`↪"ServerName", False)`

	`Call Obj.ExtendedLogProperty`
	`↪("IIS_Server_Name", "WWW", 1, "Set",`
	`↪"ServerIP", False)`

	`Call Obj.ExtendedLogProperty`
	`↪("IIS_Server_Name", "WWW", 1, "Set",`
	`↪"ServerPort", False)`

	`Call Obj.ExtendedLogProperty`
	`↪("IIS_Server_Name", "WWW", 1, "Set",`
	`↪"Method", False)`

	`Call Obj.ExtendedLogProperty`
	`↪("IIS_Server_Name", "WWW", 1, "Set",`
	`↪"URIStem", False)`

	`Call Obj.ExtendedLogProperty`
	`↪("IIS_Server_Name", "WWW", 1, "Set",`
	`↪"URISet", False)`

	`Call Obj.ExtendedLogProperty`
	`↪("IIS_Server_Name", "WWW", 1, "Set",`
	`↪"HttpStatus", False)`

	`Call Obj.ExtendedLogProperty`
	`↪("IIS_Server_Name", "WWW", 1, "Set",`
	`↪"Win32Status", False)`

	`Call Obj.ExtendedLogProperty`
	`↪("IIS_Server_Name", "WWW", 1, "Set",`
	`↪"BytesSent", False)`

	`Call Obj.ExtendedLogProperty`
	`↪("IIS_Server_Name", "WWW", 1, "Set",`
	`↪"BytesReceived", False)`

	`Call Obj.ExtendedLogProperty`
	`↪("IIS_Server_Name", "WWW", 1, "Set",`
	`↪"TimeTaken", False)`

Creating the IIsSiteManagement Class Module   255

Action	Syntax

	`Call Obj.ExtendedLogProperty`
	`↪("IIS_Server_Name", "WWW", 1, "Set",`
	`↪"ProtocolVersion", False)`

	`Call Obj.ExtendedLogProperty`
	`↪("IIS_Server_Name", "WWW", 1, "Set",`
	`↪"UserAgent", False)`

	`Call Obj.ExtendedLogProperty`
	`↪("IIS_Server_Name", "WWW", 1, "Set",`
	`↪"Cookie", False)`

	`Call Obj.ExtendedLogProperty`
	`↪("IIS_Server_Name", "WWW", 1, "Set",`
	`↪"Referrer", False)`

Query ODBC Logging Properties	`Debug.Print Obj.ODBCLogging`
	`↪("IIS_Server_Name", "WWW", 1, "Query",`
	`↪"DSN")`

	`Debug.Print Obj.ODBCLogging`
	`↪("IIS_Server_Name", "WWW", 1, "Query",`
	`↪"UserName")`

	`Debug.Print Obj.ODBCLogging`
	`↪("IIS_Server_Name", "WWW", 1, "Query",`
	`↪"Password")`

	`Debug.Print Obj.ODBCLogging`
	`↪("IIS_Server_Name", "WWW", 1, "Query",`
	`↪"TableName")`

	`Debug.Print Obj.ODBCLogging`
	`↪("IIS_Server_Name", "FTP", 1, "Query",`
	`↪"DSN")`

	`Debug.Print Obj.ODBCLogging`
	`↪("IIS_Server_Name", "FTP", 1, "Query",`
	`↪"UserName")`

	`Debug.Print Obj.ODBCLogging`
	`↪("IIS_Server_Name", "FTP", 1, "Query",`
	`↪"Password")`

	`Debug.Print Obj.ODBCLogging`
	`↪("IIS_Server_Name", "FTP", 1, "Query",`
	`↪"TableName")`

	`Debug.Print Obj.ODBCLogging`
	`↪("IIS_Server_Name", "SMTP", 1, "Query",`
	`↪"DSN")`

	`Debug.Print Obj.ODBCLogging`
	`↪("IIS_Server_Name", "SMTP", 1, "Query",`
	`↪"UserName")`

	`Debug.Print Obj.ODBCLogging`
	`↪("IIS_Server_Name", "SMTP", 1, "Query",`
	`↪"Password")`

continues ▶

Table 8.3 continued

Action	Syntax
	`Debug.Print Obj.ODBCLogging` ↪`("IIS_Server_Name", "SMTP", 1, "Query",` ↪`"TableName")`
	`Debug.Print Obj.ODBCLogging` ↪`("IIS_Server_Name", "NNTP", 1, "Query",` ↪`"DSN")`
	`Debug.Print Obj.ODBCLogging` ↪`("IIS_Server_Name", "NNTP", 1, "Query",` ↪`"UserName")`
	`Debug.Print Obj.ODBCLogging` ↪`("IIS_Server_Name", "NNTP", 1, "Query",` ↪`"Password")`
	`Debug.Print Obj.ODBCLogging` ↪`("IIS_Server_Name", "NNTP", 1, "Query",` ↪`"TableName")`
Set ODBC Logging Properties	`Call Obj.ODBCLogging("IIS_Server_Name",` ↪`"WWW", 1, "Set", "DSN", "IIS_Log")`
	`Call Obj.ODBCLogging("IIS_Server_Name",` ↪`"WWW", 1, "Set", "UserName", "IIsAdmin")`
	`Call Obj.ODBCLogging("IIS_Server_Name",` ↪`"WWW", 1, "Set", "Password",` ↪`"Superman2000")`
	`Call Obj.ODBCLogging("IIS_Server_Name",` ↪`"WWW", 1, "Set", "TableName", "WWW_Log")`
	`Call Obj.ODBCLogging("IIS_Server_Name",` ↪`"FTP", 1, "Set", "DSN", "IIS_Log")`
	`Call Obj.ODBCLogging("IIS_Server_Name",` ↪`"FTP", 1, "Set", "UserName", "IIsAdmin")`
	`Call Obj.ODBCLogging("IIS_Server_Name",` ↪`"FTP", 1, "Set", "Password",` ↪`"Superman2000")`
	`Call Obj.ODBCLogging("IIS_Server_Name",` ↪`"FTP", 1, "Set", "TableName", "FTP_Log")`
	`Call Obj.ODBCLogging("IIS_Server_Name",` ↪`"SMTP", 1, "Set", "DSN", "IIS_Log")`
	`Call Obj.ODBCLogging("IIS_Server_Name",` ↪`"SMTP", 1, "Set", "UserName", "IIsAdmin")`
	`Call Obj.ODBCLogging("IIS_Server_Name",` ↪`"SMTP", 1, "Set", "Password",` ↪`"Superman2000")`
	`Call Obj.ODBCLogging("IIS_Server_Name",` ↪`"SMTP", 1, "Set", "TableName", "SMTP_Log")`
	`Call Obj.ODBCLogging("IIS_Server_Name",` ↪`"NNTP", 1, "Set", "DSN", "IIS_Log")`

Action	Syntax
	`Call Obj.ODBCLogging("IIS_Server_Name",` ↪`"NNTP", 1, "Set", "UserName", "IIsAdmin")`
	`Call Obj.ODBCLogging("IIS_Server_Name",` ↪`"NNTP", 1, "Set", "Password",` ↪`"Superman2000")`
	`Call Obj.ODBCLogging("IIS_Server_Name",` ↪`"NNTP", 1, "Set", "TableName", "NNTP_Log")`

Enumerate Sites	`For Each Item In Obj.EnumerateSites`
	↪`("IIS_Server_Name", "WWW")`
	    `Debug.Print Item`
	`Next`

	`For Each Item In Obj.EnumerateSites`
	↪`("IIS_Server_Name", "FTP")`
	    `Debug.Print Item`
	`Next`

	`For Each Item In Obj.EnumerateSites`
	↪`("IIS_Server_Name", "SMTP")`
	    `Debug.Print Item`
	`Next`

	`For Each Item In Obj.EnumerateSites`
	↪`("IIS_Server_Name", "NNTP")`
	    `Debug.Print Item`
	`Next`

Create Sites	`Call Obj.CreateSite("IIS_Server_Name",` ↪`"WWW", "NewSiteName", "File_System_Path")`
	`Call Obj.CreateSite("IIS_Server_Name",` ↪`"FTP", "NewSiteName", "File_System_Path")`

Enumerate Directory Contents	`For Each Item In Obj.EnumerateDirectory`
	↪`("IIS_Server_Name", "WWW", 1,`
	↪`"/RelativePath")`
	    `Debug.Print Item`
	`Next`

	`For Each Item In Obj.EnumerateDirectory`
	↪`("IIS_Server_Name", "FTP", 1,`
	↪`"/RelativePath")`↪
	    `Debug.Print Item`
	`Next`

continues ▶

Table 8.3   continued

Action	Syntax

	`For Each Item In Obj.EnumerateDirectory`
	↳`("IIS_Server_Name", "SMTP", 1,`
	↳`"/RelativePath")`
	    `Debug.Print Item`
	`Next`

	`For Each Item In Obj.EnumerateDirectory`
	↳`("IIS_Server_Name", "NNTP", 1,`
	↳`"/RelativePath")`
	    `Debug.Print Item`
	`Next`

Create Virtual Directory	`Call Obj.CreateVirDir("IIS_Server_Name",` ↳`"WWW", 1, "Directory_Name",` ↳`"File_System_Path")`
	`Call Obj.CreateVirDir("IIS_Server_Name",` ↳`"FTP", 1, "Directory_Name",` ↳`"File_System_Path")`
	`Call Obj.CreateVirDir("IIS_Server_Name",` ↳`"NNTP", 1, "Directory_Name", `↳`"internal.adsi.discussion")`
Delete Virtual Directory	`Call Obj.DeleteVirDir("IIS_Server_Name",` ↳`"WWW", 1, "Directory_Name")`
	`Call Obj.DeleteVirDir("IIS_Server_Name",` ↳`"FTP", 1, "Directory_Name")`
	`Call Obj.DeleteVirDir("IIS_Server_Name",` ↳`"NNTP", 1, "Directory_Name")`
Create Web Directory Metabase Entry	`Call Obj.CreateWebDirEntry` ↳`("IIS_Server_Name", 1, "/RelativePath",` ↳`"Directory_In_File_System")`
Delete Web Directory Metabase Entry	`Call Obj.CreateWebDirEntry` ↳`("IIS_Server_Name", 1, "/RelativePath",` ↳`"Directory_In_File_System")`
Create Web File Metabase Entry	`Call Obj.DeleteWebDirEntry` ↳`("IIS_Server_Name", 1, "/RelativePath",` ↳`"File_To_Add")`
Delete Web File Metabase Entry	`Call Obj.CreateWebFileEntry` ↳`("IIS_Server_Name", 1, "/RelativePath",` ↳`"File_To_Remove")`
Start Site	`Call Obj.SiteOperations("IIS_Server_Name",` ↳`"WWW", 1, "Start")`
	`Call Obj.SiteOperations("IIS_Server_Name",` ↳`"FTP", 1, "Start")`
	`Call Obj.SiteOperations("IIS_Server_Name",` ↳`"SMTP", 1, "Start")`

Action	Syntax
Stop Site	`Call Obj.SiteOperations("IIS_Server_Name",`↪`"NNTP", 1, "Start")`
	`Call Obj.SiteOperations("IIS_Server_Name",`↪`"WWW", 1, "Stop")`
	`Call Obj.SiteOperations("IIS_Server_Name",`↪`"FTP", 1, "Stop")`
	`Call Obj.SiteOperations("IIS_Server_Name",`↪`"SMTP", 1, "Stop")`
	`Call Obj.SiteOperations("IIS_Server_Name",`↪`"NNTP", 1, "Stop")`
Pause Site	`Call Obj.SiteOperations("IIS_Server_Name",`↪`"WWW", 1, "Pause")`
	`Call Obj.SiteOperations("IIS_Server_Name",`↪`"FTP", 1, "Pause")`
	`Call Obj.SiteOperations("IIS_Server_Name",`↪`"SMTP", 1, "Pause")`
	`Call Obj.SiteOperations("IIS_Server_Name",`↪`"NNTP", 1, "Pause")`
Continue Site	`Call Obj.SiteOperations("IIS_Server_Name",`↪`"WWW", 1, "Continue")`
	`Call Obj.SiteOperations("IIS_Server_Name",`↪`"FTP", 1, "Continue")`
	`Call Obj.SiteOperations("IIS_Server_Name",`↪`"SMTP", 1, "Continue")`
	`Call Obj.SiteOperations("IIS_Server_Name",`↪`"NNTP", 1, "Continue")")`

Summary

Using the code segments found in this chapter, you can programmatically administer non-service-specific operations that affect the IIS server. Using an enumeration function, you can start at the root of the IIS namespace and show each node in the structure one layer at a time.

The IIsComputer object allows you to programmatically throttle server bandwidth for the WWW and FTP services as well as assign MIME types that will be inherited by all sites on the server.

Common to all IIS services is the ability to track user activity using industry standard log file formats. Using ADSI, you can programmatically manipulate the configuration of the log files.

Meanwhile, using the IIsContainer interface, you can programmatically create and delete WWW, FTP, SMTP, and NNTP sites. Additionally, you can create virtual directories using the programmatic methods found in this chapter. If you want to change the inherited properties for an individual virtual directory, Web directory or Web file, you must create an entry in the Metabase to block or establish a new set of properties. Programmatically manipulating these entries in the Metabase is easily performed using ADSI.

Lastly, you can programmatically manage the operation of individual sites by calling the Start, Stop, Pause, and Continue methods of the appropriate IIS service interface.

With such robust interfaces at your disposal, you will quickly find that ADSI can help you not only with enterprise automation tasks, but also with managing the impact of the explosive growth of Web technologies in your environment.

9
Programmatic Management of Web Site Properties

With the explosive growth of Web technology, the ability to manage Web environments more efficiently has become essential. Using ADSI you have over 100 properties at your disposal to manipulate the IIS Metabase, making it an extremely robust set of interfaces for automating the administration of Web environments.

In this chapter, we will look at management of the IIS Web service, including virtual site and directory binding, as well as aspects of property inheritance. We will also discuss the programmatic administration of the following:

- The Web Site, Web Operators, and Performance property sheets.
- The Home Directory and Documents property sheets.
- The Directory Security and HTTP Headers property sheets.

In this chapter, you will also continue the creation of the IIsAdmin.DLL COM server application you started in Chapter 8, "Programmatic Management of the IIS Metabase."

> **Note**
>
> *Although this chapter focuses on IIS 4.0, the structure of the Metabase in IIS 5.0 is nearly identical to that used in IIS 4.0. As a result, all code segments in this chapter can also be used with IIS 5.0 implementations.* ◆

Virtual Site Binding

In order to manipulate the properties of a site, virtual directory, or resource in the physical file system, you must first instantiate the appropriate interface required to bind the resource.

> **Note**
>
> For all examples in this chapter, you will use the default Web site installed with IIS, which should carry an index number of 1. If you want to manipulate a different site, you must already know the index number of that site. If you have not yet obtained the index number for the site, you may want to consider using one of the enumeration functions described in Chapter 8 to discover the index value assigned to the server. ♦

The following Visual Basic code will bind to the default Web site in the IIS Metabase:

```
Dim Site As IADs
Dim ServerName As String
Dim Index As Long
ServerName = "IIS_Server_Name"
Index = Site_Index_Value
Set Site = GetObject("IIS://" & ServerName & "/W3SVC/" & Index)
```

> **Tip**
>
> To bind alternate sites, simply assign the Index variable to the integer representing the site you want to bind. ♦

With the site now bound, you can manipulate the individual properties of the site.

Virtual Directory Binding

In the Metabase hierarchy, the virtual directory sits one level below the site. To bind to a virtual directory under any site, simply reference the desired site's index number, and then append the name of the virtual directory.

The following Visual Basic code demonstrates the binding of the IISHELP virtual directory under the Default Web Site:

```
Dim VirtualDirectory as IADs
Dim ServerName As String
Dim Index As Long
Dim VirtualDirectoryName as String
ServerName = "IIS_Server_Name"
Index = Site_Index_Value
VirtualDirectoryName = "Virtual_Directory_Name"
Set VirtualDirectory = GetObject("IIS://" & ServerName & "/W3SVC/" & Index &
↪"/ROOT" & VirtualDirectoryName)
```

Property Inheritance

To determine which properties can be used at each level in the IIS Metabase, consider Table 9.1.

> **Note**
>
> In Table 1.1, items shown in **bold** are of significant importance to the system administrator.
>
> + The plus symbol indicates that at least one element of the interface is supported in the namespace.
>
> - The minus symbol indicates that this interface is not supported in this namespace. ♦

Table 9.1 IIS Metabase Property Inheritance

Property	IIs Web Server	IIsWeb Virtual Directory	IIsWeb Directory	IIsWeb File
AccessExecute	+	+	+	+
AccessFlags	+	+	+	+
AccessNoRemoteExecute	+	+	+	+
AccessNoRemoteRead	+	+	+	+
AccessNoRemoteScript	+	+	+	+
AccessNoRemoteWrite	+	+	+	+
AccessRead	+	+	+	+
AccessScript	+	+	+	+
AccessSSL	+	+	+	+
AccessSSL128	+	+	+	+
AccessSSLFlags	+	+	+	+
AccessSSLMapCert	+	+	+	+
AccessSSLNegotiateCert	+	+	+	+
AccessSSLRequireCert	+	+	+	+
AccessWrite	+	+	+	+
AdminACL	+	−	−	−
AllowKeepAlive	+	−	−	−
AllowPathInfoForScriptMappings	+	−	−	−
AnonymousPasswordSync	+	+	+	+
AnonymousUserName	+	+	+	+
AnonymousUserPass	+	+	+	+
AppAllowClientDebug	+	+	−	−

continues ▶

Table 9.1 continued

Property	IIs Web Server	IIsWeb Virtual Directory	IIsWeb Directory	IIsWeb File
AppAllowDebugging	+	+	−	−
AppFriendlyName	+	+	+	−
AppIsolated	+	+	+	−
AppOopRecoverLimit	+	+	+	−
AppPackageID	+	+	+	−
AppPackageName	+	+	+	−
AppRoot	+	+	+	−
AppWamClsid	+	+	+	−
AspAllowOutOfProcComponents	+	+	+	−
AspAllowSessionState	+	+	+	−
AspBufferingOn	+	+	+	−
AspCodepage	+	+	+	−
AspEnableParentPaths	+	+	+	−
AspExceptionCatchEnable	+	+	+	−
AspLogErrorRequests	+	+	+	−
AspMemFreeFactor	+	+	+	−
AspQueueTimeout	+	+	+	−
AspScriptEngineCacheMax	+	+	+	−
AspScriptErrorMessage	+	+	+	−
AspScriptErrorSentToBrowser	+	+	+	−
AspScriptFileCacheSize	+	+	+	−
AspScriptLanguage	+	+	+	−
AspScriptTimeout	+	+	+	−
AspSessionTimeout	+	+	+	−
AuthAnonymous	+	+	+	+
AuthBasic	+	+	+	+
AuthFlags	+	+	+	+
AuthNTLM	+	+	+	+
AuthPersistence	+	+	+	+
CacheControlCustom	+	+	+	+
CacheControlMaxAge	+	+	+	+
CacheControlNoCache	+	+	+	+
CacheISAPI	+	−	−	−
CGITimeout	+	−	−	−
ConnectionTimeout	+	−	−	−
ContentIndexed	−	+	+	−

Property	IIsWebServer	IIsWebVirtualDirectory	IIsWebDirectory	IIsWebFile
CreateCGIWithNewConsole	+	+	+	+
CreateProcessAsUser	+	+	+	+
DefaultDoc	+	+	+	−
DefaultDocFooter	+	+	+	+
DefaultLogonDomain	+	+	+	+
DirBrowseFlags	+	+	+	−
DirBrowseShowDate	+	+	+	−
DirBrowseShowExtension	+	+	+	−
DirBrowseShowLongDate	+	+	+	−
DirBrowseShowSize	+	+	+	−
DirBrowseShowTime	+	+	+	−
DontLog	+	+	+	+
EnableDefaultDoc	+	+	+	−
EnableDirBrowsing	+	+	+	−
EnableDocFooter	+	+	+	+
EnableReverseDns	+	+	+	+
FrontPageWeb	+	−	−	−
HttpCustomHeaders	+	+	+	+
HttpErrors	+	+	+	+
HttpExpires	+	+	+	+
HttpPics	+	+	+	+
HttpRedirect	+	+	+	+
IPSecurity	+	+	+	+
LogExtFileBytesRecv	+	−	−	−
LogExtFileBytesSent	+	−	−	−
LogExtFileClientIp	+	−	−	−
LogExtFileComputerName	+	−	−	−
LogExtFileCookie	+	−	−	−
LogExtFileDate	+	−	−	−
LogExtFileFlags	+	−	−	−
LogExtFileHttpStatus	+	−	−	−
LogExtFileMethod	+	−	−	−
LogExtFileProtocolVersion	+	−	−	−
LogExtFileReferer	+	−	−	−
LogExtFileServerIp	+	−	−	−
LogExtFileServerPort	+	−	−	−

continues ▶

Table 9.1   continued

Property	IIs Web Server	IIsWeb Virtual Directory	IIsWeb Directory	IIsWeb File
LogExtFileSiteName	+	–	–	–
LogExtFileTime	+	–	–	–
LogExtFileTimeTaken	+	–	–	–
LogExtFileUriQuery	+	–	–	–
LogExtFileUriStem	+	–	–	–
LogExtFileUserAgent	+	–	–	–
LogExtFileUserName	+	–	–	–
LogExtFileWin32Status	+	–	–	–
LogFileDirectory	+	–	–	–
LogFilePeriod	+	–	–	–
LogFileTruncateSize	+	–	–	–
LogModuleList	–	–	–	–
LogOdbcDataSource	+	–	–	–
LogOdbcPassword	+	–	–	–
LogOdbcTableName	+	–	–	–
LogOdbcUserName	+	–	–	–
LogonMethod	+	+	+	+
LogPluginClsId	+	–	–	–
LogType	+	–	–	–
MaxBandwidth	+	–	–	–
MaxBandwidthBlocked	+	–	–	–
MaxConnections	+	–	–	–
MaxEndpointConnections	+	–	–	–
MimeMap	+	+	+	+
NetLogonWorkstation	+	–	–	–
NTAuthenticationProviders	+	–	–	–
PasswordCacheTTL	+	–	–	–
PasswordChangeFlags	+	–	–	–
PasswordExpirePrenotifyDays	+	–	–	–
Path	–	+	–	–
PoolIDCTimeout	+	+	+	+
ProcessNTCRIfLoggedOn	+	–	–	–
PutReadSize	+	+	+	+
Realm	+	+	+	+
RedirectHeaders	+	+	+	+
ScriptMaps	+	+	+	+

Property	IIs Web Server	IIsWeb Virtual Directory	IIsWeb Directory	IIsWeb File
SecureBindings	+	–	–	–
ServerAutoStart	+	–	–	–
ServerBindings	+	–	–	–
ServerComment	+	–	–	–
ServerListenBacklog	+	–	–	–
ServerListenTimeout	+	–	–	–
ServerSize	+	–	–	–
ServerState	+	–	–	–
SSIExecDisable	+	+	+	+
UNCAuthenticationPassthrough	+	+	+	+
UNCPassword	–	+	–	–
UNCUserName	–	+	–	–
UploadReadAheadSize	+	+	+	+
UseHostName	+	–	–	–

Note

For purposes of the examples in this chapter, most code segments will demonstrate manipulation of the default Web site and root virtual directory. Based on the information in the preceding table, you can easily determine which properties can be manipulated at each level in the Metabase. ✦

Programmatically Administering the Web Site Property Sheet

The Web Site property sheet, shown in Figure 9.1, allows you to manipulate the following:

- Site description
- IP address
- TCP port
- Host header name
- Number of connections allowed
- Logging options

All properties on this sheet can be manipulated using the ADSI IIS service provider.

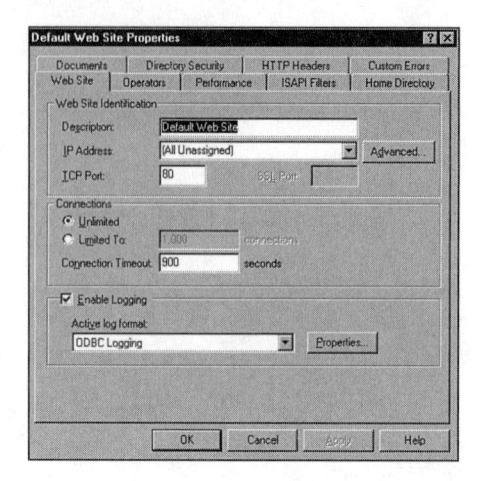

Figure 9.1 *Default Web Site Properties—Web Site property sheet.*

Web Site Identification

The Web Site Identification frame shows all properties that affect how the site is described to clients or administrative tools. In this frame, you can manipulate the following:

- ServerComment property or site description
- IP address(es) used for the site
- TCP port(s) used to access the site
- Any host header information that uniquely identifies this site

In addition, you can define the IP address and TCP port used for Secure Sockets Layer (SSL) connections. Modifying these fields is an essential step toward establishing multiple sites on a single IIS server.

Manipulating Site Description

By manipulating the ServerComment field, you can examine and modify the description assigned to the Web site. As mentioned previously, this comment field is never used for programmatic identification; it is used solely to account for the fact that people are better at remembering names rather than integers.

Querying ServerComment *Using Visual Basic*
To find the description assigned to the site, after binding to the appropriate site simply query the ServerComment property, as follows:

```
Dim Site As IADs
Dim ServerName As String
Dim Index As Long
```

```
ServerName = "IIS_Server_Name"
Index = Site_Index_Integer
Set Site = GetObject("IIS://" & ServerName & "/W3SVC/" & Index)
Debug.Print Site.ServerComment
```

Setting ServerComment *Using Visual Basic*
To set a new server comment, simply assign the ServerComment property a new value, as follows:

```
Dim Site As IADs
Dim ServerName As String
Dim Index As Long
Dim NewServerComment as String
ServerName = "IIS_Server_Name"
Index = Site_Index_Integer
NewServerComment = "New_Server_Comment_String"
Set Site = GetObject("IIS://" & ServerName & "/W3SVC/" & Index)
Site.ServerComment = NewServerComment
Site.SetInfo
```

IP Address, TCP Port and Host Header Manipulation
As shown in Figure 9.2, IIS allows you the opportunity to publish multiple Web sites on a single IP address. To use multiple Web sites on the same machine you must do one of the following:

- Use one IP address per site.
- Use a unique TCP port for each site on the same IP address.
- Use host headers to differentiate between each site on the same IP address.

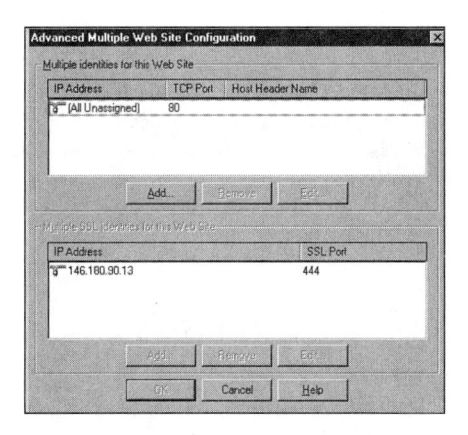

Figure 9.2 *Advanced Multiple Web Site Configuration dialog box.*

Using ADSI, you can use the ServerBindings property to manipulate these parameters. The ServerBindings field is stored as an array of strings, with each string entered in the format IP_Address:TCP_Port:Hostname.

Querying ServerBindings *Using Visual Basic*
To find out on which TCP port or from which DNS entry a particular site will respond, use the following Visual Basic code:

```
Dim Site As IADs
Dim ServerName As String
Dim SiteIndex As Long
ServerName = "IIS_Server_Name"
SiteIndex = Site_Index_Value
Set Site = GetObject("IIS://" & ServerName & "/W3SVC/" & SiteIndex)
For Each Binding In Site.ServerBindings
   Debug.Print Binding
Next
```

Setting ServerBindings *Using Visual Basic*
After formatting a string in the format IP_Address:TCP_Port:Hostname, you can create an array to change the way a site responds to an HTTP request. Use the following Visual Basic code as a guide to programmatically assign an alternate TCP port or host header to a bound site:

```
Dim Site As IADs
Dim ServerName As String
Dim SiteIndex As Long
Dim NewBindingArray as Variant
Dim ServerBindingString1 as String
Dim ServerBindingString2 as String
Dim ServerBindingString3 as String
ServerName = "IIS_Server_Name"
SiteIndex = Site_Index_Value
ServerBindingString1 = "IP_Address:TCP_Port:Hostname"
ServerBindingString2 = "IP_Address:TCP_Port:Hostname"
ServerBindingString3 = "IP_Address:TCP_Port:Hostname"
NewBindingArray = Array(ServerBindingString1, ServerBindingString2,
↪ServerBindingString3)
Set Site = GetObject("IIS://" & ServerName & "/W3SVC/" & SiteIndex)
Site.ServerBindings = NewBindingArray
Site.SetInfo
```

Secure Sockets Layer (SSL) Secure Endpoint Mapping
To set an IP address and TCP port for use with secure connections, you can manipulate the SecureBindings property. This property is nearly identical to the ServerBindings property. However, you cannot associate a host header with the site. This is not a limitation of IIS, but actually of host headers themselves. Over an SSL-encrypted connection, the host header is included

in the encrypted request, making it impossible for the browser to decipher the host header. For this reason, only the IP address and TCP port are specified for SSL connections.

Although you cannot use host headers with SSL-protected sites, if you wish to create multiple identities for an SSL-protected site, you can use an alternate TCP port setting.

> *Note*
>
> *For more information on host headers and SSL, check out the Microsoft Knowledge Base article Q187504. The Microsoft Knowledge Base can be found on Microsoft's home page, or through Microsoft TechNet or Microsoft MSDN.* ◆

Querying SecureBindings *Using Visual Basic*
To view the current configuration of your SSL-protected site, use the following Visual Basic code:

```
Dim Site As IADs
Dim ServerName As String
Dim SiteIndex As Long
ServerName = "IIS_Server_Name"
SiteIndex = Site_Index_Value
Set Site = GetObject("IIS://" & ServerName & "/W3SVC/" & SiteIndex)
For Each Binding In Site.SecureBindings
   Debug.Print Binding
Next
```

Setting SecureBindings *Using Visual Basic*
After formatting a string as IP_Address:TCP_Port:, you can create an array to be assigned to the SecureBindings property using the following Visual Basic code:

```
Dim Site As IADs
Dim ServerName As String
Dim SiteIndex As Long
Dim NewBindingArray as Variant
Dim ServerBindingString1 as String
Dim ServerBindingString2 as String
Dim ServerBindingString3 as String
ServerName = "IIS_Server_Name"
SiteIndex = Site_Index_Value
ServerBindingString1 = "IP_Address:TCP_Port:"
ServerBindingString2 = "IP_Address:TCP_Port:"
ServerBindingString3 = "IP_Address:TCP_Port:"
NewBindingArray = Array(ServerBindingString1, ServerBindingString2,
↪ServerBindingString3)
Set Site = GetObject("IIS://" & ServerName & "/W3SVC/" & SiteIndex)
Site.SecureBindings = NewBindingArray
Site.SetInfo
```

Connections

In the Connections frame of IIS 4.0 Internet Service Manager's Web Site property sheet, you can specify the maximum number of connections to the site as well as define a timeout value for all connections. This can be very useful if used after determining your host's capacity with a product such as Microsoft Homer or another capacity planning tool. In addition, it is always a good idea to time out connections to the server to improve the likelihood that new users to the site will be able to obtain a connection.

Maximum Connections

Using the MaxConnections property of the IIsWebServer object, you can find the maximum number of simultaneous connections allowed to a particular site.

> **Note**
>
> *Windows NT Workstation allows only 10 inbound connections. If you are using ADSI against a Personal Web Server (IIS on NT Workstation) the maximum number of connections will be 10.* ◆

Querying Maximum Connections Using Visual Basic
To view the maximum number of connections allowed to the bound Web site, use the following Visual Basic code:

```
Dim Site As IADs
Dim ServerName As String
Dim Index As Long
Dim RetVal as Long
ServerName = "IIS_Server_Name"
Index = Site_Index
Set Site = GetObject("IIS://" & ServerName & "/W3SVC/" & Index)
RetVal = Site.MaxConnections
Debug.Print RetVal
```

> **Note**
>
> *Unlike other ADSI properties, the* MaxConnections *property uses 2000000000 to designate an unlimited number of connections.* ◆

Programmatically Administering the Web Site Property Sheet 273

Setting Maximum Connections Using Visual Basic
Use the following Visual Basic code to establish a new value for the maximum number of connections permitted to the bound Web site:

```
Dim Site As IADs
Dim ServerName As String
Dim Index As Long
Dim NewMaxConnections as Long
ServerName = "IIS_Server_Name"
Index = Site_Index
NewMaxConnections = Maximum_Number_of_Connections
Set Site = GetObject("IIS://" & ServerName & "/W3SVC/" & Index)
Site.MaxConnections = NewMaxConnections
Site.SetInfo
```

Connection Timeout

Using the ConnectionTimeout property, you can specify the amount of time (in seconds) before a user's HTTP connection is closed.

Querying Connection Timeout Using Visual Basic
To find the number of seconds before an HTTP connection is closed, use the following Visual Basic code:

```
Dim Site As IADs
Dim ServerName As String
Dim Index As Long
Dim RetVal as Long
ServerName = "IIS_Server_Name"
Index = Site_Index
Set Site = GetObject("IIS://" & ServerName & "/W3SVC/" & Index)
RetVal = Site.ConnectionTimeout
Debug.Print RetVal
```

Setting Connection Timeout Using Visual Basic
To time out HTTP connections at a specified interval, use the following Visual Basic code:

```
Dim Site As IADs
Dim ServerName As String
Dim Index As Long
Dim ConnectionTimeout as Long
ServerName = "IIS_Server_Name"
Index = Site_Index_Value
NewConnectionTimeout = Connection_Timeout_in_Seconds
Set Site = GetObject("IIS://" & ServerName & "/W3SVC/" & Index)
Site.ConnectionTimeout = NewConnectionTimeout
Site.SetInfo
```

IIS Logging

IIS logging is used in the WWW, FTP, SNMP, and NNTP services. To configure IIS logging for your Web site, consult Chapter 8, which covers programmatic administration of the IIS logging provider. ♦

Programmatically Administering the Web Operators Property Sheet

As shown in Figure 9.3, IIS allows you to specify an Access Control List (ACL) for the site to prevent unauthorized administrative access. By default, only the local administrators' group on a server has access to the configuration of the Web site. Although you can certainly add all users to the local administrators' group to grant operator privileges, this option yields a condition where too many rights are granted to the user.

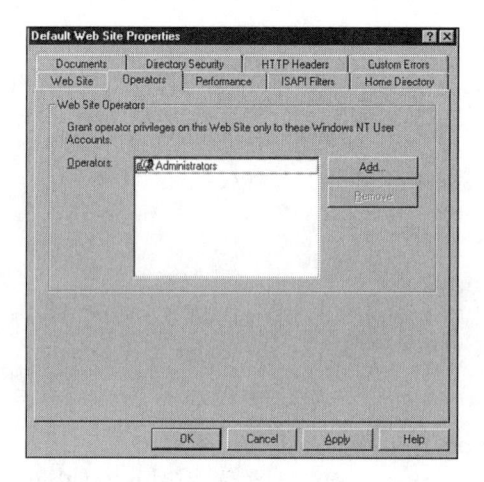

Figure 9.3 *Default Web Site Properties Configuration dialog box—Operators tab.*

Typically, security organizations strive to grant the most restrictive set of rights to a user account while still retaining the ability to perform essential job functions. To attain this model in IIS, you must create one group for each administrator type. This could be divided by site, business unit, geographic location, or any other mechanism employed in your organization to define Web site operators.

With the groups created, you can use the AdminACL property of the IIsWebServer object to set a Discretionary Access Control List (DACL) on the specific site tree in the Metabase. This will grant or deny permission to access/modify the keys according to group membership.

Querying Operators Using Visual Basic

Use the following Visual Basic code to query the currently defined site operators:

```
Dim Site As IADs
Dim ServerName As String
Dim SiteIndex As Long
ServerName = "IIS_Server_Name"
SiteIndex = Site_Index_Value
Set Site = GetObject("IIS://" & ServerName & "/W3SVC/" & SiteIndex)
Set SecurityDescriptor = Site.AdminAcl
Set DiscretionaryAcl = SecurityDescriptor.DiscretionaryAcl
For Each Item In DiscretionaryAcl
  If Item.AccessMask = 11 Or Item.AccessMask = 262315 Then
    Debug.Print Item.Trustee
  End If
Next
```

Setting a New Operator Using Visual Basic

To establish a new site operator, use the following Visual Basic code, which will create an array of entries for the ACL:

```
Dim Site As IADs
Dim ACE As Variant
Dim DiscretionaryACL As Variant
Dim ServerName As String
Dim SiteIndex As Long
Dim NewOperator As String
ServerName = "IIS_Server_Name"
SiteIndex = Site_Index_Value
NewOperator = "New_Operator_in_Format_Domain\Username"
Set Site = GetObject("IIS://" & ServerName & "/W3SVC/" & SiteIndex)
Set SecurityDescriptor = Site.AdminACL
Set DiscretionaryACL = SecurityDescriptor.DiscretionaryACL
Set ACE = CreateObject("AccessControlEntry")
ACE.Trustee = NewOperator
ACE.AccessMask = 11
DiscretionaryACL.AddAce ACE
SecurityDescriptor.DiscretionaryACL = DiscretionaryACL
Site.AdminACL = SecurityDescriptor
Site.SetInfo
```

Note

The trustee account used in the ACE must exist and be accessible. The ACE will only be added after the account has been verified. ♦

Removing an Operator Using Visual Basic

Use the following Visual Basic code to remove a specific operator Access Control Entry (ACE) from the site operators ACL:

```
Dim Site As IADs
Dim ACE As Variant
Dim DiscretionaryACL As Variant
Dim ServerName As String
Dim SiteIndex As Long
Dim OperatorToRemove As String
ServerName = "IIS_Server_Name"
SiteIndex = Site_Index_Value
OperatorToRemove = "User_Name_to_Remove"
Set Site = GetObject("IIS://" & ServerName & "/W3SVC/" & SiteIndex)
Set SecurityDescriptor = Site.AdminACL
Set DiscretionaryACL = SecurityDescriptor.DiscretionaryACL
Set ACE = CreateObject("AccessControlEntry")
ACE.Trustee = OperatorToRemove
ACE.AccessMask = 11
DiscretionaryACL.RemoveAce ACE
SecurityDescriptor.DiscretionaryACL = DiscretionaryACL
Site.AdminACL = SecurityDescriptor
Site.SetInfo
```

Programmatically Administering the Web Performance Property Sheet

There are several properties IIS uses to tune memory allocation, bandwidth usage, and connection behavior to your specifications (see Figure 9.4).

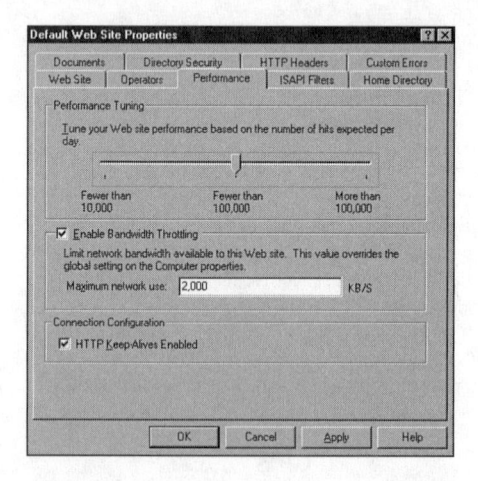

Figure 9.4 *Default Web Site Properties Configuration dialog box—Performance tab.*

Additionally, you can enable "HTTP keep-alives" to allow clients to maintain open connections to the server. This option eliminates the overhead associated with connection instantiation and tear down for each request.

In this section, you will explore the programmatic methods behind each of these configurable options.

Performance Tuning

By adjusting the Performance Tuning slider control you are actually modifying the amount of memory allocated to operate the specific site. Incorrect configuration of this option results in wasted memory resources or poor performance at the client. If your site receives significantly more hits than the number specified by this property, performance could potentially improve by allocating more memory to the site. If the site receives fewer hits than the number specified by this property, too much memory is allocated to the site. Use the logs of the live site to analyze the performance of your site and configure this setting accordingly.

Using the ServerSize property of the IIsWebServer object, you can set this value programmatically. The ServerSize property uses an integer datatype to define this property and assigns the following values to each integer, as shown in Table 9.2.

Table 9.2   ServerSize Integer Values, Settings, and Descriptions

Integer Value	Setting	Description
0	Small Site	Fewer than 10,000 requests served daily by this site
1	Medium Site	Between 10,000 and 100,000 requests served daily by this site
2	Large Site	More than 100,000 requests served daily by this site

Querying *ServerSize* Using Visual Basic

To find out the current ServerSize property configuration of the bound site, use the following Visual Basic code:

```
Dim Site As IADs
Dim ServerName As String
Dim SiteIndex As Long
ServerName = "IIS_Server_Name"
SiteIndex = Site_Index_Value
Set Site = GetObject("IIS://" & ServerName & "/W3SVC/" & SiteIndex)
Debug.Print Site.ServerSize
```

Setting *ServerSize* Using Visual Basic

To specify a new value for the `ServerSize` property, use Table 9.2 and the following Visual Basic code:

```
Dim Site As IADs
Dim ServerName As String
Dim SiteIndex As Long
Dim NewServerSize As Integer
ServerName = "IIS_Server_Name"
SiteIndex = Site_Index_Value
NewServerSize = 0
Set Site = GetObject("IIS://" & ServerName & "/W3SVC/" & SiteIndex)
Site.ServerSize = NewServerSize
Site.SetInfo
```

Enable Bandwidth Throttling

Just as you can manipulate the maximum bandwidth for the entire server, you can also manipulate individual sites by binding to the desired site, and then modifying/querying the `MaxBandwidth` property.

In certain cases, you may wish to allocate a larger percentage of available bandwidth to a specific site. This is useful when a preview and subscription site exist on the same server, or perhaps for testing purposes to determine the performance at a given transfer rate.

Querying Maximum Bandwidth for a Site Using Visual Basic

To find the current value for the `MaxBandwidth` property, use the following Visual Basic code:

```
Dim Site As IADs
Dim ServerName As String
Dim SiteIndex As Long
ServerName = "IIS_Server_Name"
SiteIndex = Site_Index_Value
Set Site = GetObject("IIS://" & ServerName & "/W3SVC/" & SiteIndex)
Debug.Print Site.MaxBandwidth
```

Setting Maximum Bandwidth for a Site Using Visual Basic

To set a new value in bytes for the `MaxBandwidth` property, use the following Visual Basic code:

```
Dim Site As IADs
Dim ServerName As String
Dim SiteIndex As Long
Dim NewMaxBandwidth As Long
ServerName = "IIS_Server_Name"
SiteIndex = Site_Index_Value
NewMaxBandwidth = Value_in_Bytes
Set Site = GetObject("IIS://" & ServerName & "/W3SVC/" & SiteIndex)
Site.MaxBandwidth = NewMaxBandwidth
Site.SetInfo
```

Connection Configuration

By default, IIS uses HTTP keep-alives to minimize the overhead associated with creating and destroying HTTP sessions for every request. Using the AllowKeepAlive property of the IIsWebServer object, you can disable or enable the use of HTTP keep-alives for a particular site. By reducing connection instantiation and destruction for each request, HTTP keep-alives will often increase performance of the site.

Querying HTTP Keep-Alive Processing Status Using Visual Basic

To find the current status of HTTP keep-alive processing, use the following Visual Basic code:

```
Dim Site As IADs
Dim ServerName As String
Dim SiteIndex As Long
ServerName = "IIS_Server_Name"
SiteIndex = Site_Index_Value
Set Site = GetObject("IIS://" & ServerName & "/W3SVC/" & SiteIndex)
Debug.Print Site.AllowKeepAlive
```

Setting HTTP Keep-Alive Processing Status Using Visual Basic

To enable or disable HTTP keep-alive processing, use the following Visual Basic code:

```
Dim Site As IADs
Dim ServerName As String
Dim SiteIndex As Long
Dim AllowKeepAlive As Boolean
ServerName = "IIS_Server_Name"
SiteIndex = Site_Index_Value
AllowKeepAlive = True
Set Site = GetObject("IIS://" & ServerName & "/W3SVC/" & SiteIndex)
Site.AllowKeepAlive = AllowKeepAlive
Site.SetInfo
```

Programmatically Administering the Home Directory Property Sheet

As shown in Figure 9.5, the configuration of a home directory path is vital to the establishment of a new Web site.

Using the properties in this section, you can determine the origin of content when accessing a resource, determine permissions and default behavior of the files and directories in the root virtual directory, and define the configuration of a Web application.

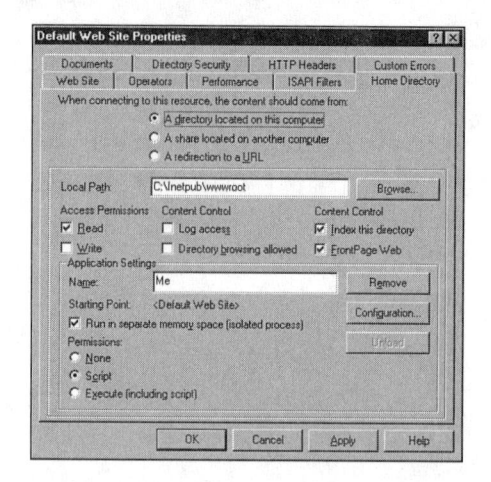

Figure 9.5 *Default Web Site Properties Configuration dialog box—Home Directory tab.*

To begin, you must determine from where the content should be derived. In IIS 4.0, you have three options:

- A directory located on this computer
- A share located on another computer
- A redirection to a URL

Local Home Directory

To access content stored on the local machine, you need only define the Path property for the Root virtual directory. To do this, simply bind the Root virtual directory for the site and assign a new value to the Path property.

Querying the Local Path Property for a Site's Root Virtual Directory Using Visual Basic

To find the current path assigned to the bound Web site, use the following Visual Basic code:

```
Dim VirtualDirectory As IADs
Dim ServerName As String
Dim Index As Long
Dim RetVal as String
ServerName = "IIS_Server_Name"
Index = Site_Index_Value
Set VirtualDirectory = GetObject("IIS://" & ServerName & "/W3SVC/" & Index & "/ROOT")
RetVal = VirtualDirectory.Path
Debug.Print RetVal
```

Modifying the Local Path Property for a Site's Root Virtual Directory Using Visual Basic

Use the following Visual Basic code to modify the path to the Root virtual directory for the default Web site:

```
Dim VirtualDirectory As IADs
Dim ServerName As String
Dim Index As Long
Dim NewVirtualDirPath As String
ServerName = "IIS_Server_Name"
Index = Site_Index_Value
NewVirtualDirPath = "New_Path_for_Site"
Set VirtualDirectory = GetObject("IIS://" & ServerName & "/W3SVC/" & Index &
Â"/ROOT")
VirtualDirectory.Path = NewVirtualDirPath
VirtualDirectory.SetInfo
```

Remote Home Directory

As shown in Figure 9.6, IIS allows you to establish a connection to a remote directory to serve the files for a particular site.

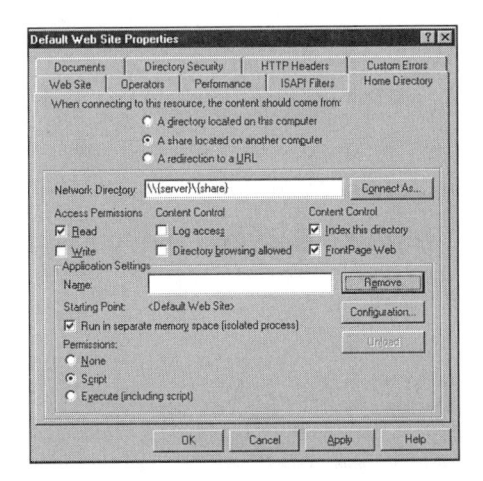

Figure 9.6 *Default Web Site Properties dialog box—Home Directory tab (remote path).*

To access content stored on a remote machine, assign the site's Root virtual directory Path property to a share name. Use the Universal Naming Convention (UNC) path for the resource (*server**share*) and define the username and password to make the connection using the UNCUserName and UNCPassword properties.

Querying the Remote Path Property and UNC Connection Information for a Site's Root Virtual Directory Using Visual Basic

Using the `Path`, `UNCUserName`, and `UNCPassword` properties, you can find the configuration settings for a remote home directory. Use the following Visual Basic code as a guide:

```
Dim VirtualDirectory As IADs
Dim ServerName As String
Dim Index As Long
Dim RetVal As String
ServerName = "IIS_Server_Name"
Index = Site_Index_Value
Set VirtualDirectory = GetObject("IIS://" & ServerName & "/W3SVC/" & Index & 
➥"/ROOT")
Debug.Print VirtualDirectory.Path
Debug.Print VirtualDirectory.UNCUserName
Debug.Print VirtualDirectory.UNCPassword
```

> **Warning**
>
> Like all password-related information stored in the IIS Metabase, the password can be viewed in clear text using ADSI. When designing your site, you should take into consideration the fact that anyone with the proper knowledge, tools, and access can compromise this account.
>
> Under no circumstances should an account with any significant level of privileges be used for the IUSR, IWAM, or UNC credentials due to this security "feature." ♦

Modifying the Remote Path Property for a Site's Root Virtual Directory Using Visual Basic

To create a new remote home directory for a site, use the following Visual Basic code:

```
Dim VirtualDirectory As IADs
Dim ServerName As String
Dim Index As Long
Dim NewVirtualDirPath As String
Dim NewVirtualDirUser As String
Dim NewVirtualDirPassword As String
ServerName = "IIS_Server_Name"
Index = Site_Index_Value
NewVirtualDirPath = "New_Path_for_Site"
NewVirtualDirUser = "UNC_Credentials_Used_To_Establish_Connection"
NewVirtualDirPassword = "UNC_Credentials_Used_To_Establish_Connection"
Set VirtualDirectory = GetObject("IIS://" & ServerName & "/W3SVC/" & Index & 
➥"/ROOT")
VirtualDirectory.Path = NewVirtualDirPath
VirtualDirectory.UNCUsername = NewVirtualDirUser
VirtualDirectory.UNCPassword = NewVirtualDirPassword
VirtualDirectory.SetInfo
```

Access Permissions and Content Control for Local and Remote Home Directories

For both the local and remote home directory site configurations, you can assign permissions, enable/disable logging, enable/disable directory browsing, allow indexing of the directory, and enable/disable FrontPage user access.

You can perform these actions by binding to the Root virtual directory and setting the appropriate Boolean value for each of the following properties:

Property	Behavior
AccessRead	Enables or disables the ability to read files in the directory.
AccessWrite	Enables or disables the ability to write files in the directory.
DontLog	Enables or disables logging of the bound directory.
EnableDirBrowsing	Enables or disables the ability to browse the virtual directory from the client.
ContentIndexed	Enables or disables indexing of the bound virtual directory.
FrontPageWeb	Enables the FrontPage manager to create the required FrontPage files. If set to disabled, the FrontPage Web support files are deleted.

Managing Access Permissions and Content Control Properties Using Visual Basic

The following Visual Basic code shows the manipulation of all Access Permissions and Content Control properties for IIS 4.0:

```
Dim VirtualDirectory As IADs
Dim ServerName As String
Dim Index As Long
ServerName = "IIS_Server_Name"
Index = Site_Index_Value
Set VirtualDirectory = GetObject("IIS://" & ServerName & "/W3SVC/" & Index & ↩
"/ROOT")
Debug.Print "Read:" & vbTab & vbTab & vbTab & VirtualDirectory.AccessRead
Debug.Print "Write:" & vbTab & vbTab & vbTab & VirtualDirectory.AccessWrite
Debug.Print "Logging Disabled: " & vbTab & VirtualDirectory.DontLog
Debug.Print "Dir Browsing: " & vbTab & vbTab & VirtualDirectory.EnableDirBrowsing
Debug.Print "Index Content: " & vbTab & VirtualDirectory.ContentIndexed
Set VirtualDirectory = GetObject("IIS://" & ServerName & "/W3SVC/" & Index)
Debug.Print "FrontPage Web:" & vbTab & vbTab & VirtualDirectory.FrontPageWeb
```

> **Warning**
>
> Notice that the `FrontPageWeb` property is defined only at the site level. An automation error will occur if you attempt to reference this property from any other location in the Metabase hierarchy. ♦

Web Application Configuration

To associate a *global.asa* file with a specific set of scripts, you can configure a virtual directory as a Web application. In addition to the ability to use global functions and variables across all scripts within the application boundaries, you can also force scripts to run in a separate memory space from the IIS service.

This can be especially useful if application developers write "misbehaving" code and you do not want to reboot the server on a regular basis. Many administrators who complain that IIS is unstable find solace by simply running custom-developed applications out-of-process from the IIS service. Although this may incur a small performance detriment, it is a worthwhile sacrifice to maintain the stability of the entire server.

After binding to a virtual directory, you can set the application name, process isolation configuration, permissions for the application, session state parameters, server-side buffering, the language used for all ASP scripts, and the timeout value for ASP scripts. On development servers, you can enable both client- and server-side ASP debugging, as well as determine the verbosity of script error messages.

Basic Application Administration

Most of the common application configuration properties can be defined using the `AppFriendlyName`, `AppRoot`, `AppIsolated`, `AccessExecute`, and `AccessRead` properties.

Querying Application Configuration Using Visual Basic

To query an existing application configuration programmatically, you can use the following Visual Basic code to display the application's attributes:

```
Dim Application as IADs
Dim ServerName As String
Dim Index As Long
ServerName = "IIS_Server_Name"
Index = Site_Index_Value
Set Application = GetObject("IIS://" & ServerName & "/W3SVC/" & Index & "/ROOT")
Debug.Print "Friendly Name:" & vbTab & vbTab & vbTab &
↪Application.AppFriendlyName
Debug.Print "Application Root:" & vbTab & vbTab & Application.AppRoot
Debug.Print "Isolated Process:" & vbTab & vbTab & Application.AppIsolated
Debug.Print "Read:" & vbTab & vbTab & vbTab & vbTab & Application.AccessRead
Debug.Print "Execute:" & vbTab & vbTab & vbTab & vbTab &
↪Application.AccessExecute
```

Setting Application Configuration Using Visual Basic

To define a new application, you can do so by configuring the appropriate properties in the following Visual Basic code:

```
Dim Application As IADs
Dim ServerName As String
Dim Index As Long
Dim ApplicationName As String
Dim Isolated As Boolean
Dim Read As Boolean
Dim Execute As Boolean
ServerName = "IIS_Server_Name"
Index = Site_Index_Value
ApplicationName = "Application_Name"
Isolated = True
Read = True
Execute = True
Set Application = GetObject("IIS://" & ServerName & "/W3SVC/" & Index & "/ROOT")
Application.AppRoot = Replace(Application.ADsPath, "IIS://" & ServerName, "/LM")
Application.AppFriendlyName = ApplicationName
Application.AppIsolated = Isolated
Application.AccessRead = Read
Application.AccessExecute = Execute
Application.SetInfo
```

Advanced Application Administration

In addition to basic application administration, you can also configure the default behavior of the application server. As shown in Figure 9.7, you can configure session timeout values, buffering, parent paths, the default language used for ASP scripts and the timeout value for ASP script execution.

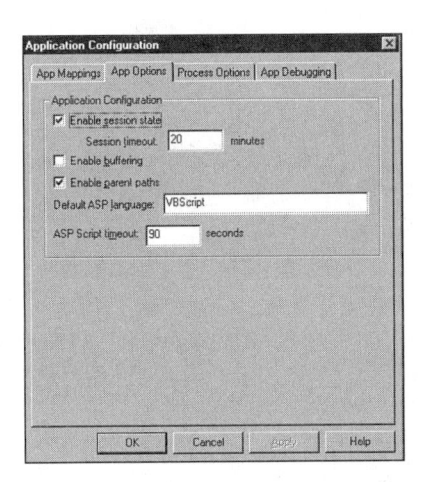

Figure 9.7 *Application Configuration dialog box—App Options tab.*

Configuring Application Options Using Visual Basic

Consider the following Visual Basic code to demonstrate the configuration of each of these properties:

```
Dim Application as IADs
Dim ServerName As String
Dim Index As Long
ServerName = "IIS_Server_Name"
Index = Site_Index_Value
Set Application = GetObject("IIS://" & ServerName & "/W3SVC/" & Index & "/ROOT")
Debug.Print "Session Timeout:" & vbTab & Application.AspSessionTimeout
Debug.Print "Buffering:" & vbTab & vbTab & Application.AspBufferingOn
Debug.Print "Parent Paths:" & vbTab & vbTab & Application.AspEnableParentPaths
Debug.Print "Script Language:" & vbTab & Application.AspScriptLanguage
Debug.Print "Script Timeout:" & vbTab & Application.AspScriptTimeout
```

Process Options Manipulation

Using ADSI, you can also configure the behavior of IIS service event logging, error handling, ASP caching, and CGI timeout values, as shown in Figure 9.8.

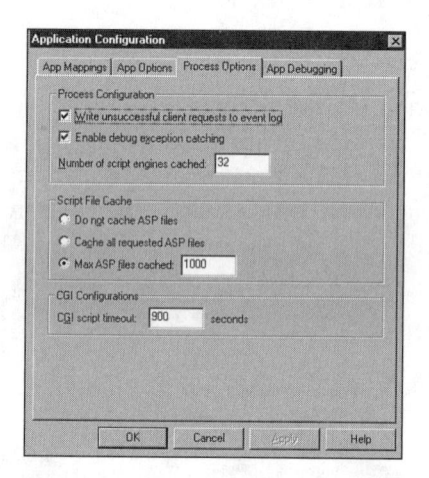

Figure 9.8 *Application Configuration dialog box—Process Options tab.*

The following Visual Basic code shows each of the properties used to manipulate the Process Options tab in the IIS 4.0 MMC ISM snap-in:

```
Dim Application as IADs
Dim ServerName As String
Dim Index As Long
ServerName = "IIS_Server_Name"
Index = Site_Index_Value
Set Application = GetObject("IIS://" & ServerName & "/W3SVC/" & Index & "/ROOT")
Debug.Print "NT Event Logging:" & vbTab & vbTab & vbTab & vbTab & vbTab &
```

Programmatically Administering the Home Directory Property Sheet

```
Application.AspLogErrorRequests
Debug.Print "Debug Exceptions:" & vbTab & vbTab & vbTab & vbTab &
Application.AspExceptionCatchEnable
Debug.Print "Script Engines Cached:" & vbTab & vbTab & vbTab &
Application.AspScriptEngineCacheMax
Debug.Print "Script File Cache:" & vbTab & vbTab & vbTab & vbTab &
Application.AspScriptFileCacheSize
Set Application = GetObject("IIS://" & ServerName & "/W3SVC/" & Index)
Debug.Print "CGI Script Timeout:" & vbTab & vbTab & vbTab & vbTab &
↪Application.CGITimeout
```

Use Table 9.3 to toggle the Script File Cache option button.

Table 9.3 Script File Cache Option Button Toggling Information

Integer	Description
0	Do not cache ASP files
-1	Cache all requested ASP files
n	Max ASP files cached

ASP Debugging Options Manipulation
In a development environment, it may be helpful to enable ASP debugging for ASP scripts to help track down issues as they arise. As shown in Figure 9.9, IIS allows you to configure both client- and server-side ASP script debugging as well as determine the nature of error messages displayed at the client.

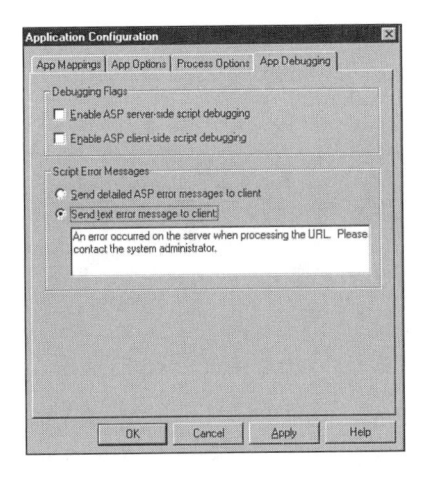

Figure 9.9 *Application Configuration dialog box—App Debugging tab.*

Manipulating ASP Debugging Option Using Visual Basic

Consider the following Visual Basic code as an example of application debug behavior manipulation:

```
Dim Application As IADs
Dim ServerName As String
Dim Index As Long
ServerName = "IIS_Server_Name"
Index = Site_Index_Value
Set Application = GetObject("IIS://" & ServerName & "/W3SVC/" & Index & "/ROOT")
Debug.Print "ASP Server-Side Debugging:" & vbTab & vbTab & vbTab &
➥Application.AppAllowDebugging
Debug.Print "ASP Client-Side Debugging:" & vbTab & vbTab & vbTab &
➥Application.AppAllowClientDebug
Debug.Print "Detailed Client Error Messages:" & vbTab & vbTab &
➥Application.AspScriptErrorSentToBrowser
If Application.AspScriptErrorSentToBrowser = False then
  Debug.Print "Error Message Text:" & vbTab & vbTab & vbTab & vbTab &
➥Application.AspScriptErrorMessage
End If
```

HTTP URL Redirection

As shown in Figure 9.10, IIS has the ability to redirect users to a new site. This can be handy in cases where the content has been moved to an alternate location or the server is in the process of being decommissioned.

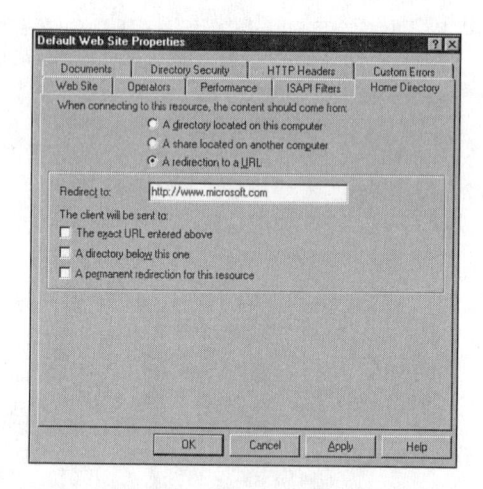

Figure 9.10 *Default Web Site Properties Configuration dialog box—Home Directory tab (URL redirection).*

Using the URL redirection option, you can redirect all requests to an alternate URL. To take advantage of this option programmatically, you assign the HttpRedirect property to the desired URL and desired behavior flags.

Quite often, you want to redirect the user to a new site by concatenating some part of the original URL to a new site while retaining all original parameters. You can perform this by using redirect variables. Variables you can use are listed in Table 9.4.

Table 9.4 Redirect Variables and Descriptions

Variable	Description
$P	Passes the original parameters to the new URL. To redirect www.site1.com?search=exact to www.site2.com?search=exact you could specify www.site2.com?$P as the redirect URL.
$Q	Passes the original parameters to the new URL. In this option, you can pass all parameters (including the question mark) to the new URL. To redirect www.site1.com?search=exact to www.site2.com?search=exact you could specify www.site2.com$Q as the redirect URL.
$S	Passes a matched suffix to the new URL. To redirect requests for /BetaSearch/Find.EXE to /Search/Find.Exe, you could specify the following redirect URL: /Search$S.
$V	Passes the requested URL without the server name. To redirect all requests from http://www.isp.net/employment/hot_jobs.asp to http://www.consulting.com/employment/hot_jobs.asp you can use the following redirect URL: http://www.consulting.com$V.
!	Do not redirect. This can be used to prevent redirecting a directory or file.

> **Tip**
>
> *URL redirection also supports the use of wildcards. Check the IIS product documentation for more information on the use of redirection wildcards.* ◆

Three options exist to configure the behavior of the URL redirection:

- **The Exact URL Entered Above.** This sends an HTTP redirect header to the specified URL. All variables and wildcards can be used with this option.
- **A Directory Below This One.** This allows you to re-map a parent directory to a child node.
- **Permanent Redirection for This Resource.** This changes the HTTP header from a 301 Temporary Redirect to a 302 Permanent Redirect. In some cases, this can be used to update the URL associated with a bookmark.

Armed with this background information, you can now begin programmatic manipulation of the URL redirect functionality of a home directory.

To perform this redirect functionality, call upon the `HttpRedirect` administrative property. This property is a single string that expects to receive data in one of two formats:

- *Destination, Flag,* (for example http://www.microsoft.com, EXACT_DESTINATION,)
- *Destination, Flag1, Flag2,* (for example http://www.microsoft.com, EXACT_DESTINATION, PERMANENT,)

With the second format, you can supply multiple flags for the same destination.

Valid flags for this property are as follows:

- EXACT_DESTINATION
- CHILD_ONLY
- PERMANENT

These flags directly correlate to the three URL redirection behavior options described previously.

Querying Current Running Redirection Status Using Visual Basic

To determine where a site has been redirected to, use the following Visual Basic code:

```
Dim Resource As IADs
Dim ServerName As String
Dim Index As Long
ServerName = "IIS_Server_Name"
Index = Site_Index_Value
Set Resource = GetObject("IIS://" & ServerName & "/W3SVC/" & Index & "/ROOT")
Debug.Print Resource.HttpRedirect
```

Setting New Resource Redirection Using Visual Basic

To establish a new resource redirection, use the following Visual Basic code:

```
Dim Resource As IADs
Dim ServerName As String
Dim SiteIndex As Long
Dim HttpRedirectString As String
ServerName = "IIS_Server_Name"
SiteIndex = Site_Index_Value
HttpRedirectString = "http://www.sitename.com,FLAG,"
Set Resource = GetObject("IIS://" & ServerName & "/W3SVC/" & SiteIndex & "/ROOT")
Resource.HttpRedirect = HttpRedirectString
Resource.SetInfo
```

Programmatically Administering the Documents Property Sheet

If a document name is not specified on the URL, IIS can be configured to automatically determine the intended document, as shown in Figure 9.11.

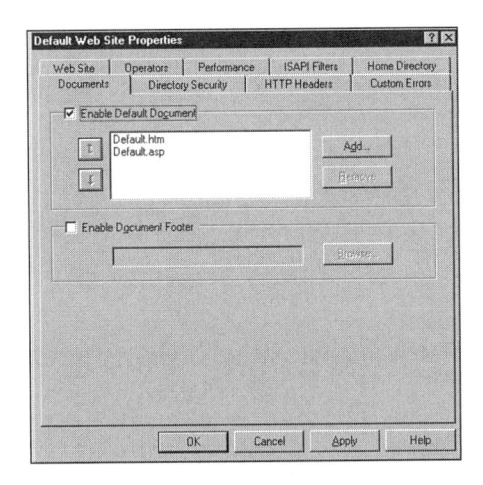

Figure 9.11 *Default Web Site Properties Configuration dialog box—Documents tab.*

In addition, you can configure IIS to attach an HTML footer to all documents transferred from your Web server to the client browser. This can be especially handy for navigation bars, copyright notices, or other legal information.

Enable Default Document

To save the user from having to know the main document for your site, you can specify the name of the document to be returned to the client when the filename is omitted from the URL.

To enable this functionality, two properties must be configured: `EnableDefaultDoc` and `DefaultDoc`. `EnableDefaultDoc` is a Boolean value describing whether the default document list should be checked or not. `DefaultDoc` is a comma-delimited list stored as a string (not in a variant array) that lists the names of documents that will be sought when the user does not specify a filename in the URL. Together, these two properties allow the user to enter a site without typing or even knowing the particular filename.

Querying *EnableDefaultDoc* Using Visual Basic

To find if a default document is in use for a specific site, use the following Visual Basic code:

```
Dim Resource As IADs
Dim ServerName As String
Dim Index As Long
ServerName = "IIS_Server_Name"
Index = Site_Index_Value
Set Resource = GetObject("IIS://" & ServerName & "/W3SVC/" & Index & "/ROOT")
Debug.Print Resource.EnableDefaultDoc
```

Setting *EnableDefaultDoc* Using Visual Basic

To set a new value for `EnableDefaultDoc`, use the following Visual Basic code:

```
Dim Resource As IADs
Dim ServerName As String
Dim SiteIndex As Long
Dim EnableDefaultDocument As Boolean
ServerName = "IIS_Server_Name"
SiteIndex = Site_Index_Value
EnableDefaultDocument = True
Set Resource = GetObject("IIS://" & ServerName & "/W3SVC/" & SiteIndex & "/ROOT")
Resource.EnableDefaultDoc = EnableDefaultDocument
Resource.SetInfo
```

Querying *DefaultDoc* Using Visual Basic

To find the default documents used for a particular site, use the following Visual Basic code to return a comma-delimited list of files:

```
Dim Resource As IADs
Dim ServerName As String
Dim Index As Long
ServerName = "IIS_Server_Name"
Index = Site_Index_Value
Set Resource = GetObject("IIS://" & ServerName & "/W3SVC/" & Index & "/ROOT")
Debug.Print Resource.DefaultDoc
```

Setting *DefaultDoc* Using Visual Basic

To set a new default document for a site, use the following Visual Basic code to pass in a comma-delimited list of documents. The order is important in the list; it determines the order in which IIS will look for the default document if more than one file in the list exists in the file system directory.

```
Dim Resource As IADs
Dim ServerName As String
Dim SiteIndex As Long
Dim DefaultDocument As String
ServerName = "IIS_Server_Name"
```

```
SiteIndex = Site_Index_Value
DefaultDocument = "default.asp,default.htm,index.html"
Set Resource = GetObject("IIS://" & ServerName & "/W3SVC/" & SiteIndex & "/ROOT")
Resource.DefaultDoc = DefaultDocument
Resource.SetInfo
```

Enable Document Footer

The document footer allows the administrator to attach an HTML-format file to all outbound HTML files from the server. This can be especially handy for navigation tool bars, legal notices, or even contact information. Unlike the DefaultDoc list, only a single file is used, and the full physical path to the file is specified in the DefaultDocFooter property.

After the DefaultDocFooter property populates the path to the HTML file, you can enable the footer by setting the EnableDocFooter property to True.

Querying *DefaultDocFooter* Using Visual Basic

To find the name of the HTML file attached to all HTML page requests, use the following Visual Basic code:

```
Dim Resource As IADs
Dim ServerName As String
Dim Index As Long
ServerName = "IIS_Server_Name"
Index = Site_Index_Value
Set Resource = GetObject("IIS://" & ServerName & "/W3SVC/" & Index & "/ROOT")
Debug.Print Resource.DefaultDocFooter
```

Setting *DefaultDocFooter* Using Visual Basic

To establish a default document footer for a site, use the following Visual Basic code:

```
Dim Resource As IADs
Dim ServerName As String
Dim SiteIndex As Long
Dim DefaultDocumentFooter As String
ServerName = "IIS_Server_Name"
SiteIndex = Site_Index_Value
DefaultDocumentFooter = "c:\legal_footers\copyright.htm"
Set Resource = GetObject("IIS://" & ServerName & "/W3SVC/" & SiteIndex & "/ROOT")
Resource.DefaultDocFooter = DefaultDocumentFooter
Resource.SetInfo
```

Querying *EnableDocFooter* Using Visual Basic

To query whether or not the document footer is enabled for a site, use the following Visual Basic code to return a Boolean value representing the status of the property:

```
Dim Resource As IADs
Dim ServerName As String
Dim Index As Long
ServerName = "IIS_Server_Name"
Index = Site_Index_Value
Set Resource = GetObject("IIS://" & ServerName & "/W3SVC/" & Index & "/ROOT")
Debug.Print Resource.EnableDocFooter
```

Setting *EnableDocFooter* Using Visual Basic

After establishing the name of the HTML file to be used, you must enable the use of the document footer by setting the `EnableDocFooter` to True if you want to attach a footer to HTML page requests. Use the following Visual Basic code to perform this task:

```
Dim Resource As IADs
Dim ServerName As String
Dim SiteIndex As Long
Dim EnableDocumentFooter As Boolean
ServerName = "IIS_Server_Name"
SiteIndex = Site_Index_Value
EnableDocumentFooter = True
Set Resource = GetObject("IIS://" & ServerName & "/W3SVC/" & SiteIndex & "/ROOT")
Resource.EnableDocFooter = EnableDocumentFooter
Resource.SetInfo
```

Programmatically Administering the Directory Security Property Sheet

Using the Directory Security properties of IIS, as shown in Figure 9.12, you can designate the authentication method(s) employed for the site as well as its SSL usage parameters, and even restrict which IP addresses and domains will have access to the file resources of the site.

Administrators who assign permissions to files and directories in the file system (rather than allowing the default Everyone—Full Control NTFS Permissions to remain) will undoubtedly agree that proper file and directory permissioning is an extremely tedious process. After the permissions on the directories have been assigned, access control is governed by membership in NT security groups.

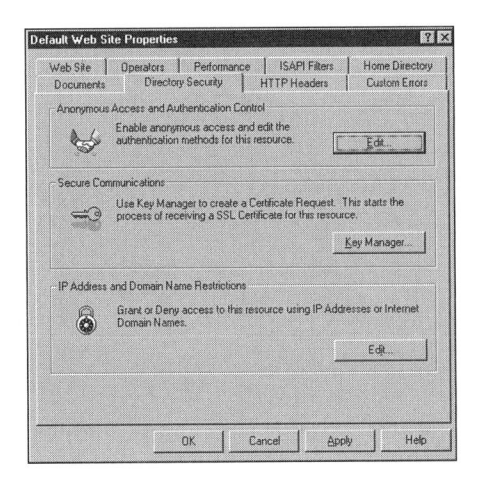

Figure 9.12 *Default Web Site Properties Configuration dialog box—Directory Security tab.*

In large distributed environments, this process becomes even more tedious; the engineers, architects, and developers creating these solutions architectures are often dependent upon another group to bring their work into reality. Such an environment requires detailed planning, many hours in a laboratory environment, and, of course, excellent documentation.

An alternative to this is to spend time in the laboratory creating a script, which, upon completion, can be easily sent to anyone in the enterprise and executed using the procedure you refined in the lab.

Authentication Methods

When it comes to IIS, there is an extremely tight coupling between NTFS permissions and the IIS authentication method used to verify user credentials. Any developer expecting flawless implementation of their latest Web application should carefully consider creating an IIS deployment package. By combining a CACLs script with the authentication control features in ADSI, implementation of a new Web application becomes more reliable and significantly less tedious.

As shown in Figure 9.13, IIS provides a graphical user interface within the Internet Service Manager to manipulate the authentication methods used for a resource. Using the AuthAnonymous, AuthBasic, AuthNTLM, and AuthFlags properties, you can programmatically manipulate the authentication method configuration.

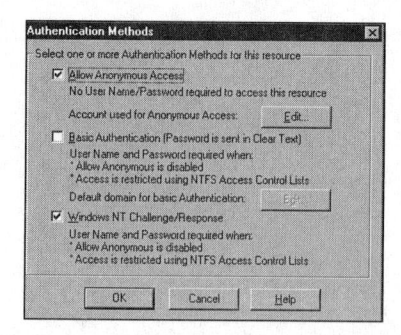

Figure 9.13 *Authentication Methods dialog box.*

Using these properties, you can enable multiple authentication methods for any given resource. When anonymous access is enabled, IIS will try to use the anonymous account before attempting to use client credentials. If the anonymous account is not authorized to access the requested resource and basic authentication is enabled on the resource, IIS will prompt the user to enter a set of credentials authorized to access the resource.

Using NTLM, if the client's installation of Internet Explorer is configured to supply credentials automatically, the user's credentials will automatically be examined to determine whether they will allow access to the resource. If not, the user is prompted for a set of credentials authorized to access the resource.

> *Note*
>
> *In environments where either Internet Explorer or Netscape Navigator (or another browser) is used, you should enable both basic and NTLM authentication methods when securing a resource to assure compatibility with all major browser types. By default, Internet Explorer will attempt to request to use NTLM authentication before prompting the user for credentials to be passed using the basic authentication method.* ◆

Querying Authentication Methods Used for a Given Resource Using Visual Basic

To find which authentication method is in place for a particular resource, use the following Visual Basic code:

```
Dim Resource As IADs
Dim ServerName As String
Dim SiteIndex As Long
ServerName = "IIS_Server_Name"
SiteIndex = Site_Index_Value
Set Resource = GetObject("IIS://" & ServerName & "/W3SVC/" & SiteIndex & "/ROOT")
```

```
Debug.Print "Authentication Methods for " & Resource.ADsPath & ":"
Debug.Print ""
Debug.Print "Anonymous Access:" & vbTab & vbTab & Resource.AuthAnonymous
If Resource.AuthAnonymous = True Then
  Debug.Print vbTab & "Anonymous User Account Name:" & vbTab & vbTab & vbTab &
  ↪vbTab & _
Resource.AnonymousUsername
  Debug.Print vbTab & "Anonymous User Account Password:" & vbTab & vbTab & vbTab
  ↪& _
Resource.AnonymousUserPass
  Debug.Print vbTab & "Anonymous User Password Synchronization:" & vbTab &
Resource.AnonymousPasswordSync
End If
Debug.Print "Basic Authentication:" & vbTab & Resource.AuthBasic
If Resource.AuthBasic = True Then
  Debug.Print vbTab & "Default Authentication Domain: " & vbTab & vbTab & vbTab &
  ↪vbTab & _
Resource.DefaultLogonDomain
End If
Debug.Print "NTLM Authentication:" & vbTab & Resource.AuthNTLM
```

Anonymous Access

To use anonymous access for a directory, you must also assign a username and password to be used to access the directory. To do this, you can modify the AnonymousUserName, AnonymousUserPass, and AnonymousPasswordSync properties, as shown in Figure 9.14.

Figure 9.14 *Anonymous User Account configuration dialog box.*

Enabling Anonymous Access Using Visual Basic

To allow anonymous access for a given resource, use the following Visual Basic code:

```
Dim Resource As IADs
Dim ServerName As String
Dim SiteIndex As Long
Dim EnableAnonymousAccess As Boolean
Dim AnonUserName as String
Dim AnonUserPassword as String
Dim AnonPasswordSync as Boolean
ServerName = "IIS_Server_Name"
SiteIndex = Site_Index_Value
EnableAnonymousAccess = True
```

```
AnonUserName = "Username_for_Anonymous_Access"
AnonUserPassword = "Password_for_Anonymous_Access_Account"
AnonPasswordSync = True
Set Resource = GetObject("IIS://" & ServerName & "/W3SVC/" & SiteIndex & "/ROOT")
Resource.AuthAnonymous = EnableAnonymousAccess
Resource.AnonymousUsername = AnonUserName
Resource.AnonymousUserPass = AnonUserPassword
Resource.AnonymousPasswordSync = AnonPasswordSync
Resource.SetInfo
```

Basic Authentication

If you must allow non-Microsoft browsers to view your site, you have no choice but to use basic authentication to secure the site. In this authentication method, the password is passed in clear text across the wire, making this a poor choice for any high security site unless SSL is used in conjunction with the basic authentication method.

As shown in Figure 9.15, in this authentication method, you can define the default domain used for authentication if the user does not specify the domain associated with the user account. Programmatically, the default domain is set using the `DefaultLogonDomain` property.

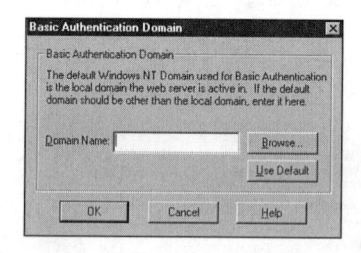

Figure 9.15 *Basic Authentication Domain dialog box.*

Enabling Basic Authentication Using Visual Basic

To enable basic authentication for a given resource, use the following Visual Basic code:

```
Dim Resource As IADs
Dim ServerName As String
Dim SiteIndex As Long
Dim EnableBasicAuth As Boolean
Dim DefaultLogonDomain as String
ServerName = "IIS_Server_Name"
SiteIndex = Site_Index_Value
EnableBasicAuth = True
DefaultLogonDomain = "Domain_Used_for_Authentication"
Set Resource = GetObject("IIS://" & ServerName & "/W3SVC/" & SiteIndex & "/ROOT")
Resource.AuthBasic= EnableBasicAuth
Resource.DefaultLogonDomain = DefaultLogonDomain
Resource.SetInfo
```

NTLM Authentication

If your enterprise has chosen Internet Explorer as the browser of choice for the organization, you should implement the NTLM authentication method for all intranet sites. In addition to eliminating the need to transmit the password across the wire in clear-text, NTLM authentication also allows credentials to be presented without user intervention.

Enabling NTLM Authentication Using Visual Basic
To enable the use of the NTLM authentication method for a given resource, use the following Visual Basic code:

```
Dim Resource As IADs
Dim ServerName As String
Dim SiteIndex As Long
Dim EnableNTLMAuth As Boolean
ServerName = "IIS_Server_Name"
SiteIndex = Site_Index_Value
EnableNTLMAuth = True
Set Resource = GetObject("IIS://" & ServerName & "/W3SVC/" & SiteIndex & "/ROOT")
Resource.AuthNTLM= EnableNTLMAuth
Resource.SetInfo
```

Secure Communications

After installing an SSL certificate using Key Manager, you can assign the key to various resources and define the client authentication behavior using programmatic methods, as shown in Figure 9.16.

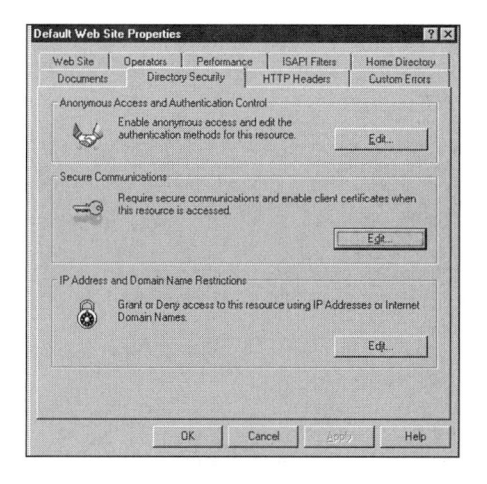

Figure 9.16 *Default Web Site Properties Configuration dialog box—Directory Security tab (SSL Certificate Installed).*

Among these options, you can require that a particular site accepts requests only across a secure channel. Additionally, you can specify that all requests to a resource are restricted to 128-bit encryption.

If clients have X.509 certificates, IIS can map NT usernames to the client certificate to assure the identity of the user. To map users to X.509 certificates, you must perform this action in the MMC. Although you cannot easily map user accounts to X.509 certificates using ADSI, you can, however, specify the default behavior (accept, deny, require) of client certificates for the resource, as shown in Figure 9.17.

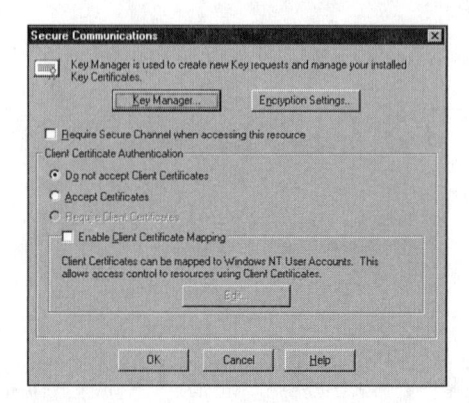

Figure 9.17 *Secure Communications dialog box.*

Querying Secure Communication Configuration Using Visual Basic

Using the following Visual Basic code, each SSL property for a given resource can be displayed:

```
Dim Resource As IADs
Dim ServerName As String
Dim SiteIndex As Long
ServerName = "IIS_Server_Name"
SiteIndex = Site_Index_Value
Set Resource = GetObject("IIS://" & ServerName & "/W3SVC/" & SiteIndex & "/ROOT")
Debug.Print "Require SSL:" & vbTab & vbTab & vbTab & vbTab & vbTab &
↪vbTab & Resource.AccessSSL
Debug.Print "Require 128-bit SSL:" & vbTab & vbTab & vbTab & vbTab & vbTab &
↪Resource.AccessSSL128
Debug.Print "Map Client Certificates to NT UserIDs:" & vbTab & vbTab &
↪Resource.AccessSSLMapCert
Debug.Print "Negotiate Client Certificates:" & vbTab & vbTab & vbTab & vbTab &
↪Resource.AccessSSLNegotiateCert
Debug.Print "Require Client Certificates:" & vbTab & vbTab & vbTab & vbTab &
↪Resource.AccessSSLRequireCert
```

Setting New Secure Communication Configuration Using Visual Basic
Using the following Visual Basic code, each available SSL property is manipulated:

```
Dim Resource As IADs
Dim ServerName As String
Dim SiteIndex As Long
ServerName = "IIS_Server_Name"
SiteIndex = Site_Index_Value
Set Resource = GetObject("IIS://" & ServerName & "/W3SVC/" & SiteIndex & "/ROOT")
Resource.AccessSSL = True
Resource.AccessSSL128 = True
Resource.AccessSSLMapCert = True
Resource.AccessSSLNegotiateCert = True
Resource.AccessSSLRequireCert = True
Resource.SetInfo
```

To re-create the behavior of the ISM dialog box, use Table 9.5.

Table 9.5 ISM Settings and Property Assignments

ISM Setting	Property Assignments
Require secure channel when accessing this resource	AccessSSL = True
Require 128-bit encryption	AccessSSL128 = True
Do not accept client certificates	AccessSSLNegotiateCert = False
Accept certificates	AccessSSLNegotiateCert = True
Require client certificates	AccessSSL = True AccessSSLNegotiateCert = True AccessSSLRequireCert = True
Enable client certificate mapping	AccessSSLMapCert = True

Restricting Access by IP Address

Using IP address restrictions, you can ensure that certain clients do not access a particular resource. To perform this task, you can configure IIS to reject all clients presenting a specific IP address in the HTTP request header if it matches the address ranges configured in the IPSecurity property, as shown in Figure 9.18.

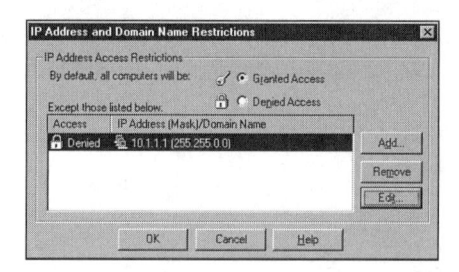

Figure 9.18 *IP Address and Domain Name Restrictions dialog box.*

Although you can also configure IIS to limit access by DNS domain, Microsoft strongly advises against this access control method because reverse DNS lookup is required for each request. If at all possible, this method should be avoided to eliminate the significant performance penalties incurred by these queries.

IP security requires construction of an array of IP addresses that are consequently assigned to one of the properties of the IPSecurity object listed in Table 9.6.

Table 9.6 IPSecurity Object Properties and Descriptions

Property	Description
IPGrant	Array of IP Addresses granted access—stored in variant array of strings in format *IPAddress, Subnet Mask*
IPDeny	Array of IP Addresses denied access—stored in variant array of strings in format *IPAddress, Subnet Mask*
DomainGrant	Array of strings representing DNS domains granted access to resources
DomainDeny	Array of strings representing DNS domains denied access to resources

Querying IP Address Restrictions Using Visual Basic

To find the current IP address and DNS domain restrictions effective for a particular site, use the following Visual Basic code:

```
Dim Site As IADs
Dim ServerName As String
Dim SiteIndex As Long
Dim IPSecurity As Variant
ServerName = "IIS_Server_Name"
SiteIndex = Site_Index_Value
Set Site = GetObject("IIS://" & ServerName & "/W3SVC/" & SiteIndex & "/ROOT")
Set IPSecurity = Site.IPSecurity
```

Programmatically Administering the Directory Security Property Sheet 303

```
    If IPSecurity.GrantByDefault Then
        Debug.Print "All addresses will be allowed, except as follows:"
        For Each Entry In IPSecurity.IPDeny
            If InStr(1, Entry, "255.255.255.255") Then
                Debug.Print vbTab & "Denied IP: " & vbTab & vbTab & Replace(Entry,
                ↪", 255.255.255.255", "")
            Else
                Debug.Print vbTab & "Denied Subnet: " & vbTab & Entry
            End If
        Next
        For Each Entry In IPSecurity.DomainDeny
            Debug.Print vbTab & "Denied Domain: " & vbTab & Entry
        Next
    Else
        Debug.Print "All addresses will be blocked, except as follows:"
        For Each Entry In IPSecurity.IPGrant
            If InStr(1, Entry, "255.255.255.255") Then
                Debug.Print vbTab & "Allowed IP: " & vbTab & vbTab &
                ↪Replace(Entry, ", 255.255.255.255", "")
            Else
                Debug.Print vbTab & "Allowed Subnet: " & vbTab & Entry
            End If
        Next
        For Each Entry In IPSecurity.DomainGrant
            Debug.Print vbTab & "Allowed Domain: " & vbTab & Entry
        Next
    End If
```

Setting New IP Address Restrictions Using Visual Basic

To create a new IP address or DNS domain restriction programmatically, use the following Visual Basic code:

```
    Dim Site As IADs
    Dim ServerName As String
    Dim SiteIndex As Long
    Dim IPSecurity As Variant
    Dim IPAddress As String
    Dim IPSubnet As String
    Dim Domain As String
    Dim ActionType As String
    ServerName = "IIS_Server_Name"
    SiteIndex = Site_Index_Value
    IPAddress = "xxx.xxx.xxx.xxx"
    IPSubnet = "xxx.xxx.xxx.xxx"
    Domain = "DNS_Domain.Name"
    ActionType = "GRANTIP"
    'ActionType = "GRANTSUBNET"
    'ActionType = "GRANTDOMAIN"
    'ActionType = "DENYIP"
    'ActionType = "DENYSUBNET"
    'ActionType = "DENYDOMAIN"
    Set Site = GetObject("IIS://" & ServerName & "/W3SVC/" & SiteIndex & "/ROOT")
```

```
Select Case ActionType
    Case "GRANTIP"
        Set IPSecurity = Site.IPSecurity
        IPSecurity.GrantByDefault = False
        Site.IPSecurity = IPSecurity
        Site.SetInfo
        IPSecurity.IPGrant = Array(IPAddress & ", 255.255.255.255")
        Site.IPSecurity = IPSecurity
        Site.SetInfo
    Case "GRANTSUBNET"
        Set IPSecurity = Site.IPSecurity
        IPSecurity.GrantByDefault = False
        IPSecurity.IPGrant = Array(IPAddress & ", " & IPSubnet)
        Site.IPSecurity = IPSecurity
        Site.SetInfo
    Case "GRANTDOMAIN"
        Set IPSecurity = Site.IPSecurity
        IPSecurity.GrantByDefault = False
        IPSecurity.DomainGrant = Array(Domain)
        Site.IPSecurity = IPSecurity
        Site.SetInfo
    Case "DENYIP"
        Set IPSecurity = Site.IPSecurity
        IPSecurity.GrantByDefault = True
        IPSecurity.IPDeny = Array(IPAddress & ", 255.255.255.255")
        Site.IPSecurity = IPSecurity
        Site.SetInfo
    Case "DENYSUBNET"
        Set IPSecurity = Site.IPSecurity
        IPSecurity.GrantByDefault = True
        IPSecurity.IPDeny = Array(IPAddress & ", " & IPSubnet)
        Site.IPSecurity = IPSecurity
        Site.SetInfo
    Case "DENYDOMAIN"
        Set IPSecurity = Site.IPSecurity
        IPSecurity.GrantByDefault = True
        IPSecurity.DomainDeny = Array(Domain)
        Site.IPSecurity = IPSecurity
        Site.SetInfo
End Select
```

> **Note**
>
> *To set a new IP address restriction, simply uncomment the desired ActionType variable assignment and verify that all associated variables have been assigned.* ◆

Programmatically Administering the HTTP Headers Property Sheet

As shown in Figure 9.19, IIS allows you to modify the contents of HTTP headers. Using ADSI, you can manipulate the `HttpExpires`, `HttpCustomHeaders`, `HttpPics`, and `MimeMap` properties to manipulate the information returned in the header of each HTML page sent to the browser.

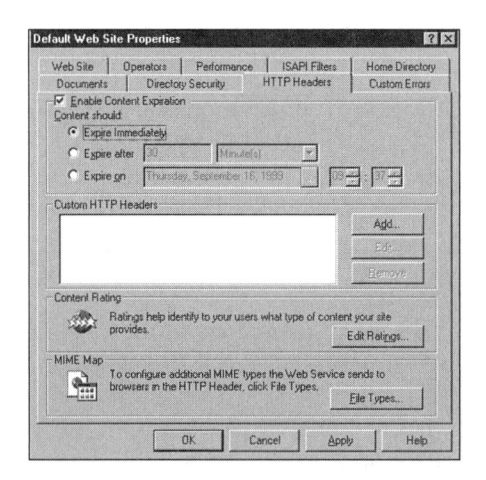

Figure 9.19 *Default Web Site Properties Configuration dialog box—HTTP Headers tab.*

These properties are useful for defining the expiration date of HTML content and defining any custom header information you want to send with all HTML transmissions. Additionally, you can define RSAC ratings for the content of individual resources to limit access to explicit content. Lastly, you can define a list of MIME types that should override the server-based MIME types.

Content Expiration

If you maintain a site that is constantly providing fresh information on a particular page, you may want to configure content expiration for a directory or group of resources. By configuring content expiration, you can prevent the client browser or caching proxy server from presenting stale data to the client. This is especially important where ASP scripts are used to access databases (assuming the developers have not already set Response.Expires=0) to guarantee that dynamic content is always generated from the query.

By default, IIS will not expire any HTTP content. To enable content expiration, you must set the HttpExpires property to a string in one of the formats found in Table 9.7.

Table 9.7 HttpExpires *Property String Definitions and Descriptions*

String Definition	Description
Null	Content expiration is disabled.
D, Hex(*time_in_seconds*)	Dynamic configuration. Defines the number of seconds until expiration. To specify content that never expires, use D,&HFFFFFFFF. To expire content immediately (recommended for ASP queries) use D, 0.
S, *UTCString*	Defines the UTC date for expiration. Use the following string as a guide: S, Fri, 10 Sep 1999 00:15:56 GMT.

Querying Current Value of Content Expiration Using Visual Basic

To find the content expiration date for the bound resource, use the following Visual Basic code:

```
Dim Resource As IADs
Dim ServerName As String
Dim Index As Long
ServerName = "IIS_Server_Name"
Index = Site_Index_Value
Set Resource = GetObject("IIS://" & ServerName & "/W3SVC/" & Index & "/ROOT")
Debug.Print Resource.HttpExpires
```

Enabling Content Expiration Using Visual Basic

To enable content expiration for a Web resource, use the following Visual Basic code:

```
Dim Resource As IADs
Dim ServerName As String
Dim SiteIndex As Long
Dim ContentExpiration As String
ServerName = "IIS_Server_Name"
SiteIndex = Site_Index_Value
ContentExpiration = "D, 0"
Set Resource = GetObject("IIS://" & ServerName & "/W3SVC/" & SiteIndex & "/ROOT")
Resource.HttpExpires = ContentExpiration
Resource.SetInfo
```

Custom HTTP Headers

To customize the header information passed to the client with each HTTP request, you can define a custom HTTP header. By assigning a list of name and value pair strings to the HttpCustomHeaders property, you can establish custom HTTP headers for a particular resource.

These strings take the format *Key: Value*.

Querying Custom HTTP Header Configurations Using Visual Basic

To find out the value of the current HTTP header configuration, you can use the following Visual Basic code:

```
Dim Resource As IADs
Dim ServerName As String
Dim Index As Long
ServerName = "IIS_Server_Name"
Index = Site_Index_Value
Set Resource = GetObject("IIS://" & ServerName & "/W3SVC/" & Index & "/ROOT")
For Each HeaderEntry in Resource.HttpCustomHeaders
    Debug.Print HeaderEntry
Next
```

Assigning a Custom HTTP Header Using Visual Basic

In addition to industry standard HTTP header information, you can also establish custom HTTP header information. Use the following Visual Basic code as a guide to perform this task:

```
Dim Resource As IADs
Dim ServerName As String
Dim Index As Long
Dim NewHeaderArray As Variant
ServerName = "IIS_Server_Name"
Index = Site_Index_Value
NewHeaderArray = Array("HeaderName: HeaderValue")
Set Resource = GetObject("IIS://" & ServerName & "/W3SVC/" & Index & "/ROOT")
Resource.HttpCustomHeaders = NewHeaderArray
Resource.SetInfo
```

> *Note*
>
> *As shown in the code segment, HTTP headers should be formatted as* Name: Value *when assembling the array.* ♦

Platform for Internet Content Selection (PICS) Ratings

Unlike other forms of mass media, the World Wide Web is an extremely easy place to publish anything from photos of your family vacation to your recent flirtations with poetry. With such a wide variety of information available at our youth's fingertips, many parents and educational institutions have been wrestling with methods to reduce the impact of explicit material on future generations. One method commonly implemented by organizations that carry explicit content utilizes PICS ratings.

If your organization has elected to rate its generally available content, you can programmatically assign ratings to any given resource using ADSI, as shown in Figure 9.20.

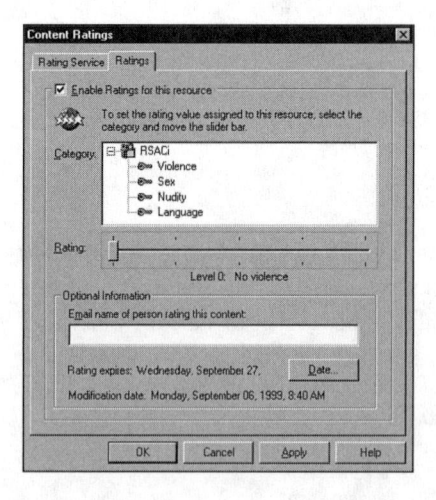

Figure 9.20 *Content Ratings dialog box.*

The RSACi service rates content is listed in Table 9.8.

Table 9.8   RSACi Service Rates Content

Criteria	Level	Description
Violence	0	No violence or sports-related violence
Violence	1	Injury to a human being
Violence	2	Destruction of realistic objects
Violence	3	Aggressive violence or death to humans
Violence	4	Rape or wanton, gratuitous violence
Sex	0	Romance or innocent kissing
Sex	1	Passionate kissing
Sex	2	Clothed sexual touching

Criteria	Level	Description
Sex	3	Non-explicit sexual acts
Sex	4	Explicit sexual acts or sex crimes
Nudity	0	None
Nudity	1	Revealing attire
Nudity	2	Partial nudity
Nudity	3	Frontal nudity
Nudity	4	Frontal nudity (qualifying as provocative display)
Language	0	None
Language	1	Mild expletives
Language	2	Moderate expletives or profanity
Language	3	Strong language or hate speech
Language	4	Crude, vulgar language, or extreme hate speech

By assigning a specially formatted string to the HttpPics property for a bound resource, you can set the PICS rating to the appropriate RSACi rating.

The format for the string is as follows:

```
"PICS-Label: (PICS-1.0 "http://www.rsac.org/ratingsv01.html" l by
➥"contact_e-mail@company.com" on "year.month.dayThour:minute-GMToffset"
➥exp "year.month.dayThour:minute-GMToffset" r (v n s n n n l n))
```

For example, consider the following data:

Creation Date	2 Jan 2000 – 01:00pm
Rating User	webmaster@dot.com
Location	Chicago
Expiration Date	2 Jun 2000
Violence	1
Nudity	1
Sex	1
Language	1

The resulting PICs label would be as follows:

```
"PICS-Label: (PICS-1.0 "http://www.rsac.org/ratingsv01.html" l by
➥"webmaster@dot.com" on "2000.0.02T13:00-0600" exp "2000.0.02T12:00-0600"
➥r (v 1 s 1 n 2 l 1))
```

Querying RSACi Ratings for a Given Resource Using Visual Basic

To find the RSACi ratings for the bound resource, use the following Visual Basic code:

```
Dim Resource As IADs
Dim ServerName As String
Dim Index As Long
Dim Entry As Variant
ServerName = "IIS_Server_Name"
Index = Site_Index_Value
Set Resource = GetObject("IIS://" & ServerName & "/W3SVC/" & Index & "/ROOT")
For Each Entry In Resource.HttpPics
    Debug.Print Entry
Next
```

Setting RSACi Rating for a Given Resource Using Visual Basic

With the background information used to form the string required to enable ratings for the resource, consider the following Visual Basic code to establish RSACi ratings for a given site:

```
Dim Resource As IADs
Dim ServerName As String
Dim Index As Long
Dim PICSLabel as String
ServerName = "IIS_Server_Name"
Index = Site_Index_Value
PICSLabel = "PICS_Format_String"
Set Resource = GetObject("IIS://" & ServerName & "/W3SVC/" & Index & "/ROOT")
Resource.HttpPics = PICSLabel
Resource.SetInfo
```

> *Note*
>
> The PICS string requires you to use a double quote as part of the string. To establish strings containing double quotes, simply double the number of quotes. An example follows:
>
> ```
> "PICS-Label: (PICS-1.0 ""http://www.rsac.org/ratingsv01.html"" 1 by
> ""webmaster@dot.com"" on ""2000.0.02T13:00-0500"" exp ""2000.0.02T12:00-
> 0500"" r (v 1 s 1 n 2 l 1))
> ```

MIME Type Management

Just as you can define MIME types at the server level, you can also override MIME types at the resource level. Using the same procedure you used to set global MIME types, you can define how you want MIME type information to be passed in the header.

Querying MIME Type Definitions for Resources Using Visual Basic
To query existing MIME type definitions for a resource, use the following Visual Basic code:

```
Dim Resource As IADs
Dim ServerName As String
Dim Index As Long
ServerName = "IIS_Server_Name"
Index = Site_Index_Value
Set Resource = GetObject("IIS://" & ServerName & "/W3SVC/" & Index & "/ROOT")
Debug.Print "Registered File Types:"
For Each MimeMapping in Resource.MimeMap
    Debug.Print "Extension: " & MimeMapping.Extension & " MIME Content Type: " &
➥MimeMapping.MimeType
Next
```

Setting MIME Type Definitions for Resources Using Visual Basic
To create a new MIME type definitions for a resource, use the following Visual Basic code:

```
Dim Resource As IADs
Dim ServerName As String
Dim Index As Long
Dim MimeMapping As Variant
Dim NewMimeMapping As Variant
Dim MimeExtension As String
Dim MimeType As String
Dim i As Integer
MimeExtension = "New_MIME_Extension"
MimeType = "New_MIME_Type"
ServerName = "IIS_Server_Name"
Index = Site_Index_Value
Set Resource = GetObject("IIS://" & ServerName & "/W3SVC/" & Index & "/ROOT")
NewMimeMapping = Resource.GetEx("MimeMap")
i = UBound(NewMimeMapping) + 1
ReDim Preserve NewMimeMapping(i)
Set NewMimeMapping(i) = CreateObject("MimeMap")
NewMimeMapping(i).MimeType = MimeType
NewMimeMapping(i).Extension = MimeExtension
Resource.PutEx ADS_PROPERTY_UPDATE, "MimeMap", NewMimeMapping
Resource.SetInfo
```

Creating the IIsWebManagement Class Module

In this section, you will continue the creation of the IIsAdmin.DLL COM server application started in Chapter 8.

Exercise 9.1   *Creating the IIsAdmin.DLL COM Server Application: The IIsWebManagement Class Module*

1. Open the IIsAdmin ActiveX DLL Visual Basic project that was started in Chapter 8. You can also download the project from http://www.newriders.com/adsi.

2. If you are adding to the IIsAdmin project, add a new class module to the project. If this is a new project, make sure to set a reference to Active DS Type Library.

3. Name the new module **IIsWebManagement**.

4. Enter the following code into the General Declarations section of the class module:

```
Public Function ManageIdentityProperty(ByVal TargetComputer As String, ByVal SiteIndex As Integer, ByVal Action
➥As String, ByVal IdentityProperty As String, Optional ByVal NewValue As Variant) As Variant
    On Error Resume Next
    Dim ArrayElement As Variant
    Dim NewElement() As Variant
    Dim i As Integer
    Dim Site As IADs
    Set Site = GetObject("IIS://" & TargetComputer & "/W3SVC/" & SiteIndex)
    Select Case UCase(Action)
        Case "QUERY"
            Select Case UCase(IdentityProperty)
                Case "SERVERCOMMENT"
                    ManageIdentityProperty = Site.ServerComment
                Case "SERVERBINDINGS"
                    For Each ArrayElement In Site.ServerBindings
                        i = UBound(NewElement) + 1
                        ReDim Preserve NewElement(i)
                        NewElement(i) = ArrayElement
                    Next
                    ManageIdentityProperty = NewElement
                Case "SECUREBINDINGS"
                    For Each ArrayElement In Site.SecureBindings
                        i = UBound(NewElement) + 1
                        ReDim Preserve NewElement(i)
                        NewElement(i) = ArrayElement
                    Next
                    ManageIdentityProperty = NewElement
                Case "MAXCONNECTIONS"
                    ManageIdentityProperty = Site.MaxConnections
                Case "CONNECTIONTIMEOUT"
                    ManageIdentityProperty = Site.ConnectionTimeout
            End Select
        Case "SET"
```

```
If NewValue <> "" Then
    Select Case UCase(IdentityProperty)
        Case "SERVERCOMMENT"
            Err.Number = 0
            Site.ServerComment = NewValue
        Case "ADDSERVERBINDING"
            If IsArray(Site.ServerBindings) Then
                For Each ArrayElement In Site.ServerBindings
                    i = UBound(NewElement) + 1
                    ReDim Preserve NewElement(i)
                    NewElement(i) = ArrayElement
                Next
                i = UBound(NewElement) + 1
                ReDim Preserve NewElement(i)
                NewElement(i) = NewValue
                Err.Number = 0
                Site.ServerBindings = NewElement
            Else
                Site.ServerBindings = Array(NewValue)
            End If
        Case "ADDSECUREBINDING"
            If IsArray(Site.SecureBindings) Then
                For Each ArrayElement In Site.SecureBindings
                    i = UBound(NewElement) + 1
                    ReDim Preserve NewElement(i)
                    NewElement(i) = ArrayElement
                Next
                i = UBound(NewElement) + 1
                ReDim Preserve NewElement(i)
                NewElement(i) = NewValue
                Err.Number = 0
                Site.SecureBindings = NewElement
            Else
                Site.SecureBindings = Array(NewValue)
            End If
        Case "REMOVEALLSERVERBINDINGS"
            Site.ServerBindings = Array("")
            Err.Number = 0
        Case "REMOVEALLSECUREBINDINGS"
            Err.Number = 0
            Site.SecureBindings = Array("")
        Case "REMOVESERVERBINDING"
            If IsArray(Site.ServerBindings) Then
                For Each ArrayElement In Site.ServerBindings
                    If ArrayElement <> NewValue Then
                        i = UBound(NewElement) + 1
                        ReDim Preserve NewElement(i)
                        NewElement(i) = ArrayElement
                    End If
                Next
                Err.Number = 0
                Site.ServerBindings = NewElement
            Else
```

continues ▶

Exercise 9.1 *continued*

```
                                If Site.ServerBindings = NewValue Then
                                    Err.Number = 0
                                    Site.ServerBindings = Array("")
                                End If
                            End If
                    Case "REMOVESECUREBINDING"
                        If IsArray(Site.SecureBindings) Then
                            For Each ArrayElement In Site.SecureBindings
                                If ArrayElement <> NewValue Then
                                    i = UBound(NewElement) + 1
                                    ReDim Preserve NewElement(i)
                                    NewElement(i) = ArrayElement
                                End If
                            Next
                            Err.Number = 0
                            Site.SecureBindings = NewElement
                        Else
                            If Site.SecureBindings = NewValue Then
                                Site.SecureBindings = Array("")
                            End If
                        End If
                    Case "MAXCONNECTIONS"
                        Site.MaxConnections = NewValue
                    Case "CONNECTIONTIMEOUT"
                        Site.ConnectionTimeout = NewValue
                End Select
                Site.SetInfo
                If Err.Number = 0 Then ManageIdentityProperty = True
            End If
    End Select
End Function

Public Function ManageOperators(ByVal TargetComputer As String, ByVal SiteIndex As Integer, ByVal Action As
⮡String, ByVal IdentityProperty As String, Optional ByVal NewValue As Variant) As Variant
    On Error Resume Next
    Dim SecurityDescriptor As Variant
    Dim DiscretionaryACL As Variant
    Dim ACE As Variant
    Dim ArrayElement As Variant
    Dim NewElement() As Variant
    Dim i As Integer
    Dim Site As IADs
    Set Site = GetObject("IIS://" & TargetComputer & "/W3SVC/" & SiteIndex)
    Set SecurityDescriptor = Site.AdminAcl
    Set DiscretionaryACL = SecurityDescriptor.DiscretionaryACL
    Select Case UCase(Action)
        Case "QUERY"
            Select Case UCase(IdentityProperty)
                Case "OPERATORS"
                    For Each ArrayElement In DiscretionaryACL
                        If ArrayElement.AccessMask = 11 Or ArrayElement.AccessMask = 262315 Then
```

Creating the IlsWebManagement Class Module   315

```
                        i = UBound(NewElement) + 1
                        ReDim Preserve NewElement(i)
                        NewElement(i) = ArrayElement.Trustee
                    End If
                Next
                ManageOperators = NewElement
        End Select
    Case "SET"
        If NewValue <> "" Then
            Select Case UCase(IdentityProperty)
                Case "NEWOPERATOR"
                    Set ACE = CreateObject("AccessControlEntry")
                    ACE.Trustee = NewValue
                    ACE.AccessMask = 11
                    DiscretionaryACL.AddAce ACE
                    SecurityDescriptor.DiscretionaryACL = DiscretionaryACL
                    Site.AdminAcl = SecurityDescriptor
                Case "REMOVEOPERATOR"
                    Set ACE = CreateObject("AccessControlEntry")
                    ACE.Trustee = NewValue
                    ACE.AccessMask = 11
                    DiscretionaryACL.RemoveAce ACE
                    SecurityDescriptor.DiscretionaryACL = DiscretionaryACL
                    Site.AdminAcl = SecurityDescriptor
            End Select
            Site.SetInfo
            If Err.Number = 0 Then ManageOperators = True
        End If
    End Select
End Function

Public Function ManageAuthenticationMethods(ByVal TargetComputer As String, ByVal SiteIndex As Integer, ByVal
↪Action As String, ByVal IdentityProperty As String, Optional ByVal NewValue As Variant) As Variant
    On Error Resume Next
    Dim Site As IADs
    Dim Resource As IADs
    Dim NewElement() As Variant
    Dim i As Integer
    Set Resource = GetObject("IIS://" & TargetComputer & "/W3SVC/" & SiteIndex & "/ROOT")
    Select Case UCase(Action)
        Case "QUERY"
            Select Case UCase(IdentityProperty)
                Case "ALLAUTHENTICATIONMETHODS"
                    i = UBound(NewElement) + 1
                    ReDim Preserve NewElement(i)
                    NewElement(i) = "Anonymous Access Enabled: " & Resource.AuthAnonymous
                    If Resource.AuthAnonymous = True Then
                        i = UBound(NewElement) + 1
                        ReDim Preserve NewElement(i)
                        NewElement(i) = "Anonymous Username: " & Resource.AnonymousUsername
                        i = UBound(NewElement) + 1
                        ReDim Preserve NewElement(i)
                        NewElement(i) = "Anonymous User Account Password: " & Resource.AnonymousUserPass
```

continues ▶

Exercise 9.1 *continued*

```
                i = UBound(NewElement) + 1
                ReDim Preserve NewElement(i)
                NewElement(i) = "Anonymous User Account Password Sync Enabled: " & _
                    Resource.AnonymousPasswordSync
            End If
            i = UBound(NewElement) + 1
            ReDim Preserve NewElement(i)
            NewElement(i) = "Basic Authentication Enabled: " & Resource.AuthBasic
            If Resource.AuthBasic = True Then
                i = UBound(NewElement) + 1
                ReDim Preserve NewElement(i)
                NewElement(i) = "Basic Authentication Default Domain: " & _
                    Resource.DefaultLogonDomain
            End If
            i = UBound(NewElement) + 1
            ReDim Preserve NewElement(i)
            NewElement(i) = "NTLM Authentication Enabled: " & Resource.AuthNTLM
            ManageAuthenticationMethods = NewElement
        Case "ANONYMOUS"
            ManageAuthenticationMethods = Resource.AuthAnonymous
        Case "BASIC"
            ManageAuthenticationMethods = Resource.AuthBasic
        Case "NTLM"
            ManageAuthenticationMethods = Resource.AuthNTLM
        Case "ANONYMOUSUSERNAME"
            ManageAuthenticationMethods = Resource.AnonymousUsername
        Case "ANONYMOUSUSERPASS"
            ManageAuthenticationMethods = Resource.AnonymousUserPass
        Case "ANONYMOUSPASSWORDSYNC"
            ManageAuthenticationMethods = Resource.AnonymousPasswordSync
        Case "DEFAULTLOGONDOMAIN"
            ManageAuthenticationMethods = Resource.DefaultLogonDomain
        End Select
    Case "SET"
        If NewValue <> "" Then
            Select Case UCase(IdentityProperty)
                Case "ANONYMOUS"
                    Resource.AuthAnonymous = NewValue
                Case "BASIC"
                    Resource.AuthBasic = NewValue
                Case "NTLM"
                    Resource.AuthNTLM = NewValue
                Case "ANONYMOUSUSERNAME"
                    Resource.AnonymousUsername = NewValue
                Case "ANONYMOUSUSERPASS"
                    Resource.AnonymousUserPass = NewValue
                Case "ANONYMOUSPASSWORDSYNC"
                    Resource.AnonymousPasswordSync = NewValue
                Case "DEFAULTLOGONDOMAIN"
                    Resource.DefaultLogonDomain = NewValue
            End Select
```

Creating the IIsWebManagement Class Module   317

```
                Resource.SetInfo
                If Err.Number = 0 Then ManageAuthenticationMethods = True
            End If
    End Select
End Function

Public Function MIMETypeManagement(ByVal TargetComputer As String, ByVal Index As Integer, ByVal Action As
➥String, Optional ByVal MIMEExtension As String, Optional ByVal MIMEType As String) As Variant
    On Error Resume Next
    Dim IIsComputer As IADs
    Set IIsComputer = GetObject("IIS://" & TargetComputer & "/W3SVC/" & Index & "/ROOT")
    Select Case UCase(Action)
        Case "ENUMERATE"
            Dim MimeMapping As Variant
            Dim NewElement() As Variant
            Dim i As Long
            For Each MimeMapping In IIsComputer.MimeMap
                i = UBound(NewElement) + 1
                ReDim Preserve NewElement(i)
                NewElement(i) = MimeMapping.Extension & vbTab & MimeMapping.MIMEType
            Next
            MIMETypeManagement = NewElement
        Case "ADD"
            If MIMEType <> "" And MIMEExtension <> "" Then
                Dim NewMimeMapping As Variant
                NewMimeMapping = IIsComputer.GetEx("MimeMap")
                i = UBound(NewMimeMapping) + 1
                ReDim Preserve NewMimeMapping(i)
                Set NewMimeMapping(i) = CreateObject("MimeMap")
                NewMimeMapping(i).MIMEType = MIMEType
                NewMimeMapping(i).Extension = MIMEExtension
                IIsComputer.PutEx ADS_PROPERTY_UPDATE, "MimeMap", NewMimeMapping
                Err.Number = 0
                IIsComputer.SetInfo
                If Err.Number = 0 Then MIMETypeManagement = True
            Else
                MIMETypeManagement = False
            End If
        Case "REMOVE"
            If MIMEExtension <> "" Then
                Dim MapToDelete As String
                Dim MimeItem As Variant
                NewMimeMapping = IIsComputer.MimeMap
                For Each MimeMapping In IIsComputer.MimeMap
                    If MimeMapping.Extension <> MIMEExtension Then
                        ReDim Preserve NewMimeMapping(i)
                        Set NewMimeMapping(i) = CreateObject("MimeMap")
                        NewMimeMapping(i).MIMEType = MimeMapping.MIMEType
                        NewMimeMapping(i).Extension = MimeMapping.Extension
                        i = i + 1
                    End If
                Next
                IIsComputer.PutEx ADS_PROPERTY_UPDATE, "MimeMap", NewMimeMapping
```

continues ▶

Exercise 9.1 *continued*

```
                Err.Number = 0
                IIsComputer.SetInfo
                If Err.Number = 0 Then MIMETypeManagement = True
            Else
                MIMETypeManagement = False
            End If
    End Select
End Function

Public Function ManageIPRestrictions(ByVal TargetComputer As String, ByVal SiteIndex As Integer, ByVal
➥RelativePath As String, ByVal Action As String, Optional ByVal RestrictAction As String, Optional ByVal
➥Restrict As String, Optional ByVal IPSubnet As String) As Variant
    On Error Resume Next
    Dim Site As IADs
    Dim IPSecurity As Variant
    Dim NewElement() As Variant
    Dim IPAddress As String
    Dim ActionType As String
    Dim Entry As Variant
    Dim i As Integer
    Set Site = GetObject("IIS://" & TargetComputer & "/W3SVC/" & SiteIndex & RelativePath)
    Select Case UCase(Action)
        Case "QUERY"
            Set IPSecurity = Site.IPSecurity
            If IPSecurity.GrantByDefault Then
                For Each Entry In IPSecurity.IPDeny
                    If InStr(1, Entry, "255.255.255.255") Then
                        i = UBound(NewElement) + 1
                        ReDim Preserve NewElement(i)
                        NewElement(i) = "Denied IP: " & Replace(Entry, ", 255.255.255.255", "")
                    Else
                        i = UBound(NewElement) + 1
                        ReDim Preserve NewElement(i)
                        NewElement(i) = "Denied Subnet: " & Entry
                    End If
                Next
                For Each Entry In IPSecurity.DomainDeny
                    i = UBound(NewElement) + 1
                    ReDim Preserve NewElement(i)
                    NewElement(i) = "Denied Domain: " & Entry
                Next
            Else
                For Each Entry In IPSecurity.IPGrant
                    If InStr(1, Entry, "255.255.255.255") Then
                        i = UBound(NewElement) + 1
                        ReDim Preserve NewElement(i)
                        NewElement(i) = "Allowed IP: " & Replace(Entry, ", 255.255.255.255", "")
                    Else
                        i = UBound(NewElement) + 1
                        ReDim Preserve NewElement(i)
                        NewElement(i) = "Allowed Subnet: " & Entry
```

Creating the IIsWebManagement Class Module   319

```
                    End If
                Next
                For Each Entry In IPSecurity.DomainGrant
                    i = UBound(NewElement) + 1
                    ReDim Preserve NewElement(i)
                    NewElement(i) = "Allowed Domain: " & Entry
                Next
            End If
            ManageIPRestrictions = NewElement
    Case "SET"
        If Restrict <> "" Then
            Select Case UCase(RestrictAction)
                Case "GRANTIP"
                    Set IPSecurity = Site.IPSecurity
                    IPSecurity.GrantByDefault = False
                    Site.IPSecurity = IPSecurity
                    Site.SetInfo
                    IPSecurity.IPGrant = Array(Restrict & ", 255.255.255.255")
                    Site.IPSecurity = IPSecurity
                    Site.SetInfo
                    If Err.Number = 0 Then ManageIPRestrictions = True
                Case "GRANTSUBNET"
                    Set IPSecurity = Site.IPSecurity
                    IPSecurity.GrantByDefault = False
                    IPSecurity.IPGrant = Array(Restrict & ", " & IPSubnet)
                    Site.IPSecurity = IPSecurity
                    Site.SetInfo
                    If Err.Number = 0 Then ManageIPRestrictions = True
                Case "GRANTDOMAIN"
                    Set IPSecurity = Site.IPSecurity
                    IPSecurity.GrantByDefault = False
                    IPSecurity.DomainGrant = Array(Restrict)
                    Site.IPSecurity = IPSecurity
                    Site.SetInfo
                    If Err.Number = 0 Then ManageIPRestrictions = True
                Case "DENYIP"
                    Set IPSecurity = Site.IPSecurity
                    IPSecurity.GrantByDefault = True
                    IPSecurity.IPDeny = Array(Restrict & ", 255.255.255.255")
                    Site.IPSecurity = IPSecurity
                    Site.SetInfo
                    If Err.Number = 0 Then ManageIPRestrictions = True
                Case "DENYSUBNET"
                    Set IPSecurity = Site.IPSecurity
                    IPSecurity.GrantByDefault = True
                    IPSecurity.IPDeny = Array(Restrict & ", " & IPSubnet)
                    Site.IPSecurity = IPSecurity
                    Site.SetInfo
                    If Err.Number = 0 Then ManageIPRestrictions = True
                Case "DENYDOMAIN"
                    Set IPSecurity = Site.IPSecurity
                    IPSecurity.GrantByDefault = True
                    IPSecurity.DomainDeny = Array(Restrict)
```

continues ▶

Exercise 9.1 *continued*

```
                            Site.IPSecurity = IPSecurity
                            Site.SetInfo
                            If Err.Number = 0 Then ManageIPRestrictions = True
                    End Select
                End If
        End Select
End Function

Public Function ManagePerformanceProperty(ByVal TargetComputer As String, ByVal SiteIndex As Integer, ByVal
➥Action As String, ByVal IdentityProperty As String, Optional ByVal NewValue As Variant) As Variant
    Dim Site As IADs
    Set Site = GetObject("IIS://" & TargetComputer & "/W3SVC/" & SiteIndex)
    Select Case UCase(Action)
        Case "QUERY"
            Select Case UCase(IdentityProperty)
                Case "SERVERSIZE"
                    ManagePerformanceProperty = Site.ServerSize
                Case "MAXBANDWIDTH"
                    ManagePerformanceProperty = Site.MaxBandwidth
                Case "ALLOWKEEPALIVE"
                    ManagePerformanceProperty = Site.AllowKeepAlive
                Case "HTTPEXPIRES"
                    Set Site = GetObject("IIS://" & TargetComputer & "/W3SVC/" & SiteIndex & "/ROOT")
                    ManagePerformanceProperty = Site.HttpExpires
            End Select
        Case "SET"
            If NewValue <> "" Then
                Select Case UCase(IdentityProperty)
                    Case "SERVERSIZE"
                        Site.ServerSize = NewValue
                    Case "MAXBANDWIDTH"
                        Site.MaxBandwidth = NewValue
                    Case "ALLOWKEEPALIVE"
                        Site.AllowKeepAlive = NewValue
                    Case "HTTPEXPIRES"
                        Set Site = GetObject("IIS://" & TargetComputer & "/W3SVC/" & SiteIndex & "/ROOT")
                        Site.HttpExpires = NewValue
                End Select
                Site.SetInfo
                If Err.Number = 0 Then ManagePerformanceProperty = True
            End If
    End Select
End Function

Public Function ManageHomeDirectoryProperty(ByVal TargetComputer As String, ByVal SiteIndex As Integer, ByVal
➥RelativePath As String, ByVal Action As String, ByVal IdentityProperty As String, Optional ByVal NewValue As
➥Variant) As Variant
    Dim Resource As IADs
    Set Resource = GetObject("IIS://" & TargetComputer & "/W3SVC/" & SiteIndex & "/ROOT" & RelativePath)
    Select Case UCase(Action)
        Case "QUERY"
```

```
            Select Case UCase(IdentityProperty)
                Case "PATH"
                    ManageHomeDirectoryProperty = Resource.Path
                Case "UNCUSERNAME"
                    ManageHomeDirectoryProperty = Resource.UNCUsername
                Case "UNCPASSWORD"
                    ManageHomeDirectoryProperty = Resource.UNCPassword
                Case "ACCESSREAD"
                    ManageHomeDirectoryProperty = Resource.AccessRead
                Case "ACCESSWRITE"
                    ManageHomeDirectoryProperty = Resource.AccessWrite
                Case "DONTLOG"
                    ManageHomeDirectoryProperty = Resource.DontLog
                Case "ENABLEDIRBROWSING"
                    ManageHomeDirectoryProperty = Resource.EnableDirBrowsing
                Case "CONTENTINDEXED"
                    ManageHomeDirectoryProperty = Resource.ContentIndexed
                Case "FRONTPAGEWEB"
                    Set Resource = GetObject(Resource.Parent)
                    ManageHomeDirectoryProperty = Resource.FrontPageWeb
                Case "HTTPREDIRECT"
                    ManageHomeDirectoryProperty = Resource.HttpRedirect
            End Select
        Case "SET"
            If NewValue <> "" Then
                Select Case UCase(IdentityProperty)
                    Case "PATH"
                        Resource.Path = NewValue
                    Case "UNCUSERNAME"
                        Resource.UNCUsername = NewValue
                    Case "UNCPASSWORD"
                        Resource.UNCPassword = NewValue
                    Case "ACCESSREAD"
                        Resource.AccessRead = NewValue
                    Case "ACCESSWRITE"
                        Resource.AccessWrite = NewValue
                    Case "DONTLOG"
                        Resource.DontLog = NewValue
                    Case "ENABLEDIRBROWSING"
                        Resource.EnableDirBrowsing = NewValue
                    Case "CONTENTINDEXED"
                        Resource.ContentIndexed = NewValue
                    Case "FRONTPAGEWEB"
                        Set Resource = GetObject(Resource.Parent)
                        Resource.FrontPageWeb = NewValue
                    Case "HTTPREDIRECT"
                        Resource.HttpRedirect = NewValue
                End Select
                Resource.SetInfo
                If Err.Number = 0 Then ManageHomeDirectoryProperty = True
            End If
    End Select
End Function
```

continues ▶

Exercise 9.1 *continued*

```
Public Function ManageApplicationProperty(ByVal TargetComputer As String, ByVal SiteIndex As Integer, ByVal
➥RelativePath As String, ByVal Action As String, ByVal IdentityProperty As String, Optional ByVal NewValue As
➥Variant) As Variant
    Dim Resource As IADs
    Set Resource = GetObject("IIS://" & TargetComputer & "/W3SVC/" & SiteIndex & "/ROOT" & RelativePath)
    Select Case UCase(Action)
        Case "QUERY"
            Select Case UCase(IdentityProperty)
                Case "APPFRIENDLYNAME"
                    ManageApplicationProperty = Resource.AppFriendlyName
                Case "APPROOT"
                    ManageApplicationProperty = Resource.AppRoot
                Case "APPISOLATED"
                    ManageApplicationProperty = Resource.AppIsolated
                Case "ACCESSREAD"
                    ManageApplicationProperty = Resource.AccessRead
                Case "ACCESSEXECUTE"
                    ManageApplicationProperty = Resource.AccessExecute
                Case "ASPSESSIONTIMEOUT"
                    ManageApplicationProperty = Resource.AspSessionTimeout
                Case "ASPBUFFERINGON"
                    ManageApplicationProperty = Resource.AspBufferingOn
                Case "ASPENABLEPARENTPATHS"
                    ManageApplicationProperty = Resource.AspEnableParentPaths
                Case "ASPSCRIPTLANGUAGE"
                    ManageApplicationProperty = Resource.AspScriptLanguage
                Case "ASPSCRIPTTIMEOUT"
                    ManageApplicationProperty = Resource.AspScriptTimeout
                Case "ASPLOGERRORREQUESTS"
                    ManageApplicationProperty = Resource.AspLogErrorRequests
                Case "ASPEXCEPTIONCATCHENABLE"
                    ManageApplicationProperty = Resource.AspExceptionCatchEnable
                Case "ASPSCRIPTENGINECACHEMAX"
                    ManageApplicationProperty = Resource.AspScriptEngineCacheMax
                Case "ASPSCRIPTFILECACHESIZE"
                    ManageApplicationProperty = Resource.AspScriptFileCacheSize
                Case "CGITIMEOUT"
                    Set Resource = GetObject(Resource.Parent)
                    ManageApplicationProperty = Resource.CGITimeout
                Case "APPALLOWDEBUGGING"
                    ManageApplicationProperty = Resource.AppAllowDebugging
                Case "APPALLOWCLIENTDEBUG"
                    ManageApplicationProperty = Resource.AppAllowClientDebug
                Case "ASPSCRIPTERRORSENTTOBROWSER"
                    ManageApplicationProperty = Resource.AspScriptErrorSentToBrowser
                Case "ASPSCRIPTERRORMESSAGE"
                    ManageApplicationProperty = Resource.AspScriptErrorMessage
            End Select
        Case "SET"
            If NewValue <> "" Then
```

```
                Select Case UCase(IdentityProperty)
                    Case "APPFRIENDLYNAME"
                        Resource.AppFriendlyName = NewValue
                    Case "APPROOT"
                        Resource.AppRoot = NewValue
                    Case "APPISOLATED"
                        Resource.AppIsolated = NewValue
                    Case "ACCESSREAD"
                        Resource.AccessRead = NewValue
                    Case "ACCESSEXECUTE"
                        Resource.AccessExecute = NewValue
                    Case "ASPSESSIONTIMEOUT"
                        Resource.AspSessionTimeout = NewValue
                    Case "ASPBUFFERINGON"
                        Resource.AspBufferingOn = NewValue
                    Case "ASPENABLEPARENTPATHS"
                        Resource.AspEnableParentPaths = NewValue
                    Case "ASPSCRIPTLANGUAGE"
                        Resource.AspScriptLanguage = NewValue
                    Case "ASPSCRIPTTIMEOUT"
                        Resource.AspScriptTimeout = NewValue
                    Case "ASPLOGERRORREQUESTS"
                        Resource.AspLogErrorRequests = NewValue
                    Case "ASPEXCEPTIONCATCHENABLE"
                        Resource.AspExceptionCatchEnable = NewValue
                    Case "ASPSCRIPTENGINECACHEMAX"
                        Resource.AspScriptEngineCacheMax = NewValue
                    Case "ASPSCRIPTFILECACHESIZE"
                        Resource.AspScriptFileCacheSize = NewValue
                    Case "CGITIMEOUT"
                        Set Resource = GetObject(Resource.Parent)
                        Resource.CGITimeout = NewValue
                    Case "APPALLOWDEBUGGING"
                        Resource.AppAllowDebugging = NewValue
                    Case "APPALLOWCLIENTDEBUG"
                        Resource.AppAllowClientDebug = NewValue
                    Case "ASPSCRIPTERRORSENTTOBROWSER"
                        Resource.AspScriptErrorSentToBrowser = NewValue
                    Case "ASPSCRIPTERRORMESSAGE"
                        Resource.AspScriptErrorMessage = NewValue
                End Select
                Resource.SetInfo
                If Err.Number = 0 Then ManageApplicationProperty = True
            End If
    End Select
End Function

Public Function ManageSSLConfigProperty(ByVal TargetComputer As String, ByVal SiteIndex As Integer, ByVal
RelativePath As String, ByVal Action As String, ByVal IdentityProperty As String, Optional ByVal NewValue As
Variant) As Variant
    Dim Resource As IADs
    Set Resource = GetObject("IIS://" & TargetComputer & "/W3SVC/" & SiteIndex & "/ROOT" & RelativePath)
    Select Case UCase(Action)
```

continues ▶

Exercise 9.1 continued

```
            Case "QUERY"
                Select Case UCase(IdentityProperty)
                    Case "ACCESSSSL"
                        ManageSSLConfigProperty = Resource.AccessSSL
                    Case "ACCESSSSL128"
                        ManageSSLConfigProperty = Resource.AccessSSL128
                    Case "ACCESSSSLMAPCERT"
                        ManageSSLConfigProperty = Resource.AccessSSLMapCert
                    Case "ACCESSSSLNEGOTIATECERT"
                        ManageSSLConfigProperty = Resource.AccessSSLNegotiateCert
                    Case "ACCESSSSLREQUIRECERT"
                        ManageSSLConfigProperty = Resource.AccessSSLRequireCert
                End Select
            Case "SET"
                If NewValue <> "" Then
                    Select Case UCase(IdentityProperty)
                        Case "ACCESSSSL"
                            Resource.AccessSSL = NewValue
                        Case "ACCESSSSL128"
                            Resource.AccessSSL128 = NewValue
                        Case "ACCESSSSLMAPCERT"
                            Resource.AccessSSLMapCert = NewValue
                        Case "ACCESSSSLNEGOTIATECERT"
                            Resource.AccessSSLNegotiateCert = NewValue
                        Case "ACCESSSSLREQUIRECERT"
                            Resource.AccessSSLRequireCert = NewValue
                    End Select
                    Resource.SetInfo
                    If Err.Number = 0 Then ManageSSLConfigProperty = True
                End If
        End Select
End Function

Public Function ManageDefaultDocumentProperty(ByVal TargetComputer As String, ByVal SiteIndex As Integer, ByVal
➥RelativePath As String, ByVal Action As String, ByVal IdentityProperty As String, Optional ByVal NewValue As
➥Variant) As Variant
    Dim Site As IADs
    Set Site = GetObject("IIS://" & TargetComputer & "/W3SVC/" & SiteIndex & "/ROOT" & RelativePath)
    Select Case UCase(Action)
        Case "QUERY"
            Select Case UCase(IdentityProperty)
                Case "ENABLEDEFAULTDOC"
                    ManageDefaultDocumentProperty = Site.EnableDefaultDoc
                Case "DEFAULTDOC"
                    ManageDefaultDocumentProperty = Site.DefaultDoc
                Case "DEFAULTDOCFOOTER"
                    ManageDefaultDocumentProperty = Site.DefaultDocFooter
                Case "ENABLEDOCFOOTER"
                    ManageDefaultDocumentProperty = Site.EnableDocFooter
            End Select
        Case "SET"
```

```
            If NewValue <> "" Then
                Select Case UCase(IdentityProperty)
                    Case "ENABLEDEFAULTDOC"
                        Site.EnableDefaultDoc = NewValue
                    Case "DEFAULTDOC"
                        Site.DefaultDoc = NewValue
                    Case "DEFAULTDOCFOOTER"
                        Site.DefaultDocFooter = NewValue
                    Case "ENABLEDOCFOOTER"
                        Site.EnableDocFooter = NewValue
                End Select
                Site.SetInfo
                If Err.Number = 0 Then ManageDefaultDocumentProperty = True
            End If
    End Select
End Function

Public Function ManageHTTPHeaderProperty(ByVal TargetComputer As String, ByVal SiteIndex As Integer, ByVal
RelativePath As String, ByVal Action As String, ByVal IdentityProperty As String, Optional ByVal NewValue As
Variant) As Variant
    On Error Resume Next
    Dim Resource As IADs
    Dim ArrayEntry As Variant
    Dim NewElement() As Variant
    Dim i As Integer
    Set Resource = GetObject("IIS://" & TargetComputer & "/W3SVC/" & SiteIndex & "/ROOT" & RelativePath)
    Select Case UCase(Action)
        Case "QUERY"
            Select Case UCase(IdentityProperty)
                Case "HTTPCUSTOMHEADERS"
                    For Each ArrayEntry In Resource.HttpCustomHeaders
                        i = UBound(NewElement) + 1
                        ReDim Preserve NewElement(i)
                        NewElement(i) = ArrayEntry
                    Next
                    ManageHTTPHeaderProperty = NewElement
                Case "PICSRATING"
                    For Each ArrayEntry In Resource.HttpPics
                        i = UBound(NewElement) + 1
                        ReDim Preserve NewElement(i)
                        NewElement(i) = ArrayEntry
                    Next
                    ManageHTTPHeaderProperty = NewElement
            End Select
        Case "SET"
            If NewValue <> "" Then
                Select Case UCase(IdentityProperty)
                    Case "HTTPCUSTOMHEADERS"
                        If IsArray(Resource.HttpCustomHeaders) Then
                            For Each ArrayEntry In Resource.HttpCustomHeaders
                                i = UBound(NewElement) + 1
                                ReDim Preserve NewElement(i)
                                NewElement(i) = ArrayEntry
```

continues ▶

Exercise 9.1 continued

```
                    Next
                    i = UBound(NewElement) + 1
                    ReDim Preserve NewElement(i)
                    NewElement(i) = NewValue
                    Resource.HttpCustomHeaders = NewElement
                    Err.Number = 0
                Else
                    Resource.HttpCustomHeaders = Array(NewValue)
                End If
            Case "PICSRATING"
                Resource.HttpPics = Array(NewValue)
        End Select
        Resource.SetInfo
        If Err.Number = 0 Then ManageHTTPHeaderProperty = True
        End If
    End Select
End Function

Public Function CreatePICSLabel(ByVal ResponsiblePartyEMail As String, ByVal ExpirationDate As Date, ByVal
➥ViolenceRating As Integer, ByVal SexRating As Integer, ByVal NudityRating As Integer, ByVal LanguageRating As
➥Integer) As String
    Dim PicsExpirationDate As String
    Dim PicsCurrentDate As String
    PicsExpirationDate = Year(ExpirationDate) & "." & (Month(ExpirationDate)) & "." & Day(ExpirationDate) &
➥"T12:00-0000"
    PicsCurrentDate = Year(Date) & "." & (Month(Date)) & "." & Day(Date) & "T12:00-0000"
    CreatePICSLabel = "PICS-Label: (PICS-1.0 ""http://www.rsac.org/ratingsv01.html"" l by """ &
➥ResponsiblePartyEMail & """ on """ & PicsCurrentDate & """ exp """ & PicsExpirationDate & """ r (v " &
➥ViolenceRating & " s " & SexRating & " n " & NudityRating & " l " & LanguageRating & "))"
End Function
```

5. Compile the code as IIsAdmin.DLL.
6. Save and close the IIsAdmin project.

Tip

You can download the Visual Basic 6.0 project or precompiled version of IIsAdmin.DLL from http://www.newriders.com/adsi. ◆

Using the Functions in IIsWebManagement

With the IIsWebManagement class module created, you can access this function from any programming language that supports OLE automation, including Visual Basic, VBScript, and JavaScript.

Tip

To instantiate the object, follow the appropriate syntax found in Chapter 3, "Container Enumeration Methods and Programmatic Domain Account Policy Manipulation."

Substitute the `IIsAdmin.IIsWebManagement` *object and class name where necessary.* ◆

Use Table 9.9 to help you use the proper syntax for each of the methods of the IIsWebManagement interface.

Table 9.9   Proper IIsWebManagement Interface Method Syntax

Action	Syntax
Query/Set Server Comment	`ManageIdentityProperty("Server_Name", 1,` ↪`"Query", "ServerComment")`
	`ManageIdentityProperty("Server_Name", 1, "Set",` ↪`"ServerComment", "Default Web Site")`
Query/Set ServerBindings	`For Each Binding In ManageIdentityProperty` ↪`("Server_Name", 1, "Query", "ServerBindings")`
	`    Debug.Print Binding`
	`Next`
	`ManageIdentityProperty("Server_Name", 1, "Set",` ↪`"AddServerBinding", "127.0.0.1:81:")`
	`ManageIdentityProperty("Server_Name", 1, "Set",` ↪`"RemoveAllServerBindings")`
	`ManageIdentityProperty("Server_Name", 1, "Set",` ↪`"RemoveServerBinding", "127.0.0.1:81:")`
Query/Set SecureBindings	`For Each Binding In ManageIdentityProperty` ↪`("Server_Name", 1, "Query", "SecureBindings")`
	`    Debug.Print Binding`
	`Next`
	`ManageIdentityProperty("Server_Name", 1, "Set",` ↪`"AddSecureBinding", "127.0.0.1:445:")`
	`ManageIdentityProperty("Server_Name", 1, "Set",` ↪`"RemoveAllSecureBindings")`

continues ▶

Table 9.9   continued

Action	Syntax
	ManageIdentityProperty("Server_Name", 1, "Set", ➥"RemoveSecureBinding", "127.0.0.1:445:")
Query/Set MaxConnections	ManageIdentityProperty("Server_Name", 1, ➥"Query", "MaxConnections")
	ManageIdentityProperty("Server_Name", 1, "Set", ➥"MaxConnections", 1000)
Query/Set Connection Timeout	ManageIdentityProperty("Server_Name", 1, ➥"Query", "ConnectionTimeout")
	ManageIdentityProperty("Server_Name", 1, "Set", ➥"ConnectionTimeout", 900)
Enumerate Site Operators	For Each Operator In ManageOperators ➥("Server_Name", 1, "Query", "Operators") Debug.Print Operator Next
Manage Site Operators	ManageOperators("Server_Name", 1, "Set", ➥"NewOperator", "Server_Name\Administrator")
	ManageOperators("Server_Name", 1, "Set", ➥"RemoveOperator", "Server_Name\Administrator")
Enumerate Authenication Methods for a Resource	For Each Item In ManageAuthenticationMethods ➥("Server_Name", 1, "Query", ➥"AllAuthenticationMethods") Debug.Print Item Next
Query Authentication Method Properties for a Given Resource	ManageAuthenticationMethods("Server_Name", 1, ➥"Query", "Anonymous")
	ManageAuthenticationMethods("Server_Name", 1, ➥"Query", "Basic")
	ManageAuthenticationMethods("Server_Name", 1, ➥"Query", "NTLM")
	ManageAuthenticationMethods("Server_Name", 1, ➥"Query", "AnonymousUserName")
	ManageAuthenticationMethods("Server_Name", 1, ➥"Query", "AnonymousUserPass")
	ManageAuthenticationMethods("Server_Name", 1, ➥"Query", "AnonymousPasswordSync")
	ManageAuthenticationMethods("Server_Name", 1, ➥"Query", "DefaultLogonDomain")

Action	Syntax
Set Authentication Method Properties for a Given Resource	`ManageAuthenticationMethods("Server_Name", 1,` ⮕`"Set", "Anonymous", False)`
	`ManageAuthenticationMethods("Server_Name", 1,` ⮕`"Set", "Basic", False)`
	`ManageAuthenticationMethods("Server_Name", 1,` ⮕`"Set", "NTLM", False)`
	`ManageAuthenticationMethods("Server_Name", 1,` ⮕`"Set", "AnonymousUserName",` ⮕`"Server_Name\IUSR_Server_Name")`
	`ManageAuthenticationMethods("Server_Name", 1,` ⮕`"Set", "AnonymousUserPass", "u327eshf2sa!")`
	`ManageAuthenticationMethods("Server_Name", 1,` ⮕`"Set", "AnonymousPasswordSync", True)`
	`ManageAuthenticationMethods("Server_Name", 1,` ⮕`"Set", "DefaultLogonDomain",` ⮕`"User_Domain_Name")`

Enumerate Site Specific MIME Types	`For Each Item In Obj.MIMETypeManagement` ⮕`("IIS_Server_Name", "Enumerate")`
	　　`Debug.Print Item`
	`Next`

Add New Site Specific MIME Type	`MIMETypeManagement("IIS_Server_Name", "Add",` ⮕`".Extension", "Application/Type")`
Remove Site Specific MIME Type	`MIMETypeManagement("IIS_Server_Name", "Remove",` ⮕` ".Extension")`

Query IP Restrictions	`For Each Item In ManageIPRestrictions` ⮕`("Server_Name", 1, "/ROOT", "Query")`
	　　`Debug.Print Item`
	`Next`

Deny All Access Except Specified IP	`ManageIPRestrictions("Server_Name", 1, "/ROOT",` ⮕ `"Set", "GrantIP", "xxx.xxx.xxx.xxx")`
Deny All Access Except Specified Subnet	`ManageIPRestrictions("Server_Name", 1, "/ROOT",` ⮕ `"Set", "GrantSubnet", "xxx.xxx.xxx.xxx",` ⮕`"xxx.xxx.xxx.0")`
Deny All Access Except Specified DNS Domain	`ManageIPRestrictions("Server_Name", 1, "/ROOT",` ⮕ `"Set", "GrantDomain", "DNS_Domain")`
Grant All Access Except Specified Address	`ManageIPRestrictions("Server_Name", 1, "/ROOT",` ⮕ `"Set", "DenyIP", "xxx.xxx.xxx.xxx")`
Grant All Access Except Specified Subnet	`ManageIPRestrictions("Server_Name", 1, "/ROOT",` ⮕ `"Set", "DenySubnet", "xxx.xxx.xxx.xxx",` ⮕`"xxx.xxx.xxx.0")`
Grant All Access Except Specified Domain	`ManageIPRestrictions("Server_Name", 1, "/ROOT",` ⮕ `"Set", "DenyDomain", "DNS_Domain")`

continues ▶

Table 9.9   continued

Action	Syntax
Query Performance Properties and HTTP Expiration	`ManagePerformanceProperty("Server_Name", 1, `↦`"Query", "ServerSize")`
	`ManagePerformanceProperty("Server_Name", 1, `↦`"Query", "MaxBandwidth")`
	`ManagePerformanceProperty("Server_Name", 1, `↦`"Query", "AllowKeepAlive")`
	`ManagePerformanceProperty("Server_Name", 1, `↦`"Query", "HttpExpires")`
Set Performance Properties and HTTP Expiration	`ManagePerformanceProperty("Server_Name", 1, `↦`"Set", "ServerSize", 1)`
	`ManagePerformanceProperty("Server_Name", 1, `↦`"Set", "MaxBandwidth", 104856)`
	`ManagePerformanceProperty("Server_Name", 1, `↦`"Set", "AllowKeepAlive", False)`
	`ManagePerformanceProperty("Server_Name", 1, `↦`"Set", "HttpExpires", "D,60")`
Query Home Directory Properties	`ManageHomeDirectoryProperty("Server_Name", 1, `↦`"","Query", "Path")`
	`ManageHomeDirectoryProperty("Server_Name", 1, `↦`"", "Query", "UNCUsername")`
	`ManageHomeDirectoryProperty("Server_Name", 1, `↦`"", "Query", "UNCUserPass")`
	`ManageHomeDirectoryProperty("Server_Name", 1, `↦`"", "Query", "AccessRead")`
	`ManageHomeDirectoryProperty("Server_Name", 1, `↦`"", "Query", "AccessWrite")`
	`ManageHomeDirectoryProperty("Server_Name", 1, `↦`"", "Query", "DontLog")`
	`ManageHomeDirectoryProperty("Server_Name", 1, `↦`"", "Query", "EnableDirBrowsing")`
	`ManageHomeDirectoryProperty("Server_Name", 1, `↦`"", "Query", "ContentIndexed")`
	`ManageHomeDirectoryProperty("Server_Name", 1, `↦`"", "Query", "FrontPageWeb")`
	`ManageHomeDirectoryProperty("Server_Name", 1, `↦`"", "Query", "HttpRedirect")`
Set Home Directory Properties	`ManageHomeDirectoryProperty("Server_Name", 1, `↦`"", "Set", "Path", "c:\inetpub\wwwroot")` ↦`[Local]`
	`ManageHomeDirectoryProperty("Server_Name", 1, `↦`"", "Set", "Path", "\\servername\share")` ↦`[Remote]`

Creating the IIsWebManagement Class Module 331

Action	Syntax
	`ManageHomeDirectoryProperty("Server_Name", 1,`↩`"", "Set", "UNCUsername", "Server_Name\`↩`administrator")`
	`ManageHomeDirectoryProperty("Server_Name", 1,`↩`"", "Set", "UNCUserPass", "sih93f91hfsNA")`
	`ManageHomeDirectoryProperty("Server_Name", 1,`↩`"", "Set", "AccessRead", True)`
	`ManageHomeDirectoryProperty("Server_Name", 1,`↩`"", "Set", "AccessWrite", True)`
	`ManageHomeDirectoryProperty("Server_Name", 1,`↩`"", "Set", "DontLog", False)`
	`ManageHomeDirectoryProperty("Server_Name", 1,`↩`"", "Set", "EnableDirBrowsing", True)`
	`ManageHomeDirectoryProperty("Server_Name", 1,`↩`"", "Set", "ContentIndexed", True)`
	`ManageHomeDirectoryProperty("Server_Name", 1,`↩`"", "Set", "FrontPageWeb", True)`
	`ManageHomeDirectoryProperty("Server_Name", 1,`↩`"", "Set", "HttpRedirect", "SiteName,FLAG")`
Query Application Properties	`ManageApplicationProperty("Server_Name", 1,`↩`"", "Query", "AppFriendlyName")`
	`ManageApplicationProperty("Server_Name", 1, "",`↩`"Query", "AppRoot")`
	`ManageApplicationProperty("Server_Name", 1, "",`↩`"Query", "AppIsolated")`
	`ManageApplicationProperty("Server_Name", 1, "",`↩`"Query", "AccessRead")`
	`ManageApplicationProperty("Server_Name", 1, "",`↩`"Query", "AccessExecute")`
	`ManageApplicationProperty("Server_Name", 1, "",`↩`"Query", "AspSessionTimeout")`
	`ManageApplicationProperty("Server_Name", 1, "",`↩`"Query", "AspBufferingOn")`
	`ManageApplicationProperty("Server_Name", 1, "",`↩`"Query", "AspEnableParentPaths")`
	`ManageApplicationProperty("Server_Name", 1, "",`↩`"Query", "AspScriptLanguage")`
	`ManageApplicationProperty("Server_Name", 1, "",`↩`"Query", "AspScriptTimeout")`
	`ManageApplicationProperty("Server_Name", 1, "",`↩`"Query", "AspLogErrorRequests")`
	`ManageApplicationProperty("Server_Name", 1, "",`↩`"Query", "AspExceptionCatchEnable")`

continues ▶

Table 9.9 continued

Action	Syntax
	`ManageApplicationProperty("Server_Name", 1, "", ` `↪"Query", "AspScriptEngineCacheMax")`
	`ManageApplicationProperty("Server_Name", 1, "", ` `↪"Query", "AspScriptFileCacheSize")`
	`ManageApplicationProperty("Server_Name", 1, "", ` `↪"Query", "CGITimeout")`
	`ManageApplicationProperty("Server_Name", 1, "", ` `↪"Query", "AppAllowDebugging")`
	`ManageApplicationProperty("Server_Name", 1, "", ` `↪"Query", "AppAllowClientDebug")`
	`ManageApplicationProperty("Server_Name", 1, "", ` `↪"Query", "AspScriptErrorSentToBrowser")`
	`ManageApplicationProperty("Server_Name", 1, "", ` `↪"Query", "AspScriptErrorMessage")`

Set Application Properties	`ManageApplicationProperty("Server_Name", 1, "", `
	`↪"Set", "AppFriendlyName", "Default`
	`↪Application")`

	`ManageApplicationProperty("Server_Name", 1, "", ` `↪"Set", "AppRoot", "/LM/W3SVC/1/ROOT")`
	`ManageApplicationProperty("Server_Name", 1, "", ` `↪"Set", "AppIsolated", False)`
	`ManageApplicationProperty("Server_Name", 1, "", ` `↪"Set", "AccessRead", False)`
	`ManageApplicationProperty("Server_Name", 1, "", ` `↪"Set", "AccessExecute", False)`
	`ManageApplicationProperty("Server_Name", 1, "", ` `↪"Set", "AspSessionTimeout", 60)`
	`ManageApplicationProperty("Server_Name", 1, "", ` `↪"Set", "AspBufferingOn", True)`
	`ManageApplicationProperty("Server_Name", 1, "", ` `↪"Set", "AspEnableParentPaths", True)`
	`ManageApplicationProperty("Server_Name", 1, "", ` `↪"Set", "AspScriptLanguage", "VBScript")`
	`ManageApplicationProperty("Server_Name", 1, "", ` `↪"Set", "AspScriptTimeout", 360)`
	`ManageApplicationProperty("Server_Name", 1, "", ` `↪"Set", "AspLogErrorRequests", False)`
	`ManageApplicationProperty("Server_Name", 1, "", ` `↪"Set", "AspExceptionCatchEnable", False)`
	`ManageApplicationProperty("Server_Name", 1, "", ` `↪"Set", "AspScriptEngineCacheMax", 60)`
	`ManageApplicationProperty("Server_Name", 1, "", ` `↪"Set", "AspScriptFileCacheSize", 1024)`

Creating the IIsWebManagement Class Module   333

Action	Syntax
	`ManageApplicationProperty("Server_Name", 1, "",` ↳`"Set", "CGITimeout", 300)`
	`ManageApplicationProperty("Server_Name", 1, "",` ↳`"Set", "AppAllowDebugging", True)`
	`ManageApplicationProperty("Server_Name", 1, "",` ↳`"Set", "AppAllowClientDebug", True)`
	`ManageApplicationProperty("Server_Name", 1, "",` ↳`"Set", "AspScriptErrorSentToBrowser", False)`
	`ManageApplicationProperty("Server_Name", 1, "",` ↳`"Set", "AspScriptErrorMessage", "An error has` ↳`occurred. Please call the corporate technical` ↳`support center at x9321")`
Query SSL COnfiguration Properties	`ManageSSLConfigProperty("Server_Name", 1, "",` ↳`"Query", "AccessSSL")`
	`ManageSSLConfigProperty("Server_Name", 1, "",` ↳`"Query", "AccessSSL128")`
	`ManageSSLConfigProperty("Server_Name", 1, "",` ↳`"Query", "AccessSSLMapCert")`
	`ManageSSLConfigProperty("Server_Name", 1, "",` ↳`"Query", "AccessSSLNegotiateCert")`
	`ManageSSLConfigProperty("Server_Name", 1, "",` ↳`"Query", "AccessSSLRequireCert")`
Set SSL Configuration Properties	`ManageSSLConfigProperty("Server_Name", 1, "",` ↳`"Set", "AccessSSL", False)`
	`ManageSSLConfigProperty("Server_Name", 1, "",` ↳`"Set", "AccessSSL128", False)`
	`ManageSSLConfigProperty("Server_Name", 1, "",` ↳`"Set", "AccessSSLMapCert", False)`
	`ManageSSLConfigProperty("Server_Name", 1, "",` ↳`"Set", "AccessSSLNegotiateCert", False)`
	`ManageSSLConfigProperty("Server_Name", 1, "",` ↳`"Set", "AccessSSLRequireCert", False)`
Query Default Document and Default Footer Properties	`ManageDefaultDocumentProperty("Server_Name", 1,` ↳`"", "Query", "DefaultDoc")`
	`ManageDefaultDocumentProperty("Server_Name", 1,` ↳`"", "Query", "EnableDefaultDoc")`
	`ManageDefaultDocumentProperty("Server_Name", 1,` ↳`"", "Query", "DefaultDocFooter")`
	`ManageDefaultDocumentProperty("Server_Name", 1,` ↳`"", "Query", "EnableDocFooter")`

continues ▶

Table 9.9   continued

Action	Syntax
Set Default Document and Default Footer Properties	`ManageDefaultDocumentProperty("Server_Name", 1, ""`, `"Set", "DefaultDoc", "default.asp")`
	`ManageDefaultDocumentProperty("Server_Name", 1, ""`, `"Set", "EnableDefaultDoc", True)`
	`ManageDefaultDocumentProperty("Server_Name", 1, ""`, `"Set", "DefaultDocFooter", "C:\Inetpub\wwwroot\LegalFooter.htm")`
	`ManageDefaultDocumentProperty("Server_Name", 1, ""`, `"Set", "EnableDocFooter", True)`
Query Custom HTTP Header Configuration	`For Each Header In ManageHTTPHeaderProperty("Server_Name", 1, "", "Query", "HttpCustomHeaders")`
	`    Debug.Print Header`
	`Next`
Add New Custom HTTP Header	`ManageHTTPHeaderProperty("Server_Name", 1, "", "Set", "HttpCustomHeaders", "CustomHeader1: True")`
Query RSACi/PICS Ratings for a Given Resource	`For Each Header In ManageHTTPHeaderProperty("Server_Name", 1, "", "Query", "PicsRating")`
	`    Debug.Print Header`
	`Next`
Set New RSACi/PICS Rating for a Given Resource	`Dim PICSLabel As String`
	`PICSLabel = CreatePICSLabel("thomas.eck@wdr.com", #1/1/2001#, 0, 0, 0, 0)`
	`ManageHTTPHeaderProperty("Server_Name", 1, "", "Set", "PicsRating", PICSLabel)`

Summary

Using the robust object model available found in ADSI's IIS service provider, you can manipulate every aspect of Web site configuration. Using ADSI and Visual Basic, you can easily manipulate the configuration of each of the following commonly used property sheets in the IIS 4.0 Internet Service Manager:

- The Web Site property sheet
- The Web Operators property sheet
- The Web Performance property sheet

- The Home Directory property sheet
- The Documents property sheet
- The Directory Security property sheet
- The HTTP Headers property sheet

Although ADSI does expose the ability to manage custom errors and ISAPI filters, the relatively small demand and significant coding complexity of these procedures does not lend well to programmatic administration. Consult the ADSI SDK, IIS Web Administration ASP code, and IIS product documentation to manipulate these properties.

Whether you simply need to configure a new site with some default property assignments or need to establish a complex site configuration, all this can be easily performed using ADSI.

10
Programmatic Management of FTP Site Properties

With the explosion of Web-based technology, technologists face the ever-mounting difficulty of finding a secure and easy method to publish data to sites. Many large ISPs and corporations use the File Transfer Protocol (FTP) to provide a relatively simplistic method to accomplish this task.

Microsoft has exposed over 60 properties to programmatically manipulate the configuration and operation of the IIS FTP service. Whether implemented as a standalone FTP site or as part of a complex Web publishing mechanism, you can use ADSI to determine property inheritance and to programmatically administer the following:

- The FTP Site property sheet
- The Security Accounts property sheet
- The Messages property sheet
- The Home Directory property sheet
- The Directory Security property sheet

This chapter covers in detail some techniques you can use to programmatically administer the IIS FTP service.

Finally, in this chapter you will complete creation of the IISAdmin.DLL COM server.

Determining Property Inheritance

To determine which properties can be used at each level in the IIS Metabase, refer to the property inheritances in Table 10.1. Using this table you can reduce automation errors during development by calling properties that are appropriate to each entry in the Metabase.

For example, as the table shows, the `ServerComment` property is available only at the IIsFTPServer level, and is not inherited by the IIsFTPVirtualDir object. If you attempt to assign a new value to the `ServerComment` property while you are bound to a site's virtual directory, an automation error occurs.

Table 10.1 Property Support for IIsFTPServer and IIsFTPVirtualDir Interfaces

Property	IIsFTPServer	IIsFTPVirtualDir
`AccessFlags`	+	+
`AccessRead`	+	+
`AccessWrite`	+	+
`AdminACL`	+	−
`AllowAnonymous`	+	−
`AnonymousOnly`	+	−
`AnonymousPasswordSync`	+	−
`AnonymousUserName`	+	−
`AnonymousUserPass`	+	−
`ConnectionTimeout`	+	−
`DefaultLogonDomain`	+	−
`DontLog`	+	+
`ExitMessage`	+	−
`GreetingMessage`	+	−
`IPSecurity`	+	+
`LogAnonymous`	+	−
`LogExtFileBytesRecv`	+	−
`LogExtFileBytesSent`	+	−
`LogExtFileClientIp`	+	−
`LogExtFileComputerName`	+	−
`LogExtFileCookie`	+	−
`LogExtFileDate`	+	−
`LogExtFileFlags`	+	−
`LogExtFileHttpStatus`	+	−
`LogExtFileMethod`	+	−
`LogExtFileProtocolVersion`	+	−
`LogExtFileReferer`	+	−
`LogExtFileServerIp`	+	−
`LogExtFileServerPort`	+	−
`LogExtFileSiteName`	+	−
`LogExtFileTime`	+	−

Property	IIsFTPServer	IIsFTPVirtualDir
LogExtFileTimeTaken	+	−
LogExtFileUriQuery	+	−
LogExtFileUriStem	+	−
LogExtFileUserAgent	+	−
LogExtFileUserName	+	−
LogExtFileWin32Status	+	−
LogFileDirectory	+	−
LogFilePeriod	+	−
LogFileTruncateSize	+	−
LogNonAnonymous	+	−
LogOdbcDataSource	+	−
LogOdbcPassword	+	−
LogOdbcTableName	+	−
LogOdbcUserName	+	−
LogPluginClsId	+	−
LogType	+	−
MaxClientsMessage	+	−
MaxConnections	+	−
MaxEndpointConnections	+	−
MSDOSDirOutput	+	−
Path	−	+
Realm	+	−
ServerAutoStart	+	−
ServerBindings	+	−
ServerComment	+	−
ServerListenBacklog	+	−
ServerListenTimeout	+	−
ServerSize	+	−
ServerState	+	−
UNCPassword	−	+
UNCUserName	+	

Programmatically Administering the FTP Site Property Sheet

The FTP site property sheet, shown in Figure 10.1, allows you to define the description, IP address, TCP port, number of connections, and logging properties for the FTP site.

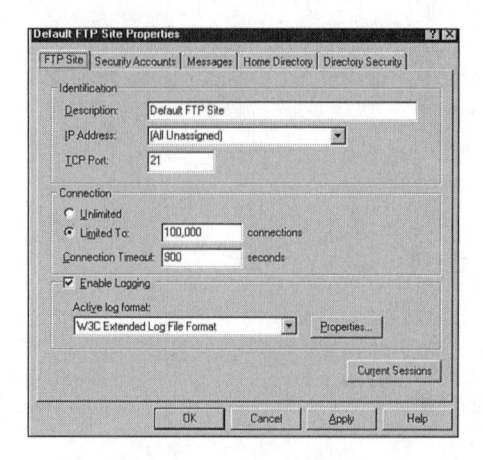

Figure 10.1 *Default FTP Site Properties dialog box—FTP Site tab.*

By manipulating the properties in this sheet, you can configure the basic identification for the site. As in an IIS Web site, you can assign a site an alternate TCP port or IP address to allow multiple FTP sites to be hosted on a single server. It is important to note, however, that unlike an IIS Web server, you do not have the ability to implement host headers. Although this may seem like a tremendously limiting factor, with a bit of creativity, this obstacle is easily overcome. By simply assigning each site a unique TCP port and creating a link to the site on a Web page, you can obtain easy access to the FTP site simply by using an HTML browser.

Manipulating Site Identification Properties

The identification frame allows you to define the server description, IP address, and TCP port to be used with the site. Each site should maintain unique values for at least two of these properties.

Manipulating the FTP Site Description

To manipulate an FTP site's description, you simply need to assign a unique value to the ServerComment property.

> *Tip*
>
> *Although you can assign non-unique values for the site description (the Metabase references sites by index number, not* ServerComment*), the use of non-unique values makes it impossible to identify one site from another and should be avoided.* ♦

Querying the ServerComment *Property Using Visual Basic*
To find the current description for an FTP site, use the following Visual Basic code:

```
Dim Site As IADs
Dim ServerName As String
Dim Index As Long
ServerName = "IIS_Server_Name"
Index = Site_Index_Integer
Set Site = GetObject("IIS://" & ServerName & "/MSFTPSVC/" & Index)
Debug.Print Site.ServerComment
```

Setting a New Value for the ServerComment *Property Using Visual Basic*
Use the following Visual Basic code to set a new description for the FTP site:

```
Dim Site As IADs
Dim ServerName As String
Dim Index As Long
Dim NewServerComment as String
ServerName = "IIS_Server_Name"
Index = Site_Index_Integer
NewServerComment = "New_Server_Comment_String"
Set Site = GetObject("IIS://" & ServerName & "/MSFTPSVC/" & Index)
Site.ServerComment = NewServerComment
Site.SetInfo
```

Manipulating IP Addresses and TCP Ports

If the IP address/TCP port pair conflicts with another site, IIS will not allow you to start the site. FTP sites cannot use host headers, thus you must use a unique IP address/TCP port combination for each site on a given machine.

To address this issue, you could use the same IP address and simply alter the TCP port assigned to each site. However, this approach causes issues for non-browser-based FTP clients because the user may not know how to connect to an FTP site running on a TCP port other than 21 in their client software.

For example, using the Windows NT command line FTP client, you cannot specify an alternate port unless you use the Open command, as follows:

```
C:\>ftp
ftp> open Server_Name 5000
Connected to Server_Name.
220 Server_Name Microsoft FTP Service (Version 4.0).
User (Server_Name:(none)): anonymous
331 Anonymous access allowed, send identity (e-mail name) as password.
Password:
230 Anonymous user logged in.
ftp>
```

Although this is certainly well within the grasp of even the least sophisticated user, many users may be used to simply specifying the FTP site name on the command line:

```
C:\>ftp server_name
```

While the use of alternate TCP ports is efficient in terms of IP address allocation, it forces the user to have a basic understanding of TCP ports and how they affect the chosen FTP client.

If you are implementing FTP sites for non-browser-based FTP clients, you can assign multiple IP addresses to any Windows NT machine with a statically assigned IP address by clicking the Advanced button while editing the properties of the TCP/IP protocol. You can then create a unique DNS entry for the IP address assigned to each individual FTP site. This allows users to simply FTP to a specific site name with little regard for non-default TCP port configurations in their client software.

No matter which approach you choose, the manipulation of the IP address and TCP port is handled by the `ServerBindings` property. This property is a variant array of strings with each string formatted as follows:

```
IP_Address:TCP_Port:
```

Querying ServerBindings *Using Visual Basic*

If you wish to find the IP address and TCP port assigned to the bound site, use the following Visual Basic code:

```
Dim Site As IADs
Dim ServerName As String
Dim SiteIndex As Long
ServerName = "IIS_Server_Name"
SiteIndex = Site_Index_Value
Set Site = GetObject("IIS://" & ServerName & "/MSFTPSVC/" & SiteIndex)
For Each Binding In Site.ServerBindings
    Debug.Print Binding
Next
```

Setting ServerBindings *Using Visual Basic*

To set the identification of the site to an alternate port or IP address, use the following Visual Basic code:

```
Dim Site As IADs
Dim ServerName As String
Dim SiteIndex As Long
Dim NewBindingArray As Variant
Dim IPAddress As String
Dim TCPPort As Long
ServerName = "IIS_Server_Name"
SiteIndex = Site_Index_Value
IPAddress = "xxx.xxx.xxx.xxx"
```

```
TCPPort = TCP_Port_Number
NewBindingArray = Array(IPAddress & ":" & TCPPort & ":")
Set Site = GetObject("IIS://" & ServerName & "/MSFTPSVC/" & SiteIndex)
Site.ServerBindings = NewBindingArray
Site.SetInfo
```

> **Note**
>
> *This code will create an array and assign it to the* `ServerBindings` *property.* ♦

Manipulating Connection Properties

To prevent over-saturation of server and network resources, you may wish to limit the number of connections to a given FTP site. If limits are imposed, you will want to define a connection timeout to allow idle connections to be recycled for use by other users.

Querying Maximum Connections Using Visual Basic

Using the `MaxConnections` property of the IIsFTPServer interface, you can find the maximum number of simultaneous connections allowed for a particular site.

Use the following Visual Basic code as a guide:

```
Dim Site As IADs
Dim ServerName As String
Dim Index As Long
Dim RetVal as Long
ServerName = "IIS_Server_Name"
Index = Site_Index
Set Site = GetObject("IIS://" & ServerName & "/MSFTPSVC/" & Index)
RetVal = Site.MaxConnections
Debug.Print RetVal
```

> **Tip**
>
> *A setting of 2000000000 allows unlimited connections to the server.* ♦

Setting Maximum Connections Using Visual Basic

To set the maximum number of connections for a given FTP site, use the following Visual Basic code:

```
Dim Site As IADs
Dim ServerName As String
Dim Index As Long
Dim NewMaxConnections as Long
ServerName = "IIS_Server_Name"
Index = Site_Index
```

```
NewMaxConnections = Maximum_Number_of_Connections
Set Site = GetObject("IIS://" & ServerName & "/MSFTPSVC/" & Index)
Site.MaxConnections = NewMaxConnections
Site.SetInfo
```

Manipulating Connection Timeout

Using the `ConnectionTimeout` property, you can specify the amount of idle time (in seconds) before a user's FTP connection is closed.

Querying Connection Timeout Using Visual Basic

To find the amount of time an FTP connection is permitted to remain idle before it is closed, use the following Visual Basic code:

```
Dim Site As IADs
Dim ServerName As String
Dim Index As Long
Dim RetVal as Long
ServerName = "IIS_Server_Name"
Index = Site_Index
Set Site = GetObject("IIS://" & ServerName & "/MSFTPSVC/" & Index)
RetVal = Site.ConnectionTimeout
Debug.Print RetVal
```

Setting Connection Timeout Using Visual Basic

To specify a new connection timeout value (in seconds) for the `ConnectionTimeout` property, use the following Visual Basic code:

```
Dim Site As IADs
Dim ServerName As String
Dim Index As Long
Dim ConnectionTimeout as Long
ServerName = "IIS_Server_Name"
Index = Site_Index_Value
NewConnectionTimeout = Connection_Timeout_in_Seconds
Set Site = GetObject("IIS://" & ServerName & "/MSFTPSVC/" & Index)
Site.ConnectionTimeout = NewConnectionTimeout
Site.SetInfo
```

Programmatically Administering the Security Accounts Property Sheet

The Security Accounts tab, shown in Figure 10.2, allows you to configure the site for anonymous access, and defines the operators allowed to modify the site configuration.

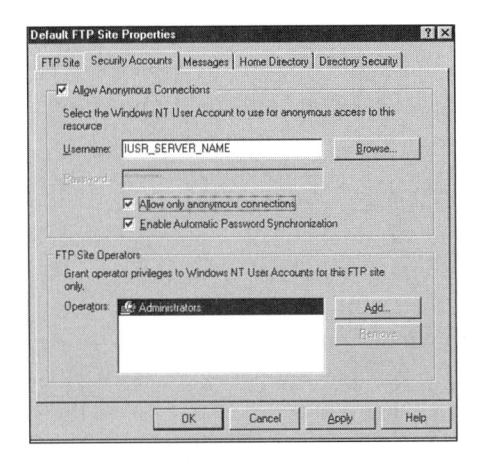

Figure 10.2 *Default FTP Site Properties dialog box—Security Accounts tab.*

Configuring Anonymous Connection

The ability to log on anonymously to a public FTP site allows external users access to resources on the FTP server without having a previously established set of credentials. If anonymous access is enabled for the site, a user can gain access to the site with the username "anonymous." In such a configuration, the calling user is given access to all files for which the defined anonymous account's access token will allow.

If you choose not to use anonymous access, the user must present a valid Windows NT username and password to gain access to the site. Access within the file system is controlled by NTFS permissions, which integrates the Windows NT security model right into the FTP server and eliminates duplication of administrative efforts.

Despite the advantages of such a configuration, Microsoft does not recommend using any account other than the anonymous user because the credentials will be passed across the network in clear text for anyone monitoring the network traffic to view.

Warning

Despite Microsoft's warnings against using non-anonymous account credentials for users, the anonymous user account username and password can be viewed in clear text through an ADSI query. In most cases, this poses a greater risk to internal security than the threat of sniffer-based attacks, therefore, the anonymous user account should always maintain extremely limited permissions in the file system. ♦

In the Allow Anonymous Connections frame, you can enable or disable anonymous access to the site, specify the account to be used for such access, deny all non-anonymous access, and enable anonymous user account password synchronization.

Allowing Anonymous Access for an FTP Site
To enable or disable the ability to use anonymous connections to an FTP site, set the appropriate Boolean value for the `AllowAnonymous` property. When set to True, the `AllowAnonymous` property enables users to access the site using the "anonymous" username. When set to False, only users with a valid Windows NT username and password (as well as the proper permissions for the resource) are allowed access.

Querying AllowAnonymous *Using Visual Basic*
To find out if an FTP site will allow anonymous connections to be established, use the following Visual Basic code:

```
Dim Site As IADs
Dim ServerName As String
Dim SiteIndex As Long
ServerName = "IIS_Server_Name"
SiteIndex = Site_Index_Value
Set Site = GetObject("IIS://" & ServerName & "/MSFTPSVC/" & SiteIndex)
Debug.Print Site.AllowAnonymous
```

Setting AllowAnonymous *Using Visual Basic*
To enable or disable the ability for users to establish anonymous connections to an FTP site, use the following Visual Basic code:

```
Dim Site As IADs
Dim ServerName As String
Dim SiteIndex As Long
ServerName = "IIS_Server_Name"
SiteIndex = Site_Index_Value
Set Site = GetObject("IIS://" & ServerName & "/MSFTPSVC/" & SiteIndex)
Site.AllowAnonymous = False
Site.SetInfo
```

Specifying Anonymous User Credential
If you enable anonymous access for the site, you must assign an account to be used to access the site. Although IIS creates an IUSR account, you can use any account you wish as long as the account has the proper NTFS permissions to traverse the file structure and to access files. In security-conscious environments, an account other than the well-known IUSR account should be used.

After you have decided upon an account to use for anonymous access, set the appropriate ACLs on each resource in the file system that will be accessed from the FTP site or virtual directory. You can then assign the account credentials to the `AnonymousUsername` and `AnonymousUserPass` properties. If you want to enable automatic password synchronization between the Metabase and the NT SAM, you can also set the `AnonymousPasswordSync` property to True.

Querying Anonymous User Credentials Using Visual Basic
To find the username and password for the account used to access the file system through an anonymous connection, use the following Visual Basic code:

```
Dim Site As IADs
Dim ServerName As String
Dim SiteIndex As Long
ServerName = "IIS_Server_Name"
SiteIndex = Site_Index_Value
Set Site = GetObject("IIS://" & ServerName & "/MSFTPSVC/" & SiteIndex)
Debug.Print Site.AnonymousUsername
Debug.Print Site.AnonymousUserPass
Debug.Print Site.AnonymousPasswordSync
```

Tip

Using the `AnonymousPasswordSync` *property, you can determine whether the password will be synchronized between the Windows NT SAM and IIS.* ◆

Setting Anonymous User Credentials Using Visual Basic
To set a new set of credentials for use by anonymous connections, use the following Visual Basic code:

```
Dim Site As IADs
Dim ServerName As String
Dim SiteIndex As Long
Dim AnonymousUserName as String
Dim AnonymousUserPassword as String
ServerName = "IIS_Server_Name"
SiteIndex = Site_Index_Value
AnonymousUserName = "Username_for_Anonymous_FTP_Access"
AnonymousUserPassword = "Password_for_Anonymous_User_Account"
Set Site = GetObject("IIS://" & ServerName & "/MSFTPSVC/" & SiteIndex)
Site.AnonymousUsername = AnonymousUserName
Site.AnonymousUserPass = AnonymousUserPassword
Site.AnonymousPasswordSync = True
Site.SetInfo
```

Configuring Anonymous Only Access

If you have anonymous access enabled, but also happen to have the proper NTFS permissions to perform an action using your own credentials, you could use your own account to access the site. This would, however, expose your password to anyone monitoring the network.

To prevent this exposure, Microsoft implemented the `AnonymousOnly` property to force FTP site users to only use the "anonymous" user account even if they have access via alternative means. In this configuration, the threat of an account compromise is limited to just the anonymous user account; a privileged account cannot be compromised using a network sniffer.

To enable this setting for a site, you simply set the `AnonymousOnly` property value to True.

Querying AnonymousOnly *Using Visual Basic*

To query whether the site will allow non-anonymous connections, use the following Visual Basic code:

```
Dim Site As IADs
Dim ServerName As String
Dim SiteIndex As Long
ServerName = "IIS_Server_Name"
SiteIndex = Site_Index_Value
Set Site = GetObject("IIS://" & ServerName & "/MSFTPSVC/" & SiteIndex)
Debug.Print Site.AnonymousOnly
```

Setting AnonymousOnly *Using Visual Basic*

To enable only anonymous connections to a site, use the following Visual Basic code:

```
Dim Site As IADs
Dim ServerName As String
Dim SiteIndex As Long
ServerName = "IIS_Server_Name"
SiteIndex = Site_Index_Value
Set Site = GetObject("IIS://" & ServerName & "/MSFTPSVC/" & SiteIndex)
Site.AnonymousOnly = True
Site.SetInfo
```

FTP Site Operators

By default, all local administrators can manage all properties in the IIS Metabase. You can define additional site operators by creating a new ACE in the ACL used to secure a site in the Metabase hierarchy.

Querying Operators Using Visual Basic
Use the following Visual Basic code to query the currently defined site operators:

```
Dim Site As IADs
Dim ServerName As String
Dim SiteIndex As Long
ServerName = "IIS_Server_Name"
SiteIndex = Site_Index_Value
Set Site = GetObject("IIS://" & ServerName & "/MSFTPSVC/" & SiteIndex)
Set SecurityDescriptor = Site.AdminAcl
Set DiscretionaryAcl = SecurityDescriptor.DiscretionaryAcl
For Each Item In DiscretionaryAcl
    If Item.AccessMask = 11 Or Item.AccessMask = 262315 Then
        Debug.Print Item.Trustee
    End If
Next
```

Creating a New Operator ACE Using Visual Basic
Use the following Visual Basic code to create a new operator ACE in the ACL:

```
Dim Site As IADs
Dim ACE As Variant
Dim DiscretionaryACL As Variant
Dim ServerName As String
Dim SiteIndex As Long
Dim NewOperator As String
ServerName = "IIS_Server_Name"
SiteIndex = Site_Index_Value
NewOperator = "New_Operator_in_Format_Domain\Username"
Set Site = GetObject("IIS://" & ServerName & "/MSFTPSVC/" & SiteIndex)
Set SecurityDescriptor = Site.AdminACL
Set DiscretionaryACL = SecurityDescriptor.DiscretionaryACL
Set ACE = CreateObject("AccessControlEntry")
ACE.Trustee = NewOperator
ACE.AccessMask = 11
DiscretionaryACL.AddAce ACE
SecurityDescriptor.DiscretionaryACL = DiscretionaryACL
Site.AdminACL = SecurityDescriptor
Site.SetInfo
```

Programmatically Administering the Messages Property Sheet

Various messages can be displayed upon successful connection or termination of an FTP session. As shown in Figure 10.3, the Messages property sheet implements three types of messages for an FTP site: Welcome, Exit, and Maximum Connections.

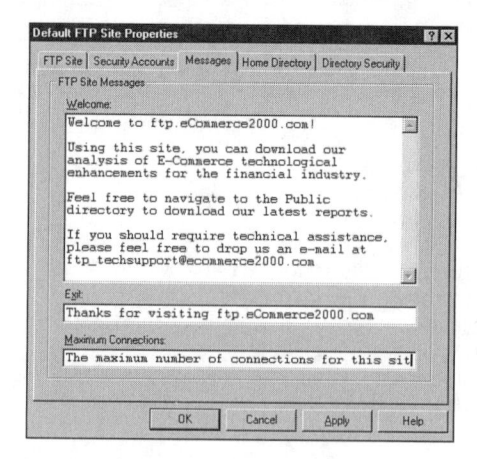

Figure 10.3 *Default FTP Site Properties dialog box—Messages tab.*

Programmatically, you can manipulate these settings by assigning values to the `GreetingMessage`, `ExitMessage`, and `MaxClientsMessage` properties.

Greeting Message

The FTP site greeting message is the message displayed immediately after successful user authentication. This value is stored in the Metabase as an array of strings assigned to the `GreetingMessage` property. Each string in the array represents an individual line of text to be displayed to the user.

```
C:\>ftp server_name
Connected to server_name.eCommerce2000.com.
220 server_name Microsoft FTP Service (Version 4.0).
User (server_name.eCommerce2000.com:(none)): anonymous
331 Anonymous access allowed, send identity (e-mail name) as password.
Password:
230-Welcome to ftp.eCommerce2000.com!
230-
230-Using this site, you can download our
230-analysis of E-Commerce technological
230-enhancements for the financial industry.
230-
230-Feel free to navigate to the Public
230-directory to download our latest reports.
230-
230-If you should require technical assistance,
230-please feel free to drop us an e-mail at
230-ftp_techsupport@ecommerce2000.com
230 Anonymous user logged in.
ftp>
```

Querying Current Greeting Message Using Visual Basic
To find the greeting message used upon a successful connection request, use the following Visual Basic code:

```
Dim Site As IADs
Dim ServerName As String
Dim SiteIndex As Long
ServerName = "IIS_Server_Name"
SiteIndex = Site_Index_Value
Set Site = GetObject("IIS://" & ServerName & "/MSFTPSVC/" & SiteIndex)
For Each MessageLine in Site.GreetingMessage
    Debug.Print MessageLine
Next
```

Setting New Greeting Message Using Visual Basic
To set a new greeting message, you must create an array of strings that will represent the message. Use the following Visual Basic code as a guide:

```
Dim Site As IADs
Dim ServerName As String
Dim SiteIndex As Long
ServerName = "IIS_Server_Name"
SiteIndex = Site_Index_Value
Set Site = GetObject("IIS://" & ServerName & "/MSFTPSVC/" & SiteIndex)
Site.GreetingMessage =
➥Array("Greeting_Line_1","Greeting_Line_2","Greeting_Line_3")
Site.SetInfo
```

Exit Message
Unlike the `GreetingMessage` property, `ExitMessage` consists of a single string displayed just before terminating the user's FTP session. If you want to implement such a feature for an FTP site, simply assign an appropriate string to the `ExitMessage` property, as follows:

```
ftp> bye
221 Thanks for visiting ftp.eCommerce2000.com
```

Querying Current Exit Message Using Visual Basic
To find the current string used upon FTP connection termination, use the following Visual Basic code:

```
Dim Site As IADs
Dim ServerName As String
Dim SiteIndex As Long
ServerName = "IIS_Server_Name"
SiteIndex = Site_Index_Value
Set Site = GetObject("IIS://" & ServerName & "/MSFTPSVC/" & SiteIndex)
Debug.Print Site.ExitMessage
```

Setting New Exit Message Using Visual Basic

To set a new message to be used upon termination of FTP client connections, use the following Visual Basic code:

```
Dim Site As IADs
Dim ServerName As String
Dim SiteIndex As Long
Dim NewExitMessageString as String
ServerName = "IIS_Server_Name"
SiteIndex = Site_Index_Value
NewExitMessageString = "FTP_Session_Termination_Text"
Set Site = GetObject("IIS://" & ServerName & "/MSFTPSVC/" & SiteIndex)
Site.ExitMessage = NewExitMessageString
Site.SetInfo
```

Maximum Connections Message

If a user accesses the site when there are no available connections, a message can be displayed to either redirect the user to a mirror site, or perhaps simply apologize for the inconvenience. You can perform such an action by assigning the `MaxClientsMessage` property a string value representing the desired message.

```
Connected to server_name.ecommerce2000.com.
421 The maximum number of connections for this site has been reached. Please
↪visit our mirror site at ftp2.ecommerce2000.com
Connection closed by remote host.
```

Querying Current Maximum Connections Message Using Visual Basic

To view the message issued to the client when the server has reached its maximum number of connections, use the following Visual Basic code:

```
Dim Site As IADs
Dim ServerName As String
Dim SiteIndex As Long
ServerName = "IIS_Server_Name"
SiteIndex = Site_Index_Value
Set Site = GetObject("IIS://" & ServerName & "/MSFTPSVC/" & SiteIndex)
Debug.Print Site.MaxClientsMessage
```

Setting New Current Maximum Connections Message Using Visual Basic

To programmatically set the value of the string issued to the client when the server has reached its maximum number of connections, use the following Visual Basic code:

```
Dim Site As IADs
Dim ServerName As String
Dim SiteIndex As Long
Dim MaxConnectionsString as String
ServerName = "IIS_Server_Name"
```

```
SiteIndex = Site_Index_Value
MaxConnectionsString = "String_Passed_To_Client_When_Maximum_Connections_Reached"
Set Site = GetObject("IIS://" & ServerName & "/MSFTPSVC/" & SiteIndex)
Site.MaxClientsMessage = MaxConnectionsString
Site.SetInfo
```

Programmatically Administering the Home Directory Property Sheet

As shown in Figure 10.4, each virtual directory utilizes a home directory to point users to the files and directories comprising the FTP site. A virtual directory can be hosted either on the FTP server itself, or on a remote share. If the remote share option is chosen, you must also specify the credentials to be used when accessing the resource.

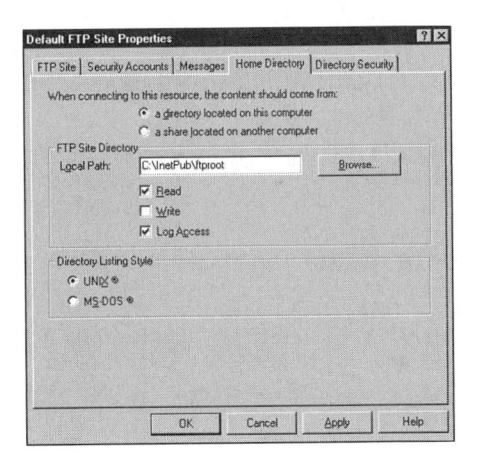

Figure 10.4 *Default FTP Site Properties dialog box—Home Directory tab (local path).*

Additionally, you can specify the access permissions for the home directory and whether the directories should utilize an MS-DOS- or UNIX-style list.

Local Home Directory

To access content stored on the local machine, only the virtual directory's Path property must be assigned a value. Although these code examples demonstrate the use of the root virtual directory, you can also easily bind another existing virtual directory.

Querying the Local Path Property for an FTP Site's Root Virtual Directory Using Visual Basic

To find the current path associated with a particular FTP site, use the following Visual Basic code as a guide:

```
Dim VirtualDirectory As IADs
Dim ServerName As String
Dim Index As Long
Dim RetVal as String
ServerName = "IIS_Server_Name"
Index = Site_Index_Value
Set VirtualDirectory = GetObject("IIS://" & ServerName & "/MSFTPSVC/" & Index & "/ROOT")
RetVal = VirtualDirectory.Path
Debug.Print RetVal
```

Modifying the Local Path Property for an FTP Site's Root Virtual Directory Using Visual Basic

To programmatically vary the path assigned to an existing FTP site, use the following Visual Basic code:

```
Dim VirtualDirectory As IADs
Dim ServerName As String
Dim Index As Long
Dim NewVirtualDirPath As String
ServerName = "IIS_Server_Name"
Index = Site_Index_Value
NewVirtualDirPath = "New_Path_for_Site"
Set VirtualDirectory = GetObject("IIS://" & ServerName & "/MSFTPSVC/" & Index & "/ROOT")
VirtualDirectory.Path = NewVirtualDirPath
VirtualDirectory.SetInfo
```

Remote Home Directory

To access content stored on a remote share, simply assign the virtual directory's path property to a valid UNC sharepoint (such as \\Server_Name\Share_Name), and define the credentials used for the connection by assigning values to UNCUserName and UNCPassword. The use of an FTP site remote home directory in the IIS 4.0 Internet Server Manager is shown in Figure 10.5.

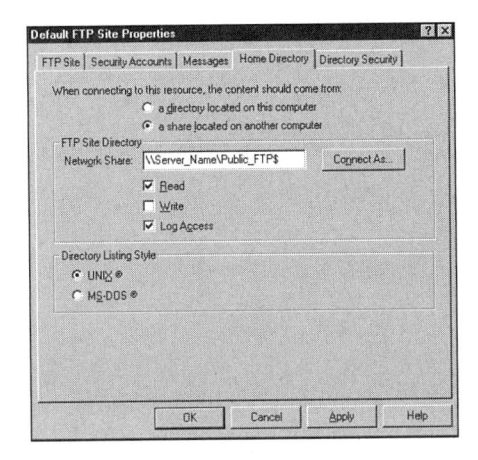

Figure 10.5 *Default FTP Site Properties dialog box—Home Directory tab (remote path).*

Querying the Remote Path Property and UNC Connection Information for a Site's Root Virtual Directory Using Visual Basic

Just as was the case with remote Web home directories, to view the credentials and path associated with a remote FTP home directory, use the following Visual Basic code:

```
Dim VirtualDirectory As IADs
Dim ServerName As String
Dim Index As Long
Dim RetVal As String
ServerName = "IIS_Server_Name"
Index = Site_Index_Value
Set VirtualDirectory = GetObject("IIS://" & ServerName & "/MSFTPSVC/" & Index &
↪"/ROOT")
Debug.Print VirtualDirectory.Path
Debug.Print VirtualDirectory.UNCUserName
Debug.Print VirtualDirectory.UNCPassword
```

Warning

Notice that you were able to obtain the username and password assigned to access the remote share. As a result of your ability to easily compromise this account information, do not use a privileged account for the UNCUserName *and* UNCPassword *properties.* ◆

Modifying the Remote Path Property for a Site's Root Virtual Directory Using Visual Basic

To programmatically establish a new remote home directory for an FTP site, use the following Visual Basic code:

```
Dim VirtualDirectory As IADs
Dim ServerName As String
Dim Index As Long
Dim NewVirtualDirPath As String
Dim NewVirtualDirUser As String
Dim NewVirtualDirPassword As String
ServerName = "IIS_Server_Name"
Index = Site_Index_Value
NewVirtualDirPath = "New_Path_for_Site"
NewVirtualDirUser = "UNC_Credentials_Used_To_Establish_Connection"
NewVirtualDirPassword = "UNC_Credentials_Used_To_Establish_Connection"
Set VirtualDirectory = GetObject("IIS://" & ServerName & "/MSFTPSVC/" & Index & _
"/ROOT")
VirtualDirectory.Path = NewVirtualDirPath
VirtualDirectory.UNCUserName = NewVirtualDirUser
VirtualDirectory.UNCPassword = NewVirtualDirPassword
VirtualDirectory.SetInfo
```

Directory Access Permissions

Although IIS uses NTFS permissions to manage access to resources, the ability to restrict permissions even further exists by assigning the appropriate Boolean value to the AccessRead and AccessWrite properties for the bound resource.

Although intended to restrict permissions for File Access Table (FAT) partitions, the AccessRead and AccessWrite properties apply only the most restrictive right when used with NTFS security. For example, if the NTFS permissions for the user account do not allow writes to the file system, regardless of the value of AccessWrite, you will not be able to write to the directory. Conversely, if the account utilized for accessing the site grants the user the ability to write to the file system, the user will only be able to write if the value of AccessWrite is assigned a True value.

In addition, you can specify by toggling the Boolean value assigned to the DontLog property whether you wish to log access to the bound resource.

Querying Directory Access Permissions and Logging Status Using Visual Basic

To determine whether a user can read or write a resource or whether the resource is subject to logging, use the following Visual Basic code:

```
Dim VirtualDirectory As IADs
Dim ServerName As String
Dim Index As Long
```

```
Dim RetVal as String
ServerName = "IIS_Server_Name"
Index = Site_Index_Value
Set VirtualDirectory = GetObject("IIS://" & ServerName & "/MSFTPSVC/" & Index &
↪"/ROOT")
Debug.Print "Read:" & vbTab & vbTab & vbTab & vbTab & VirtualDirectory.AccessRead
Debug.Print "Write:" & vbTab & vbTab & vbTab & vbTab &
↪VirtualDirectory.AccessWrite
Debug.Print "Logging Disabled: " & vbTab & vbtab & VirtualDirectory.DontLog
```

Setting Directory Access Permissions and Logging Using Visual Basic

To set these properties, simply assign the `AccessRead`, `AccessWrite`, and `DontLog` properties to the appropriate Boolean value and call the IADs `SetInfo` method, as shown in the following Visual Basic code:

```
Dim VirtualDirectory As IADs
Dim ServerName As String
Dim Index As Long
Dim RetVal as String
ServerName = "IIS_Server_Name"
Index = Site_Index_Value
Set VirtualDirectory = GetObject("IIS://" & ServerName & "/MSFTPSVC/" & Index &
↪"/ROOT")
VirtualDirectory.AccessRead = True
VirtualDirectory.AccessWrite = True
VirtualDirectory.DontLog = False
VirtualDirectory.SetInfo
```

Directory Listing Style

IIS offers two options for formatting the output from directory listings. To help illustrate and highlight the differences, consider the examples shown below.

MS-DOS directory listing style:

```
ftp> dir *.exe
200 PORT command successful.
150 Opening ASCII mode data connection for /bin/ls.
11-05-97  03:25PM              20480 aceclcab.exe
06-02-98  07:44AM              44544 clspack.exe
10-27-97  06:19PM              38784 cpsdir.exe
03-18-99  08:09PM             100864 extract.exe
09-09-99  03:16PM              26896 hh.exe
03-18-99  08:09PM              17655 iextract.exe
08-26-97  12:06PM             315904 IsUninst.exe
06-02-98  07:29AM             154112 jview.exe
06-02-98  07:41AM              42496 setdebug.exe
06-13-97  06:46AM             298496 uninst.exe
10-14-96  02:38AM              22288 welcome.exe
06-02-98  07:29AM             147456 wjview.exe
226 Transfer complete.
618 bytes received in 0.02 seconds (30.90 Kbytes/sec)
ftp>
```

UNIX directory listing style:

```
ftp> dir *.exe
200 PORT command successful.
150 Opening ASCII mode data connection for /bin/ls.
-r-xr-xr-x   1 owner    group       20480 Nov  5  1997 aceclcab.exe
-r-xr-xr-x   1 owner    group       44544 Jun  2  1998 clspack.exe
-r-xr-xr-x   1 owner    group       38784 Oct 27  1997 cpsdir.exe
-r-xr-xr-x   1 owner    group      100864 Mar 18 20:09 extract.exe
-r-xr-xr-x   1 owner    group       26896 Sep  9 15:16 hh.exe
-r-xr-xr-x   1 owner    group       17655 Mar 18 20:09 iextract.exe
-r-xr-xr-x   1 owner    group      315904 Aug 26  1997 IsUninst.exe
-r-xr-xr-x   1 owner    group      154112 Jun  2  1998 jview.exe
-r-xr-xr-x   1 owner    group       42496 Jun  2  1998 setdebug.exe
-r-xr-xr-x   1 owner    group      298496 Jun 13  1997 uninst.exe
-r-xr-xr-x   1 owner    group       22288 Oct 14  1996 welcome.exe
-r-xr-xr-x   1 owner    group      147456 Jun  2  1998 wjview.exe
226 Transfer complete.
858 bytes received in 0.29 seconds (2.96 Kbytes/sec)
```

To set the directory listing style, simply assign an appropriate Boolean value to the MSDOSDirOutput property. When set to True, the MS-DOS directory listing style is used. By default, the IIS FTP service uses MS-DOS style directory listings. In general, however, you should use the UNIX directory listing style for a more seamless presentation to users in heterogeneous computing environments.

Querying Directory Listing Style Using Visual Basic

To find out which directory listing style has been configured for use on a specific resource, use the following Visual Basic code:

```
Dim VirtualDirectory As IADs
Dim ServerName As String
Dim Index As Long
ServerName = "IIS_Server_Name"
Index = Site_Index_Value
Set VirtualDirectory = GetObject("IIS://" & ServerName & "/MSFTPSVC/" & Index)
Debug.Print VirtualDirectory.MSDOSDirOutput
```

Setting Directory Listing Style Using Visual Basic

To set the directory listing style, simply set the MSDOSDirOutput property to the appropriate Boolean value, as shown in the following Visual Basic code:

```
Dim VirtualDirectory As IADs
Dim ServerName As String
Dim Index As Long
ServerName = "IIS_Server_Name"
Index = Site_Index_Value
Set VirtualDirectory = GetObject("IIS://" & ServerName & "/MSFTPSVC/" & Index)
VirtualDirectory.MSDOSDirOutput = False
VirtualDirectory.SetInfo
```

Programmatically Administering the Directory Security Property Sheet

As shown in Figure 10.6, you can include or exclude specific sites based on IP address.

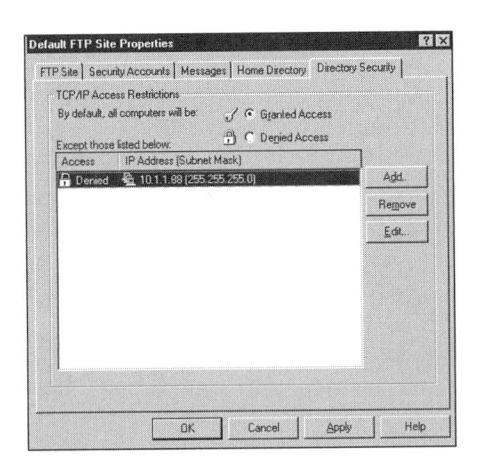

Figure 10.6 *Default FTP Site Properties dialog box—Directory Security tab.*

If your organization has requirements for "Chinese Walls" (mandated separation by regulatory agencies) between business units (as might be found between the Corporate Finance and Equities groups of an investment bank), you may want to prevent individual subnets or DNS domains from accessing specific resources on your intranet.

Although IP spoofing can compromise the effectiveness of such methods, implementing IP security can be an effective front line defense against access from an unauthorized IP address.

In a more common scenario, IP address restrictions are often imposed to ensure that development sites utilizing anonymous access are accessed only by developers. By simply inserting the IP addresses of the developer workstations into the list of machines granted access, the developers can transfer data between their client and the server with little fear that anyone else has access.

IP security requires construction of an array of IP addresses that are then consequently assigned to one of the properties of the IPSecurity object in Table 10.2.

Table 10.2   IPSecurity Properties

Property	Description
IPGrant	Array of IP Addresses granted access—stored in variant array of strings in the format *IPAddress, Subnet Mask*
IPDeny	Array of IP Addresses denied access—stored in variant array of strings in the format *IPAddress, Subnet Mask*
DomainGrant	Array of strings representing DNS domains granted access to resources
DomainDeny	Array of strings representing DNS domains denied access to resources

Armed with the basic knowledge of the operations of the IPSecurity interface, you can now examine the code used to query and set new IP address restrictions.

> **Warning**
>
> *The use of DNS domains for restricting access is not recommended because of the costly reverse DNS lookup that must take place for each request. Be sure to examine the performance of the site both before and after implementing such a restriction to ensure that performance is still reasonably acceptable.* ◆

Querying Current IP Address Restrictions Using Visual Basic

To find the current IP address and DNS domain restrictions effective for a particular site, use the following Visual Basic code:

```
Dim Site As IADs
Dim ServerName As String
Dim SiteIndex As Long
Dim IPSecurity As Variant
ServerName = "IIS_Server_Name"
SiteIndex = Site_Index_Value
Set Site = GetObject("IIS://" & ServerName & "/MSFTPSVC/" & SiteIndex & "/ROOT")
Set IPSecurity = Site.IPSecurity
If IPSecurity.GrantByDefault Then
    Debug.Print "All addresses will be allowed, except as follows:"
    For Each Entry In IPSecurity.IPDeny
        If InStr(1, Entry, "255.255.255.255") Then
            Debug.Print vbTab & "Denied IP: " & vbTab & vbTab & Replace(Entry,
              ", 255.255.255.255", "")
        Else
            Debug.Print vbTab & "Denied Subnet: " & vbTab & Entry
```

```
                End If
            Next
            For Each Entry In IPSecurity.DomainDeny
                    Debug.Print vbTab & "Denied Domain: " & vbTab & Entry
            Next
        Else
            Debug.Print "All addresses will be blocked, except as follows:"
            For Each Entry In IPSecurity.IPGrant
                    If InStr(1, Entry, "255.255.255.255") Then
                        Debug.Print vbTab & "Allowed IP: " & vbTab & vbTab &
                        ↪Replace(Entry, ", 255.255.255.255", ")
                    Else
                        Debug.Print vbTab & "Allowed Subnet: " & vbTab & Entry
                    End If
            Next
            For Each Entry In IPSecurity.DomainGrant
                    Debug.Print vbTab & "Allowed Domain: " & vbTab & Entry
            Next
        End If
```

Setting New IP Address Restrictions Using Visual Basic

To create a new IP address or DNS domain restriction programmatically, use the following Visual Basic code:

```
Dim Site As IADs
Dim ServerName As String
Dim SiteIndex As Long
Dim IPSecurity As Variant
Dim IPAddress As String
Dim IPSubnet As String
Dim Domain As String
Dim ActionType As String
ServerName = "IIS_Server_Name"
SiteIndex = Site_Index_Value
IPAddress = "xxx.xxx.xxx.xxx"
IPSubnet = "xxx.xxx.xxx.xxx"
Domain = "DNS_Domain.Name"
ActionType = "GRANTIP"
'ActionType = "GRANTSUBNET"
'ActionType = "GRANTDOMAIN"
'ActionType = "DENYIP"
'ActionType = "DENYSUBNET"
'ActionType = "DENYDOMAIN"
Select Case ActionType
    Case "GRANTIP"
        Set Site = GetObject("IIS://" & ServerName & "/MSFTPSVC/" & SiteIndex &
        ↪"/ROOT")
        Set IPSecurity = Site.IPSecurity
        IPSecurity.GrantByDefault = False
        Site.IPSecurity = IPSecurity
        Site.SetInfo
        IPSecurity.IPGrant = Array(IPAddress & ", 255.255.255.255")
        Site.IPSecurity = IPSecurity
        Site.SetInfo
```

```
            Case "GRANTSUBNET"
                Set Site = GetObject("IIS://" & ServerName & "/MSFTPSVC/" & SiteIndex &
                ➥"/ROOT")
                Set IPSecurity = Site.IPSecurity
                IPSecurity.GrantByDefault = False
                IPSecurity.IPGrant = Array(IPAddress & ", " & IPSubnet)
                Site.IPSecurity = IPSecurity
                Site.SetInfo
            Case "GRANTDOMAIN"
                Set Site = GetObject("IIS://" & ServerName & "/MSFTPSVC/" & SiteIndex &
                ➥"/ROOT")
                Set IPSecurity = Site.IPSecurity
                IPSecurity.GrantByDefault = False
                IPSecurity.DomainGrant = Array(Domain)
                Site.IPSecurity = IPSecurity
                Site.SetInfo
            Case "DENYIP"
                Set Site = GetObject("IIS://" & ServerName & "/MSFTPSVC/" & SiteIndex &
                ➥"/ROOT")
                Set IPSecurity = Site.IPSecurity
                IPSecurity.GrantByDefault = True
                IPSecurity.IPDeny = Array(IPAddress & ", 255.255.255.255")
                Site.IPSecurity = IPSecurity
                Site.SetInfo
            Case "DENYSUBNET"
                Set Site = GetObject("IIS://" & ServerName & "/MSFTPSVC/" & SiteIndex &
                ➥"/ROOT")
                Set IPSecurity = Site.IPSecurity
                IPSecurity.GrantByDefault = True
                IPSecurity.IPDeny = Array(IPAddress & ", " & IPSubnet)
                Site.IPSecurity = IPSecurity
                Site.SetInfo
            Case "DENYDOMAIN"
                Set Site = GetObject("IIS://" & ServerName & "/MSFTPSVC/" & SiteIndex &
                ➥"/ROOT")
                Set IPSecurity = Site.IPSecurity
                IPSecurity.GrantByDefault = True
                IPSecurity.DomainDeny = Array(Domain)
                Site.IPSecurity = IPSecurity
                Site.SetInfo
        End Select
```

Note

To set a new IP address restriction, simply uncomment the desired ActionType *variable assignment and verify that all associated variables have been assigned.* ◆

Creating the IIsFTPManagement Class Module

In this section, you will continue the creation of the IIsAdmin.DLL COM server application you started in Chapter 8, "Programmatic Management of the IIS Metabase."

Exercise 10.1 *Creating the IIsAdmin.DLL COM Server Application: The IIsFTPManagement Class Module*

1. Open the IIsAdmin ActiveX DLL Visual Basic project that was started in Chapter 8. You can also download the project from http://www.newriders.com/adsi.
2. If you are adding to the IIsAdmin project, add a new class module to the project. If this is a new project, be sure to set a reference to Active DS Type Library.
3. Name the new module **IIsFTPManagement**.
4. Enter the following code into the General Declarations section of the class module:

```
Public Function ManageIdentityProperties(ByVal TargetComputer As String, ByVal
↪SiteIndex As Integer, ByVal IdentityProperty As String, ByVal Action As String,
↪Optional ByVal NewValue As String) As Variant
    Dim Site As IADs
    Set Site = GetObject("IIS://" & TargetComputer & "/MSFTPSVC/" & SiteIndex)
    Select Case UCase(Action)
        Case "QUERY"
            Select Case UCase(IdentityProperty)
                Case "DESCRIPTION"
                    ManageIdentityProperties = Site.ServerComment
                Case "MAXCONNECTIONS"
                    ManageIdentityProperties = Site.MaxConnections
                Case "TIMEOUT"
                    ManageIdentityProperties = Site.ConnectionTimeout
            End Select
        Case "SET"
            If NewValue <> " " Then
                Select Case UCase(IdentityProperty)
                    Case "DESCRIPTION"
                        Site.ServerComment = NewValue
                        Site.SetInfo
                        If Err.Number = 0 Then ManageIdentityProperties =
                        ↪True
                    Case "MAXCONNECTIONS"
                        Site.MaxConnections = NewValue
                        Site.SetInfo
                        If Err.Number = 0 Then ManageIdentityProperties =
                        ↪True
                    Case "TIMEOUT"
                        Site.ConnectionTimeout = NewValue
                        Site.SetInfo
                        If Err.Number = 0 Then ManageIdentityProperties =
                        ↪True
                End Select
            End If
    End Select
End Function
```

```
Public Function ManageServerBindings(ByVal TargetComputer As String, ByVal
↪SiteIndex As Integer, ByVal Action As String, Optional ByVal Element As
↪Variant) As Variant
    On Error Resume Next
    Dim Binding As Variant
    Dim Site As IADs
    Dim NewElement() As Variant
    Dim i As Long
    Dim Entry As Variant
    Set Site = GetObject("IIS://" & TargetComputer & "/MSFTPSVC/" & SiteIndex)
    Select Case UCase(Action)
        Case "QUERY"
            If IsArray(Site.ServerBindings) = True Then
                For Each Entry In Site.ServerBindings
                    i = UBound(NewElement) + 1
                    ReDim Preserve NewElement(i)
                    NewElement(i) = Entry
                Next
                ManageServerBindings = NewElement
            Else
                ManageServerBindings = Array(Site.ServerBindings)
            End If
        Case "SET"
            If Element <> " Then
                If IsArray(Element) = True Then
                    For Each Entry In Element
                        i = UBound(NewElement) + 1
                        ReDim Preserve NewElement(i)
                        NewElement(i) = Entry
                    Next
                    Site.ServerBindings = NewElement
                Else
                    Site.ServerBindings = Array(Element)
                End If
                Site.SetInfo
                If Err.Number = 0 Then ManageServerBindings = True
            End If
    End Select
End Function

Public Function ManageSecurityProperties(ByVal TargetComputer As String, ByVal
↪SiteIndex As Integer, ByVal IdentityProperty As String, ByVal Action As String,
↪Optional ByVal NewValue As String) As Variant
    Dim Site As IADs
    Set Site = GetObject("IIS://" & TargetComputer & "/MSFTPSVC/" & SiteIndex)
    Select Case UCase(Action)
        Case "QUERY"
            Select Case UCase(IdentityProperty)
                Case "ALLOWANONYMOUS"
                    ManageSecurityProperties = Site.AllowAnonymous
                Case "ANONYMOUSUSERNAME"
                    ManageSecurityProperties = Site.AnonymousUserName
                Case "ANONYMOUSUSERPASS"
```

```
                        ManageSecurityProperties = Site.AnonymousUserPass
                    Case "ANONYMOUSPASSWORDSYNC"
                        ManageSecurityProperties = Site.AnonymousPasswordSync
                    Case "ANONYMOUSONLY"
                        ManageSecurityProperties = Site.AnonymousOnly
                End Select
        Case "SET"
            If NewValue <> " Then
                Select Case UCase(IdentityProperty)
                    Case "ALLOWANONYMOUS"
                        Site.AllowAnonymous = NewValue
                        Site.SetInfo
                        If Err.Number = 0 Then ManageSecurityProperties =
                            ↪True
                    Case "ANONYMOUSUSERNAME"
                        Site.AnonymousUserName = NewValue
                        Site.SetInfo
                        If Err.Number = 0 Then ManageSecurityProperties =
                            ↪True
                    Case "ANONYMOUSUSERPASS"
                        Site.AnonymousUserPass = NewValue
                        Site.SetInfo
                        If Err.Number = 0 Then ManageSecurityProperties =
                            ↪True
                    Case "ANONYMOUSPASSWORDSYNC"
                        Site.AnonymousPasswordSync = NewValue
                        Site.SetInfo
                        If Err.Number = 0 Then ManageSecurityProperties =
                            ↪True
                    Case "ANONYMOUSONLY"
                        Site.AnonymousOnly = NewValue
                        Site.SetInfo
                        If Err.Number = 0 Then ManageSecurityProperties =
                            ↪True
                End Select
            End If
    End Select
End Function

Public Function ManageOperators(ByVal TargetComputer As String, ByVal SiteIndex
↪As Integer, ByVal Action As String, Optional ByVal NewOperator As String) As
↪Variant
    On Error Resume Next
    Dim i As Long
    Dim Entry As Variant
    Dim NewElement() As Variant
    Dim Site As IADs
    Dim ACE As Variant
    Dim DiscretionaryACL As Variant
    Set Site = GetObject("IIS://" & TargetComputer & "/MSFTPSVC/" & SiteIndex)
    Select Case UCase(Action)
        Case "QUERY"
            Set SecurityDescriptor = Site.AdminAcl
```

```
                    Set DiscretionaryACL = SecurityDescriptor.DiscretionaryACL
                    For Each Item In DiscretionaryACL
                        If Item.AccessMask = 11 Or Item.AccessMask = 262315 Then
                            i = UBound(NewElement) + 1
                            ReDim Preserve NewElement(i)
                            NewElement(i) = Item.Trustee
                        End If
                    Next
                    ManageOperators = NewElement
                Case "SET"
                    Set SecurityDescriptor = Site.AdminAcl
                    Set DiscretionaryACL = SecurityDescriptor.DiscretionaryACL
                    Set ACE = CreateObject("AccessControlEntry")
                    ACE.Trustee = NewOperator
                    ACE.AccessMask = 11
                    DiscretionaryACL.AddAce ACE
                    SecurityDescriptor.DiscretionaryACL = DiscretionaryACL
                    Site.AdminAcl = SecurityDescriptor
                    Site.SetInfo
                    If Err.Number = 0 Then ManageOperators = True
            End Select
End Function

Public Function ManageMessageProperties(ByVal TargetComputer As String, ByVal
↪SiteIndex As Integer, ByVal IdentityProperty As String, ByVal Action As String,
↪Optional ByVal NewValue As Variant) As Variant
    On Error Resume Next
    Dim i As Long
    Dim MessageLine As Variant
    Dim NewElement() As Variant
    Dim Site As IADs
    Set Site = GetObject("IIS://" & TargetComputer & "/MSFTPSVC/" & SiteIndex)
    Select Case UCase(Action)
        Case "QUERY"
            Select Case UCase(IdentityProperty)
                Case "GREETINGMESSAGE"
                    For Each MessageLine In Site.GreetingMessage
                        i = UBound(NewElement) + 1
                        ReDim Preserve NewElement(i)
                        NewElement(i) = MessageLine
                    Next
                    ManageMessageProperties = NewElement
                Case "EXITMESSAGE"
                    ManageMessageProperties = Site.ExitMessage
                Case "MAXCLIENTSMESSAGE"
                    ManageMessageProperties = Site.MaxClientsMessage
            End Select
        Case "SET"
            If NewValue <> " Then
                Select Case UCase(IdentityProperty)
                    Case "GREETINGMESSAGE"
                        If IsArray(NewValue) = True Then
                            For Each MessageLine In NewValue
                                i = UBound(NewElement) + 1
                                ReDim Preserve NewElement(i)
```

Creating the IIsFTPManagement Class Module 367

```
                            NewElement(i) = MessageLine
                        Next
                        Site.GreetingMessage = NewElement
                    Else
                        Site.GreetingMessage = Array(NewValue)
                    End If
                    Site.SetInfo
                    If Err.Number = 0 Or Err.Number = 9 Then
                    ⇒ManageMessageProperties = True
                Case "EXITMESSAGE"
                    Site.ExitMessage = NewValue
                    Site.SetInfo
                    If Err.Number = 0 Then ManageMessageProperties =
                    ⇒True
                Case "MAXCLIENTSMESSAGE"
                    Site.MaxClientsMessage = NewValue
                    Site.SetInfo
                    If Err.Number = 0 Then ManageMessageProperties =
                    ⇒True
            End Select
        End If
    End Select
End Function

Public Function ManageDirectory(ByVal TargetComputer As String, ByVal SiteIndex
⇒As Integer, ByVal VirtualDirectoryRelativePath As String, ByVal
⇒IdentityProperty As String, ByVal Action As String, Optional ByVal NewValue As
⇒String) As Variant
    Dim VirtualDirectory As IADs
    Set VirtualDirectory = GetObject("IIS://" & TargetComputer & "/MSFTPSVC/" &
    ⇒SiteIndex & VirtualDirectoryRelativePath)
    Select Case UCase(Action)
        Case "QUERY"
            Select Case UCase(IdentityProperty)
                Case "PATH"
                    ManageDirectory = VirtualDirectory.Path
                Case "UNCUSERNAME"
                    ManageDirectory = VirtualDirectory.UNCUserName
                Case "UNCPASSWORD"
                    ManageDirectory = VirtualDirectory.UNCPassword
                Case "ACCESSREAD"
                    ManageDirectory = VirtualDirectory.AccessRead
                Case "ACCESSWRITE"
                    ManageDirectory = VirtualDirectory.AccessWrite
                Case "DONTLOG"
                    ManageDirectory = VirtualDirectory.DontLog
                Case "MSDOSDIROUTPUT"
                    ManageDirectory = VirtualDirectory.MSDOSDirOutput
            End Select
        Case "SET"
            If NewValue <> " " Then
                Select Case UCase(IdentityProperty)
                    Case "PATH"
                        VirtualDirectory.Path = NewValue
```

```
                            VirtualDirectory.SetInfo
                            If Err.Number = 0 Then ManageDirectory = True
                        Case "UNCUSERNAME"
                            VirtualDirectory.UNCUserName = NewValue
                            VirtualDirectory.SetInfo
                            If Err.Number = 0 Then ManageDirectory = True
                        Case "UNCPASSWORD"
                            VirtualDirectory.UNCPassword = NewValue
                            VirtualDirectory.SetInfo
                            If Err.Number = 0 Then ManageDirectory = True
                        Case "ACCESSREAD"
                            VirtualDirectory.AccessRead = NewValue
                            VirtualDirectory.SetInfo
                            If Err.Number = 0 Then ManageDirectory = True
                        Case "ACCESSWRITE"
                            VirtualDirectory.AccessWrite = NewValue
                            VirtualDirectory.SetInfo
                            If Err.Number = 0 Then ManageDirectory = True
                        Case "DONTLOG"
                            VirtualDirectory.DontLog = NewValue
                            VirtualDirectory.SetInfo
                            If Err.Number = 0 Then ManageDirectory = True
                        Case "MSDOSDIROUTPUT"
                            VirtualDirectory.MSDOSDirOutput = NewValue
                            VirtualDirectory.SetInfo
                            If Err.Number = 0 Then ManageDirectory = True
                    End Select
                End If
        End Select
End Function

Public Function ManageIPRestrictions(ByVal TargetComputer As String, ByVal
⇢SiteIndex As Integer, ByVal RelativePath As String, ByVal Action As String,
⇢Optional ByVal RestrictAction As String, Optional ByVal Restrict As String,
⇢Optional ByVal IPSubnet As String) As Variant
    On Error Resume Next
    Dim Site As IADs
    Dim IPSecurity As Variant
    Dim NewElement() As Variant
    Dim IPAddress As String
    Dim ActionType As String
    Set Site = GetObject("IIS://" & TargetComputer & "/MSFTPSVC/" & SiteIndex &
⇢RelativePath)
    Select Case UCase(Action)
        Case "QUERY"
            Set IPSecurity = Site.IPSecurity
            If IPSecurity.GrantByDefault Then
                For Each Entry In IPSecurity.IPDeny
                    If InStr(1, Entry, "255.255.255.255") Then
                        i = UBound(NewElement) + 1
                        ReDim Preserve NewElement(i)
                        NewElement(i) = "Denied IP: " & Replace(Entry, ",
⇢255.255.255.255", "")
```

Creating the IIsFTPManagement Class Module   369

```
                    Else
                        i = UBound(NewElement) + 1
                        ReDim Preserve NewElement(i)
                        NewElement(i) = "Denied Subnet: " & Entry
                    End If
                Next
                For Each Entry In IPSecurity.DomainDeny
                    i = UBound(NewElement) + 1
                    ReDim Preserve NewElement(i)
                    NewElement(i) = "Denied Domain: " & Entry
                Next
            Else
                For Each Entry In IPSecurity.IPGrant
                    If InStr(1, Entry, "255.255.255.255") Then
                        i = UBound(NewElement) + 1
                        ReDim Preserve NewElement(i)
                        NewElement(i) = "Allowed IP: " & Replace(Entry, ",
                        ↪255.255.255.255", ")
                    Else
                        i = UBound(NewElement) + 1
                        ReDim Preserve NewElement(i)
                        NewElement(i) = "Allowed Subnet: " & Entry
                    End If
                Next
                For Each Entry In IPSecurity.DomainGrant
                    i = UBound(NewElement) + 1
                    ReDim Preserve NewElement(i)
                    NewElement(i) = "Allowed Domain: " & Entry
                Next
            End If
            ManageIPRestrictions = NewElement
        Case "SET"
            If Restrict <> " Then
                Select Case UCase(RestrictAction)
                    Case "GRANTIP"
                        Set IPSecurity = Site.IPSecurity
                        IPSecurity.GrantByDefault = False
                        Site.IPSecurity = IPSecurity
                        Site.SetInfo
                        IPSecurity.IPGrant = Array(Restrict & ",
                        ↪255.255.255.255")
                        Site.IPSecurity = IPSecurity
                        Site.SetInfo
                        If Err.Number = 0 Then ManageIPRestrictions = True
                    Case "GRANTSUBNET"
                        Set IPSecurity = Site.IPSecurity
                        IPSecurity.GrantByDefault = False
                        IPSecurity.IPGrant = Array(Restrict & ", " & _
                        ↪IPSubnet)
                        Site.IPSecurity = IPSecurity
                        Site.SetInfo
                        If Err.Number = 0 Then ManageIPRestrictions = True
                    Case "GRANTDOMAIN"
```

```
                    Set IPSecurity = Site.IPSecurity
                    IPSecurity.GrantByDefault = False
                    IPSecurity.DomainGrant = Array(Restrict)
                    Site.IPSecurity = IPSecurity
                    Site.SetInfo
                    If Err.Number = 0 Then ManageIPRestrictions = True
                Case "DENYIP"
                    Set IPSecurity = Site.IPSecurity
                    IPSecurity.GrantByDefault = True
                    IPSecurity.IPDeny = Array(Restrict & ", 
                    ⮕255.255.255.255")
                    Site.IPSecurity = IPSecurity
                    Site.SetInfo
                    If Err.Number = 0 Then ManageIPRestrictions = True
                Case "DENYSUBNET"
                    Set IPSecurity = Site.IPSecurity
                    IPSecurity.GrantByDefault = True
                    IPSecurity.IPDeny = Array(Restrict & ", " & IPSubnet)
                    Site.IPSecurity = IPSecurity
                    Site.SetInfo
                    If Err.Number = 0 Then ManageIPRestrictions = True
                Case "DENYDOMAIN"
                    Set IPSecurity = Site.IPSecurity
                    IPSecurity.GrantByDefault = True
                    IPSecurity.DomainDeny = Array(Restrict)
                    Site.IPSecurity = IPSecurity
                    Site.SetInfo
                    If Err.Number = 0 Then ManageIPRestrictions = True
                End Select
            End If
        End Select
    End Function
```

5. Compile the code as IIsAdmin.DLL.
6. Save and close the IIsAdmin project.

Tip

If you do not want to implement your code in a COM object, you can enter the preceding code into a code module in any VB application. ◆

Tip

You can download the Visual Basic 6.0 project or a pre-compiled version of IISAdmin.DLL from http://www.newriders.com/adsi ◆

Using the Functions in IIsFTPManagement

With the IIsFTPManagement class module created, you can access this function from any programming language that supports OLE automation, including Visual Basic, VBScript, and JavaScript.

> *Tip*
>
> To instantiate the object, follow the appropriate syntax found in Chapter 3, "Container Enumeration Methods and Programmatic Domain Account Policy Manipulation." Substitute the IIsAdmin DLL name and IIsFTPManagement class name where necessary. ◆

Use Table 10.3 to help you use the proper syntax for each of the methods of the IIsFTPManagement interface.

Table 10.3   IIsFTPManagement Method Syntax

Action	Syntax
Query FTP Site Description	ManageIdentityProperties("Server_Name", ⇒1, "Description", "Query")
Set FTP Site Description	ManageIdentityProperties("Server_Name", ⇒1, "Description", "Set", ⇒"New_Description")
Query Maximum Client Connections	ManageIdentityProperties("Server_Name", ⇒1, "MaxConnections", "Query")
Set Maximum Client Connections	ManageIdentityProperties("Server_Name", ⇒1, "MaxConnections", "Set", 100)
Query Connection Timeout	ManageIdentityProperties("Server_Name", ⇒1, "Timeout", "Query")
Set Connection Timeout	ManageIdentityProperties("Server_Name", ⇒1, "Timeout", "Set", "300")
Query FTP Site IP Address and TCP Port	For Each Item In ⇒ManageServerBindings("Server_Name", 1, ⇒"Query") Debug.Print Item Next
Set FTP Site IP Address and TCP Port	ManageServerBindings("Server_Name", 1, ⇒"Set", "xxx.xxx.xxx.xxx:tcp_port")
Query Anonymous Access Allowed	ManageSecurityProperties("Server_Name", ⇒1, "AllowAnonymous", "Query")
Set Anonymous Access Allowed	ManageSecurityProperties("Server_Name", ⇒1, "AllowAnonymous", "Set", True)
Query User Name Used for Anonymous Access	ManageSecurityProperties("Server_Name", ⇒ 1, "AnonymousUserName", "Query")
Set User Name Used for Anonymous Access	ManageSecurityProperties("Server_Name", ⇒ 1, "AnonymousUserName", "Set", ⇒"Username")

Table 10.3 continued

Action	Syntax
Query Password Used for Anonymous Access	`ManageSecurityProperties("Server_Name",` ↪ `1, "AnonymousUserPass", "Query")`
Set Password Used for Anonymous Access	`ManageSecurityProperties("Server_Name",` ↪`1, "AnonymousUserPass", "Set",` ↪`"Password")`
Query Password Synchronization Configuration	`ManageSecurityProperties("Server_Name",` ↪`1, "AnonymousPasswordSync", "Query")`
Set Password Synchronization Configuration	`ManageSecurityProperties("Server_Name",` ↪`1, "AnonymousPasswordSync", "Set", True)`
Query Anonymous Access Only	`ManageSecurityProperties("Server_Name",` ↪`1, "AnonymousOnly", "Query")`
Set Anonymous Access Only	`ManageSecurityProperties("Server_Name",` ↪`1, "AnonymousOnly", "Set", True)`

Query Site Operators	`For Each Item In ManageOperators`
	↪`("Server_Name", 1, "Query")`
	
	`    Debug.Print Item`
	`Next`

Add Site Operator	`ManageOperators("Server_Name", 1, "Set",` ↪`"User_Name")`

Query FTP Site Greeting Message	`For Each Item In ManageMessageProperties`
	↪`("Server_Name", 1, "GreetingMessage",`
	↪`"Query")`
	
	`    Debug.Print Item`
	`Next`

Set New FTP Site Greeting Message	`ManageMessageProperties("Server_Name", 1,` ↪`"GreetingMessage", "Set",` ↪`Array("Line1", "Line2", "Line3"))`
Query FTP Site Exit Message	`ManageMessageProperties("Server_Name", 1,` ↪`"ExitMessage", "Query")`
Set FTP Site Exit Message	`ManageMessageProperties("Server_Name", 1,` ↪`"ExitMessage", "Set", "Exit_Message")`
Query Maximum Clients Message	`ManageMessageProperties("Server_Name", 1,` ↪`"MaxClientsMessage", "Query")`
Set Maximum Clients Message	`ManageMessageProperties("Server_Name", 1,` ↪`"MaxClientsMessage", "set", "too many` ↪`users right now")`
Query Virtual Directory Path	`ManageDirectory("Server_Name", 1,` ↪`"/ROOT", "Path", "Query")`
Set Virtual Directory Path	`ManageDirectory("Server_Name", 1,` ↪`"/ROOT", "Path", "Set", "C:\")`
Query Remote Virtual Directory UNC User Name	`ManageDirectory("Server_Name", 1,` ↪`"/ROOT", "UNCUserName", "Query")`
Set Remote Virtual Directory UNC User Name	`ManageDirectory("Server_Name", 1,` ↪`"/ROOT", "UNCUserName", "Set",` ↪`"User_Name")`

Action	Syntax
Query Remote Virtual Directory UNC User Password	`ManageDirectory("Server_Name", 1,` `↪"/ROOT", "UNCPassword", "Query")`

Set Remote Virtual Directory UNC User Password	`ManageDirectory("Server_Name", 1,`
	`↪"/ROOT", "UNCPassword", "Set",`
	`↪"User_Password")`

Query Virtual Directory Read Access Permission	`ManageDirectory("Server_Name", 1,` `↪"/ROOT", "AccessRead", "Query")`
Set Virtual Directory Read Access Permission	`ManageDirectory("Server_Name", 1,` `↪"/ROOT", "AccessRead", "Set", False)`
Query Virtual Directory Write Access Permission	`ManageDirectory("Server_Name", 1,` `↪"/ROOT", "AccessWrite", "Query")`
Set Virtual Directory Write Access Permission	`ManageDirectory("Server_Name", 1,` `↪"/ROOT", "AccessWrite", "Set", False)`
Query Virtual Directory Logging	`ManageDirectory("Server_Name", 1,` `↪"/ROOT", "DontLog", "Query")`
Set Virtual Directory Logging	`ManageDirectory("Server_Name", 1,` `↪"/ROOT", "DontLog", "Set", True)`
Query Virtual Directory Directory Listing Style	`ManageDirectory("Server_Name", 1, "",` `↪"MSDOSDirOutput", "Query")`
Set Virtual Directory Directory Listing Style	`ManageDirectory("Server_Name", 1, "",` `↪"MSDOSDirOutput", "Set", True)`

Query IP Restrictions	`For Each Item In ManageIPRestrictions`
	`↪("Server_Name", 1, "/ROOT", "Query")`
	`    Debug.Print Item`
	`Next`

Deny All Access Except Specified IP	`ManageIPRestrictions("Server_Name", 1,`
	`↪"/ROOT", "Set", "GrantIP",`
	`↪"xxx.xxx.xxx.xxx")`

Deny All Access Except Specified Subnet	`ManageIPRestrictions("Server_Name", 1,`
	`↪"/ROOT", "Set", "GrantSubnet",`
	`↪"xxx.xxx.xxx.xxx", "xxx.xxx.xxx.0")`

Deny All Access Except Specified DNS Domain	`ManageIPRestrictions("Server_Name", 1,`
	`↪"/ROOT", "Set", "GrantDomain",`
	`↪"DNS_Domain")`

Grant All Access Except Specified Address	`ManageIPRestrictions("Server_Name", 1,`
	`↪"/ROOT", "Set", "DenyIP",`
	`↪"xxx.xxx.xxx.xxx")`

Grant All Access Except Specified Subnet	`ManageIPRestrictions("Server_Name", 1,`
	`↪"/ROOT", "Set", "DenySubnet",`
	`↪"xxx.xxx.xxx.xxx", "xxx.xxx.xxx.0")`

Grant All Access Except Specified Domain	`ManageIPRestrictions("Server_Name", 1,`
	`↪"/ROOT", "Set", "DenyDomain",`
	`↪"DNS_Domain")`

Summary

Using the ADSI techniques presented in this chapter, you can easily perform basic FTP site configuration tasks, including manipulation of the site's identification, number of connections, and logging format.

To reduce the risks associated with network protocol analysis-type attacks, Microsoft recommends the use of only anonymous connections to your site. Although this may protect against attacks from hackers sniffing the network, it opens up the potential for an attacker to obtain the credentials used for the anonymous user account using ADSI. Before selecting your FTP site security configuration, you should carefully analyze the area that presents the greatest threat to the integrity of the data hosted on the site.

Unique to the FTP site is the ability to define custom client messages upon instantiation, termination, and denial of a connection. In addition to the ability to host files locally or on a remote file share, you can also configure the directory listing style presented to the client using the MSDOSDirOutput property. In similar fashion to other IIS services, you can selectively grant and deny access to the site based on IP address or DNS domain.

Using the programmatic techniques presented in this chapter and a little bit of imagination, you can create easy-to-use administrative applications that allow the user to create her own FTP site from a Web page. Shifting the administrative burden from administrators to users can allow a more proactive approach to administration and free you to perform more interesting and complex duties for the organization.

Part IV

Exploring the ADSI Service Providers: LDAP

11 Programmatic Management of LDAP Infrastructures

12 Programmatic Management of the Windows 2000 Active Directory

11

Programmatic Management of LDAP Infrastructures

The Lightweight Directory Access Protocol (LDAP) provides an Internet Engineering Task Force (IETF) RFC-based standard to store user, organizational, and application configuration information for any LDAP-compliant client to access. With the proliferation of HTML-based products and sites in recent years, LDAP has become the standard directory access protocol for many application and operating system vendors, including Netscape, Entrust, and Microsoft.

In this chapter, you will learn how LDAP fits into the enterprise computing model and how ADSI and LDAP are related. Specifically, this chapter briefly examines LDAP technology and terminology and discusses available LDAP APIs, as well as several commercial products that employ LDAP directories.

In addition, you will learn how to:

- Manipulate an LDAP directory using ADSI.
- Enumerate an LDAP namespace using ADSI.
- Search an LDAP namespace using the ActiveX Data Objects (ADO).
- Manage Microsoft Exchange mailboxes and distribution lists using ADSI's LDAP provider.

You will also take a look at the installation of Netscape's Directory Server product and the Airius sample directory in a hands-on exercise. From this exercise, you will establish a common namespace, which will enable you to test the code segments found throughout the chapter on the sample directory.

A Brief Overview of LDAP Technology and Terminology

The technology and architecture behind LDAP are extremely broad topics that cannot be covered sufficiently within the context of this book. To truly understand LDAP, you may want to examine the resources listed in Appendix B, "ADSI 2.5 Programmer's Reference," and balance your theoretical studies with practical, hands-on experience by utilizing one of the many LDAP server products.

With the caveat that this section is not intended to be a comprehensive discussion of LDAP, we can examine some of the more elemental properties of its specification.

What Is LDAP?

Based on the X.500 directory standard, LDAP is a common language that all LDAP-enabled clients and servers can use to communicate. Although originally proposed as a front-end for X.500 directories to help reduce the complexity of implementing client applications, LDAP has instead dwarved the growth of X.500 directories. This explosion of LDAP use is due in part to its directory specification's relative simplicity.

Timothy Howe, the primary author of the original LDAP specification proposals, has defined four models to establish the standard for the directory access protocol. These models are as follows:

- **Information Model.** Defines the data that can be placed in the directory.
- **Naming Model.** Defines the organization of the namespace.
- **Functional Model.** Defines the methods for accessing and updating data.
- **Security Model.** Defines the methods that should be employed to protect the directory from unauthorized access.

The Informational Model: What Can Be Placed into an LDAP Directory?

In large, distributed enterprises, a central repository of employee information is essential to enable quick access to telephone numbers and user account information, and even to establish a common X.509 certificate store. Most enterprises house employee information in various systems, such as the human resources database, the NT SAM, and even local file servers and workstations. However, with an LDAP directory, you no longer need to design applications to query disparate systems, and you can store information about any object.

Meanwhile, if your enterprise houses data on multiple database vendor platforms (such as Oracle, Sybase, and Microsoft SQL Server), implementation of an LDAP infrastructure can also reduce or eliminate the need to maintain the client libraries required to access each database type. This, in turn, significantly reduces support issues and system installation complexity.

With the flexibility provided in an LDAP infrastructure, a developer creating an enterprise telephone directory, for example, can simply query the LDAP directory to derive the information required to create the telephone directory. The developer thus avoids performing a direct query to the appropriate data store(s), eliminating the need to establish data source names (DSNs) and to install libraries for each vendor's database implementation. In addition, in the telephone directory example, the developer can create an infrastructure to pull information directly from the phone system switch and employee database to ensure that a current telephone directory is always maintained without any administration.

Storing information in the directory, meanwhile, is made simple through the use of entries and attributes. An *entry* defines any entity of interest, whether it is an entire organization, a department, an employee, or even a single machine. Within any entry, *attributes* are defined to describe the entity. An enterprise user is typically defined by his full name (common name (cn) and surname (sn) attributes) and, optionally, by the relevant associated department, office location, telephone number, and/or manager information.

Within each entry, a required attribute that defines the entry type is stored in the ObjectClass attribute. Depending on an object's class, several mandatory and optional attributes are also defined. For example, if an entry's class is person, the cn attribute is one of the attributes required to identify that entry.

With a bit of development work, you can extend the LDAP attributes from those specified in default server installations. This allows you to customize the directory to your organization's specific requirements. Note, however, that most directory experts recommend against modifying the directory schema because these customizations can make it difficult to consolidate directories if business entities merge at a later date.

The Naming Model: How Is the Data Organized?

LDAP utilizes a hierarchical data model to organize its directory. Within this model, few restrictions exist as to how the data is placed. This freedom allows you to construct a directory that is nearly flat, is organized geographically or by business unit, or follows any other organizational method that suits the needs of the enterprise.

To store and access the data, you must have a way to reference its location in the directory. LDAP utilizes either a *distinguished name (DN)* or a *relative distinguished name (RDN)* to identify entries in the directory. Another hierarchical directory service that uses DNs and RDNs is the NT file system. Within this directory structure, if you want to run notepad.exe from the command line (pretend for a moment that the %systemroot%/system32 directory is not in the path), you can use two methods to reference the application name. One method is to use the application's DN to run the application, as follows:

```
C:\WinNT\System32\notepad.exe
```

Although this first method is very efficient for accessing data when the full path is known, you might occasionally need to verify the existence of the application before running the image. To do this, you can instead execute a series of commands to navigate to the proper folder, as follows:

```
C:\>cd WinNT
C:\WinNT>cd System32
C:\WinNT\System32>notepad.exe
```

Using this method, notepad.exe can be considered an RDN. To access the file, you must be bound to the container holding the object you want to access. In this method, the location of notepad.exe is relative to its parent container.

In LDAP directories, a DN is typically used to quickly navigate to a specific directory location. An object is then created or removed using the directory's RDN.

Also fundamental to directory creation is the *organization unit (OU)*, which allows the directory administrator to create logical groupings of directory entries.

The Functional Model: Accessing and Updating Data

The functional model defines how entries are added, modified, and removed from the directory. In addition, this model defines the techniques used to search and compare items in the directory (through interrogation operations) and determines the identity of users attempting to access the underlying data (through authentication and control operations).

Within the functional model, you can also establish a *filter*. LDAP filters are used to limit a result set, much like the WHERE clause in a SELECT statement is used in ANSI-SQL. Filter definitions are created using the LDAP search syntax, which can be non-intuitive for those unfamiliar with its definition. Although you can use LDAP filter syntax to limit result sets, the ADsDSOObject provider for ADO allows you to use ANSI SQL syntax against LDAP namespaces. An example of using ADO to search an LDAP namespace will be discussed in the later section "Using ADO to Search an LDAP Directory."

The Security Model: Controlling Unauthorized Access to Entries and Attributes

Oddly enough, the LDAP security model does not define a standard to establish a common access control model. Instead, the standard leaves this to the directory implementor to determine and maintain. The RFC does, however, define the authentication procedure used for the connection-oriented LDAP protocol.

It should be noted that each LDAP server implements security a bit differently. Netscape's server product, for example, allows not only entries in the directory to be secured, but attributes as well. Due to the relatively open specification used in this model, vendor documentation should be used to determine how the specification was implemented in each product.

Available LDAP APIs

The LDAP Data Interchange Format (LDIF) files allow for great flexibility in implementing new entries and modifying existing entries. However, to help fuel the proliferation of LDAP-based directories via developer support of the standard, a software development kit (SDK) is needed.

RFC-1823 defines the LDAP C API for LDAP v2, whereas a standard SDK is emerging for version 3 LDAP directories. It is important to note that the SDK defined by the standards documents proposes only the API structure and leaves SDK implementation up to the reader of the RFC.

Several companies and organizations have implemented these SDKs, which are freely available from the Web in both binary and open-source formats. See Appendix B for the resource locations if you have experience with the C programming language or maintain a more than casual curiosity about the LDAP SDK standard proposal.

For those who are not C programmers, these SDKs do little to clarify programmatic LDAP directory manipulation. Meanwhile, managing an enterprise directory by editing text files is rather daunting by today's GUI-reliant standards. However, to bring programmatic manipulation of LDAP directories to the masses, several companies have created Java, Perl, C++, and Visual Basic implementations of the LDAP SDK.

Of particular interest and relevance to this text is Microsoft's implementation, which is contained within ADSI.

Commercial Products Supporting LDAP

As you are by now aware, ADSI is a relatively simple API used for managing multiple namespaces. By examining which products utilize an LDAP directory to store application information, you can also determine which products can be manipulated using ADSI.

At the time of this writing, the following products and Internet directories (among others not listed here) can be queried using ADSI's LDAP provider:

- Microsoft Windows 2000 (covered in Chapter 12, "Programmatic Management of the Windows 2000 Active Directory")
- Microsoft Exchange Versions 5.5 and higher
- Microsoft Site Server 3.0 (with Site Server Service Pack 2)
- Netscape Directory Server
- The BigFoot (ldap.bigfoot.com), InfoSpace (ldap.infospace.com), SwitchBoard (ldap.switchboard.com), VeriSign (directory.verisign.com), WhoWhere (ldap.whowhere.com) and Yahoo (ldap.yahoo.com) Internet directories
- Entrust PKI

Additionally, the Directory-Enabled Network standard proposals initiated by Cisco and Microsoft promise to deliver integration of network devices into LDAP directories.

LDAP directory implementation can serve as the much-needed bridge between systems by providing a common language and structure for storing application data, configuration parameters, and user information. Meanwhile, LDAP provides the capability for single-signon and a central X.509 certificate repository, which will be useful as e-commerce technologies continue to emerge.

Applied Theory: Installing the Netscape Directory Server

Netscape's Directory Server product allows you to import the namespace of a fictitious company, called Airius, as a sample directory. Complete the following exercise to obtain and install the Netscape Directory Server product so that we can explore directory manipulation with a common directory structure.

Exercise 11.1 *Installing Netscape Directory Server 4.11*

> **Warning**
>
> Before beginning this exercise, be sure that a valid DNS domain has been entered in the TCP/IP protocol properties page of your NT Server. ♦

1. To begin, obtain the D411DIU.EXE file from
   http://www.iplanet.com/downloads/testdrive/index.html.
2. After the D411DIU.EXE file has been transferred, run the D411DIU.EXE image on a Windows NT Server 4.0 machine to unpack the distribution and begin the server installation process.
3. After passing the introductory dialog boxes in the installation wizard, you will be presented with an option to install Netscape Servers or the Netscape Console product. Select the Netscape Servers option for installation on a server.
4. Next, you will be presented with three options to select the installation type. Choose Custom.
5. Install the server images and libraries in any directory.
6. Install all options except the Netscape Directory Server 4.1 Synch Service. This configuration should not require any modification to the default selections.
7. Configure the Directory Server instance to be the configuration directory server (default).
8. Choose the Store Data in this Directory Server option button (default).
9. Use the defaults for the Directory Server 4.1 Server Settings dialog box. By default, the Server Identifier should hold the NetBIOS name of the server and the server port should be set to port 389 (the LDAP default TCP port). Also by default, the suffix should hold the value of the current DNS domain (previously configured from Control Panel, Network, Protocols tab, TCP/IP Protocol, Properties, DNS tab) prefixed by o=.

> **Tip**
>
> If the fields in the dialog box are blank, terminate the installation process and make sure that the DNS domain has been set in the TCP/IP Protocol properties dialog box. The server installation will fail if this step has not yet been taken.

10. Enter a password for the administrative console credential. ♦

continues ▶

Exercise 11.1 *continued*

> **Note**
>
> The Administration Domain should match the Windows NT DNS domain configuration. ◆

11. Enter a password for the Directory Manager credential. This credential is vital to your ability to programmatically manage the directory, so be sure to either use a credential you will remember or store a written copy of the information in a secure location.

> **Note**
>
> Do not configure the server to be a supplier or consumer for replication (default). ◆

12. Next, you will be presented with the option to install the sample organizational structure. By default, this is checked and should remain as such because we wish to use a common directory for the code samples in this section. You should also populate the database by selecting the Populate with Sample Database option. By default, this option is *not* selected, so be sure to verify this setting before continuing.
13. Skip past the Disable Schema Checking dialog box.
14. If this server has multiple IP addresses assigned to it, enter the IP address you wish to use for the administration server. In most cases, the default should be acceptable.
15. Next, enter the password for the administration server user. This account is used to log in to the Netscape Console, which is a Java-based utility for managing your directory server.

> **Note**
>
> A random port number is assigned to the administration server instance. You can modify it to use any TCP port. However, in most cases it is best to choose a standard TCP port to be used for all LDAP servers across the enterprise. ◆

16. After clicking Next for the administration port dialog box, a summary screen is presented. Verify all settings and click Next to begin the installation process.

17. When the file copy process is completed, you will be presented with the option to restart your computer. If all other applications have been closed or left in a safe state, click Finish to exit the wizard and reboot the server.

    Upon return of a ready state for the server, the installation of Netscape Directory Server 4.11 and the Airius sample namespace will be complete.

With the installation of a non-production LDAP directory server completed, you can now explore the programmatic management of an LDAP directory using ADSI.

> **Note**
>
> *All code segments in this chapter will use the Airius sample database for query and manipulation. With a common directory established, you can test the code provided in each example code segment without modification.* ✦

Manipulating an LDAP Directory Using ADSI

Unlike the Windows NT and IIS ADSI providers, which are constrained by an established directory structure, the open architecture of an LDAP directory allows infinite variations on the design of the namespace. Because of such flexibility, some organizations may choose flat structures, whereas others might opt for extremely deep hierarchical schemes utilizing geographical or functionally based organizational units to organize their entries.

You must understand the architecture of your particular directory implementation to properly bind to entries in the directory. For an example of how a binding string relates to the directory structure, consider Figure 11.1 and both of the following related binding strings.

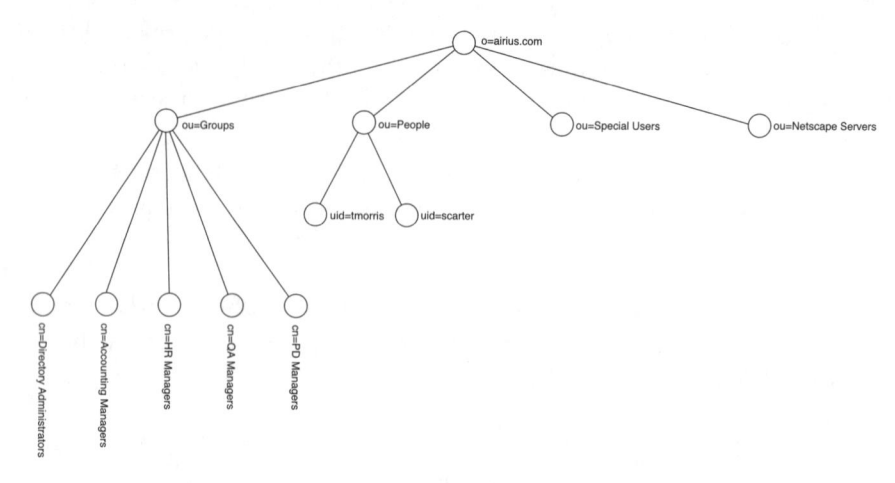

Figure 11.1 *Relatively flat hierarchical directory architecture used in the Airius sample database.*

To bind to the user object `scarter`, use either of the following ADSI binding strings:

Big-Endian form:
```
Set Obj =
GetObject("LDAP://LDAP_ServerName/O=airius.com/OU=People/UID=scarter")
```

Little-Endian form (default):
```
Set Obj = GetObject("LDAP://LDAP_ServerName:TCP_Port/UID=scarter,
➥OU=People, O=airius.com")
```

Notice in Big-Endian form, you start from the top of the structure and work your way down to the smallest element, which in this case happens to be a user object. Conversely, Little-Endian form starts at the smallest element, the user object in this case, and navigates up the directory back to the root of the tree. Although Little-Endian form is the default returned by ADSI queries, many people find Big-Endian form a bit more intuitive when binding to objects in the directory.

> **Note**
>
> *If you have an LDAP server installed on an alternate port, you must use Little-Endian form with ADSI.* ◆

Discovering the Architecture of an Existing LDAP Directory Using Visual Basic

To properly bind to an LDAP directory, you must know the relationship between parent and child objects for each entry in the directory. If you do not want to ask the LDAP directory project team for a detailed sketch of the topology of the directory, use the following Visual Basic code to programmatically derive a map:

```
Dim Container As IADsContainer
Dim Entry As IADs
Dim StartingPoint As String

'StartingPoint = "/ou=People"

Set Container = GetObject("LDAP://LDAP_SERVER/o=airius.com" & StartingPoint)

For Each Entry In Container
    Debug.Print "Entry Name: " & Entry.Name & vbTab & vbTab & "Class: " & 
    ↪Entry.Class
Next
```

By changing the starting point, you can enumerate all child entries beneath the point chosen in the binding string. This can be useful for displaying all entries in, for example, the People or Groups containers.

> **Warning**
>
> *Enumeration processes can be extremely CPU intensive when run on containers with significantly large quantities (20,000 or more) of entries. If your organization has implemented a relatively flat directory architecture, you should take this into account when designing your LDAP client application.* ◆

Querying Entry Attributes with ADSI Using Anonymous Access in Visual Basic

To query an entry's attributes, you can typically bind to the entry and use the IAD's Get method to query each desired attribute. If your LDAP server allows anonymous read access to the directory, you can use the following Visual Basic code as a guide to query the entry's attributes:

```
On Error Resume Next
Dim Container As IADsContainer
Dim User As IADs
Set Container = GetObject("LDAP://LDAP_SERVER/o=airius.com/ou=People")
For Each User In Container
    Debug.Print "UserID: " & vbTab & User.Get("uid") & vbTab & "Common Name: " & 
    ↪User.Get("cn") & vbTab & "Surname: " & User.Get("sn")
Next
```

> **Note**
>
> *In this example, you are simply querying the mandatory properties (*cn *and* sn *attributes) of an entry of type inetOrgPerson.* ◆

Querying Entry Attributes with ADSI Using Alternate Credentials in Visual Basic

If you must access an entry that either is blocked from general access or whose attributes have access control items assigned, you must use the OpenDSObject method of the IADsOpenDSObject interface to define a set of credentials to use for directory access.

For Netscape Directory Servers, this account is typically defined as cn=directory manager, although it can be changed at installation time to any value valid for a common name entry.

Use the following code to bind to the directory as cn=directory manager and query the mandatory attributes of an entry of type inetOrgPerson:

```
On Error Resume Next
Dim dso As IADsOpenDSObject
Dim Container As IADsContainer
Dim User As IADs
Set dso = GetObject("LDAP:")
Set Container = dso.OpenDSObject("LDAP://LDAP_SERVER/o=airius.com/ou=People",
➥"cn=Directory Manager", "l@undrym@t1974", 0)

For Each User In Container
    Debug.Print "UserID: " & vbTab & User.Get("uid") & vbTab & "Common Name: " &
    ➥User.Get("cn") & vbTab & "Surname: " & User.Get("sn")
Next
```

Modifying Entry Attributes Using ADSI in Visual Basic

To set an attribute value of an existing directory entry, simply use the Put method of the IAD's interface. To successfully perform this task, you must be bound to the directory as a user with directory modification privileges. As in the authenticated access query in the preceding example, specifying the directory manager account credentials as an argument of the IADsOpenDSObject interface's OpenDSObject method will allow you to modify the directory. Use the following Visual Basic code to change the sn attribute of a user named uid=aknutson from Knutson to McNally:

```
Dim dso As IADsOpenDSObject
Dim Container As IADsContainer
Dim User As IADs
Set dso = GetObject("LDAP:")
Set Container = dso.OpenDSObject("LDAP://LDAP_SERVER/o=airius.com/ou=People",
➥"cn=Directory Manager", "l@undrym@t1974", 0)
Set User = Container.GetObject("inetorgperson", "uid=aknutson")
User.Put "sn", "McNally"
User.SetInfo
```

Creating a New Entry Using ADSI in Visual Basic

To create a new entry in the directory, you must have several pieces of information about the entry and its parent container, including the following:

- The credentials required to update the directory (such as the credentials for the directory manager account)
- The path to the Parent container in which you wish to create the entry
- The class of the object to be created
- The mandatory properties for the object class of the entry you want to create

Consider the following Visual Basic code example, which creates a new entry named uid=teck of type inetOrgPerson in the People organizational unit:

```
Dim dso As IADsOpenDSObject
Dim Container As IADsContainer
Dim User As IADs
Dim ClassArray As Variant

Set dso = GetObject("LDAP:")
Set Container = dso.OpenDSObject("LDAP://LDAP_SERVER/o=airius.com/ou=People",
➥"cn=Directory Manager", "l@undrym@t1974", 0)

Set User = Container.Create("inetorgperson", "uid=teck")
ClassArray = Array("inetOrgPerson", "person", "top", "organizationalPerson")

User.Put "objectClass", ClassArray
User.Put "cn", "Thomas Eck"
User.Put "sn", "Eck"
User.SetInfo
```

Removing an Entry Using ADSI in Visual Basic

To remove an existing entry in the directory, simply call the Delete method of the IAD's interface, with the name of the entry and its class specified as arguments.

Consider the following Visual Basic code to remove the entry created in the previous example:

```
Dim dso As IADsOpenDSObject
Dim Container As IADsContainer
Set dso = GetObject("LDAP:")
Set Container = dso.OpenDSObject("LDAP://LDAP_SERVER/o=airius.com/ou=People",
➥"cn=Directory Manager", "l@undrym@t1974", 0)
Call Container.Delete("inetorgperson", "uid=teck")
```

Using ADO to Search an LDAP Directory Using Visual Basic

With the Windows NT provider, you were often forced to combine conditionals with enumeration functions to find data in the namespace. The LDAP provider allows you to use alternate methods for searching the namespace, such as *IDirectorySearch* (non-automation languages only) and *ADO*. With ADO at your command, you can use enumeration functions for what they are truly intended: enumerating subordinate entries.

Using ADO against an LDAP directory is incredibly fast and returns an ADO recordset that can be easily displayed record by record using a *While...Wend* loop. An additional advantage to using ADO and the ADsDSOObject provider is that you can use ANSI-SQL syntax to search the LDAP directory, thus avoiding the need to learn LDAP filter syntax (a true blessing indeed!).

> **Note**
>
> To use the following code sample, you must have ADO installed on your development workstation. You can obtain the ADO libraries by downloading the Microsoft Data Access Components from http://www.microsoft.com/data.
>
> After you have run the setup routine, you must set a reference to the library in Visual Basic by selecting the Project menu and clicking the References...entry. When the References dialog box appears, simply select Microsoft ADO 2.X Library. ◆

Use the following Visual Basic code to search the Airius sample directory for all users with their sn attribute assigned to Carter:

```
Dim Connection As ADODB.Connection
Dim RS As ADODB.Recordset
Dim Entry As String
Dim Index As Long
Index = 0
Set Connection = New ADODB.Connection
Connection.Provider = "ADsDSOObject"
Connection.Open "ADSI"

Set RS = Connection.Execute("SELECT cn,telephonenumber FROM
➥'LDAP://LDAP_SERVER/o=airius.com/ou=people' WHERE sn='carter'")

While Not RS.EOF
    For i = 0 To RS.Fields.Count - 1
        If RS.Fields(i).Type = adVariant And Not (IsNull(RS.Fields(i).Value))
➥Then
            For j = LBound(RS.Fields(i).Value) To UBound(RS.Fields(i).Value)
                Entry = Entry & RS.Fields(i).Value(j) & vbTab
```

```
                Next j
            Else
                Entry = Entry & RS.Fields(i).Value & vbTab
            End If
            
            If Index = RS.Fields.Count - 1 Then
                Debug.Print Entry
            End If
            Index = Index + 1
        Next i
        Entry = ""
        Index = 0
        RS.MoveNext
    Wend
```

Managing Microsoft Exchange Mailboxes and Distribution Lists Using ADSI's LDAP Provider

Using ADSI's LDAP provider against a Microsoft Exchange 5.5 (or higher) server, you can query and manipulate the directory configuration, create and remove mailboxes, as well as manage distribution lists. Using these programmatic methods, you can, for example, automate the creation of a mailbox when a new user account request is fulfilled.

In most organizations, the distribution list owner must authorize the addition or removal of list members. Using ADSI's LDAP provider, you can instead delegate the responsibility for managing distribution lists to the list owner by implementing a Web front-end for list management.

In this section, we will take a look at the programmatic techniques you can employ to perform such tasks using Visual Basic, the ADSI LDAP provider, and the Microsoft ADSI resource kit ADsSecurity.DLL for managing Exchange directory security.

Creating a New Exchange Mailbox Using Visual Basic

When the Exchange Administrator is installed, an NT account creation automatically starts a Graphical User Interface (GUI) to allow simultaneous creation of an Exchange mailbox. Using programmatic methods, you lose the integration of the Exchange mailbox creation GUI. However, you can use ADSI's LDAP provider to programmatically create a mailbox and associate it with a Windows NT user domain account.

> **Note**
>
> *Before continuing, be sure that the NT account used to log in to the development workstation has been assigned the right to modify the Exchange database. The necessary rights are granted to the default Exchange roles: Permissions Admin and Service Account Admin.* ♦

Use the following Visual Basic code to programmatically create an Exchange mailbox:

```
Dim ExchangeServerName As String
Dim ExchangeServerOrganization As String
Dim ExchangeServerSite As String
Dim Mailbox As IADs
Dim MailboxParentContainer as IADs
Dim MailboxRelativePath As String
Dim MailboxDisplayName As String
Dim MailboxFirstName As String
Dim MailboxLastName As String
Dim MailboxMiddleInitial As String
Dim MailboxAlias As String
Dim MTA As String
Dim MDB As String
Dim MailboxSMTPAddress As String
Dim MailboxX400Address As String
Dim MailboxCCMailAddress As String
Dim MailboxMSMailAddress As String
Dim NTUserAccountToAssociate As String
Dim UserDomain As String
Dim SID As New ADsSID
Dim Security As New ADsSecurity
Dim SecurityDescriptor As IADsSecurityDescriptor
Dim DiscretionaryACL As IADsAccessControlList
Dim AccessControlEntry As New AccessControlEntry

ExchangeServerName = "EXCHANGE_SERVER"
ExchangeServerOrganization = "ADSITest"
ExchangeServerSite = "Macmillan"
MailboxRelativePath = ""
MailboxDisplayName = "Eck, Thomas E."
MailboxFirstName = "Thomas"
MailboxLastName = "Eck"
MailboxMiddleInitial = "E"
MailboxAlias = "Thomas.Eck"
UserDomain = "UserDomain"
NTUserAccountToAssociate = "teck"

MTA = "cn=Microsoft MTA,cn=" & ExchangeServerName &
↪",cn=Servers,cn=Configuration,ou=" & ExchangeServerSite & ",o=" &
↪ExchangeServerOrganization
MDB = "cn=Microsoft Private MDB,cn=" & ExchangeServerName &
↪",cn=Servers,cn=Configuration,ou=" & ExchangeServerSite & ",o=" &
↪ExchangeServerOrganization
MailboxSMTPAddress = MailboxAlias & "@" & ExchangeServerSite & "." &
↪ExchangeServerOrganization & ".com"
MailboxX400Address = "c=US;a= ;p=" & ExchangeServerOrganization & ";o=" &
↪ExchangeServerSite & ";s=" & MailboxLastName & ";g=" & MailboxFirstName & ";i="
↪& MailboxMiddleInitial
MailboxCCMailAddress = MailboxLastName & ", " & MailboxFirstName & " at " &
↪ExchangeServerSite
MailboxMSMailAddress = UCase(ExchangeServerOrganization & "/" &
↪ExchangeServerSite & "/" & MailboxAlias)
```

Managing Microsoft Exchange Mailboxes and Distribution Lists Using ADSI's LDAP Provider

```
Set MailboxParentContainer = GetObject("LDAP://" & ExchangeServerName & "/o=" &
➥ExchangeServerOrganization & "/ou=" & ExchangeServerSite & "/cn=Recipients" &
➥MailboxRelativePath)
Set Mailbox = MailboxParentContainer.Create("organizationalPerson", "cn=" &
➥MailboxAlias)

Mailbox.Put "mailPreferenceOption", 0
Mailbox.Put "givenName", MailboxFirstName
Mailbox.Put "sn", MailboxLastName
Mailbox.Put "cn", MailboxDisplayName
Mailbox.Put "uid", MailboxAlias
Mailbox.Put "Home-MTA", MTA
Mailbox.Put "Home-MDB", MDB
Mailbox.Put "mail", MailboxSMTPAddress
Mailbox.Put "MAPI-Recipient", True
Mailbox.Put "rfc822Mailbox", MailboxSMTPAddress
Mailbox.Put "textEncodedORAddress", MailboxX400Address
Mailbox.PutEx ADS_PROPERTY_APPEND, "otherMailbox", Array("CCMAIL$" &
➥MailboxCCMailAddress, "MS$" & MailboxMSMailAddress)

SID.SetAs ADS_SID_WINNT_PATH, "WinNT://" & UserDomain & "/" &
➥NTUserAccountToAssociate & ",user"
sidHex = SID.GetAs(ADS_SID_HEXSTRING)
Mailbox.Put "Assoc-NT-Account", sidHex
Mailbox.SetInfo

Set SecurityDescriptor = Security.GetSecurityDescriptor(Mailbox.ADsPath)
Set DiscretionaryACL = SecurityDescriptor.DiscretionaryACL
AccessControlEntry.AceType = ADS_ACETYPE_ACCESS_ALLOWED
AccessControlEntry.Trustee = UserDomain & "\" & MailboxAlias
AccessControlEntry.AccessMask = ADS_RIGHT_EXCH_MAIL_SEND_AS Or
➥ADS_RIGHT_EXCH_MAIL_RECEIVE_AS Or ADS_RIGHT_EXCH_MODIFY_USER_ATT
DiscretionaryACL.AddAce AccessControlEntry
SecurityDescriptor.DiscretionaryACL = DiscretionaryACL
Security.SetSecurityDescriptor SecurityDescriptor
```

> *Note*
>
> *In this example, references are made to the ADsSid and ADsSecurity interfaces. Both interfaces are contained in ADSSECURITY.DLL, available from* http://www.newriders.com/adsi *and* http://www.microsoft.com/adsi.
>
> *After obtaining the required DLL, you must register it using the REGSVR32 utility from a command prompt:*
>
>   REGSVR32 ADsSecurity.DLL
>
> *Depending on the configuration of your machine, you may also be able to register the DLL simply by double-clicking it in the Windows Explorer.*
>
> *You must also set a reference in the Visual Basic IDE to this DLL by clicking the References... item from the Project menu and selecting the* "ADsSecurity 2.5 Type Library" *entry.* ◆

Removing an Existing Exchange Mailbox Using Visual Basic

To remove an existing Microsoft Exchange Mailbox, use the following Visual Basic code:

```
Dim ExchangeServerName As String
Dim ExchangeServerOrganization As String
Dim ExchangeServerSite As String
Dim MailboxParentContainer As IADsContainer
Dim MailboxRelativePath As String
Dim MailboxToRemove As String

ExchangeServerName = "EXCHANGE_SERVER"
ExchangeServerOrganization = "ADSITest"
ExchangeServerSite = "Macmillan"
MailboxRelativePath = ""
MailboxToRemove = "Thomas.Eck"

Set MailboxParentContainer = GetObject("LDAP://" & ExchangeServerName & "/o=" &
➥ExchangeServerOrganization & "/ou=" & ExchangeServerSite & "/cn=Recipients" &
➥MailboxRelativePath)

Call MailboxParentContainer.Delete("organizationalPerson", "cn=" &
➥MailboxToRemove)
```

Adding a Distribution List Member Using Visual Basic

If your organization utilizes a set of distribution lists that is assigned to users based on their role, location, or department (such as DL_Permanent_Employees, DL_Chicago, DL_Senior_Management, or DL_Research_Development), you can automate the addition of users to the list using ADSI's LDAP provider and Visual Basic. This is demonstrated in the following Visual Basic code segment:

```
Dim ExchangeServerName As String
Dim ExchangeServerOrganization As String
Dim ExchangeServerSite As String
Dim DistributionList As IADs
Dim DistributionListName As String
Dim DistributionListRelativePath As String
Dim DLMemberMailboxName As String

ExchangeServerName = "EXCHANGE_SERVER"
ExchangeServerOrganization = "ADSITest"
ExchangeServerSite = "Macmillan"
DistributionListRelativePath = ""
DistributionListName = "DL_Research_Development"
DLMemberMailboxName = "Thomas.Eck"

Set DistributionList = GetObject("LDAP://" & ExchangeServerName & "/o=" &
➥ExchangeServerOrganization & "/ou=" & ExchangeServerSite & "/cn=Recipients" &
➥DistributionListRelativePath & "/cn=" & DistributionListName)
```

```
DistributionList.Add ("LDAP://" & ExchangeServerName & "/o=" &
➥ExchangeServerOrganization & "/ou=" & ExchangeServerSite & "/cn=Recipients" &
➥"/cn=" & DLMemberMailboxName)

DistributionList.SetInfo
```

Removing a Distribution List Member Using Visual Basic

To remove an existing member from a distribution list, use the following Visual Basic code:

```
Dim ExchangeServerName As String
Dim ExchangeServerOrganization As String
Dim ExchangeServerSite As String
Dim DistributionList As IADs
Dim DistributionListName As String
Dim DistributionListRelativePath As String
Dim DLMemberMailboxName As String

ExchangeServerName = "EXCHANGE_SERVER"
ExchangeServerOrganization = "ADSITest"
ExchangeServerSite = "Macmillan"
DistributionListRelativePath = ""
DistributionListName = "DL_Engineering"
DLMemberMailboxName = "Thomas.Eck"

Set DistributionList = GetObject("LDAP://" & ExchangeServerName & "/o=" &
➥ExchangeServerOrganization & "/ou=" & ExchangeServerSite & "/cn=Recipients" &
➥DistributionListRelativePath & "/cn=" & DistributionListName)

DistributionList.Remove ("LDAP://" & ExchangeServerName & "/o=" &
➥ExchangeServerOrganization & "/ou=" & ExchangeServerSite & "/cn=Recipients" &
➥"/cn=" & DLMemberMailboxName)

DistributionList.SetInfo
```

Determining the Distribution List Owner Using Visual Basic

To transfer the administrative burden for maintaining distribution lists to the list owner, use the following Visual Basic code to first determine the owner of an existing list:

```
Dim ExchangeServerName As String
Dim ExchangeServerOrganization As String
Dim ExchangeServerSite As String
Dim DistributionList As IADs
Dim DistributionListName As String
Dim DistributionListRelativePath As String

ExchangeServerName = "EXCHANGE_SERVER"
ExchangeServerOrganization = "ADSITest"
ExchangeServerSite = "Macmillan"
DistributionListRelativePath = ""
```

```
DistributionListName = "DL_Senior_Management"

Set DistributionList = GetObject("LDAP://" & ExchangeServerName & "/o=" & _
ExchangeServerOrganization & "/ou=" & ExchangeServerSite & "/cn=Recipients" & _
DistributionListRelativePath & "/cn=" & DistributionListName)

Debug.Print DistributionList.Owner
```

> **Note**
>
> *ADSI can programmatically manipulate many common administrative tasks within the Exchange directory. Examine the ADSI25.CHM help file (available from* http://www.microsoft.com/adsi) *to learn more about ADSI ability to manage Microsoft Exchange Server.* ◆

Creating the LDAPObjectManagement Class Module

In this section, you will begin an exercise that will yield the creation of the LDAPAdmin.DLL COM server.

Exercise 11.2 *Creating the LDAPAdmin.DLL COM Server Application: The LDAPObjectManagement Module.*

1. Create a new ActiveX DLL Visual Basic project.
2. Set a reference to the Active DS Type Library by clicking the Project menu, selecting References[el], and placing a checkmark next to the "Active DS Type Library" entry. Also set a reference to the "Microsoft ADO". Click the OK command button to exit the References–Project1 dialog box.
3. Rename Project1 as **LDAPAdmin**.
4. Rename the Class1 class module as **LDAPObjectManagement**.
5. Enter the following code into the General Declarations section of the class module:

```
Public Function ModifyObjectAttribute(ByVal ObjectDistinguishedName As String, _
ByVal DirectoryAdminUsername As String, ByVal DirectoryAdminPassword As String, _
ByVal AttributeName As String, ByVal NewAttributeValue As Variant) As Boolean
    Dim dso As IADsOpenDSObject
    Dim Obj As IADs

    Set dso = GetObject("LDAP:")
    Set Obj = dso.OpenDSObject(ObjectDistinguishedName, DirectoryAdminUsername, DirectoryAdminPassword, 0)

    Call Obj.Put(AttributeName, NewAttributeValue)

    Obj.SetInfo
```

Creating the LDAPObjectManagement Class Module 397

```
    If Err.Number = 0 Then ModifyObjectAttribute = True
End Function

Public Function CreateNewLDAPObject(ByVal ParentContainerDistinguishedName As
String, ByVal DirectoryAdminUsername As String, ByVal DirectoryAdminPassword As
String, ByVal ObjectRelativeName As String, ByVal ObjectClass As String, Optional
ByVal MandatoryAttributeName1 As String, Optional ByVal MandatoryAttributeValue1
As Variant, Optional ByVal MandatoryAttributeName2 As String, Optional ByVal
MandatoryAttributeValue2 As Variant, Optional ByVal MandatoryAttributeName3 As
String, Optional ByVal MandatoryAttributeValue3 As Variant, Optional ByVal
MandatoryAttributeName4 As String, Optional ByVal MandatoryAttributeValue4 As
Variant, Optional ByVal MandatoryAttributeName5 As String, Optional ByVal
MandatoryAttributeValue5 As Variant) As Boolean
    Dim dso As IADsOpenDSObject
    Dim Obj As IADs
    Dim ParentObj As IADs

    Set dso = GetObject("LDAP:")
    Set ParentObj = dso.OpenDSObject(ParentContainerDistinguishedName,
DirectoryAdminUsername, DirectoryAdminPassword, 0)

    Set Obj = ParentObj.Create(ObjectClass, ObjectRelativeName)

    If MandatoryAttributeName1 <> "" Then
        Obj.Put MandatoryAttributeName1, MandatoryAttributeValue1
    End If

    If MandatoryAttributeName2 <> "" Then
        Obj.Put MandatoryAttributeName2, MandatoryAttributeValue2
    End If

    If MandatoryAttributeName3 <> "" Then
        Obj.Put MandatoryAttributeName3, MandatoryAttributeValue3
    End If

    If MandatoryAttributeName4 <> "" Then
        Obj.Put MandatoryAttributeName4, MandatoryAttributeValue4
    End If

    If MandatoryAttributeName5 <> "" Then
        Obj.Put MandatoryAttributeName5, MandatoryAttributeValue5
    End If

    Obj.SetInfo

    If Err.Number = 0 Then CreateNewLDAPObject = True

End Function

Public Function RemoveLDAPObject(ByVal ParentContainerDistinguishedName As
String, ByVal DirectoryAdminUsername As String, ByVal DirectoryAdminPassword As
String, ByVal ObjectRelativeName As String, ByVal ObjectClass As String) As
Boolean
```

continues ▶

Exercise 11.2 *continued*

```
    Dim dso As IADsOpenDSObject
    Dim Obj As IADs
    Dim ParentObj As IADs

    Set dso = GetObject("LDAP:")
    Set ParentObj = dso.OpenDSObject(ParentContainerDistinguishedName,
DirectoryAdminUsername, DirectoryAdminPassword, 0)

    Call ParentObj.Delete(ObjectClass, ObjectRelativeName)

    If Err.Number = 0 Then RemoveLDAPObject = True

End Function

Public Function EnumerateLDAPContainer(ByVal ContainerDistinguishedName As
String, ByVal DirectoryAdminUsername As String, ByVal DirectoryAdminPassword As
String) As Variant
    On Error Resume Next
    Dim dso As IADsOpenDSObject
    Dim Obj As IADs
    Dim Item As IADs
    Dim Counter As Long
    Dim ReturnArray() As Variant

    Set dso = GetObject("LDAP:")
    Set Obj = dso.OpenDSObject(ContainerDistinguishedName,
DirectoryAdminUsername, DirectoryAdminPassword, 0)

    For Each Item In Obj
        Counter = UBound(ReturnArray) + 1
        ReDim Preserve ReturnArray(Counter)
        ReturnArray(Counter) = Item.Name
    Next
    EnumerateLDAPContainer = ReturnArray
End Function

Public Function SearchLDAPNamespace(ByVal SQLStmt As String) As Variant
    On Error Resume Next
    Dim Connection As ADODB.Connection
    Dim RS As ADODB.Recordset
    Dim Entry As String
    Dim Index As Long
    Dim ReturnArray() As Variant
    Dim Counter As Long

    Index = 0
    Set Connection = New ADODB.Connection
    Connection.Provider = "ADsDSOObject"
    Connection.Open "ADSI"

    'Example SQLStmt: SELECT cn,telephonenumber FROM
```

```
            'LDAP://LDAP_SERVER/o=airius.com/ou=people' WHERE sn='carter'
            Set RS = Connection.Execute(SQLStmt)

        While Not RS.EOF
            For i = 0 To RS.Fields.Count - 1
                If RS.Fields(i).Type = adVariant And Not (IsNull(RS.Fields(i).Value))
    Then
                    For j = LBound(RS.Fields(i).Value) To UBound(RS.Fields(i).Value)
                        Entry = Entry & RS.Fields(i).Value(j) & vbTab
                    Next j
                Else
                    Entry = Entry & RS.Fields(i).Value & vbTab
                End If

                If Index = RS.Fields.Count - 1 Then
                    Counter = UBound(ReturnArray) + 1
                    ReDim Preserve ReturnArray(Counter)
                    ReturnArray(Counter) = Entry
                End If
                Index = Index + 1
            Next i
            Entry = ""
            Index = 0
            RS.MoveNext
        Wend
        SearchLDAPNamespace = ReturnArray
    End Function
```

6. Compile the code as LDAPAdmin.DLL.
7. Save and close the LDAPAdmin project.

> *Tip*
>
> *If you do not want to share your code between applications, you can enter the preceding code into a code module in any Visual Basic application.* ♦

> *Tip*
>
> *You can download the Visual Basic 6.0 project or precompiled version of LDAPAdmin.DLL from* http://www.newriders.com/adsi. ♦

Using the Functions in LDAPObjectManagement

With the LDAPObjectManagement class module created, you can access the functions contained in the class module from any programming language that supports OLE automation including Visual Basic, VBScript, and JavaScript.

> **Tip**
>
> *To instantiate the object, follow the appropriate syntax found in Chapter 3, "Container Enumeration Methods and Programmatic Domain Account Policy Manipulation." Substitute the LDAPObjectManagement class name where necessary.* ◆

Use Table 11.1 to help you use the proper syntax for each of the methods of the LDAPObjectManagement interface.

Table 11.1   LDAPObjectManatement Method Syntax

Action	Syntax
Modify Object Attribute	ModifyObjectAttribute("LDAP://Directory_ ↪Server/o=airius.com/ou=people/uid=jlutz", ↪"cn=directory manager", "l@undrym@t1962", ↪"sn", "London")
Create Generic Object in Namespace	Debug.Print CreateNewLDAPObject LDAP ↪("LDAP://Directory_Server/o=airius.com/ ↪ou=people", "cn=directory manager", ↪"l@undrym@t1962", "uid=teck", ↪"inetOrgPerson", "cn", "Thomas Eck", ↪"sn", "Eck", "givenName", "Thomas")
Enumerate Container Object	For Each Item In EnumerateLDAPContainer ↪("LDAP://Directory_Server/o=airius. ↪com/ou=people", "cn=directory ↪manager", "l@undrym@t1962") Debug.Print Item Next
Remove LDAP Object From Namespace	Debug.Print RemoveLDAPObject ↪("LDAP://Directory_Server/o= ↪airius.com/ou=people", "cn=directory ↪manager", "l@undrym@t1962", ↪"uid=eckth", "inetOrgPerson")
Search LDAP Namespace By Namespace	For Each ObjName In SearchLDAP Attribute ↪Value ("SELECT cn,telephonenumber FROM ↪'LDAP://Directory_Server/ ↪o=airius.com/ou=people' WHERE ↪sn='carter'") Debug.Print ObjName Next

Creating the ExchangeObjectMgt Class Module

In this section, you will begin an exercise that will yield the creation of the MSExchAdmin.DLL COM server.

Exercise 11.3 *Creating the MSExchAdmin.DLL COM Server Application: The ExchangeObjectMgt Module*

1. Create a new ActiveX DLL Visual Basic project.

2. Set a reference to the Active DS Type Library by clicking the Project menu, selecting References..., and placing a checkmark next to the "Active DS Type Library" entry. Click the OK command button to exit the References–Project1 dialog box.

3. Rename Project1 as **MSExchAdmin**.

4. Rename the Class1 class module as **ExchangeObjectMgt**.

5. Enter the following code into the General Declarations section of the class module:

```
Public Function CreateExchangeMailbox(ByVal ExchangeServerName As String, ByVal
ExchangeServerOrganization As String, ByVal ExchangeServerSite As String, ByVal
MailboxRelativePath As String, ByVal MailboxDisplayName As String, ByVal
MailboxFirstName As String, ByVal MailboxLastName As String, ByVal
MailboxMiddleInitial As String, ByVal MailboxAlias As String, ByVal UserDomain As
String, ByVal NTUserAccountToAssociate As String) As Boolean
    Dim Mailbox As IADs
    Dim MailboxParentContainer As IADs
    Dim MTA As String
    Dim MDB As String
    Dim MailboxSMTPAddress As String
    Dim MailboxX400Address As String
    Dim MailboxCCMailAddress As String
    Dim MailboxMSMailAddress As String
    Dim SID As New ADsSID
    Dim Security As New ADsSecurity
    Dim SecurityDescriptor As IADsSecurityDescriptor
    Dim DiscretionaryACL As IADsAccessControlList
    Dim AccessControlEntry As New AccessControlEntry

    MTA = "cn=Microsoft MTA,cn=" & ExchangeServerName &
",cn=Servers,cn=Configuration,ou=" & ExchangeServerSite & ",o=" &
ExchangeServerOrganization
    MDB = "cn=Microsoft Private MDB,cn=" & ExchangeServerName &
",cn=Servers,cn=Configuration,ou=" & ExchangeServerSite & ",o=" &
ExchangeServerOrganization
    MailboxSMTPAddress = MailboxAlias & "@" & ExchangeServerSite & "." &
ExchangeServerOrganization & ".com"
    MailboxX400Address = "c=US;a= ;p=" & ExchangeServerOrganization & ";o=" &
ExchangeServerSite & ";s=" & MailboxLastName & ";g=" & MailboxFirstName & ";i=" &
MailboxMiddleInitial
    MailboxCCMailAddress = MailboxLastName & ", " & MailboxFirstName & " at " &
ExchangeServerSite
```

continues ▶

Exercise 11.3 *continued*

```
        MailboxMSMailAddress = UCase(ExchangeServerOrganization & "/" &
ExchangeServerSite & "/" & MailboxAlias)

        Set MailboxParentContainer = GetObject("LDAP://" & ExchangeServerName & "/o="
& ExchangeServerOrganization & "/ou=" & ExchangeServerSite & "/cn=Recipients" &
MailboxRelativePath)
        Set Mailbox = MailboxParentContainer.Create("organizationalPerson", "cn=" &
MailboxAlias)

        Mailbox.Put "mailPreferenceOption", 0
        Mailbox.Put "givenName", MailboxFirstName
        Mailbox.Put "sn", MailboxLastName
        Mailbox.Put "cn", MailboxDisplayName
        Mailbox.Put "uid", MailboxAlias
        Mailbox.Put "Home-MTA", MTA
        Mailbox.Put "Home-MDB", MDB
        Mailbox.Put "mail", MailboxSMTPAddress
        Mailbox.Put "MAPI-Recipient", True
        Mailbox.Put "rfc822Mailbox", MailboxSMTPAddress
        Mailbox.Put "textEncodedORAddress", MailboxX400Address
        Mailbox.PutEx ADS_PROPERTY_APPEND, "otherMailbox", Array("CCMAIL$" &
MailboxCCMailAddress, "MS$" & MailboxMSMailAddress)

        SID.SetAs ADS_SID_WINNT_PATH, "WinNT://" & UserDomain & "/" &
NTUserAccountToAssociate & ",user"
        sidHex = SID.GetAs(ADS_SID_HEXSTRING)
        Mailbox.Put "Assoc-NT-Account", sidHex
        Mailbox.SetInfo

        Set SecurityDescriptor = Security.GetSecurityDescriptor(Mailbox.ADsPath)
        Set DiscretionaryACL = SecurityDescriptor.DiscretionaryACL
        AccessControlEntry.AceType = ADS_ACETYPE_ACCESS_ALLOWED
        AccessControlEntry.Trustee = UserDomain & "\" & MailboxAlias
        AccessControlEntry.AccessMask = ADS_RIGHT_EXCH_MAIL_SEND_AS Or
ADS_RIGHT_EXCH_MAIL_RECEIVE_AS Or ADS_RIGHT_EXCH_MODIFY_USER_ATT
        DiscretionaryACL.AddAce AccessControlEntry
        SecurityDescriptor.DiscretionaryACL = DiscretionaryACL
        Security.SetSecurityDescriptor SecurityDescriptor

        If Err.Number = 0 Then CreateExchangeMailbox = True
End Function

Public Function RemoveExchangeMailbox(ByVal ExchangeServerName As String, ByVal
ExchangeServerOrganization As String, ByVal ExchangeServerSite As String, ByVal
MailboxRelativePath As String, ByVal MailboxToRemove As String) As Boolean
        Dim MailboxParentContainer As IADsContainer
        Set MailboxParentContainer = GetObject("LDAP://" & ExchangeServerName & "/o="
& ExchangeServerOrganization & "/ou=" & ExchangeServerSite & "/cn=Recipients" &
MailboxRelativePath)
        Call MailboxParentContainer.Delete("organizationalPerson", "cn=" &
MailboxToRemove)
```

Creating the ExchangeObjectMgt Class Module   403

```
        If Err.Number = 0 Then RemoveExchangeMailbox = True
End Function

Public Function AddExchangeDLMember(ByVal ExchangeServerName As String, ByVal
ExchangeServerOrganization As String, ByVal ExchangeServerSite As String, ByVal
DistributionListRelativePath As String, ByVal DistributionListName As String,
ByVal DLMemberMailboxName As String) As Boolean
        Dim DistributionList As IADs
        Set DistributionList = GetObject("LDAP://" & ExchangeServerName & "/o=" &
ExchangeServerOrganization & "/ou=" & ExchangeServerSite & "/cn=Recipients/cn=" &
DistributionListName)

        DistributionList.Add ("LDAP://" & ExchangeServerName & "/o=" &
ExchangeServerOrganization & "/ou=" & ExchangeServerSite & "/cn=Recipients" &
"/cn=" & DLMemberMailboxName)

        DistributionList.SetInfo

        If Err.Number = 0 Then AddExchangeDLMember = True
End Function

Public Function RemoveExchangeDLMember(ByVal ExchangeServerName As String, ByVal
ExchangeServerOrganization As String, ByVal ExchangeServerSite As String, ByVal
DistributionListRelativePath As String, ByVal DistributionListName As String,
ByVal DLMemberMailboxName As String) As Boolean
        Dim DistributionList As IADs
        Set DistributionList = GetObject("LDAP://" & ExchangeServerName & "/o=" &
ExchangeServerOrganization & "/ou=" & ExchangeServerSite & "/cn=Recipients" &
DistributionListRelativePath & "/cn=" & DistributionListName)

        DistributionList.Remove ("LDAP://" & ExchangeServerName & "/o=" &
ExchangeServerOrganization & "/ou=" & ExchangeServerSite & "/cn=Recipients" &
"/cn=" & DLMemberMailboxName)

        DistributionList.SetInfo

        If Err.Number = 0 Then RemoveExchangeDLMember = True
End Function

Public Function DetermineExchangeDLOwner(ByVal ExchangeServerName As String,
ByVal ExchangeServerOrganization As String, ByVal ExchangeServerSite As String,
ByVal DistributionListRelativePath As String, ByVal DistributionListName As
String) As String
        Dim DistributionList As IADs
        Set DistributionList = GetObject("LDAP://" & ExchangeServerName & "/o=" &
ExchangeServerOrganization & "/ou=" & ExchangeServerSite & "/cn=Recipients" &
DistributionListRelativePath & "/cn=" & DistributionListName)

        DetermineExchangeDLOwner = DistributionList.Owner
End Function
```

6. Compile the code as MSExchAdmin.DLL.
7. Save and close the MSExchAdmin project.

> *Tip*
>
> *If you do not want to share your code between applications, you can enter the preceding code into a code module in any Visual Basic application.* ♦

> *Tip*
>
> *You can download the Visual Basic 6.0 project or precompiled version of MSExchAdmin.DLL from* http://www.newriders.com/adsi. ♦

Using the Functions in ExchangeObjectMgt

With the ExchangeObjectMgt class module created, you can access the functions contained in the class module from any programming language that supports OLE automation, including Visual Basic, VBScript, and JavaScript.

> *Tip*
>
> *To instantiate the object, follow the appropriate syntax found in Chapter 3. Substitute the ExchangeObjectMgt class name where necessary.* ♦

Use the Table 11.2 to help you use the proper syntax for each of the methods of the ExchangeObjectMgt interface.

Table 11.2 ExchangeObjectMgt Method Syntax

Action	Syntax
Create a New Exchange Mailbox	Debug.Print CreateExchangeMailbox ↳("Exchange_Server", "ADSITest", ↳"Macmillan", "", "Milan Kundera", ↳"Milan", "Kundera", "-", ↳"Milan.Kundera", "UserDomain", ↳"mkundera")
Remove an Existing Exchange Mailbox	Debug.Print RemoveExchangeMailbox ↳("Exchange_Server", "ADSITest", ↳"Macmillan", "", "Milan.Kundera")
Add an Existing Mailbox as Member of an Existing Distribution List	Debug.Print AddExchangeDLMember ↳("Exchange_Server", "ADSITest", ↳"Macmillan", "", ↳"DL_Senior_Management", ↳"Julian.Barnes")
Remove Member from Distribution List	Debug.Print RemoveExchangeDLMember ↳("Exchange_Server", "ADSITest", ↳"Macmillan", "", ↳"DL_Senior_Management", ↳"Milan.Kundera")

Action	Syntax

`Determine Distribution List Owner`	`Debug.Print DetermineExchangeDLOwner`
	`➥("Exchange_Server", "ADSITest",`
	`➥"Macmillan", "",`
	`➥"DL_Senior_Management")`

Summary

As enterprises strive to solve issues arising from the need for disparate systems to interoperate, an LDAP-based enterprise directory can often suit such purposes efficiently. Based on IETF RFC proposals, the LDAP standard offers solutions to the following issues:

- The type of data that can be stored (the information model)
- The organization of the data (the naming model)
- The methods for accessing and updating data in the directory (the functional model)
- The protection of data (the security model)

The LDAP standard is supported in many major Windows NT applications, including Microsoft Windows 2000, Microsoft Exchange Server 5.5 and higher, Microsoft Site Server 3.0, Netscape Directory Server, many major Internet directories (Yahoo, BigFoot, WhoWhere, VeriSign, and so on), and even some network hardware devices.

To modify the data in the directory, you may import and export LDIF files, or you may freely obtain several SDKs from various vendors and organizations.

Using Microsoft's LDAP provider (contained within the ADSI libraries), you can programmatically access and manipulate data in an LDAP directory. In addition to performing standard binding operations, you can easily enumerate container objects and search the namespace using standard ANSI-SQL syntax in the `Execute` method of an ADO connection object.

In addition to managing native LDAP directory servers, Microsoft's adoption of the LDAP standard in several Microsoft BackOffice products allows programmatic manipulation of Exchange mailboxes and distribution lists, as well as other administrative tasks.

In the future, vendors will likely use the LDAP directory standard to store application configuration data to allow seamless integration of applications running on various vendor platforms. As LDAP directories proliferate, system architects and developers may quickly, easily, and seamlessly bridge the gaps that exist between systems of varying vendors, and simplify development and administrative efforts.

12

Programmatic Management of the Windows 2000 Active Directory

Despite the massive overhaul Microsoft prescribed for the Windows NT operating system in the final release of Windows 2000, many of the programmatic techniques described previously in this text remain relatively unaffected by the changes to the operating system.

The Active Directory drastically modifies the way we look at user and group objects at the enterprise level, with its implementation of Lightweight Diectory Access Protocol's (LDAP's) distinguished name standards. However, on workstations and member servers, you must use ADSI's Windows NT provider to manage local accounts and groups. Furthermore, even on Windows 2000 AD Domain Controllers, you can still use the Windows NT provider to perform most of the common management tasks for users and groups.

In this chapter, you will explore the use of the ADSI LDAP service provider within an Active Directory infrastructure. You will look at basic Active Directory terminology and the service provider support available for ADSI interfaces.

In addition, you will learn how to do the following:

- Bind to objects in the Active Directory.
- Manipulate objects in the Active Directory.
- Manipulate Active Directory object security.

Active Directory Terminology Primer

Critics of the Windows NT platform have often regarded the Windows NT SAM's inability to scale to enterprise requirements as a flaw that has prevented Windows NT from entering the enterprise operating system market. Although there is still debate over the viability of Windows NT as an enterprise computing platform, even the harshest critic will find it difficult to criticize the scalability and attribute-level security found in the Active Directory.

Based on the LDAP Request For Comments (RFCs), the Active Directory provides system architects with a central location to store enterprise information for everything from employee data to configuration of network devices.

> *Tip*
>
> *Several of the concepts found in this chapter overlap with those found in Chapter 11, "Programmatic Management of LDAP Infrastructures." If you haven't yet read Chapter 11 and are new to either LDAP or the Active Directory, this chapter may be a bit easier to digest after reading that chapter's background information.* ◆

Although the Active Directory is indeed based on the LDAP RFCs, Microsoft's use of several terms differ from traditional LDAP nomenclature. Thus, it is essential that you understand the following before you attempt to use ADSI to manipulate the Active Directory:

- **Attribute.** Attributes are the characteristics of each object and are defined by the schema definitions for each object's class. Attributes can also be referred to as *properties* of an object; the terms are interchangable.

- **Domain.** A domain defines the boundaries for security, administration, and replication processes. A domain can run in either native mode (all Windows 2000 domain controllers) or mixed mode (a combination of both Windows NT and Windows 2000 domain controllers). Native mode domains have significant advantages related to group administration, including the ability to nest groups and to create universal groups. Additionally, it is important to note that the first domain established is the root domain, which, at the time of this writing, cannot be renamed.

- **Forest.** A forest is a collection of trees that do not share a common root domain name. Trees within the same forest share information through automatically established trust relationships. A common use of a forest might be to separate loosely related business entities, while still retaining a common global catalog, configuration, and schema.

- **Global catalog.** The global catalog is a central repository for frequently used information, derived by creating a partial replica of every object in the directory. Each partial replica object is composed from a specific subset of each full object's attributes. As a result, the global catalog allows a user to quickly search an entire forest for a particular object, and stores information pointing to the actual location of an object in the forest to allow quick navigation to the desired object. As with many of the other terms in this chapter, the global catalog is specific to the Active Directory.
- **Globally Unique Identifier (GUID).** A GUID is a 128-bit number that is statistically improbable to be anything other than unique within any given namespace. This identifier is used to uniquely and permanently identify objects; it can never be changed even after relocating an object elsewhere in the namespace. Even if an object is renamed, the GUID does not change. This stability enables you to permanently identify an object's association with another object in the directory.
- **Object.** An object is simply an entry in the directory of a specific class. A group object, for example, is an entry in the directory that has values for all mandatory properties as defined by the schema definition for the group class. Additionally, an object can allow various optional properties to describe the object; these optional properties are also based on the schema definition for the particular object's class. This term is synonymous with *entries* as defined in the LDAP chapter.
- **Organizational unit (OU).** An organizational unit is a container used to hold objects in a domain to allow logical groupings of objects along geographical, functional, or administrative boundaries. OUs are especially important to establish delegated administration: it is recommended to delegate rights only at the OU level and allow all child objects to inherit the permissions assigned to their parent container object. Additionally, OUs allow you to eliminate the use of the multiple master user domain model, which is currently found in many large Windows NT implementations.
- **Site.** A site defines the boundaries of high-speed IP connectivity to help optimize replication traffic and increase the probability of successful authentication. Although stored in the Active Directory, sites are not part of LDAP standard nomenclature.
- **Tree.** If two domains share the same root name, the hierarchical structure created by such an arrangement is referred to as a tree. Two-way transitive trust relationships are defined automatically between individual domains within a tree. To understand this concept, consider that a company might have individual domains for Engineering, Sales, and Marketing; because all three entities are part of the same root domain name, they establish a tree.

- **User principal name (UPN).** The UPN is formed by default from the concatenation of the user's logon name and the DNS name of the domain in which the user object resides. This name is one of several methods that can be used to uniquely identify the user object for login or identification purposes. Microsoft chose the structure of the UPN to match that of an Internet email address so that enterprises that have established unique email names for their employees can allow employees to log on using their email aliases.

> **Note**
>
> As with the LDAP and Visual Basic discussions presented in this text, this section is not intended as a comprehensive discussion of the Active Directory and its many intricacies.
>
> Please see Appendix C, "Further Reading," for a list of references to other resources on Microsoft Active Directory technology. ◆

Binding to Objects in the Active Directory

Although the Active Directory transforms the way we think about user domains and other enterprise entities, operations at the workstation and member server level continue to use the Windows NT (WinNT:) ADSI service provider. For example, to create a user account on a member server, you can follow the same code used to create accounts in the Windows NT model. When you want to create a user account that would have once resided in the user domain, you should instead use the ADSI LDAP service provider to add an object to the Active Directory.

Use the code segments in this chapter as a guide to update the binding string used for any code that manipulates user accounts, computer accounts, groups, or print queues in a Windows 2000 directory. In most cases, only the binding string must be changed to specify the object's location in the Active Directory's hierarchical data structure.

> **Using ADSI Edit to Examine the Active Directory**
>
> Using the ADSI Edit MMC snap-in, you can view and edit objects in the Active Directory at an extremely low level. This tool duplicates much of the functionality provided by the MMC snap-ins included in the Administrative Tools folder. ADSI Edit is also extremely useful for viewing the object classes and mandatory and optional properties for each object class, as well as for viewing the contents and hierarchical structure of the domain naming context, schema, and configuration containers.◆

Binding to the Root DS Entry (RootDSE) Using Visual Basic

As part of RFC 2251, the LDAP standard requires all LDAP directories to maintain a set of properties that any user can query to find various key characteristics about the directory. These characteristics include the server's current time, the LDAP server name, and the server's DNS host name. This information is stored in the RootDSE and maintains each property as an attribute of the object.

To view these properties using Visual Basic, use the following code segment:

```
Dim RootDSE As IADs
Set RootDSE = GetObject("LDAP://RootDSE")

Debug.Print "Current Time: " & RootDSE.Get("CurrentTime")

Debug.Print "SubSchemaSubEntry: " & RootDSE.Get("SubSchemaSubEntry")

Debug.Print "DsServiceName: " & RootDSE.Get("DsServiceName")

For Each Item In RootDSE.Get("NamingContexts")
     Debug.Print "Naming Context: " & Item
Next

Debug.Print "Default Naming Context: " & RootDSE.Get("DefaultNamingContext")

Debug.Print "Schema Naming Context: " & RootDSE.Get("SchemaNamingContext")

Debug.Print "Configuration Naming Context: " &
➥RootDSE.Get("ConfigurationNamingContext")

Debug.Print "Root Domain Naming Context: " &
➥RootDSE.Get("RootDomainNamingContext")

For Each Item In RootDSE.Get("SupportedControl")
     Debug.Print "Supported Control: " & Item
Next

For Each Item In RootDSE.Get("SupportedLDAPVersion")
     Debug.Print "Supported LDAP Version: " & Item
Next

Debug.Print "Highest Committed USN: " & RootDSE.Get("HighestCommittedUSN")

For Each Item In RootDSE.Get("SupportedSASLMechanisms")
     Debug.Print "Supported SASL Mechanism: " & Item
Next

Debug.Print "DNS Host Name: " & RootDSE.Get("DnsHostName")

Debug.Print "LDAP Service Name: " & RootDSE.Get("LdapServiceName")

Debug.Print "Server Name: " & RootDSE.Get("ServerName")
```

Using the RootDSE *DefaultNamingContext* Attribute to Bind to an Active Directory Object Using Current Credentials in Visual Basic

To avoid having to hard-code distinguished names in your code, you can often use the default naming context to derive the name of the domain you are logged in to at run-time.

The following Visual Basic code will return the distinguished name of the current user's domain at run-time:

```
Dim DefaultDomain as IADs
Dim RootDSE as IADs
Set RootDSE = GetObject("LDAP://RootDSE")
Set DefaultDomain = GetObject("LDAP://" & RootDSE.Get("DefaultNamingContext"))
```

Tip

This code should form the basis for all binding operations performed on the current user's domain; it eliminates the need for the user to specify a server/domain name or credentials at run-time. ♦

Note

In the previous example, you establish a binding at the domain level. However, you can specify any point in the hierarchy by inserting the relative distinguished names of the structure between the LDAP:// *string and the RootDSE.Get statement.* ♦

Binding to an Active Directory Object Using Alternate Credentials

To bind to the Active Directory using a set of credentials other than those used on the client, you can use the IADsOpenDSObject interface to bind with an alternate username and password, as shown in the following Visual Basic code segment:

```
Dim DSO As IADsOpenDSObject
Dim Obj As IADs
Dim AdsPath As String
Dim AlternateUser_UPN As String
Dim AlternateUser_Password As String

AdsPath =
↪"LDAP://Server_Name.ResearchDevelopment.TestInfra/cn=Users,dc=ResearchDevelopment↪
↪,dc=TestInfra"
AlternateUser_UPN = "thomas.eck@ResearchDevelopment.TestInfra"
AlternateUser_Password = "P0l1t1c@l@rs0ni$t"

Set DSO = GetObject("LDAP:")
Set Obj = DSO.OpenDSObject(AdsPath, AlternateUser_UPN, AlternateUser_Password,
ADS_SECURE_AUTHENTICATION)
```

> **Note**
>
> *In the preceding example, you are binding to a completely different domain, although you can use the same code to specify an alternate user who can access restricted attributes in the same domain. Whenever possible, derive the default naming context programmatically, as shown in this example.*
>
> *In some cases, you might want to use alternate credentials only after a call to GetObject has failed due to the user's credentials. To implement such a scenario, use a conditional to test whether* `Err.Number` *equals 0. If* `Err.Number` *returns anything other than a 0 after the binding is attempted, you can execute the above code, prompting the user for his credentials at run-time.*◆

Searching the Entire Forest Using the Global Catalog and Visual Basic

If you are unsure of a specific item's location in the forest, you can use the following Visual Basic code to perform a search of the Global Catalog:

```
Dim Container As IADsContainer
Dim GC As IADs
Dim ADsPath As String
Dim Obj As Variant
Dim Conn As ADODB.Connection
Dim Command As ADODB.Command
Dim RS As ADODB.Recordset
Dim SQLStmt As String

'Change the SQL statement below to display objects that reflect the
specified criteria
SQLStmt = "SELECT cn, distinguishedName FROM '" & ADsPath & "' WHERE
objectCategory = 'person' AND objectClass = 'user'"
Set Container = GetObject("GC:")
For Each Obj In Container
Set GC = Obj
Next
ADsPath = GC.ADsPath
Set Conn = New ADODB.Connection
Set Command = New ADODB.Command
Conn.Provider = "ADsDSOObject"
Conn.Open

Set Command.ActiveConnection = Conn
Set RS = Conn.Execute(SQLStmt)

While Not RS.EOF
Debug.Print RS.Fields("cn") & vbTab & RS.Fields("distinguishedName")
RS.MoveNext
Wend
RS.Close
Conn.Close
```

By simply changing the SQL statement, you can return the ADsPath of any desired object anywhere in the forest.

Determining Which Object Attributes Are Replicated to the Global Catalog Using Visual Basic

To find out which attributes are replicated to the global catalog, use ADO to query the schema container for all objects maintaining a True Boolean condition for the `isMemberOfPartialAttributeSet` *attribute.*

The following Visual Basic code segment exemplifies this process:

```
Dim Connection As ADODB.Connection
Dim RS As ADODB.Recordset
Dim Entry As String
Dim Index As Long
Dim RootDSE As IADs
Dim SchemaContainer As IADs

Index = 0
Set Connection = New ADODB.Connection
Connection.Provider = "ADsDSOObject"
Connection.Open "ADSI"

Set RootDSE = GetObject("LDAP://RootDSE")
Set SchemaContainer = GetObject("LDAP://" & RootDSE.Get("SchemaNamingContext"))

Set RS = Connection.Execute("SELECT cn FROM '" & SchemaContainer.AdsPath & "'
➥where isMemberOfPartialAttributeSet = TRUE AND objectCategory =
➥'attributeSchema'")

While Not RS.EOF
    For i = 0 To RS.Fields.Count - 1
        If RS.Fields(i).Type = adVariant And Not (IsNull(RS.Fields(i).Value))
➥Then
            For j = LBound(RS.Fields(i).Value) To UBound(RS.Fields(i).Value)
                Entry = Entry & RS.Fields(i).Value(j) & vbTab
            Next j
        Else
            Entry = Entry & RS.Fields(i).Value & vbTab
        End If

        If Index = RS.Fields.Count - 1 Then
            Debug.Print Entry
        End If
        Index = Index + 1
    Next i
    Entry = ""
    Index = 0
    RS.MoveNext
Wend ◆
```

> **Note**
>
> *You must set a reference to the Microsoft ActiveX Data Objects type library before running the preceding code!* ♦

Manipulating Objects in the Active Directory

To create an object in the directory, you must first create an object of a specific class and then assign values to the mandatory attributes of the object before writing it to the directory. From this procedure, one can quickly conclude that the only thing differentiating one object from another within the directory is the class of the object and the attributes values assigned to each object.

Armed with this knowledge, you can easily enumerate, create, and remove objects in the directory using generic code syntax, and change the attribute assignments as appropriate for each object created.

Displaying All User Class Objects in the Active Directory Using Visual Basic

To enumerate all user objects in a particular container in the Active Directory, use a variation of the following Visual Basic code:

```
Dim RootDSE As IADs
Dim UserContainer As IADsContainer
Dim User As IADs
Dim RelativePathFromDomainToUserContainer As String

RelativePathFromDomainToUserContainer = "ou=user accounts,"

Set RootDSE = GetObject("LDAP://RootDSE")
Set UserContainer = GetObject("LDAP://" & RelativePathFromDomainToUserContainer & RootDSE.Get("DefaultNamingContext"))
UserContainer.Filter = Array("User")

For Each User In UserContainer
    Debug.Print User.AdsPath
Next
```

> **Note**
>
> *In the previous example you are using the IADsContainer* Filter *property to display objects belonging only to the User class.* ♦

Displaying All Group Class Objects in the Active Directory Using Visual Basic

By changing the IADsContainer `Filter` property value assignment (and potentially, the relative path to the groups you want to enumerate) you can display all groups defined in a particular container.

An example of such a procedure is shown in the following Visual Basic code segment:

```
Dim RootDSE As IADs
Dim GroupContainer As IADsContainer
Dim Group As IADs
Dim RelativePathFromDomainToGroupContainer As String

RelativePathFromDomainToGroupContainer = "ou=Groups,ou=Chicago,"

Set RootDSE = GetObject("LDAP://RootDSE")
Set GroupContainer = GetObject("LDAP://" & RelativePathFromDomainToGroupContainer
↪& RootDSE.Get("defaultNamingContext"))

GroupContainer.Filter = Array("Group")

For Each Group In GroupContainer
    Debug.Print Group.AdsPath
Next
```

Displaying All Computer Class Objects in the Active Directory Using Visual Basic

To display all computer accounts in a particular container, use the following Visual Basic code:

```
Dim RootDSE As IADs
Dim ComputerAccountContainer As IADsContainer
Dim ComputerAccount As IADs
Dim RelativePathFromDomainToComputerContainer As String

RelativePathFromDomainToComputerContainer = "ou=Workstations,ou=Computer
↪Accounts,ou=Chicago"

Set RootDSE = GetObject("LDAP://RootDSE")
Set ComputerAccountContainer = GetObject("LDAP://" &
↪RelativePathFromDomainToComputerContainer & RootDSE.Get("defaultNamingContext"))

ComputerAccountContainer.Filter = Array("Computer")

For Each ComputerAccount In ComputerAccountContainer
    Debug.Print ComputerAccount.AdsPath
Next
```

Creating Objects in the Active Directory

As in a traditional LDAP directory, to create objects in the Active Directory, you must know several pieces of information, including the following:

- The desired location in the directory
- The class of the object to be created
- The appropriate values for the mandatory attributes for the selected class

To help determine which attributes are required for each object class, consider Table 12.1, which describes the most commonly created objects in the Active Directory:

Table 12.1 Mandatory attributes for common object classes used in the Active Directory

Object Class	Mandatory Attribute(s)	Attribute Datatype(s)
computer	cn	String
	sAMAccountName	String
contact	cn	String
container	cn	String
group	cn	String
	groupType	Integer
	sAMAccountName	String
locality	l	String
organizationalUnit	ou	String
printQueue	cn	String
	shortServerName	String
	serverName	String
	printerName	String
	versionNumber	Integer
	uNCName	String
user	cn	String
	sAMAccountName	String

Creating Objects in the Active Directory Using Visual Basic

Use the following Visual Basic code as a guide to create any object in the Active Directory:

```
Dim RootDSE As IADs
Dim Container As IADsContainer
Dim RelativePathToObject As String
Dim ObjectClass As String
```

```
Dim ObjectName As String
Dim NewObject As IADs
Dim MandatoryProperty1_Name As String
Dim MandatoryProperty1_Value As String
'Define more mandatory properties as needed

RelativePathToObject = "ou=administrators,"
ObjectClass = "user"
ObjectRelativeName = "cn=TestAdmin"
MandatoryProperty1_Name = "sAMAccountName"
MandatoryProperty1_Value = "TestAdmin"
'If you dimensioned additional mandatory properties, assign them here

Set RootDSE = GetObject("LDAP://RootDSE")
Set Container = GetObject("LDAP://" & RelativePathToObject &
↪RootDSE.Get("defaultNamingContext"))
Set NewObject = Container.Create(ObjectClass, ObjectRelativeName)

NewObject.Put MandatoryProperty1_Name, MandatoryProperty1_Value
'Assign additional mandatory properties to the object here

NewObject.SetInfo
```

Note

To create groups, computer accounts, or user accounts in the Active Directory, follow the code found in Chapter 3, "Container Enumeration Methods and Programmatic Domain Account Policy Manipulation," used to create each respective object type (after the binding operation takes place and the sAMAccountName has been set).

To create these objects on Windows 2000 member servers or workstations, simply follow the code used for Windows NT infrastructures. ◆

Displaying Object Classes and Associated Mandatory Attributes Using Visual Basic

To find the mandatory properties of a class for any existing object in the directory, use the following Visual Basic code:

```
Dim RootDSE As IADs
Dim ObjectName As IADs
Dim ObjectClass As IADs
Dim RelativePath As String
Dim Obj As IADs
Dim MandatoryProperty As Variant

RelativePath = "cn=System,"

Set RootDSE = GetObject("LDAP://RootDSE")
ADsPath = "LDAP://" & RelativePath & RootDSE.Get("DefaultNamingContext")
```

```
Set ObjectName = GetObject(ADsPath)
Debug.Print "Object Name: " & ObjectName.Name
Debug.Print "Object Class: " & ObjectName.Class
Set ObjectClass = GetObject(ObjectName.Schema)
For Each MandatoryProperty In ObjectClass.MandatoryProperties
    Debug.Print vbTab & MandatoryProperty
Next
```

Removing Objects from the Active Directory Using Visual Basic

To remove objects from the Active Directory, you must know the object class, relative name of the object, and the distinguished path to the object.

Use the following Visual Basic code as a guide to remove any object from the Active Directory:

```
Dim RootDSE As IADs
Dim Container As IADsContainer
Dim RelativePathToObject As String
Dim ObjectClass As String
Dim ObjectName As String

RelativePathToObject = "ou=administrators,"
ObjectClass = "user"
ObjectRelativeName = "cn=TestAdmin"

Set RootDSE = GetObject("LDAP://RootDSE")
Set Container = GetObject("LDAP://" & RelativePathToObject &
➥RootDSE.Get("DefaultNamingContext"))

Call Container.Delete(ObjectClass, ObjectRelativeName)
```

Deleting an Entire Branch of a Directory Tree Using Visual Basic

Using ADSI's IADsDeleteOps interface, you can prune an entire subtree from the directory tree. The IADsDeleteOps interface allows you to remove an object and all its child objects using a single line of code.

Use the following Visual Basic code to delete the Print Queues organizational unit from the base of the tree:

```
Dim RootDSE As IADs
Dim Container As IADsDeleteOps
Dim RelativePathToObject As String
RelativePathToObject = "ou=Print Queues,"
Set RootDSE = GetObject("LDAP://RootDSE")
Set Container = GetObject("LDAP://" & RelativePathToObject &
➥RootDSE.Get("DefaultNamingContext"))

Container.DeleteObject (0)
```

Renaming Objects in the Active Directory Using Visual Basic

To rename an object in the Active Directory, you can use the IADsContainer MoveHere method. Although designed for moving objects from one location of the directory to another, when the origin and destination containers are equivalent, and a new relative name for the object is specified, the object is renamed.

To rename any object in the Active Directory, use the following Visual Basic code as a guide:

```
Dim Container as IADsContainer
Dim NewObjectName as IADs
Set Container = GetObject("LDAP://ou=Admins,dc=eCommerce2000,dc=com")
Set NewObjectName =
↪Container.MoveHere("LDAP://cn=Administrator,ou=Admins,dc=eCommerce2000,dc=com",
"cn=DMZAdmin")
```

> **Warning**
>
> *IADsDeleteOps can do* significant *amounts of damage if improperly executed in the namespace. Be careful when granting rights to users to allow use of this interface.* ◆

Moving Objects Within a Tree Using Visual Basic

To use the IADsContainer MoveHere method to move an object, bind to the destination container and then specify the object to be moved into the container object as an argument to the MoveHere method, as shown in the following Visual Basic code segment:

```
Dim Container as IADsContainer
Dim NewObjectName as IADs
Set Container = GetObject("LDAP://ou=Users,dc=eCommerce2000,dc=com")
Set NewObjectName =
↪Container.MoveHere("LDAP://cn=DMZAdmin,ou=Admins,dc=eCommerce2000,dc=com",
↪vbNullString)
```

> **Tip**
>
> *You can move and rename an object simultaneously by passing the new object name as the second argument of the IADsContainer* MoveHere *method.* ◆

> **Warning**
>
> *Because VBScript does not have a constant value equivalent to vbNullString, you must explicitly name the relative name of the object (such as cn=DMZAdmin) as the second argument of the IADsContainer* MoveHere *method.* ◆

Managing Security for Objects in the Active Directory

In response to critical analysis regarding the granularity of the administrative model implemented in Windows NT, Microsoft's efforts with the Active Directory are sure to please administrators eager to break free of the chains binding them to the most mundane administrative tasks. This newfound freedom comes at the cost of additional complexity to the design and programmatic manipulation of the entries in the directory. However, most will agree that such complexity is a worthwhile compromise to gain the additional features and benefits derived from having such fine granularity to the administrative model.

> **Warning**
>
> *Programmatic administration of the security descriptors for Active Directory objects is not a topic that should be tackled by those new to the Active Directory or Visual Basic. To successfully achieve a working security model, you often must pass a properly formatted schemaIDGuid for either an object class or attribute definition.*
>
> *To perform this task, you can use a custom DLL included with the sample code associated with this text, found at* http://www.newriders.com/adsi. ◆

Security administration of objects in the directory uses the following basic flow to assign establish permissions on an object:

1. Bind to an object in the directory.
2. Open the object's security descriptor.
3. Obtain the discretionary access control list (DACL) from the security descriptor.
4. Create a new access control entry (ACE.)
5. Assign the appropriate constants to the fields in the ACE.
6. Assign a trustee to the ACE.
7. Write the ACE to the DACL.
8. Write the DACL to the Security Descriptor.
9. Write the update back to the Active Directory.

Based on the constants assigned within the properties of the access control entry, you can determine whether child objects should inherit the permissions assigned to the parent object. You can also specify whether the permissions will be inherited by all objects or will affect just a single object class or attribute definition.

After you understand how the security descriptors are manipulated programmatically, you can manipulate the most powerful security feature of the Active Directory: the delegation of administrative authority.

By managing security down to the attribute level, you can create an administrative model in which specific groups of users can manage a very small subset of properties for all users in a particular container. Imagine how much you would reduce administrative burden if you could create a Web page wherein users could manage their own user information, such as department, telephone extension, address, and so on. The number of solutions you can implement by taking advantage of attribute-level security descriptors is limited only by the design of your directory and by your own creativity.

Constants Used in ACEs

To configure the ACE for an object in the Active Directory, you must reference the proper constant representing the right you wish to grant, the type of access control entry, and the inheritance scope for the ACE.

Directory Object Access Rights

To specify the rights for an object in the Active Directory, you can assign any of the constants found in Table 12.2 to the `AccessMask` ACE field.

Table 12.2   Access Mask Property Flags

Constant	Value	Description
Full Control Access	-1	To specify full control, set the value of the sAccessMask ACE field to –1.
ADS_RIGHT_DS_CREATE_CHILD	0x1	Grants the ability to create child objects. All objects can be created unless the ObjectType field in the ACE contains a valid schemaIDGuid for an object class.
ADS_RIGHT_DS_DELETE_CHILD	0x2	Grants the ability to delete child objects of all classes, unless the ObjectType contains a valid schemaIDGuid for an object class.
ADS_RIGHT_ACTRL_DS_LIST	0x4	Grants the ability to list all child objects.
ADS_RIGHT_DS_SELF	0x8	Grants the ability to list the object itself.
ADS_RIGHT_DS_READ_PROP	0x10	Grants the ability to read object properties. Setting the ObjectType to a valid property or property set GUID restricts the grant to a specific property or property set.

Constant	Value	Description
ADS_RIGHT_DS_WRITE_PROP	0x20	Grants the ability to write object properties. Can be restricted using the ObjectType ACE member. Setting the ObjectType to a valid property or property set GUID restricts the grant to a specific property or property set.
ADS_RIGHT_DS_DELETE_TREE	0x40	Grants the ability to delete the object and all associated child objects.
ADS_RIGHT_DS_LIST_OBJECT	0x80	Can be used to show or hide an object from user view.
ADS_RIGHT_DS_CONTROL_ACCESS	0x100	Grants the ability to perform an operation restricted by an extended access right. Must specify a rights GUID identifying a controlAccessRight object in the Extended-Rights container in the configuration partition (naming context).
ADS_RIGHT_DELETE	0x10000	Grants the right to delete the object.
ADS_RIGHT_READ_CONTROL	0x20000	Grants the right to read the object's security descriptor.
ADS_RIGHT_WRITE_DAC	0x40000	Grants the right to modify the discretionary access control list.
ADS_RIGHT_OWNER	0x80000	Grants the right to take ownership of an object.
ADS_RIGHT_SYNCHRONIZE	0x100000	Enables the object to be used for synchronization.
ADS_RIGHT_ACCESS_SYSTEM_SECURITY	0x1000000	Grants the right to manipulate the object's SACL.
ADS_RIGHT_GENERIC_ALL	0x10000000	Grants the right to create or delete child objects and subtrees, read and write all properties, and add or remove the object from the directory.
ADS_RIGHT_GENERIC_EXECUTE	0x20000000	Grants the ability to list the object's children.
ADS_RIGHT_GENERIC_WRITE	0x40000000	Grants the right to write to the DACL and all properties, as well as to remove the object from the directory.
ADS_RIGHT_GENERIC_READ	0x80000000	Grants the right to read the security descriptor, all properties, and any children of the object.

Access Control Entry Types

To specify the type of ACE used in an Active Directory object access control list (ACL), assign one of the constants in Table 12.3 to the `AceType` ACE field.

Table 12.3 AceType *Flag Values*

Constant	Value	Description
ADS_ACETYPE_ACCESS_ALLOWED	0	Access allowed, no object class discrimination
ADS_ACETYPE_ACCESS_DENIED	0x1	Access denied, no object class discrimination
ADS_ACETYPE_SYSTEM_AUDIT	0x2	System type ACE, no object class discrimination
ADS_ACETYPE_ACCESS_ALLOWED_OBJECT	0x5	Access allowed for objects defined by `ObjectType` or `InheritedObjectType`
ADS_ACETYPE_ACCESS_DENIED_OBJECT	0x6	Access denied for objects defined by `ObjectType` or `InheritedObjectType`
ADS_ACETYPE_SYSTEM_AUDIT_OBJECT	0x7	System type ACE, applied only to objects defined by `ObjectType` or `InheritedObjectType`

Security Propagation and Inheritance

To define the scope of inheritance and the use of system audit messages, assign one of the constants in Table 12.4 to an ACE's `AceFlags` field.

Table 12.4 AceFlags *Flag Values*

Constant	Value	Description
ADS_ACEFLAG_INHERIT_ACE	0x2	Child objects inherit the ACE unless the ADS_ACEFLAG_NO_PROPAGATE_INHERIT_ACE flag has been set.
ADS_ACEFLAG_NO_PROPAGATE_INHERIT_ACE	0x4	The ACEs for all child objects will not contain this ACE.
ADS_ACEFLAG_INHERIT_ONLY_ACE	0x8	Specifies the ACE to be inherited for child objects, but is not subject to the ACE itself.
ADS_ACEFLAG_INHERITED_ACE	0x10	System controlled bit to determine whether the ACE was derived from the parent object.
ADS_ACEFLAG_VALID_INHERIT_FLAGS	0x1f	System controlled bit to determine whether inherit flags are valid.

Constant	Value	Description
ADS_ACEFLAG_SUCCESSFUL_ACCESS	0x40	Used with SACL ACEs to generate a successful audit message.
ADS_ACEFLAG_FAILED_ACCESS	0x80	Used with SACL ACEs to generate a failed audit message.

ObjectType Constants

To restrict an ACE to a particular class of objects (or even an individual object class attribute) assign the schemaIDGuid associated with the object class to the ACE's `ObjectType` field and then assign one of the constants in Table 12.5 to the `Flags` field in the ACE.

Table 12.5   ACE Flags Flag Values

Constant	Value	Description
ADS_FLAG_OBJECT_TYPE_PRESENT	0x1	Indicates that the ObjectType field has been populated with a schemaIDGuid and that the ObjectType GUID should be used.
ADS_FLAG_INHERITED_OBJECT_TYPE_PRESENT	0x2	Indicates that the InheritedObjectType field has been populated with a schemaIDGuid and that the InheritedObjectType GUID should be used.

Basic Active Directory Security Administration

Every object in the Active Directory maintains a security descriptor that can be manipulated programmatically using Visual Basic. In this section, we'll explore basic manipulation of an object's security descriptor, including enumeration of the defined access control entries in an access control list, addition of an access control entry that only applies to the bound object's ACL, and removal of ACEs.

Enumerating the ACEs Within an Active Directory ACL Using Visual Basic

To enumerate the ACEs within the ACL of an object's security descriptor, use the following Visual Basic code:

```
Dim Obj As IADs
Dim ACE As AccessControlEntry
Dim DiscretionaryACL As AccessControlList
Dim SecurityDescriptor As IADsSecurityDescripter
Dim ObjectDistinguishedName As String
```

```
ObjectDistinguishedName = "ou=Admins,dc=eCommerce2000,dc=com"

Set Obj = GetObject("LDAP:// " & ObjectDistinguishedName)
Set SecurityDescriptor = Obj.Get("ntSecurityDescriptor")
Set DiscretionaryACL = SecurityDescriptor.DiscretionaryACL

For Each ACE In DiscretionaryACL
    Debug.Print ACE.Trustee
    If (ACE.AccessMask And ADS_RIGHT_DELETE) <> 0 Then
        If (ACE.ObjectType = "" And ACE.InheritedObjectType = "") Then
            Debug.Print vbTab & "ADS_RIGHT_DELETE"
        Else
            If ACE.InheritedObjectType = "" Then
                Debug.Print vbTab & "ADS_RIGHT_DELETE for SchemaIDGuid: " &
➥ACE.ObjectType
            Else
                Debug.Print vbTab & "Inherited ADS_RIGHT_DELETE for SchemaIDGuid:
➥" & ACE.InheritedObjectType
            End If
        End If
    End If

    If (ACE.AccessMask And ADS_RIGHT_READ_CONTROL) <> 0 Then
        If (ACE.ObjectType = "" And ACE.InheritedObjectType = "") Then
            Debug.Print vbTab & "ADS_RIGHT_READ_CONTROL"
        Else
            If ACE.InheritedObjectType = "" Then
                Debug.Print vbTab & "ADS_RIGHT_READ_CONTROL for SchemaIDGuid: " &
➥ACE.ObjectType
            Else
                Debug.Print vbTab & "Inherited ADS_RIGHT_READ_CONTROL for
➥SchemaIDGuid: " & ACE.InheritedObjectType
            End If
        End If
    End If

    If (ACE.AccessMask And ADS_RIGHT_WRITE_DAC) <> 0 Then
        If (ACE.ObjectType = "" And ACE.InheritedObjectType = "") Then
            Debug.Print vbTab & "ADS_RIGHT_WRITE_DAC"
        Else
            If ACE.InheritedObjectType = "" Then
                Debug.Print vbTab & "ADS_RIGHT_WRITE_DAC for SchemaIDGuid: " &
➥ACE.ObjectType
            Else
                Debug.Print vbTab & "Inherited ADS_RIGHT_WRITE_DAC for
➥SchemaIDGuid: " & ACE.InheritedObjectType
            End If
        End If
    End If

    If (ACE.AccessMask And ADS_RIGHT_WRITE_OWNER) <> 0 Then
        If (ACE.ObjectType = "" And ACE.InheritedObjectType = "") Then
            Debug.Print vbTab & "ADS_RIGHT_WRITE_OWNER"
```

```
        Else
            If ACE.InheritedObjectType = "" Then
                Debug.Print vbTab & "ADS_RIGHT_WRITE_OWNER for SchemaIDGuid: " &
➥ACE.ObjectType
            Else
                Debug.Print vbTab & "Inherited ADS_RIGHT_WRITE_OWNER for
➥SchemaIDGuid: " & ACE.InheritedObjectType
            End If
        End If
    End If

    If (ACE.AccessMask And ADS_RIGHT_SYNCHRONIZE) <> 0 Then
        If (ACE.ObjectType = "" And ACE.InheritedObjectType = "") Then
            Debug.Print vbTab & "ADS_RIGHT_SYNCHRONIZE"
        Else
            If ACE.InheritedObjectType = "" Then
                Debug.Print vbTab & "ADS_RIGHT_SYNCHRONIZE for SchemaIDGuid: " &
➥ACE.ObjectType
            Else
                Debug.Print vbTab & "Inherited ADS_RIGHT_SYNCHRONIZE for
➥SchemaIDGuid: " & ACE.InheritedObjectType
            End If
        End If
    End If

    If (ACE.AccessMask And ADS_RIGHT_ACCESS_SYSTEM_SECURITY) <> 0 Then
        If (ACE.ObjectType = "" And ACE.InheritedObjectType = "") Then
            Debug.Print vbTab & "ADS_RIGHT_ACCESS_SYSTEM_SECURITY"
        Else
            If ACE.InheritedObjectType = "" Then
                Debug.Print vbTab & "ADS_RIGHT_ACCESS_SYSTEM_SECURITY for
➥SchemaIDGuid: " & ACE.ObjectType
            Else
                Debug.Print vbTab & "Inherited ADS_RIGHT_ACCESS_SYSTEM_SECURITY
➥for SchemaIDGuid: " & ACE.InheritedObjectType
            End If
        End If
    End If

    If (ACE.AccessMask And ADS_RIGHT_GENERIC_READ) <> 0 Then
        If (ACE.ObjectType = "" And ACE.InheritedObjectType = "") Then
            Debug.Print vbTab & "ADS_RIGHT_GENERIC_READ"
        Else
            If ACE.InheritedObjectType = "" Then
                Debug.Print vbTab & "ADS_RIGHT_GENERIC_READ for SchemaIDGuid: " &
➥ACE.ObjectType
            Else
                Debug.Print vbTab & "Inherited ADS_RIGHT_GENERIC_READ for
➥SchemaIDGuid: " & ACE.InheritedObjectType
            End If
        End If
    End If
```

```
        If (ACE.AccessMask And ADS_RIGHT_GENERIC_WRITE) <> 0 Then
            If (ACE.ObjectType = "" And ACE.InheritedObjectType = "") Then
                Debug.Print vbTab & "ADS_RIGHT_GENERIC_WRITE"
            Else
                If ACE.InheritedObjectType = "" Then
                    Debug.Print vbTab & "ADS_RIGHT_GENERIC_WRITE for SchemaIDGuid: "
↪& ACE.ObjectType
                Else
                    Debug.Print vbTab & "Inherited ADS_RIGHT_GENERIC_WRITE for
↪SchemaIDGuid: " & ACE.InheritedObjectType
                End If
            End If
        End If

        If (ACE.AccessMask And ADS_RIGHT_GENERIC_EXECUTE) <> 0 Then
            If (ACE.ObjectType = "" And ACE.InheritedObjectType = "") Then
                Debug.Print vbTab & "ADS_RIGHT_GENERIC_EXECUTE"
            Else
                If ACE.InheritedObjectType = "" Then
                    Debug.Print vbTab & "ADS_RIGHT_GENERIC_EXECUTE for SchemaIDGuid:
↪" & ACE.ObjectType
                Else
                    Debug.Print vbTab & "Inherited ADS_RIGHT_GENERIC_EXECUTE for
↪SchemaIDGuid: " & ACE.InheritedObjectType
                End If
            End If
        End If

        If (ACE.AccessMask And ADS_RIGHT_GENERIC_ALL) <> 0 Then
            If (ACE.ObjectType = "" And ACE.InheritedObjectType = "") Then
                Debug.Print vbTab & "ADS_RIGHT_GENERIC_ALL"
            Else
                If ACE.InheritedObjectType = "" Then
                    Debug.Print vbTab & "ADS_RIGHT_GENERIC_ALL for SchemaIDGuid: " &
↪ACE.ObjectType
                Else
                    Debug.Print vbTab & "Inherited ADS_RIGHT_GENERIC_ALL for
↪SchemaIDGuid: " & ACE.InheritedObjectType
                End If
            End If
        End If

        If (ACE.AccessMask And ADS_RIGHT_DS_CREATE_CHILD) <> 0 Then
            If (ACE.ObjectType = "" And ACE.InheritedObjectType = "") Then
                Debug.Print vbTab & "ADS_RIGHT_DS_CREATE_CHILD"
            Else
                If ACE.InheritedObjectType = "" Then
                    Debug.Print vbTab & "ADS_RIGHT_DS_CREATE_CHILD for SchemaIDGuid:
↪" & ACE.ObjectType
                Else
                    Debug.Print vbTab & "Inherited ADS_RIGHT_DS_CREATE_CHILD for
↪SchemaIDGuid: " & ACE.InheritedObjectType
                End If
```

```
            End If
        End If
        
        If (ACE.AccessMask And ADS_RIGHT_DS_DELETE_CHILD) <> 0 Then
            If (ACE.ObjectType = "" And ACE.InheritedObjectType = "") Then
                Debug.Print vbTab & "ADS_RIGHT_DS_DELETE_CHILD"
            Else
                If ACE.InheritedObjectType = "" Then
                    Debug.Print vbTab & "ADS_RIGHT_DS_DELETE_CHILD for SchemaIDGuid:
↳" & ACE.ObjectType
                Else
                    Debug.Print vbTab & "Inherited ADS_RIGHT_DS_DELETE_CHILD for
↳SchemaIDGuid: " & ACE.InheritedObjectType
                End If
            End If
        End If
        
        If (ACE.AccessMask And ADS_RIGHT_ACTRL_DS_LIST) <> 0 Then
            If (ACE.ObjectType = "" And ACE.InheritedObjectType = "") Then
                Debug.Print vbTab & "ADS_RIGHT_ACTRL_DS_LIST"
            Else
                If ACE.InheritedObjectType = "" Then
                    Debug.Print vbTab & "ADS_RIGHT_ACTRL_DS_LIST for SchemaIDGuid: "
↳& ACE.ObjectType
                Else
                    Debug.Print vbTab & "Inherited ADS_RIGHT_ACTRL_DS_LIST for
↳SchemaIDGuid: " & ACE.InheritedObjectType
                End If
            End If
        End If
        
        If (ACE.AccessMask And ADS_RIGHT_DS_SELF) <> 0 Then
            If (ACE.ObjectType = "" And ACE.InheritedObjectType = "") Then
                Debug.Print vbTab & "ADS_RIGHT_DS_SELF"
            Else
                If ACE.InheritedObjectType = "" Then
                    Debug.Print vbTab & "ADS_RIGHT_DS_SELF for SchemaIDGuid: " &
↳ACE.ObjectType
                Else
                    Debug.Print vbTab & "Inherited ADS_RIGHT_DS_SELF for
↳SchemaIDGuid: " & ACE.InheritedObjectType
                End If
            End If
        End If
        
        If (ACE.AccessMask And ADS_RIGHT_DS_READ_PROP) <> 0 Then
            If (ACE.ObjectType = "" And ACE.InheritedObjectType = "") Then
                Debug.Print vbTab & "ADS_RIGHT_DS_READ_PROP"
            Else
                If ACE.InheritedObjectType = "" Then
                    Debug.Print vbTab & "ADS_RIGHT_DS_READ_PROP for SchemaIDGuid: " &
↳ACE.ObjectType
                Else
```

```
                    Debug.Print vbTab & "Inherited ADS_RIGHT_DS_READ_PROP for
➥SchemaIDGuid: " & ACE.InheritedObjectType
            End If
        End If
    End If

    If (ACE.AccessMask And ADS_RIGHT_DS_WRITE_PROP) <> 0 Then
        If (ACE.ObjectType = "" And ACE.InheritedObjectType = "") Then
            Debug.Print vbTab & "ADS_RIGHT_DS_WRITE_PROP"
        Else
            If ACE.InheritedObjectType = "" Then
                Debug.Print vbTab & "ADS_RIGHT_DS_WRITE_PROP for SchemaIDGuid: "
➥& ACE.ObjectType
            Else
                Debug.Print vbTab & "Inherited ADS_RIGHT_DS_WRITE_PROP for
➥SchemaIDGuid: " & ACE.InheritedObjectType
            End If
        End If
    End If

    If (ACE.AccessMask And ADS_RIGHT_DS_DELETE_TREE) <> 0 Then
        If (ACE.ObjectType = "" And ACE.InheritedObjectType = "") Then
            Debug.Print vbTab & "ADS_RIGHT_DS_DELETE_TREE"
        Else
            If ACE.InheritedObjectType = "" Then
                Debug.Print vbTab & "ADS_RIGHT_DS_DELETE_TREE for SchemaIDGuid: "
➥& ACE.ObjectType
            Else
                Debug.Print vbTab & "Inherited ADS_RIGHT_DS_DELETE_TREE for
➥SchemaIDGuid: " & ACE.InheritedObjectType
            End If
        End If
    End If

    If (ACE.AccessMask And ADS_RIGHT_DS_LIST_OBJECT) <> 0 Then
        If (ACE.ObjectType = "" And ACE.InheritedObjectType = "") Then
            Debug.Print vbTab & "ADS_RIGHT_DS_LIST_OBJECT"
        Else
            If ACE.InheritedObjectType = "" Then
                Debug.Print vbTab & "ADS_RIGHT_DS_LIST_OBJECT for SchemaIDGuid: "
➥& ACE.ObjectType
            Else
                Debug.Print vbTab & "Inherited ADS_RIGHT_DS_LIST_OBJECT for
➥SchemaIDGuid: " & ACE.InheritedObjectType
            End If
        End If
    End If

    If (ACE.AccessMask And ADS_RIGHT_DS_CONTROL_ACCESS) <> 0 Then
        If (ACE.ObjectType = "" And ACE.InheritedObjectType = "") Then
            Debug.Print vbTab & "ADS_RIGHT_DS_CONTROL_ACCESS"
        Else
```

```
            If ACE.InheritedObjectType = "" Then
                Debug.Print vbTab & "ADS_RIGHT_DS_CONTROL_ACCESS for
➥SchemaIDGuid: " & ACE.ObjectType
            Else
                Debug.Print vbTab & "Inherited ADS_RIGHT_DS_CONTROL_ACCESS for
➥SchemaIDGuid: " & ACE.InheritedObjectType
            End If
        End If
    End If
Next
```

Adding an ACE to an Active Directory Object ACL Using Visual Basic

To add a new ACE to the ACL of an object's security descriptor, use the following Visual Basic code and the tables used for ACE field flag values (refer to the section "Constants Used in ACEs") as a guide:

```
Dim Obj As IADs
Dim SecurityDescriptor As IADsSecurityDescriptor
Dim ACE As AccessControlEntry
Dim DACL As AccessControlList

Set Obj = GetObject("LDAP://ou=Admins,dc=eCommerce2000,dc=com")

Set SecurityDescriptor = Obj.Get("ntSecurityDescriptor")
Set DACL = SecurityDescriptor.DiscretionaryACL
Set ACE = CreateObject("AccessControlEntry")
ACE.AccessMask = ADS_RIGHT_DELETE Or ADS_RIGHT_GENERIC_READ Or
ADS_RIGHT_GENERIC_WRITE
ACE.AceFlags = ADS_ACEFLAG_NO_PROPAGATE_INHERIT_ACE
ACE.AceType = ADS_ACETYPE_ACCESS_ALLOWED
ACE.Trustee = "eCommerce2000\DMZAdmin"
DACL.AddAce ACE
SecurityDescriptor.DiscretionaryACL = DACL
Obj.Put "ntSecurityDescriptor", Array(SecurityDescriptor)
Obj.SetInfo
```

Removing an ACE from an Active Directory Object ACL Using Visual Basic

Use the following Visual Basic code to remove all ACEs for a particular trustee:

```
Dim Obj As IADs
Dim ACE As AccessControlEntry
Dim DACL As AccessControlList
Dim SecurityDescriptor As IADsSecurityDescriptor

Set Obj = GetObject("LDAP://cn=Guest,ou=users, dc=eCommerce2000,dc=com")
Set SecurityDescriptor = Obj.Get("ntSecurityDescriptor")
Set DACL = SecurityDescriptor.DiscretionaryACL

For Each ACE In DACL
    If UCase(ACE.Trustee) = "ECOMMERCE2000\GUEST" Then
        DACL.RemoveAce ACE
```

```
        End If
Next

SecurityDescriptor.DiscretionaryACL = DACL
Obj.Put "ntSecurityDescriptor", Array(SecurityDescriptor)
Obj.SetInfo
```

> *Tip*
>
> Although the previous code example indiscriminately removes an ACE based on the trustee's name, you can design a conditional to remove an ACE based on `ObjectType` or `AccessMask` constants. ♦

Advanced Topics in Active Directory Security Manipulation

The true power of the Active Directory is found in the Directory's ability to create ACLs for security descriptors at the attribute level, and its ability to delegate administrative privileges for objects in the directory.

A key element to creating a delegation model for the Active Directory is based on the concept of *inheritance*. Just as you can propagate an ACL throughout the entire file structure in the file system, the Active Directory allows you to specify permissions for a parent object and allow child objects to *inherit* the ACL.

By assigning the `ADS_ACEFLAG_INHERIT_ACE` constant to the `AceFlags` field in the ACE, you can allow or disallow the ability for child objects to inherit the permissions assigned to the parent object.

To establish a delegation model, you can assign trustees the ability to create and remove child objects, or even create and remove specific types of objects. To make this work effectively, you typically assign permissions to a container object (such as an OU) to establish the ability to manage child entities in the directory.

To take this a step further, because Windows 2000's Active Directory allows attribute-level permissions to be assigned, you can even specify specific object attributes that trustees can manipulate.

Adding an ACE to an Active Directory OU ACL with Inheritance to All Child Objects Using Visual Basic

As shown in the following Visual Basic code, by simply changing the `AceFlags` field value assignment, you can allow child objects to inherit the permissions assigned to parent objects in the directory:

```
Dim Obj As IADs
Dim SecurityDescriptor As IADsSecurityDescriptor
Dim ACE As AccessControlEntry
Dim DACL As AccessControlList
```

```
Set Obj = GetObject("LDAP://ou=Admins,dc=eCommerce2000,dc=com")

Set SecurityDescriptor = Obj.Get("ntSecurityDescriptor")
Set DACL = SecurityDescriptor.DiscretionaryACL
Set ACE = CreateObject("AccessControlEntry")
ACE.AccessMask = ADS_RIGHT_GENERIC_READ
ACE.AceFlags = ADS_ACEFLAG_INHERIT_ACE
ACE.AceType = ADS_ACETYPE_ACCESS_ALLOWED
ACE.Trustee = "eCommerce2000\DMZAdmin"
DACL.AddAce ACE
SecurityDescriptor.DiscretionaryACL = DACL
Obj.Put "ntSecurityDescriptor", Array(SecurityDescriptor)
Obj.SetInfo
```

Adding an ACE to an Active Directory OU ACL with Inheritance to a Single Class of Child Objects Using Visual Basic

To allow a user to manipulate a subset of object classes, you can specify the allowed (or denied) object class in an ACE within the ACL assigned to the security descriptor for the OU.

For example, creating an access control entry based on an object class definition can be useful if you want a user to be able to create and delete objects belonging only to the Group object class. In this scenario, this user can create and remove groups within the particular OU, but cannot create any other type of object in the container.

Assigning the schemaIDGuid of the desired object class to the ObjectType field in the ACE and assigning the ACE's Flags field to ADS_FLAG_OBJECT_TYPE_PRESENT perform specification of a particular object class.

The schemaIDGuid is defined in the schema container of the directory; however, to use the GUID in the ObjectType field, a string must be created and assigned in the form {xxxxxxxx-xxxx-xxxx-xxxx-xxxxxxxxxxxx}.

After obtaining and formatting the proper GUID for the object class (usually done in combination with the StringFromGUID2 API call), you can use the following Visual Basic code to guide your efforts to create an application that will restrict object manipulation to a single object class:

```
Dim Obj As IADs
Dim SecurityDescriptor As IADsSecurityDescriptor
Dim ACE As AccessControlEntry
Dim DACL As AccessControlList

Set Obj = GetObject("LDAP://ou=Admins,dc=eCommerce2000,dc=com")

Set SecurityDescriptor = Obj.Get("ntSecurityDescriptor")
Set DACL = SecurityDescriptor.DiscretionaryACL
Set ACE = CreateObject("AccessControlEntry")
ACE.AccessMask = ADS_RIGHT_DS_DELETE_TREE
ACE.AceFlags = ADS_ACEFLAG_INHERIT_ACE
```

```
ACE.AceType = ADS_ACETYPE_ACCESS_ALLOWED_OBJECT
ACE.Flags = ADS_FLAG_OBJECT_TYPE_PRESENT
ACE.ObjectType = "{BF967A9C-0DE6-11D0-A285-00AA003049E2}"

ACE.Trustee = "eCommerce2000\DMZAdmin"
DACL.AddAce ACE
SecurityDescriptor.DiscretionaryACL = DACL
Obj.Put "ntSecurityDescriptor", Array(SecurityDescriptor)
Obj.SetInfo
```

> **Note**
>
> The GUID used in the previous example was for group objects.
>
> If you prefer not to hard-code GUIDs into your application, you can download the COM-based GetSchemaIDGuid.DLL from http://www.newriders.com/adsi to programmatically derive the GUID for a particular object class. ♦

Removing an ACE from an Active Directory OU ACL with Inheritance to a Single Class of Child Objects Using Visual Basic

To remove an ACE that has been assigned to restrict object manipulation to a specific class, simply use a conditional to match the `ObjectType` and `Trustee` fields during the enumeration process, as shown in the following Visual Basic code segment:

```
Dim Obj As IADs
Dim ACE As AccessControlEntry
Dim DACL As AccessControlList
Dim SecurityDescriptor As Variant

Set Obj = GetObject("LDAP://ou=Admins,dc=eCommerce2000,dc=com")
Set SecurityDescriptor = Obj.Get("ntSecurityDescriptor")
Set DACL = SecurityDescriptor.DiscretionaryACL

For Each ACE In DACL
    If ((UCase(ACE.Trustee) = "ECOMMERCE2000\DMZADMIN") and (ACE.ObjectType =
➥"{BF967A9C-0DE6-11D0-A285-00AA003049E2}")) Then
        DACL.RemoveAce ACE
    End If
Next

SecurityDescriptor.DiscretionaryACL = DACL
Obj.Put "ntSecurityDescriptor", Array(SecurityDescriptor)
Obj.SetInfo
```

Adding an ACE to an Active Directory OU ACL with Inheritance to a Single Property for an Object Class Using Visual Basic

Just as you can restrict manipulation of objects based on object class, you can also specify which attributes a user has the right to read and modify. Once again, you simply need to assign the schemaIDGuid for the desired property to the `ObjectType` field and set the `AccessMask` field to `ADS_RIGHT_DS_READ_PROP` or `ADS_RIGHT_DS_WRITE_PROP`.

The following Visual Code segment allows users to write their own `telephoneNumber` attribute for objects in the Users container:

```
Dim Obj As IADs
Dim SecurityDescriptor As IADsSecurityDescriptor
Dim ACE As AccessControlEntry
Dim DACL As AccessControlList

Set Obj = GetObject("LDAP://ou=Admins,dc=eCommerce2000,dc=com")

Set SecurityDescriptor = Obj.Get("ntSecurityDescriptor")
Set DACL = SecurityDescriptor.DiscretionaryACL
Set ACE = CreateObject("AccessControlEntry")
ACE.AccessMask = ADS_RIGHT_DS_READ_PROP Or ADS_RIGHT_DS_WRITE_PROP
ACE.AceFlags = ADS_ACEFLAG_INHERIT_ACE
ACE.AceType = ADS_ACETYPE_ACCESS_ALLOWED_OBJECT
ACE.ObjectType = "{BF967A49-0DE6-11D0-A285-00AA003049E2}"
ACE.Trustee = "NT AUTHORITY\SELF"
DACL.AddAce ACE
SecurityDescriptor.DiscretionaryACL = DACL
Obj.Put "ntSecurityDescriptor", Array(SecurityDescriptor)
Obj.SetInfo
```

Creating the ADObjectManagement Class Module

In this section, you will begin an exercise that will ultimately yield the creation of the ADAdmin.DLL COM server.

Exercise 12.1   *Creating the ADAdmin.DLL COM Server Application: The ADObject Management Module.*

1. Create a new ActiveX DLL Visual Basic project.
2. Set a reference to the Active DS Type Library by clicking the Project menu, selecting References..., and placing a checkmark next to the "Active DS Type Library" entry. Click the OK command button to exit the References–Project1 dialog box.
3. Rename Project1 as **ADAdmin**.
4. Rename the Class1 class module as **ADObjectManagement**.

continues ▶

Exercise 12.1 *continued*

5. Enter the following code into the General Declarations section of the class module:

```
Public Function RootDSEntries(ByVal PropertyName As String) As Variant
    On Error Resume Next
    Dim RootDSE As IADs
    Dim RetVal As Variant
    Dim RetArray() As Variant
    Dim i As Long
    Set RootDSE = GetObject("LDAP://RootDSE")
    RetVal = RootDSE.Get(PropertyName)
    If IsArray(RetVal) Then
        For Each Item In RetVal
            i = UBound(RetArray) + 1
            ReDim Preserve RetArray(i)
            RetArray(i) = PropertyName & ": " & Item
        Next
        RootDSEntries = RetArray
    Else
        RootDSEntries = PropertyName & ": " & RootDSE.Get(PropertyName)
    End If
End Function

Public Function EnumerateContainer(ByVal ObjectClass As String, ByVal
➥RelativePathToObject As String) As Variant
    On Error Resume Next
    Dim RootDSE As IADs
    Dim UserContainer As IADsContainer
    Dim User As IADs
    Dim RetArray() As Variant
    Dim i As Long
    Dim Obj As Variant

    Set RootDSE = GetObject("LDAP://RootDSE")
    Set UserContainer = GetObject("LDAP://" & RelativePathToObject &
➥RootDSE.Get("DefaultNamingContext"))

    UserContainer.Filter = Array(ObjectClass)

    For Each Obj In UserContainer
        i = UBound(RetArray) + 1
        ReDim Preserve RetArray(i)
        RetArray(i) = Obj.Name
    Next

    EnumerateContainer = RetArray

End Function

Public Function RemoveADObject(ByVal RelativePathToObject As String, ByVal
➥ObjectClass As String, ByVal ObjectRelativeName As String) As Boolean
    Dim RootDSE As IADs
    Dim Container As IADsContainer
```

```
    Set RootDSE = GetObject("LDAP://RootDSE")
    Set Container = GetObject("LDAP://" & RelativePathToObject & _
➥RootDSE.Get("DefaultNamingContext"))
    Call Container.Delete(ObjectClass, ObjectRelativeName)
    If Err.Number = 0 Then RemoveADObject = True
End Function

Public Function DeleteADBranch(ByVal RelativePathToObject As String) As Boolean
    Dim RootDSE As IADs
    Dim Container As IADsDeleteOps
    Set RootDSE = GetObject("LDAP://RootDSE")
    Set Container = GetObject("LDAP://" & RelativePathToObject & _
➥RootDSE.Get("DefaultNamingContext"))
    Container.DeleteObject (0)
    If Err.Number = 0 Then DeleteADBranch = True
End Function

Public Function MoveRenameADObject(ByVal RelativePathToNewLocation As String, _
➥ByVal OriginalObjectRelativePath As String, Optional ByVal NewObjectName As _
➥String) As Boolean
    Dim RootDSE As IADs
    Dim Container As IADsContainer
    Set RootDSE = GetObject("LDAP://RootDSE")
    Set Container = GetObject("LDAP://" & RelativePathToNewLocation & _
RootDSE.Get("DefaultNamingContext"))
    If NewObjectName = "" Then NewObjectName = vbNullString
    Call Container.MoveHere(OriginalObjectRelativePath, NewObjectName)

    If Err.Number = 0 Then MoveRenameADObject = True
End Function

Public Function RemoveADACE(ByVal RelativeObjectPath As String, ByVal _
TrusteeToRemove As String) As Boolean
    Dim Obj As IADs
    Dim ACE As AccessControlEntry
    Dim DACL As AccessControlList
    Dim SecurityDescriptor As Variant
    Dim RootDSE As IADs

    Set RootDSE = GetObject("LDAP://RootDSE")
    Set Obj = GetObject("LDAP://" & RelativeObjectPath & _
➥RootDSE.Get("DefaultNamingContext"))
    Set SecurityDescriptor = Obj.Get("ntSecurityDescriptor")
    Set DACL = SecurityDescriptor.DiscretionaryACL

    For Each ACE In DACL
        If UCase(ACE.Trustee) = UCase(TrusteeToRemove) Then
            DACL.RemoveAce ACE
        End If
    Next

    SecurityDescriptor.DiscretionaryACL = DACL
    Obj.Put "ntSecurityDescriptor", Array(SecurityDescriptor)
```

continues ▶

Exercise 12.1 *continued*

```
        Obj.SetInfo
        If Err.Number = 0 Then RemoveADACE = True
    End Function

    Public Function EnumerateAclAces(ByVal RelativeObjectPath As String) As Variant
        On Error Resume Next
        Dim Obj As IADs
        Dim RootDSE As IADs
        Dim ACE As AccessControlEntry
        Dim DiscretionaryACL As AccessControlList
        Dim SecurityDescriptor As Variant
        Dim ObjectDistinguishedName As String
        Dim RetArray() As Variant
        Dim i As Long

        Set RootDSE = GetObject("LDAP://RootDSE")
        Set Obj = GetObject("LDAP://" & RelativeObjectPath &
    ⇨RootDSE.Get("DefaultNamingContext"))
        Set SecurityDescriptor = Obj.Get("ntSecurityDescriptor")
        Set DiscretionaryACL = SecurityDescriptor.DiscretionaryACL
        i = 1

        For Each ACE In DiscretionaryACL
            i = UBound(RetArray) + 1
            ReDim Preserve RetArray(i)
            RetArray(i) = ACE.Trustee
            If (ACE.AccessMask And ADS_RIGHT_DELETE) <> 0 Then
                If (ACE.ObjectType = "" And ACE.InheritedObjectType = "") Then
                    i = UBound(RetArray) + 1
                    ReDim Preserve RetArray(i)
                    RetArray(i) = vbTab & "ADS_RIGHT_DELETE"
                Else
                    If ACE.InheritedObjectType = "" Then
                        i = UBound(RetArray) + 1
                        ReDim Preserve RetArray(i)
                        RetArray(i) = vbTab & "ADS_RIGHT_DELETE for SchemaIDGuid: " &
    ⇨ACE.ObjectType
                    Else
                        i = UBound(RetArray) + 1
                        ReDim Preserve RetArray(i)
                        RetArray(i) = vbTab & "Inherited ADS_RIGHT_DELETE for
    ⇨SchemaIDGuid: " & ACE.InheritedObjectType
                    End If
                End If
            End If

            If (ACE.AccessMask And ADS_RIGHT_READ_CONTROL) <> 0 Then
                If (ACE.ObjectType = "" And ACE.InheritedObjectType = "") Then
                    i = UBound(RetArray) + 1
                    ReDim Preserve RetArray(i)
                    RetArray(i) = vbTab & "ADS_RIGHT_READ_CONTROL"
```

Creating the ADObjectManagement Class Module 439

```
            Else
                If ACE.InheritedObjectType = "" Then
                    i = UBound(RetArray) + 1
                    ReDim Preserve RetArray(i)
                    RetArray(i) = vbTab & "ADS_RIGHT_READ_CONTROL for
➥SchemaIDGuid: " & ACE.ObjectType
                Else
                    i = UBound(RetArray) + 1
                    ReDim Preserve RetArray(i)
                    RetArray(i) = vbTab & "Inherited ADS_RIGHT_READ_CONTROL for
➥SchemaIDGuid: " & ACE.InheritedObjectType
                End If
            End If
        End If

        If (ACE.AccessMask And ADS_RIGHT_WRITE_DAC) <> 0 Then
            If (ACE.ObjectType = "" And ACE.InheritedObjectType = "") Then
                i = UBound(RetArray) + 1
                ReDim Preserve RetArray(i)
                RetArray(i) = vbTab & "ADS_RIGHT_WRITE_DAC"
            Else
                If ACE.InheritedObjectType = "" Then
                    i = UBound(RetArray) + 1
                    ReDim Preserve RetArray(i)
                    RetArray(i) = vbTab & "ADS_RIGHT_WRITE_DAC for SchemaIDGuid:
➥" & ACE.ObjectType
                Else
                    i = UBound(RetArray) + 1
                    ReDim Preserve RetArray(i)
                    RetArray(i) = vbTab & "Inherited ADS_RIGHT_WRITE_DAC for
➥SchemaIDGuid: " & ACE.InheritedObjectType
                End If
            End If
        End If

        If (ACE.AccessMask And ADS_RIGHT_WRITE_OWNER) <> 0 Then
            If (ACE.ObjectType = "" And ACE.InheritedObjectType = "") Then
                i = UBound(RetArray) + 1
                ReDim Preserve RetArray(i)
                RetArray(i) = vbTab & "ADS_RIGHT_WRITE_OWNER"
            Else
                If ACE.InheritedObjectType = "" Then
                    i = UBound(RetArray) + 1
                    ReDim Preserve RetArray(i)
                    RetArray(i) = vbTab & "ADS_RIGHT_WRITE_OWNER for
➥SchemaIDGuid: " & ACE.ObjectType
                Else
                    i = UBound(RetArray) + 1
                    ReDim Preserve RetArray(i)
                    RetArray(i) = vbTab & "Inherited ADS_RIGHT_WRITE_OWNER for
➥SchemaIDGuid: " & ACE.InheritedObjectType
                End If
            End If
```

continues ▶

Exercise 12.1 *continued*

```
            End If

            If (ACE.AccessMask And ADS_RIGHT_SYNCHRONIZE) <> 0 Then
                If (ACE.ObjectType = "" And ACE.InheritedObjectType = "") Then
                    i = UBound(RetArray) + 1
                    ReDim Preserve RetArray(i)
                    RetArray(i) = vbTab & "ADS_RIGHT_SYNCHRONIZE"
                Else
                    If ACE.InheritedObjectType = "" Then
                        i = UBound(RetArray) + 1
                        ReDim Preserve RetArray(i)
                        RetArray(i) = vbTab & "ADS_RIGHT_SYNCHRONIZE for
⇝SchemaIDGuid: " & ACE.ObjectType
                    Else
                        i = UBound(RetArray) + 1
                        ReDim Preserve RetArray(i)
                        RetArray(i) = vbTab & "Inherited ADS_RIGHT_SYNCHRONIZE for
⇝SchemaIDGuid: " & ACE.InheritedObjectType
                    End If
                End If
            End If

            If (ACE.AccessMask And ADS_RIGHT_ACCESS_SYSTEM_SECURITY) <> 0 Then
                If (ACE.ObjectType = "" And ACE.InheritedObjectType = "") Then
                    i = UBound(RetArray) + 1
                    ReDim Preserve RetArray(i)
                    RetArray(i) = vbTab & "ADS_RIGHT_ACCESS_SYSTEM_SECURITY"
                Else
                    If ACE.InheritedObjectType = "" Then
                        i = UBound(RetArray) + 1
                        ReDim Preserve RetArray(i)
                        RetArray(i) = vbTab & "ADS_RIGHT_ACCESS_SYSTEM_SECURITY for
⇝SchemaIDGuid: " & ACE.ObjectType
                    Else
                        i = UBound(RetArray) + 1
                        ReDim Preserve RetArray(i)
                        RetArray(i) = vbTab & "Inherited
⇝ADS_RIGHT_ACCESS_SYSTEM_SECURITY for SchemaIDGuid: " & ACE.InheritedObjectType
                    End If
                End If
            End If

            If (ACE.AccessMask And ADS_RIGHT_GENERIC_READ) <> 0 Then
                If (ACE.ObjectType = "" And ACE.InheritedObjectType = "") Then
                    i = UBound(RetArray) + 1
                    ReDim Preserve RetArray(i)
                    RetArray(i) = vbTab & "ADS_RIGHT_GENERIC_READ"
                Else
                    If ACE.InheritedObjectType = "" Then
                        i = UBound(RetArray) + 1
                        ReDim Preserve RetArray(i)
```

Creating the ADObjectManagement Class Module 441

```
                    RetArray(i) = vbTab & "ADS_RIGHT_GENERIC_READ for
↪SchemaIDGuid: " & ACE.ObjectType
                Else
                    i = UBound(RetArray) + 1
                    ReDim Preserve RetArray(i)
                    RetArray(i) = vbTab & "Inherited ADS_RIGHT_GENERIC_READ for
↪SchemaIDGuid: " & ACE.InheritedObjectType
                End If
            End If
        End If

        If (ACE.AccessMask And ADS_RIGHT_GENERIC_WRITE) <> 0 Then
            If (ACE.ObjectType = "" And ACE.InheritedObjectType = "") Then
                i = UBound(RetArray) + 1
                ReDim Preserve RetArray(i)
                RetArray(i) = vbTab & "ADS_RIGHT_GENERIC_WRITE"
            Else
                If ACE.InheritedObjectType = "" Then
                    i = UBound(RetArray) + 1
                    ReDim Preserve RetArray(i)
                    RetArray(i) = vbTab & "ADS_RIGHT_GENERIC_WRITE for
↪SchemaIDGuid: " & ACE.ObjectType
                Else
                    i = UBound(RetArray) + 1
                    ReDim Preserve RetArray(i)
                    RetArray(i) = vbTab & "Inherited ADS_RIGHT_GENERIC_WRITE for
↪SchemaIDGuid: " & ACE.InheritedObjectType
                End If
            End If
        End If

        If (ACE.AccessMask And ADS_RIGHT_GENERIC_EXECUTE) <> 0 Then
            If (ACE.ObjectType = "" And ACE.InheritedObjectType = "") Then
                i = UBound(RetArray) + 1
                ReDim Preserve RetArray(i)
                RetArray(i) = vbTab & "ADS_RIGHT_GENERIC_EXECUTE"
            Else
                If ACE.InheritedObjectType = "" Then
                    i = UBound(RetArray) + 1
                    ReDim Preserve RetArray(i)
                    RetArray(i) = vbTab & "ADS_RIGHT_GENERIC_EXECUTE for
↪SchemaIDGuid: " & ACE.ObjectType
                Else
                    i = UBound(RetArray) + 1
                    ReDim Preserve RetArray(i)
                    RetArray(i) = vbTab & "Inherited ADS_RIGHT_GENERIC_EXECUTE
↪for SchemaIDGuid: " & ACE.InheritedObjectType
                End If
            End If
        End If

        If (ACE.AccessMask And ADS_RIGHT_GENERIC_ALL) <> 0 Then
            If (ACE.ObjectType = "" And ACE.InheritedObjectType = "") Then
```

continues ▶

Exercise 12.1 *continued*

```
                    i = UBound(RetArray) + 1
                    ReDim Preserve RetArray(i)
                    RetArray(i) = vbTab & "ADS_RIGHT_GENERIC_ALL"
                Else
                    If ACE.InheritedObjectType = "" Then
                        i = UBound(RetArray) + 1
                        ReDim Preserve RetArray(i)
                        RetArray(i) = vbTab & "ADS_RIGHT_GENERIC_ALL for
➥SchemaIDGuid: " & ACE.ObjectType
                    Else
                        i = UBound(RetArray) + 1
                        ReDim Preserve RetArray(i)
                        RetArray(i) = vbTab & "Inherited ADS_RIGHT_GENERIC_ALL for
➥SchemaIDGuid: " & ACE.InheritedObjectType
                    End If
                End If
            End If

            If (ACE.AccessMask And ADS_RIGHT_DS_CREATE_CHILD) <> 0 Then
                If (ACE.ObjectType = "" And ACE.InheritedObjectType = "") Then
                    i = UBound(RetArray) + 1
                    ReDim Preserve RetArray(i)
                    RetArray(i) = vbTab & "ADS_RIGHT_DS_CREATE_CHILD"
                Else
                    If ACE.InheritedObjectType = "" Then
                        i = UBound(RetArray) + 1
                        ReDim Preserve RetArray(i)
                        RetArray(i) = vbTab & "ADS_RIGHT_DS_CREATE_CHILD for
➥SchemaIDGuid: " & ACE.ObjectType
                    Else
                        i = UBound(RetArray) + 1
                        ReDim Preserve RetArray(i)
                        RetArray(i) = vbTab & "Inherited ADS_RIGHT_DS_CREATE_CHILD
➥for SchemaIDGuid: " & ACE.InheritedObjectType
                    End If
                End If
            End If

            If (ACE.AccessMask And ADS_RIGHT_DS_DELETE_CHILD) <> 0 Then
                If (ACE.ObjectType = "" And ACE.InheritedObjectType = "") Then
                    i = UBound(RetArray) + 1
                    ReDim Preserve RetArray(i)
                    RetArray(i) = vbTab & "ADS_RIGHT_DS_DELETE_CHILD"
                Else
                    If ACE.InheritedObjectType = "" Then
                        i = UBound(RetArray) + 1
                        ReDim Preserve RetArray(i)
                        RetArray(i) = vbTab & "ADS_RIGHT_DS_DELETE_CHILD for
➥SchemaIDGuid: " & ACE.ObjectType
                    Else
                        i = UBound(RetArray) + 1
```

```
                    ReDim Preserve RetArray(i)
                    RetArray(i) = vbTab & "Inherited ADS_RIGHT_DS_DELETE_CHILD
↪for SchemaIDGuid: " & ACE.InheritedObjectType
                End If
            End If
        End If

        If (ACE.AccessMask And ADS_RIGHT_ACTRL_DS_LIST) <> 0 Then
            If (ACE.ObjectType = "" And ACE.InheritedObjectType = "") Then
                i = UBound(RetArray) + 1
                ReDim Preserve RetArray(i)
                RetArray(i) = vbTab & "ADS_RIGHT_ACTRL_DS_LIST"
            Else
                If ACE.InheritedObjectType = "" Then
                    i = UBound(RetArray) + 1
                    ReDim Preserve RetArray(i)
                    RetArray(i) = vbTab & "ADS_RIGHT_ACTRL_DS_LIST for
↪SchemaIDGuid: " & ACE.ObjectType
                Else
                    i = UBound(RetArray) + 1
                    ReDim Preserve RetArray(i)
                    RetArray(i) = vbTab & "Inherited ADS_RIGHT_ACTRL_DS_LIST for
↪SchemaIDGuid: " & ACE.InheritedObjectType
                End If
            End If
        End If

        If (ACE.AccessMask And ADS_RIGHT_DS_SELF) <> 0 Then
            If (ACE.ObjectType = "" And ACE.InheritedObjectType = "") Then
                i = UBound(RetArray) + 1
                ReDim Preserve RetArray(i)
                RetArray(i) = vbTab & "ADS_RIGHT_DS_SELF"
            Else
                If ACE.InheritedObjectType = "" Then
                    i = UBound(RetArray) + 1
                    ReDim Preserve RetArray(i)
                    RetArray(i) = vbTab & "ADS_RIGHT_DS_SELF for SchemaIDGuid: "
↪& ACE.ObjectType
                Else
                    i = UBound(RetArray) + 1
                    ReDim Preserve RetArray(i)
                    RetArray(i) = vbTab & "Inherited ADS_RIGHT_DS_SELF for
↪SchemaIDGuid: " & ACE.InheritedObjectType
                End If
            End If
        End If

        If (ACE.AccessMask And ADS_RIGHT_DS_READ_PROP) <> 0 Then
            If (ACE.ObjectType = "" And ACE.InheritedObjectType = "") Then
                i = UBound(RetArray) + 1
                ReDim Preserve RetArray(i)
                RetArray(i) = vbTab & "ADS_RIGHT_DS_READ_PROP"
```

continues ▶

Exercise 12.1   *continued*

```
                Else
                    If ACE.InheritedObjectType = "" Then
                        i = UBound(RetArray) + 1
                        ReDim Preserve RetArray(i)
                        RetArray(i) = vbTab & "ADS_RIGHT_DS_READ_PROP for
➥SchemaIDGuid: " & ACE.ObjectType
                    Else
                        i = UBound(RetArray) + 1
                        ReDim Preserve RetArray(i)
                        RetArray(i) = vbTab & "Inherited ADS_RIGHT_DS_READ_PROP for
➥SchemaIDGuid: " & ACE.InheritedObjectType
                    End If
                End If
            End If

            If (ACE.AccessMask And ADS_RIGHT_DS_WRITE_PROP) <> 0 Then
                If (ACE.ObjectType = "" And ACE.InheritedObjectType = "") Then
                    i = UBound(RetArray) + 1
                    ReDim Preserve RetArray(i)
                    RetArray(i) = vbTab & "ADS_RIGHT_DS_WRITE_PROP"
                Else
                    If ACE.InheritedObjectType = "" Then
                        i = UBound(RetArray) + 1
                        ReDim Preserve RetArray(i)
                        RetArray(i) = vbTab & "ADS_RIGHT_DS_WRITE_PROP for
➥SchemaIDGuid: " & ACE.ObjectType
                    Else
                        i = UBound(RetArray) + 1
                        ReDim Preserve RetArray(i)
                        RetArray(i) = vbTab & "Inherited ADS_RIGHT_DS_WRITE_PROP for
➥SchemaIDGuid: " & ACE.InheritedObjectType
                    End If
                End If
            End If

            If (ACE.AccessMask And ADS_RIGHT_DS_DELETE_TREE) <> 0 Then
                If (ACE.ObjectType = "" And ACE.InheritedObjectType = "") Then
                    i = UBound(RetArray) + 1
                    ReDim Preserve RetArray(i)
                    RetArray(i) = vbTab & "ADS_RIGHT_DS_DELETE_TREE"
                Else
                    If ACE.InheritedObjectType = "" Then
                        i = UBound(RetArray) + 1
                        ReDim Preserve RetArray(i)
                        RetArray(i) = vbTab & "ADS_RIGHT_DS_DELETE_TREE for
➥SchemaIDGuid: " & ACE.ObjectType
                    Else
                        i = UBound(RetArray) + 1
                        ReDim Preserve RetArray(i)
                        RetArray(i) = vbTab & "Inherited ADS_RIGHT_DS_DELETE_TREE for
➥SchemaIDGuid: " & ACE.InheritedObjectType
                    End If
```

Creating the ADObjectManagement Class Module   445

```
                End If
            End If

            If (ACE.AccessMask And ADS_RIGHT_DS_LIST_OBJECT) <> 0 Then
                If (ACE.ObjectType = "" And ACE.InheritedObjectType = "") Then
                    i = UBound(RetArray) + 1
                    ReDim Preserve RetArray(i)
                    RetArray(i) = vbTab & "ADS_RIGHT_DS_LIST_OBJECT"
                Else
                    If ACE.InheritedObjectType = "" Then
                        i = UBound(RetArray) + 1
                        ReDim Preserve RetArray(i)
                        RetArray(i) = vbTab & "ADS_RIGHT_DS_LIST_OBJECT for
➥SchemaIDGuid: " & ACE.ObjectType
                    Else
                        i = UBound(RetArray) + 1
                        ReDim Preserve RetArray(i)
                        RetArray(i) = vbTab & "Inherited ADS_RIGHT_DS_LIST_OBJECT for
➥SchemaIDGuid: " & ACE.InheritedObjectType
                    End If
                End If
            End If

            If (ACE.AccessMask And ADS_RIGHT_DS_CONTROL_ACCESS) <> 0 Then
                If (ACE.ObjectType = "" And ACE.InheritedObjectType = "") Then
                    i = UBound(RetArray) + 1
                    ReDim Preserve RetArray(i)
                    RetArray(i) = vbTab & "ADS_RIGHT_DS_CONTROL_ACCESS"
                Else
                    If ACE.InheritedObjectType = "" Then
                        i = UBound(RetArray) + 1
                        ReDim Preserve RetArray(i)
                        RetArray(i) = vbTab & "ADS_RIGHT_DS_CONTROL_ACCESS for
➥SchemaIDGuid: " & ACE.ObjectType
                    Else
                        i = UBound(RetArray) + 1
                        ReDim Preserve RetArray(i)
                        RetArray(i) = vbTab & "Inherited ADS_RIGHT_DS_CONTROL_ACCESS
➥for SchemaIDGuid: " & ACE.InheritedObjectType
                    End If
                End If
            End If
    Next
    EnumerateAclAces = RetArray
End Function

Public Function CreateGenericADObject(ByVal RelativePathToObject As String, ByVal
➥ObjectClass As String, ByVal ObjectRelativeName As String, Optional ByVal
➥MandatoryPropertyName As String, Optional ByVal MandatoryPropertyValue As
➥Variant, Optional ByVal MandatoryPropertyName2 As String, Optional ByVal
➥MandatoryPropertyValue2 As Variant, Optional ByVal MandatoryPropertyName3 As
➥String, Optional ByVal MandatoryPropertyValue3 As Variant, Optional ByVal
```

continues ▶

Exercise 12.1 *continued*

```
        ⮠MandatoryPropertyName4 As String, Optional ByVal MandatoryPropertyValue4 As
        ⮠Variant, Optional ByVal MandatoryPropertyName5 As String, Optional ByVal
        ⮠MandatoryPropertyValue5 As Variant, Optional ByVal MandatoryPropertyName6 As
        ⮠String, Optional ByVal MandatoryPropertyValue6 As Variant, Optional ByVal
        ⮠MandatoryPropertyName7 As String, Optional ByVal MandatoryPropertyValue7 As
        ⮠Variant, Optional ByVal MandatoryPropertyName8 As String, Optional ByVal
        ⮠MandatoryPropertyValue8 As Variant) As Boolean
            Dim RootDSE As IADs
            Dim Container As IADsContainer
            Set RootDSE = GetObject("LDAP://RootDSE")
            Set Container = GetObject("LDAP://" & RelativePathToObject &
        ⮠RootDSE.Get("DefaultNamingContext"))
            Set NewObject = Container.Create(ObjectClass, ObjectRelativeName)

            If MandatoryPropertyName <> "" Then
                Call NewObject.Put(MandatoryPropertyName, MandatoryPropertyValue)
            End If

            If MandatoryPropertyName2 <> "" Then
                Call NewObject.Put(MandatoryPropertyName2, MandatoryPropertyValue2)
            End If

            If MandatoryPropertyName3 <> "" Then
                Call NewObject.Put(MandatoryPropertyName3, MandatoryPropertyValue3)
            End If

            If MandatoryPropertyName4 <> "" Then
                Call NewObject.Put(MandatoryPropertyName4, MandatoryPropertyValue4)
            End If

            If MandatoryPropertyName5 <> "" Then
                Call NewObject.Put(MandatoryPropertyName5, MandatoryPropertyValue5)
            End If

            If MandatoryPropertyName6 <> "" Then
                Call NewObject.Put(MandatoryPropertyName6, MandatoryPropertyValue6)
            End If

            If MandatoryPropertyName7 <> "" Then
                Call NewObject.Put(MandatoryPropertyName7, MandatoryPropertyValue7)
            End If

            If MandatoryPropertyName8 <> "" Then
                Call NewObject.Put(MandatoryPropertyName8, MandatoryPropertyValue8)
            End If

            NewObject.SetInfo

            If Err.Number = 0 Then CreateADObject = True
        End Function

        Public Function SetOptionalProperty(ObjectRelativeName As String,
        ⮠OptionalPropertyName As String, OptionalPropertyValue As Variant) As Boolean
            Dim RootDSE As IADs
```

```
    Dim Obj As IADs
    Set RootDSE = GetObject("LDAP://RootDSE")
    Set Obj = GetObject("LDAP://" & ObjectRelativeName &
↪RootDSE.Get("DefaultNamingContext"))

    Call Obj.Put(OptionalPropertyName, OptionalPropertyValue)

    Obj.SetInfo

    If Err.Number = 0 Then SetOptionalProperty = True
End Function

Public Function ADSObjectSecurity(ByVal RelativeObjectPath As String, ByVal
↪TrusteeName As String, ByVal AllowAccess As Boolean, ByVal InheritenceType As
↪String, Optional ByVal SchemaIDGuid As String = "ALL", Optional ByVal
↪Generic_All As Boolean, Optional ByVal Generic_Read As Boolean, Optional ByVal
↪Generic_Write As Boolean, Optional ByVal DS_Create_Child As Boolean, Optional
↪ByVal DS_Delete_Child As Boolean, Optional ByVal Delete As Boolean, Optional
↪ByVal Read_Control As Boolean, Optional ByVal Write_DAC As Boolean, Optional
↪ByVal Write_Owner As Boolean, Optional ByVal Synchronize As Boolean, Optional
↪ByVal Access_System_Security As Boolean, Optional ByVal ACtrl_DS_List As
↪Boolean, Optional ByVal DS_Self As Boolean, Optional ByVal DS_Read_Prop As
↪Boolean, Optional ByVal DS_Write_Prop As Boolean, Optional ByVal DS_Delete_Tree
↪As Boolean, Optional ByVal DS_List_Object As Boolean, Optional ByVal
↪DS_Control_Access As Boolean) As Boolean

    Dim Obj As IADs
    Dim SecurityDescriptor As Variant
    Dim ACE As AccessControlEntry
    Dim DACL As AccessControlList
    Dim RootDSE As IADs
    Dim AccessMask As Long

    Set RootDSE = GetObject("LDAP://RootDSE")
    Set Obj = GetObject("LDAP://" & RelativeObjectPath &
↪RootDSE.Get("DefaultNamingContext"))
    Set SecurityDescriptor = Obj.Get("ntSecurityDescriptor")
    Set DACL = SecurityDescriptor.DiscretionaryACL
    Set ACE = CreateObject("AccessControlEntry")

    If FullControl = True Then
        AccessMask = -1
    End If

    If Delete = True Then
        AccessMask = AccessMask Or ADS_RIGHT_DELETE
    End If

    If Read_Control = True Then
        AccessMask = AccessMask Or ADS_RIGHT_READ_CONTROL
    End If

    If Write_DAC = True Then
        AccessMask = AccessMask Or ADS_RIGHT_WRITE_DAC
```

continues ▶

Exercise 12.1 *continued*

```
        End If

        If Write_Owner = True Then
            AccessMask = AccessMask Or ADS_RIGHT_WRITE_OWNER
        End If

        If Synchronize = True Then
            AccessMask = AccessMask Or ADS_RIGHT_SYNCHRONIZE
        End If

        If Access_System_Security = True Then
            AccessMask = AccessMask Or ADS_RIGHT_ACCESS_SYSTEM_SECURITY
        End If

        If Generic_Read = True Then
            AccessMask = AccessMask Or ADS_RIGHT_GENERIC_READ
        End If

        If Generic_Write = True Then
            AccessMask = AccessMask Or ADS_RIGHT_GENERIC_WRITE
        End If

        If Generic_All = True Then
            AccessMask = AccessMask Or ADS_RIGHT_GENERIC_ALL
        End If

        If DS_Create_Child = True Then
            AccessMask = AccessMask Or ADS_RIGHT_DS_CREATE_CHILD
        End If

        If DS_Delete_Child = True Then
            AccessMask = AccessMask Or ADS_RIGHT_DS_DELETE_CHILD
        End If

        If ACtrl_DS_List = True Then
            AccessMask = AccessMask Or ADS_RIGHT_ACTRL_DS_LIST
        End If

        If DS_Self = True Then
            AccessMask = AccessMask Or ADS_RIGHT_DS_SELF
        End If

        If DS_Read_Prop = True Then
            AccessMask = AccessMask Or ADS_RIGHT_DS_READ_PROP
        End If

        If DS_Write_Prop = True Then
            AccessMask = AccessMask Or ADS_RIGHT_DS_WRITE_PROP
        End If

        If DS_Delete_Tree = True Then
            AccessMask = AccessMask Or ADS_RIGHT_DS_DELETE_TREE
        End If
```

```
        If DS_List_Object = True Then
            AccessMask = AccessMask Or ADS_RIGHT_DS_LIST_OBJECT
        End If

        If DS_Control_Access = True Then
            AccessMask = AccessMask Or ADS_RIGHT_DS_CONTROL_ACCESS
        End If

        ACE.AccessMask = AccessMask

        Select Case UCase(InheritenceType)
            Case "NONE"

            Case "INHERIT"
                ACE.AceFlags = ADS_ACEFLAG_INHERIT_ACE
            Case "INHERIT_ONLY"
                ACE.AceFlags = ADS_ACEFLAG_INHERIT_ONLY_ACE
            Case "NO_PROPAGATE"
                ACE.AceFlags = ADS_ACEFLAG_NO_PROPAGATE_INHERIT_ACE
        End Select

        If AllowAccess = True Then
            If UCase(SchemaIDGuid) = "ALL" Then
                ACE.AceType = ADS_ACETYPE_ACCESS_ALLOWED
            Else
                ACE.AceType = ADS_ACETYPE_ACCESS_ALLOWED_OBJECT
                ACE.ObjectType = SchemaIDGuid
                ACE.Flags = ADS_FLAG_OBJECT_TYPE_PRESENT
            End If
        Else
            If UCase(SchemaIDGuid) = "ALL" Then
                ACE.AceType = ADS_ACETYPE_ACCESS_DENIED
            Else
                ACE.AceType = ADS_ACETYPE_ACCESS_DENIED_OBJECT
                ACE.ObjectType = SchemaIDGuid
                ACE.Flags = ADS_FLAG_OBJECT_TYPE_PRESENT
            End If
        End If

        ACE.Trustee = UCase(TrusteeName)

        DACL.AddAce ACE
        SecurityDescriptor.DiscretionaryACL = DACL
        Obj.Put "ntSecurityDescriptor", Array(SecurityDescriptor)
        Obj.SetInfo
        If Err.Number = 0 Then ADSObjectSecurity = True
    End Function
```

6. Compile the code as ADAdmin.DLL.
7. Save and close the ADAdmin project.

Tip

If you do not want to share your code between applications, you can enter the preceding code into a code module in any Visual Basic application. ♦

> **Tip**
>
> You can download the Visual Basic 6.0 project or precompiled version of ADAdmin.DLL from http://www.newriders.com/adsi. ◆

Using the Functions in ADObjectManagement

With the ADObjectManagement class module created, you can access the functions contained in the class module from any programming language that supports OLE automation, including Visual Basic, VBScript, and JavaScript.

> **Tip**
>
> To instantiate the object, follow the appropriate syntax found in Chapter 3. Substitute the ADObjectManagement class name where necessary. ◆

Use Table 12.6 to help you use the proper syntax for each of the methods of the ADObjectManagement interface.

Table 12.6   *ADObjectManagement Method Syntax*

Action	Syntax
Query RootDSE Properties	`Debug.Print RootDSEntries("CurrentTime")`
	`Debug.Print RootDSEntries` `↳("SubSchemaSubEntry")`
	`Debug.Print RootDSEntries("DsServiceName")`

	`For Each Element In RootDSEntries`
	`↳("NamingContexts")`
	    `Debug.Print Element`
	`Next`

	`Debug.Print RootDSEntries` `↳("DefaultNamingContext")`
	`Debug.Print RootDSEntries` `↳("SchemaNamingContext")`
	`Debug.Print RootDSEntries` `↳("ConfigurationNamingContext")`
	`Debug.Print RootDSEntries` `↳("RootDomainNamingContext")`

	`For Each Element In RootDSEntries`
	`↳("SupportedControl")`
	    `Debug.Print Element`
	`Next`

Creating the ADObjectManagement Class Module   451

Action	Syntax

	`For Each Element In RootDSEntries`
	↪`("SupportedLDAPVersion")`
	    `Debug.Print Element`
	`Next`
	`Debug.Print RootDSEntries`
	↪`("HighestCommittedUSN")`
	`For Each Element In RootDSEntries`
	↪`("SupportedSASLMechanisms")`
	    `Debug.Print Element`
	`Next`
	`Debug.Print RootDSEntries("DnsHostName")`
	`Debug.Print RootDSEntries("LdapServiceName")`
	`Debug.Print RootDSEntries("ServerName")`

Enumerate Container Elements	`For Each Element In EnumerateContainer`
	↪`("user", "CN=Users,")`
	    `Debug.Print Element`
	`Next`

Remove AD Object from Directory	`Debug.Print RemoveADObject("cn=Users,",` ↪`"user", "cn=IWAM_SERVERNAME")`
Remove AD Branch	`Debug.Print DeleteADBranch` ↪`("ou=Printer_Queues,")`
Move AD Object	`Debug.Print MoveRenameADObject` ↪`("ou=DelegatedAdmins,", "LDAP://cn=Admin1,` ↪`cn=Users,dc=crash,dc=burn")`
Rename AD Object	`Debug.Print MoveRenameADObject` ↪`("ou=DelegatedAdmins,", "LDAP://cn=Admin1,` ↪`cn=users,dc=crash,dc=burn", "cn=DMZAdmin")`
Remove AD ACE	`Debug.Print RemoveADACE("cn=JunkObject,` ↪`ou=DelegatedAdmins,", "Crash\Guest")`

Enumerate ACEs in an AD Object ACL	`For Each ACE In EnumerateAclAces("cn=Users,")`
	    `Debug.Print ACE`
	`Next`

Create AD Object	`Debug.Print CreateADObject("ou=TestOU,",` ↪`"user", "cn=TestUsr1", "sAMAccountName",` ↪`"testUsr1")`
Populate AD Object Attribute	`Debug.Print SetOptionalProperty` ↪`("cn=TEck,ou=Users,", "sn", "Eck")`

continues ▶

Table 12.6   continued

Action	Syntax
Set Full Control Security for AD Object	`Debug.Print ADSObjectSecurity("ou=Users,",`⤦`"Crash\OUAdmin", False, "Inherit", "all",`⤦`True)`
Allow Trustee To Create User Objects in Container	`Debug.Print ADSObjectSecurity`⤦`("ou=Users,", "Crash\UserAdmin",`⤦`True, "Inherit", "{BF967ABA-0DE6-11D0-`⤦`A285-00AA003049E2}", False, False,`⤦`False, True, True)`

Summary

Using the ADSI LDAP service provider, you can programmatically manipulate Active Directory objects, attributes, and security descriptors in Windows 2000.

When creating a binding string, consider using the RootDSE, which allows you to determine the default naming context for a current user session. This can be a vital operation if you want the user to perform administration without specifying alternate credentials.

Using the IADsOpenDSObject interface, you can bind to the Active Directory with alternate credentials and specify the type of authentication to be used. This can be handy for managing domains in other forests or temporarily elevating the privilege of an operation without user intervention.

To aid performance and usability in large enterprise environments, Windows 2000 maintains a partial replica of the data in the directory in the global catalog. By binding to the global catalog, you can perform forest-wide searches and derive the data directly from the global catalog. If the attribute you want to query is not found in the global catalog, you can also derive the original location of the replicated object using the catalog.

By simply changing the object class within a generic object creation code segment, you can create entries in the directory of any type. This, of course, assumes that you have assigned all mandatory attributes before attempting to write the object into the directory. An object's class also allows you to use the IADsContainer `Filter` property to return a specific subset of objects when querying the directory.

Using the IADsDeleteOps interface, you can prune away entire branches of the directory structure. If you prefer not to delete an object but rather move it to a new location, you can use the IADsContainer `MoveHere` method to move or rename an object in the directory.

Lastly, ADSI allows you to fully manipulate the security descriptor for objects in the Active Directory to either establish security on a single object or establish an ACE for all child objects. Modifying the security descriptor on an OU and allowing objects with specific schemaIDGuid values to inherit the parent ACE can implement a delegation model that can allow administration down to the attribute level.

Combining the WinNT:, IIS:, and LDAP: ADSI service providers, you can programmatically manipulate almost every namespace-related element of a native or mixed mode Windows 2000 domain.

Whether you are attempting to decentralize administration, enforce specific standards in the enterprise, or simply reduce the repetition of a particular task, programmatic manipulation of the Active Directory and related namespaces will free you from some of the mundane tasks that plague your workday.

Part V

Appendixes

A   **VBScript Code Reference**

B   **ADSI 2.5 Programmer's Reference**

C   **Further Reading**

      Index

Appendix A
VBScript Code Reference

Although the recommended approach for developing distributed applications remains the use of Visual Basic-developed Component Object Model (COM) objects, there may be occasions in which it is infeasible to do so. If you want to leave the Visual Basic environment for your development efforts, this appendix lists the code segments presented in each chapter of this text in VBScript form for easy inclusion into an Internet Information Server Active Server Page.

To obviate the need for typing each example individually, you can download an electronic copy of this appendix from http://www.newriders.com/adsi.

Chapter 3: Container Management Code

Enumerating Domains Using a VBScript Active Server Page

```
Dim NameSpace
Dim Domain
Set NameSpace = GetObject("WinNT:")
For Each Domain in Namespace
    Response.Write Domain.Name & "<BR>"
Next
```

Querying *AutoUnlockInterval* Using a VBScript Active Server Page

```
Dim Domain
Dim DomainName
DomainName = "Domain_To_Manage"
Set Domain = GetObject("WinNT://" & DomainName)
Response.Write Domain.AutoUnlockInterval
```

Setting a New Value for *AutoUnlockInterval* Using a VBScript Active Server Page

```
Dim Domain
Dim DomainName
Dim NewValue
DomainName = "Domain_To_Manage"
Set Domain = GetObject("WinNT://" & DomainName)
NewValue = 3600
Domain.AutoUnlockInterval = NewValue
Domain.SetInfo
Response.Write Err.Number
```

Querying *LockoutObservationInterval* Using a VBScript Active Server Page

```
Dim Domain
Dim DomainName
DomainName = "Domain_To_Manage"
Set Domain = GetObject("WinNT://" & DomainName)
Response.Write Domain.LockOutObservationInterval
```

Setting a New Value for *LockoutObservationInterval* Using a VBScript Active Server Page

```
Dim Domain
Dim DomainName
Dim NewValue
DomainName = "Domain_To_Manage"
Set Domain = GetObject("WinNT://" & DomainName)

NewValue = 1800
Domain.LockoutObservationInterval = NewValue
Domain.SetInfo
```

Querying *MaxBadPasswordsAllowed* Using a VBScript Active Server Page

```
Dim Domain
Dim DomainName
DomainName = "Domain_To_Manage"
Set Domain = GetObject("WinNT://" & DomainName)
Response.Write Domain.MaxBadPasswordsAllowed
```

Setting a New Value for *MaxBadPasswordsAllowed* Using a VBScript Active Server Page

```
Dim Domain
Dim DomainName
Dim NewValue
DomainName = "Domain_To_Manage"
Set Domain = GetObject("WinNT://" & DomainName)
NewValue = 5
Domain.MaxBadPasswordsAllowed = NewValue
Domain.SetInfo
```

Querying *MaxPasswordAge* Using a VBScript Active Server Page

```
Dim Domain
Dim DomainName
DomainName = "Domain_To_Manage"
Set Domain = GetObject("WinNT://" & DomainName)
Response.Write ((Domain.MaxPasswordAge) / 86400)
```

Setting a New Value for *MaxPasswordAge* Using a VBScript Active Server Page

```
Dim Domain
Dim DomainName
Dim NewValue
DomainName = "Domain_Name_To_Manage"
Set Domain = GetObject("WinNT://" & DomainName)
NewValue = 2592000
Domain.MaxPasswordAge = NewValue
Domain.SetInfo
```

Querying *MinPasswordAge* Using a VBScript Active Server Page

```
Dim Domain
Dim DomainName
DomainName = "Domain_To_Manage"
Set Domain = GetObject("WinNT://" & DomainName)
Response.Write ((Domain.MinPasswordAge) / 86400)
```

Setting a New Value for *MinPasswordAge* Using a VBScript Active Server Page

```
Dim Domain
Dim DomainName
Dim NewValue
DomainName = "Domain_To_Manage"
Set Domain = GetObject("WinNT://" & DomainName)
NewValue = 0
Domain.MinPasswordAge = NewValue
Domain.SetInfo
```

Querying *MinPasswordLength* Using a VBScript Active Server Page

```
Dim Domain
Dim DomainName
DomainName = "Domain_To_Manage"
Set Domain = GetObject("WinNT://" & DomainName)
Response.Write Domain.MinPasswordLength
```

Setting a New Value for *MinPasswordLength* Using a VBScript Active Server Page

```
Dim Domain
Dim DomainName
Dim NewValue
DomainName = "Domain_To_Manage"
Set Domain = GetObject("WinNT://" & DomainName)
NewValue = 7
Domain.MinPasswordLength = NewValue
Domain.SetInfo
```

Querying *PasswordHistoryLength* Using a VBScript Active Server Page

```
Dim Domain
Dim DomainName
DomainName = "Domain_To_Manage"
Set Domain = GetObject("WinNT://" & DomainName)
Response.Write Domain.PasswordHistoryLength
```

Setting a New Value for *PasswordHistoryLength* Using a VBScript Active Server Page

```
Dim Domain
Dim DomainName
Dim NewValue
DomainName = "Domain_To_Manage"
Set Domain = GetObject("WinNT://" & DomainName)
NewValue = 3
Domain.PasswordHistoryLength = NewValue
Domain.SetInfo
```

Enumerating a Generic Container Using a VBScript Active Server Page

```
Dim Container
Dim ContainerName
Dim LeafObject
ContainerName = "Container_Name"
Set Container = GetObject("WinNT://" & ContainerName)
For Each LeafObject in Container
    Response.Write LeafObject.Name & "<BR>"
Next
```

Enumerating User Accounts Using a VBScript Active Server Page

```
Dim Container
Dim ContainerName
Dim User
ContainerName = "Domain_To_Manage"
Set Container = GetObject("WinNT://" & ContainerName)
Container.Filter = Array("User")
For Each User in Container
    Response.Write User.Name & "<BR>"
Next
```

Enumerating Computer Accounts Using a VBScript Active Server Page

```
Dim Container
Dim ContainerName
Dim Computer
ContainerName = "Domain_To_Manage"
Set Container = GetObject("WinNT://" & ContainerName)
Container.Filter = Array("Computer")
For Each Computer in Container
    Response.Write Computer.Name & "<BR>"
Next
```

Enumerating Groups Using a VBScript Active Server Page

```
Dim Container
Dim ContainerName
Dim Group
ContainerName = "Domain_To_Manage"
Set Container = GetObject("WinNT://" & ContainerName)
Container.Filter = Array("Group")
For Each Group in Container
    Response.Write Group.Name & "<BR>"
Next
```

Adding a New Computer Account Using a VBScript Active Server Page

```
Dim Container
Dim ContainerName
Dim ComputerAccount
Dim Computer
Dim NewComputer
ContainerName = "Domain_To_Manage"
Set Container = GetObject("WinNT://" & ContainerName)
NewComputer = "Computer_Account_To_Create"
Set Computer = Container.Create("Computer", UCase(NewComputer))
Computer.SetInfo
```

```
Set ComputerAccount = GetObject("WinNT://" & ContainerName & "/" & NewComputer &
↪"$,user")
ComputerAccount.Put "UserFlags", (ComputerAccount.Get("UserFlags") Or &H1000)
ComputerAccount.SetPassword (LCase(NewComputer))
ComputerAccount.SetInfo
```

Removing a Computer Account Using a VBScript Active Server Page

```
Dim Container
Dim ContainerName
Dim ComputerToRemove
ContainerName = "Domain_To_Manage"
Set Container = GetObject("WinNT://" & ContainerName)
ComputerToRemove = "Computer_To_Remove"
Call Container.Delete("Computer", ComputerToRemove)
```

Adding a New User Account Using a VBScript Active Server Page

```
Dim Container
Dim ContainerName
Dim User
Dim NewUser
ContainerName = "Domain_To_Manage"
NewUser = "User_Account_To_Create"
Set Container = GetObject("WinNT:// " & ContainerName)
Set User = Container.Create("User", NewUser)
User.SetInfo
```

Removing a User Account Using a VBScript Active Server Page

```
Dim Container
Dim ContainerName
Dim UserToRemove
ContainerName = "Domain_To_Manage"
UserToRemove = "User_Account_To_Remove"
Set Container = GetObject("WinNT://" & ContainerName)
Call Container.Delete("User", UserToRemove)
```

Renaming a User Account Using a VBScript Active Server Page

```
Dim Container
Dim ContainerName
Dim OldName
Dim User
Dim NewUser
Dim NewName
OldName = "Old_Account_Name"
NewName = "New_Account_Name"
ContainerName = "Domain_To_Manage"
```

```
Set Container = GetObject("WinNT://" & ContainerName)
Set User = GetObject("WinNT://" & ContainerName & "/" & OldName & ",user")
Set NewUser = Container.MoveHere(User.ADsPath, NewName)
Set User = Nothing
```

Adding a New Local Group Using a VBScript Active Server Page

```
Dim Container
Dim ContainerName
Dim Group
Dim NewGroup
ContainerName = "Domain_To_Manage"
NewGroup = "Requested_Groupname"
Set Container = GetObject("WinNT:// " & ContainerName)
Set Group = Container.Create("Group", NewGroup)
Group.Put "groupType", ADS_GROUP_TYPE_LOCAL_GROUP
Group.SetInfo
```

Adding a New Global Group Using a VBScript Active Server Page

```
Dim Container
Dim ContainerName
Dim Group
Dim NewGroup
ContainerName = "Domain_To_Manage"
NewGroup = "Requested_Groupname"
Set Container = GetObject("WinNT://" & ContainerName)
Set Group = Container.Create("Group", NewGroup)
Group.Put "groupType", ADS_GROUP_TYPE_GLOBAL_GROUP
Group.SetInfo
```

Removing a Group Using a VBScript Active Server Page

```
Dim Container
Dim ContainerName
Dim GroupToRemove
ContainerName = "Domain_To_Manage"
GroupToRemove = "Group_To_Remove"
Set Container = GetObject("WinNT://" & ContainerName)
Call Container.Delete("Group", GroupToRemove)
```

Chapter 4: User Management Code

Querying the User *FullName* Property Using a VBScript Active Server Page

```
Dim User
Dim UserName
Dim UserDomain
UserDomain = "Domain_To_Manage"
```

```
UserName = "Target_User_Name"
Set User = GetObject("WinNT:// " & UserDomain & "/" & UserName & ",user")
Response.Write User.Fullname
```

Setting a New Value for the User *FullName* Property Using a VBScript Active Server Page

```
Dim User
Dim UserName
Dim UserDomain
Dim NewFullName
UserDomain = "Domain_To_Manage"
UserName = "Target_User_Name"
NewFullName = "New_Value_For_Full_Name_Field"
Set User = GetObject("WinNT://" & UserDomain & "/" & UserName & ",user")
User.Fullname = NewFullname
User.SetInfo
```

Querying the *Description* Property Using a VBScript Active Server Page

```
Dim User
Dim UserName
Dim UserDomain
UserDomain = "Domain_To_Manage"
UserName = "Target_User_Name"
Set User = GetObject("WinNT://" & UserDomain & "/" & UserName & ",user")
Response.Write User.Description
```

Setting a New Value for the *Description* Property Using a VBScript Active Server Page

```
Dim User
Dim UserName
Dim UserDomain
Dim NewDescription
UserDomain = "Domain_To_Manage"
UserName = "Target_User_Name"
NewDescription = "New_Value_For_Description_Field"
Set User = GetObject("WinNT://" & UserDomain & "/" & UserName & ",user")
User.Description = NewDescription
User.SetInfo
```

Querying Individual Elements of a Comma-Delimited *Description* Field Using a VBScript Active Server Page

```
Dim User
Dim UserName
Dim UserDomain
Dim Delimiter
```

```
Dim RetVal
Dim FirstDelim
Dim DescriptionLength
Dim ParsedElement
Dim TerminalCondition

UserDomain = "Domain_To_Manage"
UserName = "Target_User_Name"
Delimiter = "|"
Set User = GetObject("WinNT://" & UserDomain & "/" & UserName & ",user")
RetVal = User.Description
StartPosition = 1
While TerminalCondition <> True
    FirstDelim = InStr(1, RetVal, Delimiter)
    If FirstDelim = 0 Then
        TerminalCondition = True
    Else
        DescriptionLength = Len(RetVal)
        ParsedElement = Left(RetVal, FirstDelim - 1)
        Response.Write Trim(ParsedElement) & "<BR>"
        RetVal = Right(RetVal, (DescriptionLength - FirstDelim))
    End If
Wend
```

Setting a New Value for a User Password Using a VBScript Active Server Page

```
Dim User
Dim UserName
Dim UserDomain
Dim NewPassword
UserDomain = "Domain_To_Manage"
UserName = "Target_User_Name"
NewPassword = "Superm@n99"
Set User = GetObject("WinNT://" & UserDomain & "/" & UserName & ",user")
Call User.SetPassword(NewPassword)
User.SetInfo
```

Changing a User Password Using a VBScript Active Server Page

```
Dim User
Dim UserName
Dim UserDomain
Dim NewPassword
Dim OldPassword
UserDomain = "Domain_To_Manage"
UserName = "Target_User_Name"
NewPassword = "Superm@n26"
OldPassword = "B@tm@n74!"
Set User = GetObject("WinNT://" & UserDomain & "/" & UserName & ",user")
Call User.ChangePassword(OldPassword, NewPassword)
User.SetInfo
```

Querying the Value of a User Flag Using a VBScript Active Server Page

```
Dim User
Dim UserName
Dim UserDomain
Dim Flags
UserDomain = "Domain_To_Manage"
UserName = "Target_User_Name"
Set User = GetObject("WinNT://" & UserDomain & "/" & UserName & ",user")
Flags = User.Get("UserFlags")
If (Flags And &H10000) <> 0 Then
    Response.Write "The specified user account is configured so that the password
    ↪never expires."
End If
```

Toggling a User Flag Using a VBScript Active Server Page

```
Dim User
Dim UserName
Dim UserDomain
Dim Flags
UserDomain = "Domain_To_Manage"
UserName = "Target_User_Name"
Set User = GetObject("WinNT://" & UserDomain & "/" & UserName & ",user")
Flags = User.Get("UserFlags")
User.Put "UserFlags", (Flags Xor &H10000)
User.SetInfo
```

Querying the User Must Change Password at Next Logon Status Flag Using a VBScript Active Server Page

```
Dim User
Dim UserName
Dim UserDomain
Dim PasswordExpired
UserDomain = "Domain_To_Manage"
UserName = "Target_User_Name"
Set User = GetObject("WinNT://" & UserDomain & "/" & UserName & ",user")
PasswordExpired= User.Get("PasswordExpired")
If PasswordExpired = 1 Then
    Response.Write "The user account is configured so that the password must be
    ↪changed on next logon."
Else
    Response.Write "The user will NOT be required to change the account password on
    ↪next logon."
End If
```

Setting a New Value for the User Must Change Password at Next Logon Status Flag Using a VBScript Active Server Page

```
Dim User
Dim UserName
Dim UserDomain
Dim PasswordExpired
UserDomain = "Domain_To_Manage"
UserName = "Target_User_Name"
Set User = GetObject("WinNT://" & UserDomain & "/" & UserName & ",user")
User.Put "PasswordExpired", 1
User.SetInfo
```

Querying the User Cannot Change Password Status Flag Using a VBScript Active Server Page

```
Dim User
Dim UserName
Dim UserDomain
Dim Flags
UserDomain = "Domain_To_Manage"
UserName = "Target_User_Name"
Set User = GetObject("WinNT://" & UserDomain & "/" & UserName & ",user")
Flags = User.Get("UserFlags")
If (Flags And &H00040) <> 0 Then
    Response.Write "The specified user account is configured so that the password
    ↳cannot be changed."
End If
```

Setting the Value for the User Cannot Change Password Status Flag Using a VBScript Active Server Page

```
Dim User
Dim UserName
Dim UserDomain
Dim Flags
UserDomain = "Domain_To_Manage"
UserName = "Target_User_Name"
Set User = GetObject("WinNT://" & UserDomain & "/" & UserName & ",user")
Flags = User.Get("UserFlags")
User.Put "UserFlags", Flags OR &H00040
User.SetInfo
```

Toggling the Value for the User Cannot Change Password Status Flag Using a VBScript Active Server Page

```
Dim User
Dim UserName
Dim UserDomain
Dim Flags
UserDomain = "Domain_To_Manage"
```

```
UserName = "Target_User_Name"
Set User = GetObject("WinNT://" & UserDomain & "/" & UserName & ",user")
Flags = User.Get("UserFlags")
User.Put "UserFlags", Flags XOR &H00040
User.SetInfo
```

Querying the Password Never Expires Status Flag Using a VBScript Active Server Page

```
Dim User
Dim UserName
Dim UserDomain
Dim Flags
UserDomain = "Domain_To_Manage"
UserName = "Target_User_Name"
Set User = GetObject("WinNT://" & UserDomain & "/" & UserName & ",user")
Flags = User.Get("UserFlags")
If (Flags And &H10000) <> 0 Then
    Response.Write "The specified user account is configured so that the password
    ↳never expires."
End If
```

Setting the Password Never Expires Status Flag Using a VBScript Active Server Page

```
Dim User
Dim UserName
Dim UserDomain
Dim Flags
UserDomain = "Domain_To_Manage"
UserName = "Target_User_Name"
Set User = GetObject("WinNT://" & UserDomain & "/" & UserName & ",user")
Flags = User.Get("UserFlags")
User.Put "UserFlags", Flags OR &H10000
User.SetInfo
```

Toggling the Password Never Expires Status Flag Using a VBScript Active Server Page

```
Dim User
Dim UserName
Dim UserDomain
Dim Flags
UserDomain = "Domain_To_Manage"
UserName = "Target_User_Name"
Set User = GetObject("WinNT://" & UserDomain & "/" & UserName & ",user")
Flags = User.Get("UserFlags")
User.Put "UserFlags", Flags XOR &H10000
User.SetInfo
```

Querying the Account Disabled Status Flag Using a VBScript Active Server Page and the *AccountDisabled* Property

```
Dim User
Dim UserName
Dim UserDomain
UserDomain = "Domain_To_Manage"
UserName = "Target_User_Name"
Set User = GetObject("WinNT://" & UserDomain & "/" & UserName & ",user")
Response.Write User.AccountDisabled
```

Setting a New Value for the Account Disabled Status Flag Using a VBScript Active Server Page and the *AccountDisabled* Property

```
Dim User
Dim UserName
Dim UserDomain
UserDomain = "Domain_To_Manage"
UserName = "Target_User_Name"
Set User = GetObject("WinNT://" & UserDomain & "/" & UserName & ",user")
User.AccountDisabled = True
User.SetInfo
```

Enumerating a Domain to Report all Disabled Accounts Using a VBScript Active Server Page

```
Dim Domain
Dim DomainName
Dim UserAccount
Dim Counter
Counter = 0
DomainName = "Domain_To_Manage"
Set Domain = GetObject("WinNT://" & DomainName)
Domain.Filter = Array("User")
Response.Write "The following accounts are disabled in domain: " & Domain.Name &
↳"<BR>"
For Each UserAccount In Domain
    If UserAccount.AccountDisabled = True Then
        Response.Write UserAccount.Name & "<BR>"
        Counter = Counter + 1
    End If
Next
If Counter = 1 Then
    Response.Write "Only 1 user account in the " & Domain.Name & " domain is
    ↳disabled." & "<BR>"
Else
    Response.Write Counter & " user accounts are disabled in the " & Domain.Name & "
    ↳domain." & "<BR>"
End If
```

Querying the Account Locked Out Status Flag Using a VBScript Active Server Page and the *IsAccountLocked* Property

```
Dim User
Dim UserName
Dim UserDomain
UserDomain = "Domain_To_Manage"
UserName = "Target_User_Name"
Set User = GetObject("WinNT://" & UserDomain & "/" & UserName & ",user")
Response.Write User.IsAccountLocked
```

Unlocking a User Account Using a VBScript Active Server Page and the *IsAccountLocked* Property

```
Dim User
Dim UserName
Dim UserDomain
UserDomain = "Domain_To_Manage"
UserName = "Target_User_Name"
Set User = GetObject("WinNT://" & UserDomain & "/" & UserName & ",user")
If User.IsAccountLocked = True Then
    User.IsAccountLocked = False
    User.SetInfo
End If
```

Resetting All Locked-Out User Accounts for a Domain Using a VBScript Active Server Page

```
Dim Domain
Dim UserAccount
Dim Counter
Dim DomainName
Counter = 0
DomainName = "Domain_To_Manage"
Set Domain = GetObject("WinNT://" & DomainName)
Domain.Filter = Array("User")
For Each UserAccount In Domain
    If UserAccount.IsAccountLocked = True Then
        Response.Write UserAccount.Name & "<BR>"
        UserAccount.IsAccountLocked = False
        UserAccount.SetInfo
        Counter = Counter + 1
    End If
Next
If Counter = 1 Then
    Response.Write "Only 1 user account in the " & Domain.Name & " domain was
        ↪unlocked." & "<BR>"
Else
    Response.Write Counter & " user accounts were unlocked in the " & Domain.Name &
        ↪" domain." & "<BR>"
End If
```

Querying the User Profile Path Using a VBScript Active Server Page

```
Dim User
Dim UserName
Dim UserDomain
UserDomain = "Domain_To_Manage"
UserName = "Target_User_Name"
Set User = GetObject("WinNT://" & UserDomain & "/" & UserName & ",user")
Response.Write User.Profile
```

Setting a New User Profile Path Using a VBScript Active Server Page

```
Dim User
Dim UserName
Dim UserDomain
Dim NewValue
UserDomain = "Domain_To_Manage"
UserName = "Target_User_Name"
NewValue = "New_User_Profile_Path"
Set User = GetObject("WinNT://" & UserDomain & "/" & UserName & ",user")
User.Profile = NewValue
User.SetInfo
```

Querying the *LoginScript* Property Using a VBScript Active Server Page

```
Dim User
Dim UserName
Dim UserDomain
UserDomain = "Domain_To_Manage"
UserName = "Target_User_Name"
Set User = GetObject("WinNT://" & UserDomain & "/" & UserName & ",user")
Response.Write User.LoginScript
```

Setting the *LoginScript* Property Using a VBScript Active Server Page

```
Dim User
Dim UserName
Dim UserDomain
Dim NewValue
UserDomain = "Domain_To_Manage"
UserName = "Target_User_Name"
Set User = GetObject("WinNT://" & UserDomain & "/" & UserName & ",user")
NewValue = "NewLoginScript.CMD"
User.LoginScript = NewValue
User.SetInfo
```

Querying the Home Directory Path Using a VBScript Active Server Page

```
Dim User
Dim UserName
Dim UserDomain
UserDomain = "Domain_To_Manage"
UserName = "Target_User_Name"
Set User = GetObject("WinNT://" & UserDomain & "/" & UserName & ",user")
Response.Write User.HomeDirectory
```

Setting a New Home Directory Path Using a VBScript Active Server Page

```
Dim User
Dim UserName
Dim UserDomain
Dim NewValue
UserDomain = "Domain_To_Manage"
UserName = "Target_User_Name"
NewValue = "New_Home_Directory_Path_Value"
Set User = GetObject("WinNT://" & UserDomain & "/" & UserName & ",user")

User.HomeDirectory = NewValue
User.SetInfo
```

Querying the Home Directory Mapping Using a VBScript Active Server Page

```
Dim User
Dim UserName
Dim UserDomain
UserDomain = "Domain_To_Manage"
UserName = "Target_User_Name"
Set User = GetObject("WinNT://" & UserDomain & "/" & UserName & ",user")
Response.Write User.Get("HomeDirDrive")
```

Setting a New Home Directory Mapping Using a VBScript Active Server Page

```
Dim User
Dim UserName
Dim UserDomain
Dim NewValue
UserDomain = "Domain_To_Manage"
UserName = "Target_User_Name"
NewValue = "New_Value_For_Home_Directory_Drive"
Set User = GetObject("WinNT://" & UserDomain & "/" & UserName & ",user")
User.Put("HomeDirDrive"), NewValue
User.SetInfo
```

Querying User Logon Hours Using a VBScript Active Server Page

```
Dim User
Dim UserName
Dim UserDomain
Dim TimeEntry
Dim Restriction
UserDomain = "Domain_To_Manage"
UserName = "Target_User_Name"
Set User = GetObject("WinNT://" & UserDomain & "/" & UserName & ",user")
For Each TimeEntry In User.LoginHours
    If TimeEntry < 255 Then Restriction = 1
Next
If Restriction = 1 Then
    Response.Write "User account " & UserDomain & "\" & UserName & " has time
    ↪restrictions placed upon it."
Else
    Response.Write "There are no time restrictions affecting user account " &
    ↪UserDomain & "\" & UserName & "."
End If
```

Querying Login Workstations Using a VBScript Active Server Page

```
On Error Resume Next
Dim User
Dim UserName
Dim UserDomain
Dim Workstation
UserDomain = "Domain_To_Manage"
UserName = "Target_User_Name"
Set User = GetObject("WinNT://" & UserDomain & "/" & UserName & ",user")
If User.LoginWorkstations = "" then
    For Each Workstation in User.LoginWorkstations
        Response.Write Workstation & "<BR>"
    Next
Else
    Response.Write User.LoginWorkstations & "<BR>"
End If
```

Adding a New Login Workstation to the *LoginWorkstations* Property Using a VBScript Active Server Page

```
On Error Resume Next
Dim User
Dim UserName
Dim UserDomain
Dim Workstation
Dim NewElement()
Dim i
Dim NewValue
```

```
UserDomain = "Domain_To_Manage"
UserName = "Target_User_Name"
NewValue = "New_Machine_To_Add"
Set User = GetObject("WinNT://" & UserDomain & "/" & UserName & ",user")
If User.LoginWorkstations = "" Then
    For Each Workstation In User.LoginWorkstations
        i = UBound(NewElement) + 1
        ReDim Preserve NewElement(i)
        NewElement(i) = Workstation
    Next
    i = UBound(NewElement) + 1
    ReDim Preserve NewElement(i)
    NewElement(i) = NewValue
    User.LoginWorkstations = NewElement
    User.SetInfo
Else
    User.LoginWorkstations = Array(NewValue)
    User.SetInfo
End If
```

Removing an Existing Login Workstation from the *LoginWorkstations* Property Using a VBScript Active Server Page

```
On Error Resume Next
Dim User
Dim UserName
Dim UserDomain
Dim Workstation
Dim NewElement()
Dim i
Dim NewValue
UserDomain = "Domain_To_Manage"
UserName = "Target_User_Name"
NewValue = "Machine_To_Remove"
Set User = GetObject("WinNT://" & UserDomain & "/" & UserName & ",user")
If User.LoginWorkstations = "" Then
    For Each Workstation In User.LoginWorkstations
        If NewValue <> Workstation Then
            i = UBound(NewElement) + 1
            ReDim Preserve NewElement(i)
            NewElement(i) = Workstation
        End If
    Next
    User.LoginWorkstations = NewElement
    User.SetInfo
Else
    If NewValue <> User.LoginWorkstations Then
        User.LoginWorkstations = Array(NewValue)
    Else
        User.LoginWorkstations = Array("")
    End If
    User.SetInfo
End If
```

Querying the Account Expiration Date Using a VBScript Active Server Page

```
On Error Resume Next
Dim User
Dim UserName
Dim UserDomain
Dim AccountExpirationDate
UserDomain = "Domain_To_Manage"
UserName = "Target_User_Name"
Set User = GetObject("WinNT://" & UserDomain & "/" & UserName & ",user")
AccountExpirationDate = User.AccountExpirationDate
Response.Write AccountExpirationDate
```

Setting the Account Expiration Date Using a VBScript Active Server Page

```
Dim User
Dim UserName
Dim UserDomain
Dim AccountExpirationDate
UserDomain = "Domain_To_Manage"
UserName = "Target_User_Name"
Set User = GetObject("WinNT://" & UserDomain & "/" & UserName & ",user")
AccountExpirationDate = #mm/dd/yyyy#
User.AccountExpirationDate = AccountExpirationDate
User.SetInfo
```

Querying the Account Type Using a VBScript Active Server Page

```
Dim User
Dim UserName
Dim UserDomain
Dim Flags
UserDomain = "Domain_To_Manage"
UserName = "Target_User_Name"
Set User = GetObject("WinNT://" & UserDomain & "/" & UserName & ",user")
Flags = User.Get("UserFlags")
If (Flags And &H100) <> 0 Then
     Response.Write "Local Account"
Else
     Response.Write "Global Account"
End If
```

Configuring a Global Account as a Local Account Using a VBScript Active Server Page

```
Dim User
Dim UserName
Dim UserDomain
Dim Flags
UserDomain = "Domain_To_Manage"
UserName = "Target_User_Name"
Set User = GetObject("WinNT://" & UserDomain & "/" & UserName & ",user")
Flags = User.Get("UserFlags")
If (Flags And &H200) <> 0 Then
    User.Put "UserFlags", Flags Xor &H200
    User.SetInfo
    Flags = User.Get("UserFlags")
    User.Put "UserFlags", Flags Xor &H100
    User.SetInfo
End If
```

Configuring a Local Account as a Global Account Using a VBScript Active Server Page

```
Dim User
Dim UserName
Dim UserDomain
Dim Flags
UserDomain = "Domain_To_Manage"
UserName = "Target_User_Name"
Set User = GetObject("WinNT://" & UserDomain & "/" & UserName & ",user")
Flags = User.Get("UserFlags")
If (Flags And &H100) <> 0 Then
    User.Put "UserFlags", Flags Xor &H100
    User.SetInfo
    Flags = User.Get("UserFlags")
    User.Put "UserFlags", Flags Xor &H200
    User.SetInfo
End If
```

Querying the *BadLoginCount* Property Using a VBScript Active Server Page

```
On Error Resume Next
Dim User
Dim UserName
Dim UserDomain
UserDomain = "Domain_To_Manage"
UserName = "Target_User_Name"
Set User = GetObject("WinNT://" & UserDomain & "/" & UserName & ",user")
Response.Write User.BadLoginCount
```

Querying *LastLogin* for a Given Machine Using a VBScript Active Server Page

```
On Error Resume Next
Dim User
Dim UserName
Dim UserDomain
UserDomain = "Domain_To_Manage"
UserName = "Target_User_Name"
Set User = GetObject("WinNT://" & UserDomain & "/" & UserName & ",user")
Response.Write User.LastLogin
```

Querying *LastLogoff* for a Given Machine Using a VBScript Active Server Page

```
Dim User
Dim UserName
Dim UserDomain
UserDomain = "Domain_To_Manage"
UserName = "Target_User_Name"
Set User = GetObject("WinNT://" & UserDomain & "/" & UserName & ",user")
Response.Write User.LastLogoff
```

Querying *PasswordMinimumLength* for a User Account Using a VBScript Active Server Page

```
Dim User
Dim UserName
Dim UserDomain
UserDomain = "Domain_To_Manage"
UserName = "Target_User_Name"
Set User = GetObject("WinNT://" & UserDomain & "/" & UserName & ",user")
Response.Write User.PasswordMinimumLength
```

Querying *PasswordRequired* for a User Account Using a VBScript Active Server Page

```
Dim User
Dim UserName
Dim UserDomain
UserDomain = "Domain_To_Manage"
UserName = "Target_User_Name"
Set User = GetObject("WinNT://" & UserDomain & "/" & UserName & ",user")
Response.Write User.PasswordRequired
```

Setting *PasswordRequired* for a User Account Using a VBScript Active Server Page

```
Dim User
Dim UserName
Dim UserDomain
Dim NewValue
UserDomain = "Domain_To_Manage"
UserName = "Target_User_Name"
Set User = GetObject("WinNT://" & UserDomain & "/" & UserName & ",user")
NewValue = New_Boolean_Value_For_PasswordRequired
User.PasswordRequired = NewValue
User.SetInfo
```

Querying User Password Age Using a VBScript Active Server Page

```
Dim Group
Dim GroupName
Dim GroupDomain
Dim User
GroupDomain = "Domain_To_Manage"
GroupName = "Domain Admins"
Set Group = GetObject("WinNT://" & GroupDomain & "/" & GroupName & ",group")
For Each Member In Group.Members
    Set User = GetObject("WinNT://" & GroupDomain & "/" & Member.Name & ",user")
    If User.Get("PasswordAge") > 2592000 Then
        If (User.Get("UserFlags") And &H10000) = 0 Then
            Response.Write Member.Name & "<BR>"
            'If you wish to perform a query only, comment out the following two
            ↪lines:
            User.Put "PasswordExpired", CLng(1)
            User.SetInfo
        End If
    End If
Next
```

Detecting Machines No Longer in the Resource Domain Using a VBScript Active Server Page

```
Dim Container
Dim TargetDomain
Dim Member
Dim Computer
TargetDomain = "Domain_In_Which_To_Find_Old_Machine_Accounts"
Set Container = GetObject("WinNT://" & TargetDomain)
Container.Filter = Array("Computer")
For Each Member In Container
    Set Computer = GetObject("WinNT://" & TargetDomain & "/" & Member.Name &
    ↪"$,user")
```

```
        If Computer.Get("PasswordAge") > 15552000 Then
            Response.Write Computer.ADsPath & " " & Computer.Get("PasswordAge") &
            ➥"<BR>"
        End If
Next
```

Chapter 5: Group Management Code

Adding Users to a Group Using a VBScript Active Server Page

```
Dim Group
Dim GroupName
Dim GroupDomain
Dim User
Dim UserName
Dim UserDomain
GroupName = "Target_Group_Name"
GroupDomain = "Target_Group_Domain"
UserName = "Target_User_Name"
UserDomain = "Target User Domain"
Set User = GetObject("WinNT://" & UserDomain & "/" & UserName & ",user")
Set Group = GetObject("WinNT://" & GroupDomain & "/" & GroupName & ",group")
Group.Add(User.ADsPath)
Group.SetInfo
```

Removing Users from a Group Using a VBScript Active Server Page

```
Dim Group
Dim GroupName
Dim GroupDomain
Dim User
Dim UserName
Dim UserDomain
GroupName = "Target_Group_Name"
GroupDomain = "Target_Group_Domain"
UserName = "Target_User_Name"
UserDomain = "Target User Domain"
Set User = GetObject("WinNT://" & UserDomain & "/" & UserName & ",user")
Set Group = GetObject("WinNT://" & GroupDomain & "/" & GroupName & ",group")
Group.Remove(User.ADsPath)
Group.SetInfo
```

Enumerating Members of a Group Using a VBScript Active Server Page

```
Dim Group
Dim GroupName
Dim GroupDomain
GroupName = "Target_Group_Name"
GroupDomain = "Target_Group_Domain"
Set Group = GetObject("WinNT://" & GroupDomain & "/" & GroupName & ",group")
For Each Member in Group.Members
    Response.Write Member.Name & "<BR>"
Next
```

Querying User Membership in a Group Using a VBScript Active Server Page

```
Dim Group
Dim GroupName
Dim GroupDomain
Dim User
Dim UserName
Dim UserDomain
GroupName = "Target_Group_Name"
GroupDomain = "Target_Group_Domain"
UserName = "Target_User_Name"
UserDomain = "Domain_To_Manage"
Set User = GetObject("WinNT://" & UserDomain & "/" & UserName & ",user")
Set Group = GetObject("WinNT://" & GroupDomain & "/" & GroupName & ",group")
Response.Write Group.IsMember(User.ADsPath)
```

Querying Group Description Field Value Using a VBScript Active Server Page

```
Dim Group
Dim GroupName
Dim GroupDomain
GroupDomain = "Target_Group_Domain"
GroupName = "Target_Group_Name"
Set Group = GetObject("WinNT://" & GroupDomain & "/" & GroupName & ",group")
Response.Write Group.Description
```

Setting New Group Description Field Value Using a VBScript Active Server Page

```
Dim Group
Dim GroupName
Dim GroupDomain
GroupDomain = "Target_Group_Domain"
GroupName = "Target_Group_Name"
```

```
GroupDescription = "Target_Group_Description"
Set Group = GetObject("WinNT://" & GroupDomain & "/" & GroupName & ",group")
Group.Description = GroupDescription
Group.SetInfo
```

Enumerating Individual User Group Membership Using a VBScript Active Server Page

```
Dim User
Dim Group
Dim UserDomain
Dim UserName
UserDomain = "Domain_To_Manage"
UserName = "Target_User_Name"
Set User = GetObject("WinNT://" & UserDomain & "/" & UserName & ",user")
For Each Group in User.Groups
    Response.Write Group.Name & "<BR>"
Next
```

Chapter 6: Computer and Service Management Code

Querying the Computer Owner Using VBScript Active Server Page

```
Dim Computer
Dim ComputerName
Dim ComputerDomain
ComputerDomain = "Domain_To_Manage"
ComputerName = "Target_Computer_Name"
Set Computer= GetObject("WinNT://" & ComputerDomain & "/" & ComputerName &
↪",computer")
Response.Write Computer.Owner
```

Querying the Registered Organization Using a VBScript Active Server Page

```
Dim Computer
Dim ComputerName
Dim ComputerDomain
ComputerDomain = "Domain_To_Manage"
ComputerName = "Target_Computer_Name"
Set Computer= GetObject("WinNT://" & ComputerDomain & "/" & ComputerName &
↪",computer")
Response.Write Computer.Division
```

Querying the Computer Operating System Using VBScript Active Server Page

```
Dim Computer
Dim ComputerName
Dim ComputerDomain
ComputerDomain = "Domain_To_Manage"
ComputerName = "Target_Computer_Name"
Set Computer= GetObject("WinNT://" & ComputerDomain & "/" & ComputerName &
➥",computer")
Response.Write Computer.OperatingSystem
```

Querying the Computer Operating System Version Using a VBScript Active Server Page

```
Dim Computer
Dim ComputerName
Dim ComputerDomain
ComputerDomain = "Domain_To_Manage"
ComputerName = "Target_Computer_Name"
Set Computer= GetObject("WinNT://" & ComputerDomain & "/" & ComputerName &
➥",computer")
Response.Write Computer.OperatingSystemVersion
```

Querying the Computer Processor Type Using a VBScript Active Server Page

```
Dim Computer
Dim ComputerName
Dim ComputerDomain
ComputerDomain = "Domain_To_Manage"
ComputerName = "Target_Computer_Name"
Set Computer= GetObject("WinNT://" & ComputerDomain & "/" & ComputerName &
➥",computer")
Response.Write Computer.Processor
```

Querying the Installed HAL on Windows NT Using a VBScript Active Server Page

```
Dim Computer
Dim ComputerName
Dim ComputerDomain
ComputerDomain = "Domain_To_Manage"
ComputerName = "Target_Computer_Name"
Set Computer= GetObject("WinNT://" & ComputerDomain & "/" & ComputerName &
➥",computer")
Response.Write Computer.ProcessorCount
```

Enumerating Installed Services on a Specific Computer Using a VBScript Active Server Page

```
Dim Computer
Dim ComputerName
Dim ComputerDomain
Dim Service
ComputerDomain = "Domain_To_Manage"
ComputerName = "Target_Computer_Name"
Set Computer = GetObject("WinNT://" & ComputerDomain & "/" & ComputerName &
➥",computer")
Computer.Filter = Array("service")
For Each Service In Computer
    Response.Write Service.Name & "<BR>"
Next
```

Querying Service Dependencies Using a VBScript Active Server Page

```
On Error Resume Next
Dim Computer
Dim ComputerName
Dim ComputerDomain
Dim Service
Dim TargetService
TargetService = "Target_Service_Name"
ComputerDomain = "Domain_To_Manage"
ComputerName = "Target_Computer_Name"
Set Computer = GetObject("WinNT://" & ComputerDomain & "/" & ComputerName &
➥",computer")
Set Service = Computer.GetObject("service", TargetService)
If IsArray(Service.Dependencies) = True Then
    Dim Entry
    For Each Entry In Service.Dependencies
        Response.Write Entry & "<BR>"
    Next
Else
    Response.Write Service.Dependencies & "<BR>"
End If
```

Setting a New Service Dependency Using a VBScript Active Server Page

```
On Error Resume Next
Dim Computer
Dim Service
Dim NewElement()
Dim i
Dim EmptyArray
Dim DependencyAlreadyExists
Dim ComputerDomain
Dim TargetComputer
```

```vbscript
Dim TargetService
Dim NewDependency
TargetService = "Target_Service_Name"
ComputerDomain = "Domain_To_Manage"
TargetComputer = "Target_Computer_Name"
NewDependency = "mssqlserver"
Set Computer = GetObject("WinNT://" & ComputerDomain & "/" & TargetComputer & _
",computer")
Set Service = Computer.GetObject("service", TargetService)
If IsArray(Service.Dependencies) = True Then
    Dim Entry
    For Each Entry In Service.Dependencies
        i = UBound(NewElement) + 1
        ReDim Preserve NewElement(i)
        NewElement(i) = Entry
        If Entry = "" Then EmptyArray = 1
        If Entry = NewDependency Then DependencyAlreadyExists = 1
    Next
    If EmptyArray = 1 Then
        Service.Dependencies = Array(NewDependency)
        Service.SetInfo
    Else
        If DependencyAlreadyExists <> 1 Then
            i = UBound(NewElement) + 1
            ReDim Preserve NewElement(i)
            NewElement(i) = NewDependency
            Service.Dependencies = NewElement
            Service.SetInfo
        End If
    End If
Else
    If Service.Dependencies <> NewDependency Then
        Service.Dependencies = Array(Service.Dependencies, NewDependency)
        Service.SetInfo
    End If
End If
```

Querying Service Display Name Using a VBScript Active Server Page

```vbscript
Dim Computer
Dim ComputerName
Dim ComputerDomain
Dim Service
Dim TargetService
TargetService = "Target_Service_Name"
ComputerDomain = "Domain_To_Manage"
ComputerName = "Target_Computer_Name"
Set Computer = GetObject("WinNT://" & ComputerDomain & "/" & ComputerName & _
",computer")
Set Service = Computer.GetObject("service", TargetService)
Response.Write Service.DisplayName
```

Determining the Programmatic Name of a Service from the Display Name Using a VBScript Active Server Page

```
Dim Computer
Dim ComputerName
Dim ComputerDomain
Dim StringToFind
Dim Service
ComputerDomain = "Domain_To_Manage"
ComputerName = "Target_Computer_Name"
StringToFind = "Display_Name_To_Find"
Set Computer = GetObject("WinNT://" & ComputerDomain & "/" & ComputerName &
↪",computer")
Computer.Filter = Array("service")
For Each Service In Computer
    If InStr(Service.DisplayName, StringToFind) <> 0 Then
        Response.Write Service.Name; " = "; Service.DisplayName & "<BR>"
    End If
Next
```

Setting a New Service Display Name Using a VBScript Active Server Page

```
Dim Computer
Dim ComputerName
Dim ComputerDomain
Dim Service
Dim TargetService
Dim NewDisplayName
TargetService = "Target_Service_Name"
ComputerDomain = "Domain_To_Manage"
ComputerName = "Target_Computer_Name"
NewDisplayName = "New_Service_Display_Name"
Set Computer = GetObject("WinNT://" & ComputerDomain & "/" & ComputerName &
↪",computer")
Set Service = Computer.GetObject("service", TargetService)
Service.DisplayName = NewDisplayName
Service.SetInfo
```

Querying Host Computer Property Using a VBScript Active Server Page

```
Dim Computer
Dim ComputerName
Dim ComputerDomain
Dim Service
Dim TargetService
TargetService = "Target_Service_Name"
ComputerDomain = "Domain_To_Manage"
ComputerName = "Target_Computer_Name"
Set Computer = GetObject("WinNT://" & ComputerDomain & "/" & ComputerName &
↪",computer")
Set Service = Computer.GetObject("service", TargetService)
Response.Write Service.HostComputer
```

Querying Service Executable Path Using a VBScript Active Server Page

```
Dim Computer
Dim ComputerName
Dim ComputerDomain
Dim Service
Dim TargetService
TargetService = "Target_Service_Name"
ComputerDomain = "Domain_To_Manage"
ComputerName = "Target_Computer_Name"
Set Computer = GetObject("WinNT://" & ComputerDomain & "/" & ComputerName &
↵",computer")
Set Service = Computer.GetObject("service", TargetService)
Response.Write Service.Path
```

Setting New Service Executable Path Using a VBScript Active Server Page

```
Dim Computer
Dim ComputerName
Dim ComputerDomain
Dim Service
Dim TargetService
Dim NewServicePath
TargetService = "Target_Service_Name"
ComputerDomain = "Domain_To_Manage"
ComputerName = "Target_Computer_Name"
NewServicePath = "New_Path_To_Executable"
Set Computer = GetObject("WinNT://" & ComputerDomain & "/" & ComputerName &
↵",computer")
Set Service = Computer.GetObject("service", TargetService)
Service.Path = NewServicePath
Service.SetInfo
```

Querying Service Account Name Using a VBScript Active Server Page

```
Dim Computer
Dim ComputerName
Dim ComputerDomain
Dim Service
Dim TargetService
TargetService = "Target_Service_Name"
ComputerDomain = "Domain_To_Manage"
ComputerName = "Target_Computer_Name"
Set Computer = GetObject("WinNT://" & ComputerDomain & "/" & ComputerName &
↵",computer")
Set Service = Computer.GetObject("service", TargetService)
Response.Write Service.ServiceAccountName
```

Querying Service Start Type Using a VBScript Active Server Page

```
Dim Computer
Dim ComputerName
Dim ComputerDomain
Dim Service
Dim TargetService
TargetService = "Target_Service_Name"
ComputerDomain = "Domain_To_Manage"
ComputerName = "Target_Computer_Name"
Set Computer = GetObject("WinNT://" & ComputerDomain & "/" & ComputerName &
↵",computer")
Set Service = Computer.GetObject("service", TargetService)
Select Case Service.StartType
     Case 0
          Response.Write "BOOT"
     Case 1
          Response.Write "SYSTEM"
     Case 2
          Response.Write "AUTOMATIC"
     Case 3
          Response.Write "MANUAL"
     Case 4
          Response.Write "DISABLED"
End Select
```

Setting Service Start Type Using a VBScript Active Server Page

```
Dim Computer
Dim ComputerName
Dim ComputerDomain
Dim Service
Dim TargetService
TargetService = "Target_Service_Name"
ComputerDomain = "Domain_To_Manage"
ComputerName = "Target_Computer_Name"
Set Computer = GetObject("WinNT://" & ComputerDomain & "/" & ComputerName &
↵",computer")
Set Service = Computer.GetObject("service", TargetService)
'Use 4 to disable the service, 3 for Manual startup or 2 to AutoStart the service
Service.StartType = 4
Service.SetInfo
```

Enumerating Service Status Using a VBScript Active Server Page

```
Dim Computer
Dim ComputerName
Dim ComputerDomain
Dim Service
Dim ServiceStatus
ComputerDomain = "Domain_To_Manage"
ComputerName = "Target_Computer_Name"
```

```
Set Computer = GetObject("WinNT://" & ComputerDomain & "/" & ComputerName &
↪",computer")
Computer.Filter = Array("service")
For Each Service In Computer
    Select Case Service.Status
        Case 1
            ServiceStatus = "Stopped"
        Case 2
            ServiceStatus = "Start Pending"
        Case 3
            ServiceStatus = "Stop Pending"
        Case 4
            ServiceStatus = "Running"
        Case 5
            ServiceStatus = "Continue_Pending"
        Case 6
            ServiceStatus = "Pause_Pending"
        Case 7
            ServiceStatus = "Paused"
        Case 8
            ServiceStatus = "Error"
    End Select
    Response.Write Service.Name & ServiceStatus & "<BR>"
Next
```

Starting a Service Using a VBScript Active Server Page

```
Dim Computer
Dim ComputerName
Dim ComputerDomain
Dim Service
Dim TargetService
TargetService = "Target_Service_Name"
ComputerDomain = "Domain_To_Manage"
ComputerName = "Target_Computer_Name"
Set Computer = GetObject("WinNT://" & ComputerDomain & "/" & ComputerName &
↪",computer")
Set Service = Computer.GetObject("service", TargetService)
If Service.Status = 1 Then
    Service.Start
    Response.Write "The " & Service.Name & " service has been started." & "<BR>"
Else
    If Service.Status = 4 Then
        Response.Write "The " & Service.Name & " service is already started." &
        ↪"<BR>"
    Else
        Response.Write "The " & Service.Name & " service could not be started." &
        ↪"<BR>"
    End If
End If
```

Stopping a Service Using a VBScript Active Server Page

```
Dim Computer
Dim ComputerName
Dim ComputerDomain
Dim Service
Dim TargetService
TargetService = "Target_Service_Name"
ComputerDomain = "Domain_To_Manage"
ComputerName = "Target_Computer_Name"
Set Computer = GetObject("WinNT://" & ComputerDomain & "/" & ComputerName &
↪",computer")
Set Service = Computer.GetObject("service", TargetService)
If Service.Status = 4 Then
    Service.Stop
    Response.Write "The " & Service.Name & " service has been stopped." & "<BR>"
Else
    If Service.Status = 1 then
        Response.Write "The " & Service.Name & " service is already stopped." &
        ↪"<BR>"
    Else
        Response.Write "The " & Service.Name & " service could not be stopped." &
        ↪"<BR>"
    End If
End If
```

Pausing a Service Using a VBScript Active Server Page

```
Dim Computer
Dim ComputerName
Dim ComputerDomain
Dim Service
Dim TargetService
TargetService = "Target_Service_Name"
ComputerDomain = "Domain_To_Manage"
ComputerName = "Target_Computer_Name"
Set Computer = GetObject("WinNT://" & ComputerDomain & "/" & ComputerName &
↪",computer")
Set Service = Computer.GetObject("service", TargetService)
If Service.Status = 4 Then
    Service.Pause
    Response.Write "The " & Service.Name & " service has been paused." & "<BR>"
Else
    If Service.Status = 7 Then
        Response.Write "The " & Service.Name & " service is already paused." &
        ↪"<BR>"
    Else
        Response.Write "The " & Service.Name & " service could not be paused." &
        ↪"<BR>"
    End If
End If
```

Continuing a Paused Service Using a VBScript Active Server Page

```
Dim Computer
Dim ComputerName
Dim ComputerDomain
Dim Service
Dim TargetService
TargetService = "Target_Service_Name"
ComputerDomain = "Domain_To_Manage"
ComputerName = "Target_Computer_Name"
Set Computer = GetObject("WinNT://" & ComputerDomain & "/" & ComputerName &
➥",computer")
Set Service = Computer.GetObject("service", TargetService)
If Service.Status = 7 Then
    Service.Continue
    Response.Write "The " & Service.Name & " service has been unpaused." & "<BR>"
Else
    If Service.Status = 4 Then
        Response.Write "The " & Service.Name & " service is already running." &
        ➥"<BR>"
    End If
End If
```

Setting New Service Password Using VBScript Active Server Page

```
Dim Computer
Dim ComputerName
Dim ComputerDomain
Dim Service
Dim TargetService
Dim NewPassword
TargetService = "Target_Service_Name"
ComputerDomain = "Domain_To_Manage"
ComputerName = "Target_Computer_Name"
NewPassword = "New_Password"
Set Computer = GetObject("WinNT://" & ComputerDomain & "/" & ComputerName &
➥",computer")
Set Service = Computer.GetObject("service", TargetService)
Service.SetPassword(NewPassword)
Service.SetInfo
```

Chapter 7: File and Print Service Management Code

Enumerating Shares on a System Using a VBScript Active Server Page

```
Dim FileService
Dim FileShare
Dim ComputerName
Dim ComputerDomain
```

```
ComputerDomain = "Domain_To_Manage"
ComputerName = "Target_Computer_Name"
Set FileService = GetObject("WinNT://" & ComputerDomain & "/" & ComputerName &
↪"/LanmanServer")
For Each FileShare In FileService
     Response.Write FileShare.Name & "<BR>"
Next
```

Binding to a Specific File Share Using A VBScript Active Server Page

```
Dim FileShare
Dim ComputerName
Dim ComputerDomain
Dim ShareName
ComputerDomain = "Domain_To_Manage"
ComputerName = "Target_Computer_Name"
ShareName = "Target_Share_Name"
Set FileShare = GetObject("WinNT://" & ComputerDomain & "/" & ComputerName &
↪"/LanmanServer/" & ShareName)
```

Querying the File Share Current User Count Using a VBScript Active Server Page

```
Dim FileShare
Dim ComputerName
Dim ComputerDomain
Dim ShareName
ComputerDomain = "Domain_To_Manage"
ComputerName = "Target_Computer_Name"
ShareName = "Target_Share_Name"
Set FileShare = GetObject("WinNT://" & ComputerDomain & "/" & ComputerName &
↪"/LanmanServer/" & ShareName)
Response.Write FileShare.CurrentUserCount
```

Querying the File Share Description (Comment Field) Using a VBScript Active Server Page

```
Dim FileShare
Dim ComputerName
Dim ComputerDomain
Dim ShareName
ComputerDomain = "Domain_To_Manage"
ComputerName = "Target_Computer_Name"
ShareName = "Target_Share_Name"
Set FileShare = GetObject("WinNT://" & ComputerDomain & "/" & ComputerName &
↪"/LanmanServer/" & ShareName)
Response.Write FileShare.Description
```

Setting a New File Share Description Using a VBScript Active Server Page

```
Dim FileShare
Dim ComputerName
Dim ComputerDomain
Dim ShareName
Dim NewFileShareDescription
ComputerDomain = "Domain_To_Manage"
ComputerName = "Target_Computer_Name"
ShareName = "Target_Share_Name"
NewFileShareDescription = "New_File_Share_Description"
Set FileShare = GetObject("WinNT://" & ComputerDomain & "/" & ComputerName & ↵"/LanmanServer/" & ShareName)
FileShare.Description = NewFileShareDescription
FileShare.SetInfo
```

Querying the File Share Host Computer Using a VBScript Active Server Page

```
Dim FileShare
Dim ComputerName
Dim ComputerDomain
Dim ShareName
ComputerDomain = "Domain_To_Manage"
ComputerName = "Target_Computer_Name"
ShareName = "Target_Share_Name"
Set FileShare = GetObject("WinNT://" & ComputerDomain & "/" & ComputerName & ↵"/LanmanServer/" & ShareName)
Response.Write FileShare.HostComputer
```

Querying the File Share Maximum Users Property Value Using a VBScript Active Server Page

```
Dim FileShare
Dim ComputerName
Dim ComputerDomain
Dim ShareName
ComputerDomain = "Domain_To_Manage"
ComputerName = "Target_Computer_Name"
ShareName = "Target_Share_Name"
Set FileShare = GetObject("WinNT://" & ComputerDomain & "/" & ComputerName & ↵"/LanmanServer/" & ShareName)
Response.Write FileShare.MaxUserCount
```

Setting a New Value for the File Share Maximum Users Property Value Using a VBScript Active Server Page

```
Dim FileShare
Dim ComputerName
Dim ComputerDomain
Dim ShareName
Dim NewFileShareMaximumUsers
ComputerDomain = "Domain_To_Manage"
ComputerName = "Target_Computer_Name"
ShareName = "Target_Share_Name"
NewFileShareMaximumUsers = Maximum_Users_Value
Set FileShare = GetObject("WinNT://" & ComputerDomain & "/" & ComputerName & _
"/LanmanServer/" & ShareName)
FileShare.MaxUserCount = NewFileShareMaximumUsers
FileShare.SetInfo
```

Querying the File Share Path Property Value Using a VBScript Active Server Page

```
Dim FileShare
Dim ComputerName
Dim ComputerDomain
Dim ShareName
ComputerDomain = "Domain_To_Manage"
ComputerName = "Target_Computer_Name"
ShareName = "Target_Share_Name"
Set FileShare = GetObject("WinNT://" & ComputerDomain & "/" & ComputerName & _
"/LanmanServer/" & ShareName)
Response.Write FileShare.Path
```

Creating a Share Programmatically Using a VBScript Active Server Page

```
Dim Container
Dim FileShare
Dim ComputerName
Dim ComputerDomain
Dim ShareName
Dim NewFileSharePath
Dim NewFileShareDescription
ComputerDomain = "Domain_To_Manage"
ComputerName = "Target_Computer_Name"
ShareName = "Target_Share_Name"
NewFileSharePath = "Path_To_Share"
NewFileShareDescription = "File_Share_Comment"
Set Container = GetObject("WinNT://" & ComputerDomain & "/" & ComputerName & _
"/LanmanServer")
Set FileShare = Container.Create("fileshare", ShareName)
FileShare.Path = NewFileSharePath
FileShare.Description = NewFileShareDescription
FileShare.MaxUserCount = -1
FileShare.SetInfo
```

Removing a Share Using a VBScript Active Server Page

```
Dim Container
Dim ComputerName
Dim ComputerDomain
Dim ShareName
ComputerDomain = "Domain_To_Manage"
ComputerName = "Target_Computer_Name"
ShareName = "Target_Share_Name"
Set Container = GetObject("WinNT://" & ComputerDomain & "/" & ComputerName &
↪"/LanmanServer")
Call Container.Delete("fileshare", ShareName)
```

Enumerating User Sessions Using a VBScript Active Server Page

```
Dim FileService
Dim ComputerName
Dim ComputerDomain
Dim Session
ComputerDomain = "Domain_To_Manage"
ComputerName = "Target_Computer_Name"
Set FileService = GetObject("WinNT://" & ComputerDomain & "/" & ComputerName &
↪"/LanmanServer")
For Each Session In FileService.Sessions
    Response.Write "Session Name:" & Session.Name & " established by User: " &
    ↪Session.User & _
" from Computer: " & Session.Computer & " Connect Time: " & Session.ConnectTime & _
" Idle Time: " & Session.IdleTime & "<BR>"
Next
```

Managing Individual Sessions Using a VBScript Active Server Page

```
Dim FileService
Dim ComputerName
Dim ComputerDomain
Dim Session
Dim Collection
Dim UserSessionName
Dim UserSession
ComputerDomain = "Domain_To_Manage"
ComputerName = "Target_Computer_Name"
UserSessionName = "Target_Session"
Set FileService = GetObject("WinNT://" & ComputerDomain & "/" & ComputerName &
↪"/LanmanServer")
Set Collection = FileService.Sessions
Set UserSession = Collection.GetObject(UserSessionName)
```

Disconnecting a Single User Session Using a VBScript Active Server Page

```
Dim FileService
Dim ComputerName
Dim ComputerDomain
Dim Session
Dim Collection
Dim UserSessionName
ComputerDomain = "Domain_To_Manage"
ComputerName = "Target_Computer_Name"
UserSessionName = "Target_Session"
Set FileService = GetObject("WinNT://" & ComputerDomain & "/" & ComputerName & _
➥"/LanmanServer")
Set Collection = FileService.Sessions
Collection.Remove (UserSessionName)
```

Disconnecting All User Sessions Using a VBScript Active Server Page

```
Dim FileService
Dim ComputerName
Dim ComputerDomain
Dim Session
Dim Collection
ComputerDomain = "Domain_To_Manage"
ComputerName = "Target_Computer_Name"
Set FileService = GetObject("WinNT://" & ComputerDomain & "/" & ComputerName & _
➥"/LanmanServer")
Set Collection = FileService.Sessions
For Each Session In Collection
     Collection.Remove (Session.Name)
Next
```

Enumerating Open Resources Using a VBScript Active Server Page

```
Dim FileService
Dim ComputerName
Dim ComputerDomain
Dim Resource
ComputerDomain = "Domain_To_Manage"
ComputerName = "Target_Computer_Name"
Set FileService = GetObject("WinNT://" & ComputerDomain & "/" & ComputerName & _
➥"/LanmanServer")
For Each Resource In FileService.Resources
    Response.Write "ResourceID: " & Resource.Name & " Resource: " & Resource.Path & _
    ➥" Opened by: " & _
Resource.User & " Lock Count: " & Resource.LockCount & "<BR>"
Next
```

Examining the Properties of a Single Open Resource Using a VBScript Active Server Page

```
Dim FileService
Dim ComputerName
Dim ComputerDomain
Dim ResourceUser
Dim ResourcePath
Dim Resource
Dim Collection
ComputerDomain = "Domain_To_Manage"
ComputerName = "Target_Computer_Name"
ResourceUser = "Target_Username"
Set FileService = GetObject("WinNT://" & ComputerDomain & "/" & ComputerName & "/LanmanServer")
Set Collection = FileService.Resources
Response.Write "User " & ResourceUser & " has the following resources open:" & "<BR>" For Each Resource In Collection
    If Resource.User = ResourceUser Then
        Response.Write Resource.Path & "<BR>"
    End If
Next
```

Enumerating Print Queues Using a VBScript Active Server Page

```
Dim ComputerName
Dim ComputerDomain
Dim Container
Dim PrintQueue
ComputerDomain = "Domain_To_Manage"
ComputerName = "Target_Computer_Name"
Set Container = GetObject("WinNT://" & ComputerDomain & "/" & ComputerName)
Container.Filter = Array("PrintQueue")
For Each PrintQueue In Container
    Response.Write PrintQueue.Name & "<BR>"
Next
```

Binding a Specific Print Queue Using a VBScript Active Server Page

```
Dim ComputerName
Dim ComputerDomain
Dim PrintQueueName
Dim PrintQueue
ComputerDomain = "Domain_To_Manage"
ComputerName = "Target_Computer_Name"
PrintQueueName = "Target_Print_Queue"
Set PrintQueue = GetObject("WinNT://" & ComputerDomain & "/" & ComputerName & "/" & PrintQueueName)
```

Querying Single-Valued Print Queue Properties Using a VBScript Active Server Page

```
Dim ComputerName
Dim ComputerDomain
Dim PrintQueueName
Dim PrintQueue
ComputerDomain = "Domain_To_Manage"
ComputerName = "Target_Computer_Name"
PrintQueueName = "Target_Print_Queue"
Set PrintQueue = GetObject("WinNT://" & ComputerDomain & "/" & ComputerName & "/" &
➥PrintQueueName)
Response.Write PrintQueue.Model
```

Querying Multi-Valued Print Queue Properties Using a VBScript Active Server Page

```
Dim ComputerName
Dim ComputerDomain
Dim PrintQueueName
Dim PrintQueue
Dim Item
ComputerDomain = "Domain_To_Manage"
ComputerName = "Target_Computer_Name"
PrintQueueName = "Target_Print_Queue"
Set PrintQueue = GetObject("WinNT://" & ComputerDomain & "/" & ComputerName & "/" &
➥PrintQueueName)
If IsArray(PrintQueue.PrintDevices) Then
    For Each Item In PrintQueue.PrintDevices
        Response.Write Item & "<BR>"
    Next
Else
    Response.Write PrintQueue.PrintDevices & "<BR>"
End If
```

Querying Queue Status Using a VBScript Active Server Page

```
Dim PrintQueue
Dim ComputerName
Dim ComputerDomain
Dim PrintQueueName
ComputerDomain = "Domain_To_Manage"
ComputerName = "Target_Computer_Name"
PrintQueueName = "Target_Print_Queue"
Set PrintQueue = GetObject("WinNT://" & ComputerDomain & "/" & ComputerName & "/" &
➥PrintQueueName)
Response.Write PrintQueue.Status
```

Pausing a Print Queue Using a VBScript Active Server Page

```
Dim PrintQueue
Dim ComputerName
Dim ComputerDomain
Dim PrintQueueName
ComputerDomain = "Domain_To_Manage"
ComputerName = "Target_Computer_Name"
PrintQueueName = "Target_Print_Queue"
Set PrintQueue = GetObject("WinNT://" & ComputerDomain & "/" & ComputerName & "/" &
➥PrintQueueName)
PrintQueue.Pause
```

Resuming a Print Queue Using a VBScript Active Server Page

```
Dim PrintQueue
Dim ComputerName
Dim ComputerDomain
Dim PrintQueueName
ComputerDomain = "Domain_To_Manage"
ComputerName = "Target_Computer_Name"
PrintQueueName = "Target_Print_Queue"
Set PrintQueue = GetObject("WinNT://" & ComputerDomain & "/" & ComputerName & "/" &
➥PrintQueueName)
PrintQueue.Resume
```

Enumerating Print Jobs in a Print Queue Using a VBScript Active Server Page

```
Dim PrintQueue
Dim ComputerName
Dim ComputerDomain
Dim PrintQueueName
Dim PrintJob
ComputerDomain = "Domain_To_Manage"
ComputerName = "Target_Computer_Name"
PrintQueueName = "Target_Print_Queue"
Set PrintQueue = GetObject("WinNT://" & ComputerDomain & "/" & ComputerName & "/" &
PrintQueueName)
For Each PrintJob in PrintQueue.PrintJobs
    Response.Write PrintJob.Name & " " & PrintJob.Description & " " & PrintJob.User
    ➥& " " & PrintJob.TotalPages & "<BR>"
Next
```

Changing the Priority of a Queued Print Job for a Specific Username Using a VBScript Active Server Page

```
Dim PrintQueue
Dim ComputerName
Dim ComputerDomain
Dim PrintQueueName
Dim PrintJob
```

```
Dim UserToPrioritize
ComputerDomain = "Domain_To_Manage"
ComputerName = "Target_Computer_Name"
PrintQueueName = "Target_Print_Queue"
UserToPrioritize = "User_To_Elevate_Priority"
Set PrintQueue = GetObject("WinNT://" & ComputerDomain & "/" & ComputerName & "/" &
➥PrintQueueName)
For Each PrintJob in PrintQueue.PrintJobs
    If PrintJob.User = UserToPrioritize Then
        PrintJob.Priority = 99
        PrintJob.SetInfo
    End If
Next
```

Removing Jobs from the Print Queue Using a VBScript Active Server Page

```
Dim PrintQueue
Dim PrintJob
Dim ComputerName
Dim ComputerDomain
Dim PrintQueueName
Dim Collection
Dim UserToRemove
ComputerDomain = "Domain_To_Manage"
ComputerName = "Target_Computer_Name"
PrintQueueName = "Target_Print_Queue"
UserToRemove = "User_To_Remove_From_Queue"
Set PrintQueue = GetObject("WinNT://" & ComputerDomain & "/" & ComputerName & "/" &
➥PrintQueueName)
Set Collection = PrintQueue.PrintJobs
For Each PrintJob In PrintQueue.PrintJobs
    If PrintJob.User = UserToRemove Then
        Collection.Remove (CStr(PrintJob.Name))
    End If
Next
```

Purging All Print Job Entries from the Queue Using a VBScript Active Server Page

```
Dim PrintQueue
Dim ComputerName
Dim ComputerDomain
Dim PrintQueueName
ComputerDomain = "Domain_To_Manage"
ComputerName = "Target_Computer_Name"
PrintQueueName = "Target_Print_Queue"
Set PrintQueue = GetObject("WinNT://" & ComputerDomain & "/" & ComputerName & "/" &
➥PrintQueueName)
PrintQueue.Purge
```

Chapter 8: IIS Site Operations Code

Backing Up the IIS Metabase Using a VBScript Active Server Page

```
Dim IisComputer
Dim Flags
Dim TargetComputer
TargetComputer = "Target_Server_Name"
Flags = (MD_BACKUP_SAVE_FIRST Or MD_BACKUP_FORCE_BACKUP)
Set IIsComputer = GetObject("IIS://" & TargetComputer)
IIsComputer.Backup "MyBackup10", MD_BACKUP_NEXT_VERSION, Flags
```

Enumerating Existing Backups Using a VBScript Active Server Page

```
On Error Resume Next
Dim IIsComputer
Dim TargetComputer
Dim Version
Dim Index
Dim TermCond
Dim Location
Dim UTCDate
TargetComputer = "Target_Server_Name"
Set IIsComputer = GetObject("IIS://" & TargetComputer)
Do While TermCond <> 1
  IIsComputer.EnumBackups "", Index, Version, Location, UTCDate
  If Err.Number <> 0 Then
    Exit Do
  End If
  Response.Write Location & " Version: " & Version & " " & UTCDate & "<BR>"
  Index = Index + 1
Loop
```

Restoring an Existing Metabase Backup Using a VBScript Active Server Page

```
Dim IIsComputer
Dim TargetComputer
Dim BackupLocation
TargetComputer = "Target_Server_Name"
BackupLocation = "Backup_Location_On_Target_Server"
Set IIsComputer = GetObject("IIS://" & TargetComputer)
IIsComputer.Restore BackupLocation, MD_BACKUP_HIGHEST_VERSION, 0
```

Deleting an Existing Metabase Backup Using a VBScript Active Server Page

```
Dim IIsComputer
Dim TargetComputer
Dim BackupLocation
TargetComputer = "Target_Server_Name"
BackupLocation = "Backup_Location"
Set IIsComputer = GetObject("IIS://" & TargetComputer)
IIsComputer.DeleteBackup BackupLocation, MD_BACKUP_HIGHEST_VERSION
```

Querying *MaxBandwidth* Using a VBScript Active Server Page

```
Dim IIsComputer
Dim TargetComputer
Dim RetVal
TargetComputer = "Target_Server_Name"
Set IIsComputer = GetObject("IIS://" & TargetComputer)
Response.Write IIsComputer.MaxBandwidth
```

Setting a New Value for *MaxBandwidth* Using a VBScript Active Server Page

```
Dim IIsComputer
Dim TargetComputer
Dim NewValue
TargetComputer = "Target_Server_Name"
NewValue = New_Throttle_Value_In_Bytes
Set IIsComputer = GetObject("IIS://" & TargetComputer)
IIsComputer.MaxBandwidth = NewValue
IIsComputer.SetInfo
```

Viewing the List of Current Server-Defined MIME Type Mappings Using a VBScript Active Server Page

```
Dim IIsComputer
Dim TargetComputer
Dim MimeMapping
TargetComputer = "Target_Server_Name"
Set IIsComputer = GetObject("IIS://" & TargetComputer & "/MimeMap")
Response.Write "Registered File Types:" & "<BR>"
For Each MimeMapping in IISComputer.MimeMap
   Response.Write "Extension: " & MimeMapping.Extension & " MIME Content Type: " &
   ➥MimeMapping.MimeType & "<BR>"
Next
```

Adding a New Server-Defined MIME Mapping Using a VBScript Active Server Page

```
Dim IIsComputer
Dim TargetComputer
Dim MimeMapping
Dim NewMimeMapping
Dim MimeExtension
Dim MimeType
Dim i
TargetComputer = "Target_Server_Name"
MimeExtension = "New_MIME_Extension"
MimeType = "New_MIME_Type"
Set IIsComputer = GetObject("IIS://" & TargetComputer & "/MimeMap")
NewMimeMapping = IIsComputer.GetEx("MimeMap")
i = UBound(NewMimeMapping) + 1
ReDim Preserve NewMimeMapping(i)
Set NewMimeMapping(i) = CreateObject("MimeMap")
NewMimeMapping(i).MimeType = MimeType
NewMimeMapping(i).Extension = MimeExtension
IIsComputer.PutEx ADS_PROPERTY_UPDATE, "MimeMap", NewMimeMapping
IIsComputer.SetInfo
```

Removing a Server-Defined MIME Mapping Using a VBScript Active Server Page

```
Dim IIsComputer
Dim TargetComputer
Dim MimeMapping
Dim MapToDelete
Dim NewMimeMapping
Dim i
MapToDelete = "Extension_To_Delete_From_MIME_Map"
TargetComputer = "Target_Server_Name"
Set IIsComputer = GetObject("IIS://" & TargetComputer & "/MimeMap")
NewMimeMapping = IIsComputer.MimeMap
For Each MimeMapping In IIsComputer.MimeMap
    If MimeMapping.Extension <> MapToDelete Then
        ReDim Preserve NewMimeMapping(i)
          Set NewMimeMapping(i) = CreateObject("MimeMap")
        NewMimeMapping(i).MimeType = MimeMapping.MimeType
        NewMimeMapping(i).Extension = MimeMapping.Extension
        i = i + 1
    End If
Next
Dim MimeItem
For Each MimeItem In NewMimeMapping
    Response.Write MimeItem.MimeType & "<BR>"
Next
IIsComputer.PutEx ADS_PROPERTY_UPDATE, "MimeMap", NewMimeMapping
'IIsComputer.SetInfo
```

Querying Current Logging Status Using a VBScript Active Server Page

```
Dim Site
Dim ServerName
Dim SiteIndex
ServerName = "IIS_Server_Name"
SiteIndex = Site_Index_Value
Set Site = GetObject("IIS://" & ServerName & "/W3SVC/" & SiteIndex)
Response.Write Site.LogType
```

Setting Logging Status Using a VBScript Active Server Page

```
Dim Site
Dim ServerName
Dim SiteIndex
ServerName = "IIS_Server_Name"
SiteIndex = Site_Index_Value
Set Site = GetObject("IIS://" & ServerName & "/W3SVC/" & SiteIndex)
Site.LogType = 1
Site.SetInfo
```

Querying Active Log Format Using a VBScript Active Server Page

```
Dim Site
Dim Log
Dim ServerName
Dim SiteIndex
ServerName = "IIS_Server_Name"
SiteIndex = Site_Index_Value
Set Site = GetObject("IIS://" & ServerName & "/W3SVC/" & SiteIndex)
Set Log = GetObject("IIS://" & ServerName & "/logging")
For Each Item In Log
  If Site.LogPluginCLSID = Item.LogModuleID Then
    Response.Write Item.Name & "<BR>"
  End If
Next
```

Setting Active Log Format Using a VBScript Active Server Page

```
Dim Site
Dim Log
Dim ServerName
Dim SiteIndex
Dim NewLogFormatName
ServerName = "IIS_Server_Name"
SiteIndex = Site_Index_Value
NewLogFormatName = "NCSA Common Log File Format"
'NewLogFormatName = "ODBC Logging"
'NewLogFormatName = "Microsoft IIS Log File Format"
'NewLogFormatName = "W3C Extended Log File Format"
```

```
Set Site = GetObject("IIS://" & ServerName & "/W3SVC/" & SiteIndex)
Set Log = GetObject("IIS://" & ServerName & "/logging")
For Each Item In Log
    If Item.Name = NewLogFormatName Then
        Site.LogPluginCLSID = Item.LogModuleID
        Site.SetInfo
    End If
Next
```

Querying New Log Time Period Using a VBScript Active Server Page

```
Dim Site
Dim ServerName
Dim SiteIndex
ServerName = "IIS_Server_Name"
SiteIndex = Site_Index_Value
Set Site = GetObject("IIS://" & ServerName & "/W3SVC/" & SiteIndex)
Response.Write Site.LogFilePeriod
```

Setting New Log Time Period Using a VBScript Active Server Page

```
Dim Site
Dim ServerName
Dim SiteIndex
Dim NewLogFilePeriod
ServerName = "IIS_Server_Name"
SiteIndex = Site_Index_Value
NewLogFilePeriod = 1
Set Site = GetObject("IIS://" & ServerName & "/W3SVC/" & SiteIndex)
Site.LogFilePeriod = NewLogFilePeriod
Site.SetInfo
```

Querying Maximum Log File Size Using a VBScript Active Server Page

```
Dim Site
Dim ServerName
Dim SiteIndex
ServerName = "IIS_Server_Name"
SiteIndex = Site_Index_Value
Set Site = GetObject("IIS://" & ServerName & "/W3SVC/" & SiteIndex)
Response.Write Site.LogFileTruncateSize
```

Setting Maximum Log File Size Using a VBScript Active Server Page

```
Dim Site
Dim ServerName
Dim SiteIndex
Dim NewLogFileSize
ServerName = "IIS_Server_Name"
```

```
SiteIndex = Site_Index_Value
NewLogFileSize = 1048576
Set Site = GetObject("IIS://" & ServerName & "/W3SVC/" & SiteIndex)
Site.LogFileTruncateSize = NewLogFileSize
Site.SetInfo
```

Querying Extended Logging Options Using a VBScript Active Server Page

```
Dim Site
Dim ServerName
Dim SiteIndex
ServerName = "IIS_Server_Name"
SiteIndex = Site_Index_Value
Set Site = GetObject("IIS://" & ServerName & "/W3SVC/" & SiteIndex)
Response.Write "Log Date: " & Site.LogExtFileDate & "<BR>"
Response.Write "Log Time: " & Site.LogExtFileTime & "<BR>"
Response.Write "Log Client IP Address: " & Site.LogExtFileClientIp & "<BR>"
Response.Write "Log User Name: " & Site.LogExtFileUserName & "<BR>"
Response.Write "Log Service Name: " & Site.LogExtFileSiteName & "<BR>"
Response.Write "Log Server Name: " & Site.LogExtFileComputerName & "<BR>"
Response.Write "Log Server IP: " & Site.LogExtFileServerIp & "<BR>"
Response.Write "Log Server Port: " & Site.LogExtFileServerPort & "<BR>"
Response.Write "Log Method: " & Site.LogExtFileMethod & "<BR>"
Response.Write "Log URI Stem: " & Site.LogExtFileUriStem & "<BR>"
Response.Write "Log URI Query: " & Site.LogExtFileUriQuery & "<BR>"
Response.Write "Log Http Status: " & Site.LogExtFileHttpStatus & "<BR>"
Response.Write "Log Win32 Status: " & Site.LogExtFileWin32Status & "<BR>"
Response.Write "Log Bytes Sent: " & Site.LogExtFileBytesSent & "<BR>"
Response.Write "Log Bytes Received: " & Site.LogExtFileBytesRecv & "<BR>"
Response.Write "Log Time Taken: " & Site.LogExtFileTimeTaken & "<BR>"
Response.Write "Log Protocol Version: " & Site.LogExtFileProtocolVersion & "<BR>"
Response.Write "Log User Agent: " & Site.LogExtFileUserAgent & "<BR>"
Response.Write "Log Cookie: " & Site.LogExtFileCookie & "<BR>"
Response.Write "Log Referrer: " & Site.LogExtFileReferer & "<BR>"
```

Setting Extended Logging Options Using a VBScript Active Server Page

```
Dim Site
Dim ServerName
Dim SiteIndex
ServerName = "IIS_Server_Name"
SiteIndex = Site_Index_Value
Set Site = GetObject("IIS://" & ServerName & "/W3SVC/" & SiteIndex)
Site.LogExtFileDate = True
Site.LogExtFileTime = True
Site.LogExtFileClientIp = True
Site.LogExtFileUserName = True
Site.LogExtFileSiteName = True
Site.LogExtFileComputerName = True
```

```
Site.LogExtFileServerIp = True
Site.LogExtFileServerPort = True
Site.LogExtFileMethod = True
Site.LogExtFileUriStem = True
Site.LogExtFileUriQuery = True
Site.LogExtFileHttpStatus = True
Site.LogExtFileWin32Status = True
Site.LogExtFileBytesSent = True
Site.LogExtFileBytesRecv = True
Site.LogExtFileTimeTaken = True
Site.LogExtFileProtocolVersion = True
Site.LogExtFileUserAgent = True
Site.LogExtFileCookie = True
Site.LogExtFileReferer = True
Site.SetInfo
```

Querying ODBC Logging Information Using a VBScript Active Server Page

```
Dim Site
Dim ServerName
Dim SiteIndex
ServerName = "IIS_Server_Name"
SiteIndex = Site_Index_Value
Set Site = GetObject("IIS://" & ServerName & "/W3SVC/" & SiteIndex)
Response.Write Site.LogOdbcDataSource & "<BR>"
Response.Write Site.LogOdbcPassword & "<BR>"
Response.Write Site.LogOdbcTableName & "<BR>"
Response.Write Site.LogOdbcUserName & "<BR>"
```

Setting ODBC Logging Information Using a VBScript Active Server Page

```
Dim Site
Dim ServerName
Dim SiteIndex
Dim ODBC_DSN
Dim DBPassword
Dim TableName
Dim UserName
ODBC_DSN = "Name_of_Data_Source_to_Use_With_ODBC_Logging"
DBPassword = "DB_Access_Credential"
TableName = "Logging_Table_in_DB"
UserName = "DB_Access_Credential"
ServerName = "IIS_Server_Name"
SiteIndex = Site_Index_Value
Set Site = GetObject("IIS://" & ServerName & "/W3SVC/" & SiteIndex)
Site.LogOdbcDataSource = ODBC_DSN
Site.LogOdbcPassword = DBPassword
Site.LogOdbcTableName = TableName
Site.LogOdbcUserName = UserName
Site.SetInfo
```

Enumerating WWW Virtual Sites on an IIS Server Using a VBScript Active Server Page

```
Dim Parent
Dim Child
Dim ServerName
ServerName = "IIS_Server_Name"
Set Parent = GetObject("IIS://" & ServerName & "/W3SVC")
For Each Child In Parent
    If IsNumeric(Child.Name) then
            Response.Write "ProgrammaticID: " & Child.Name & "Friendly Name: " & Child.ServerComment & "<BR>"
    End If
Next
```

Enumerating FTP Virtual Sites on an IIS Server Using a VBScript Active Server Page

```
Dim Parent
Dim Child
Dim ServerName
ServerName = "IIS_Server_Name"
Set Parent = GetObject("IIS://" & ServerName & "/MSFTPSVC")
For Each Child In Parent
    If IsNumeric(Child.Name) Then
        Response.Write Child.Name & " - " & Child.ServerComment & "<BR>"
    End If
Next
```

Finding the Index Number for a Site Based on the *ServerComment* Property Using a VBScript Active Server Page

```
Dim Sites
Dim Site
Dim SearchTerm
Dim Counter
Dim IndexValue
Dim ServerName
SearchTerm = "Site_Description_String"
ServerName = "IIS_Server_Name"
Counter = 0
Set Sites = GetObject("IIS:\\" & ServerName & "\w3svc")
For Each Site In Sites
    If IsNumeric(Site.Name) Then
        If LCase(Site.ServerComment) = LCase(SearchTerm) Then
            Counter = Counter + 1
            IndexValue = Site.Name
        End If
    End If
Next
```

```
    Select Case Counter
        Case 0
            Response.Write "The referenced site could not be found.  Please enter a
            ⇒new search term." & "<BR>"
        Case 1
            Response.Write "The index value for site '" & SearchTerm & "' is " &
            ⇒IndexValue & "<BR>"
        Case Is > 1
            Response.Write "More than one site uses the value '" & SearchTerm & "' for
            ⇒the &" _
            ; "ServerComments property.  Assure all values are unique before
continuing." & "<BR>"
    End Select
```

Creating a New Web Site Using a VBScript Active Server Page

```
        On Error Resume Next
        Dim Parent
        Dim Child
        Dim NewSite
        Dim NewRoot
        Dim ServerName
        Dim Index
        Dim SiteName
        Dim SitePath
        SiteName = "Friendly_Site_Name"
        ServerName = "IIS_Server_Name"
        SitePath = "Site_Path"
        Set Parent = GetObject("IIS://" & ServerName & "/W3SVC")
        For Each Child In Parent
            If IsNumeric(Child.Name) Then
                If Index < Child.Name Then
                    Index = Child.Name
                End If
            End If
        Next
        Index = Index + 1
        Set NewSite = Parent.Create("IIsWebServer", Index)
        NewSite.ServerComment = SiteName
        NewSite.SetInfo
        Set NewRoot = NewSite.Create("IIsWebVirtualDir", "Root")
        NewRoot.Path = SitePath
        NewRoot.SetInfo
```

Creating a New FTP Site Using a VBScript Active Server Page

```
        Dim Parent
        Dim Child
        Dim NewSite
        Dim NewRoot
        Dim ServerName
        Dim Index
```

```
        Dim SiteName
        Dim SitePath
        Dim SiteIPAddress
        Dim SiteTCPPort
        SiteName = "Friendly_Site_Name"
        ServerName = "IIS_Server_Name"
        SitePath = "Site_Path"
        SiteIPAddress = ""
        SiteTCPPort = "21"
        'SiteIPAddress = "xxx.xxx.xxx.xxx"
        'SiteTCPPort = "TCP_Port_for_Server"
        Set Parent = GetObject("IIS://" & ServerName & "/MSFTPSVC")
        For Each Child In Parent
            If IsNumeric(Child.Name) Then
                If Index < Child.Name Then
                    Index = Child.Name
                End If
            End If
        Next
        Index = Index + 1
        Set NewSite = Parent.Create("IIsFTPServer", Index)
        NewSite.ServerComment = SiteName
        NewSite.ServerBindings = Array(SiteIPAddress & ":" & SiteTCPPort & ":")
        NewSite.SetInfo
        Set NewRoot = NewSite.Create("IIsFTPVirtualDir", "Root")
        NewRoot.Path = SitePath
        NewRoot.SetInfo
```

Deleting a Site Using the *ServerComment* Property Using a VBScript Active Server Page

```
        Dim Sites
        Dim Site
        Dim SearchTerm
        Dim Counter
        Dim IndexValue
        Dim ServerName
        SearchTerm = "Site_Description_String"
        ServerName = "IIS_Server_Name"
        Counter = 0
        Set Sites = GetObject("IIS:\\" & ServerName & "\w3svc")
        For Each Site In Sites
            If IsNumeric(Site.Name) Then
                If LCase(Site.ServerComment) = LCase(SearchTerm) Then
                    Counter = Counter + 1
                    IndexValue = Site.Name
                End If
            End If
        Next
        Select Case Counter
            Case 0
                Response.Write "The referenced site could not be found.  Please enter a
                ↳new search term."
```

```
            Case 1
                Call Sites.Delete("IIsWebServer", IndexValue)
                Set Sites = Nothing
                Response.Write "Site '" & SearchTerm & "' was deleted successfully."
            Case Is > 1
                Response.Write "More than one site uses the value '" & SearchTerm & "' for
                ↪the " _
; "ServerComments property.  Assure all values are unique before continuing."
        End Select
```

Deleting an FTP Site Using a VBScript Active Server Page

```
        Dim Sites
        Dim Site
        Dim SearchTerm
        Dim Counter
        Dim IndexValue
        Dim ServerName
        SearchTerm = "Site_Description_String"
        ServerName = "IIS_Server_Name"
        Counter = 0
        Set Sites = GetObject("IIS:\\" & ServerName & "\MSFTPSVC")
        For Each Site In Sites
            If IsNumeric(Site.Name) Then
                If LCase(Site.ServerComment) = LCase(SearchTerm) Then
                    Counter = Counter + 1
                    IndexValue = Site.Name
                End If
            End If
        Next
        Select Case Counter
            Case 0
                Response.Write "The referenced site could not be found.  Please enter a
new search term."
            Case 1
                Call Sites.Delete("IIsFTPServer", IndexValue)
                Set Sites = Nothing
                Response.Write "Site '" & SearchTerm & "' was deleted successfully."
            Case Is > 1
                Response.Write "More than one site uses the value '" & SearchTerm & "' for
                ↪the " & ServerComments & _
" property.  Assure all values are unique before continuing."
        End Select
```

Creating a New Virtual Directory Using a VBScript Active Server Page

```
        Dim Parent
        Dim NewVDir
        Dim ServerName
        Dim VDirPath
        Dim VDirName
        Dim Index
```

```
ServerName = "IIS_Server_Name"
VDirPath = "Path_for_New_Virtual_Directory"
VDirName = "Name_For_Virtual_Directory"
Index = Site_Index_Integer
Set Parent = GetObject("IIS://" & ServerName & "/W3SVC/" & Index & "/ROOT")
Set NewVDir = Parent.Create("IIsWebVirtualDir", VDirName)
NewVDir.SetInfo
NewVDir.Path = VDirPath
NewVDir.SetInfo
```

Creating a New FTP Virtual Directory Using a VBScript Active Server Page

```
Dim Parent
Dim NewVDir
Dim ServerName
Dim VDirPath
Dim VDirName
Dim Index
ServerName = "IIS_Server_Name"
VDirPath = "Path_for_New_Virtual_Directory"
VDirName = "Name_For_Virtual_Directory"
Index = Site_Index_Integer
Set Parent = GetObject("IIS://" & ServerName & "/MSFTPSVC/" & Index & "/ROOT")
Set NewVDir = Parent.Create("IIsFTPVirtualDir", VDirName)
NewVDir.SetInfo
NewVDir.Path = VDirPath
NewVDir.SetInfo
```

Removing an Existing Virtual Directory Using a VBScript Active Server Page

```
Dim Parent
Dim ServerName
Dim VDirName
Dim Index
ServerName = "IIS_Server_Name"
VDirName = "Name_For_Virtual_Directory"
Index = Site_Index_Value
Set Parent = GetObject("IIS://" & ServerName & "/W3SVC/" & Index & "/ROOT")
Call Parent.Delete("IIsWebVirtualDir", VDirName)
Set Parent = Nothing
```

Removing an Existing FTP Virtual Directory Using a VBScript Active Server Page

```
Dim Parent
Dim ServerName
Dim VDirName
Dim Index
ServerName = "IIS_Server_Name"
```

```
VDirName = "Name_For_Virtual_Directory
Index = Site_Index_Value
Set Parent = GetObject("IIS://" & ServerName & "/MSFTPSVC/" & Index & "/ROOT")
Call Parent.Delete("IIsFTPVirtualDir", VDirName)
```

Managing Web Directories and Files Using a VBScript Active Server Page

```
Dim VirtualDirectory
Dim ServerName
Dim Index
ServerName = "IIS_Server_Name"
Index = Site_Index_Value
Set VirtualDirectory = GetObject("IIS://" & ServerName & "/W3SVC/" & Index & "/ROOT")
For Each Item In VirtualDirectory
    Response.Write Item.Name & "<BR>"
Next
```

Adding an Entry in the Metabase for a File System Directory Using a VBScript Active Server Page

```
Dim VirtualDirectory
Dim WebDir
Dim ServerName
Dim FileName
Dim Index
Dim VirtualDirectoryName
ServerName = "IIS_Server_Name"
DirName = "Directory_Name_To_Enter"
Index = Site_Index
Set VirtualDirectory = GetObject("IIS://" & ServerName & "/W3SVC/" & Index & "/ROOT")
Set WebDir = VirtualDirectory.Create("IIsWebDirectory", DirName)
WebDir.SetInfo
```

Adding an Entry in the Metabase for a File in the File System Using a VBScript Active Server Page

```
Dim VirtualDirectory
Dim WebFile
Dim ServerName
Dim FileName
Dim Index
Dim VirtualDirectoryName
ServerName = "IIS_Server_Name"
FileName = "File_Name_To_Enter"
Index = Site_Index
Set VirtualDirectory = GetObject("IIS://" & ServerName & "/W3SVC/" & Index & "/ROOT")
Set WebFile = VirtualDirectory.Create("IIsWebFile", FileName)
WebFile.SetInfo
```

Querying Site Status Using a VBScript Active Server Page

```
Dim Site
Dim ServerName
Dim Index
ServerName = "IIS_Server_Name"
Index = Site_Index_Value
Set Site = GetObject("IIS://" & ServerName & "/W3SVC/" & Index)
Select Case Site.ServerState
    Case 1
        Response.Write "Starting"
    Case 2
        Response.Write "Started"
    Case 3
        Response.Write "Stopping"
    Case 4
        Response.Write "Stopped"
    Case 5
        Response.Write "Pausing"
    Case 6
        Response.Write "Paused"
    Case 7
        Response.Write "Continuing"
End Select
```

Starting a Site Using a VBScript Active Server Page

```
Dim Site
Dim ServerName
Dim Index
ServerName = "IIS_Server_Name"
Index = Site_Index_Value
Set Site = GetObject("IIS://" & ServerName & "/W3SVC/" & Index)
If Site.ServerState = 4 or Site.ServerState = 3 Then
   Site.Start
   Response.Write "Request to start site " & Site.ServerComment & " was issued."
End If
```

Stopping a Site Using a VBScript Active Server Page

```
Dim Site
Dim ServerName
Dim Index
ServerName = "IIS_Server_Name"
Index = Site_Index_Value
Set Site = GetObject("IIS://" & ServerName & "/W3SVC/" & Index)
If Site.ServerState = 2 or Site.ServerState = 1 Then
   Site.Stop
   Response.Write "Request to stop site " & Site.ServerComment & " was issued."
End If
```

Pausing a Site Using a VBScript Active Server Page

```
Dim Site
Dim ServerName
Dim Index
ServerName = "IIS_Server_Name"
Index = Site_Index_Value
Set Site = GetObject("IIS://" & ServerName & "/W3SVC/" & Index)
If Site.ServerState = 1 or Site.ServerState = 2 Then
   Site.Pause
   Response.Write "Request to pause site " & Site.ServerComment & " was issued."
End If
```

Continuing a Paused Site Using a VBScript Active Server Page

```
Dim Site
Dim ServerName
Dim Index
ServerName = "IIS_Server_Name"
Index = Site_Index_Value
Set Site = GetObject("IIS://" & ServerName & "/W3SVC/" & Index)
If Site.ServerState = 6 or Site.ServerState = 5 Then
   Site.Continue
   Response.Write "Request to continue paused site " & Site.ServerComment & " was
   ↪issued."
End If
```

Chapter 9: IIS Web Site Operations Code

Querying *ServerComment* Using a VBScript Active Server Page

```
Dim Site
Dim ServerName
Dim Index
ServerName = "IIS_Server_Name"
Index = Site_Index_Integer
Set Site = GetObject("IIS://" & ServerName & "/W3SVC/" & Index)
Response.Write Site.ServerComment
```

Setting *ServerComment* Using a VBScript Active Server Page

```
Dim Site
Dim ServerName
Dim Index
Dim NewServerComment
ServerName = "IIS_Server_Name"
Index = Site_Index_Integer
NewServerComment = "New_Server_Comment_String"
Set Site = GetObject("IIS://" & ServerName & "/W3SVC/" & Index)
Site.ServerComment = NewServerComment
Site.SetInfo
```

Querying *ServerBindings* Using a VBScript Active Server Page

```
Dim Site
Dim ServerName
Dim SiteIndex
ServerName = "IIS_Server_Name"
SiteIndex = Site_Index_Value
Set Site = GetObject("IIS://" & ServerName & "/W3SVC/" & SiteIndex)
For Each Binding In Site.ServerBindings
  Response.Write Binding & "<BR>"
Next
```

Setting *ServerBindings* Using a VBScript Active Server Page

```
Dim Site
Dim ServerName
Dim SiteIndex
Dim NewBindingArray
Dim ServerBindingString1
Dim ServerBindingString2
Dim ServerBindingString3
ServerName = "IIS_Server_Name"
SiteIndex = Site_Index_Value
ServerBindingString1 = "IP_Address:TCP_Port:Hostname"
ServerBindingString2 = "IP_Address:TCP_Port:Hostname"
ServerBindingString3 = "IP_Address:TCP_Port:Hostname"
NewBindingArray = Array(ServerBindingString1, ServerBindingString2,
↪ServerBindingString3)
Set Site = GetObject("IIS://" & ServerName & "/W3SVC/" & SiteIndex)
Site.ServerBindings = NewBindingArray
Site.SetInfo
```

Querying *SecureBindings* Using a VBScript Active Server Page

```
Dim Site
Dim ServerName
Dim SiteIndex
ServerName = "IIS_Server_Name"
SiteIndex = Site_Index_Value
Set Site = GetObject("IIS://" & ServerName & "/W3SVC/" & SiteIndex)
For Each Binding In Site.SecureBindings
  Response.Write Binding & "<BR>"
Next
```

Setting *SecureBindings* Using a VBScript Active Server Page

```
Dim Site
Dim ServerName
Dim SiteIndex
Dim NewBindingArray
Dim ServerBindingString1
Dim ServerBindingString2
```

```
Dim ServerBindingString3
ServerName = "IIS_Server_Name"
SiteIndex = Site_Index_Value
ServerBindingString1 = "IP_Address:TCP_Port:Hostname"
ServerBindingString2 = "IP_Address:TCP_Port:Hostname"
ServerBindingString3 = "IP_Address:TCP_Port:Hostname"
NewBindingArray = Array(ServerBindingString1, ServerBindingString2,
↪ServerBindingString3)
Set Site = GetObject("IIS://" & ServerName & "/W3SVC/" & SiteIndex)
Site.SecureBindings = NewBindingArray
Site.SetInfo
```

Querying Maximum Connections Using a VBScript Active Server Page

```
Dim Site
Dim ServerName
Dim Index
Dim RetVal
ServerName = "IIS_Server_Name"
Index = Site_Index
Set Site = GetObject("IIS://" & ServerName & "/W3SVC/" & Index)
RetVal = Site.MaxConnections
Response.Write RetVal
```

Setting Maximum Connections Using a VBScript Active Server Page

```
Dim Site
Dim ServerName
Dim Index
Dim NewMaxConnections
ServerName = "IIS_Server_Name"
Index = Site_Index
NewMaxConnections = Maximum_Number_of_Connections
Set Site = GetObject("IIS://" & ServerName & "/W3SVC/" & Index)
Site.MaxConnections = NewMaxConnections
Site.SetInfo
```

Querying Connection Timeout Using a VBScript Active Server Page

```
Dim Site
Dim ServerName
Dim Index
Dim RetVal
ServerName = "IIS_Server_Name"
Index = Site_Index
Set Site = GetObject("IIS://" & ServerName & "/W3SVC/" & Index)
RetVal = Site.ConnectionTimeout
Response.Write RetVal
```

Setting Connection Timeout Using a VBScript Active Server Page

```
Dim Site
Dim ServerName
Dim Index
Dim ConnectionTimeout
ServerName = "IIS_Server_Name"
Index = Site_Index_Value
NewConnectionTimeout = Connection_Timeout_in_Seconds
Set Site = GetObject("IIS://" & ServerName & "/W3SVC/" & Index)
Site.ConnectionTimeout = NewConnectionTimeout
Site.SetInfo
```

Querying Operators Using a VBScript Active Server Page

```
Dim Site
Dim ServerName
Dim SiteIndex
ServerName = "IIS_Server_Name"
SiteIndex = Site_Index_Value
Set Site = GetObject("IIS://" & ServerName & "/W3SVC/" & SiteIndex)
Set SecurityDescriptor = Site.AdminAcl
Set DiscretionaryAcl = SecurityDescriptor.DiscretionaryAcl
For Each Item In DiscretionaryAcl
  If Item.AccessMask = 11 Or Item.AccessMask = 262315 Then
    Response.Write Item.Trustee & "<BR>"
  End If
Next
```

Setting a New Operator Using a VBScript Active Server Page

```
Dim Site
Dim ACE
Dim DiscretionaryACL
Dim ServerName
Dim SiteIndex
Dim NewOperator
ServerName = "IIS_Server_Name"
SiteIndex = Site_Index_Value
NewOperator = "New_Operator_in_Format_Domain\Username"
Set Site = GetObject("IIS://" & ServerName & "/W3SVC/" & SiteIndex)
Set SecurityDescriptor = Site.AdminACL
Set DiscretionaryACL = SecurityDescriptor.DiscretionaryACL
Set ACE = CreateObject("AccessControlEntry")
ACE.Trustee = NewOperator
ACE.AccessMask = 11
DiscretionaryACL.AddAce ACE
SecurityDescriptor.DiscretionaryACL = DiscretionaryACL
Site.AdminACL = SecurityDescriptor
Site.SetInfo
```

Removing an Operator Using a VBScript Active Server Page

```
Dim Site
Dim ACE
Dim DiscretionaryACL
Dim ServerName
Dim SiteIndex
Dim OperatorToRemove
ServerName = "IIS_Server_Name"
SiteIndex = Site_Index_Value
OperatorToRemove = "User_Name_to_Remove"
Set Site = GetObject("IIS://" & ServerName & "/W3SVC/" & SiteIndex)
Set SecurityDescriptor = Site.AdminACL
Set DiscretionaryACL = SecurityDescriptor.DiscretionaryACL
Set ACE = CreateObject("AccessControlEntry")
ACE.Trustee = OperatorToRemove
ACE.AccessMask = 11
DiscretionaryACL.RemoveAce ACE
SecurityDescriptor.DiscretionaryACL = DiscretionaryACL
Site.AdminACL = SecurityDescriptor
Site.SetInfo
```

Querying *ServerSize* Using a VBScript Active Server Page

```
Dim Site
Dim ServerName
Dim SiteIndex
ServerName = "IIS_Server_Name"
SiteIndex = Site_Index_Value
Set Site = GetObject("IIS://" & ServerName & "/W3SVC/" & SiteIndex)
Response.Write Site.ServerSize
```

Setting *ServerSize* Using a VBScript Active Server Page

```
Dim Site
Dim ServerName
Dim SiteIndex
Dim NewServerSize
ServerName = "IIS_Server_Name"
SiteIndex = Site_Index_Value
NewServerSize = 0
Set Site = GetObject("IIS://" & ServerName & "/W3SVC/" & SiteIndex)
Site.ServerSize = NewServerSize
Site.SetInfo
```

Querying Maximum Bandwidth for a Site Using a VBScript Active Server Page

```
Dim Site
Dim ServerName
Dim SiteIndex
ServerName = "IIS_Server_Name"
SiteIndex = Site_Index_Value
Set Site = GetObject("IIS://" & ServerName & "/W3SVC/" & SiteIndex)
Response.Write Site.MaxBandwidth
```

Setting Maximum Bandwidth for a Site Using a VBScript Active Server Page

```
Dim Site
Dim ServerName
Dim SiteIndex
Dim NewMaxBandwidth
ServerName = "IIS_Server_Name"
SiteIndex = Site_Index_Value
NewMaxBandwidth = Value_in_Bytes
Set Site = GetObject("IIS://" & ServerName & "/W3SVC/" & SiteIndex)
Site.MaxBandwidth = NewMaxBandwidth
Site.SetInfo
```

Querying HTTP Keep-Alive Processing Status Using a VBScript Active Server Page

```
Dim Site
Dim ServerName
Dim SiteIndex
ServerName = "IIS_Server_Name"
SiteIndex = Site_Index_Value
Set Site = GetObject("IIS://" & ServerName & "/W3SVC/" & SiteIndex)
Response.Write Site.AllowKeepAlive
```

Setting HTTP Keep-Alive Processing Status Using a VBScript Active Server Page

```
Dim Site
Dim ServerName
Dim SiteIndex
Dim AllowKeepAlive
ServerName = "IIS_Server_Name"
SiteIndex = Site_Index_Value
AllowKeepAlive = True
Set Site = GetObject("IIS://" & ServerName & "/W3SVC/" & SiteIndex)
Site.AllowKeepAlive = AllowKeepAlive
Site.SetInfo
```

Querying the Local Path Property for a Site's Root Virtual Directory Using a VBScript Active Server Page

```
Dim VirtualDirectory
Dim ServerName
Dim Index
Dim RetVal
ServerName = "IIS_Server_Name"
Index = Site_Index_Value
Set VirtualDirectory = GetObject("IIS://" & ServerName & "/W3SVC/" & Index &
↪"/ROOT")
RetVal = VirtualDirectory.Path
Response.Write RetVal
```

Modifying the Local Path Property for a Site's Root Virtual Directory Using a VBScript Active Server Page

```
Dim VirtualDirectory
Dim ServerName
Dim Index
Dim NewVirtualDirPath
ServerName = "IIS_Server_Name"
Index = Site_Index_Value
NewVirtualDirPath = "New_Path_for_Site"
Set VirtualDirectory = GetObject("IIS://" & ServerName & "/W3SVC/" & Index &
↪"/ROOT")
VirtualDirectory.Path = NewVirtualDirPath
VirtualDirectory.SetInfo
```

Querying the Remote Path Property and UNC Connection Information for a Site's Root Virtual Directory Using a VBScript Active Server Page

```
Dim VirtualDirectory
Dim ServerName
Dim Index
Dim RetVal
ServerName = "IIS_Server_Name"
Index = Site_Index_Value
Set VirtualDirectory = GetObject("IIS://" & ServerName & "/W3SVC/" & Index &
↪"/ROOT")
Response.Write VirtualDirectory.Path & "<BR>"
Response.Write VirtualDirectory.UNCUserName & "<BR>"
Response.Write VirtualDirectory.UNCPassword
```

Modifying the Remote Path Property for a Site's Root Virtual Directory Using a VBScript Active Server Page

```
Dim VirtualDirectory
Dim ServerName
Dim Index
Dim NewVirtualDirPath
Dim NewVirtualDirUser
Dim NewVirtualDirPassword
ServerName = "IIS_Server_Name"
Index = Site_Index_Value
NewVirtualDirPath = "New_Path_for_Site"
NewVirtualDirUser = "UNC_Credentials_Used_To_Establish_Connection"
NewVirtualDirPassword = "UNC_Credentials_Used_To_Establish_Connection"
Set VirtualDirectory = GetObject("IIS://" & ServerName & "/W3SVC/" & Index &
↪"/ROOT")
VirtualDirectory.Path = NewVirtualDirPath
VirtualDirectory.UNCUsername = NewVirtualDirUser
VirtualDirectory.UNCPassword = NewVirtualDirPassword
VirtualDirectory.SetInfo
```

Managing Access Permissions and Content Control Properties Using a VBScript Active Server Page

```
Dim VirtualDirectory
Dim ServerName
Dim Index
ServerName = "IIS_Server_Name"
Index = Site_Index_Value
Set VirtualDirectory = GetObject("IIS://" & ServerName & "/W3SVC/" & Index &
↪"/ROOT")
Response.Write "Read:" & VirtualDirectory.AccessRead & "<BR>"
Response.Write "Write:" & VirtualDirectory.AccessWrite & "<BR>"
Response.Write "Logging Disabled: " & VirtualDirectory.DontLog & "<BR>"
Response.Write "Dir Browsing: " & VirtualDirectory.EnableDirBrowsing & "<BR>"
Response.Write "Index Content: " & VirtualDirectory.ContentIndexed & "<BR>"
Set VirtualDirectory = GetObject("IIS://" & ServerName & "/W3SVC/" & Index)
Response.Write "FrontPage Web:" & VirtualDirectory.FrontPageWeb
```

Querying Application Configuration Using a VBScript Active Server Page

```
Dim Application
Dim ServerName
Dim Index
ServerName = "IIS_Server_Name"
Index = Site_Index_Value
Set Application = GetObject("IIS://" & ServerName & "/W3SVC/" & Index & "/ROOT")
Response.Write "Friendly Name:" & Application.AppFriendlyName & "<BR>"
```

```
Response.Write "Application Root:" & Application.AppRoot & "<BR>"
Response.Write "Isolated Process:" & Application.AppIsolated & "<BR>"
Response.Write "Read:" & Application.AccessRead & "<BR>"
Response.Write "Execute:" & Application.AccessExecute
```

Setting Application Configuration Using a VBScript Active Server Page

```
Dim Application
Dim ServerName
Dim Index
Dim ApplicationName
Dim Isolated
Dim Read
Dim Execute
ServerName = "IIS_Server_Name"
Index = Site_Index_Value
ApplicationName = "Application_Name"
Isolated = True
Read = True
Execute = True
Set Application = GetObject("IIS://" & ServerName & "/W3SVC/" & Index & "/ROOT")
Application.AppRoot = Replace(Application.ADsPath, "IIS://" & ServerName, "/LM")
Application.AppFriendlyName = ApplicationName
Application.AppIsolated = Isolated
Application.AccessRead = Read
Application.AccessExecute = Execute
Application.SetInfo
```

Configuring Application Options Using a VBScript Active Server Page

```
Dim Application
Dim ServerName
Dim Index
ServerName = "IIS_Server_Name"
Index = Site_Index_Value
Set Application = GetObject("IIS://" & ServerName & "/W3SVC/" & Index & "/ROOT")
Response.Write "Session Timeout:" & Application.AspSessionTimeout & "<BR>"
Response.Write "Buffering:" & Application.AspBufferingOn & "<BR>"
Response.Write "Parent Paths:" & Application.AspEnableParentPaths & "<BR>"
Response.Write "Script Language:" & Application.AspScriptLanguage & "<BR>"
Response.Write "Script Timeout:" & Application.AspScriptTimeout
```

Manipulating Process Options Using a VBScript Active Server Page

```
Dim Application
Dim ServerName
Dim Index
ServerName = "IIS_Server_Name"
Index = Site_Index_Value
Set Application = GetObject("IIS://" & ServerName & "/W3SVC/" & Index & "/ROOT")
Response.Write "NT Event Logging:" & Application.AspLogErrorRequests & "<BR>"
Response.Write "Debug Exceptions:" & Application.AspExceptionCatchEnable & "<BR>"
Response.Write "Script Engines Cached:" & Application.AspScriptEngineCacheMax &
↪"<BR>"
Response.Write "Script File Cache:" & Application.AspScriptFileCacheSize & "<BR>"
Set Application = GetObject("IIS://" & ServerName & "/W3SVC/" & Index)
Response.Write "CGI Script Timeout:" & Application.CGITimeout
```

Manipulating the ASP Debugging Option Using a VBScript Active Server Page

```
Dim Application
Dim ServerName
Dim Index
ServerName = "IIS_Server_Name"
Index = Site_Index_Value
Set Application = GetObject("IIS://" & ServerName & "/W3SVC/" & Index & "/ROOT")
Response.Write "ASP Server-Side Debugging:" & Application.AppAllowDebugging & "<BR>"
Response.Write "ASP Client-Side Debugging:" & Application.AppAllowClientDebug &
↪"<BR>"
Response.Write "Detailed Client Error Messages:" &
Application.AspScriptErrorSentToBrowser & "<BR>"
If Application.AspScriptErrorSentToBrowser = False then
  Response.Write "Error Message Text:" & Application.AspScriptErrorMessage & "<BR>"
End If
```

Querying Current Running Redirection Status Using a VBScript Active Server Page

```
Dim Resource
Dim ServerName
Dim Index
ServerName = "IIS_Server_Name"
Index = Site_Index_Value
Set Resource = GetObject("IIS://" & ServerName & "/W3SVC/" & Index & "/ROOT")
Response.Write Resource.HttpRedirect
```

Setting New Resource Redirection Using a VBScript Active Server Page

```
Dim Resource
Dim ServerName
Dim SiteIndex
Dim HttpRedirectString
ServerName = "IIS_Server_Name"
SiteIndex = Site_Index_Value
HttpRedirectString = "http://www.sitename.com,FLAG,"
Set Resource = GetObject("IIS://" & ServerName & "/W3SVC/" & SiteIndex & "/ROOT")
Resource.HttpRedirect = HttpRedirectString
Resource.SetInfo
```

Querying *EnableDefaultDoc* Using a VBScript Active Server Page

```
Dim Resource
Dim ServerName
Dim Index
ServerName = "IIS_Server_Name"
Index = Site_Index_Value
Set Resource = GetObject("IIS://" & ServerName & "/W3SVC/" & Index & "/ROOT")
Response.Write Resource.EnableDefaultDoc
```

Setting *EnableDefaultDoc* Using a VBScript Active Server Page

```
Dim Resource
Dim ServerName
Dim SiteIndex
Dim EnableDefaultDocument
ServerName = "IIS_Server_Name"
SiteIndex = Site_Index_Value
EnableDefaultDocument = True
Set Resource = GetObject("IIS://" & ServerName & "/W3SVC/" & SiteIndex & "/ROOT")
Resource.EnableDefaultDoc = EnableDefaultDocument
Resource.SetInfo
```

Querying *DefaultDoc* Using a VBScript Active Server Page

```
Dim Resource
Dim ServerName
Dim Index
ServerName = "IIS_Server_Name"
Index = Site_Index_Value
Set Resource = GetObject("IIS://" & ServerName & "/W3SVC/" & Index & "/ROOT")
Response.Write Resource.DefaultDoc
```

Setting *DefaultDoc* Using a VBScript Active Server Page

```
Dim Resource
Dim ServerName
Dim SiteIndex
Dim DefaultDocument
ServerName = "IIS_Server_Name"
SiteIndex = Site_Index_Value
DefaultDocument = "default.asp,default.htm,index.html"
Set Resource = GetObject("IIS://" & ServerName & "/W3SVC/" & SiteIndex & "/ROOT")
Resource.DefaultDoc = DefaultDocument
Resource.SetInfo
```

Querying *DefaultDocFooter* Using a VBScript Active Server Page

```
Dim Resource
Dim ServerName
Dim Index
ServerName = "IIS_Server_Name"
Index = Site_Index_Value
Set Resource = GetObject("IIS://" & ServerName & "/W3SVC/" & Index & "/ROOT")
Response.Write Resource.DefaultDocFooter
```

Setting *DefaultDocFooter* Using a VBScript Active Server Page

```
Dim Resource
Dim ServerName
Dim SiteIndex
Dim DefaultDocumentFooter
ServerName = "IIS_Server_Name"
SiteIndex = Site_Index_Value
DefaultDocumentFooter = "c:\legal_footers\copyright.htm"
Set Resource = GetObject("IIS://" & ServerName & "/W3SVC/" & SiteIndex & "/ROOT")
Resource.DefaultDocFooter = DefaultDocumentFooter
Resource.SetInfo
```

Querying *EnableDocFooter* Using a VBScript Active Server Page

```
Dim Resource
Dim ServerName
Dim Index
ServerName = "IIS_Server_Name"
Index = Site_Index_Value
Set Resource = GetObject("IIS://" & ServerName & "/W3SVC/" & Index & "/ROOT")
Response.Write Resource.EnableDocFooter
```

Setting *EnableDocFooter* Using a VBScript Active Server Page

```
Dim Resource
Dim ServerName
Dim SiteIndex
Dim EnableDocumentFooter
ServerName = "IIS_Server_Name"
SiteIndex = Site_Index_Value
EnableDocumentFooter = True
Set Resource = GetObject("IIS://" & ServerName & "/W3SVC/" & SiteIndex & "/ROOT")
Resource.EnableDocFooter = EnableDocumentFooter
Resource.SetInfo
```

Querying Authentication Methods Used for a Given Resource Using a VBScript Active Server Page

```
Dim Resource
Dim ServerName
Dim SiteIndex
ServerName = "IIS_Server_Name"
SiteIndex = Site_Index_Value
Set Resource = GetObject("IIS://" & ServerName & "/W3SVC/" & SiteIndex & "/ROOT")
Response.Write "Authentication Methods for " & Resource.ADsPath & ":"
Response.Write "<BR>"
Response.Write "Anonymous Access:" & Resource.AuthAnonymous & "<BR>"
If Resource.AuthAnonymous = True Then
  Response.Write "Anonymous User Account Name:" & _
Resource.AnonymousUsername & "<BR>"
  Response.Write "Anonymous User Account Password:" & _
Resource.AnonymousUserPass & "<BR>"
  Response.Write "Anonymous User Password Synchronization:" &
Resource.AnonymousPasswordSync & "<BR>"
End If
Response.Write "Basic Authentication:" & Resource.AuthBasic & "<BR>"
If Resource.AuthBasic = True Then
  Response.Write "Default Authentication Domain: " & _
Resource.DefaultLogonDomain & "<BR>"
End If
Response.Write "NTLM Authentication:" & Resource.AuthNTLM
```

Enabling Anonymous Access Using a VBScript Active Server Page

```
Dim Resource
Dim ServerName
Dim SiteIndex
Dim EnableAnonymousAccess
Dim AnonUserName
Dim AnonUserPassword
Dim AnonPasswordSync
ServerName = "IIS_Server_Name"
SiteIndex = Site_Index_Value
```

```
EnableAnonymousAccess = True
AnonUserName = "Username_for_Anonymous_Access"
AnonUserPassword = "Password_for_Anonymous_Access_Account"
AnonPasswordSync = True
Set Resource = GetObject("IIS://" & ServerName & "/W3SVC/" & SiteIndex & "/ROOT")
Resource.AuthAnonymous = EnableAnonymousAccess
Resource.AnonymousUsername = AnonUserName
Resource.AnonymousUserPass = AnonUserPassword
Resource.AnonymousPasswordSync = AnonPasswordSync
Resource.SetInfo
```

Enabling Basic Authentication Using a VBScript Active Server Page

```
Dim Resource
Dim ServerName
Dim SiteIndex
Dim EnableBasicAuth
Dim DefaultLogonDomain
ServerName = "IIS_Server_Name"
SiteIndex = Site_Index_Value
EnableBasicAuth = True
DefaultLogonDomain = "Domain_Used_for_Authentication"
Set Resource = GetObject("IIS://" & ServerName & "/W3SVC/" & SiteIndex & "/ROOT")
Resource.AuthBasic= EnableBasicAuth
Resource.DefaultLogonDomain = DefaultLogonDomain
Resource.SetInfo
```

Enabling NTLM Authentication Using a VBScript Active Server Page

```
Dim Resource
Dim ServerName
Dim SiteIndex
Dim EnableNTLMAuth
ServerName = "IIS_Server_Name"
SiteIndex = Site_Index_Value
EnableNTLMAuth = True
Set Resource = GetObject("IIS://" & ServerName & "/W3SVC/" & SiteIndex & "/ROOT")
Resource.AuthNTLM= EnableNTLMAuth
Resource.SetInfo
```

Querying Secure Communication Configuration Using a VBScript Active Server Page

```
Dim Resource
Dim ServerName
Dim SiteIndex
ServerName = "IIS_Server_Name"
SiteIndex = Site_Index_Value
```

```
Set Resource = GetObject("IIS://" & ServerName & "/W3SVC/" & SiteIndex & "/ROOT")
Response.Write "Require SSL:" & Resource.AccessSSL & "<BR>"
Response.Write "Require 128-bit SSL:" & Resource.AccessSSL128 & "<BR>"
Response.Write "Map Client Certificates to NT UserIDs:" & Resource.AccessSSLMapCert
    & "<BR>"
Response.Write "Negotiate Client Certificates:" & Resource.AccessSSLNegotiateCert &
    "<BR>"
Response.Write "Require Client Certificates:" & Resource.AccessSSLRequireCert &
    "<BR>"
```

Setting New Secure Communication Configuration Using a VBScript Active Server Page

```
Dim Resource
Dim ServerName
Dim SiteIndex
ServerName = "IIS_Server_Name"
SiteIndex = Site_Index_Value
Set Resource = GetObject("IIS://" & ServerName & "/W3SVC/" & SiteIndex & "/ROOT")
Resource.AccessSSL = True
Resource.AccessSSL128 = True
Resource.AccessSSLMapCert = True
Resource.AccessSSLNegotiateCert = True
Resource.AccessSSLRequireCert = True
Resource.SetInfo
```

Querying IP Address Restrictions Using a VBScript Active Server Page

```
Dim Site
Dim ServerName
Dim SiteIndex
Dim IPSecurity
ServerName = "IIS_Server_Name"
SiteIndex = Site_Index_Value
Set Site = GetObject("IIS://" & ServerName & "/W3SVC/" & SiteIndex & "/ROOT")
Set IPSecurity = Site.IPSecurity
If IPSecurity.GrantByDefault Then
    Response.Write "All addresses will be allowed, except as follows:" & "<BR>"
    For Each Entry In IPSecurity.IPDeny
        If InStr(1, Entry, "255.255.255.255") Then
            Response.Write "Denied IP: " & Replace(Entry, ", ", 255.255.255.255",
                ↵"") & "<BR>"
        Else
            Response.Write "Denied Subnet: " & Entry & "<BR>"
        End If
    Next
    For Each Entry In IPSecurity.DomainDeny
        Response.Write "Denied Domain: " & Entry & "<BR>"
    Next
Else
```

```
            Response.Write "All addresses will be blocked, except as follows:" & "<BR>"
            For Each Entry In IPSecurity.IPGrant
                If InStr(1, Entry, "255.255.255.255") Then
                    Response.Write "Allowed IP: " & Replace(Entry, ", 255.255.255.255",
                    ↳"") & "<BR>"
                Else
                    Response.Write "Allowed Subnet: " & Entry & "<BR>"
                End If
            Next
            For Each Entry In IPSecurity.DomainGrant
                Response.Write "Allowed Domain: " & Entry & "<BR>"
            Next
        End If
```

Setting New IP Address Restrictions Using a VBScript Active Server Page

```
Dim Site
Dim ServerName
Dim SiteIndex
Dim IPSecurity
Dim IPAddress
Dim IPSubnet
Dim Domain
Dim ActionType
ServerName = "IIS_Server_Name"
SiteIndex = Site_Index_Value
IPAddress = "xxx.xxx.xxx.xxx"
IPSubnet = "xxx.xxx.xxx.xxx"
Domain = "DNS_Domain.Name"
ActionType = "GRANTIP"
'ActionType = "GRANTSUBNET"
'ActionType = "GRANTDOMAIN"
'ActionType = "DENYIP"
'ActionType = "DENYSUBNET"
'ActionType = "DENYDOMAIN"
Set Site = GetObject("IIS://" & ServerName & "/W3SVC/" & SiteIndex & "/ROOT")
Select Case ActionType
    Case "GRANTIP"
        Set IPSecurity = Site.IPSecurity
        IPSecurity.GrantByDefault = False
        Site.IPSecurity = IPSecurity
        Site.SetInfo
        IPSecurity.IPGrant = Array(IPAddress & ", 255.255.255.255")
        Site.IPSecurity = IPSecurity
        Site.SetInfo
    Case "GRANTSUBNET"
        Set IPSecurity = Site.IPSecurity
        IPSecurity.GrantByDefault = False
        IPSecurity.IPGrant = Array(IPAddress & ", " & IPSubnet)
        Site.IPSecurity = IPSecurity
        Site.SetInfo
```

```
        Case "GRANTDOMAIN"
            Set IPSecurity = Site.IPSecurity
            IPSecurity.GrantByDefault = False
            IPSecurity.DomainGrant = Array(Domain)
            Site.IPSecurity = IPSecurity
            Site.SetInfo
        Case "DENYIP"
            Set IPSecurity = Site.IPSecurity
            IPSecurity.GrantByDefault = True
            IPSecurity.IPDeny = Array(IPAddress & ", 255.255.255.255")
            Site.IPSecurity = IPSecurity
            Site.SetInfo
        Case "DENYSUBNET"
            Set IPSecurity = Site.IPSecurity
            IPSecurity.GrantByDefault = True
            IPSecurity.IPDeny = Array(IPAddress & ", " & IPSubnet)
            Site.IPSecurity = IPSecurity
            Site.SetInfo
        Case "DENYDOMAIN"
            Set IPSecurity = Site.IPSecurity
            IPSecurity.GrantByDefault = True
            IPSecurity.DomainDeny = Array(Domain)
            Site.IPSecurity = IPSecurity
            Site.SetInfo
    End Select
```

Querying Current Value of Content Expiration Using a VBScript Active Server Page

```
    Dim Resource
    Dim ServerName
    Dim Index
    ServerName = "IIS_Server_Name"
    Index = Site_Index_Value
    Set Resource = GetObject("IIS://" & ServerName & "/W3SVC/" & Index & "/ROOT")
    Response.Write Resource.HttpExpires
```

Enabling Content Expiration Using a VBScript Active Server Page

```
    Dim Resource
    Dim ServerName
    Dim SiteIndex
    Dim ContentExpiration
    ServerName = "IIS_Server_Name"
    SiteIndex = Site_Index_Value
    ContentExpiration = "D, 0"
    Set Resource = GetObject("IIS://" & ServerName & "/W3SVC/" & SiteIndex & "/ROOT")
    Resource.HttpExpires = ContentExpiration
    Resource.SetInfo
```

Querying Custom HTTP Header Configurations Using a VBScript Active Server Page

```
Dim Resource
Dim ServerName
Dim Index
ServerName = "IIS_Server_Name"
Index = Site_Index_Value
Set Resource = GetObject("IIS://" & ServerName & "/W3SVC/" & Index & "/ROOT")
For Each HeaderEntry in Resource.HttpCustomHeaders
   Response.Write HeaderEntry & "<BR>"
Next
```

Assigning a Custom HTTP Header Using a VBScript Active Server Page

```
Dim Resource
Dim ServerName
Dim Index
Dim NewHeaderArray
ServerName = "IIS_Server_Name"
Index = Site_Index_Value
NewHeaderArray = Array("HeaderName: HeaderValue")
Set Resource = GetObject("IIS://" & ServerName & "/W3SVC/" & Index & "/ROOT")
Resource.HttpCustomHeaders = NewHeaderArray
Resource.SetInfo
```

Querying RSACi Rating for a Given Resource Using a VBScript Active Server Page

```
Dim Resource
Dim ServerName
Dim Index
Dim Entry
ServerName = "IIS_Server_Name"
Index = Site_Index_Value
Set Resource = GetObject("IIS://" & ServerName & "/W3SVC/" & Index & "/ROOT")
For Each Entry In Resource.HttpPics
     Response.Write Entry & "<BR>"
Next
```

Setting RSACi Rating for a Given Resource Using a VBScript Active Server Page

```
Dim Resource
Dim ServerName
Dim Index
Dim PICSLabel
ServerName = "IIS_Server_Name"
```

```
Index = Site_Index_Value
PICSLabel = "PICS_Format_String"
Set Resource = GetObject("IIS://" & ServerName & "/W3SVC/" & Index & "/ROOT")
Resource.HttpPics = PICSLabel
Resource.SetInfo
```

Querying MIME Type Definitions for Resources Using a VBScript Active Server Page

```
Dim Resource
Dim ServerName
Dim Index
ServerName = "IIS_Server_Name"
Index = Site_Index_Value
Set Resource = GetObject("IIS://" & ServerName & "/W3SVC/" & Index & "/ROOT")
Response.Write "Registered File Types:" & "<BR>"
For Each MimeMapping in Resource.MimeMap
    Response.Write "Extension: " & MimeMapping.Extension & " MIME Content Type: " & _
    MimeMapping.MimeType & "<BR>"
Next
```

Setting MIME Type Definitions for Resources Using a VBScript Active Server Page

```
Dim Resource
Dim ServerName
Dim Index
Dim MimeMapping
Dim NewMimeMapping
Dim MimeExtension
Dim MimeType
Dim i
MimeExtension = "New_MIME_Extension"
MimeType = "New_MIME_Type"
ServerName = "IIS_Server_Name"
Index = Site_Index_Value
Set Resource = GetObject("IIS://" & ServerName & "/W3SVC/" & Index & "/ROOT")
NewMimeMapping = Resource.GetEx("MimeMap")
i = UBound(NewMimeMapping) + 1
ReDim Preserve NewMimeMapping(i)
Set NewMimeMapping(i) = CreateObject("MimeMap")
NewMimeMapping(i).MimeType = MimeType
NewMimeMapping(i).Extension = MimeExtension
Resource.PutEx ADS_PROPERTY_UPDATE, "MimeMap", NewMimeMapping
Resource.SetInfo
```

Chapter 10: IIS FTP Site Operations Code

Querying the *ServerComment* Property Using a VBScript Active Server Page

```
Dim Site
Dim ServerName
Dim Index
ServerName = "IIS_Server_Name"
Index = Site_Index_Integer
Set Site = GetObject("IIS://" & ServerName & "/MSFTPSVC/" & Index)
Response.Write Site.ServerComment
```

Setting a New Value for the *ServerComment* Property Using a VBScript Active Server Page

```
Dim Site
Dim ServerName
Dim Index
Dim NewServerComment
ServerName = "IIS_Server_Name"
Index = Site_Index_Integer
NewServerComment = "New_Server_Comment_String"
Set Site = GetObject("IIS://" & ServerName & "/MSFTPSVC/" & Index)
Site.ServerComment = NewServerComment
Site.SetInfo
```

Querying *ServerBindings* Using a VBScript Active Server Page

```
Dim Site
Dim ServerName
Dim SiteIndex
ServerName = "IIS_Server_Name"
SiteIndex = Site_Index_Value
Set Site = GetObject("IIS://" & ServerName & "/MSFTPSVC/" & SiteIndex)
For Each Binding In Site.ServerBindings
    Response.Write Binding & "<BR>"
Next
```

Setting *ServerBindings* Using a VBScript Active Server Page

```
Dim Site
Dim ServerName
Dim SiteIndex
Dim NewBindingArray
Dim IPAddress
Dim TCPPort
ServerName = "IIS_Server_Name"
SiteIndex = Site_Index_Value
```

```
IPAddress = "xxx.xxx.xxx.xxx"
TCPPort = TCP_Port_Number
NewBindingArray = Array(IPAddress & ":" & TCPPort & ":")
Set Site = GetObject("IIS://" & ServerName & "/MSFTPSVC/" & SiteIndex)
Site.ServerBindings = NewBindingArray
Site.SetInfo
```

Querying Maximum Connections Using a VBScript Active Server Page

```
Dim Site
Dim ServerName
Dim Index
Dim RetVal
ServerName = "IIS_Server_Name"
Index = Site_Index
Set Site = GetObject("IIS://" & ServerName & "/MSFTPSVC/" & Index)
RetVal = Site.MaxConnections
Response.Write RetVal
```

Setting Maximum Connections Using a VBScript Active Server Page

```
Dim Site
Dim ServerName
Dim Index
Dim NewMaxConnections
ServerName = "IIS_Server_Name"
Index = Site_Index
NewMaxConnections = Maximum_Number_of_Connections
Set Site = GetObject("IIS://" & ServerName & "/MSFTPSVC/" & Index)
Site.MaxConnections = NewMaxConnections
Site.SetInfo
```

Querying Connection Timeout Using a VBScript Active Server Page

```
Dim Site
Dim ServerName
Dim Index
Dim RetVal
ServerName = "IIS_Server_Name"
Index = Site_Index
Set Site = GetObject("IIS://" & ServerName & "/MSFTPSVC/" & Index)
RetVal = Site.ConnectionTimeout
Response.Write RetVal
```

Setting Connection Timeout Using a VBScript Active Server Page

```
Dim Site
Dim ServerName
Dim Index
Dim ConnectionTimeout
ServerName = "IIS_Server_Name"
Index = Site_Index_Value
NewConnectionTimeout = Connection_Timeout_in_Seconds
Set Site = GetObject("IIS://" & ServerName & "/MSFTPSVC/" & Index)
Site.ConnectionTimeout = NewConnectionTimeout
Site.SetInfo
```

Querying *AllowAnonymous* Using a VBScript Active Server Page

```
Dim Site
Dim ServerName
Dim SiteIndex
ServerName = "IIS_Server_Name"
SiteIndex = Site_Index_Value
Set Site = GetObject("IIS://" & ServerName & "/MSFTPSVC/" & SiteIndex)
Response.Write Site.AllowAnonymous
```

Setting *AllowAnonymous* Using a VBScript Active Server Page

```
Dim Site
Dim ServerName
Dim SiteIndex
ServerName = "IIS_Server_Name"
SiteIndex = Site_Index_Value
Set Site = GetObject("IIS://" & ServerName & "/MSFTPSVC/" & SiteIndex)
Site.AllowAnonymous = False
Site.SetInfo
```

Querying Anonymous User Credentials Using a VBScript Active Server Page

```
Dim Site
Dim ServerName
Dim SiteIndex
ServerName = "IIS_Server_Name"
SiteIndex = Site_Index_Value
Set Site = GetObject("IIS://" & ServerName & "/MSFTPSVC/" & SiteIndex)
Response.Write Site.AnonymousUsername & "<BR>"
Response.Write Site.AnonymousUserPass & "<BR>"
Response.Write Site.AnonymousPasswordSync
```

Setting Anonymous User Credentials Using a VBScript Active Server Page

```
Dim Site
Dim ServerName
Dim SiteIndex
Dim AnonymousUserName
Dim AnonymousUserPassword
ServerName = "IIS_Server_Name"
SiteIndex = Site_Index_Value
AnonymousUserName = "Username_for_Anonymous_FTP_Access"
AnonymousUserPassword = "Password_for_Anonymous_User_Account"
Set Site = GetObject("IIS://" & ServerName & "/MSFTPSVC/" & SiteIndex)
Site.AnonymousUsername = AnonymousUserName
Site.AnonymousUserPass = AnonymousUserPassword
Site.AnonymousPasswordSync = True
Site.SetInfo
```

Querying *AnonymousOnly* Using a VBScript Active Server Page

```
Dim Site
Dim ServerName
Dim SiteIndex
ServerName = "IIS_Server_Name"
SiteIndex = Site_Index_Value
Set Site = GetObject("IIS://" & ServerName & "/MSFTPSVC/" & SiteIndex)
Response.Write Site.AnonymousOnly
```

Setting *AnonymousOnly* Using a VBScript Active Server Page

```
Dim Site
Dim ServerName
Dim SiteIndex
ServerName = "IIS_Server_Name"
SiteIndex = Site_Index_Value
Set Site = GetObject("IIS://" & ServerName & "/MSFTPSVC/" & SiteIndex)
Site.AnonymousOnly = True
Site.SetInfo
```

Querying Operators Using a VBScript Active Server Page

```
Dim Site
Dim ServerName
Dim SiteIndex
ServerName = "IIS_Server_Name"
SiteIndex = Site_Index_Value
Set Site = GetObject("IIS://" & ServerName & "/MSFTPSVC/" & SiteIndex)
Set SecurityDescriptor = Site.AdminAcl
Set DiscretionaryAcl = SecurityDescriptor.DiscretionaryAcl
For Each Item In DiscretionaryAcl
```

```
        If Item.AccessMask = 11 Or Item.AccessMask = 262315 Then
            Response.Write Item.Trustee & "<BR>"
        End If
    Next
```

Creating a New Operator Using a VBScript Active Server Page

```
    Dim Site
    Dim ACE
    Dim DiscretionaryACL
    Dim ServerName
    Dim SiteIndex
    Dim NewOperator
    ServerName = "IIS_Server_Name"
    SiteIndex = Site_Index_Value
    NewOperator = "New_Operator_in_Format_Domain\Username"
    Set Site = GetObject("IIS://" & ServerName & "/MSFTPSVC/" & SiteIndex)
    Set SecurityDescriptor = Site.AdminACL
    Set DiscretionaryACL = SecurityDescriptor.DiscretionaryACL
    Set ACE = CreateObject("AccessControlEntry")
    ACE.Trustee = NewOperator
    ACE.AccessMask = 11
    DiscretionaryACL.AddAce ACE
    SecurityDescriptor.DiscretionaryACL = DiscretionaryACL
    Site.AdminACL = SecurityDescriptor
    Site.SetInfo
```

Querying Current Greeting Message Using a VBScript Active Server Page

```
    Dim Site
    Dim ServerName
    Dim SiteIndex
    ServerName = "IIS_Server_Name"
    SiteIndex = Site_Index_Value
    Set Site = GetObject("IIS://" & ServerName & "/MSFTPSVC/" & SiteIndex)
    For Each MessageLine in Site.GreetingMessage
        Response.Write MessageLine & "<BR>"
    Next
```

Setting a New Greeting Message Using a VBScript Active Server Page

```
    Dim Site
    Dim ServerName
    Dim SiteIndex
    ServerName = "IIS_Server_Name"
    SiteIndex = Site_Index_Value
    Set Site = GetObject("IIS://" & ServerName & "/MSFTPSVC/" & SiteIndex)
    Site.GreetingMessage = Array("Greeting_Line_1","Greeting_Line_2","Greeting_Line_3")
    Site.SetInfo
```

Querying Current Exit Message Using a VBScript Active Server Page

```
Dim Site
Dim ServerName
Dim SiteIndex
ServerName = "IIS_Server_Name"
SiteIndex = Site_Index_Value
Set Site = GetObject("IIS://" & ServerName & "/MSFTPSVC/" & SiteIndex)
Response.Write Site.ExitMessage
```

Setting a New Exit Message Using a VBScript Active Server Page

```
Dim Site
Dim ServerName
Dim SiteIndex
Dim NewExitMessageString
ServerName = "IIS_Server_Name"
SiteIndex = Site_Index_Value
NewExitMessageString = "FTP_Session_Termination_Text"
Set Site = GetObject("IIS://" & ServerName & "/MSFTPSVC/" & SiteIndex)
Site.ExitMessage = NewExitMessageString
Site.SetInfo
```

Querying Current Maximum Connections Message Using a VBScript Active Server Page

```
Dim Site
Dim ServerName
Dim SiteIndex
ServerName = "IIS_Server_Name"
SiteIndex = Site_Index_Value
Set Site = GetObject("IIS://" & ServerName & "/MSFTPSVC/" & SiteIndex)
Response.Write Site.MaxClientsMessage
```

Setting a New Current Maximum Connections Message Using a VBScript Active Server Page

```
Dim Site
Dim ServerName
Dim SiteIndex
Dim MaxConnectionsString
ServerName = "IIS_Server_Name"
SiteIndex = Site_Index_Value
MaxConnectionsString = "String_Passed_To_Client_When_Maximum_Connections_Reached"
Set Site = GetObject("IIS://" & ServerName & "/MSFTPSVC/" & SiteIndex)
Site.MaxClientsMessage = MaxConnectionsString
Site.SetInfo
```

Querying the Local Path Property for an FTP Site's Root Virtual Directory Using a VBScript Active Server Page

```
Dim VirtualDirectory
Dim ServerName
Dim Index
Dim RetVal
ServerName = "IIS_Server_Name"
Index = Site_Index_Value
Set VirtualDirectory = GetObject("IIS://" & ServerName & "/MSFTPSVC/" & Index &
↪"/ROOT")
RetVal = VirtualDirectory.Path
Response.Write RetVal
```

Modifying the Local Path Property for an FTP Site's Root Virtual Directory Using a VBScript Active Server Page

```
Dim VirtualDirectory
Dim ServerName
Dim Index
Dim NewVirtualDirPath
ServerName = "IIS_Server_Name"
Index = Site_Index_Value
NewVirtualDirPath = "New_Path_for_Site"
Set VirtualDirectory = GetObject("IIS://" & ServerName & "/MSFTPSVC/" & Index &
↪"/ROOT")
VirtualDirectory.Path = NewVirtualDirPath
VirtualDirectory.SetInfo
```

Querying the Remote Path Property and UNC Connection Information for a Site's Root Virtual Directory Using a VBScript Active Server Page

```
Dim VirtualDirectory
Dim ServerName
Dim Index
Dim RetVal
ServerName = "IIS_Server_Name"
Index = Site_Index_Value
Set VirtualDirectory = GetObject("IIS://" & ServerName & "/MSFTPSVC/" & Index &
↪"/ROOT")
Response.Write VirtualDirectory.Path & "<BR>"
Response.Write VirtualDirectory.UNCUserName & "<BR>"
Response.Write VirtualDirectory.UNCPassword
```

Modifying the Remote Path Property for a Site's Root Virtual Directory Using a VBScript Active Server Page

```
Dim VirtualDirectory
Dim ServerName
Dim Index
Dim NewVirtualDirPath
Dim NewVirtualDirUser
Dim NewVirtualDirPassword
ServerName = "IIS_Server_Name"
Index = Site_Index_Value
NewVirtualDirPath = "New_Path_for_Site"
NewVirtualDirUser = "UNC_Credentials_Used_To_Establish_Connection"
NewVirtualDirPassword = "UNC_Credentials_Used_To_Establish_Connection"
Set VirtualDirectory = GetObject("IIS://" & ServerName & "/MSFTPSVC/" & Index &
➥"/ROOT")
VirtualDirectory.Path = NewVirtualDirPath
VirtualDirectory.UNCUserName = NewVirtualDirUser
VirtualDirectory.UNCPassword = NewVirtualDirPassword
VirtualDirectory.SetInfo
```

Querying Directory Access Permissions and Logging Status Using a VBScript Active Server Page

```
Dim VirtualDirectory
Dim ServerName
Dim Index
Dim RetVal
ServerName = "IIS_Server_Name"
Index = Site_Index_Value
Set VirtualDirectory = GetObject("IIS://" & ServerName & "/MSFTPSVC/" & Index &
➥"/ROOT")
Response.Write "Read:" & VirtualDirectory.AccessRead & "<BR>"
Response.Write "Write:" & VirtualDirectory.AccessWrite & "<BR>"
Response.Write "Logging Disabled: " & VirtualDirectory.DontLog
```

Setting Directory Access Permissions and Logging Using a VBScript Active Server Page

```
Dim VirtualDirectory
Dim ServerName
Dim Index
Dim RetVal
ServerName = "IIS_Server_Name"
Index = Site_Index_Value
Set VirtualDirectory = GetObject("IIS://" & ServerName & "/MSFTPSVC/" & Index &
➥"/ROOT")
VirtualDirectory.AccessRead = True
VirtualDirectory.AccessWrite = True
VirtualDirectory.DontLog = False
VirtualDirectory.SetInfo
```

Querying Directory Listing Style Using a VBScript Active Server Page

```
Dim VirtualDirectory
Dim ServerName
Dim Index
ServerName = "IIS_Server_Name"
Index = Site_Index_Value
Set VirtualDirectory = GetObject("IIS://" & ServerName & "/MSFTPSVC/" & Index)
Response.Write VirtualDirectory.MSDOSDirOutput
```

Setting Directory Listing Style Using a VBScript Active Server Page

```
Dim VirtualDirectory
Dim ServerName
Dim Index
ServerName = "IIS_Server_Name"
Index = Site_Index_Value
Set VirtualDirectory = GetObject("IIS://" & ServerName & "/MSFTPSVC/" & Index)
VirtualDirectory.MSDOSDirOutput = False
VirtualDirectory.SetInfo
```

Querying Current IP Address Restrictions Using a VBScript Active Server Page

```
Dim Site
Dim ServerName
Dim SiteIndex
Dim IPSecurity
ServerName = "IIS_Server_Name"
SiteIndex = Site_Index_Value
Set Site = GetObject("IIS://" & ServerName & "/MSFTPSVC/" & SiteIndex & "/ROOT")
Set IPSecurity = Site.IPSecurity
If IPSecurity.GrantByDefault Then
    Response.Write "All addresses will be allowed, except as follows:" & "<BR>"
    For Each Entry In IPSecurity.IPDeny
        If InStr(1, Entry, "255.255.255.255") Then
            Response.Write "Denied IP: " & Replace(Entry, ", 255.255.255.255",
            ⮡"") & "<BR>"
        Else
            Response.Write "Denied Subnet: " & Entry & "<BR>"
        End If
    Next
    For Each Entry In IPSecurity.DomainDeny
        Response.Write "Denied Domain: " & Entry & "<BR>"
    Next
Else
    Response.Write "All addresses will be blocked, except as follows:" & "<BR>"
    For Each Entry In IPSecurity.IPGrant
        If InStr(1, Entry, "255.255.255.255") Then
            Response.Write "Allowed IP: " & Replace(Entry, ", 255.255.255.255",
            ⮡"") & "<BR>"
        Else
```

Setting New IP Address Restrictions Using a VBScript Active Server Page

```
                Response.Write "Allowed Subnet: " & Entry & "<BR>"
            End If
        Next
        For Each Entry In IPSecurity.DomainGrant
                Response.Write "Allowed Domain: " & Entry & "<BR>"
        Next
    End If
```

```
Dim Site
Dim ServerName
Dim SiteIndex
Dim IPSecurity
Dim IPAddress
Dim IPSubnet
Dim Domain
Dim ActionType
ServerName =
SiteIndex = Site_Index_Value
IPAddress = "xxx.xxx.xxx.xxx"
IPSubnet = "xxx.xxx.xxx.xxx"
Domain = "DNS_Domain.Name"
ActionType = "GRANTIP"
'ActionType = "GRANTSUBNET"
'ActionType = "GRANTDOMAIN"
'ActionType = "DENYIP"
'ActionType = "DENYSUBNET"
'ActionType = "DENYDOMAIN"
Select Case ActionType
    Case "GRANTIP"
        Set Site = GetObject("IIS://" & ServerName & "/MSFTPSVC/" & SiteIndex &
        ↵"/ROOT")
        Set IPSecurity = Site.IPSecurity
        IPSecurity.GrantByDefault = False
        Site.IPSecurity = IPSecurity
        Site.SetInfo
        IPSecurity.IPGrant = Array(IPAddress & ", 255.255.255.255")
        Site.IPSecurity = IPSecurity
        Site.SetInfo
    Case "GRANTSUBNET"
        Set Site = GetObject("IIS://" & ServerName & "/MSFTPSVC/" & SiteIndex &
        ↵"/ROOT")
        Set IPSecurity = Site.IPSecurity
        IPSecurity.GrantByDefault = False
        IPSecurity.IPGrant = Array(IPAddress & ", " & IPSubnet)
        Site.IPSecurity = IPSecurity
        Site.SetInfo
    Case "GRANTDOMAIN"
        Set Site = GetObject("IIS://" & ServerName & "/MSFTPSVC/" & SiteIndex &
        ↵"/ROOT")
```

```
            Set IPSecurity = Site.IPSecurity
            IPSecurity.GrantByDefault = False
            IPSecurity.DomainGrant = Array(Domain)
            Site.IPSecurity = IPSecurity
            Site.SetInfo
        Case "DENYIP"
            Set Site = GetObject("IIS://" & ServerName & "/MSFTPSVC/" & SiteIndex &
            ↳"/ROOT")
            Set IPSecurity = Site.IPSecurity
            IPSecurity.GrantByDefault = True
            IPSecurity.IPDeny = Array(IPAddress & ", 255.255.255.255")
            Site.IPSecurity = IPSecurity
            Site.SetInfo
        Case "DENYSUBNET"
            Set Site = GetObject("IIS://" & ServerName & "/MSFTPSVC/" & SiteIndex &
            ↳"/ROOT")
            Set IPSecurity = Site.IPSecurity
            IPSecurity.GrantByDefault = True
            IPSecurity.IPDeny = Array(IPAddress & ", " & IPSubnet)
            Site.IPSecurity = IPSecurity
            Site.SetInfo
        Case "DENYDOMAIN"
            Set Site = GetObject("IIS://" & ServerName & "/MSFTPSVC/" & SiteIndex &
            ↳"/ROOT")
            Set IPSecurity = Site.IPSecurity
            IPSecurity.GrantByDefault = True
            IPSecurity.DomainDeny = Array(Domain)
            Site.IPSecurity = IPSecurity
            Site.SetInfo
    End Select
```

Chapter 11: LDAP Infrastructure Management Code

Discovering the Architecture of an Existing LDAP Directory Using a VBScript Active Server Page

```
Dim Container
Dim Entry
Dim StartingPoint

'StartingPoint = "/ou=People"

Set Container = GetObject("LDAP://LDAP_SERVER/o=airius.com" & StartingPoint)

For Each Entry In Container
    Response.Write "Entry Name: " & Entry.Name & "Class: " & Entry.Class & "<BR>"
Next
```

Querying Entry Attributes with ADSI Using Anonymous Access in a VBScript Active Server Page

```
On Error Resume Next
Dim Container
Dim User
Set Container = GetObject("LDAP://LDAP_SERVER/o=airius.com/ou=People")
For Each User In Container
    Response.Write "UserID: " & User.Get("uid") & "Common Name: " & User.Get("cn")
    ↪& "Surname: " & User.Get("sn") & "<BR>"
Next
```

Querying Entry Attributes with ADSI Using Alternate Credentials in a VBScript Active Server Page

```
On Error Resume Next
Dim dso
Dim Container
Dim User
Set dso = GetObject("LDAP:")
Set Container = dso.OpenDSObject("LDAP://LDAP_SERVER/o=airius.com/ou=People",
"cn=Directory Manager", "l@undrym@t1974", 0)

For Each User In Container
    Response.Write "UserID: " & User.Get("uid") & "Common Name: " & User.Get("cn")
    ↪& "Surname: " & User.Get("sn") & "<BR>"
Next
```

Modifying Entry Attributes Using ADSI Using a VBScript Active Server Page

```
Dim dso
Dim Container
Dim User
Set dso = GetObject("LDAP:")
Set Container = dso.OpenDSObject("LDAP://LDAP_SERVER/o=airius.com/ou=People",
↪"cn=Directory Manager", "l@undrym@t1974", 0)
Set User = Container.GetObject("inetorgperson", "uid=aknutson")
User.Put "sn", "McNally"
User.SetInfo
```

Creating a New Entry Using ADSI In a VBScript Active Server Page

```
Dim dso
Dim Container
Dim User
Set dso = GetObject("LDAP:")
Set Container = dso.OpenDSObject("LDAP://LDAP_SERVER/o=airius.com/ou=People",
↪"cn=Directory Manager", "l@undrym@t1974", 0)
```

```
Set User = Container.Create("inetorgperson", "uid=teck")

User.Put "cn", "Thomas Eck"
User.Put "sn", "Eck"
User.SetInfo
```

Removing an Entry Using ADSI In a VBScript Active Server Page

```
Dim dso
Dim Container
Set dso = GetObject("LDAP:")
Set Container = dso.OpenDSObject("LDAP://LDAP_SERVER/o=airius.com/ou=People",
➥"cn=Directory Manager", "1@undrym@t1974", 0)
Call Container.Delete("inetorgperson", "uid=teck")
```

Using ADO to Search an LDAP Directory Using a VBScript Active Server Page

```
Dim Connection
Dim RS
Dim Entry
Dim Index
Index = 0
Set Connection = Server.CreateObject("ADODB.Connection")
Connection.Provider = "ADsDSOObject"
Connection.Open "ADSI"

Set RS = Connection.Execute("SELECT cn,telephonenumber FROM
➥'LDAP://LDAP_SERVER/o=airius.com/ou=people' WHERE sn='carter'")

While Not RS.EOF
    For i = 0 To RS.Fields.Count - 1
        If RS.Fields(i).Type = adVariant And Not (IsNull(RS.Fields(i).Value)) Then
            For j = LBound(RS.Fields(i).Value) To UBound(RS.Fields(i).Value)
                Entry = Entry & RS.Fields(i).Value(j) & vbTab
            Next j
        Else
            Entry = Entry & RS.Fields(i).Value & vbTab
        End If

        If Index = RS.Fields.Count - 1 Then
            Response.Write Entry & "<BR>"
        End If
        Index = Index + 1
    Next i
    Entry = ""
    Index = 0
    RS.MoveNext
Wend
```

Creating a New Exchange Mailbox Using a VBScript Active Server Page

```
Dim ExchangeServerName
Dim ExchangeServerOrganization
Dim ExchangeServerSite
Dim Mailbox
Dim MailboxParentContainer
Dim MailboxRelativePath
Dim MailboxDisplayName
Dim MailboxFirstName
Dim MailboxLastName
Dim MailboxMiddleInitial
Dim MailboxAlias
Dim MTA
Dim MDB
Dim MailboxSMTPAddress
Dim MailboxX400Address
Dim MailboxCCMailAddress
Dim MailboxMSMailAddress
Dim NTUserAccountToAssociate
Dim UserDomain
Dim SID
Dim Security
Dim SecurityDescriptor
Dim DiscretionaryACL
Dim AccessControlEntry

ExchangeServerName = "EXCHANGE_SERVER"
ExchangeServerOrganization = "ADSITest"
ExchangeServerSite = "Macmillan"
MailboxRelativePath = ""
MailboxDisplayName = "Eck, Thomas E."
MailboxFirstName = "Thomas"
MailboxLastName = "Eck"
MailboxMiddleInitial = "E"
MailboxAlias = "Thomas.Eck"
UserDomain = "UserDomain"
NTUserAccountToAssociate = "teck"

MTA = "cn=Microsoft MTA,cn=" & ExchangeServerName &
",cn=Servers,cn=Configuration,ou=" & ExchangeServerSite & ",o=" &
➥ExchangeServerOrganization
MDB = "cn=Microsoft Private MDB,cn=" & ExchangeServerName &
➥",cn=Servers,cn=Configuration,ou=" & ExchangeServerSite & ",o=" &
➥ExchangeServerOrganization
MailboxSMTPAddress = MailboxAlias & "@" & ExchangeServerSite & "." &
➥ExchangeServerOrganization & ".com"
MailboxX400Address = "c=US;a= ;p=" & ExchangeServerOrganization & ";o=" &
➥ExchangeServerSite & ";s=" & MailboxLastName & ";g=" & MailboxFirstName & ";i=" &
➥MailboxMiddleInitial
MailboxCCMailAddress = MailboxLastName & ", " & MailboxFirstName & " at " &
➥ExchangeServerSite
```

```
MailboxMSMailAddress = UCase(ExchangeServerOrganization & "/" & ExchangeServerSite &
➥"/" & MailboxAlias)

Set MailboxParentContainer = GetObject("LDAP://" & ExchangeServerName & "/o=" &
➥ExchangeServerOrganization & "/ou=" & ExchangeServerSite & "/cn=Recipients" &
➥MailboxRelativePath)
Set Mailbox = MailboxParentContainer.Create("organizationalPerson", "cn=" &
➥MailboxAlias)

Mailbox.Put "mailPreferenceOption", 0
Mailbox.Put "givenName", MailboxFirstName
Mailbox.Put "sn", MailboxLastName
Mailbox.Put "cn", MailboxDisplayName
Mailbox.Put "uid", MailboxAlias
Mailbox.Put "Home-MTA", MTA
Mailbox.Put "Home-MDB", MDB
Mailbox.Put "mail", MailboxSMTPAddress
Mailbox.Put "MAPI-Recipient", True
Mailbox.Put "rfc822Mailbox", MailboxSMTPAddress
Mailbox.Put "textEncodedORAddress", MailboxX400Address
Mailbox.PutEx ADS_PROPERTY_APPEND, "otherMailbox", Array("CCMAIL$" &
➥MailboxCCMailAddress, "MS$" & MailboxMSMailAddress)

SID.SetAs ADS_SID_WINNT_PATH, "WinNT://" & UserDomain & "/" &
➥NTUserAccountToAssociate & ",user"
sidHex = SID.GetAs(ADS_SID_HEXSTRING)
Mailbox.Put "Assoc-NT-Account", sidHex
Mailbox.SetInfo

Set SecurityDescriptor = Security.GetSecurityDescriptor(Mailbox.ADsPath)
Set DiscretionaryACL = SecurityDescriptor.DiscretionaryACL
AccessControlEntry.AceType = ADS_ACETYPE_ACCESS_ALLOWED
AccessControlEntry.Trustee = UserDomain & "\" & MailboxAlias
AccessControlEntry.AccessMask = ADS_RIGHT_EXCH_MAIL_SEND_AS Or
➥ADS_RIGHT_EXCH_MAIL_RECEIVE_AS Or ADS_RIGHT_EXCH_MODIFY_USER_ATT
DiscretionaryACL.AddAce AccessControlEntry
SecurityDescriptor.DiscretionaryACL = DiscretionaryACL
Security.SetSecurityDescriptor SecurityDescriptor
```

Removing an Existing Exchange Mailbox Using a VBScript Active Server Page

```
Dim ExchangeServerName
Dim ExchangeServerOrganization
Dim ExchangeServerSite
Dim MailboxParentContainer
Dim MailboxRelativePath
Dim MailboxToRemove

ExchangeServerName = "EXCHANGE_SERVER"
ExchangeServerOrganization = "ADSITest"
ExchangeServerSite = "Macmillan"
```

```
MailboxRelativePath = ""
MailboxToRemove = "Thomas.Eck"

Set MailboxParentContainer = GetObject("LDAP://" & ExchangeServerName & "/o=" & _
ExchangeServerOrganization & "/ou=" & ExchangeServerSite & "/cn=Recipients" & _
MailboxRelativePath)

Call MailboxParentContainer.Delete("organizationalPerson", "cn=" & MailboxToRemove)
```

Adding a Distribution List Member Using a VBScript Active Server Page

```
Dim ExchangeServerName
Dim ExchangeServerOrganization
Dim ExchangeServerSite
Dim DistributionList
Dim DistributionListName
Dim DistributionListRelativePath
Dim DLMemberMailboxName

ExchangeServerName = "EXCHANGE_SERVER"
ExchangeServerOrganization = "ADSITest"
ExchangeServerSite = "Macmillan"
DistributionListRelativePath = ""
DistributionListName = "DL_Research_Development"
DLMemberMailboxName = "Thomas.Eck"

Set DistributionList = GetObject("LDAP://" & ExchangeServerName & "/o=" & _
ExchangeServerOrganization & "/ou=" & ExchangeServerSite & "/cn=Recipients" & _
DistributionListRelativePath & "/cn=" & DistributionListName)

DistributionList.Add ("LDAP://" & ExchangeServerName & "/o=" & _
ExchangeServerOrganization & "/ou=" & ExchangeServerSite & "/cn=Recipients" & _
"/cn=" & DLMemberMailboxName)

DistributionList.SetInfo
```

Removing a Distribution List Member Using a VBScript Active Server Page

```
Dim ExchangeServerName
Dim ExchangeServerOrganization
Dim ExchangeServerSite
Dim DistributionList
Dim DistributionListName
Dim DistributionListRelativePath
Dim DLMemberMailboxName

ExchangeServerName = "EXCHANGE_SERVER"
ExchangeServerOrganization = "ADSITest"
ExchangeServerSite = "Macmillan"
```

```
DistributionListRelativePath = ""
DistributionListName = "DL_Engineering"
DLMemberMailboxName = "Thomas.Eck"

Set DistributionList = GetObject("LDAP://" & ExchangeServerName & "/o=" &
➥ExchangeServerOrganization & "/ou=" & ExchangeServerSite & "/cn=Recipients" &
➥DistributionListRelativePath & "/cn=" & DistributionListName)

DistributionList.Remove ("LDAP://" & ExchangeServerName & "/o=" &
➥ExchangeServerOrganization & "/ou=" & ExchangeServerSite & "/cn=Recipients" &
➥"/cn=" & DLMemberMailboxName)

DistributionList.SetInfo
```

Determining the Distribution List Owner Using a VBScript Active Server Page

```
Dim ExchangeServerName
Dim ExchangeServerOrganization
Dim ExchangeServerSite
Dim DistributionList
Dim DistributionListName
Dim DistributionListRelativePath

ExchangeServerName = "EXCHANGE_SERVER"
ExchangeServerOrganization = "ADSITest"
ExchangeServerSite = "Macmillan"
DistributionListRelativePath = ""
DistributionListName = "DL_Senior_Management"

Set DistributionList = GetObject("LDAP://" & ExchangeServerName & "/o=" &
➥ExchangeServerOrganization & "/ou=" & ExchangeServerSite & "/cn=Recipients" &
➥DistributionListRelativePath & "/cn=" & DistributionListName)

Response.Write DistributionList.Owner
```

Chapter 12: Windows 2000 Management Code

Binding to the Root DS Entry (RootDSE) Using a VBScript Active Server Page

```
Dim RootDSE
Set RootDSE = GetObject("LDAP://RootDSE")

Response.Write "Current Time: " & RootDSE.Get("CurrentTime") & "<BR>"

Response.Write "SubSchemaSubEntry: " & RootDSE.Get("SubSchemaSubEntry") & "<BR>"

Response.Write "DsServiceName: " & RootDSE.Get("DsServiceName") & "<BR>"
```

```
For Each Item In RootDSE.Get("NamingContexts")
     Response.Write "Naming Context: " & Item & "<BR>"
Next

Response.Write "Default Naming Context: " & RootDSE.Get("DefaultNamingContext") &
↪"<BR>"

Response.Write "Schema Naming Context: " & RootDSE.Get("SchemaNamingContext") &
↪"<BR>"

Response.Write "Configuration Naming Context: " &
↪RootDSE.Get("ConfigurationNamingContext") & "<BR>"

Response.Write "Root Domain Naming Context: " &
↪RootDSE.Get("RootDomainNamingContext") & "<BR>"

For Each Item In RootDSE.Get("SupportedControl")
     Response.Write "Supported Control: " & Item & "<BR>"
Next

For Each Item In RootDSE.Get("SupportedLDAPVersion")
     Response.Write "Supported LDAP Version: " & Item & "<BR>"
Next

Response.Write "Highest Committed USN: " & RootDSE.Get("HighestCommittedUSN") &
↪"<BR>"

For Each Item In RootDSE.Get("SupportedSASLMechanisms")
     Response.Write "Supported SASL Mechanism: " & Item & "<BR>"
Next

Response.Write "DNS Host Name: " & RootDSE.Get("DnsHostName") & "<BR>"

Response.Write "LDAP Service Name: " & RootDSE.Get("LdapServiceName") & "<BR>"

Response.Write "Server Name: " & RootDSE.Get("ServerName") & "<BR>"
```

Using the RootDSE DefaultNamingContext Attribute to Bind to an Active Directory Object Using Current Credentials In a VBScript Active Server Page

```
Dim DefaultDomain
Dim RootDSE
Set RootDSE = GetObject("LDAP://RootDSE")
Set DefaultDomain = GetObject("LDAP://" & RootDSE.Get("DefaultNamingContext"))
```

Binding to an Active Directory Object Using Alternate Credentials In a VBScript Active Server Page

```
Dim DSO
Dim Obj
Dim AdsPath
Dim AlternateUser_UPN
Dim AlternateUser_Password

AdsPath =
➥"LDAP://Server_Name.ResearchDevelopment.TestInfra/cn=Users,dc=ResearchDevelopment,
➥dc=TestInfra"
AlternateUser_UPN = "thomas.eck@ResearchDevelopment.TestInfra"
AlternateUser_Password = "P0l1t1c@l@rs0ni$t"

Set DSO = GetObject("LDAP:")
Set Obj = DSO.OpenDSObject(AdsPath, AlternateUser_UPN, AlternateUser_Password,
➥ADS_SECURE_AUTHENTICATION)
```

Determining Which Object Attributes Are Replicated to the Global Catalog Using a VBScript Active Server Page

```
Dim Connection
Dim RS
Dim Entry
Dim Index
Dim RootDSE
Dim SchemaContainer

Index = 0
Set Connection = New ADODB.Connection
Connection.Provider = "ADsDSOObject"
Connection.Open "ADSI"

Set RootDSE = GetObject("LDAP://RootDSE")
Set SchemaContainer = GetObject("LDAP://" & RootDSE.Get("SchemaNamingContext"))

Set RS = Connection.Execute("SELECT cn FROM '" & SchemaContainer.AdsPath & "' where
➥isMemberOfPartialAttributeSet = TRUE AND objectCategory = 'attributeSchema'")

While Not RS.EOF
    For i = 0 To RS.Fields.Count - 1
        If RS.Fields(i).Type = adVariant And Not (IsNull(RS.Fields(i).Value)) Then
            For j = LBound(RS.Fields(i).Value) To UBound(RS.Fields(i).Value)
                Entry = Entry & RS.Fields(i).Value(j) & vbTab
            Next j
        Else
            Entry = Entry & RS.Fields(i).Value & vbTab
        End If
```

```
            If Index = RS.Fields.Count - 1 Then
                Response.Write Entry & "<BR>"
            End If
            Index = Index + 1
        Next i
        Entry = ""
        Index = 0
        RS.MoveNext
Wend
```

Displaying All User Class Objects in the Active Directory Using a VBScript Active Server Page

```
Dim RootDSE
Dim UserContainer
Dim User
Dim RelativePathFromDomainToUserContainer

RelativePathFromDomainToUserContainer = "ou=user accounts,"

Set RootDSE = GetObject("LDAP://RootDSE")
Set UserContainer = GetObject("LDAP://" & RelativePathFromDomainToUserContainer & _
➥RootDSE.Get("DefaultNamingContext"))
UserContainer.Filter = Array("User")

For Each User In UserContainer
    Response.Write User.AdsPath & "<BR>"
Next
```

Displaying All Group Class Objects in the Active Directory Using a VBScript Active Server Page

```
Dim RootDSE
Dim GroupContainer
Dim Group
Dim RelativePathFromDomainToGroupContainer

RelativePathFromDomainToGroupContainer = "ou=Groups,ou=Chicago,"

Set RootDSE = GetObject("LDAP://RootDSE")
Set GroupContainer = GetObject("LDAP://" & RelativePathFromDomainToGroupContainer & _
➥RootDSE.Get("defaultNamingContext"))

GroupContainer.Filter = Array("Group")

For Each Group In GroupContainer
    Response.Write Group.AdsPath & "<BR>"
Next
```

Displaying All Computer Class Objects in the Active Directory Using a VBScript Active Server Page

```
Dim RootDSE
Dim ComputerAccountContainer
Dim ComputerAccount
Dim RelativePathFromDomainToComputerContainer

RelativePathFromDomainToComputerContainer = "ou=Workstations,ou=Computer
➥Accounts,ou=Chicago"

Set RootDSE = GetObject("LDAP://RootDSE")
Set ComputerAccountContainer = GetObject("LDAP://" &
RelativePathFromDomainToComputerContainer & RootDSE.Get("defaultNamingContext"))

ComputerAccountContainer.Filter = Array("Computer")

For Each ComputerAccount In ComputerAccountContainer
    Response.Write ComputerAccount.AdsPath & "<BR>"
Next
```

Creating Objects in the Active Directory Using a VBScript Active Server Page

```
Dim RootDSE
Dim Container
Dim RelativePathToObject
Dim ObjectClass
Dim ObjectName
Dim NewObject
Dim MandatoryProperty1_Name
Dim MandatoryProperty1_Value
'Define more mandatory properties as needed

RelativePathToObject = "ou=administrators,"
ObjectClass = "user"
ObjectRelativeName = "cn=TestAdmin"
MandatoryProperty1_Name = "SAMAccountName"
MandatoryProperty1_Value = "TestAdmin"
'If you dimensioned additional mandatory properties, assign them here

Set RootDSE = GetObject("LDAP://RootDSE")
Set Container = GetObject("LDAP://" & RelativePathToObject &
➥RootDSE.Get("defaultNamingContext"))
Set NewObject = Container.Create(ObjectClass, ObjectRelativeName)

NewObject.Put MandatoryProperty1_Name, MandatoryProperty1_Value
'Assign additional mandatory properties to the object here

NewObject.SetInfo
```

Displaying Object Classes and Associated Mandatory Attributes Using a VBScript Active Server Page

```
Dim RootDSE
Dim ObjectName
Dim ObjectClass
Dim RelativePath
Dim Obj
Dim MandatoryProperty

RelativePath = "cn=System,"

Set RootDSE = GetObject("LDAP://RootDSE")
ADsPath = "LDAP://" & RelativePath & RootDSE.Get("DefaultNamingContext")

Set ObjectName = GetObject(ADsPath)
Response.Write "Object Name: " & ObjectName.Name & "<BR>"
Response.Write "Object Class: " & ObjectName.Class & "<BR>"
Set ObjectClass = GetObject(ObjectName.Schema)
For Each MandatoryProperty In ObjectClass.MandatoryProperties
    Response.Write MandatoryProperty & "<BR>"
Next
```

Removing Objects from the Active Directory Using a VBScript Active Server Page

```
Dim RootDSE
Dim Container
Dim RelativePathToObject
Dim ObjectClass
Dim ObjectName

RelativePathToObject = "ou=administrators,"
ObjectClass = "user"
ObjectRelativeName = "cn=TestAdmin"

Set RootDSE = GetObject("LDAP://RootDSE")
Set Container = GetObject("LDAP://" & RelativePathToObject & ↵RootDSE.Get("DefaultNamingContext"))

Call Container.Delete(ObjectClass, ObjectRelativeName)
```

Deleting an Entire Branch of a Directory Tree Using a VBScript Active Server Page

```
Dim RootDSE
Dim Container
Dim RelativePathToObject
RelativePathToObject = "ou=Print Queues,"
Set RootDSE = GetObject("LDAP://RootDSE")
```

```
Set Container = GetObject("LDAP://" & RelativePathToObject &
RootDSE.Get("DefaultNamingContext"))

Container.DeleteObject (0)
```

Renaming Objects in the Active Directory Using a VBScript Active Server Page

```
Dim Container
Dim NewObjectName
Set Container = GetObject("LDAP://ou=Admins,dc=eCommerce2000,dc=com")
Set NewObjectName =
Container.MoveHere("LDAP://cn=Administrator,ou=Admins,dc=eCommerce2000,dc=com",
➥"cn=DMZAdmin")
```

Moving Objects Within a Tree Using a VBScript Active Server Page

```
Dim Container
Dim NewObjectName
Set Container = GetObject("LDAP://ou=Users,dc=eCommerce2000,dc=com")
Set NewObjectName =
Container.MoveHere("LDAP://cn=DMZAdmin,ou=Admins,dc=eCommerce2000,dc=com",
➥"cn=DMZAdmin")
```

Enumerating the ACEs Within an Active Directory ACL Using a VBScript Active Server Page

```
Dim Obj
Dim ACE
Dim DiscretionaryACL
Dim SecurityDescriptor
Dim ObjectDistinguishedName

ObjectDistinguishedName = "ou=Admins,dc=eCommerce2000,dc=com"

Set Obj = GetObject("LDAP://" & ObjectDistinguishedName)
Set SecurityDescriptor = Obj.Get("ntSecurityDescriptor")
Set DiscretionaryACL = SecurityDescriptor.DiscretionaryACL

For Each ACE In DiscretionaryACL
    Response.Write ACE.Trustee & "<BR>"
    If (ACE.AccessMask And ADS_RIGHT_DELETE) <> 0 Then
        If (ACE.ObjectType = "" And ACE.InheritedObjectType = "") Then
            Response.Write "ADS_RIGHT_DELETE" & "<BR>"
        Else
            If ACE.InheritedObjectType = "" Then
                Response.Write "ADS_RIGHT_DELETE for SchemaIDGuid: " &
                    ➥ACE.ObjectType & "<BR>"
            Else
```

```vbscript
                Response.Write "Inherited ADS_RIGHT_DELETE for SchemaIDGuid: " & _
                ➥ACE.InheritedObjectType & "<BR>"
            End If
        End If
    End If

    If (ACE.AccessMask And ADS_RIGHT_READ_CONTROL) <> 0 Then
        If (ACE.ObjectType = "" And ACE.InheritedObjectType = "") Then
            Response.Write "ADS_RIGHT_READ_CONTROL" & "<BR>"
        Else
            If ACE.InheritedObjectType = "" Then
                Response.Write "ADS_RIGHT_READ_CONTROL for SchemaIDGuid: " & _
                ➥ACE.ObjectType & "<BR>"
            Else
                Response.Write "Inherited ADS_RIGHT_READ_CONTROL for SchemaIDGuid: " _
                ➥& ACE.InheritedObjectType & "<BR>"
            End If
        End If
    End If

    If (ACE.AccessMask And ADS_RIGHT_WRITE_DAC) <> 0 Then
        If (ACE.ObjectType = "" And ACE.InheritedObjectType = "") Then
            Response.Write "ADS_RIGHT_WRITE_DAC" & "<BR>"
        Else
            If ACE.InheritedObjectType = "" Then
                Response.Write "ADS_RIGHT_WRITE_DAC for SchemaIDGuid: " & _
                ➥ACE.ObjectType & "<BR>"
            Else
                Response.Write "Inherited ADS_RIGHT_WRITE_DAC for SchemaIDGuid: " & _
                ➥ACE.InheritedObjectType & "<BR>"
            End If
        End If
    End If

    If (ACE.AccessMask And ADS_RIGHT_WRITE_OWNER) <> 0 Then
        If (ACE.ObjectType = "" And ACE.InheritedObjectType = "") Then
            Response.Write "ADS_RIGHT_WRITE_OWNER" & "<BR>"
        Else
            If ACE.InheritedObjectType = "" Then
                Response.Write "ADS_RIGHT_WRITE_OWNER for SchemaIDGuid: " & _
                ➥ACE.ObjectType & "<BR>"
            Else
                Response.Write "Inherited ADS_RIGHT_WRITE_OWNER for SchemaIDGuid: " _
                ➥& ACE.InheritedObjectType & "<BR>"
            End If
        End If
    End If

    If (ACE.AccessMask And ADS_RIGHT_SYNCHRONIZE) <> 0 Then
        If (ACE.ObjectType = "" And ACE.InheritedObjectType = "") Then
            Response.Write "ADS_RIGHT_SYNCHRONIZE" & "<BR>"
        Else
            If ACE.InheritedObjectType = "" Then
```

```
                Response.Write "ADS_RIGHT_SYNCHRONIZE for SchemaIDGuid: " &
                ➥ACE.ObjectType & "<BR>"
            Else
                Response.Write "Inherited ADS_RIGHT_SYNCHRONIZE for SchemaIDGuid: "
                ➥& ACE.InheritedObjectType & "<BR>"
            End If
        End If
    End If
End If

If (ACE.AccessMask And ADS_RIGHT_ACCESS_SYSTEM_SECURITY) <> 0 Then
    If (ACE.ObjectType = "" And ACE.InheritedObjectType = "") Then
        Response.Write "ADS_RIGHT_ACCESS_SYSTEM_SECURITY" & "<BR>"
    Else
        If ACE.InheritedObjectType = "" Then
            Response.Write "ADS_RIGHT_ACCESS_SYSTEM_SECURITY for SchemaIDGuid: "
            ➥& ACE.ObjectType & "<BR>"
        Else
            Response.Write "Inherited ADS_RIGHT_ACCESS_SYSTEM_SECURITY for
            ➥SchemaIDGuid: " & ACE.InheritedObjectType & "<BR>"
        End If
    End If
End If

If (ACE.AccessMask And ADS_RIGHT_GENERIC_READ) <> 0 Then
    If (ACE.ObjectType = "" And ACE.InheritedObjectType = "") Then
        Response.Write "ADS_RIGHT_GENERIC_READ" & "<BR>"
    Else
        If ACE.InheritedObjectType = "" Then
            Response.Write "ADS_RIGHT_GENERIC_READ for SchemaIDGuid: " &
            ➥ACE.ObjectType & "<BR>"
        Else
            Response.Write "Inherited ADS_RIGHT_GENERIC_READ for SchemaIDGuid: "
            ➥& ACE.InheritedObjectType & "<BR>"
        End If
    End If
End If

If (ACE.AccessMask And ADS_RIGHT_GENERIC_WRITE) <> 0 Then
    If (ACE.ObjectType = "" And ACE.InheritedObjectType = "") Then
        Response.Write "ADS_RIGHT_GENERIC_WRITE" & "<BR>"
    Else
        If ACE.InheritedObjectType = "" Then
            Response.Write "ADS_RIGHT_GENERIC_WRITE for SchemaIDGuid: " &
            ➥ACE.ObjectType & "<BR>"
        Else
            Response.Write "Inherited ADS_RIGHT_GENERIC_WRITE for SchemaIDGuid:
            ➥" & ACE.InheritedObjectType & "<BR>"
        End If
    End If
End If

If (ACE.AccessMask And ADS_RIGHT_GENERIC_EXECUTE) <> 0 Then
    If (ACE.ObjectType = "" And ACE.InheritedObjectType = "") Then
        Response.Write "ADS_RIGHT_GENERIC_EXECUTE" & "<BR>"
    Else
```

```vbscript
            If ACE.InheritedObjectType = "" Then
                Response.Write "ADS_RIGHT_GENERIC_EXECUTE for SchemaIDGuid: " & _
                    ACE.ObjectType & "<BR>"
            Else
                Response.Write "Inherited ADS_RIGHT_GENERIC_EXECUTE for _
                    SchemaIDGuid: " & ACE.InheritedObjectType & "<BR>"
            End If
        End If
End If

If (ACE.AccessMask And ADS_RIGHT_GENERIC_ALL) <> 0 Then
    If (ACE.ObjectType = "" And ACE.InheritedObjectType = "") Then
        Response.Write "ADS_RIGHT_GENERIC_ALL" & "<BR>"
    Else
        If ACE.InheritedObjectType = "" Then
            Response.Write "ADS_RIGHT_GENERIC_ALL for SchemaIDGuid: " & _
                ACE.ObjectType & "<BR>"
        Else
            Response.Write "Inherited ADS_RIGHT_GENERIC_ALL for SchemaIDGuid: " _
                & ACE.InheritedObjectType & "<BR>"
        End If
    End If
End If

If (ACE.AccessMask And ADS_RIGHT_DS_CREATE_CHILD) <> 0 Then
    If (ACE.ObjectType = "" And ACE.InheritedObjectType = "") Then
        Response.Write "ADS_RIGHT_DS_CREATE_CHILD" & "<BR>"
    Else
        If ACE.InheritedObjectType = "" Then
            Response.Write "ADS_RIGHT_DS_CREATE_CHILD for SchemaIDGuid: " & _
                ACE.ObjectType & "<BR>"
        Else
            Response.Write "Inherited ADS_RIGHT_DS_CREATE_CHILD for _
                SchemaIDGuid: " & ACE.InheritedObjectType & "<BR>"
        End If
    End If
End If

If (ACE.AccessMask And ADS_RIGHT_DS_DELETE_CHILD) <> 0 Then
    If (ACE.ObjectType = "" And ACE.InheritedObjectType = "") Then
        Response.Write "ADS_RIGHT_DS_DELETE_CHILD" & "<BR>"
    Else
        If ACE.InheritedObjectType = "" Then
            Response.Write "ADS_RIGHT_DS_DELETE_CHILD for SchemaIDGuid: " & _
                ACE.ObjectType & "<BR>"
        Else
            Response.Write "Inherited ADS_RIGHT_DS_DELETE_CHILD for _
                SchemaIDGuid: " & ACE.InheritedObjectType & "<BR>"
        End If
    End If
End If

If (ACE.AccessMask And ADS_RIGHT_ACTRL_DS_LIST) <> 0 Then
    If (ACE.ObjectType = "" And ACE.InheritedObjectType = "") Then
        Response.Write "ADS_RIGHT_ACTRL_DS_LIST" & "<BR>"
    Else
```

```
            If ACE.InheritedObjectType = "" Then
                Response.Write "ADS_RIGHT_ACTRL_DS_LIST for SchemaIDGuid: " &
                ➥ACE.ObjectType & "<BR>"
            Else
                Response.Write "Inherited ADS_RIGHT_ACTRL_DS_LIST for SchemaIDGuid:
                ➥" & ACE.InheritedObjectType & "<BR>"
            End If
        End If
    End If

    If (ACE.AccessMask And ADS_RIGHT_DS_SELF) <> 0 Then
        If (ACE.ObjectType = "" And ACE.InheritedObjectType = "") Then
            Response.Write "ADS_RIGHT_DS_SELF" & "<BR>"
        Else
            If ACE.InheritedObjectType = "" Then
                Response.Write "ADS_RIGHT_DS_SELF for SchemaIDGuid: " &
                ➥ACE.ObjectType & "<BR>"
            Else
                Response.Write "Inherited ADS_RIGHT_DS_SELF for SchemaIDGuid: " &
                ➥ACE.InheritedObjectType & "<BR>"
            End If
        End If
    End If
If (ACE.AccessMask And ADS_RIGHT_DS_READ_PROP) <> 0 Then
        If (ACE.ObjectType = "" And ACE.InheritedObjectType = "") Then
            Response.Write "ADS_RIGHT_DS_READ_PROP" & "<BR>"
        Else
            If ACE.InheritedObjectType = "" Then
                Response.Write "ADS_RIGHT_DS_READ_PROP for SchemaIDGuid: " &
                ➥ACE.ObjectType & "<BR>"
            Else
                Response.Write "Inherited ADS_RIGHT_DS_READ_PROP for SchemaIDGuid: "
                ➥& ACE.InheritedObjectType & "<BR>"
            End If
        End If
    End If

    If (ACE.AccessMask And ADS_RIGHT_DS_WRITE_PROP) <> 0 Then
        If (ACE.ObjectType = "" And ACE.InheritedObjectType = "") Then
            Response.Write "ADS_RIGHT_DS_WRITE_PROP" & "<BR>"
        Else
            If ACE.InheritedObjectType = "" Then
                Response.Write "ADS_RIGHT_DS_WRITE_PROP for SchemaIDGuid: " &
                ➥ACE.ObjectType & "<BR>"
            Else
                Response.Write "Inherited ADS_RIGHT_DS_WRITE_PROP for SchemaIDGuid:
                ➥" & ACE.InheritedObjectType & "<BR>"
            End If
        End If
    End If

    If (ACE.AccessMask And ADS_RIGHT_DS_DELETE_TREE) <> 0 Then
        If (ACE.ObjectType = "" And ACE.InheritedObjectType = "") Then
            Response.Write "ADS_RIGHT_DS_DELETE_TREE" & "<BR>"
        Else
```

```
            If ACE.InheritedObjectType = "" Then
                Response.Write "ADS_RIGHT_DS_DELETE_TREE for SchemaIDGuid: " & _
                ➥ACE.ObjectType & "<BR>"
            Else
                Response.Write "Inherited ADS_RIGHT_DS_DELETE_TREE for SchemaIDGuid:
                ➥" & ACE.InheritedObjectType & "<BR>"
            End If
        End If
    End If

    If (ACE.AccessMask And ADS_RIGHT_DS_LIST_OBJECT) <> 0 Then
        If (ACE.ObjectType = "" And ACE.InheritedObjectType = "") Then
            Response.Write "ADS_RIGHT_DS_LIST_OBJECT" & "<BR>"
        Else
            If ACE.InheritedObjectType = "" Then
                Response.Write "ADS_RIGHT_DS_LIST_OBJECT for SchemaIDGuid: " & _
                ➥ACE.ObjectType & "<BR>"
            Else
                Response.Write "Inherited ADS_RIGHT_DS_LIST_OBJECT for SchemaIDGuid:
                ➥" & ACE.InheritedObjectType & "<BR>"
            End If
        End If
    End If

    If (ACE.AccessMask And ADS_RIGHT_DS_CONTROL_ACCESS) <> 0 Then
        If (ACE.ObjectType = "" And ACE.InheritedObjectType = "") Then
            Response.Write "ADS_RIGHT_DS_CONTROL_ACCESS" & "<BR>"
        Else
            If ACE.InheritedObjectType = "" Then
                Response.Write "ADS_RIGHT_DS_CONTROL_ACCESS for SchemaIDGuid: " & _
                ➥ACE.ObjectType & "<BR>"
            Else
                Response.Write "Inherited ADS_RIGHT_DS_CONTROL_ACCESS for
                ➥SchemaIDGuid: " & ACE.InheritedObjectType & "<BR>"
            End If
        End If
    End If
Next
```

Adding an ACE to an Active Directory Object ACL Using a VBScript Active Server Page

```
Dim Obj
Dim SecurityDescriptor
Dim ACE
Dim DACL

Set Obj = GetObject("LDAP://ou=ou=Admins,dc=eCommerce2000,dc=com")

Set SecurityDescriptor = Obj.Get("ntSecurityDescriptor")
Set DACL = SecurityDescriptor.DiscretionaryACL
Set ACE = CreateObject("AccessControlEntry")
```

```
ACE.AccessMask = ADS_RIGHT_DELETE Or ADS_RIGHT_GENERIC_READ Or
ADS_RIGHT_GENERIC_WRITE
ACE.AceFlags = ADS_ACEFLAG_NO_PROPAGATE_INHERIT_ACE
ACE.AceType = ADS_ACETYPE_ACCESS_ALLOWED
ACE.Trustee = "eCommerce2000\DMZAdmin"
DACL.AddAce ACE
SecurityDescriptor.DiscretionaryACL = DACL
Obj.Put "ntSecurityDescriptor", Array(SecurityDescriptor)
Obj.SetInfo
```

Removing an ACE from an Active Directory Object ACL Using a VBScript Active Server Page

```
Dim Obj
Dim ACE
Dim DACL
Dim SecurityDescriptor

Set Obj = GetObject("LDAP://cn=Guest,ou=users, dc=eCommerce2000,dc=com")
Set SecurityDescriptor = Obj.Get("ntSecurityDescriptor")
Set DACL = SecurityDescriptor.DiscretionaryACL

For Each ACE In DACL
    If UCase(ACE.Trustee) = "ECOMMERCE2000\GUEST" Then
        DACL.RemoveAce ACE
    End If
Next

SecurityDescriptor.DiscretionaryACL = DACL
Obj.Put "ntSecurityDescriptor", Array(SecurityDescriptor)
Obj.SetInfo
```

Adding an ACE to an Active Directory Organizational Unit ACL with Inheritance to All Child Objects Using a VBScript Active Server Page

```
Dim Obj
Dim SecurityDescriptor
Dim ACE
Dim DACL

Set Obj = GetObject("LDAP://ou=Admins,dc=eCommerce2000,dc=com")

Set SecurityDescriptor = Obj.Get("ntSecurityDescriptor")
Set DACL = SecurityDescriptor.DiscretionaryACL
Set ACE = CreateObject("AccessControlEntry")
ACE.AccessMask = ADS_RIGHT_GENERIC_READ
ACE.AceFlags = ADS_ACEFLAG_INHERIT_ACE
ACE.AceType = ADS_ACETYPE_ACCESS_ALLOWED
ACE.Trustee = "eCommerce2000\DMZAdmin"
```

```
DACL.AddAce ACE
SecurityDescriptor.DiscretionaryACL = DACL
Obj.Put "ntSecurityDescriptor", Array(SecurityDescriptor)
Obj.SetInfo
```

Adding an ACE to an Active Directory Organizational Unit ACL with Inheritance to a Single Class of Child Objects Using a VBScript Active Server Page

```
Dim Obj
Dim SecurityDescriptor
Dim ACE
Dim DACL

Set Obj = GetObject("LDAP://ou=Admins,dc=eCommerce2000,dc=com")

Set SecurityDescriptor = Obj.Get("ntSecurityDescriptor")
Set DACL = SecurityDescriptor.DiscretionaryACL
Set ACE = CreateObject("AccessControlEntry")
ACE.AccessMask = ADS_RIGHT_DS_DELETE_TREE
ACE.AceFlags = ADS_ACEFLAG_INHERIT_ACE

ACE.AceType = ADS_ACETYPE_ACCESS_ALLOWED_OBJECT
ACE.Flags = ADS_FLAG_OBJECT_TYPE_PRESENT
ACE.ObjectType = "{BF967A9C-0DE6-11D0-A285-00AA003049E2}"

ACE.Trustee = "eCommerce2000\DMZAdmin"
DACL.AddAce ACE
SecurityDescriptor.DiscretionaryACL = DACL
Obj.Put "ntSecurityDescriptor", Array(SecurityDescriptor)
Obj.SetInfo
```

Removing an ACE from an Active Directory Organizational Unit ACL with Inheritance to a Single Class of Child Objects Using a VBScript Active Server Page

```
Dim Obj
Dim ACE
Dim DACL
Dim SecurityDescriptor

Set Obj = GetObject("LDAP://ou=Admins,dc=eCommerce2000,dc=com")
Set SecurityDescriptor = Obj.Get("ntSecurityDescriptor")
Set DACL = SecurityDescriptor.DiscretionaryACL

For Each ACE In DACL
    If ((UCase(ACE.Trustee) = "ECOMMERCE2000\DMZADMIN") and (ACE.ObjectType =
    ➥"{BF967A9C-0DE6-11D0-A285-00AA003049E2}")) Then
        DACL.RemoveAce ACE
```

```
    End If
Next

SecurityDescriptor.DiscretionaryACL = DACL
Obj.Put "ntSecurityDescriptor", Array(SecurityDescriptor)
Obj.SetInfo
```

Adding an ACE to an Active Directory Organizational Unit ACL with Inheritance to a Single Property for an Object Class Using a VBScript Active Server Page

```
Dim Obj
Dim SecurityDescriptor
Dim ACE
Dim DACL

Set Obj = GetObject("LDAP://ou=Admins,dc=eCommerce2000,dc=com")

Set SecurityDescriptor = Obj.Get("ntSecurityDescriptor")
Set DACL = SecurityDescriptor.DiscretionaryACL
Set ACE = CreateObject("AccessControlEntry")
ACE.AccessMask = ADS_RIGHT_DS_READ_PROP Or ADS_RIGHT_DS_WRITE_PROP
ACE.AceFlags = ADS_ACEFLAG_INHERIT_ACE
ACE.AceType = ADS_ACETYPE_ACCESS_ALLOWED_OBJECT
ACE.ObjectType = "{BF967A49-0DE6-11D0-A285-00AA003049E2}"
ACE.Trustee = "NT AUTHORITY\SELF"
DACL.AddAce ACE
SecurityDescriptor.DiscretionaryACL = DACL
Obj.Put "ntSecurityDescriptor", Array(SecurityDescriptor)
Obj.SetInfo
```

Appendix B
ADSI 2.5 Programmer's Reference

No matter how comprehensive a text may be, it is impossible to cover every programming scenario. To help remedy that problem, this appendix looks at the object model employed for each major ADSI interface.

Listed in this appendix are tables that include descriptions, provider support definitions, information about whether a property is read-only, usage syntax for each method, and the data type returned for every commonly used property and method in the ADSI object model. Additionally, any required constants or flags are defined for each associated interface.

AccessControlEntry Interface

AccessControlEntry::AccessMask

Description	Specifies access permissions
Provider Support	LDAP
Data Type	Long
Read-Only?	No

AccessControlEntry::AccessMask Flag Values

Flag	Value
ADS_RIGHT_DS_CREATE_CHILD	0x1
ADS_RIGHT_DS_DELETE_CHILD	0x2
ADS_RIGHT_ACTRL_DS_LIST	0x4
ADS_RIGHT_DS_SELF	0x8
ADS_RIGHT_DS_READ_PROP	0x10
ADS_RIGHT_DS_WRITE_PROP	0x20

continues ▶

▶ *continued*

Flag	Value
ADS_RIGHT_DS_DELETE_TREE	0x40
ADS_RIGHT_DS_LIST_OBJECT	0x80
ADS_RIGHT_DS_CONTROL_ACCESS	0x100
ADS_RIGHT_DELETE	0x10000
ADS_RIGHT_READ_CONTROL	0x20000
ADS_RIGHT_WRITE_DAC	0x40000
ADS_RIGHT_WRITE_OWNER	0x80000
ADS_RIGHT_SYNCHRONIZE	0x100000
ADS_RIGHT_ACCESS_SYSTEM_SECURITY	0x1000000
ADS_RIGHT_GENERIC_ALL	0x10000000
ADS_RIGHT_GENERIC_EXECUTE	0x20000000
ADS_RIGHT_GENERIC_WRITE	0x40000000
ADS_RIGHT_GENERIC_READ	0x80000000

AccessControlEntry::AceFlags

Description	Indicates whether the ACE is inherited or defines a specific object type
Provider Support	LDAP
Data Type	Long
Read-Only?	No

AccessControlEntry::AceFlags Flag Values

Flag	Value
ADS_ACEFLAG_INHERIT_ACE	0x2
ADS_ACEFLAG_NO_PROPAGATE_INHERIT_ACE	0x4
ADS_ACEFLAG_INHERIT_ONLY_ACE	0x8
ADS_ACEFLAG_INHERITED_ACE	0x10
ADS_ACEFLAG_VALID_INHERIT_FLAGS	0x1f
ADS_ACEFLAG_SUCCESSFUL_ACCESS	0x40
ADS_ACEFLAG_FAILED_ACCESS	0x80

AccessControlEntry::AceType

Description	Indicates the type of ACE
Provider Support	LDAP
Data Type	Long
Read-Only?	No

AccessControlEntry::AceType Flag Values

Flag	Value
ADS_ACETYPE_ACCESS_ALLOWED	0
ADS_ACETYPE_ACCESS_DENIED	0x1
ADS_ACETYPE_SYSTEM_AUDIT	0x2
ADS_ACETYPE_ACCESS_ALLOWED_OBJECT	0x5
ADS_ACETYPE_ACCESS_DENIED_OBJECT	0x6
ADS_ACETYPE_SYSTEM_AUDIT_OBJECT	0x7

AccessControlEntry::Flags

Description	Indicates the use of an inherited or explicitly defined object type
Provider Support	LDAP
Data Type	Long
Read-Only?	No

AccessControlEntry::Flags Flag Values

Flag	Value
ADS_FLAG_OBJECT_TYPE_PRESENT	0x1
ADS_FLAG_INHERITED_OBJECT_TYPE_PRESENT	0x2

AccessControlEntry::InheritedObjectType

Description	A GUID representing the schemaIDGuid for an object class. This value is used to restrict the scope of the ACE to this particular class of objects. In this case, the restriction is inherited from the parent container.
Provider Support	LDAP
Data Type	String
Read-Only?	No

AccessControlEntry::ObjectType

Description	A GUID representing the schemaIDGuid for an object class. This value is used to restrict the scope of the ACE to this particular class of objects.
Provider Support	LDAP
Data Type	String
Read-Only?	No

> **Note**
>
> To find the schemaIDGuid for any object defined in the schema container, use the following Visual Basic code:

```
Private Type GUID
    Data(15) As Byte
End Type

Public Function GetSchemaIDGuid(ByVal ObjectClass As String) As String
    Dim RootDSE As IADs
    Dim SchemaIDGuidObject As IADs
    Dim ADsPath As String
    Dim lGuid As GUID
    Dim GetGUID As String
    Dim i As Byte
    Dim Element As Variant
    Dim GUIDString1 As String
    Dim GUIDString2 As String
    Dim GUIDString3 As String
    Dim GUIDString4 As String
    Dim GUIDString5 As String
    Set RootDSE = GetObject("LDAP://RootDSE")
    ADsPath = "LDAP://CN=" & ObjectClass & "," & _
    RootDSE.Get("SchemaNamingContext")
    Set SchemaIDGuidObject = GetObject(ADsPath)
    i = 0
    For Each Element In SchemaIDGuidObject.Get("SchemaIDGuid")
        lGuid.Data(i) = Element
        i = i + 1
    Next
    For i = 0 To 3
        If (lGuid.Data(3 - i) < 16) Then
            GUIDString1 = GUIDString1 & "0"
        End If
        GUIDString1 = GUIDString1 & Hex(lGuid.Data(3 - i))
    Next i
    For i = 0 To 1
        If (lGuid.Data(5 - i) < 16) Then
            GUIDString2 = GUIDString2 & "0"
        End If
        GUIDString2 = GUIDString2 & Hex(lGuid.Data(5 - i))
```

```
        Next i
        For i = 0 To 1
            If (lGuid.Data(7 - i) < 16) Then
                GUIDString3 = GUIDString3 & "0"
            End If
            GUIDString3 = GUIDString3 & Hex(lGuid.Data(7 - i))
        Next i
        For i = 0 To 1
            If (lGuid.Data(8 + i) < 16) Then
                GUIDString4 = GUIDString4 & "0"
            End If
            GUIDString4 = GUIDString4 & Hex(lGuid.Data(8 + i))
        Next i
        For i = 0 To 5
            If (lGuid.Data(10 + i) < 16) Then
                GUIDString5 = GUIDString5 & "0"
            End If
            GUIDString5 = GUIDString5 & Hex(lGuid.Data(10 + i))
        Next i
        GetSchemaIDGuid = "{" & GUIDString1 & "-" & GUIDString2 & "-" & GUIDString3 &
    "-" & GUIDString4 & "-" & GUIDString5 & "}"
    End Function
```

With the previous procedure in place in your project, you can simply pass the name of any object class or attribute found in the schema container and receive the schemaIDGuid as a properly formatted string. ◆

AccessControlEntry::Trustee

Description	Associates this ACE with an object in the directory
Provider Support	LDAP
Data Type	String
Read-Only?	No

Note

Trustees can be defined in an access control entry using the following format:

   DOMAIN\Trustee_Object

For example, to add a trustee named NBURN in the CRASH domain, the string passed would be CRASH\NBURN.

You can also pass the trustee name in by SID, well-known security principal, group, or the object's distinguished name. ◆

AccessControlList

AccessControlList::AceCount
Description	Defines the number of ACEs in an ACL
Provider Support	LDAP
Data Type	Long
Read-Only?	No

AccessControlList::AclRevision
Description	Specifies the ACL revision number
Provider Support	LDAP
Data Type	Long
Read-Only?	No

AccessControlList::AddAce
Description	Adds an access control entry object to the ACL
Provider Support	LDAP
Syntax	`AddAce(AccessControlEntry As Object)`
Data Type	None

AccessControlList::CopyAccessList
Description	Copies an ACL to another location
Provider Support	LDAP
Syntax	`CopyAccessList()`
Data Type	Object

AccessControlList::RemoveAce
Description	Removes an access control entry from the ACL
Provider Support	LDAP
Syntax	`RemoveAce(AccessControlEntry As Object)`
Data Type	None

IADs Interface

IADs::ADsPath

Description	Returns the distinguished name of the bound object
Provider Support	LDAP, WinNT
Data Type	String
Read-Only?	Yes

IADs::Class

Description	Returns the object class definition of the bound object
Provider Support	LDAP, WinNT
Data Type	String
Read-Only?	Yes

IADs::Get

Description	Retrieves a value from a namespace by name
Provider Support	LDAP, WinNT
Syntax	`Get(Name As String)`
Data Type	Variant

IADs::GetEx

Description	Retrieves a single value from a multi-valued attribute
Provider Support	LDAP, WinNT
Syntax	`GetEx(Name As String)`
Data Type	Variant

IADs::GetInfo

Description	Loads all property values into the cache
Provider Support	LDAP, WinNT
Syntax	`GetInfo()`
Data Type	None

IADs::GetInfoEx

Description	Loads specific properties into the cache
Provider Support	LDAP, WinNT
Syntax	`GetInfoEx(Properties As Variant, Reserved as Long)`
Data Type	None

IADs::GUID

Description	Returns the GUID of the bound object
Provider Support	LDAP, WinNT
Data Type	String
Read-Only?	Yes

IADs::Name

Description	Returns the relative name of the bound object
Provider Support	LDAP, WinNT
Data Type	String
Read-Only?	Yes

IADs::Parent

Description	Returns the ADsPath of the parent object
Provider Support	LDAP, WinNT
Data Type	String
Read-Only?	Yes

IADs::Put

Description	Allows population of a single attribute by name
Provider Support	LDAP, WinNT
Syntax	`Put(Name As String, Property As Variant)`
Data Type	None

IADs::PutEx

Description	Allows population of a multi-valued property by name
Provider Support	LDAP, WinNT
Syntax	`PutEx(ControlCode As Long, Name As String, Property As Variant)`
Data Type	None

IADs::Schema

Description	Returns the ADsPath to the schema class object for the bound object
Provider Support	LDAP, WinNT
Data Type	String
Read-Only?	Yes

IADs::SetInfo

Description	Writes the current properties held in the cache to the directory
Provider Support	LDAP, WinNT
Syntax	`SetInfo()`
Data Type	None

IADsCollection

IADsCollection::Add

Description	Adds an element to a collection
Provider Support	Not supported in WinNT provider
Syntax	`Add(Name As String, Item As Variant)`
Data Type	None

IADsCollection::GetObject

Description	Retrieves an element from the collection
Provider Support	WinNT
Syntax	`GetObject(Name As String)`
Data Type	Variant

IADsCollection::Remove

Description	Removes an element from the collection
Provider Support	WinNT
Syntax	`Remove(ItemToRemoved As String)`
Data Type	None

IADsComputer

IADsComputer::ADsPath

Description	Returns the distinguished name of the bound object
Provider Support	WinNT
Data Type	String
Read-Only?	Yes

IADsComputer::Class

Description	Returns the object class definition of the bound object
Provider Support	WinNT
Data Type	String
Read-Only?	Yes

IADsComputer::ComputerID

Description	Returns the GUID used to identify the bound computer
Provider Support	Not supported in WinNT provider
Data Type	String
Read-Only?	Yes

IADsComputer::Department

Description	Retrieves/manipulates the associated department for the bound computer object
Provider Support	Not supported in WinNT provider
Data Type	String
Read-Only?	No

IADsComputer::Description

Description	Free-text description of the bound computer object
Provider Support	WinNT
Data Type	String
Read-Only?	No

IADsComputer::Division

Description	Free-text field to describe the division associated with the bound computer object
Provider Support	Not supported in WinNT provider
Data Type	String
Read-Only?	No

IADsComputer::Get

Description	Retrieves a value from a namespace by name
Provider Support	WinNT
Syntax	`Get(Name As String)`
Data Type	Variant

IADsComputer::GetEx

Description	Retrieves a single value from a multi-valued attribute
Provider Support	WinNT
Syntax	`GetEx(Name As String)`
Data Type	Variant

IADsComputer::GetInfo

Description	Loads all property values into the cache
Provider Support	WinNT
Syntax	`GetInfo()`
Data Type	None

IADsComputer::GetInfoEx

Description	Loads specific properties into the cache
Provider Support	WinNT
Syntax	`GetInfoEx(Properties As Variant, Reserved As Long)`
Data Type	None

IADsComputer::GUID

Description	Returns the GUID of the bound object
Provider Support	WinNT
Data Type	String
Read-Only?	Yes

IADsComputer::Location

Description	Free-text field used to associate a physical location with the bound computer object
Provider Support	Not supported in WinNT provider
Data Type	String
Read-Only?	No

IADsComputer::MemorySize

Description	Describes the RAM installed on a system
Provider Support	Not supported in WinNT provider
Data Type	String
Read-Only?	No

IADsComputer::Model

Description	Describes the make and model of the bound computer object
Provider Support	Not supported in WinNT provider
Data Type	String
Read-Only?	No

IADsComputer::Name

Description	Returns the relative name of the bound object
Provider Support	WinNT
Data Type	String
Read-Only?	Yes

IADsComputer::NetAddresses

Description	Describes binding information for the computer object
Provider Support	Not supported in WinNT provider
Data Type	Variant
Read-Only?	No

IADsComputer::OperatingSystem

Description	Describes the operating system in use on the bound computer object
Provider Support	WinNT
Data Type	String
Read-Only?	No

IADsComputer::OperatingSystemVersion

Description	Describes the version of the operating system used on the bound computer object
Provider Support	WinNT
Data Type	String
Read-Only?	No

IADsComputer::Owner

Description	Describes the licensed user of the bound computer object
Provider Support	WinNT
Data Type	String
Read-Only?	No

IADsComputer::Parent

Description	Returns the ADsPath of the parent object
Provider Support	WinNT
Data Type	String
Read-Only?	Yes

IADsComputer::PrimaryUser

Description	Describes the primary user of the bound computer object
Provider Support	Not supported in WinNT provider
Data Type	String
Read-Only?	No

IADsComputer::Processor

Description	Describes the type of processor used on the bound computer object
Provider Support	WinNT
Data Type	String
Read-Only?	No

IADsComputer::ProcessorCount

Description	Describes the HAL in use on the bound computer object or the number of processors installed for non-Windows NT/2000 machines
Provider Support	WinNT
Data Type	String
Read-Only?	No

IADsComputer::Put

Description	Allows population of a single attribute by name
Provider Support	WinNT
Syntax	Put(Name As String, Property As Variant)
Data Type	None

IADsComputer::PutEx

Description	Allows population of a multi-valued property by name
Provider Support	WinNT
Syntax	PutEx(ControlCode As Long, Name As String, Property As Variant)
Data Type	None

IADsComputer::Role

Description	Describes the role of the computer (workstation/server)
Provider Support	Not supported in WinNT provider
Data Type	String
Read-Only?	No

IADsComputer::Schema

Description	Returns the ADsPath to the schema class object for the bound object
Provider Support	WinNT
Data Type	String
Read-Only?	Yes

IADsComputer::SetInfo

Description	Writes the current properties held in the cache to the directory
Provider Support	WinNT
Syntax	`SetInfo()`
Data Type	None

IADsComputer::Site

Description	Returns the GUID for the site associated with the bound computer object
Provider Support	Not supported in WinNT provider
Data Type	String
Read-Only?	Yes

IADsComputer::StorageCapacity

Description	Describes the disk space in MB for the bound computer object
Provider Support	Not supported in WinNT provider
Data Type	String
Read-Only?	No

IADsContainer

IADsContainer::CopyHere

Description	Copies an object to an alternate location in the directory
Provider Support	LDAP, WinNT
Syntax	`CopyHere(SourceName As String, NewName As String)`
Data Type	Object

IADsContainer::Count

Description	Returns the number of objects in the container
Provider Support	Not supported in LDAP or WinNT provider
Data Type	Long
Read-Only?	Yes

IADsContainer::Create

Description	Creates a new object of a specific class in the directory
Provider Support	LDAP, WinNT
Syntax	`Create(ClassName As String, RelativeName As String)`
Data Type	Object

IADsContainer::Delete

Description	Removes an object from the directory
Provider Support	LDAP, WinNT
Syntax	`Delete(ClassName As String, RelativeName As String)`
Data Type	None

IADsContainer::Filter

Description	Establishes an object class filter for container enumeration functions
Provider Support	LDAP, WinNT
Data Type	Variant
Read-Only?	No

IADsContainer::GetObject

Description	Establishes an interface to a specified object
Provider Support	LDAP, WinNT
Syntax	`GetObject(ClassName As String, RelativeName As String)`
Data Type	Object

IADsContainer::Hints

    Description   Determines which properties should be loaded
    Provider Support   LDAP
    Data Type   Variant
    Read-Only?   No

IADsContainer::MoveHere

    Description   Moves (or renames) an object within the directory
    Provider Support   LDAP, WinNT
    Syntax   `MoveHere(SourceName As String, NewName As String)`
    Data Type   Object

IADsDeleteOps Interface

IADsDeleteOps::DeleteObject

    Description   Deletes an object (and all child objects) from the directory
    Provider Support   LDAP
    Syntax   `DeleteObject(Flags As Long)`
    Data Type   None

IADsDomain

IADsDomain::ADsPath

    Description   Returns the distinguished name of the bound object
    Provider Support   WinNT
    Data Type   String
    Read-Only?   Yes

IADsDomain::AutoUnlockInterval

    Description   Establishes the minimum amount of time that must elapse before an account lockout condition is automatically reset
    Provider Support   WinNT
    Data Type   Long
    Read-Only?   No

IADsDomain::Class

Description	Returns the object class definition of the bound object
Provider Support	WinNT
Data Type	String
Read-Only?	Yes

IADsDomain::Get

Description	Retrieves a value from a namespace by name
Provider Support	WinNT
Syntax	`Get(Name As String)`
Data Type	Variant

IADsDomain::GetEx

Description	Retrieves a single value from a multi-valued attribute
Provider Support	WinNT
Syntax	`GetEx(Name As String)`
Data Type	Variant

IADsDomain::GetInfo

Description	Loads all property values into the cache
Provider Support	WinNT
Syntax	`GetInfo()`
Data Type	None

IADsDomain::GetInfoEx

Description	Loads specific properties into the cache
Provider Support	WinNT
Syntax	`GetInfoEx(Properties As Variant, Reserved As Long)`
Data Type	None

IADsDomain::GUID

Description	Returns the GUID of the bound object
Provider Support	WinNT
Data Type	String
Read-Only?	Yes

IADsDomain::IsWorkgroup

Description	Returns a Boolean value representing whether the bound object is part of a workgroup
Provider Support	Not supported in WinNT provider
Data Type	Boolean
Read-Only?	Yes

IADsDomain::LockoutObservationInterval

Description	Establishes the amount of time in which a user's bad password attempts will increment the bad login counter
Provider Support	WinNT
Data Type	Long
Read-Only?	No

IADsDomain::MaxBadPasswordsAllowed

Description	Establishes the number of bad password attempts before an account is locked out
Provider Support	WinNT
Data Type	Long
Read-Only?	No

IADsDomain::MaxPasswordAge

Description	Determines the time interval for which a user may retain a password
Provider Support	WinNT
Data Type	Long
Read-Only?	No

IADsDomain::MinPasswordAge

Description	Determines the minimum amount of time a user must retail a password
Provider Support	WinNT
Data Type	Long
Read-Only?	No

IADsDomain::MinPasswordLength

Description	Establishes the minimum length a user may use for his or her password
Provider Support	WinNT
Data Type	Long
Read-Only?	No

IADsDomain::Name

Description	Returns the relative name of the bound object
Provider Support	WinNT
Data Type	String
Read-Only?	Yes

IADsDomain::Parent

Description	Returns the ADsPath of the parent object
Provider Support	WinNT
Data Type	String
Read-Only?	Yes

IADsDomain::PasswordAttributes

Description	Establishes password restrictions
Provider Support	Not supported in WinNT provider
Data Type	Long
Read-Only?	No

IADsDomain::PasswordHistoryLength

Description	Determines the number of passwords that will be retained to prevent reuse of a previously used password
Provider Support	WinNT
Data Type	Long
Read-Only?	No

IADsDomain::Put

Description	Allows population of a single attribute by name
Provider Support	WinNT
Syntax	`Put(Name As String, Property As Variant)`
Data Type	None

IADsDomain::PutEx

Description	Allows population of a multi-valued property by name
Provider Support	WinNT
Syntax	`PutEx(ControlCode As Long, Name As String, Property As Variant)`
Data Type	None

IADsDomain::Schema

Description	Returns the ADsPath to the schema class object for the bound object
Provider Support	WinNT
Data Type	String
Read-Only?	Yes

IADsDomain::SetInfo

Description	Writes the current properties held in the cache to the directory
Provider Support	WinNT
Syntax	`SetInfo()`
Data Type	None

IADsFileService

IADsFileService::ADsPath

Description	Returns the distinguished name of the bound object
Provider Support	WinNT
Data Type	String
Read-Only?	Yes

IADsFileService::Class

Description	Returns the object class definition of the bound object
Provider Support	WinNT
Data Type	String
Read-Only?	Yes

IADsFileService::Dependencies

Description	Establishes the names of the services or load groups that must also be loaded to start this service
Provider Support	WinNT
Data Type	Variant
Read-Only?	No

IADsFileService::Description

Description	Establishes the description of the file service
Provider Support	WinNT
Data Type	String
Read-Only?	No

IADsFileService::DisplayName

Description	Establishes the display name of the service
Provider Support	WinNT
Data Type	String
Read-Only?	No

IADsFileService::ErrorControl

Description	Establishes the actions to be taken upon service failure
Provider Support	WinNT
Data Type	Long
Read-Only?	No

IADsFileService::ErrorControl Flag Values

Flag	Value
ADS_SERVICE_ERROR_IGNORE	0x00000000
ADS_SERVICE_ERROR_NORMAL	0x00000001
ADS_SERVICE_ERROR_SEVERE	0x00000002
ADS_SERVICE_ERROR_CRITICAL	0x00000003

IADsFileService::Get

Description	Retrieves a value from a namespace by name
Provider Support	WinNT
Syntax	`Get(Name As String)`
Data Type	Variant

IADsFileService::GetEx

Description	Retrieves a single value from a multi-valued attribute
Provider Support	WinNT
Syntax	`GetEx(Name As String)`
Data Type	Variant

IADsFileService::GetInfo

Description	Loads all property values into the cache
Provider Support	WinNT
Syntax	`GetInfo()`
Data Type	None

IADsFileService::GetInfoEx

Description	Loads specific properties into the cache
Provider Support	WinNT
Syntax	`GetInfoEx(Properties As Variant, Reserved as Long)`
Data Type	None

IADsFileService::GUID

Description	Returns the GUID of the bound object
Provider Support	WinNT
Data Type	String
Read-Only?	Yes

IADsFileService::HostComputer

Description	Establishes the host of the currently bound service
Provider Support	WinNT
Data Type	String
Read-Only?	No

IADsFileService::LoadOrderGroup

Description	Establishes the load order group used with the currently bound service
Provider Support	WinNT
Data Type	String
Read-Only?	No

IADsFileService::MaxUserCount

Description	Specifies the maximum number of users allowed to concurrently access the service
Provider Support	WinNT
Data Type	Long
Read-Only?	No

IADsFileService::Name

Description	Returns the relative name of the bound object
Provider Support	WinNT
Data Type	String
Read-Only?	Yes

IADsFileService::Parent

Description	Returns the ADsPath of the parent object
Provider Support	WinNT
Data Type	String
Read-Only?	Yes

IADsFileService::Path

Description	Establishes the path of the executable associated with the bound service
Provider Support	WinNT
Data Type	String
Read-Only?	No

IADsFileService::Put

Description	Allows population of a single attribute by name
Provider Support	WinNT
Syntax	`Put(Name As String, Property As Variant)`
Data Type	None

IADsFileService::PutEx

Description	Allows population of a multi-valued property by name
Provider Support	WinNT
Syntax	`PutEx(ControlCode As Long, Name As String, Property As Variant)`
Data Type	None

IADsFileService::Schema

Description	Returns the ADsPath to the schema class object for the bound object
Provider Support	WinNT
Data Type	String
Read-Only?	Yes

IADsFileService::ServiceAccountName

Description	Establishes the username of the user account to be used with the service
Provider Support	WinNT
Data Type	String
Read-Only?	No

IADsFileService::ServiceAccountPath

Description	Establishes the ADsPath to the user account to be used for service authentication
Provider Support	WinNT
Data Type	String
Read-Only?	No

IADsFileService::ServiceType

Description	Establishes the process type in which the bound service will be run
Provider Support	WinNT
Data Type	Long
Read-Only?	No

IADsFileService::ServiceType Flag Values

Flag	Value
ADS_SERVICE_KERNAL_DRIVER	0x00000001
ADS_SERVICE_FILE_SYSTEM_DRIVER	0x00000002
ADS_SERVICE_OWN_PROCESS	0x00000010
ADS_SERVICE_SHARE_PROCESS	0x00000020

IADsFileService::SetInfo

Description	Writes the current properties held in the cache to the directory
Provider Support	WinNT
Syntax	SetInfo()
Data Type	None

IADsFileService::StartType

Description	Establishes how the service will start
Provider Support	WinNT
Data Type	Long
Read-Only?	No

IADsFileService::StartType Flag Values

Flag	Value
ADS_SERVICE_BOOT_START	0
ADS_SERVICE_SYSTEM_START	1
ADS_SERVICE_AUTO_START	2
ADS_SERVICE_DEMAND_START	3
ADS_SERVICE_DISABLED	4

IADsFileService::StartupParameters

Description	Establishes the arguments passed to the service at startup
Provider Support	WinNT
Data Type	Long
Read-Only?	No

IADsFileService::Version

Description	Establishes version information for the service
Provider Support	WinNT
Data Type	String
Read-Only?	No

IADsFileServiceOperations

IADsFileServiceOperations::ADsPath

Description	Returns the distinguished name of the bound object
Provider Support	WinNT
Data Type	String
Read-Only?	Yes

IADsFileServiceOperations::Class

    Description   Returns the object class definition of the bound object
    Provider Support   WinNT
    Data Type   String
    Read-Only?   Yes

IADsFileServiceOperations::Continue

    Description   Resumes a previously paused service
    Provider Support   WinNT
    Syntax   `Continue()`
    Data Type   None

IADsFileServiceOperations::Get

    Description   Retrieves a value from a namespace by name
    Provider Support   WinNT
    Syntax   `Get(Name As String)`
    Data Type   Variant

IADsFileServiceOperations::GetEx

    Description   Retrieves a single value from a multi-valued attribute
    Provider Support   WinNT
    Syntax   `GetEx(Name As String)`
    Data Type   Variant

IADsFileServiceOperations::GetInfo

    Description   Loads all property values into the cache
    Provider Support   WinNT
    Syntax   `GetInfo()`
    Data Type   None

IADsFileServiceOperations::GetInfoEx

    Description   Loads specific properties into the cache
    Provider Support   WinNT
    Syntax   `GetInfoEx(Properties As Variant, Reserved As Long)`
    Data Type   None

IADsFileServiceOperations::GUID

Description	Returns the GUID of the bound object
Provider Support	WinNT
Data Type	String
Read-Only?	Yes

IADsFileServiceOperations::Name

Description	Returns the relative name of the bound object
Provider Support	WinNT
Data Type	String
Read-Only?	Yes

IADsFileServiceOperations::Parent

Description	Returns the ADsPath of the parent object
Provider Support	WinNT
Data Type	String
Read-Only?	Yes

IADsFileServiceOperations::Pause

Description	Pauses a running service
Provider Support	WinNT
Syntax	`Pause()`
Data Type	None

IADsFileServiceOperations::Put

Description	Allows population of a single attribute by name
Provider Support	WinNT
Syntax	`Put(Name As String, Property As String)`
Data Type	None

IADsFileServiceOperations::PutEx

Description	Allows population of a multi-valued property by name
Provider Support	WinNT
Syntax	`PutEx(ControlCode As Long, Name As String, Property As Variant)`
Data Type	None

IADsFileServiceOperations::Resources

Description	Establishes an interface to the collection object representing the open resources for the bound object
Provider Support	WinNT
Syntax	`Resources()`
Data Type	IADsCollection

IADsFileServiceOperations::Schema

Description	Returns the ADsPath to the schema class object for the bound object
Provider Support	WinNT
Data Type	String
Read-Only?	Yes

IADsFileServiceOperations::Sessions

Description	Establishes an interface to the collection object containing open user sessions for the bound object
Provider Support	WinNT
Syntax	`Sessions()`
Data Type	IADsCollection

IADsFileServiceOperations::SetInfo

Description	Writes the current properties held in the cache to the directory
Provider Support	WinNT
Syntax	`SetInfo()`
Data Type	None

IADsFileServiceOperations::SetPassword

Description	Sets a new password to be used for the service account
Provider Support	WinNT
Syntax	`SetPassword(NewPassword As String)`
Data Type	None

IADsFileServiceOperations::Start

Description	Starts a stopped service
Provider Support	WinNT
Syntax	Start()
Data Type	None

IADsFileServiceOperations::Status

Description	Returns the status of the currently bound service
Provider Support	WinNT
Data Type	Long
Read-Only?	Yes

IADsFileServiceOperations::Status Flag Values

Flag	Value
ADS_SERVICE_STOPPED	0x00000001
ADS_SERVICE_START_PENDING	0x00000002
ADS_SERVICE_STOP_PENDING	0x00000003
ADS_SERVICE_RUNNING	0x00000004
ADS_SERVICE_CONTINUE_PENDING	0x00000005
ADS_SERVICE_PAUSE_PENDING	0x00000006
ADS_SERVICE_PAUSED	0x00000007
ADS_SERVICE_ERROR	0x00000008

IADsFileServiceOperations::Stop

Description	Stops a running service
Provider Support	WinNT
Syntax	Stop()
Data Type	None

IADsFileShare

IADsFileShare::ADsPath

Description	Returns the distinguished name of the bound object
Provider Support	WinNT
Data Type	String
Read-Only?	Yes

IADsFileShare::Class

Description	Returns the object class definition of the bound object
Provider Support	WinNT
Data Type	String
Read-Only?	Yes

IADsFileShare::CurrentUserCount

Description	Returns the number of current users
Provider Support	WinNT
Data Type	Long
Read-Only?	Yes

IADsFileShare::Description

Description	Establishes the description for a file share
Provider Support	WinNT
Data Type	String
Read-Only?	No

IADsFileShare::Get

Description	Retrieves a value from a namespace by name
Provider Support	WinNT
Syntax	`Get(Name As String)`
Data Type	Variant

IADsFileShare::GetEx

Description	Retrieves a single value from a multi-valued attribute
Provider Support	WinNT
Syntax	`GetEx(Name As String)`
Data Type	Variant

IADsFileShare::GetInfo

Description	Loads all property values into the cache
Provider Support	WinNT
Syntax	`GetInfo()`
Data Type	None

IADsFileShare::GetInfoEx

Description	Loads specific properties into the cache
Provider Support	WinNT
Syntax	`GetInfoEx(Properties As Variant, Reserved As Long)`
Data Type	None

IADsFileShare::GUID

Description	Returns the GUID of the bound object
Provider Support	WinNT
Data Type	String
Read-Only?	Yes

IADsFileShare::HostComputer

Description	Establishes the ADsPath to the computer hosting the file share
Provider Support	WinNT
Data Type	String
Read-Only?	No

IADsFileShare::MaxUserCount

Description	Establishes the maximum number of users permitted on the file share
Provider Support	WinNT
Data Type	Long
Read-Only?	No

IADsFileShare::Name

Description	Returns the relative name of the bound object
Provider Support	WinNT
Data Type	String
Read-Only?	Yes

IADsFileShare::Parent

Description	Returns the ADsPath of the parent object
Provider Support	WinNT
Data Type	String
Read-Only?	Yes

IADsFileShare::Path

Description	Establishes the file system path to the file share
Provider Support	WinNT
Data Type	String
Read-Only?	No

IADsFileShare::Put

Description	Allows population of a single attribute by name
Provider Support	WinNT
Syntax	`Put(Name As String, Property As Variant)`
Data Type	None

IADsFileShare::PutEx

Description	Allows population of a multi-valued property by name
Provider Support	WinNT
Syntax	`PutEx(ControlCode As Long, Name As String, Property As Variant)`
Data Type	None

IADsFileShare::Schema

Description	Returns the ADsPath to the schema class object for the bound object
Provider Support	WinNT
Data Type	String
Read-Only?	Yes

IADsFileShare::SetInfo

Description	Writes the current properties held in the cache to the directory
Provider Support	WinNT
Syntax	`SetInfo()`
Data Type	None

IADsGroup

IADsGroup::Add

Description	Adds a directory object to the bound group
Provider Support	LDAP, WinNT
Syntax	`Add(NewItem As String)`
Data Type	None

IADsGroup::ADsPath

Description	Returns the distinguished name of the bound object
Provider Support	LDAP, WinNT
Data Type	String
Read-Only?	Yes

IADsGroup::Class

Description	Returns the object class definition of the bound object
Provider Support	LDAP, WinNT
Data Type	String
Read-Only?	Yes

IADsGroup::Description

Description	Establishes the description for the bound group
Provider Support	LDAP, WinNT
Data Type	String
Read-Only?	No

IADsGroup::Get

Description	Retrieves a value from a namespace by name
Provider Support	LDAP, WinNT
Syntax	`Get(Name As String)`
Data Type	Variant

IADsGroup::GetEx
Description	Retrieves a single value from a multi-valued attribute
Provider Support	LDAP, WinNT
Syntax	`GetEx(Name As String)`
Data Type	Variant

IADsGroup::GetInfo
Description	Loads all property values into the cache
Provider Support	LDAP, WinNT
Syntax	`GetInfo()`
Data Type	None

IADsGroup::GetInfoEx
Description	Loads specific properties into the cache
Provider Support	LDAP, WinNT
Syntax	`GetInfoEx(Properties As Variant, Reserved As Long)`
Data Type	None

IADsGroup::GUID
Description	Returns the GUID of the bound object
Provider Support	LDAP, WinNT
Data Type	String
Read-Only?	Yes

IADsGroup::IsMember
Description	When passed the ADsPath of a user or group object determines whether the object is part of the bound group
Provider Support	LDAP, WinNT
Syntax	`IsMember(Member As String)`
Data Type	Boolean

IADsGroup::Members
Description	Returns an array of strings representing the members of the currently bound group
Provider Support	LDAP, WinNT
Syntax	`Members()`
Data Type	IADsMembers

IADsGroup::Name

Description	Returns the relative name of the bound object
Provider Support	LDAP, WinNT
Data Type	String
Read-Only?	Yes

IADsGroup::Parent

Description	Returns the ADsPath of the parent object
Provider Support	LDAP, WinNT
Data Type	String
Read-Only?	Yes

IADsGroup::Put

Description	Allows population of a single attribute by name
Provider Support	LDAP, WinNT
Syntax	`Put(Name As String, Property As Variant)`
Data Type	None

IADsGroup::PutEx

Description	Allows population of a multi-valued property by name
Provider Support	LDAP, WinNT
Syntax	`PutEx(ControlCode As Long, Name As String, Property As Variant)`
Data Type	None

IADsGroup::Remove

Description	Removes a directory object from the currently bound group
Provider Support	LDAP, WinNT
Syntax	`Remove(ItemToBeRemoved As String)`
Data Type	None

IADsGroup::Schema

Description	Returns the ADsPath to the schema class object for the bound object
Provider Support	LDAP, WinNT
Data Type	String
Read-Only?	Yes

IADsGroup::SetInfo

Description	Writes the current properties held in the cache to the directory
Provider Support	LDAP, WinNT
Syntax	SetInfo()
Data Type	None

IADsLocality

IADsLocality::ADsPath

Description	Returns the distinguished name of the bound object
Provider Support	LDAP
Data Type	String
Read-Only?	Yes

IADsLocality::Class

Description	Returns the object class definition of the bound object
Provider Support	LDAP
Data Type	String
Read-Only?	Yes

IADsLocality::Description

Description	Establishes the description for the locality object
Provider Support	LDAP
Data Type	String
Read-Only?	No

IADsLocality::Get
    Description   Retrieves a value from a namespace by name
    Provider Support   LDAP
    Syntax   `Get(Name As String)`
    Data Type   Variant

IADsLocality::GetEx
    Description   Retrieves a single value from a multi-valued attribute
    Provider Support   LDAP
    Syntax   `GetEx(Name As String)`
    Data Type   Variant

IADsLocality::GetInfo
    Description   Loads all property values into the cache
    Provider Support   LDAP
    Syntax   `GetInfo()`
    Data Type   None

IADsLocality::GetInfoEx
    Description   Loads specific properties into the cache
    Provider Support   LDAP
    Syntax   `GetInfoEx(Properties As Variant, Reserved as Long)`
    Data Type   None

IADsLocality::GUID
    Description   Returns the GUID of the bound object
    Provider Support   LDAP
    Data Type   String
    Read-Only?   Yes

IADsLocality::LocalityName
    Description   Establishes the name of the geographical region
    Provider Support   LDAP
    Data Type   String
    Read-Only?   No

IADsLocality::Name

Description	Returns the relative name of the bound object
Provider Support	LDAP
Data Type	String
Read-Only?	Yes

IADsLocality::Parent

Description	Returns the ADsPath of the parent object
Provider Support	LDAP
Data Type	String
Read-Only?	Yes

IADsLocality::PostalAddress

Description	Establishes the postal address associated with the locality object
Provider Support	LDAP
Data Type	String
Read-Only?	No

IADsLocality::Put

Description	Allows population of a single attribute by name
Provider Support	LDAP
Syntax	Put(Name As String, Property As Variant)
Data Type	None

IADsLocality::PutEx

Description	Allows population of a multi-valued property by name
Provider Support	LDAP
Syntax	PutEx(ControlCode As Long, Name As String, Property As Variant)
Data Type	None

IADsLocality::Schema

    Description   Returns the ADsPath to the schema class object for the bound object
    Provider Support   LDAP
    Data Type   String
    Read-Only?   Yes

IADsLocality::SeeAlso

    Description   Establishes a list of other relevant objects that also describe the bound locality object
    Provider Support   LDAP
    Data Type   Variant
    Read-Only?   No

IADsLocality::SetInfo

    Description   Writes the current properties held in the cache to the directory
    Provider Support   LDAP
    Syntax   `SetInfo( )`
    Data Type   None

IADsMembers

IADsMembers:Count

    Description   Returns the number of members in the selection
    Provider Support   Supported only in LDAP provider GroupCollection
    Data Type   String
    Read-Only?   Yes

IADsMembers:Filter

    Description   Establishes a filter for the selection
    Provider Support   LDAP, WinNT
    Data Type   String
    Read-Only?   No

IADsO Interface

IADsO::ADsPath

Description	Returns the distinguished name of the bound object
Provider Support	LDAP
Data Type	String
Read-Only?	Yes

IADsO::Class

Description	Returns the object class definition of the bound object
Provider Support	LDAP
Data Type	String
Read-Only?	Yes

IADsO::Description

Description	Establishes the description for an organization (often this is the name of the company)
Provider Support	LDAP
Data Type	String
Read-Only?	No

IADsO::FaxNumber

Description	Establishes the fax number for the organization
Provider Support	LDAP
Data Type	String
Read-Only?	No

IADsO::Get

Description	Retrieves a value from a namespace by name
Provider Support	LDAP
Syntax	Get(Name As String)
Data Type	Variant

IADsO::GetEx

Description	Retrieves a single value from a multi-valued attribute
Provider Support	LDAP
Syntax	`GetEx(Name As String)`
Data Type	Variant

IADsO::GetInfo

Description	Loads all property values into the cache
Provider Support	LDAP
Syntax	`GetInfo()`
Data Type	None

IADsO::GetInfoEx

Description	Loads specific properties into the cache
Provider Support	LDAP
Syntax	`GetInfoEx(Properties As Variant, Reserved as Long)`
Data Type	None

IADsO::GUID

Description	Returns the GUID of the bound object
Provider Support	LDAP
Data Type	String
Read-Only?	Yes

IADsO::LocalityName

Description	Establishes the location of the organization
Provider Support	LDAP
Data Type	String
Read-Only?	No

IADsO::Name

Description	Returns the relative name of the bound object
Provider Support	LDAP
Data Type	String
Read-Only?	Yes

IADsO::Parent

Description	Returns the ADsPath of the parent object
Provider Support	LDAP
Data Type	String
Read-Only?	Yes

IADsO::PostalAddress

Description	Establishes the postal address for the organization
Provider Support	LDAP
Data Type	String
Read-Only?	No

IADsO::Put

Description	Allows population of a single attribute by name
Provider Support	LDAP
Syntax	Put(Name As String, Property As Variant)
Data Type	None

IADsO::PutEx

Description	Allows population of a multi-valued property by name
Provider Support	LDAP
Syntax	PutEx(ControlCode As Long, Name As String, Property As Variant)
Data Type	None

IADsO::Schema

Description	Returns the ADsPath to the schema class object for the bound object
Provider Support	LDAP
Data Type	String
Read-Only?	Yes

IADsO::SeeAlso

Description	Establishes a list of other information relevant to the organization
Provider Support	LDAP
Data Type	Variant
Read-Only?	No

IADsO::SetInfo

Description	Writes the current properties held in the cache to the directory
Provider Support	LDAP
Syntax	SetInfo()
Data Type	None

IADsO::TelephoneNumber

Description	Establishes the telephone number for the organization
Provider Support	LDAP
Data Type	String
Read-Only?	No

IADsOU Interface

IADsOU::ADsPath

Description	Returns the distinguished name of the bound object
Provider Support	LDAP
Data Type	String
Read-Only?	Yes

IADsOU::BusinessCategory

Description	Establishes the functional description for the business unit
Provider Support	LDAP
Data Type	String
Read-Only?	No

IADsOU::Class

Description	Returns the object class definition of the bound object
Provider Support	LDAP
Data Type	String
Read-Only?	Yes

IADsOU::Description

Description	Establishes the description for the organizational unit
Provider Support	LDAP
Data Type	String
Read-Only?	No

IADsOU::FaxNumber

Description	Establishes the fax number for the organizational unit
Provider Support	LDAP
Data Type	String
Read-Only?	No

IADsOU::Get

Description	Retrieves a value from a namespace by name
Provider Support	LDAP
Syntax	Get(Name As String)
Data Type	Variant

IADsOU::GetEx

Description	Retrieves a single value from a multi-valued attribute
Provider Support	LDAP
Syntax	GetEx(Name As String)
Data Type	Variant

IADsOU::GetInfo

Description	Loads all property values into the cache
Provider Support	LDAP
Syntax	GetInfo()
Data Type	None

IADsOU::GetInfoEx

Description	Loads specific properties into the cache
Provider Support	LDAP
Syntax	`GetInfoEx(Properties As Variant, Reserved as Long)`
Data Type	None

IADsOU::GUID

Description	Returns the GUID of the bound object
Provider Support	LDAP
Data Type	String
Read-Only?	Yes

IADsOU::LocalityName

Description	Establishes the physical location of the organizational unit
Provider Support	LDAP
Data Type	String
Read-Only?	No

IADsOU::Name

Description	Returns the relative name of the bound object
Provider Support	LDAP
Data Type	String
Read-Only?	Yes

IADsOU::Parent

Description	Returns the ADsPath of the parent object
Provider Support	LDAP
Data Type	String
Read-Only?	Yes

IADsOU::PostalAddress

Description	Establishes the postal address for the organizational unit
Provider Support	LDAP
Data Type	String
Read-Only?	No

IADsOU::Put

Description	Allows population of a single attribute by name
Provider Support	LDAP
Syntax	`Put(Name As String, Property As Variant)`
Data Type	None

IADsOU::PutEx

Description	Allows population of a multi-valued property by name
Provider Support	LDAP
Syntax	`PutEx(ControlCode As Long, Name As String, Property As Variant)`
Data Type	None

IADsOU::Schema

Description	Returns the ADsPath to the schema class object for the bound object
Provider Support	LDAP
Data Type	String
Read-Only?	Yes

IADsOU::SeeAlso

Description	Establishes a list of other information relevant to the organizational unit
Provider Support	LDAP
Data Type	Variant
Read-Only?	No

IADsOU::SetInfo

Description	Writes the current properties held in the cache to the directory
Provider Support	LDAP
Syntax	`SetInfo()`
Data Type	None

IADsOU::TelephoneNumber

Description	Establishes the telephone number associated with the organizational unit
Provider Support	LDAP
Data Type	String
Read-Only?	No

IADsOpenDSObject

IADsOpenDSObject::OpenDSObject

Description	Allows alternate credentials to be used when connecting to a directory
Provider Support	LDAP, WinNT
Syntax	`OpenDSObject(DnName As String, UserName As String, Password As String, Reserved As Long)`
Data Type	Object

IADsPrintJob

IADsPrintJob::ADsPath

Description	Returns the distinguished name of the bound object
Provider Support	WinNT
Data Type	String
Read-Only?	Yes

IADsPrintJob::Class

Description	Returns the object class definition of the bound object
Provider Support	WinNT
Data Type	String
Read-Only?	Yes

IADsPrintJob::Description

Description	Establishes the description for the print job
Provider Support	WinNT
Data Type	String
Read-Only?	No

IADsPrintJob::Get

Description	Retrieves a value from a namespace by name
Provider Support	WinNT
Syntax	`Get(Name As String)`
Data Type	Variant

IADsPrintJob::GetEx

Description	Retrieves a single value from a multi-valued attribute
Provider Support	WinNT
Syntax	`GetEx(Name As String)`
Data Type	Variant

IADsPrintJob::GetInfo

Description	Loads all property values into the cache
Provider Support	WinNT
Syntax	`GetInfo()`
Data Type	None

IADsPrintJob::GetInfoEx

Description	Allows population of a single attribute by name
Provider Support	WinNT
Syntax	`GetInfoEx(Properties As Variant, Reserved As Long)`
Data Type	None

IADsPrintJob::GUID

Description	Returns the GUID of the bound object
Provider Support	WinNT
Data Type	String
Read-Only?	Yes

IADsPrintJob::HostPrintQueue

Description	Returns the ADsPath of the hosting print queue
Provider Support	WinNT
Data Type	String
Read-Only?	Yes

IADsPrintJob::Name

Description	Returns the relative name of the bound object
Provider Support	WinNT
Data Type	String
Read-Only?	Yes

IADsPrintJob::Notify

Description	Establishes the name of the user to be notified when the job completes
Provider Support	WinNT
Data Type	String
Read-Only?	No

IADsPrintJob::NotifyPath

Description	Establishes the ADsPath of the user object to be notified
Provider Support	WinNT
Data Type	String
Read-Only?	No

IADsPrintJob::Parent

Description	Returns the ADsPath of the parent object
Provider Support	WinNT
Data Type	String
Read-Only?	Yes

IADsPrintJob::Priority

Description	Establishes the priority of the print job
Provider Support	WinNT
Data Type	Long
Read-Only?	No

IADsPrintJob::Put

Description	Allows population of a single attribute by name
Provider Support	WinNT
Syntax	`Put(Name As String, Property As Variant)`
Data Type	None

IADsPrintJob::PutEx

Description	Allows population of a multi-valued property by name
Provider Support	WinNT
Syntax	PutEx(ControlCode As Long, Name As String, Property As Variant)
Data Type	None

IADsPrintJob::Schema

Description	Returns the ADsPath to the schema class object for the bound object
Provider Support	WinNT
Data Type	String
Read-Only?	Yes

IADsPrintJob::SetInfo

Description	Writes the current properties held in the cache to the directory
Provider Support	WinNT
Syntax	SetInfo()
Data Type	None

IADsPrintJob::Size

Description	Returns the size of the print job in bytes
Provider Support	WinNT
Data Type	Long
Read-Only?	Yes

IADsPrintJob::StartTime

Description	Establishes the earliest time the print job can be printed
Provider Support	WinNT
Data Type	Date
Read-Only?	No

IADsPrintJob::TimeSubmitted

Description	Returns the time the job was submitted to the queue
Provider Support	WinNT
Data Type	Date
Read-Only?	Yes

IADsPrintJob::TotalPages

Description	Returns the number of pages in the job
Provider Support	WinNT
Data Type	Long
Read-Only?	Yes

IADsPrintJob::UntilTime

Description	Establishes the latest time the job is allowed to print
Provider Support	WinNT
Data Type	Date
Read-Only?	No

IADsPrintJob::User

Description	Returns the name of the user who submitted the job to the queue
Provider Support	WinNT
Data Type	String
Read-Only?	Yes

IADsPrintJob::UserPath

Description	Returns the path to the user object that submitted the job to the queue
Provider Support	WinNT
Data Type	String
Read-Only?	Yes

IADsPrintJobOperations

IADsPrintJobOperations::ADsPath

Description	Returns the distinguished name of the bound object
Provider Support	WinNT
Data Type	String
Read-Only?	Yes

IADsPrintJobOperations::Class

Description	Returns the object class definition of the bound object
Provider Support	WinNT
Data Type	String
Read-Only?	Yes

IADsPrintJobOperations::Get

Description	Retrieves a value from a namespace by name
Provider Support	WinNT
Syntax	`Get(Name As String)`
Data Type	Variant

IADsPrintJobOperations::GetEx

Description	Retrieves a single value from a multi-valued attribute
Provider Support	WinNT
Syntax	`GetEx(Name As String)`
Data Type	Variant

IADsPrintJobOperations::GetInfo

Description	Loads all property values into the cache
Provider Support	WinNT
Syntax	`GetInfo()`
Data Type	None

IADsPrintJobOperations::GetInfoEx

Description	Loads specific properties into the cache
Provider Support	WinNT
Syntax	`GetInfoEx(Properties As Variant, Reserved As Long)`
Data Type	None

IADsPrintJobOperations::GUID

Description	Returns the GUID of the bound object
Provider Support	WinNT
Data Type	String
Read-Only?	Yes

IADsPrintJobOperations::Name

Description	Returns the relative name of the bound object
Provider Support	WinNT
Data Type	String
Read-Only?	Yes

IADsPrintJobOperations::PagesPrinted

Description	Returns the total number of pages printed for the bound print job
Provider Support	WinNT
Data Type	Long
Read-Only?	Yes

IADsPrintJobOperations::Parent

Description	Returns the ADsPath of the parent object
Provider Support	WinNT
Data Type	String
Read-Only?	Yes

IADsPrintJobOperations::Pause

Description	Pauses printing of the current job
Provider Support	WinNT
Syntax	`Pause()`
Data Type	None

IADsPrintJobOperations::Position

Description	Establishes the position of the current print job within the print queue
Provider Support	WinNT
Data Type	Long
Read-Only?	No

IADsPrintJobOperations::Put

Description	Allows population of a single attribute by name
Provider Support	WinNT
Syntax	`Put(Name As String, Property As Variant)`
Data Type	None

IADsPrintJobOperations::PutEx

Description	Allows population of a multi-valued property by name
Provider Support	WinNT
Syntax	`PutEx(ControlCode As Long, Name as String, Property As Variant)`
Data Type	None

IADsPrintJobOperations::Resume

Description	Resumes printing of the bound print job
Provider Support	WinNT
Syntax	`Resume`
Data Type	None

IADsPrintJobOperations::Schema

Description	Returns the ADsPath to the schema class object for the bound object
Provider Support	WinNT
Data Type	String
Read-Only?	Yes

IADsPrintJobOperations::SetInfo

Description	Writes the current properties held in the cache to the directory
Provider Support	WinNT
Syntax	`SetInfo()`
Data Type	None

IADsPrintJobOperations::Status

Description	Returns the status of the currently bound print job
Provider Support	WinNT
Data Type	Long
Read-Only?	Yes

IADsPrintJobOperations::Status Return Values

Flag	Value
ADS_JOB_PAUSED	0x00000001
ADS_JOB_ERROR	0x00000002
ADS_JOB_DELETING	0x00000004
ADS_JOB_PRINTING	0x00000010
ADS_JOB_OFFLINE	0x00000020
ADS_JOB_PAPEROUT	0x00000040
ADS_JOB_PRINTED	0x00000080
ADS_JOB_DELETED	0x00000100

IADsPrintJobOperations::TimeElapsed

Description	Returns the time elapsed (in seconds) since the job was serviced
Provider Support	WinNT
Data Type	Long
Read-Only?	Yes

IADsPrintQueue

IADsPrintQueue::ADsPath

Description	Returns the distinguished name of the bound object
Provider Support	LDAP, WinNT
Data Type	String
Read-Only?	Yes

IADsPrintQueue::BannerPage

Description	Establishes the file system path to the file to be used as a separator page
Provider Support	LDAP, WinNT
Data Type	String
Read-Only?	No

IADsPrintQueue::Class

Description	Returns the object class definition of the bound object
Provider Support	LDAP, WinNT
Data Type	String
Read-Only?	Yes

IADsPrintQueue::Datatype

Description	Establishes the datatype processed by the bound print queue
Provider Support	WinNT
Data Type	String
Read-Only?	No

IADsPrintQueue::DefaultJobPriority

Description	Establishes the priority assigned by default to all print jobs in the queue
Provider Support	WinNT
Data Type	Long
Read-Only?	No

IADsPrintQueue::Description

Description	Establishes the description for the print queue
Provider Support	LDAP, WinNT
Data Type	String
Read-Only?	No

IADsPrintQueue::Get

Description	Retrieves a value from a namespace by name
Provider Support	LDAP, WinNT
Syntax	`Get(Name As String)`
Data Type	Variant

IADsPrintQueue::GetEx

Description	Retrieves a single value from a multi-valued attribute
Provider Support	LDAP, WinNT
Syntax	`GetEx(Name As String)`
Data Type	Variant

IADsPrintQueue::GetInfo

Description	Loads all property values into the cache
Provider Support	LDAP, WinNT
Syntax	`GetInfo()`
Data Type	None

IADsPrintQueue::GetInfoEx

Description	Loads specific properties into the cache
Provider Support	LDAP, WinNT
Syntax	`GetInfoEx(Properties As Variant, Reserved as Long)`
Data Type	None

IADsPrintQueue::GUID

Description	Returns the GUID of the bound object
Provider Support	LDAP, WinNT
Data Type	String
Read-Only?	Yes

IADsPrintQueue::Location

Description	Establishes the physical description for the print queue location
Provider Support	LDAP, WinNT
Data Type	String
Read-Only?	No

IADsPrintQueue::Model

Description	Establishes the name of the driver associated with the bound print queue
Provider Support	LDAP, WinNT
Data Type	String
Read-Only?	No

IADsPrintQueue::Name

Description	Returns the relative name of the bound object
Provider Support	LDAP, WinNT
Data Type	String
Read-Only?	Yes

IADsPrintQueue::NetAddresses

Description	Establishes binding information
Provider Support	Not supported in WinNT or LDAP provider
Data Type	Variant
Read-Only?	No

IADsPrintQueue::Parent

Description	Returns the ADsPath of the parent object
Provider Support	LDAP, WinNT
Data Type	String
Read-Only?	Yes

IADsPrintQueue::PrintDevices

Description	Establishes the names of print devices the bound queue will use to service print jobs
Provider Support	LDAP, WinNT
Data Type	Variant
Read-Only?	No

IADsPrintQueue::PrinterPath

Description	Establishes the path of a printer
Provider Support	LDAP
Data Type	String
Read-Only?	No

IADsPrintQueue::PrintProcessor

Description	Establishes the print processing engine to be used with the bound queue
Provider Support	WinNT
Data Type	String
Read-Only?	No

IADsPrintQueue::Priority

Description	Establishes the priority for the job queue for connected devices
Provider Support	LDAP, WinNT
Data Type	Long
Read-Only?	No

IADsPrintQueue::Put

Description	Allows population of a single attribute by name
Provider Support	LDAP, WinNT
Syntax	`Put(Name As String, Property As Variant)`
Data Type	None

IADsPrintQueue::PutEx

Description	Allows population of a multi-valued property by name
Provider Support	LDAP, WinNT
Syntax	`PutEx(ControlCode As Long, Name As String, Property As Variant)`
Data Type	None

IADsPrintQueue::Schema

Description	Returns the ADsPath to the schema class object for the bound object
Provider Support	LDAP, WinNT
Data Type	String
Read-Only?	Yes

IADsPrintQueue::SetInfo

Description	Writes the current properties held in the cache to the directory
Provider Support	LDAP, WinNT
Syntax	`SetInfo()`
Data Type	None

IADsPrintQueue::StartTime

Description	Establishes the start time for which the bound queue is allowed to service jobs
Provider Support	LDAP, WinNT
Data Type	Date
Read-Only?	No

IADsPrintQueue::UntilTime

Description	Establishes the end time for which the bound queue is allowed to service jobs
Provider Support	LDAP, WinNT
Data Type	Date
Read-Only?	No

IADsPrintQueueOperations

IADsPrintQueueOperations::ADsPath

Description	Returns the distinguished name of the bound object
Provider Support	LDAP, WinNT
Data Type	String
Read-Only?	Yes

IADsPrintQueueOperations::Class

Description	Returns the object class definition of the bound object
Provider Support	LDAP, WinNT
Data Type	String
Read-Only?	Yes

IADsPrintQueueOperations::Get

Description	Retrieves a value from a namespace by name
Provider Support	LDAP, WinNT
Syntax	`Get(Name As String)`
Data Type	Variant

IADsPrintQueueOperations::GetEx

Description	Retrieves a single value from a multi-valued attribute
Provider Support	LDAP, WinNT
Syntax	`GetEx(Name As String)`
Data Type	Variant

IADsPrintQueueOperations::GetInfo

Description	Loads all property values into the cache
Provider Support	LDAP, WinNT
Syntax	`GetInfo()`
Data Type	None

IADsPrintQueueOperations::GetInfoEx

Description	Loads specific properties into the cache
Provider Support	LDAP, WinNT
Syntax	GetInfoEx(Properties As Variant, Reserved as Long)
Data Type	None

IADsPrintQueueOperations::GUID

Description	Returns the GUID of the bound object
Provider Support	LDAP, WinNT
Data Type	String
Read-Only?	Yes

IADsPrintQueueOperations::Name

Description	Returns the relative name of the bound object
Provider Support	LDAP, WinNT
Data Type	String
Read-Only?	Yes

IADsPrintQueueOperations::Parent

Description	Returns the ADsPath of the parent object
Provider Support	LDAP, WinNT
Data Type	String
Read-Only?	Yes

IADsPrintQueueOperations::Pause

Description	Pauses operation of the bound print queue
Provider Support	LDAP, WinNT
Syntax	Pause()
Data Type	None

IADsPrintQueueOperations::PrintJobs

Description	Returns a collection of print jobs currently held in the bound queue
Provider Support	LDAP, WinNT
Syntax	PrintJobs()
Data Type	IADsCollection

IADsPrintQueueOperations::Purge

Description	Purges all jobs from the currently bound queue
Provider Support	LDAP, WinNT
Syntax	`Purge()`
Data Type	None

IADsPrintQueueOperations::Put

Description	Allows population of a single attribute by name
Provider Support	LDAP, WinNT
Syntax	`Put(Name As String, Property As Variant)`
Data Type	None

IADsPrintQueueOperations::PutEx

Description	Allows population of a multi-valued property by name
Provider Support	LDAP, WinNT
Syntax	`PutEx(ControlCode As Long, Name As String, Property As Variant)`
Data Type	None

IADsPrintQueueOperations::Resume

Description	Resumes a print queue from a previously paused state
Provider Support	LDAP, WinNT
Syntax	`Resume()`
Data Type	None

IADsPrintQueueOperations::Schema

Description	Returns the ADsPath to the schema class object for the bound object
Provider Support	LDAP, WinNT
Data Type	String
Read Only?	Yes

IADsPrintQueueOperations::SetInfo

Description	Writes the current properties held in the cache to the directory
Provider Support	LDAP, WinNT
Syntax	`SetInfo()`
Data Type	None

IADsPrintQueueOperations::Status

Description	Returns the current status of the print queue
Provider Support	LDAP, WinNT
Data Type	Long
Read-Only?	Yes

IADsPrintQueueOperations::Status Return Values

Flag	Value
ADS_PRINTER_PAUSED	0x00000001
ADS_PRINTER_PENDING_DELETION	0x00000002
ADS_PRINTER_ERROR	0x00000003
ADS_PRINTER_PAPER_JAM	0x00000004
ADS_PRINTER_PAPER_OUT	0x00000005
ADS_PRINTER_MANUAL_FEED	0x00000006
ADS_PRINTER_PAPER_PROBLEM	0x00000007
ADS_PRINTER_OFFLINE	0x00000008
ADS_PRINTER_IO_ACTIVE	0x00000100
ADS_PRINTER_BUSY	0x00000200
ADS_PRINTER_PRINTING	0x00000400
ADS_PRINTER_OUTPUT_BIN_FULL	0x00000800
ADS_PRINTER_NOT_AVAILABLE	0x00001000
ADS_PRINTER_WAITING	0x00002000
ADS_PRINTER_PROCESSING	0x00004000
ADS_PRINTER_INITIALIZING	0x00008000
ADS_PRINTER_WARMING_UP	0x00010000
ADS_PRINTER_TONER_LOW	0x00020000
ADS_PRINTER_NO_TONER	0x00040000
ADS_PRINTER_PAGE_PUNT	0x00080000
ADS_PRINTER_USER_INTERVENTION	0x00100000

Flag	Value
ADS_PRINTER_OUT_OF_MEMORY	0x00200000
ADS_PRINTER_DOOR_OPEN	0x00400000
ADS_PRINTER_SERVER_UNKNOWN	0x00800000
ADS_PRINTER_POWER_SAVE	0x01000000

IADsResource

IADsResource::ADsPath

Description	Returns the distinguished name of the bound object
Provider Support	WinNT
Data Type	String
Read-Only?	Yes

IADsResource::Class

Description	Returns the object class definition of the bound object
Provider Support	WinNT
Data Type	String
Read-Only?	Yes

IADsResource::Get

Description	Retrieves a value from a namespace by name
Provider Support	WinNT
Syntax	`Get(Name As String)`
Data Type	Variant

IADsResource::GetEx

Description	Retrieves a single value from a multi-valued attribute
Provider Support	WinNT
Syntax	`GetEx(Name As String)`
Data Type	Variant

IADsResource::GetInfo

Description	Loads all property values into the cache
Provider Support	WinNT
Syntax	`GetInfo()`
Data Type	None

IADsResource::GetInfoEx
    Description   Loads specific properties into the cache
    Provider Support   WinNT
    Syntax   `GetInfoEx(Properties As Variant, Reserved as Long)`
    Data Type   None

IADsResource::GUID
    Description   Returns the GUID of the bound object
    Provider Support   WinNT
    Data Type   String
    Read-Only?   Yes

IADsResource::LockCount
    Description   Returns the number of locks established on a resource
    Provider Support   WinNT
    Data Type   Long
    Read-Only?   Yes

IADsResource::Name
    Description   Returns the relative name of the bound object
    Provider Support   WinNT
    Data Type   String
    Read-Only?   Yes

IADsResource::Parent
    Description   Returns the ADsPath of the parent object
    Provider Support   WinNT
    Data Type   String
    Read-Only?   Yes

IADsResource::Path
    Description   Returns the file system path of the bound resource
    Provider Support   WinNT
    Data Type   String
    Read-Only?   Yes

IADsResource::Put

Description	Allows population of a single attribute by name
Provider Support	WinNT
Syntax	`Put(Name As String, Property As Variant)`
Data Type	None

IADsResource::PutEx

Description	Allows population of a multi-valued property by name
Provider Support	WinNT
Syntax	`PutEx(ControlCode As Long, Name As String, Property As Variant)`
Data Type	None

IADsResource::Schema

Description	Returns the ADsPath to the schema class object for the bound object
Provider Support	WinNT
Data Type	String
Read-Only?	Yes

IADsResource::SetInfo

Description	Writes the current properties held in the cache to the directory
Provider Support	WinNT
Syntax	`SetInfo()`
Data Type	None

IADsResource::User

Description	Returns the name of the user for the currently bound resource
Provider Support	WinNT
Data Type	String
Read-Only?	Yes

IADsResource::UserPath

Description	Returns the ADsPath of the user associated with the currently bound resource
Provider Support	WinNT
Data Type	String
Read-Only?	Yes

IADsService

IADsService::ADsPath

Description	Returns the distinguished name of the bound object
Provider Support	WinNT
Data Type	String
Read-Only?	Yes

IADsService::Class

Description	Returns the object class definition of the bound object
Provider Support	WinNT
Data Type	String
Read-Only?	Yes

IADsService::Dependencies

Description	Establishes the names of the services or load groups that must also be loaded to start this service
Provider Support	WinNT
Data Type	Variant
Read-Only?	No

IADsService::DisplayName

Description	Establishes the display name of the service
Provider Support	WinNT
Data Type	Name
Read-Only?	No

IADsService::ErrorControl

Description	Establishes the actions to be taken upon service failure
Provider Support	WinNT
Data Type	Long
Read-Only?	No

IADsService::ErrorControl Flag Values

Flag	Value
ADS_SERVICE_ERROR_IGNORE	0x00000000
ADS_SERVICE_ERROR_NORMAL	0x00000001
ADS_SERVICE_ERROR_SEVERE	0x00000002
ADS_SERVICE_ERROR_CRITICAL	0x00000003

IADsService::Get

Description	Retrieves a value from a namespace by name
Provider Support	WinNT
Syntax	`Get(Name As String)`
Data Type	Variant

IADsService::GetEx

Description	Retrieves a single value from a multi-valued attribute
Provider Support	WinNT
Syntax	`GetEx(Name As String)`
Data Type	Variant

IADsService::GetInfo

Description	Loads all property values into the cache
Provider Support	WinNT
Syntax	`GetInfo()`
Data Type	None

IADsService::GetInfoEx
Description	Loads specific properties into the cache
Provider Support	WinNT
Syntax	GetInfoEx(Properties As Variant, Reserved as Long)
Data Type	None

IADsService::GUID
Description	Returns the GUID of the bound object
Provider Support	WinNT
Data Type	String
Read-Only?	Yes

IADsService::HostComputer
Description	Establishes the host of the currently bound service
Provider Support	WinNT
Data Type	String
Read-Only?	No

IADsService::LoadOrderGroup
Description	Establishes the load order group used with the currently bound service
Provider Support	WinNT
Data Type	String
Read-Only?	No

IADsService::Name
Description	Returns the relative name of the bound object
Provider Support	WinNT
Data Type	String
Read-Only?	Yes

IADsService::Parent
Description	Returns the ADsPath of the parent object
Provider Support	WinNT
Data Type	String
Read-Only?	Yes

IADsService::Path

Description	Establishes the path of the executable associated with the bound service
Provider Support	WinNT
Data Type	String
Read-Only?	No

IADsService::Put

Description	Allows population of a single attribute by name
Provider Support	WinNT
Syntax	`Put(Name As String, Property As Variant)`
Data Type	None

IADsService::PutEx

Description	Allows population of a multi-valued property by name
Provider Support	WinNT
Syntax	`PutEx(ControlCode As Long, Name As String, Property As Variant)`
Data Type	None

IADsService::Schema

Description	Returns the ADsPath to the schema class object for the bound object
Provider Support	WinNT
Data Type	String
Read-Only?	Yes

IADsService::ServiceAccountName

Description	Establishes the username of the user account to be used with the service
Provider Support	WinNT
Data Type	String
Read-Only?	No

IADsService::ServiceAccountPath

Description	Establishes the ADsPath to the user account to be used for service authentication
Provider Support	WinNT
Data Type	String
Read-Only?	No

IADsService::ServiceType

Description	Establishes the process type in which the bound service will be run
Provider Support	WinNT
Data Type	Long
Read-Only?	No

IADsService::ServiceType Flag Values

Flag	Value
ADS_SERVICE_KERNAL_DRIVER	0x00000001
ADS_SERVICE_FILE_SYSTEM_DRIVER	0x00000002
ADS_SERVICE_OWN_PROCESS	0x00000010
ADS_SERVICE_SHARE_PROCESS	0x00000020

IADsService::SetInfo

Description	Writes the current properties held in the cache to the directory
Provider Support	WinNT
Syntax	SetInfo()
Data Type	None

IADsService::StartType

Description	Establishes how the service will start
Provider Support	WinNT
Data Type	Long
Read-Only?	No

IADsService::StartType Flag Values

Flag	Value
ADS_SERVICE_BOOT_START	0
ADS_SERVICE_SYSTEM_START	1
ADS_SERVICE_AUTO_START	2
ADS_SERVICE_DEMAND_START	3
ADS_SERVICE_DISABLED	4

IADsService::StartupParameters

Description	Establishes the arguments passed to the service at startup
Provider Support	WinNT
Data Type	String
Read-Only?	No

IADsService::Version

Description	Establishes version information for the service
Provider Support	WinNT
Data Type	String
Read-Only?	No

IADsServiceOperations

IADsServiceOperations::ADsPath

Description	Returns the distinguished name of the bound object
Provider Support	WinNT
Data Type	String
Read-Only?	Yes

IADsServiceOperations::Class

Description	Returns the object class definition of the bound object
Provider Support	WinNT
Data Type	String
Read-Only?	Yes

IADsServiceOperations::Continue

Description	Resumes a previously paused service
Provider Support	WinNT
Syntax	`Continue()`
Data Type	None

IADsServiceOperations::Get

Description	Retrieves a value from a namespace by name
Provider Support	WinNT
Syntax	`Get(Name As String)`
Data Type	Variant

IADsServiceOperations::GetEx

Description	Retrieves a single value from a multi-valued attribute
Provider Support	WinNT
Syntax	`GetEx(Name As String)`
Data Type	Variant

IADsServiceOperations::GetInfo

Description	Loads all property values into the cache
Provider Support	WinNT
Syntax	`GetInfo()`
Data Type	None

IADsServiceOperations::GetInfoEx

Description	Loads specific properties into the cache
Provider Support	WinNT
Syntax	`GetInfoEx(Properties As Variant, Reserved as Long)`
Data Type	None

IADsServiceOperations::GUID

Description	Returns the GUID of the bound object
Provider Support	WinNT
Data Type	String
Read-Only?	Yes

IADsServiceOperations::Name

Description	Returns the relative name of the bound object
Provider Support	WinNT
Data Type	String
Read-Only?	Yes

IADsServiceOperations::Parent

Description	Returns the ADsPath of the parent object
Provider Support	WinNT
Data Type	String
Read-Only?	Yes

IADsServiceOperations::Pause

Description	Pauses a running service
Provider Support	WinNT
Syntax	Pause()
Data Type	None

IADsServiceOperations::Put

Description	Allows population of a single attribute by name
Provider Support	WinNT
Syntax	Put(Name As String, Property As Variant)
Data Type	None

IADsServiceOperations::PutEx

Description	Allows population of a multi-valued property by name
Provider Support	WinNT
Syntax	PutEx(ControlCode As Long, Name As String, Property As Variant)
Data Type	None

IADsServiceOperations::Schema

Description	Returns the ADsPath to the schema class object for the bound object
Provider Support	WinNT
Data Type	String
Read-Only?	Yes

IADsServiceOperations::SetInfo

Description	Writes the current properties held in the cache to the directory
Provider Support	WinNT
Syntax	SetInfo()
Data Type	None

IADsServiceOperations::SetPassword

Description	Sets a new password to be used for the service account
Provider Support	WinNT
Syntax	SetPassword(NewPassword As String)
Data Type	None

IADsServiceOperations::Start

Description	Starts a stopped service
Provider Support	WinNT
Syntax	Start()
Data Type	None

IADsServiceOperations::Status

Description	Returns the status of the currently bound service
Provider Support	WinNT
Data Type	Long
Read-Only?	Yes

IADsServiceOperations::Status Return Values

Flag	Value
ADS_SERVICE_STOPPED	0x00000001
ADS_SERVICE_START_PENDING	0x00000002
ADS_SERVICE_STOP_PENDING	0x00000003
ADS_SERVICE_RUNNING	0x00000004
ADS_SERVICE_CONTINUE_PENDING	0x00000005
ADS_SERVICE_PAUSE_PENDING	0x00000006
ADS_SERVICE_PAUSED	0x00000007
ADS_SERVICE_ERROR	0x00000008

IADsServiceOperations::Stop

Description	Stops a running service
Provider Support	WinNT
Syntax	Stop()
Data Type	None

IADsSession

IADsSession::ADsPath

Description	Returns the distinguished name of the bound object
Provider Support	WinNT
Data Type	String
Read-Only?	Yes

IADsSession::Class

Description	Returns the object class definition of the bound object
Provider Support	String
Data Type	String
Read-Only?	Yes

IADsSession::Computer

Description	Returns the name of the client machine
Provider Support	WinNT
Data Type	String
Read-Only?	Yes

IADsSession::ComputerPath

Description	Returns the ADsPath to the client machine
Provider Support	WinNT
Data Type	String
Read-Only?	Yes

IADsSession::ConnectTime

Description	Returns the number of minutes elapsed since the session was started
Provider Support	WinNT
Data Type	Long
Read-Only?	Yes

IADsSession::Get

Description	Retrieves a value from a namespace by name
Provider Support	WinNT
Syntax	`Get(Name As String)`
Data Type	Variant

IADsSession::GetEx

Description	Retrieves a single value from a multi-valued attribute
Provider Support	WinNT
Syntax	`GetEx(Name As String)`
Data Type	Variant

IADsSession::GetInfo

Description	Loads all property values into the cache
Provider Support	WinNT
Syntax	`GetInfo()`
Data Type	None

IADsSession::GetInfoEx

Description	Loads specific properties into the cache
Provider Support	WinNT
Syntax	`GetInfoEx(Properties As Variant, Reserved as Long)`
Data Type	None

IADsSession::GUID

Description	Returns the GUID of the bound object
Provider Support	WinNT
Data Type	String
Read-Only?	Yes

IADsSession::IdleTime

Description	Returns the number of minutes the session has been idle
Provider Support	WinNT
Data Type	Long
Read-Only?	Yes

IADsSession::Name

Description	Returns the relative name of the bound object
Provider Support	WinNT
Data Type	String
Read-Only?	Yes

IADsSession::Parent

Description	Returns the ADsPath of the parent object
Provider Support	WinNT
Data Type	String
Read-Only?	Yes

IADsSession::Put

Description	Allows population of a single attribute by name
Provider Support	WinNT
Syntax	`Put(Name As String, Property As Variant)`
Data Type	None

IADsSession::PutEx

Description	Allows population of a multi-valued property by name
Provider Support	WinNT
Syntax	`PutEx(ControlCode As Long, Name As String, Property As Variant)`
Data Type	None

IADsSession::Schema

Description	Returns the ADsPath to the schema class object for the bound object
Provider Support	WinNT
Data Type	String
Read-Only?	Yes

IADsSession::SetInfo

Description	Writes the current properties held in the cache to the directory
Provider Support	WinNT
Syntax	SetInfo()
Data Type	None

IADsSession::User

Description	Returns the name of the session user
Provider Support	WinNT
Data Type	String
Read-Only?	Yes

IADsSession::UserPath

Description	Returns the ADsPath to the session user object
Provider Support	WinNT
Data Type	String
Read-Only?	Yes

IADsUser

IADsUser::AccountDisabled

Description	Establishes whether an account is enabled or disabled
Provider Support	LDAP, WinNT
Data Type	Boolean
Read-Only?	No

IADsUser::AccountExpirationDate

Description	Establishes the time and date when the bound user account will expire
Provider Support	LDAP, WinNT
Data Type	Date
Read-Only?	No

IADsUser::ADsPath

Description	Returns the distinguished name of the bound object
Provider Support	LDAP, WinNT
Data Type	String
Read-Only?	Yes

IADsUser::BadLoginAddress

Description	Gets the intruder's node address (Novell)
Provider Support	Not Supported in LDAP or WinNT Providers
Data Type	String
Read-Only?	Yes

IADsUser::BadLoginCount

Description	Returns the number of bad login attempts since the counter was last reset
Provider Support	LDAP, WinNT
Data Type	Long
Read-Only?	Yes

IADsUser::ChangePassword

Description	Changes the password for the bound user object. Assumes the old password is known, so no administrative rights are needed to perform this action.
Provider Support	LDAP, WinNT
Syntax	`ChangePassword(OldPassword As String, NewPassword As String)`
Data Type	None

IADsUser::Class

Description	Returns the object class definition of the bound object
Provider Support	LDAP, WinNT
Data Type	String
Read-Only?	Yes

IADsUser::Department

Description	Establishes the name of the department or organizational unit associated with the user object
Provider Support	LDAP
Data Type	String
Read-Only?	No

IADsUser::Description

Description	Establishes a description for the user object
Provider Support	LDAP, WinNT
Data Type	String
Read-Only?	No

IADsUser::Division

Description	Establishes the division within the organization associated with the user object
Provider Support	LDAP
Data Type	String
Read-Only?	No

IADsUser::EmailAddress

Description	Establishes the email address associated with the user object
Provider Support	LDAP
Data Type	String
Read-Only?	No

IADsUser::EmployeeID

Description	Establishes the employee identification number associated with the user object
Provider Support	LDAP
Data Type	String
Read-Only?	No

IADsUser::FaxNumber

Description	Establishes the user's fax number
Provider Support	LDAP
Data Type	String
Read-Only?	No

IADsUser::FirstName

Description	Establishes the user's first name
Provider Support	LDAP
Data Type	String
Read-Only?	No

IADsUser::FullName

Description	Establishes the user's full name
Provider Support	LDAP, WinNT
Data Type	String
Read-Only?	No

IADsUser::Get

Description	Retrieves a value from a namespace by name
Provider Support	LDAP, WinNT
Syntax	`Get(Name As String)`
Data Type	Variant

IADsUser::GetEx

Description	Retrieves a single value from a multi-valued attribute
Provider Support	LDAP, WinNT
Syntax	`GetEx(Name As String)`
Data Type	Variant

IADsUser::GetInfo

Description	Loads all property values into the cache
Provider Support	LDAP, WinNT
Syntax	`GetInfo()`
Data Type	None

IADsUser::GetInfoEx

Description	Loads specific properties into the cache
Provider Support	LDAP, WinNT
Syntax	`GetInfoEx(Properties As Variant, Reserved as Long)`
Data Type	None

IADsUser::GraceLoginsAllowed

Description	Establishes the number of logins allowed before the user must change the password associated with the account. This property is available only for Novell service providers.
Provider Support	Not supported in LDAP or WinNT providers
Data Type	Long
Read-Only?	No

IADsUser::GraceLoginsRemaining

Description	Establishes the number of grace logins remaining. This property is available only for Novell service providers.
Provider Support	Not supported in LDAP or WinNT providers
Data Type	Long
Read-Only?	No

IADsUser::Groups

Description	Establishes group membership for the bound user object
Provider Support	LDAP, WinNT
Syntax	`Groups()`
Data Type	IADsMembers

IADsUser::GUID

Description	Returns the GUID of the bound object
Provider Support	LDAP, WinNT
Data Type	String
Read-Only?	Yes

IADsUser::HomeDirectory

Description	Establishes the path to the user's home directory
Provider Support	LDAP, WinNT
Data Type	String
Read-Only?	No

IADsUser::HomePage

Description	Establishes the URL for the user's home page
Provider Support	LDAP
Data Type	String
Read-Only?	No

IADsUser::IsAccountLocked

Description	Establishes whether the account is locked out
Provider Support	LDAP, WinNT
Data Type	Boolean
Read-Only?	No (although this property cannot set to True)

IADsUser::Languages

Description	Establishes an array of languages associated with the user object
Provider Support	Not supported in LDAP or WinNT providers
Data Type	Variant
Read-Only?	No

IADsUser::LastFailedLogin

Description	Returns the time and date of the last failed network login
Provider Support	LDAP
Data Type	Date
Read-Only?	Yes

IADsUser::LastLogin

Description	Returns the time and date of the last successful network login
Provider Support	LDAP, WinNT
Data Type	Date
Read-Only?	Yes

IADsUser::LastLogoff

Description	Returns the time and date for the last network logoff
Provider Support	LDAP, WinNT
Data Type	Date
Read-Only?	Yes

IADsUser::LastName

Description	Establishes the last name associated with the user object
Provider Support	LDAP
Data Type	String
Read-Only?	No

IADsUser::LoginHours

Description	Establishes the time periods for which the user object is granted access
Provider Support	LDAP, WinNT
Data Type	Variant
Read-Only?	No

IADsUser::LoginScript

Description	Establishes the path to the login script associated with the user object
Provider Support	LDAP, WinNT
Data Type	String
Read-Only?	No

IADsUser::LoginWorkstations

Description	Establishes an array of workstations or server from which the user object is permitted to authenticate
Provider Support	LDAP, WinNT
Data Type	Variant
Read-Only?	No

IADsUser::Manager

Description	Establishes the name of the user's manager
Provider Support	LDAP
Data Type	String
Read-Only?	No

IADsUser::MaxLogins

Description	Establishes the number of simultaneous logins for Novell systems
Provider Support	Not supported in LDAP or WinNT providers
Data Type	Long
Read-Only?	No

IADsUser::MaxStorage

Description	Establishes the maximum amount of disk space (in kilobytes) a user account may maintain
Provider Support	LDAP, WinNT
Data Type	Long
Read-Only?	No

IADsUser::Name

Description	Returns the relative name of the bound object
Provider Support	LDAP, WinNT
Data Type	String
Read-Only?	Yes

IADsUser::NamePrefix

Description	Establishes the name prefix associated with the user object (such as Mr., Mrs., or Dr.)
Provider Support	LDAP
Data Type	String
Read-Only?	No

IADsUser::NameSuffix

Description	Establishes the suffix associated with a user object (such as Jr., Sr., or III)
Provider Support	LDAP
Data Type	String
Read-Only?	No

IADsUser::OfficeLocations

Description	Establishes the user's office location(s)
Provider Support	LDAP
Data Type	Variant (Note: Active Directory supports only a single office location)
Read-Only?	No

IADsUser::OtherName

Description	Establishes an additional name for the user, such as a middle name
Provider Support	LDAP
Data Type	String
Read-Only?	No

IADsUser::Parent

Description	Returns the ADsPath of the parent object
Provider Support	LDAP, WinNT
Data Type	String
Read-Only?	Yes

IADsUser::PasswordExpirationDate

    Description   Establishes the date for which the user account will expire
    Provider Support   LDAP, WinNT
    Data Type   Date
    Read-Only?   No

IADsUser::PasswordLastChanged

    Description   Returns the time and date for the last password change event associated with the user object
    Provider Support   LDAP
    Data Type   Date
    Read-Only?   Yes

IADsUser::PasswordMinimumLength

    Description   Establishes the minimum password length allowed for the user object
    Provider Support   LDAP, WinNT
    Data Type   Long
    Read-Only?   No

IADsUser::PasswordRequired

    Description   Establishes the user's ability or inability to use a blank password
    Provider Support   LDAP, WinNT
    Data Type   Boolean
    Read-Only?   No

IADsUser::Picture

    Description   An OctetString array containing an image
    Provider Support   LDAP
    Data Type   Variant
    Read-Only?   No

IADsUser::PostalAddresses

Description	Establishes the postal addresses associated with the user object. The address should be defined as six elements of 30 bytes each, containing the street address, an optional second address line, city or locality, state or province, postal/zip code, and country.
Provider Support	LDAP
Data Type	Variant
Read-Only?	No

IADsUser::PostalCodes

Description	Establishes an array of postal codes. In Active Directory, this value is single valued.
Provider Support	LDAP
Data Type	Variant
Read-Only?	No

IADsUser::Profile

Description	Establishes the path to the user's profile directory
Provider Support	LDAP, WinNT
Data Type	String
Read-Only?	No

IADsUser::Put

Description	Allows population of a single attribute by name
Provider Support	LDAP, WinNT
Syntax	Put(Name As String, Property As Variant)
Data Type	None

IADsUser::PutEx

Description	Allows population of a multi-valued property by name
Provider Support	LDAP, WinNT
Syntax	PutEx(ControlCode As Long, Name As String, Property As Variant)
Data Type	None

IADsUser::RequireUniquePassword

Description	Establishes a flag to indicate whether the user must maintain a unique password from those stored in the password history
Provider Support	LDAP
Data Type	Boolean
Read-Only?	No

IADsUser::Schema

Description	Returns the ADsPath to the schema class object for the bound object
Provider Support	LDAP, WinNT
Data Type	String
Read-Only?	Yes

IADsUser::SeeAlso

Description	Establishes an array of additional objects that describe the currently bound user object
Provider Support	LDAP
Data Type	Variant
Read-Only?	No

IADsUser::SetInfo

Description	Writes the current properties held in the cache to the directory
Provider Support	LDAP, WinNT
Syntax	`SetInfo()`
Data Type	None

IADsUser::SetPassword

Description	Establishes a new password for the user object without knowing the old password. Requires administrative rights to set successfully.
Provider Support	LDAP, WinNT
Syntax	`SetPassword(NewPassword As String)`
Data Type	None

IADsUser::TelephoneHome

Description	Establishes an array of telephone numbers that are associated with the user object. In Active Directory, this property is single valued.
Provider Support	LDAP
Data Type	Variant
Read-Only?	No

IADsUser::TelephoneMobile

Description	Establishes an array of telephone numbers that are associated with the user object. In Active Directory, this property is single valued.
Provider Support	LDAP
Data Type	Variant
Read-Only?	No

IADsUser::TelephoneNumber

Description	Establishes an array of telephone numbers that are associated with the user object. In Active Directory, this property is single valued.
Provider Support	LDAP
Data Type	Variant
Read-Only?	No

IADsUser::TelephonePager

Description	Establishes an array of telephone numbers that are associated with the user object. In Active Directory, this property is single valued.
Provider Support	LDAP
Data Type	Variant
Read-Only?	No

IADsUser::Title

Description	Establishes the user's title
Provider Support	LDAP
Data Type	String
Read-Only?	No

Custom WinNT Properties

The following WinNT custom properties are available using the Get and Put methods of the IADs interface.

IADsUser::HomeDirDrive

Description	Establishes the drive letter used to map the user's home directory
Provider Support	WinNT
Data Type	String
Read-Only?	No

IADsUser::ObjectSID

Description	Establishes the security identifier associated with the user object
Provider Support	WinNT
Data Type	Octet String
Read-Only?	No

IADsUser::Parameters

Description	Allows access to custom fields in the parameters field in the SAM. Terminal Server/Citrix profile path and RAS settings are usually stored in this field, along with any other OEM modifications to a user's SAM record.
Provider Support	WinNT
Data Type	String
Read-Only?	No

IADsUser::PasswordAge

Description	Returns the password age for the currently bound user object
Provider Support	WinNT
Data Type	Time
Read-Only?	No

IADsUser::PasswordExpired

Description	Returns an integer representing whether the account password has expired
Provider Support	WinNT
Data Type	Long
Read-Only?	No

IADsUser::PrimaryGroupID

Description	Establishes the primary group identification number for the user object
Provider Support	WinNT
Data Type	Long
Read-Only?	No

IADsUser::UserFlags

Description	Establishes various custom configurations for the user account as defined in ADS_USER_FLAG
Provider Support	WinNT
Data Type	Long
Read-Only?	No

IADsUser::UserFlags Flag Values

Flag	Value	Description
ADS_UF_SCRIPT	0x0001	Executes logon script
ADS_UF_ACCOUNTDISABLE	0x0002	Disables account
ADS_UF_HOMEDIR_REQUIRED	0x0003	Requires home directory
ADS_UF_LOCKOUT	0x0010	Account locked out
ADS_UF_PASSWD_NOTREQD	0x0020	Does not require password
ADS_UF_PASSWD_CANT_CHANGE	0x0040	Disallows user's ability to change password
ADS_UF_ENCRYPTED_TEXT_PASSWORD_ALLOWED	0x0080	Allows user to send encrypted password
ADS_UF_TEMP_DUPLICATE_ACCOUNT	0x0100	Local user account
ADS_UF_NORMAL_ACCOUNT	0x0200	Typical user account
ADS_UF_INTERDOMAIN_TRUST_ACCOUNT	0x0800	Establishes permit to trust account

Flag	Value	Description
ADS_UF_WORKSTATION_TRUST_ACCOUNT	0x1000	Computer account
ADS_UF_SERVER_TRUST_ACCOUNT	0x2000	BDC computer account
ADS_UF_DONTEXPIREPASSWORD	0x10000	Does not force password to expire
ADS_UF_MNS_LOGON_ACCOUNT	0x20000	MNS Logon account
ADS_UF_SMARTCARD_REQUIRED	0x40000	Requires use of a smart card for logon
ADS_UF_TRUSTED_FOR_DELEGATION	0x80000	Trusts account for Kerberos delegation
ADS_UF_NOT_DELEGATED	0x100000	Does not allow user security context to be delegated to a service

WinNTSystemInfo

To use the WinNTSystemInfo interface from a Windows 2000 client, use the following Visual Basic code as a guide:

```
Dim WinNTSysInfo as WinNTSystemInfo
Set WinNTSysInfo = New WinNTSystemInfo
Debug.Print WinNTSysInfo.ComputerName
Debug.Print WinNTSysInfo.DomainName
Debug.Print WinNTSysInfo.PDC
Debug.Print WinNTSysInfo.UserName
```

WinNTSystemInfo::ComputerName

Description	Returns the name of the client computer
Provider Support	Windows 2000 clients only
Data Type	String
Read-Only?	Yes

WinNTSystemInfo::DomainName

Description	Returns the current domain of the client computer
Provider Support	Windows 2000 clients only
Data Type	String
Read-Only?	Yes

WinNTSystemInfo::PDC

Description	Returns the name of the PDC or PDC emulator associated with the client machine domain
Provider Support	Windows 2000 clients only
Data Type	String
Read-Only?	Yes

WinNTSystemInfo::UserName

Description	Returns the username logged into the client machine
Provider Support	Windows 2000 clients only
Data Type	String
Read-Only?	Yes

Appendix C
Further Reading

The references in this appendix can help you learn more about the underlying technologies you might encounter during your explorations of programmatic administration of enterprise environments.

> **Tip**
>
> *The World Wide Web is an extremely dynamic environment, providing an outlet for updated information of products whose documentation may change without notice.*
>
> *If a link listed in this reference section is no longer functioning, check* http://www.newriders.com/adsi *for an updated link.* ◆

Active Directory Design and Administration

For those interested in learning more about the design and administration of an Active Directory Service implementation, there are many resources, both in print and on the Web, to help you increase the depth of your knowledge on the topic.

Web Resources

The following URLs are excellent sources of information on the Active Directory Service:

Active Directory Overview Whitepaper:

> http://www.microsoft.com/windows/server/Technical/directory/ADarch.asp

Microsoft Windows 2000 Technical Information:

> http://www.microsoft.com/windows/server/Technical/default.asp

Print Resources

The following books are excellent sources of information on the Active Directory:

Blum, Daniel. 1999. *Understanding the Active Directory Service*. Redmond: Microsoft Press. ISBN: 1572317213

Cone, Eric, Jon Boggs, and Sergio Perez. 1999. *Planning for Windows 2000*. Indianapolis: New Riders. ISBN: 0735700486

Schwartz, Richard. 1999. *Windows 2000: Active Directory Survival Guide*. New York: John Wiley & Sons. ISBN: 047135600X

Sheresh, Beth and Doug. 1999. *Understanding Directory Services*. Indianapolis: New Riders. ISBN: 0735700486

Active Directory Service Interfaces (ADSI)

Due to the growing popularity of ADSI, there are several Web sites and print resources you may want to use to supplement your work with this book.

Web Resources

Whether you want to download ADSI and its supporting files from Microsoft or view a third-party ADSI scripting site, there are many resources on the Web to help guide you along your journey to efficient programmatic namespace manipulation using ADSI.

Microsoft Resources

The following URLs allow you to download the base ADSI libraries for Windows NT and 9x machines, as well as ADSI support documentation:
Root ADSI Site:

    http://www.microsoft.com/adsi

ADSI Download Site (includes libraries, the ADSI SDK and the ADSI Resource Kit):

    http://www.microsoft.com/ntserver/nts/downloads/other/ADSI25/default.asp

> **Note**
>
> The ADSI Resource Kit is contained as part of the ADSI SDK. ♦

ADSI 2.5 Help File:

    http://www.microsoft.com/ntserver/downloads/bin/nts/adsi25.chm

Third-Party Resources
If you want to view third-party material on ADSI scripting (or join a listserv) the following sites may be helpful:

15 Seconds:
> http://www.15seconds.com/focus/ADSI.htm

Win32 Scripting:
> http://cwashington.netreach.net/script_repository/adsifaq.asp

Print Resources
The following books are excellent sources of information on the Active Directory Service Interfaces:

Hahn, Stephen. 1998. *ADSI ASP Programmer's Reference*. Birmingham, UK: Wrox Press. ISBN: 186100169X

Kirkpatrick, Gil. 1999. *Active Directory Programming*. Indianapolis: SAMS. ISBN: 0672315874

Robinson, Simon. 1999. *Professional ADSI Programming*. Birmingham, UK: Wrox Press. ISBN: 1861002262

Active Server Page (ASP) Scripting
If you are new to ASP, there are many resources, both on the Web and in print, to enhance your understanding of Active Server Page scripting.

Web Resources
The following URLs are excellent sources of information on ASP scripting:

15 Seconds:
> http://www.15seconds.com/focus/ADSI.htm

ASP Alliance:
> http://www.aspalliance.com

ASP Hole:
> http://www.asphole.com

ASP Today:
> http://www.asptoday.com

developer.com:
> http://www.developer.com

Learn ASP:
> http://www.learnasp.com

Microsoft MSDN:
> http://msdn.microsoft.com

Win32 Scripting:
> http://cwashington.netreach.net/script_repository/adsifaq.asp

Print Resources

The following books are excellent sources of information on ASP scripting:

Anderson, Richard, Chris Blexrud, Andrea Chiarelli, et al. 1999. *Professional Active Server Pages 3.0*. Birmingham, UK: Wrox Press. ISBN: 1861002610

Walther, Stephen. 1999. *Active Server Pages 2.0: Unleashed*. Indianapolis: SAMS. ISBN: 0672316137

ActiveX Data Objects

If you want to search an LDAP namespace, you can take advantage of the ActiveX Data Objects (ADO). Although the topic is covered relatively thoroughly in MSDN, there are additional sources of information on ADO found in both electronic and print format.

Web Resources

You might want to consider the following URLs to answer any questions regarding ADO:

DevX – Ask the IT Professionals:
> http://www.inquiry.com

Microsoft Universal Data Access:
> http://www.microsoft.com/data

Print Resources

The following texts do an excellent job of covering developer use of ADO:

Sussman, David. 1999. *ADO 2.1 Programmer's Reference*. Birmingham, UK: Wrox Press. ISBN: 1861002688

Wille, Christoph. 2000. *Teach Yourself ADO 2.5 in 21 Days*. Indianapolis: SAMS. ISBN: 0672318733

Lightweight Directory Access Protocol (LDAP)

For those deploying LDAP servers in the enterprise or wanting to better understand the foundational technology used in the Active Directory, there are several excellent sources of information in both electronic and print formats.

Web Resources
The following URLs present the LDAP standards and the administration of one of the most popular production LDAP server products in use today:
Search the RFC Index for LDAP:
> http://www.rfc-editor.org/rfcsearch.html

Netscape Directory Server Documentation:
> http://devedge.netscape.com/docs/manuals/index.html?content=directory.html

University of Michigan LDAP Project:
> http://www.umich.edu/~dirsvcs/ldap/

Print Resources
The following print resources are often quoted as quintessential reading for those working with LDAP namespaces:

Howes, Timothy and Mark Smith. 1998. *Understanding and Deploying LDAP Directory Services*. Indianapolis: Macmillan Technical Publishing. ISBN: 1578700701

Wilcox, Mark. 1999. *Implementing LDAP*. Birmingham, UK: Wrox Press Ltd. ISBN: 1861002211

Visual Basic
For many administrators, the use of Visual Basic will be a fairly sizable leap into the world of development. There should be little cause for concern, however, because Visual Basic is one of the easiest languages to learn and is well supported by third-party Web and print resources.

Web Resources
The following URLs may be helpful for those working with Visual Basic or VBScript:
ASP Zone:
> http://www.aspzone.com

developer.com:
> http://www.developer.com

DevX:
> http://www.devx.com

DevX inquiry.com:
> http://www.inquiry.com

Microsoft MSDN Library:
> http://www.msdn.com

VBScript Language Reference:
> http://msdn.microsoft.com/scripting/default.htm?/scripting/VBScript/doc/VBSTOCAlt.htm

Visual Basic Web Directory:
> http://www.vb-web-directory.com/

Print Resources

The following print resources on Visual Basic development are available for readers at any level of understanding:

Appleman, Dan. 1998. *Developing COM/ActiveX Components with Visual Basic 6*. Indianapolis: SAMS. ISBN: 1562765760

Halvorson, Michael. 1998. *Microsoft Visual Basic 6.0 Professional Step by Step*. Redmond: Microsoft Press. ISBN: 1572318090

Lhotka, Rockford. 1999. *Visual Basic 6.0 Business Objects*. Birmingham, UK: Wrox Press. ISBN: 186100107X

McKinney, Bruce. 1997. *Hardcore Visual Basic*, Second Edition. Redmond: Microsoft Press. ISBN: 1572314222

Pattison, Ted. 1998. *Programming Distributed Application with COM and Microsoft Visual Basic 6.0*. Redmond: Microsoft Press. ISBN: 1572319615

Wright, Peter. 1998. *Beginning Visual Basic 6*. Birmingham, UK: Wrox Press. ISBN: 1861001053

Index

A

abstraction, 5-8
access control. *See also* authentication
  local and remote home directories, 283-284, 521
  Web Operators property sheet, 274-275
access control entries. *See* ACEs
access control list. *See* ACL
AccessControlEntry interface, 565
  AccessMask property, 565-566
  AceFlags property, 566
  AceType property, 567
  Flags property, 567
  InheritedObjectType property, 567
  ObjectType property, 568-569
  Trustee property, 569
AccessControlList interface, 570
  AceCount property, 570
  AclRevision property, 570
  AddAce method, 570
  CopyAccessList method, 570
  RemoveAce method, 570
AccessExecute property (Home Directory property sheet), 284
AccessMask ACE field (flags), 422-423
AccessMask property (AccessControlEntry interface), 565-566
AccessRead property
  FTP service management, 356
  Home Directory property sheet, 283-284

AccessWrite property
  FTP service management, 356
  Home Directory property sheet, 283
Account Disabled status flag, 83-85, 469
Account Information dialog box, 95
Account Locked-Out status flag, 85-87, 470
account lockout
  bad login attempts, resetting, 47-49, 458-459
  resetting, 46-47, 457-458
Account Policy dialog box, 44-45
account type, querying, 97, 475
AccountDisabled property (IADsUser interface), 84-85, 469, 646
AccountExpirationDate property (IADsUser interface), 95-96, 475, 647
accounts. *See also* user accounts
  computer accounts
    creating/deleting, 56-57, 461-462
    enumeration, 55, 461
  machine accounts
    not in resource domain, detecting, 478
    password age, querying, 103-105
    removing inactive, 103-105
AceCount property (AccessControlList interface), 570

AceFlags ACE field (flags), 424-425
AceFlags property
(AccessControlEntry interface), 566
ACEs (access control entries),
123, 422
  adding to ACL, 431, 560
    inheritance for all child objects,
    432-433, 561
    inheritance for single attributes,
    435, 563
    inheritance for single child object
    class, 433-434, 562
  constants, 422-424
  enumerating, 425-431, 555-560
  removing from ACL, 431-432, 561
    inheritance for single child object
    class, 434, 562
AceType ACE field (flags), 424
AceType property
(AccessControlEntry interface), 567
ACL (access control list), 123, 425
  adding ACEs to, 431, 560
    inheritance for all child objects,
    432-433, 561
    inheritance for single attributes,
    435, 563
    inheritance for single child object
    class, 433-434, 562
  enumerating ACEs within,
    425-431, 555-560
  removing ACEs from,
    431-432, 561
    inheritance for single child
    object class, 434, 562
AclRevision property
(AccessControlList interface), 570
Active Directory
  design/administration resources,
    663-664
  development of, 4
  directory trees, deleting branches,
    419, 554

  global catalog, binding, 415, 551-552
  migrating from SAM to, 17
  objects
    attribute replication in global
    catalog, 414
    binding, 410-413, 549-551
    computer class objects,
    enumerating, 416, 553
    creating, 415-418, 553
    finding mandatory attributes,
    418-419, 554
    group class objects, enumerating,
    416, 552
    mandatory attributes, 417
    moving, 420, 555
    removing, 419, 554
    renaming, 420, 555
    user class objects, enumerating,
    415, 552
  security, 421-422, 425
    adding ACEs to ACL, 431, 560
    constants for ACEs, 422-424
    enumerating ACEs, 425-431,
    555-560
    inheritance, 424-425, 432-435,
    561-563
    removing ACEs from ACL,
    431-432, 561
  terminology, 408-410
Active Directory Service Interfaces.
  See ADSI
active log format (IIS site logging),
  214-215, 503-504
Active Server Pages. *See* ASP
ActiveX Data Objects. *See* ADO
ActiveX DLL. *See* COM, servers
Add method
  IADsCollection interface, 573
  IADsGroup interface, 599
AddAce method (AccessControlList
  interface), 570

alternate credentials   671

adding. *See also* creating
    entries to Web directories,
        232-233, 512
    MIME-type mappings, 210, 502
    users to groups, 117, 479
addresses. *See* IP addresses
administration
    Active Directory resources, 663-664
    COM servers
        creating, 28-31
        instantiating from ASP, 32-33
        testing, 31-32
    delegation model, creating, 34-38
    interaction between ADSI and
        Visual Basic, 27-28
ADO (ActiveX Data Objects),
    390, 545
    resources, 666
    searching LDAP directories,
        390-391, 545
ADObjectManagement class module
    creating, 435-450
    functions, 450-452
ADSI (Active Directory Service
    Interfaces), 4
    abstraction, 5-8
    development of, 3-5
    installing, 22-23
    interaction with Visual Basic for
        administrative tasks, 27-28
    interface support, 14-16
    as migration tool, 17
    performance, compared to
        native-API calls, 8
    practical applications, 8-9
        *automated system management,
            10-11*
        *business workflow processes,
            9-10*
        enforcing naming standards, 10
        namespace queries, 13
        property caching, 11-13
        security, 14
    resources, 664-665
    test environment, importance of, 26
ADSI Edit MMC snap-in, 410
ADsPath property, 117
    IADs interface, 571
    IADsComputer interface, 574
    IADsDomain interface, 581
    IADsFileService interface, 585
    IADsFileServiceOperations
        interface, 591
    IADsFileShare interface, 595
    IADsGroup interface, 599
    IADsLocality interface, 602
    IADsO interface, 606
    IADsOU interface, 609
    IADsPrintJob interface, 613
    IADsPrintJobOperations
        interface, 618
    IADsPrintQueue interface, 622
    IADsPrintQueueOperations
        interface, 627
    IADsResource interface, 631
    IADsService interface, 634
    IADsServiceOperations
        interface, 639
    IADsSession interface, 643
    IADsUser interface, 647
advanced log format
    ASCII-based log providers, 216
    IIS site logging, 216-217
    log file size, 217-218, 504-505
    log time period, 217, 504
AllowAnonymous property (FTP
    service management), 346, 535
AllowKeepAlive property (Web
    Performance property sheet),
    279, 519
alternate credentials, binding Active
    Directory objects with, 412-413, 551

And operator (user status flags), 78
anonymous access (Directory Security property sheet), 297-298, 526
anonymous FTP connections, 345-346
　account credentials, 346-347, 535-536
　anonymous only access, 348, 536
　enabling/disabling access, 346, 535
AnonymousOnly property (FTP service management), 348, 536
AnonymousPasswordSync property
　Directory Security property sheet, 297
　FTP service management, 346-347, 535-536
AnonymousUserName property
　Directory Security property sheet, 297
　FTP service management, 346-347, 535-536
AnonymousUserPass property
　Directory Security property sheet, 297
　FTP service management, 346-347, 535-536
APIs, LDAP, 381
AppFriendlyName property (Home Directory property sheet), 284
AppIsolated property (Home Directory property sheet), 284
application logic, separating from business logic, 21-22
AppRoot property (Home Directory property sheet), 284
architecture of LDAP directories, determining, 387, 543
ASCII-based log providers (IIS site logging), 216

ASP (Active Server Pages), 20
　disadvantages of, 20-21
　instantiating COM servers, 32-33
　instantiating NTContainerManagement class module, 65
　resources, 665-666
　scripts, Web application configuration, 284-288, 521-523
attributes (Active Directory)
　finding for objects, 418-419, 554
　inheritance, 435, 563
　list of, 417
　replication in global catalog, 414
　terminology, 408
attributes (LDAP)
　entries, 379
　modifying, 388, 544
　querying
　　alternate credentials, 388, 544
　　anonymous access, 387-388, 544
AuthAnonymous property (Directory Security property sheet), 295
AuthBasic property (Directory Security property sheet), 295
authentication. *See also* access control
　ADSI practical applications, 14
　Directory Security property sheet, 295-299, 526-527
AuthFlags property (Directory Security property sheet), 295
AuthNTLM property (Directory Security property sheet), 295
automated system management (ADSI practical applications), 10-11
AutoUnlockInterval property (IADsDomain interface), 46-47, 457-458, 581

B

BackupFlags parameter, 206
BackupLocation parameter, 206
backups
    IIS Metabase, 206-207, 500
        deleting, 208, 501
        enumeration, 207, 500
        restoring, 207, 500
    IIsComputer
        deleting, 208, 501
        enumeration, 207
        restoring, 207, 500
BackupVersion parameter, 206
bad login attempts
    querying, 99, 476
    resetting count, 47-49, 458-459
BadLoginAddress property (IADsUser interface), 647
BadLoginCount property (IADsUser interface), 99, 476, 647
bandwidth
    IIsComputer, manipulating, 208-209, 501
    MaxBandwidth property (Web Performance property sheet), 278, 519
BannerPage property (IADsPrintQueue interface), 622
basic authentication (Directory Security property sheet), 298, 527
Big-Endian form, binding LDAP objects, 386
binding
    domains, 45-46
    global catalog (Active Directory), 415, 551-552
    groups, 116
    LanmanServer, 162
    to LDAP objects, 385-386
    objects (Active Directory), 410
        RootDSE, 411-413, 549-551
    print queues, 175, 496
    to specific files, 163, 491
    user objects, 72
    virtual directory binding, 262
    virtual site binding, 262
bitwise operators (user status flags), 78
business logic, separating from application logic, 21-22
business workflow processes (ADSI practical applications), 9-10
BusinessCategory property (IADsOU interface), 609

C

caching model, 11-13
ChangePassword method (IADsUser interface), 647
changing priority of print jobs (print queues), 181, 498
child objects (Active Directory), inheritance, 432-434, 561-562
class modules
    ADObjectManagement
        creating, 435-450
        functions, 450-452
    ExchangeObjectMgt
        creating, 401-404
        functions, 404-405
    IIsFTPManagement
        creating, 362-370
        functions, 371-373
    IIsSiteManagement
        creating, 236-249
        functions, 249
        method syntax, 250-259

674   class modules

IIsWebManagement
   creating, 312-326
   functions, 326-334
LDAPObjectManagement
   creating, 396-399
   functions, 399-400
NTComputerManagement
   functions, 156-158
   IADsComputer, 150-155
   IADsService, 150-155
   IADsServiceOperations, 150-155
NTContainerManagement
   creating, 60-64
   functions, 64
   instantiating, 65
   method syntax, 67-68
NTGroupManagement, 126-127
   functions, 128
NTResouceManagement, 184-194
   functions, 194-196, 200
NTUserManagement
   creating, 105-110
   functions, 111-113

Class property
IADs interface, 571
IADsComputer interface, 574
IADsDomain interface, 582
IADsFileService interface, 586
IADsFileServiceOperations
   interface, 592
IADsFileShare interface, 596
IADsGroup interface, 599
IADsLocality interface, 602
IADsO interface, 606
IADsOU interface, 610
IADsPrintJob interface, 613
IADsPrintJobOperations
   interface, 618
IADsPrintQueue interface, 622
IADsPrintQueueOperations
   interface, 627

IADsResource interface, 631
IADsService interface, 634
IADsServiceOperations
   interface, 639
IADsSession interface, 643
IADsUser interface, 648

COM (Component Object Model), 19
advantages of Visual Basic, 21-22
objects, shadowing business
   workflow processes, 9
servers
   administrative delegation model,
     creating, 34-38
   ADObjectManagement class
     module, creating, 435-450
   creating, 28-31
   ExchangeObjectMgt class
     module, creating, 401-404
   IIsFTPManagement class
     module, creating, 362-370
   IIsWebManagement class
     module, creating, 312-326
   instantiating from ASP, 32-33
   LDAPObjectManagement class
     module, creating, 396-399
   NTContainerManagement class
     module, creating, 60-64
   NTUserManagement class
     module, creating, 105-110
   testing, 31-32

command-line utilities, limitations of, 3-4

Component Object Model. *See* **COM**

computer accounts
creating/deleting, 56-57, 461-462
enumeration, 55, 461

computer class objects (Active Directory), enumerating, 416, 553

computer owner (IADsComputer), querying, 132, 481

computer processors (IADsComputer), querying, 482
computer properties (IADsComputer), querying, 131
Computer property (IADsSession interface), 643
ComputerID property (IADsComputer interface), 574
ComputerName property (WinNTSystemInfo interface), 661
ComputerPath property (IADsSession interface), 643
configuring
  ODBC logging, 222
  Visual Basic development environment, 23-26
ConnectionTimeout property
  FTP service management, 344, 534-535
  Web Site property sheet, 273-274, 516-517
ConnectTime property (IADsSession interface), 644
constants (ACEs), 422-424
containers
  creating/deleting objects, 55-56
    computer accounts, 56-57, 461-462
    groups, 59-60, 463
    user accounts, 57-59, 462-463
  enumeration, 53-54, 460
  filters, 54-55
content control (local and remote home directories), 283-284, 521
content expiration (HTTP Headers property sheet), 305-306, 530
content rating (HTTP Headers property sheet), 308-310, 531-532
ContentIndexed property (Home Directory property sheet), 283

Continue method
  IADsFileServiceOperations interface, 592
  IADsServiceOperations interface, 640
converting days to seconds, 49
CopyAccessList method (AccessControlList interface), 570
CopyHere method (IADsContainer interface), 579
Count property
  IADsContainer interface, 580
  IADsMembers interface, 605
Create method (IADsContainer interface), 55, 580
creating
  administrative delegation model, 34-38
  ADObjectManagement class module, 435-450
  COM servers, 28-31
  ExchangeObjectMgt class module, 401-404
  IIsFTPManagement class module, 362-370
  IIsWebManagement class module, 312-326
  LDAPObjectManagement class module, 396-399
  NTContainerManagement class module, 60-64
  NTResourceManagement class module, 184-194
  NTUserManagement class module, 105-110
  objects in containers, 55-56
    computer accounts, 56-57, 461-462
    groups, 59-60, 463
    user accounts, 57-59, 462-463
  Visual Basic project template, 23-26
  Web site operators, 275, 517

CurrentUserCount property
    IADsFileShare interface, 596
    querying, 163, 491
custom HTTP headers (HTTP Headers property sheet), 307, 531

D

databases. *See also* directory services
    schema, extending, 6
Datatype property (IADsPrintQueue interface), 622
datatypes, advantages of Visual Basic, 20
days, converting to seconds, 49
DCOM (Distributed Component Object Model), 34
default documents (Web sites), enabling, 291-293, 524
default naming context, binding Active Directory objects with, 412, 550
DefaultDoc property (Documents property sheet), 291-293, 524-525
DefaultDocFooter property (Documents property sheet), 293-294, 525
DefaultJobPriority property (IADsPrintQueue interface), 622
DefaultLogonDomain property (Directory Security property sheet), 298
delegation model, creating, 34-38
Delete method (IADsContainer interface), 55, 580
DeleteObject method (IADsDeleteOps interface), 581

deleting
    ACEs from ACL, 431-432, 561
        with inheritance for single child object class, 434, 562
    directory subtrees (Active Directory), 419, 554
    distribution list members (Exchange), 395, 548
    Exchange mailboxes, 394, 547
    FTP sites (IIS site management), 229, 510
    FTP virtual directories (IIS site management), 231, 511
    IIS Metabase backups, 208, 501
    IIsComputer backups, 208, 501
    inactive machine accounts, 103-105
    LDAP entries, 389, 545
    MIME-type mappings, 211-212, 502
    objects (Active Directory), 419, 554
    objects in containers, 55-56
        computer accounts, 56-57, 461-462
        groups, 59-60, 463
        user accounts, 57-59, 462-463
    print jobs, 182, 499
    shares, 168, 494
    sites (ServerComment property), 227-228, 509
    user account expiration dates, 96
    users from groups, 117-118, 479
    virtual directories (IIS site management), 230, 511
    Web site operators, 276, 518
Department property
    IADsComputer interface, 574
    IADsUser interface, 648
Dependencies property
    IADsFileService interface, 586
    IADsService interface, 634

domains 677

Description property
  IADsComputer interface, 574
  IADsFileService interface, 586
  IADsFileShare interface, 596
  IADsGroup interface, 599
  IADsLocality interface, 602
  IADsO interface, 606
  IADsOU interface, 610
  IADsPrintJob interface, 613
  IADsPrintQueue interface, 623
  IADsUser interface, 74-75, 464-465, 648
design, Active Directory resources, 663-664
directories. *See* LDAP; virtual directories; Web directories
directory access permissions (FTP service management), 356-357, 540
directory listing style (FTP service management), 357-358, 541
Directory Security property sheet (FTP service), 359-362, 541-543
Directory Security property sheet (WWW service), 294-295
  authentication methods, 295-299, 526-527
  IP address restrictions, 301-304, 528-530
  secure communcations, 299-301, 527-528
Directory Server (Netscape), installing, 382-385
directory services. *See also* databases
  abstraction, 5-8
  Active Directory, development of, 4
directory structures, 123
directory trees (Active Directory), deleting branches, 419, 554
disabled user accounts in domains, 84
disconnecting user sessions, 171, 495

DisplayName property
  IADsFileService interface, 586
  IADsService interface, 634
distinguished names (DNs), 380
Distributed Component Object Model (DCOM), 34
distribution lists (Exchange)
  adding members, 394-395, 548
  determining owner, 395-396, 549
  removing members, 395, 548
Division property
  IADsComputer interface, 575
  IADsUser interface, 648
DNs (distinguished names), 380
document footers (Web sites), enabling, 293-294, 525
Documents property sheet (WWW service), 291
  default document, enabling, 291-293, 524
  document footer, enabling, 293-294, 525
DomainDeny property (IPSecurity interface), 302, 360
DomainGrant property (IPSecurity interface), 302, 360
DomainName property (WinNTSystemInfo interface), 661
domains
  Active Directory terminology, 408
  containers, enumeration, 53-54, 460
  creating/deleting objects, 55-56
    computer accounts, 56-57, 461-462
    groups, 59-60, 463
    user accounts, 57-59, 462-463
  disabled user accounts, 84
  enumeration, 44, 457
  filters, 54-55

678　domains

properties
　Account Policy dialog box, 44-45
　AutoUnlockInterval, 46-47, 457-458
　binding, 45-46
　LockoutObservationInterval, 47, 458
　MaxBadPasswordsAllowed, 47-49, 458-459
　MaxPasswordAge, 49, 459
　MinPasswordAge, 50, 459
　MinPasswordLength, 51-52, 460
　PasswordHistoryLength, 52-53, 460
DontLog property
　FTP service management, 356
　Home Directory property sheet, 283

E

EmailAddress property (IADsUser interface), 648
EmployeeID property (IADsUser interface), 649
EnableDefaultDoc property (Documents property sheet), 291-293, 524
EnableDirBrowsing property (Home Directory property sheet), 283
EnableDocFooter property (Documents property sheet), 293-294, 525
enabling
　default documents (Web sites), 291-293, 524
　document footers (Web sites), 293-294, 525
　IIS site logging, 213-214, 503

encryption (SAM), SYSKEY utility, 51
entries (LDAP), 379
　creating, 389, 544
　determining directory architecture, 387, 543
　modifying attributes, 388, 544
　querying attributes
　　alternate credentials, 388, 544
　　anonymous access, 387-388, 544
　removing, 389, 545
entries (Web directories), adding to, 232-233, 512
enumeration
　ACEs, 425-431, 555-560
　computer class objects (Active Directory), 416, 553
　containers, 53-54, 460
　　filters, 54-55
　domains, 44, 457
　group class objects (Active Directory), 416, 552
　groups, 118, 480
　IADsService, installed services, 135-136, 483
　IADsServiceOperations, service status, 145-146, 487-488
　IIS Metabase, backups, 207, 500
　IIS site management
　　FTP, 224, 507
　　WWW, 223, 507
　IIsComputer, backups, 207
　open resources, 172-173, 495
　print queues, 175, 496
　　print jobs, 179-181, 498
　shares, 162-163, 490
　user class objects (Active Directory), 415, 552
　user group membership, 122-123, 481
　user sessions, 169-170, 494

environment profiles, user
    accounts, 87
  home directory mapping, 90, 472
  home directory path, 89, 472
  LoginScript property, 89, 471
  profile paths, 471
error handling, user account
    expiration dates, 96
ErrorControl property
  IADsFileService interface, 586-587
  IADsService interface, 635
examining IIS Metabase structure,
    204-205
Exchange mailbox management, 391
  adding distribution list members,
    394-395, 548
  creating mailboxes, 391-393,
    546-547
  determining distribution list owner,
    395-396, 549
  removing distribution list members,
    395, 548
  removing mailboxes, 394, 547
ExchangeObjectMgt class module
  creating, 401-404
  functions, 404-405
exercises
  ADObjectManagement
    creating, 435-450
    functions, 450-452
  ExchangeObjectMgt
    creating, 401-404
    functions, 404-405
  IIsFTPManagement
    creating, 362-370
    functions, 371-373
  IIsSiteManagement
    creating, 236-249
    functions, 249
    method syntax, 250-259

  IIsWebManagement
    creating, 312-326
    functions, 326-334
  LDAPObjectManagement
    creating, 396-399
    functions, 399-400
  NTComputerManagement
    functions, 156, 158
    IADsComputer, 150-155
    IADsService, 150-155
    IADsServiceOperations, 150-155
  NTContainerManagement
    creating, 60-64
    functions, 64
    instantiating, 65
    method syntax, 67-68
  NTGroupManagement, 126-127
    functions, 128
  NTResoucManagement, 184-194
    functions, 194-196, 200
  NTUserManagement
    creating, 105-110
    functions, 111-113
ExitMessage property (FTP service
    management), 351-352, 538
expiration date of user accounts
  querying, 95-96, 475
  setting, 96
expiration of passwords, resetting,
    49, 459

F

FaxNumber property
  IADsO interface, 606
  IADsOU interface, 610
  IADsUser interface, 649
file resources, managing, 162
  CurrentUserCount, querying,
    163, 491

file share descriptions
    querying, 164-165, 491
    setting, 165, 492
file share host computers, querying,
    165, 492
file share maximum users
    property values
    querying, 166, 492
    setting, 167, 493
file share path property values,
    querying, 167, 493
LanmanServer, binding, 162
shares
    creating programmatically,
        168, 493
    enumerating, 162-163, 490
    removing, 168, 494
specific files, binding to, 163, 491
file sessions, managing, 169
    disconnecting user sessions,
        171, 495
    enumerating user sessions,
        169-170, 494
    individual sessions, 170, 494
file share descriptions
    querying, 164-165, 491
    setting, 165, 492
file share host computers, querying,
    165, 492
file share maximum users
    property values
    querying, 166, 492
    setting, 167, 493
file share path property values,
    querying, 167, 493
file-system security, inheritance
    structures, 124-126
File Transfer Protocol. *See* FTP
files, binding to specific, 163, 491

Filter property
    IADsContainer interface,
        54-55, 580
    IADsMembers interface, 605
filters
    enumeration, 54-55
    LDAP, 380
finding index numbers for sites (IIS
    site management), 225, 507-508
FirstName property (IADsUser
    interface), 649
flags. *See* status flags
Flags property (AccessControlEntry
    interface), 567
forests (Active Directory)
    searching global catalog, 413-414
    terminology, 408
FrontPageWeb property (Home
    Directory property sheet), 283
FTP (File Transfer Protocol), IIS site
    management
    creating FTP sites, 227, 508-509
    deleting FTP sites, 229, 510
    enumeration, 224, 507
    virtual directories, 230, 511
FTP service management, 337
    Directory Security property sheet,
        359-362, 541-543
    FTP site property sheet, 339-340
        connection timeout, 344, 534-535
        IP addresses and TCP ports,
            341-343, 533-534
        maximum connections,
            343-344, 534
        site description, 340-341, 533
    Home Directory property
        sheet, 353
        directory access permissions,
            356-357, 540
        directory listing style,
            357-358, 541

local home directory path,
  353-354, 539
remote home directory path,
  354-356, 539-540
Messages property sheet, 349-350
  exit messages, 351-352, 538
  greeting messages, 350-351, 537
  maximum connections messages,
    352-353, 538
property inheritance table, 337-339
Security Accounts property sheet,
  344-345
  anonymous connections,
    345-348, 535-536
  site operators, 348-349, 536-537

FTP site property sheet, 339-340
connection timeout, 344, 534-535
IP addresses and TCP ports,
  341-343, 533-534
maximum connections,
  343-344, 534
site description, 340-341, 533

**FullName property (IADsUser
interface), 73-74, 463-464, 649**

functional model, LDAP, 380-381

functions
ADObjectManagement class
  module, 450-452
ExchangeObjectMgt class module,
  404-405
IIsFTPManagement class module,
  371-373
IIsSiteManagement class
  module, 249
IIsWebManagement class module,
  326-334
LDAPObjectManagement class
  module, 399-400
NTComputerManagement class
  module, 156-158
NTContainerManagement class
  module, 64

NTGroupManagement class
  module, 128
NTResourceManagement class
  module, 194-196, 200
NTUserManagement class module,
  111-113

G

Get method
IADs interface, 571
IADsComputer interface, 575
IADsDomain interface, 582
IADsFileService interface, 587
IADsFileServiceOperations
  interface, 592
IADsFileShare interface, 596
IADsGroup interface, 599
IADsLocality interface, 603
IADsO interface, 606
IADsOU interface, 610
IADsPrintJob interface, 614
IADsPrintJobOperations
  interface, 618
IADsPrintQueue interface, 623
IADsPrintQueueOperations
  interface, 627
IADsResource interface, 631
IADsService interface, 635
IADsServiceOperations
  interface, 640
IADsSession interface, 644
IADsUser interface, 649

GetEx method
IADs interface, 571
IADsComputer interface, 575
IADsDomain interface, 582
IADsFileService interface, 587
IADsFileServiceOperations
  interface, 592

IADsFileShare interface, 596
IADsGroup interface, 600
IADsLocality interface, 603
IADsO interface, 607
IADsOU interface, 610
IADsPrintJob interface, 614
IADsPrintJobOperations
  interface, 618
IADsPrintQueue interface, 623
IADsPrintQueueOperations
  interface, 627
IADsResource interface, 631
IADsService interface, 635
IADsServiceOperations
  interface, 640
IADsSession interface, 644
IADsUser interface, 649

GetInfo method
  IADs interface, 12-13, 571
  IADsComputer interface, 575
  IADsDomain interface, 582
  IADsFileService interface, 587
  IADsFileServiceOperations
    interface, 592
  IADsFileShare interface, 596
  IADsGroup interface, 600
  IADsLocality interface, 603
  IADsO interface, 607
  IADsOU interface, 610
  IADsPrintJob interface, 614
  IADsPrintJobOperations
    interface, 618
  IADsPrintQueue interface, 623
  IADsPrintQueueOperations
    interface, 627
  IADsResource interface, 631
  IADsService interface, 635
  IADsServiceOperations
    interface, 640
  IADsSession interface, 644
  IADsUser interface, 650

GetInfoEx method
  IADs interface, 572
  IADsComputer interface, 575
  IADsDomain interface, 582
  IADsFileService interface, 587
  IADsFileServiceOperations
    interface, 592
  IADsFileShare interface, 597
  IADsGroup interface, 600
  IADsLocality interface, 603
  IADsO interface, 607
  IADsOU interface, 611
  IADsPrintJob interface, 614
  IADsPrintJobOperations
    interface, 619
  IADsPrintQueue interface, 623
  IADsPrintQueueOperations
    interface, 628
  IADsResource interface, 632
  IADsService interface, 636
  IADsServiceOperations
    interface, 640
  IADsSession interface, 644
  IADsUser interface, 650

GetObject method
  IADsCollection interface, 573
  IADsContainer interface, 580

global accounts
  changing local accounts to, 98, 476
  changing to local accounts, 97-98, 476

global catalog (Active Directory)
  binding, 415, 551-552
  object attribute replication, 414
  searching, 413-414
  terminology, 409

global groups
  creating, 59-60, 463
  enumeration, 55

Globally Unique Identifier (GUID),
  Active Directory terminology, 409

GraceLoginsAllowed property
  (IADsUser interface), 650

GraceLoginsRemaining property
  (IADsUser interface), 650
GreetingMessage property (FTP
  service management), 350-351, 537
group class objects (Active Directory),
  enumerating, 416, 552
group description field values
  querying, 120-121, 480
  setting new values, 121, 480
groups
  binding, 116
  creating/deleting, 59-60, 463
  enumeration, 55, 118, 461, 480
  file-system security, managing,
    123-124
  user membership, querying,
    118-119, 480
  users
    adding, 117, 479
    removing, 117-118, 479
Groups method (IADsUser
  interface), 650
GUID (Globally Unique Identifier),
  Active Directory terminology, 409
GUID property
  IADs interface, 572
  IADsComputer interface, 575
  IADsDomain interface, 582
  IADsFileService interface, 588
  IADsFileServiceOperations
    interface, 593
  IADsFileShare interface, 597
  IADsGroup interface, 600
  IADsLocality interface, 603
  IADsO interface, 607
  IADsOU interface, 611
  IADsPrintJob interface, 614
  IADsPrintJobOperations
    interface, 619
  IADsPrintQueue interface, 623

IADsPrintQueueOperations
  interface, 628
IADsResource interface, 632
IADsService interface, 636
IADsServiceOperations
  interface, 640
IADsSession interface, 644
IADsUser interface, 651

H

HAL (IADsComputer), querying,
  134, 482
Hints property (IADsContainer
  interface), 581
home directory mapping (user
  accounts), 90, 472
home directory path (user accounts),
  89, 472
Home Directory property sheet (FTP
  service), 353
  directory access permissions,
    356-357, 540
  directory listing style, 357-358, 541
  local home directory path,
    353-354, 539
  remote home directory path,
    354-356, 539-540
Home Directory property sheet
  (WWW service), 279-280
  access permissions and content
    control, 283-284, 521
  local home directories,
    280-281, 520
  remote home directories, 281-282,
    520-521
  URL redirection, 288-290, 523-524
  Web application configuration,
    284-288, 521-523

HomeDirDrive property (IADsUser interface), 659
HomeDirectory property (IADsUser interface), 651
HomePage property (IADsUser interface), 651
host headers (secure connections), 270
HostComputer property
    IADsFileService interface, 588
    IADsFileShare interface, 597
    IADsService interface, 636
        querying, 140, 485
HostPrintQueue property (IADsPrintJob interface), 614
HTTP Headers property sheet (WWW service), 305
    content expiration, 305-306, 530
    content rating, 308-310, 531-532
    custom HTTP headers, 307, 531
    MIME type information, 310-311, 532
HTTP keep-alives, AllowKeepAlive property (Web Performance property sheet), 279, 519
HttpCustomHeaders property (HTTP Headers property sheet), 307, 531
HttpExpires property (HTTP Headers property sheet), 305-306, 530
HttpPics property (HTTP Headers property sheet), 308-310, 531-532
HttpRedirect property (Home Directory property sheet), 288-290, 523-524

I

IADs interface, 571
    ADsPath property, 571
    Class property, 571
    Get method, 571
    GetEx method, 571
    GetInfo method, 12-13, 571
    GetInfoEx method, 572
    GUID property, 572
    Name property, 572
    Parent property, 572
    Put method, 572
    PutEx method, 572
    Schema property, 573
    SetInfo method, 12-13, 573
IADsCollection interface, 573
    Add method, 573
    GetObject method, 573
    Remove method, 573
IADsComputer interface, 574
    ADsPath property, 574
    Class property, 574
    computer owner, querying, 132, 481
    computer processors, querying, 482
    computer properties, querying, 131
    ComputerID property, 574
    Department property, 574
    Description property, 574
    Division property, 575
    Get method, 575
    GetEx method, 575
    GetInfo method, 575
    GetInfoEx method, 575
    GUID property, 575
    HAL, querying, 134, 482
    Location property, 576
    MemorySize property, 576
    Model property, 576
    Name property, 576
    NetAddresses property, 576
    NTComputerManagement class module, 150-155
    operating systems, querying, 133, 482
    OperatingSystem property, 577

OperatingSystemVersion
   property, 577
organizations (registered), querying,
   132, 481
Owner property, 577
Parent property, 577
PrimaryUser property, 577
Processor property, 578
ProcessorCount property, 578
Put method, 578
PutEx method, 578
Role property, 578
Schema property, 579
SetInfo method, 579
Site property, 579
StorageCapacity property, 579
IADsContainer interface, 579
   CopyHere method, 579
   Count property, 580
   Create method, 55, 580
   Delete method, 55, 580
   Filter property, 54-55, 580
   GetObject method, 580
   Hints property, 581
   MoveHere method, 58, 581
IADsDeleteOps interface, 581
   DeleteObject method, 581
IADsDomain interface, 581
   ADsPath property, 581
   AutoUnlockInterval property,
      46-47, 457-458, 581
   Class property, 582
   Get method, 582
   GetEx method, 582
   GetInfo method, 582
   GetInfoEx method, 582
   GUID property, 582
   IsWorkgroup property, 583
   LockoutObservationInterval
      property, 47, 458, 583
   MaxBadPasswordsAllowed
      property, 47-49, 458-459, 583

MaxPasswordAge property, 49,
   459, 583
MinPasswordAge property, 50,
   459, 583
MinPasswordLength property,
   51-52, 460, 584
Name property, 584
Parent property, 584
PasswordAttributes property, 584
PasswordHistoryLength property,
   52-53, 460, 584
Put method, 585
PutEx method, 585
Schema property, 585
SetInfo method, 585
IADsFileService interface, 585
   ADsPath property, 585
   Class property, 586
   Dependencies property, 586
   Description property, 586
   DisplayName property, 586
   ErrorControl property, 586-587
   Get method, 587
   GetEx method, 587
   GetInfo method, 587
   GetInfoEx method, 587
   GUID property, 588
   HostComputer property, 588
   LoadOrderGroup property, 588
   MaxUserCount property, 588
   Name property, 588
   Parent property, 589
   Path property, 589
   Put method, 589
   PutEx method, 589
   Schema property, 589
   ServiceAccountName property, 590
   ServiceAccountPath property, 590
   ServiceType property, 590
   SetInfo method, 590
   StartType property, 591
   StartupParemeters property, 591
   Version property, 591

IADsFileServiceOperations interface, 591
   ADsPath property, 591
   Class property, 592
   Continue method, 592
   Get method, 592
   GetEx method, 592
   GetInfo method, 592
   GetInfoEx method, 592
   GUID property, 593
   Name property, 593
   Parent property, 593
   Pause method, 593
   Put method, 593
   PutEx method, 593
   Resources method, 594
   Schema property, 594
   Sessions method, 594
   SetInfo method, 594
   SetPassword method, 594
   Start method, 595
   Status property, 595
   Stop method, 595
IADsFileShare interface, 595
   ADsPath property, 595
   Class property, 596
   CurrentUserCount property, 596
   Description property, 596
   Get method, 596
   GetEx method, 596
   GetInfo method, 596
   GetInfoEx method, 597
   GUID property, 597
   HostComputer property, 597
   MaxUserCount property, 597
   Name property, 597
   Parent property, 597
   Path property, 598
   Put method, 598
   PutEx method, 598
   Schema property, 598
   SetInfo method, 598

IADsGroup interface, 599
   Add method, 599
   ADsPath property, 599
   Class property, 599
   Description property, 599
   Get method, 599
   GetEx method, 600
   GetInfo method, 600
   GetInfoEx method, 600
   GUID property, 600
   IsMember method, 600
   Members method, 600
   Name property, 601
   namespace, 115
   Parent property, 601
   Put method, 601
   PutEx method, 601
   Remove method, 601
   Schema property, 602
   SetInfo method, 602
IADsLocality interface, 602
   ADsPath property, 602
   Class property, 602
   Description property, 602
   Get method, 603
   GetEx method, 603
   GetInfo method, 603
   GetInfoEx method, 603
   GUID property, 603
   LocalityName property, 603
   Name property, 604
   Parent property, 604
   PostalAddress property, 604
   Put method, 604
   PutEx method, 604
   Schema property, 605
   SeeAlso property, 605
   SetInfo method, 605
IADsMembers interface, 605
   Count property, 605
   Filter property, 605

IADsO interface, 606
  ADsPath property, 606
  Class property, 606
  Description property, 606
  FaxNumber property, 606
  Get method, 606
  GetEx method, 607
  GetInfo method, 607
  GetInfoEx method, 607
  GUID property, 607
  LocalityName property, 607
  Name property, 607
  Parent property, 608
  PostalAddress property, 608
  Put method, 608
  PutEx method, 608
  Schema property, 608
  SeeAlso property, 609
  SetInfo method, 609
  TelephoneNumber property, 609
IADsOpenDSObject interface, 613
  OpenDSObject method, 388, 544, 613
IADsOU interface, 609
  ADsPath property, 609
  BusinessCategory property, 609
  Class property, 610
  Description property, 610
  FaxNumber property, 610
  Get method, 610
  GetEx method, 610
  GetInfo method, 610
  GetInfoEx method, 611
  GUID property, 611
  LocalityName property, 611
  Name property, 611
  Parent property, 611
  PostalAddress property, 611
  Put method, 612
  PutEx method, 612
  Schema property, 612
  SeeAlso property, 612
  SetInfo method, 612
  TelephoneNumber property, 613
IADsPrintJob interface, 182, 613
  ADsPath property, 613
  Class property, 613
  Description property, 613
  Get method, 614
  GetEx method, 614
  GetInfo method, 614
  GetInfoEx method, 614
  GUID property, 614
  HostPrintQueue property, 614
  Name property, 615
  Notify property, 615
  NotifyPath property, 615
  Parent property, 615
  Priority property, 615
  Put method, 615
  PutEx method, 616
  Schema property, 616
  SetInfo method, 616
  Size property, 616
  StartTime property, 616
  TimeSubmitted property, 617
  TotalPages property, 617
  UntilTime property, 617
  User property, 617
  UserPath property, 617
IADsPrintJobOperations interface, 618
  ADsPath property, 618
  Class property, 618
  Get method, 618
  GetEx method, 618
  GetInfo method, 618
  GetInfoEx method, 619
  GUID property, 619
  Name property, 619
  PagesPrinted property, 619
  Parent property, 619
  Pause method, 619
  Position property, 620
  Put method, 620

PutEx method, 620
Resume method, 620
Schema property, 620
SetInfo method, 621
Status property, 621
TimeElapsed property, 621

IADsPrintQueue interface, 622
  ADsPath property, 622
  BannerPage property, 622
  Class property, 622
  Datatype property, 622
  DefaultJobPriority property, 622
  Description property, 623
  Get method, 623
  GetEx method, 623
  GetInfo method, 623
  GetInfoEx method, 623
  GUID property, 623
  Location property, 624
  Model property, 624
  Name property, 624
  NetAddresses property, 624
  Parent property, 624
  PrintDevices property, 625
  PrinterPath property, 625
  PrintProcessor property, 625
  Priority property, 625
  Put method, 625
  PutEx method, 626
  Schema property, 626
  SetInfo method, 626
  StartTime property, 626
  UntilTime property, 626

IADsPrintQueueOperations interface, 627
  ADsPath property, 627
  Class property, 627
  Get method, 627
  GetEx method, 627
  GetInfo method, 627
  GetInfoEx method, 628
  GUID property, 628
  Name property, 628
  Parent property, 628
  Pause method, 628
  PrintJobs method, 628
  Purge method, 629
  Put method, 629
  PutEx method, 629
  Resume method, 629
  Schema property, 629
  SetInfo method, 630
  Status property, 630-631

IADsResource interface, 631
  ADsPath property, 631
  Class property, 631
  Get method, 631
  GetEx method, 631
  GetInfo method, 631
  GetInfoEx method, 632
  GUID property, 632
  LockCount property, 632
  Name property, 632
  Parent property, 632
  Path property, 632
  Put method, 633
  PutEx method, 633
  Schema property, 633
  SetInfo method, 633
  User property, 633
  UserPath property, 634

IADsService interface, 135, 634
  ADsPath property, 634
  Class property, 634
  Dependencies property, 634
  DisplayName property, 634
  enumeration, installed services, 135-136, 483
  ErrorControl property, 635
  Get method, 635
  GetEx method, 635
  GetInfo method, 635
  GetInfoEx method, 636
  GUID property, 636

IADsSession interface 689

HostComputer property, 636
   querying, 140, 485
LoadOrderGroup property, 636
Name property, 636
NTComputerManagement class
   module, 150-155
Parent property, 636
Path property, 637
Put method, 637
PutEx method, 637
Schema property, 637
service account names, querying,
   142-143, 486
service dependencies
   querying, 136-137, 483
   setting, 137-138, 483-484
service display names
   querying, 138-140, 484-485
   setting, 140, 485
service executable path
   querying, 141, 486
   setting, 141, 486
service start types
   querying, 143-144, 487
   setting, 144, 487
ServiceAccountName property, 637
ServiceAccountPath property, 638
ServiceType property, 638
SetInfo method, 638
StartType property, 638-639
StartupParameters property, 639
Version property, 639

**IADsServiceOperations interface, 135,
145, 639**
ADsPath property, 639
Class property, 639
Continue method, 640
Get method, 640
GetEx method, 640
GetInfo method, 640
GetInfoEx method, 640

GUID property, 640
Name property, 641
NTComputerManagement class
   module, 150-155
Parent property, 641
passwords, setting, 149, 490
Pause method, 641
Put method, 641
PutEx method, 641
Schema property, 641
service status, enumeration,
   145-146, 487-488
services
   pausing, 148, 489-490
   starting, 146, 488
   stopping, 147, 489
SetInfo method, 642
SetPassword method, 642
Start method, 642
Status property, 642
Stop method, 643

IADsSession interface, 643
ADsPath property, 643
Class property, 643
Computer property, 643
ComputerPath property, 643
ConnectTime property, 644
Get method, 644
GetEx method, 644
GetInfo method, 644
GetInfoEx method, 644
GUID property, 644
IdleTime property, 645
Name property, 645
Parent property, 645
Put method, 645
PutEx method, 645
Schema property, 646
SetInfo method, 646
User property, 646
UserPath property, 646

IADsUser interface, 72-73, 646
  AccountDisabled property, 84-85, 469, 646
  AccountExpirationDate property, 95-96, 475, 647
  ADsPath property, 647
  BadLoginAddress property, 647
  BadLoginCount property, 99, 476, 647
  ChangePassword method, 647
  Class property, 648
  Department property, 648
  Description property, 74-75, 464-465, 648
  Division property, 648
  EmailAddress property, 648
  EmployeeID property, 649
  FaxNumber property, 649
  FirstName property, 649
  FullName property, 73-74, 463-464, 649
  Get method, 649
  GetEx method, 649
  GetInfo method, 650
  GetInfoEx method, 650
  GraceLoginsAllowed property, 650
  GraceLoginsRemaining property, 650
  Groups method, 650
  GUID property, 651
  HomeDirDrive property, 659
  HomeDirectory property, 651
  HomePage property, 651
  IsAccountLocked property, 85-87, 470, 651
  Languages property, 651
  LastFailedLogin property, 651
  LastLogin property, 100, 477, 652
  LastLogoff property, 100, 477, 652
  LastName property, 652
  LoginHours property, 652
  LoginScript property, 89, 471, 652
  LoginWorkstations property, 92-95, 473-474, 653
  Manager property, 653
  MaxLogins property, 653
  MaxStorage property, 653
  Name property, 653
  NamePrefix property, 654
  NameSuffix property, 654
  ObjectSID property, 659
  OfficeLocations property, 654
  OtherName property, 654
  Parameters property, 659
  Parent property, 654
  PasswordAge property, 102-105, 478, 659
  PasswordExpirationDate property, 655
  PasswordExpired property, 660
  PasswordLastChanged property, 655
  PasswordMinimumLength property, 101, 477, 655
  PasswordRequired property, 101-102, 477-478, 655
  Picture property, 655
  PostalAddresses property, 656
  PostalCodes property, 656
  PrimaryGroupID property, 660
  Profile property, 656
  Put method, 656
  PutEx method, 656
  RequireUniquePassword property, 657
  Schema property, 657
  SeeAlso property, 657
  SetInfo method, 657
  SetPassword method, 657
  TelephoneHome property, 658
  TelephoneMobile property, 658
  TelephoneNumber property, 658
  TelephonePager property, 658
  Title property, 658
  UserFlags property, 660-661

IdleTime property (IADsSession
  interface), 645
IIS (Internet Information Server) 4.0, 203
IIS Log Replay utility, 213
IIS Metabase, 203-204
  backups, 206-207, 500
    deleting, 208, 501
    enumeration, 207, 500
    restoring, 207, 500
  Directory Security property sheet,
  294-295
    authentication methods,
    295-299, 526-527
    IP address restrictions, 301-304,
    528-530
    secure communications,
    299-301, 527-528
  Documents property sheet, 291
    default document, enabling,
    291-293, 524
    document footer, enabling,
    293-294, 525
  entries, adding, 232-233, 512
  Home Directory property sheet,
  279-280
    access permissions and content
    control, 283-284, 521
    local home directories,
    280-281, 520
    remote home directories,
    281-282, 520-521
    URL redirection, 288-290,
    523-524
    Web application configuration,
    284-288, 521-523
  HTTP Headers property sheet, 305
    content expiration, 305-306, 530
    content rating, 308-310,
    531-532
    custom HTTP headers, 307, 531
    MIME type information,
    310-311, 532

IIsComputer object, 206
  property inheritance, 263-267
  structure, examining, 204-205
  Web Operators property sheet,
  274-275
    creating operators, 275, 517
    querying operators, 275, 517
    removing operators, 276, 518
  Web Performance property sheet,
  276-277
    AllowKeepAlive property,
    279, 519
    MaxBandwidth property,
    278, 519
    ServerSize property,
    277-278, 518
  Web Site property sheet, 267-268
    Connections frame, 272-274,
    516-517
    Web Site Identification frame,
    268-271, 514-516
IIS site logging, 213
  active log format, 214-215,
  503-504
  advanced log format, 216-217
    ASCII-based log providers, 216
  enabling, 213-214, 503
  log time period
    querying, 217, 504
    setting, 217, 504
  ODBC logging, 220-222, 506
  provider support, 213
  W3C Extended Log File Format,
  218-220, 505-506
IIS site management, 223
  creating new sites, 225-226, 508
  deleting sites with ServerComment
    property, 227-228, 509
  FTP enumeration, 224, 507
  FTP sites
    creating, 227, 508-509
    deleting, 229, 510

FTP virtual directories
  creating, 230, 511
  deleting, 231, 511
index numbers for sites, finding, 225, 507-508
virtual directories
  creating, 229-230, 510
  deleting, 230, 511
Web directories, managing, 231, 512
WWW enumeration, 223, 507
IIsComputer object, 206
  backups
    deleting, 208, 501
    enumeration, 207
    restoring, 207, 500
  bandwidth, manipulating, 208-209, 501
IIsFTPManagement class module
  creating, 362-370
  functions, 371-373
IIsSiteManagement class module
  creating, 236-249
  functions, 249
  method syntax, 250-259
IIsWebManagement class module
  creating, 312-326
  functions, 326-334
inactive machine accounts, removing, 103-105
index numbers (IIS site management), finding, 225, 507-508
informational model (LDAP), 378-379
inheritance
  Active Directory security, 424-425, 432
    all child objects, 432-433, 561
    single attributes, 435, 563
    single child object class, 433-434, 562

properties
  FTP service, 337-339
  IIS Metabase, 263-267
structures, file-system security, 124-126
InheritedObjectType property (AccessControlEntry interface), 567
installing
  ADSI, 22-23
  MDAC (Microsoft Data Access Components), 23
  Netscape Directory Server, 382-385
  Visual Basic, 23
instantiating
  COM servers from ASP, 32-33
  NTContainerManagement class module, 65
interface support, ADSI, 14-16
Internet Information Server 4.0, 203
IP addresses
  FTP service management, 341-343, 533-534
  publishing multiple Web sites, 269-270, 515
  restrictions
    Directory Security property sheet, 301-304, 528-530
    FTP service management, 359-362, 541-543
IPDeny property (IPSecurity interface), 302, 360
IPGrant property (IPSecurity interface), 302, 360
IPSecurity interface, properties, 302, 360
IsAccountLocked property (IADsUser interface), 85-87, 470, 651
IsMember method, 118-120
  IADsGroup interface, 600
IsWorkgroup property (IADsDomain interface), 583

J-K

JavaScript Active Server Page, instantiating NTContainerManagement class module, 65

keep-alives (HTTP), Web Performance property sheet, 279, 519

L

Languages property (IADsUser interface), 651
LanmanServer, binding, 162
last login attempt, querying, 100, 477
last logoff attempt, querying, 100, 477
LastFailedLogin property (IADsUser interface), 651
LastLogin property (IADsUser interface), 100, 477, 652
LastLogoff property (IADsUser interface), 100, 477, 652
LastName property (IADsUser interface), 652
LDAP (Lightweight Directory Access Protocol), 377
  binding to objects, 385-386
  commercial support for, 382
  creating entries, 389, 544
  determining directory architecture, 387, 543
  Exchange mailbox management, 391
    adding distribution list members, 394-395, 548
    creating mailboxes, 391-393, 546-547
    determining distribution list owner, 395-396, 549
    removing distribution list members, 395, 548
    removing mailboxes, 394, 547
  functional model, 380-381
  informational model, 378-379
  modifying entry attributes, 388, 544
  naming model, 379-380
  overview, 378
  querying entry attributes
    alternate credentials, 388, 544
    anonymous access, 387-388, 544
  removing entries, 389, 545
  resources, 666-667
  SDKs, 381
  searching with ADO, 390-391, 545
  security model, 381
LDAPObjectManagement class module
  creating, 396-399
  functions, 399-400
Lightweight Directory Access Protocol. *See* LDAP
Little-Endian form, binding LDAP objects, 386
LoadOrderGroup property
  IADsFileService interface, 588
  IADsService interface, 636
local accounts
  changing global accounts to, 97-98, 476
  changing to global accounts, 98, 476
local groups
  creating, 59, 463
  enumeration, 55
local home directories (Home Directory property sheet), 280-281, 520
  access permissions and content control, 283-284, 521

local home directory path (FTP service management), 353-354, 539
LocalityName property
   IADsLocality interface, 603
   IADsO interface, 607
   IADsOU interface, 611
Location property
   IADsComputer interface, 576
   IADsPrintQueue interface, 624
LockCount property (IADsResource interface), 632
LockoutObservationInterval property (IADsDomain interface), 47, 458, 583
lockouts
   bad login attempts, resetting, 47-49, 458-459
   resetting, 46-47, 457-458
   user accounts, 85-87, 470
log file size (advanced log format), 217-218, 504-505
log time period
   querying, 217, 504
   setting, 217, 504
LogFilePeriod property, 217
LogFileTruncateSize property, 217
logging (IIS site logging), 213
   active log format, 214-215, 503-504
   advanced log format, 216-217
      ASCII-based log providers, 216
   enabling, 213-214, 503
   log time period
      querying, 217, 504
      setting, 217, 504
   ODBC logging, 220-222, 506
   provider support, 213
   W3C Extended Log File Format, 218-220, 505-506
login attempts, resetting count for bad attempts, 47-49, 458-459

login hours (user accounts), 91-92, 473
login workstations (user accounts), 92-95, 473-474
LoginHours property (IADsUser interface), 652
logins
   bad login attempts, querying, 99, 476
   last login attempt, querying, 100, 477
   last logoff attempt, querying, 100, 477
LoginScript property (IADsUser interface), 89, 471, 652
LoginWorkstations property (IADsUser interface), 92-95, 473-474, 653
LogPluginCLSID property, 214
logs, advanced format, 217-218, 504-505

M

machine accounts
   not in resource domain, detecting, 478
   password age, querying, 103-105
   removing inactive, 103-105
mailboxes (Exchange), management, 391
   adding distribution list members, 394-395, 548
   creating mailboxes, 391-393, 546-547
   determining distribution list owner, 395-396, 549
   removing distribution list members, 395, 548
   removing mailboxes, 394, 547

Manager property (IADsUser interface), 653
managing
  Exchange mailboxes, 391
    adding distribution list members, 394-395, 548
    creating mailboxes, 391-393, 546-547
    determining distribution list owner, 395-396, 549
    removing distribution list members, 395, 548
    removing mailboxes, 394, 547
  file resources, 162
    binding LanmanServer, 162
    binding to specific files, 163, 491
    creating shares programmatically, 168, 493
    enumerating shares, 162-163, 490
    querying CurrentUserCount, 163, 491
    querying file share descriptions, 164-165, 491
    querying file share host computers, 165, 492
    querying file share maximum users property values, 166, 492
    querying file share path property values, 167, 493
    removing shares, 168, 494
    setting file share descriptions, 165, 492
    setting file share maximum users property values, 167, 493
  file sessions, 169
    disconnecting user sessions, 171, 495
    enumerating user sessions, 169-170, 494
    individual sessions, 170, 494
  file-system security with groups, 123-124
  IIS sites, 223
    creating new sites, 225-226, 508
    deleting sites with ServerComment property, 227-228, 509
    FTP enumeration, 224, 507
    FTP sites, creating/deleting, 227-229, 508-510
    FTP virtual directories, creating/deleting, 230-231, 511
    index numbers for sites, finding, 225, 507-508
    virtual directories, creating/ deleting, 229-230, 510-511
    Web directories, managing, 231, 512
    WWW enumeration, 223, 507
  open resources, 172-174, 495-496
  print queues, 174, 177
    binding print queues, 175, 496
    changing priority of queued print jobs, 181, 498
    enumerating print jobs, 179-181, 498
    enumerating print queues, 175, 496
    pausing print queues, 179, 498
    purging print jobs, 183, 499
    querying print queues, 176-177, 497
    querying queue status, 177-178, 497
    removing print jobs, 182, 499
    resuming print queues, 179, 498
  Web directories (IIS site management), 231, 512
manipulating
  bandwidth (IIsComputer), 208-209, 501
  sites, 233

mapping MIME types, 210
MaxBadPasswordsAllowed property (IADsDomain interface), 47-49, 458-459, 583
MaxBandwidth property, 209
  Web Performance property sheet, 278, 519
MaxClientsMessage property (FTP service management), 352-353, 538
MaxConnections property
  FTP service management, 343-344, 534
  Web Site property sheet, 272-273, 516
MaxLogins property (IADsUser interface), 653
MaxPasswordAge property (IADsDomain interface), 49, 459, 583
MaxStorage property (IADsUser interface), 653
MaxUserCount property
  IADsFileService interface, 588
  IADsFileShare interface, 597
MDAC (Microsoft Data Access Components), installing, 23
Members method (IADsGroup interface), 600
memory, Web site performance tuning, 277-278, 518
MemorySize property (IADsComputer interface), 576
Messages property sheet (FTP service), 349-350
  exit messages, 351-352, 538
  greeting messages, 350-351, 537
  maximum connections messages, 352-353, 538
Metabase. *See* IIS Metabase

MetaEdit utility, 204
methods
  AccessControlList interface
    AddAce, 570
    CopyAccessList, 570
    RemoveAce, 570
  IADs interface
    Get, 571
    GetEx, 571
    GetInfo, 12-13, 571
    GetInfoEx, 572
    Put, 572
    PutEx, 572
    SetInfo, 12-13, 573
  IADsCollection interface
    Add, 573
    GetObject, 573
    Remove, 573
  IADsComputer interface
    Get, 575
    GetEx, 575
    GetInfo, 575
    GetInfoEx, 575
    Put, 578
    PutEx, 578
    SetInfo, 579
  IADsContainer interface
    CopyHere, 579
    Create, 55, 580
    Delete, 55, 580
    GetObject, 580
    MoveHere, 58, 581
  IADsDeleteOps interface, *DeleteObject,* 581
  IADsDomain interface
    Get, 582
    GetEx, 582
    GetInfo, 582
    GetInfoEx, 582
    Put, 585
    PutEx, 585
    SetInfo, 585

IADsFileService interface
  Get, 587
  GetEx, 587
  GetInfo, 587
  GetInfoEx, 587
  Put, 589
  PutEx, 589
  SetInfo, 590
IADsFileServiceOperations interface
  Continue, 592
  Get, 592
  GetEx, 592
  GetInfo, 592
  GetInfoEx, 592
  Pause, 593
  Put, 593
  PutEx, 593
  Resources, 594
  Sessions, 594
  SetInfo, 594
  SetPassword, 594
  Start, 595
  Stop, 595
IADsFileShare interface
  Get, 596
  GetEx, 596
  GetInfo, 596
  GetInfoEx, 597
  Put, 598
  PutEx, 598
  SetInfo, 598
IADsGroup interface
  Add, 599
  Get, 599
  GetEx, 600
  GetInfo, 600
  GetInfoEx, 600
  IsMember, 600
  Members, 600
  Put, 601
  PutEx, 601
  Remove, 601
  SetInfo, 602
IADsLocality interface
  Get, 603
  GetEx, 603
  GetInfo, 603
  GetInfoEx, 603
  Put, 604
  PutEx, 604
  SetInfo, 605
IADsO interface
  Get, 606
  GetEx, 607
  GetInfo, 607
  GetInfoEx, 607
  Put, 608
  PutEx, 608
  SetInfo, 609
IADsOpenDSObject interface,
  OpenDSObject, 388, 544, 613
IADsOU interface
  Get, 610
  GetEx, 610
  GetInfo, 610
  GetInfoEx, 611
  Put, 612
  PutEx, 612
  SetInfo, 612
IADsPrintJob interface
  Get, 614
  GetEx, 614
  GetInfo, 614
  GetInfoEx, 614
  Put, 615
  PutEx, 616
  SetInfo, 616
IADsPrintJobOperations interface
  Get, 618
  GetEx, 618
  GetInfo, 618
  GetInfoEx, 619

Pause, 619
Put, 620
PutEx, 620
Resume, 620
SetInfo, 621
IADsPrintQueue interface
  Get, 623
  GetEx, 623
  GetInfo, 623
  GetInfoEx, 623
  Put, 625
  PutEx, 626
  SetInfo, 626
IADsPrintQueueOperations interface
  Get, 627
  GetEx, 627
  GetInfo, 627
  GetInfoEx, 628
  Pause, 628
  PrintJobs, 628
  Purge, 629
  Put, 629
  PutEx, 629
  Resume, 629
  SetInfo, 630
IADsResource interface
  Get, 631
  GetEx, 631
  GetInfo, 631
  GetInfoEx, 632
  Put, 633
  PutEx, 633
  SetInfo, 633
IADsService interface
  Get, 635
  GetEx, 635
  GetInfo, 635
  GetInfoEx, 636
  Put, 637
  PutEx, 637
  SetInfo, 638

IADsServiceOperations interface
  Continue, 640
  Get, 640
  GetEx, 640
  GetInfo, 640
  GetInfoEx, 640
  Pause, 641
  Put, 641
  PutEx, 641
  SetInfo, 642
  SetPassword, 642
  Start, 642
  Stop, 643
IADsSession interface
  Get, 644
  GetEx, 644
  GetInfo, 644
  GetInfoEx, 644
  Put, 645
  PutEx, 645
  SetInfo, 646
IADsUser interface
  ChangePassword, 647
  Get, 649
  GetEx, 649
  GetInfo, 650
  GetInfoEx, 650
  Groups, 650
  Put, 656
  PutEx, 656
  SetInfo, 657
  SetPassword, 657
IIsSiteManagement class module, syntax, 250-259
IsMember, 118-120
NTContainerManagement class module, syntax, 67-68

Microsoft Data Access Components (MDAC), installing, 23

Microsoft Exchange. *See* **Exchange mailbox management**

Microsoft Management Console (MMC), 203
Microsoft Transaction Server (MTS), 34
　administrative delegation model, creating, 34-38
migration, Windows NT 4.0 to Windows 2000, 17
MIME mappings, 210
　adding, 210, 502
　removing, 211-212, 502
　viewing, 210, 501
MIME type information (HTTP Headers property sheet), 310-311, 532
MimeExtension variable, 211
MimeType variable, 211
minimum password length, querying, 101, 477
MinPasswordAge property (IADsDomain interface), 50, 459, 583
MinPasswordLength property (IADsDomain interface), 51-52, 460, 584
MMC (Microsoft Management Console), 203
Model property
　IADsComputer interface, 576
　IADsPrintQueue interface, 624
MoveHere method (IADsContainer interface), 58, 581
moving objects (Active Directory), 420, 555
MSDOSDirOutput property (FTP service management), 358
MTS (Microsoft Transaction Server), 34
　administrative delegation model, creating, 34-38

multi-tier development, advantages of Visual Basic, 20-21
multiple Web sites, publishing on one IP address, 269-270, 515

N

Name property
　IADs interface, 572
　IADsComputer interface, 576
　IADsDomain interface, 584
　IADsFileService interface, 588
　IADsFileServiceOperations interface, 593
　IADsFileShare interface, 597
　IADsGroup interface, 601
　IADsLocality interface, 604
　IADsO interface, 607
　IADsOU interface, 611
　IADsPrintJob interface, 615
　IADsPrintJobOperations interface, 619
　IADsPrintQueue interface, 624
　IADsPrintQueueOperations interface, 628
　IADsResource interface, 632
　IADsService interface, 636
　IADsServiceOperations interface, 641
　IADsSession interface, 645
　IADsUser interface, 653
NamePrefix property (IADsUser interface), 654
namespaces
　abstraction layer, 5-8
　domains, enumeration, 44, 457
　IADsGroup interface, 115
　queries (ADSI practical applications), 13

NameSuffix property (IADsUser interface), 654
naming model (LDAP), 379-380
naming standards, enforcing (ADSI practical applications), 10
native-API calls, performance compared to ADSI, 8
NetAddresses property
   IADsComputer interface, 576
   IADsPrintQueue interface, 624
Netscape Directory Server, installing, 382-385
Notify property (IADsPrintJob interface), 615
NotifyPath property (IADsPrintJob interface), 615
NTComputerManagement class module
   functions, 156-158
   IADsComputer, 150-155
   IADsService, 150-155
   IADsServiceOperations, 150-155
NTContainerManagement class module
   creating, 60-64
   functions, 64
   instantiating, 65
   method syntax, 67-68
NTGroupManagement class module, 126-127
   functions, 128
NTLM authentication (Directory Security property sheet), 299, 527
NTResourceManagement class module, 184-194
   functions, 194-196, 200
NTUserManagement class module
   creating, 105-110
   functions, 111-113

O

objects (Active Directory)
   attribute replication in global catalog, 414
   binding, 410
      RootDSE, 411-413, 549-551
   computer class objects, enumerating, 416, 553
   creating, 415-418, 553
   finding mandatory attributes, 418-419, 554
   group class objects, enumerating, 416, 552
   mandatory attributes, 417
   moving, 420, 555
   removing, 419, 554
   renaming, 420, 555
   security, 421-422, 425
      adding ACEs to ACL, 431, 560
      constants for ACEs, 422-424
      enumerating ACEs, 425-431, 555-560
      inheritance, 432-435, 561-563
      removing ACEs from ACL, 431-432, 561
   terminology, 409
   user class objects, enumerating, 415, 552
objects (COM), shadowing business workflow processes, 9
objects (IIsComputer), 206
   backups
      deleting, 208, 501
      enumeration, 207
      restoring, 207, 500
   bandwidth, manipulating, 208-209, 501
objects (user), binding, 72
ObjectSID property (IADsUser interface), 659
ObjectType ACE field (flags), 425

PasswordExpired property 701

ObjectType property
(AccessControlEntry interface),
568-569
ODBC logging
configuring, 222
IIS site logging, 220-222, 506
OfficeLocations property (IADsUser
interface), 654
OLE-DB provider, ADSI as, 13
open resources, managing,
172-174, 496
enumeration, 172-173, 495
OpenDSObject method
(IADsOpenDSObject interface), 388,
544, 613
operating systems (IADsComputer),
querying, 133, 482
OperatingSystem property
(IADsComputer interface), 577
OperatingSystemVersion property
(IADsComputer interface), 577
operators. *See* Web Operators
property sheet
Or bitwise operator (user status
flags), 78
organizational units (OUs), 380
Active Directory terminology, 409
organizations (registered), querying
(IADsComputer), 132, 481
OtherName property (IADsUser
interface), 654
OUs (organizational units), 380
Active Directory terminology, 409
owner of distribution list (Exchange),
determining, 395-396, 549
Owner property (IADsComputer
interface), 577

P

PagesPrinted property
(IADsPrintJobOperations
interface), 619
Parameters property, 98
IADsUser interface, 659
Parent property
IADs interface, 572
IADsComputer interface, 577
IADsDomain interface, 584
IADsFileService interface, 589
IADsFileServiceOperations
interface, 593
IADsFileShare interface, 597
IADsGroup interface, 601
IADsLocality interface, 604
IADsO interface, 608
IADsOU interface, 611
IADsPrintJob interface, 615
IADsPrintJobOperations
interface, 619
IADsPrintQueue interface, 624
IADsPrintQueueOperations
interface, 628
IADsResource interface, 632
IADsService interface, 636
IADsServiceOperations
interface, 641
IADsSession interface, 645
IADsUser interface, 654
Password Never Expires status flag,
83, 468
PasswordAge property (IADsUser
interface), 102-105, 478, 659
PasswordAttributes property
(IADsDomain interface), 584
PasswordExpirationDate property
(IADsUser interface), 655
PasswordExpired property (IADsUser
interface), 660

**PasswordHistoryLength property
(IADsDomain interface), 52-53,
460, 584**
**PasswordLastChanged property
(IADsUser interface), 655**
**PasswordMinimumLength property
(IADsUser interface), 101, 477, 655**
**PasswordRequired property (IADsUser
interface), 101-102, 477-478, 655**
passwords
age, querying, 102-105, 478
bad login attempts, resetting count,
47-49, 458-459
expiration, resetting, 49, 459
IADsServiceOperations, setting,
149, 490
maximum age, 49, 459
minimum age, 50, 459
minimum length, 51-52, 460
querying, 101, 477
number stored for each user,
52-53, 460
requirements
querying, 101, 477
setting, 102, 478
security considerations, 282
user accounts, 76
changing, 77, 465
determining, 76
*Password Never Expires status
flag, 83, 468*
setting new, 76, 465
*User Cannot Change Password
status flag, 81, 467-468*
*User Must Change Password at
Next Logon status flag, 79-80,
466-467*
Path property
FTP service management,
353-354, 539
Home Directory property sheet,
280-282, 520-521

IADsFileService interface, 589
IADsFileShare interface, 598
IADsResource interface, 632
IADsService interface, 637
Pause method
IADsFileServiceOperations
interface, 593
IADsPrintJobOperations
interface, 619
IADsPrintQueueOperations
interface, 628
IADsServiceOperations
interface, 641
pausing
print queues, 179, 498
services (IADsServiceOperations),
148, 489-490
sites, 235-236, 514
**PDC property (WinNTSystemInfo
interface), 662**
performance
native-API calls versus ADSI, 8
ServerSize property (Web
Performance property sheet),
277-278, 518
permissions. *See also* security,
Active Directory
FTP directories (FTP service
management), 356-357, 540
local and remote home directories,
283-284, 521
**PICS rating (HTTP Headers property
sheet), 308-310, 531-532**
**Picture property (IADsUser
interface), 655**
**Position property
(IADsPrintJobOperations
interface), 620**
PostalAddress property
IADsLocality interface, 604
IADsO interface, 608

properties   703

IADsOU interface, 611
IADsUser interface, 656
PostalCodes property (IADsUser interface), 656
practical applications of ADSI, 8-9
   automated system management, 10-11
   business workflow processes, 9-10
   enforcing naming standards, 10
   namespace queries, 13
   property caching, 11-13
   security, 14
PrimaryGroupID property (IADsUser interface), 660
PrimaryUser property (IADsComputer interface), 577
print queues, 174, 177
   binding, 175, 496
   enumerating, 175, 496
   pausing, 179, 498
   print jobs
      changing priority of, 181, 498
      enumerating, 179-181, 498
      purging, 183, 499
      removing, 182, 499
   querying, 176-177, 497
   resuming, 179, 498
   status, querying, 177-178, 497
PrintDevices property (IADsPrintQueue interface), 625
PrinterPath property (IADsPrintQueue interface), 625
PrintJobs method (IADsPrintQueueOperations interface), 628
PrintProcessor property (IADsPrintQueue interface), 625
Priority property
   IADsPrintJob interface, 615
   IADsPrintQueue interface, 625

privileges, Web Operators property sheet, 274-275
Processor property (IADsComputer interface), 578
ProcessorCount property (IADsComputer interface), 578
profile paths (user accounts), 471
Profile property (IADsUser interface), 656
project template (Visual Basic), creating, 23-26
properties
   AccessControlEntry interface
      AccessMask, 565-566
      AceFlags, 566
      AceType, 567
      Flags, 567
      InheritedObjectType, 567
      ObjectType, 568-569
      Trustee, 569
   AccessControlList interface
      AceCount, 570
      AclRevision, 570
   Active Directory terminology, 408
   containers, Filter, 54-55
   Directory Security property sheet
      AnonymousPasswordSync, 297
      AnonymousUserName, 297
      AnonymousUserPass, 297
      AuthAnonymous, 295
      AuthBasic, 295
      AuthFlags, 295
      AuthNTLM, 295
      DefaultLogonDomain, 298
   Documents property sheet
      DefaultDoc, 291-293, 524-525
      DefaultDocFooter, 293-294, 525
      EnableDefaultDoc, 291-293, 524
      EnableDocFooter, 293-294, 525

domains
  Account Policy dialog box,
    44-45
  AutoUnlockInterval, 46-47,
    457-458
  binding, 45-46
  LockoutObservationInterval,
    47, 458
  MaxBadPasswordsAllowed,
    47-49, 458-459
  MaxPasswordAge, 49, 459
  MinPasswordAge, 50, 459
  MinPasswordLength, 51-52, 460
  PasswordHistoryLength,
    52-53, 460
FTP service management
  AccessRead, 356
  AccessWrite, 356
  AllowAnonymous, 346, 535
  AnonymousOnly, 348, 536
  AnonymousPasswordSync,
    346-347, 535-536
  AnonymousUserName, 346-347,
    535-536
  AnonymousUserPass, 346-347,
    535-536
  ConnectionTimeout, 344,
    534-535
  DontLog, 356
  ExitMessage, 351-352, 538
  GreetingMessage, 350-351, 537
  MaxClientsMessage,
    352-353, 538
  MaxConnections, 343-344, 534
  MSDOSDirOutput, 358
  Path, 353-354, 539
  property inheritance table,
    337-339
  ServerBindings, 341-343,
    533-534
  ServerComment, 340-341, 533

  UNCPassword, 354-356,
    539-540
  UNCUserName, 354-356,
    539-540
Home Directory property sheet
  AccessExecute, 284
  AccessRead, 283-284
  AccessWrite, 283
  AppFriendlyName, 284
  AppIsolated, 284
  AppRoot, 284
  ContentIndexed, 283
  DontLog, 283
  EnableDirBrowsing, 283
  FrontPageWeb, 283
  HttpRedirect, 288-290, 523-524
  Path, 280-282, 520-521
  UNCPassword, 282
  UNCUserName, 282
HTTP Headers property sheet
  HttpCustomHeaders, 307, 531
  HttpExpires, 305-306, 530
  HttpPics, 308-310, 531-532
IADs interface
  ADsPath, 571
  Class, 571
  GUID, 572
  Name, 572
  Parent, 572
  Schema, 573
IADsComputer interface
  ADsPath, 574
  Class, 574
  ComputerID, 574
  Department, 574
  Description, 574
  Division, 575
  GUID, 575
  Location, 576
  MemorySize, 576
  Model, 576
  Name, 576

properties

NetAddresses, 576
OperatingSystem, 577
OperatingSystemVersion, 577
Owner, 577
Parent, 577
PrimaryUser, 577
Processor, 578
ProcessorCount, 578
Role, 578
Schema, 579
Site, 579
StorageCapacity, 579
IADsContainer interface
   Count, 580
   Filter, 54-55, 580
   Hints, 581
IADsDomain interface
   ADsPath, 581
   AutoUnlockInterval, 46-47, 457-458, 581
   Class, 582
   GUID, 582
   IsWorkgroup, 583
   LockoutObservationInterval, 47, 458, 583
   MaxBadPasswordsAllowed, 47-48, 458-459, 583
   MaxPasswordAge, 49, 459, 583
   MinPasswordAge, 50, 459, 583
   MinPasswordLength, 51-52, 460, 584
   Name, 584
   Parent, 584
   PasswordAttributes, 584
   PasswordHistoryLength, 52-53, 460, 584
   Schema, 585
IADsFileService interface
   ADsPath, 585
   Class, 586
   Dependencies, 586
   Description, 586
   DisplayName, 586
   ErrorControl, 586-587
   GUID, 588
   HostComputer, 588
   LoadOrderGroup, 588
   MaxUserCount, 588
   Name, 588
   Parent, 589
   Path, 589
   Schema, 589
   ServiceAccountName, 590
   ServiceAccountPath, 590
   ServiceType, 590
   StartType, 591
   StartupParameters, 591
   Version, 591
IADsFileServiceOperations interface
   ADsPath, 591
   Class, 592
   GUID, 593
   Name, 593
   Parent, 593
   Schema, 594
   Status, 595
IADsFileShare interface
   ADsPath, 595
   Class, 596
   CurrentUserCount, 596
   Description, 596
   GUID, 597
   HostComputer, 597
   MaxUserCount, 597
   Name, 597
   Parent, 597
   Path, 598
   Schema, 598
IADsGroup interface
   ADsPath, 599
   Class, 599
   Description, 599
   GUID, 600
   Name, 601

Parent, 601
Schema, 602
IADsLocality interface
  ADsPath, 602
  Class, 602
  Description, 602
  GUID, 603
  LocalityName, 603
  Name, 604
  Parent, 604
  PostalAddress, 604
  Schema, 605
  SeeAlso, 605
IADsMembers interface
  Count, 605
  Filter, 605
IADsO interface
  ADsPath, 606
  Class, 606
  Description, 606
  FaxNumber, 606
  GUID, 607
  LocalityName, 607
  Name, 607
  Parent, 608
  PostalAddress, 608
  Schema, 608
  SeeAlso, 609
  TelephoneNumber, 609
IADsOU interface
  ADsPath, 609
  BusinessCategory, 609
  Class, 610
  Description, 610
  FaxNumber, 610
  GUID, 611
  LocalityName, 611
  Name, 611
  Parent, 611
  PostalAddress, 611
  Schema, 612

SeeAlso, 612
TelephoneNumber, 613
IADsPrintJob interface
  ADsPath, 613
  Class, 613
  Description, 613
  GUID, 614
  HostPrintQueue, 614
  Name, 615
  Notify, 615
  NotifyPath, 615
  Parent, 615
  Priority, 615
  Schema, 616
  Size, 616
  StartTime, 616
  TimeSubmitted, 617
  TotalPages, 617
  UntilTime, 617
  User, 617
  UserPath, 617
IADsPrintJobOperations interface
  ADsPath, 618
  Class, 618
  GUID, 619
  Name, 619
  PagesPrinted, 619
  Parent, 619
  Position, 620
  Schema, 620
  Status, 621
  TimeElapsed, 621
IADsPrintQueue interface
  ADsPath, 622
  BannerPage, 622
  Class, 622
  Datatype, 622
  DefaultJobPriority, 622
  Description, 623
  GUID, 623
  Location, 624
  Model, 624

Name, 624
NetAddresses, 624
Parent, 624
PrintDevices, 625
PrinterPath, 625
PrintProcessor, 625
Priority, 625
Schema, 626
StartTime, 626
UntilTime, 626
IADsPrintQueueOperations
 interface
    ADsPath, 627
    Class, 627
    GUID, 628
    Name, 628
    Parent, 628
    Schema, 629
    Status, 630-631
IADsResource interface
    ADsPath, 631
    Class, 631
    GUID, 632
    LockCount, 632
    Name, 632
    Parent, 632
    Path, 632
    Schema, 633
    User, 633
    UserPath, 634
IADsService interface
    ADsPath, 634
    Class, 634
    Dependencies, 634
    DisplayName, 634
    ErrorControl, 635
    GUID, 636
    HostComputer, 140, 485, 636
    LoadOrderGroup, 636
    Name, 636
    Parent, 636
    Path, 637

Schema, 637
ServiceAccountName, 637
ServiceAccountPath, 638
ServiceType, 638
StartType, 638-639
StartupParameters, 639
Version, 639
IADsServiceOperations interface
    ADsPath, 639
    Class, 639
    GUID, 640
    Name, 641
    Parent, 641
    Schema, 641
    Status, 642
IADsSession interface
    ADsPath, 643
    Class, 643
    Computer, 643
    ComputerPath, 643
    ConnectTime, 644
    GUID, 644
    IdleTime, 645
    Name, 645
    Parent, 645
    Schema, 646
    User, 646
    UserPath, 646
IADsUser interface
    AccountDisabled, 84-85,
     469, 646
    AccountExpirationDate, 95-96,
     475, 647
    ADsPath, 647
    BadLoginAddress, 647
    BadLoginCount, 99, 476, 647
    Class, 648
    Department, 648
    Description, 74-75,
     464-465, 648
    Division, 648
    EmailAddress, 648

EmployeeID, 649
FaxNumber, 649
FirstName, 649
FullName, 73-74, 463-464, 649
GraceLoginsAllowed, 650
GraceLoginsRemaining, 650
GUID, 651
HomeDirDrive, 659
HomeDirectory, 651
HomePage, 651
IsAccountLocked, 85-87, 470, 651
Languages, 651
LastFailedLogin, 651
LastLogin, 100, 477, 652
LastLogoff, 100, 477, 652
LastName, 652
LoginHours, 652
LoginScript, 89, 471, 652
LoginWorkstations, 92-95, 473-474, 653
Manager, 653
MaxLogins, 653
MaxStorage, 653
Name, 653
NamePrefix, 654
NameSuffix, 654
ObjectSID, 659
OfficeLocations, 654
OtherName, 654
Parameters, 659
Parent, 654
PasswordAge, 102-105, 478, 659
PasswordExpirationDate, 655
PasswordExpired, 660
PasswordLastChanged, 655
PasswordMinimumLength, 101, 477, 655
PasswordRequired, 101-102, 477-478, 655
Picture, 655
PostalAddress, 656
PostalCodes, 656
PrimaryGroupID, 660
Profile, 656
RequireUniquePassword, 657
Schema, 657
SeeAlso, 657
TelephoneHome, 658
TelephoneMobile, 658
TelephoneNumber, 658
TelephonePager, 658
Title, 658
UserFlags, 660-661
IIS Metabase, inheritance, 263-267
IPSecurity interface, 302, 360
LogFilePeriod, 217
LogFileTruncateSize, 217
LogPluginCLSID, 214
MaxBandwidth, 209
Parameters, 98
ServerBindings, 226
ServerComment, 224
   index numbers, finding, 225, 507-508
   sites, deleting, 227-228, 509
ServerState, 233
user accounts, 72-73
   AccountDisabled, 84-85, 469
   Description, 74-75, 464-465
   FullName, 73-74, 463-464
   IsAccountLocked, 85, 87, 470
   LoginScript, 89, 471
Web Performance property sheet
   AllowKeepAlive, 279, 519
   MaxBandwidth, 278, 519
   ServerSize, 277-278, 518
Web Site property sheet
   ConnectionTimeout, 273-274, 516-517
   MaxConnections, 272-273, 516

SecureBindings, 270-271,
    515-516
ServerBindings, 269-270, 515
ServerComment, 268-269, 514
WinNTSystemInfo interface
    ComputerName, 661
    DomainName, 661
    PDC, 662
    UserName, 662
property caching model, 11-13
property sheets (FTP service)
    Directory Security property sheet,
        359-362, 541-543
    FTP site property sheet, 339-340
        connection timeout, 344,
            534-535
        IP addresses and TCP ports,
            341-343, 533-534
        maximum connections,
            343-344, 534
        site description, 340-341, 533
    Home Directory property
        sheet, 353
        directory access permissions,
            356-357, 540
        directory listing style,
            357-358, 541
        local home directory path,
            353-354, 539
        remote home directory path,
            354-356, 539-540
    Messages property sheet, 349-350
        exit messages, 351-352, 538
        greeting messages, 350-351, 537
        maximum connections messages,
            352-353, 538
    Security Accounts property sheet,
        344-345
        anonymous connections, 345-348,
            535-536
        site operators, 348-349, 536-537

property sheets (WWW service)
    Directory Security property sheet,
        294-295
        authentication methods,
            295-299, 526-527
        IP address restrictions, 301-304,
            528-530
        secure communications, 299-301,
            527-528
    Documents property sheet, 291
        default document, enabling,
            291-293, 524
        document footer, enabling,
            293-294, 525
    Home Directory property sheet,
        279-280
        *access permissions and content
            control*, 283-284, 521
        local home directories,
            280-281, 520
        remote home directories,
            281-282, 520-521
        URL redirection, 288-290,
            523-524
        Web application configuration,
            284-288, 521-523
    HTTP Headers property sheet, 305
        content expiration, 305-306, 530
        content rating, 308-310,
            531-532
        custom HTTP headers, 307, 531
        MIME type information,
            310-311, 532
    Web Operators property sheet,
        274-275
        creating operators, 275, 517
        querying operators, 275, 517
        removing operators, 276, 518
    Web Performance property sheet,
        276-277
        AllowKeepAlive property,
            279, 519

710 property sheets

MaxBandwidth property,
278, 519
ServerSize property,
277-278, 518
Web Site property sheet, 267-268
Connections frame, 272-274,
516-517
Web Site Identification frame,
268-271, 514-516
provider support, IIS site logging, 213
publishing multiple Web sites on one IP address, 269-270, 515
Purge method (IADsPrintQueueOperations interface), 629
purging print jobs, 183, 499
Put method
IADs interface, 572
IADsComputer interface, 578
IADsDomain interface, 585
IADsFileService interface, 589
IADsFileServiceOperations
interface, 593
IADsFileShare interface, 598
IADsGroup interface, 601
IADsLocality interface, 604
IADsO interface, 608
IADsOU interface, 612
IADsPrintJob interface, 615
IADsPrintJobOperations
interface, 620
IADsPrintQueue interface, 625
IADsPrintQueueOperations
interface, 629
IADsResource interface, 633
IADsService interface, 637
IADsServiceOperations
interface, 641
IADsSession interface, 645
IADsUser interface, 656

PutEx method
IADs interface, 572
IADsComputer interface, 578
IADsDomain interface, 585
IADsFileService interface, 589
IADsFileServiceOperations
interface, 593
IADsFileShare interface, 598
IADsGroup interface, 601
IADsLocality interface, 604
IADsO interface, 608
IADsOU interface, 612
IADsPrintJob interface, 616
IADsPrintJobOperations
interface, 620
IADsPrintQueue interface, 626
IADsPrintQueueOperations
interface, 629
IADsResource interface, 633
IADsService interface, 637
IADsServiceOperations
interface, 641
IADsSession interface, 645
IADsUser interface, 656

Q

querying
account expiration dates,
95-96, 475
bad login attempts, 99, 476
computer owner (IADsComputer),
132, 481
computer processors
(IADsComputer), 482
computer properties
(IADsComputer), 131
CurrentUserCount, 163, 491
file share descriptions,
164-165, 491

file share host computers, 165, 492
file share maximum users property values, 166, 492
file share path property values, 167, 493
group description field values, 120-121, 480
groups, user membership, 118-119, 480
HAL (IADsComputer), 134, 482
host computer property (IADsService), 140, 485
last login attempt, 100, 477
last logoff attempt, 100, 477
log time period (IIS site logging), 217, 504
minimum password length, 101, 477
namespaces (ADSI practical applications), 13
operating systems (IADsComputer), 133, 482
organizations (registered), IADsComputer, 132, 481
password age, 102-105, 478
password requirements, 101, 477
print queues, 176-177, 497
  status, 177-178, 497
seconds, converting to days, 49
service account names (IADsService), 142-143, 486
service dependencies (IADsService), 136-137, 483
service display names (IADsService), 138-140, 484-485
service executable path (IADsService), 141, 486
service start types (IADsService), 143-144, 487
sites, status, 234, 513
user accounts, account type, 97, 475
Web site operators, 275, 517

R

RDNs (relative distinguished names), 380
redirect variables, 289
redirection (URL), Home Directory property sheet, 288-290, 523-524
relative distinguished names (RDNs), 380
remote home directories (Home Directory property sheet), 281-282, 520-521
  access permissions and content control, 283-284, 521
remote home directory path (FTP service management), 354-356, 539-540
Remove method
  IADsCollection interface, 573
  IADsGroup interface, 601
RemoveAce method (AccessControlList interface), 570
removing. *See* deleting
renaming
  objects (Active Directory), 420, 555
  user accounts, 57-59, 462-463
replication, object attributes in global catalog, 414
requirements, Visual Basic development environment, 22-23
RequireUniquePassword property (IADsUser interface), 657
resources
  Active Directory design and administration, 663-664
  ADO, 666
  ADSI, 664-665
  ASP, 665-666
  LDAP, 666-667
  Visual Basic, 667

Resources method
(IADsFileServiceOperations
interface), 594
ResourceUser variable, 174
restoring backups
  IIS Metabase, 207, 500
  IIsComputer, 207, 500
restrictions, IP addresses (Directory
  Security property sheet), 301-304,
  528-530
Resume method
  IADsPrintJobOperations
    interface, 620
  IADsPrintQueueOperations
    interface, 629
resuming print queues, 179, 498
rights. *See* access control;
  privileges; security
Role property (IADsComputer
  interface), 578
RootDSE, binding, 411, 549-550
  alternate credentials, 412-413, 551
  default naming context, 412, 550
RSACi content rating (HTTP Headers
  property sheet), 308-310, 531-532

S

SAM (Security Account Manager), 17
  encryption, SYSKEY utility, 51
  migrating to Active Directory, 17
schema, extending, 6
Schema property
  IADs interface, 573
  IADsComputer interface, 579
  IADsDomain interface, 585
  IADsFileService interface, 589
  IADsFileServiceOperations
    interface, 594

IADsFileShare interface, 598
IADsGroup interface, 602
IADsLocality interface, 605
IADsO interface, 608
IADsOU interface, 612
IADsPrintJob interface, 616
IADsPrintJobOperations
  interface, 620
IADsPrintQueue interface, 626
IADsPrintQueueOperations
  interface, 629
IADsResource interface, 633
IADsService interface, 637
IADsServiceOperations
  interface, 641
IADsSession interface, 646
IADsUser interface, 657
scope of inheritance (Active Directory
  security), 424-425
scripting languages
  ASP resources, 665-666
  command-line utilities, limitations, 3-4
SDKs (software development kits), 381
searching. *See also* querying
  global catalog, 413-414
  LDAP directories with ADO,
    390-391, 545
seconds, converting to days, 49
secure communications (Directory
  Security property sheet), 299-301,
  527-528
Secure Sockets Layer (SSL), endpoint
  mapping, 270-271, 515-516
SecureBindings property (Web Site
  property sheet), 270-271, 515-516
security
  Active Directory, 421-422, 425
    adding ACEs to ACL, 431, 560
    constants for ACEs, 422-424
    enumerating ACEs, 425-431,
      555-560

servers 713

inheritance, 424-425, 432-435, 561-563
removing ACEs from ACL, 431-432, 561
administrative delegation model, creating, 34-38
ADSI practical applications, 14
Directory Security property sheet, 294-295, 359-362, 541-543
  authentication methods, 295-299, 526-527
  IP address restrictions, 301-304, 528-530
  secure communications, 299-301, 527-528
encryption (SAM), SYSKEY utility, 51
file systems
  inheritance structures, 124-126
  managing with groups, 123-124
passwords, 76
  age, querying, 102-105, 478
  bad login attempts, resetting count, 47-49, 458-459
  changing, 77, 465
  determining, 76
  expiration, resetting, 49, 459
  IADsServiceOperations, 149, 490
  maximum age, 49, 459
  minimum age, 50, 459
  minimum length, 51-52, 101, 460, 477
  number stored for each user, 52-53, 460
  Password Never Expires status flag, 83, 468
  requirements, 101-102, 477-478
  security considerations, 282
  setting new, 76, 465
  User Cannot Change Password status flag, 81, 467-468
  User Must Change Password at Next Logon status flag, 79-80, 466-467
privileges (Web Operators property sheet), 274-275
Security Account Manager. *See* SAM
Security Accounts property sheet (FTP service), 344-345
  anonymous FTP connections, 345-346
    account credentials, 346-347, 535-536
    anonymous only access, 348, 536
    enabling/disabling access, 346, 535
  site operators, 348-349, 536-537
security model, LDAP, 381
SeeAlso property
  IADsLocality interface, 605
  IADsO interface, 609
  IADsOU interface, 612
  IADsUser interface, 657
ServerBindings property, 226
  FTP service management, 341-343, 533-534
  Web Site property sheet, 269-270, 515
ServerComment property, 224
  FTP service management, 340-341, 533
  index numbers, finding, 225, 507-508
  sites, deleting, 227-228, 509
  Web Site property sheet, 268-269, 514
servers, COM
  administrative delegation model, creating, 34-38
  ADObjectManagement class module, creating, 435-450

714 servers

creating, 28-31
ExchangeObjectMgt class module, creating, 401-404
IIsFTPManagement class module, creating, 362-370
IIsWebManagement class module, creating, 312-326
instantiating from ASP, 32-33
LDAPObjectManagement class module, creating, 396-399
NTContainerManagement class module, creating, 60-64
NTUserManagement class module, creating, 105-110
testing, 31-32

ServerSize property (Web Performance property sheet), 277-278, 518

ServerState property, 233

service account names (IADsService), querying, 142-143, 486

service dependencies (IADsService)
 querying, 136-137, 483
 setting, 137-138, 483-484

service display names (IADsService)
 querying, 138-140, 484-485
 setting, 140, 485

service executable path (IADsService)
 querying, 141, 486
 setting, 141, 486

service start types (IADsService)
 querying, 143-144, 487
 setting, 144, 487

service status (IADsServiceOperations), enumeration, 145-146, 487-488

ServiceAccountName property
 IADsFileService interface, 590
 IADsService interface, 637

ServiceAccountPath property
 IADsFileService interface, 590
 IADsService interface, 638

services (IADsServiceOperations)
 pausing, 148, 489-490
 starting, 146, 488
 stopping, 147, 489

ServiceType property
 IADsFileService interface, 590
 IADsService interface, 638

Sessions method (IADsFileServiceOperations interface), 594

SetInfo method
 IADs interface, 12-13, 573
 IADsComputer interface, 579
 IADsDomain interface, 585
 IADsFileService interface, 590
 IADsFileServiceOperations interface, 594
 IADsFileShare interface, 598
 IADsGroup interface, 602
 IADsLocality interface, 605
 IADsO interface, 609
 IADsOU interface, 612
 IADsPrintJob interface, 616
 IADsPrintJobOperations interface, 621
 IADsPrintQueue interface, 626
 IADsPrintQueueOperations interface, 630
 IADsResource interface, 633
 IADsService interface, 638
 IADsServiceOperations interface, 642
 IADsSession interface, 646
 IADsUser interface, 657

SetPassword method
 IADsFileServiceOperations interface, 594
 IADsServiceOperations interface, 642
 IADsUser interface, 657

system management 715

shares
  creating programmatically, 168, 493
  enumerating, 162-163, 490
  removing, 168, 494
single-signon (ADSI practical applications), 14
site management. *See* IIS site management
site operators (FTP service management), 348-349, 536-537
Site property (IADsComputer interface), 579
sites. *See also* Web sites
  Active Directory terminology, 409
  manipulating, 233
  pausing, 235-236, 514
  querying status, 234, 513
  starting, 235, 513
  stopping, 235, 513
Size property (IADsPrintJob interface), 616
software development kits (SDKs), 381
SSL (Secure Sockets Layer), endpoint mapping, 270-271, 515-516
Start method
  IADsFileServiceOperations interface, 595
  IADsServiceOperations interface, 642
starting
  services (IADsServiceOperations), 146, 488
  sites, 235, 513
StartTime property
  IADsPrintJob interface, 616
  IADsPrintQueue interface, 626
StartType property
  IADsFileService interface, 591
  IADsService interface, 638-639

StartupParameters property
  IADsFileService interface, 591
  IADsService interface, 639
status flags, user accounts, 77-78
  Account Disabled, 83-85, 469
  Account Locked-Out, 85-87, 470
  determining value of, 78, 466
  Password Never Expires, 83, 468
  toggling, 79, 466
  User Cannot Change Password, 81, 467-468
  User Must Change Password at Next Logon, 79-80, 466-467
Status property
  IADsFileServiceOperations interface, 595
  IADsPrintJobOperations interface, 621
  IADsPrintQueueOperations interface, 630-631
  IADsServiceOperations interface, 642
Stop method
  IADsFileServiceOperations interface, 595
  IADsServiceOperations interface, 643
stopping
  services (IADsServiceOperations), 147, 489
  sites, 235, 513
StorageCapacity property (IADsComputer interface), 579
structure (IIS Metabase), examining, 204-205
SYSKEY utility (SAM encryption), 51
system management, automated (ADSI practical applications), 10-11

T

TAPI (Telephony Application
  Programming Interface), 6
TCP ports (FTP service management),
  341-343, 533-534
TelephoneHome property (IADsUser
  interface), 658
TelephoneMobile property (IADsUser
  interface), 658
TelephoneNumber property
  IADsO interface, 609
  IADsOU interface, 613
  IADsUser interface, 658
TelephonePager property (IADsUser
  interface), 658
Telephony Application Programming
  Interface (TAPI), 6
templates (Visual Basic projects),
  creating, 23-26
terminology, Active Directory, 408-410
test environment, importance of, 26
testing COM servers, 31-32
TimeElapsed property
  (IADsPrintJobOperations
  interface), 621
timeouts, ConnectionTimeout property
  (Web Site property sheets), 273-274,
  516-517
TimeSubmitted property
  (IADsPrintJob interface), 617
Title property (IADsUser
  interface), 658
toggling user status flags, 79, 466
TotalPages property (IADsPrintJob
  interface), 617
trees (Active Directory
  terminology), 409
troubleshooting COM object
  instantiation from ASP, 33
Trustee property (AccessControlEntry
  interface), 569

U

UNCPassword property
  FTP service management, 354-356,
    539-540
  Home Directory property
    sheet, 282
UNCUserName property
  FTP service management, 354-356,
    539-540
  Home Directory property
    sheet, 282
UntilTime property
  IADsPrintJob interface, 617
  IADsPrintQueue interface, 626
UPN (user principal name),
  Active Directory terminology, 410
URL redirection (Home Directory
  property sheet), 288-290, 523-524
user accounts. *See also* accounts; users
  Account Information dialog
    box, 95
  account type, querying, 97, 475
  administrative delegation model,
    creating, 34-38
  bad login attempts, querying,
    99, 476
  creating/deleting/renaming, 57-59,
    462-463
  enumeration, 54, 461
  environment profiles, 87
    home directory mapping,
      90, 472
    home directory path, 89, 472
    LoginScript property, 89, 471
    profile paths, 471
  expiration date
    querying, 95-96, 475
    setting, 96
  global accounts, changing to local
    accounts, 97-98, 476
  last login attempt, querying,
    100, 477

last logoff attempt, querying,
   100, 477
local accounts, changing to global
   accounts, 98, 476
login hours, 91-92, 473
login workstations, 92-95, 473-474
minimum password length,
   querying, 101, 477
Parameters property, 98
password age, querying,
   102-105, 478
password requirements
   querying, 101, 477
   setting, 102, 478
passwords, 76
   changing, 77, 465
   determining, 76
   setting new, 76, 465
properties, 72-73
   Description, 74-75, 464-465
   FullName, 73-74, 463-464
status flags, 77-78
   Account Disabled, 83-85, 469
   Account Locked-Out,
      85-87, 470
   determining value of, 78, 466
   Password Never Expires,
      83, 468
   toggling, 79, 466
   User Cannot Change Password,
      81, 467-468
   User Must Change Password at
      Next Logon, 79-80, 466-467
User Cannot Change Password status
   flag, 81, 467-468
user class objects (Active Directory),
   enumeration, 415, 552
user group membership, enumeration,
   122-123, 481
User Must Change Password at Next
   Logon status flag, 79-80, 466-467
user objects, binding, 72

user principal name (UPN),
   Active Directory terminology, 410
User property
   IADsPrintJob interface, 617
   IADsResource interface, 633
   IADsSession interface, 646
user sessions
   disconnecting, 171, 495
   enumerating, 169-170, 494
UserFlags property (IADsUser
   interface), 660-661
UserName property
   (WinNTSystemInfo interface), 662
UserPath property
   IADsPrintJob interface, 617
   IADsResource interface, 634
   IADsSession interface, 646
users. *See also* user accounts
   adding to groups, 117, 479
   querying group membership,
      118-119, 480
   removing from groups,
      117-118, 479
utilities
   command-line, limitations of, 3-4
   IIS Log Replay, 213
   MetaEdit, 204

V

variables
   MimeExtension, 211
   MimeType, 211
   redirect variables, 289
   ResourceUser, 174
VBScript, disadvantages of, 20
VBScript Active Server Page, instantiating NTContainerManagement class module, 65

Version property
IADsFileService interface, 591
IADsService interface, 639
viewing MIME-type mappings, 210, 501
virtual directories
FTP service management
local home directory path, 353-354, 539
remote home directory path, 354-356, 539-540
IIS site management
creating, 229-230, 510
creating FTP virtual directories, 230, 511
deleting, 230, 511
deleting FTP sites, 231, 511
virtual directory binding, 262
virtual site binding, 262
Visual Basic
advantages of, 20
COM, 21-22
datatype definitions, 20
multi-tier development, 20-21
COM servers
creating, 28-31
instantiating from ASP, 32-33
testing, 31-32
development environment
configuring, 23-26
requirements, 22-23
installing, 23
instantiating NTContainerManagement class module, 65
interaction with ADSI for administrative tasks, 27-28
resources, 667
test environment, importance of, 26

W-Z

W3C Extended Log File Format (IIS site logging), 218-220, 505-506
Web application configuration (Home Directory property sheet), 284-288, 521-523
Web directories
entries, adding, 232-233, 512
IIS site management, managing, 231, 512
Web Operators property sheet, 274-275
creating operators, 275, 517
querying operators, 275, 517
removing operators, 276, 518
Web Performance property sheet, 276-277
AllowKeepAlive property, 279, 519
MaxBandwidth property, 278, 519
ServerSize property, 277-278, 518
Web Site property sheet, 267-268
Connections frame, 272
ConnectionTimeout property, 273-274, 516-517
MaxConnections property, 272-273, 516
Web Site Identification frame, 268
SecureBindings property, 270-271, 515-516
ServerBindings property, 269-270, 515
ServerComment property, 268-269, 514
Web sites. *See also* **IIS Metabase; sites**
IIS Metabase property inheritance, 263-267
IIS site management, creating, 225-226, 508
performance tuning, memory, 277-278, 518
publishing multiple on one IP address, 269-270, 515

ServerComment property, deleting, 227-228, 509
virtual directory binding, 262
virtual site binding, 262
Web-based applications, shadowing business workflow processes, 9
Windows 2000, migrating from Windows NT 4.0 to, 17
Windows NT 4.0, migrating to Windows 2000, 17
WinNTSystemInfo interface, 661
  ComputerName property, 661
  DomainName property, 661
  PDC property, 662
  UserName property, 662
workflow processes (ADSI practical applications), 9-10
WWW (IIS site management), enumeration, 223, 507
WWW service (IIS Metabase), 203-204
  backups, 206-207, 500
    deleting, 208, 501
    enumeration, 207, 500
    restoring, 207, 500
  Directory Security property sheet, 294-295
    authentication methods, 295-299, 526-527
    IP address restrictions, 301-304, 528-530
    secure communications, 299-301, 527-528
  Documents property sheet, 291
    default document, enabling, 291-293, 524
    document footer, enabling, 293-294, 525
  entries, adding, 232-233, 512

Home Directory property sheet, 279-280
  access permissions and content control, 283-284, 521
  local home directories, 280-281, 520
  remote home directories, 281-282, 520-521
  URL redirection, 288-290, 523-524
  Web application configuration, 284-288, 521-523
  HTTP Headers property sheet, 305
    content expiration, 305-306, 530
    content rating, 308-310, 531-532
    custom HTTP headers, 307, 531
    MIME type information, 310-311, 532
  IIsComputer object, 206
  property inheritance, 263-267
  structure, examining, 204-205
  Web Operators property sheet, 274-275
    creating operators, 275, 517
    querying operators, 275, 517
    removing operators, 276, 518
  Web Performance property sheet, 276-277
    AllowKeepAlive property, 279, 519
    MaxBandwidth property, 278, 519
    ServerSize property, 277-278, 518
  Web Site property sheet, 267-268
    Connections frame, 272-274, 516-517
    Web Site Identification frame, 268-271, 514-516

Xor operator (user status flags), 78

The Circle Series from MTP

April 1998

Richard Puckett: *Windows NT Automated Deployment and Customization*
ISBN: 1-57870-045-0

Tim Hill: *Windows NT Shell Scripting*
ISBN: 1-57870-047-7

May 1998

Gene Henriksen: *Windows NT and UNIX Integration*
ISBN: 1-57870-048-5

November 1998

PeterViscarola/Anthony Mason: *Windows NT Device Driver Development*
ISBN: 1-57870-058-2

Steve Thomas: *Windows NT Heterogeneous Networking*
ISBN: 1-57870-064-7

Todd Mathers/Shawn Genoway: *Windows NT Thin Client Solutions: Implementing Terminal Server and Citrix MetaFrame*
ISBN: 1-57870-065-5

January 1999

David Roth: *Win32 Perl Programming: The Standard Extensions*
ISBN: 1-57870-067-1

February 1999

Gregg Branham: *Windows NT Domain Architecture*
ISBN: 1-57870-112-0

August 1999

Sean Deuby: *Windows 2000 Server: Planning and Migration*
ISBN: 1-57870-023-X

September 1999

David Iseminger: *Windows 2000 Quality of Service*
ISBN: 1-57870-115-5

October 1999

Tim Hill: *Windows Script Host*
ISBN: 1-57870-139-2

Paul Hinsberg: *Windows NT Applications: Measuring and Optimizing Performance*
ISBN: 1-57870-176-7

William Zack: *Windows 2000 and Mainframe Integration*
ISBN: 1-57870-200-3

Windows NT/2000 ADSI Scripting for System Administration provides ready-to-implement Visual Basic code segments for the following administrative tasks:

Chapter 3, "Container Enumeration Methods and Programmatic Domain Acount Policy Manipulation":
- Enumerating Domains (44)
- Manipulating Domain Properties (46-52)
- Enumerating Computer and User Accounts in a Domain (54-55)
- Enumerating Local and Global Groups in a Domain (55)
- Adding and Removing Computer Accounts to a Domain (56-57)
- Adding, Removing, and Renaming User Accounts in a Domain (57-58)
- Adding and Removing Groups in a Domain (59-60)
- Creating a COM Object for Domain Manipulation (60)

Chapter 4, "Programmatic User Account Manipulation":
- Manipulating User Account Properties (73-97)
- Querying the BadLoginCount Property for a User Account (99)
- Querying the LastLogin Property for a User Account (100)
- Querying the LastLogoff Property for a User Account (100)
- Manipulating the MinimumPasswordLength Property for a User Account (101)
- Manipulating the PasswordRequired Property for a User Account (101)
- Querying the Password Age Property for User and Computer Accounts (103)
- Creating a COM Object for Manipulating User Account Properties (105)

Chapter 5, "Programmatic Group Manipulation":
- Adding User Accounts to Groups (117)
- Removing User Accounts from Groups (118)
- Enumerating Group Members (118)
- Querying Group Membership Using the IsMember Method (119)
- Manipulating Group Descriptions (121)
- Enumerating the Groups Associated with a User Account (122)
- Creating a COM Object for Group Manipulation (126)

Chapter 6, "Programmatic Computer and Service Manipulation":
- Querying the Computer Owner (132)
- Querying the Registered Organization (132)
- Querying the Operating System (133)
- Querying the Operating System Version (133)
- Querying the Processor Type (134)
- Querying the Installed HAL (134)
- Enumerating Installed Services (136)
- Manipulating Service Dependencies (137)
- Manipulating the Display Name for a Service (139)
- Querying the Host Computer for a Service (141)
- Manipulating the Service Path for a Service (141-142)
- Querying the Service Account Name for a Service (143)
- Manipulating the Service Start Type for a Service (144)
- Enumerating Service Status (145)
- Programmatically Starting a Service (147)
- Programmatically Stopping a Service (147)
- Programmatically Pausing a Service (148)

- Programmatically Continuing a Service (148)
- Setting a New Service Account Password (149)
- Creating a COM Object for Computer Management (150)

Chapter 7, "Programmatic File and Print Resource Management":
- Enumerating Existing Shares (page 163)
- Querying File Share User Count (164)
- Manipulating File Share Descriptions (165)
- Manipulating Maximum File Share Users (166)
- Querying the Current Path to a Share (167)
- Creating/Removing Shares Programmatically (168)
- Enumerating File Sessions (170)
- Disconnecting a User Session (171)
- Enumerating Open Resources (173)
- Examining the Properties of a Single Open Resource (174)
- Enumerating Print Queues (175)
- Examining Print Queue Properties (176-177)
- Querying Queue Status (177)
- Pausing a Print Queue (179)
- Resuming a Print Queue (179)
- Enumerating Print Queue Jobs (180)
- Manipulating Print Job Operations (182)
- Removing Print Jobs from a Queue (183)
- Purging All Jobs from the Queue (183)
- Creating a COM Object for Print Management (184)

Chapter 8, "Programmatic Management of the IIS Metabase":
- Programmatic Metabase Backup Management (207-208)
- Manipulating IIS Maximum Bandwidth (209)
- Manipulating MIME Mappings (210-212)
- Manipulating IIS Logging (214-222)
- Enumerating Virtual Sites (223-224)
- Manipulating Site Descriptions Programmatically (225)
- Creating a New Site Programmatically (226-227)
- Deleting Sites (228-229)
- Creating/Removing Virtual Directories (230-231)
- Managing Web Files and Directories (232-233)
- Querying Site Status (234)
- Starting a Site (235)
- Stopping a Site (235)
- Pausing a Site (236)
- Continuing a Paused Site (236)
- Creating a for IIS Site Management (236)

Chapter 9, "Programmatic Management of Web Site Properties":
- Manipulating the Web Site Property Sheet (267-274)
- Manipulating the Web Operators Property Sheet (274-276)
- Manipulating the Web Performance Property Sheet (276-279)
- Manipulating the Home Directory Property Sheet (279-290)
- Manipulating the Documents Property Sheet (291-294)